THE OXFORD ILLUSTRATED HISTORY OF

THE ROMAN WORLD

Edited by
JOHN BOARDMAN
JASPER GRIFFIN
OSWYN MURRAY

OXFORD
UNIVERSITY PRESS

OXFORD
UNIVERSITY PRESS

Great Clarendon Street, Oxford OX2 6DP
Oxford University Press is a department of the University of Oxford.
It furthers the University's objective of excellence in research, scholarship,
and education by publishing worldwide in

Oxford New York

Auckland Bangkok Buenos Aires Cape Town Chennai
Dar es Salaam Delhi Hong Kong Istanbul Karachi Kolkata
Kuala Lumpur Madrid Melbourne Mexico City Mumbai
Nairobi São Paulo Shanghai Taipei Tokyo Toronto

Oxford is a registered trade mark of Oxford University Press
in the UK and in certain other countries

First published 1986 by Oxford University Press
First issued in two volumes as an Oxford University Press paperback
and as a simultaneous hardback 1988
Reissued 2001

British Library Cataloguing in Publication Data
The Oxford history of the classical world
Vol. 2. The Roman World
1. Classical antiquity to 200
I. Boardman, John, 1927– II. Griffin, Jasper
III. Murray, Oswyn
938

Library of Congress Cataloging in Publication Data
Data available
ISBN-13: 978-0-19-285436-0
ISBN-10: 0-19-285436-4

7 9 10 8 6

Printed in Great Britain by Ashford Colour Press Ltd,
Gosport, Hants.

THE OXFORD ILLUSTRATED HISTORY OF

THE ROMAN WORLD

The seventeen scholars who have contributed to *The Oxford Illustrated History of the Roman World* are all distinguished authorities in their field. They are:

MICHAEL CRAWFORD, University College, London, *Early Rome and Italy*

ELIZABETH RAWSON, Corpus Christi College, Oxford, *The Expansion of Rome*

P. G. McC. BROWN, Trinity College, Oxford, *The First Roman Literature*

MIRIAM GRIFFIN, Somerville College, Oxford, *Cicero and Rome*

ROBIN NISBET, Corpus Christi College, Oxford, *The Poets of the Late Republic*

DAVID STOCKTON, Brasenose College, Oxford, *The Founding of the Empire*

NICHOLAS PURCELL, St John's College, Oxford, *The Arts of Government*

R. O. A. M. LYNE, Balliol College, Oxford, *Augustan Poetry and Society*

JASPER GRIFFIN, Balliol College, Oxford, *Virgil*

ANDREW LINTOTT, Worcester College, Oxford, *Roman Historians*

DONALD RUSSELL, St John's College, Oxford, *The Arts of Prose: The Early Empire*

RICHARD JENKYNS, Lady Margaret Hall, Oxford, *Silver Latin Poetry and the Latin Novel*

ANTHONY MEREDITH, Campion Hall, Oxford, *Later Philosophy*

ROGER LING, University of Manchester, *The Arts of Living*

JOHN MATTHEWS, Queen's College, Oxford, *Roman Life and Society*

R. J. A. WILSON, Trinity College, Dublin, *Roman Art and Architecture*

HENRY CHADWICK, Peterhouse, Cambridge, *Envoi: On Taking Leave of Antiquity*

CONTENTS

LIST OF COLOUR PLATES

LIST OF MAPS

ACKNOWLEDGEMENTS

THE editors wish to express their thanks to the many institutions and individuals named in the List of Illustrations for provision of photographs and drawings, and permission to use them; and to Philippa Lewis who did the picture research. A special debt of gratitude is owed to Roger Ling who undertook the main responsibility for the choice of illustrations in this volume. Oswyn Murray compiled the Chronological Charts. The Index was compiled by Peter Tickler. Many members of the Press have devoted their skills to the creation of this volume, but our principal debt must be to the authors for their patient co-operation.

NOTE

The Oxford History of the Classical World was originally published as one volume. For this Oxford Paperback edition, it appears as two books: *Greece and the Hellenistic World* and *The Roman World*. Where a cross-reference refers to *Greece and the Hellenistic World,* this is given as (for example): Vol. 1, p. 100.

Introduction

JASPER GRIFFIN

THIS book tells the story of the rise of Rome from its origins as a cluster of villages on the hills round the Forum to the possession of an empire which unified the Mediterranean world and a great deal besides. At its height the Roman Empire stretched from Northumberland to Algeria, from Portugal to Syria, from the Rhine to the Nile: it comprised the whole or part of the territory of what are now thirty sovereign states, and it was not until 1870 that Italy, for instance, achieved again the unity which Rome had imposed before the birth of Christ. The memory of that lost unity has haunted the mind of Europe.

The idea of Rome has given to the West several distinct myths, each full of resonance. There is the image of the stern and upright generals and consuls of the Republican period, great conquerors devoted to the service of their country. These were men like Cato, who after governing a province in Spain sold his horse so that the state should not have to bear the cost of transporting it back to Italy, and like Cincinnatus, who when the Senate summoned him to serve again as supreme commander was found hard at work ploughing his fields. Such a man deserved to have a great American city named after him. Their wives were women like Cornelia, mother of the Gracchi, who when a visitor displayed her jewellery called in her sons and said 'These are my jewels', and, later, Arria Paeta, who when the Emperor ordered her husband to commit suicide showed the way by stabbing herself with the words 'Look, it doesn't hurt'.

In later literature we find such figures in the tragedies of Corneille, and in Shakespeare's Brutus. Swift, in the third part of *Gulliver's Travels*, sends his hero to an island of necromancers, who at his desire call up the mighty dead. Gulliver tells us: 'I was struck with a profound veneration at the Sight of *Brutus*; and could easily discover the most consummate Virtue, the greatest intrepidity and Firmness of Mind, the truest Love of his Country, and general Benevolence for Mankind in every Lineament of his Countenance'. He goes on to say, 'I desired that the Senate of *Rome* might appear before me in one large Chamber, and a modern Representative, in Counterview, in another. The first seemed to be an Assembly of Heroes and Demy-Gods; the other a knot of Pedlars, Pick-pockets, Highwaymen and Bullies ...' In art we see such grand Romans depicted in the paintings of David: such subjects as Lucius Brutus condemning his own sons to death for treason to the Republic, and Horatius killing his country's enemy, although he is betrothed to his own sister.

In time the Republic gave place to an Empire. On the one hand the flamboyant personalities of the early Emperors, and the opulence of Imperial Rome, have created an ineffaceable picture of luxury and cruelty, which found expression in Flaubert, Gautier, and Victor Hugo, in *The Last Days of Pompeii*, and in Hollywood spectaculars from *Spartacus* to *Ben Hur*. But there also was the contrasting image: the straight and endless Roman roads which dominated the face of Europe, the matchless efficiency of the legions, and an Empire which brought peace for generations to a world where such a thing has at all times been far rarer than gold. Poems and stories of Kipling give that idea powerful expression: a self-denying and loyal military and administrative machine, protecting civilization from the barbarians across the frontier.

There have, of course, been other great civilizations in the history of the world. Ancient China, for instance, was an empire which lasted longer than Rome, and which produced great art and literature. But ancient Rome, with ancient Greece, has a special claim on the West, because our own culture has grown directly out of it. The remembrance was never lost that European society was the successor to an impressive earlier culture, even when, as we see from works like the medieval *Gesta Romanorum* (old stories collected and given Christian morals, often strikingly inappropriate) all sense of realistic history might be so completely vanished that in one story we find the Emperor Claudius marrying his daughter to the philosopher Socrates, who one day in the forest meets King Alexander. Rome was always a model for imitation and emulation, and thus two ideas were inbuilt: first, that one's own society was not the first in history; and second, that high civilization, once achieved, could be lost.

The Latin language, like Greek, belongs to the great Indo-European family which spread, in the course of many centuries, from an original centre somewhere south of the Caucasus into India, Iran, and Europe. The ancestors of the Romans must include many people who entered Italy from the north, probably not in one single group, reaching the site of Rome by about 1000 B C. There they mingled with other peoples: we can dimly discern different words and even different burial customs of elements later called 'Latin' and 'Sabine'. Until about 600 B C we find separate settlements on the Roman hills, that on the Palatine being traditionally the oldest. In the course of the sixth century the settlements amalgamated into one, and from then on Rome may be said to exist. Its traditional foundation date, 21 April 753 BC, with most of what we are told by later antiquity about Rome's early period, is essentially myth rather than history; but the tradition that Romulus, the founder, established a 'refuge' (*asylum*) to welcome refugees and outcasts to his new city may reflect a truth about the miscellaneous population of early Rome.

The city was much influenced by the Etruscans, a mysterious people then at their zenith in central Italy. They modified the Indo-European inheritance considerably. It was their influence, for instance, that explains the triad of deities worshipped on the Capitol: Jupiter, Juno, and Minerva. That makes sense only in Etruscan terms. From Etruria also came the elaborate systems for discovering the divine purposes by means of omens, which were officially practised by Roman magistrates. Even their own names came to follow an alien pattern, the Indo-European single name (Menelaus, Siegfried), giving place to a complex style (Marcus Tullius Cicero). Etruria also transmitted the influence of Greece, especially in the visual arts.

Rome proved exceptional in aggressiveness and aptitude for war. Long years of campaigning reduced all of peninsular Italy to Roman domination by the early third century B C. The conquering city adopted many Greek refinements: her early coinage, for instance, is purely Greek in appearance. It was also hospitable to immigrants from other Italian communities, and generous in bestowing citizenship (but without the vote) on whole areas of Italy. Rome exacted tribute from subject Italian peoples in the form of soldiers; at the end of their military service they were settled in 'colonies', new towns which retained something of a military character, and which were intended to hold down and guarantee the security of conquered territories. The whole process made for a uniquely efficient machine for conquest.

Early Rome was characterized by a powerful public opinion, a strong public spirit, and a marked distaste for eccentricity and individualism. Despite the cultural influence of Greece, there was a powerful current of suspicion and dislike of highbrow foreign ways. A man should not lose touch with the soil, and the country was a morally better place than the town. The 'way of the ancestors' (*mos maiorum*) possessed a great moral force, and within the family, at least in the upper class, the father enjoyed a degree of power over his sons, even when they were grown men, which astonished the Greeks, and which is reflected in many stories of fathers who put their own sons to death and were admired for doing so. It is not difficult to imagine the stress produced in Romans by such pressures, and it is tempting to connect it with the double Roman obsession, on the one hand with parricide, and on the other with *pietas*, dutiful behaviour to parents, the archetype of which was the figure of Aeneas, founder of Rome, carrying his old father on his shoulders out of burning Troy. The anxiety engendered by such conflicts within the psyche, issuing in restless energy, might be part of the explanation for that astonishing fact, which seemed to the Romans themselves to be explicable only by constant divine favour: that this city, not particularly well sited or obviously well endowed, conquered the world.

Roman art and literature alike present the men of the Republic as tight-lipped, tight-fisted, and resolute. Such qualities as *parsimonia, severitas, frugalitas, simplicitas,* constantly praised, tell their own story; as does the moral ascendency of a man like Cato, the quintessential peasant farmer magnified into a senator and consul. The names of many Roman grandees poignantly reveal their peasant origin. Cincinnatus and Calvus ('Curly' and 'Baldy'), Capito and Naso ('Big-head' and 'Nosey'),

Crassus and Macer ('Fatty' and 'Skinny'), Flaccus and Bibulus ('Floppy' and 'The Drinker'), are the names of Roman consuls and poets, the inheritors of Etruscan kingly regalia and Greek aesthetic refinement.

Our richest and clearest evidence is for the late Republic, when the system was visibly breaking down, and when the old safeguards could no longer restrain the magnates from looting the provinces and even marching with armies on Rome in pursuit of their own aggrandisement. It is tempting to suppose that the reality had always been as venal and as ruthless. Yet it is clear that there had really been a change. When for twenty years Hannibal led an invincible army about Italy urging Rome's Italian allies to revolt, the great majority of them stood firm; not much more than a hundred years later their grievances drove them to make war on Rome themselves. Roman justice and self-restraint, the public spirit which impressed Greeks when they met it in the second century B C, were not a myth.

The conquests of Alexander spread the language, architecture, and art of Greece as far to the East as India; the rise of Rome led eventually to the whole Mediterranean world and its 'fringe', as far as Britain, Romania, and Iraq, sharing in one recognizable culture with two great languages, Greek and Latin. Anything like modern nationalism was strikingly ineffective, and the Empire was not held down by force: for most of the first century A D, for instance, there was only one legion stationed in North Africa, and none at all in Spain. The Imperial administration insisted on two things: taxes must be paid, and law and order must be maintained. In most other respects the running of life was left to the cities, that is to say to the upper class who by their rank and wealth reckoned to run the cities. Culture was urban, literate, and remarkably uniform. The same books were studied by schoolboys all over this huge world, and whether in Provence, Turkey, or North Africa, cities arose whose layout and temples and public buildings shared the same repertory of forms and decorations. The silver on the table, the mosaics on the floor, the under-floor heating: a uniformity of style existed which is only now returning to our world.

That style was not, of course, all-inclusive. It was the creation of a leisured class, and Berber tribesmen or Illyrian goatherds doubtless felt little sympathy with it. The Empire must have depended on unfree labour to a much greater extent than Greece; and the slums of Rome show that many of the free urban poor lived lives of great poverty. Yet Rome was extraordinary among slave-owning societies in that slaves were constantly freed in great numbers, and the moment they were freed they became citizens. More than half of the thousands of epitaphs extant from imperial Rome are of freedmen and freedwomen. The poor citizen had the great public baths, public squares, parks, and forums, in which he reckoned to spend far more time out of his house than is normal in the colder and damper north.

Still darker aspects are not to be glossed over: the slave trade, infanticide, the gladiatorial shows, absolute power which could be in the hands of irresponsible or unbalanced men. Caligula and Nero, the spectacle of bloodshed and the sinister opulence of the orgy, have haunted the imagination of Europe. One of the ways in which the Roman Empire is interesting is that it shows certain sides of human nature developed to their fullest extent: 'Remember', Caligula used to say to people, 'that I can do anything to anybody.' The past is the laboratory in which human nature can be studied with security, perhaps the only way it can really be studied at all.

The ancients believed in the power and significance of great individuals. The daemonic Alcibiades, the imperturbable and ironic Socrates, the vehement Alexander: these stand beside such Romans as the all-conquering Caesar, the gallant but profligate Mark Antony, the demented aesthete Nero. The will to power incarnated in great individuals, the qualities of resolution, magnanimity, and pride: the ancients saw events very much in such terms. Such qualities as pride and magnanimity are essentially un-Christian. In the Middle Ages, and still more in the Renaissance, such pagan virtues, which Christian Europe had in reality by no means renounced, could be glorified in the persons and stories of the ancient world. Important human qualities which Christianity seemed to leave out, or which it rejected, could be depicted with sympathy in Achilles or Caesar, Helen or Cleopatra; in the rational suicide of Seneca or the passionate suicide of Dido.

The incompatibility of some pagan virtues with Christianity draws attention to an important aspect of the scope of this book. Jews and Christians are in principle not included—the *Envoi* looks forward to Christian Europe. Judaism and Christianity do not belong in a History of the Classical World because they were too separate, too unclassical. The presuppositions of Jewish literature were essentially different from those of Greece and Rome, and so were its characteristic forms. Rome could come to terms with Judaism, which was at least an ancestral cult, if a bizarre one, more easily than with Christianity, which was not even respectably ancient, and which in vital respects contradicted the fundamental nature of the pagan state. Other-worldliness, celibacy, refusal to take an oath or offer the regular sacrifices—all this was more than official Rome could stomach, while the uncouth literary form of Christian writings, and their outlandish message, repelled the educated class: to the Greeks it seemed foolishness, St Paul admits of the Gospel. Yet there was a perspective in which, at least later, the classical world could be seen as necessary for the universal acceptance of the Christian revelation. The glorification of Socrates' condemnation and death as being a martyrdom, a triumph, which was proclaimed with all the literary genius of Plato, and accepted by the educated of Greece and Rome alike, prepared the way for the understanding of the Passion of Christ. The Roman Empire had pacified and united the world in time for the Gospel to be proclaimed everywhere. Rome the Imperial City became Rome the Holy City, and her bishops took the old Roman title of Supreme Pontiff. The universal claims of Rome assumed a sacerdotal form, but the continuity is obvious.

The classical tradition, a large fraction of the history of the West, is too vast a theme to be more than glanced at here. Greece and Rome provided the languages of the Western and Eastern Churches, when the unity imposed on the Mediterranean world finally broke in half with Rome's fall, and they continued to be the vehicle of intellectual communication for many centuries. The eastern Empire continued to call itself 'Roman' to its end, in 1453, but it did so in Greek. Some of ancient literature survived, including many masterpieces, although much more was lost. After great struggles and doubts on the part of Fathers of the Church it was widely, though never universally, accepted that the pagan classics could be read and taught by Christians. Virgil and Terence continued for a thousand years to be fundamental texts at schools in the West.

The idea of Rome never lost its fascination. Charlemagne went to the inconvenient Italian city to be crowned Emperor, and the struggle for and against a Roman Empire with universal claims dominated the history of Italy and Germany for hundreds of years. Napoleon revived it again, and Mussolini claimed to have 'restored the fasces' (whence 'fascists') and reconstituted an Empire for Rome. Shakespeare explored the dilemmas of power more deeply in his Roman tragedies than in his English history plays; Kipling, in some of his best poems and stories, took the Roman Empire as a paradigm of the British Raj. In the sphere of political reality the same idea can be seen. The trial of Warren Hastings for oppression and extortion in India was felt by all the participants to be an echo of the celebrated trials of Roman governors like Verres, denounced by Cicero. The word 'proconsul' was unselfconsciously applied to British colonial administrators.

The founders of new constitutions often took Roman models: thus there are Senates in France, Ireland, Italy, and the United States. The radical political wing could also find Roman models. French Revolutionaries took names like Gracchus, and claimed the inheritance of the tyrannicide Brutus and the Roman Republic. A German revolutionary movement named itself after the rebellious slave Spartacus; a left-wing magazine in Britain is still called *Tribune*. The Roman Church, of course, re-enacted the claims of the Empire on a different plane.

For the arts the influence of antiquity had three aspects: subject matter, form, and spirit. The myths of Greece were the other great subject of Renaissance art, along with Christian themes; the myths of Ovid were painted by Titian and Correggio, Rubens and Poussin; Mantegna, Piranesi, and David created visual images of Rome. Michelangelo began his career as a sculptor by creating works so closely modelled on ancient models that they passed as genuine antiques. The genres of ancient literature, too, lived on. Pastorals and epics, elegies and satires sprang up in every European language; the Italian musicians and patrons who created the first operas were trying to reconstruct the musical drama of antiquity; before Greek tragedy was understood, the rhetorical melodramas of Seneca were a formative influence on the tragedy which blossomed with Marlowe and Shakespeare. In another art the triumphal arch, the Doric, Ionic, and Corinthian capitals, the fountains with marble nymphs and river gods, the ornamental urns, all proliferated through the cities. The spirit is even more pervasive. David's Marat stabbed in his bath recalls the philosophical suicides of Rome; the grand manner of Raphael and Milton is inseparable from their classical studies; Dante claimed Virgil as his master, and for all the enormous difference of their styles the claim clearly expresses an important truth.

The English language itself is distinguished from its cousins in the Germanic branch of the Indo-European family by the very large number of words which have come into it from Latin and, to a lesser extent, from Greek; some directly, others through French or Italian. People sometimes talk as if such words were always massive and abstruse, like 'psychiatry' or 'prelapsarian', and indeed the vocabulary of abstract thought, of science and culture, is especially full of them. But the following sample of twenty-five may remind the reader that many short and basic words have the same source: act, art, beauty, colour, crime, fact, fate, fork, hour, human, idea, justice, language, law, matter, music, nature, number, place, reason, school, sense, sex, space, time.

Every generation approaches classical antiquity in a different way, draws different lessons from it, finds different things about it interesting. It is hoped that this book will help contemporary readers to understand something of its continuing significance and fascination.

A
B
C

● Virunum

R. DANUBE

TRANSPADANA

VENETIA

Aquileia

● Tergeste

PANNONIA

Mediolanum

a

Verona

Patavium

HISTRIA

DALMATIA

a

● Sirmio

Cremona

● Mantua

Bedriacum

● Parma

R. PADUS

Placentia

AEMILIA

● Pola

● Genua

Ravenna

Salonae (Split)

R. RUBICON

Carrara

Ariminum

Pisa

Faesulae

R. ARNUS

Florentia

Ancona

Volterra

UMBRIA

Arretium

b

Populonia

Vetulonia

Cortona

Iguvium

PICENUM

b

Clusium

Perusia

Volsinii

Asculum

Spoletium

SABINES

Aleria

Volci

Cosa

Falerii

R. TIBER

Alba

Fucens

CORSICA

Tarquinii

Veii

Corfinium

R. LIRIS

SAMNIUM

Rome

Praeneste

LATIUM

Ostia

Arpinum

Luceria

Sipontum

APULIA

Velitrae

Fregellae

Antium

CAMPANIA

Cales

Cannae

Barium

Minturnae

Capua

Beneventum

Olbia

Neapolis

Nola

c

Cumae

MT. VESUVIUS

Brundisium

ISCHIA

Puteoli

Pompeii

Tarentum

CALABRIA

c

Paestum

Metapontum

SARDINIA

LUCANIA

Heraclea

Velia

(Elea)

Laus

Thurii

Caralis

Terina

Croton

BRUTTIUM

N

Hipponium

Lipara

Medma

Messana

Locri

Tyndaris

Rhegium

Panormus

d

Segesta

Himera

Tauromenium

d

Lilybaeum

MT. ETNA

Altitude in metres

Selinus

SICILY

Centuripae

Enna

Catana

Over 1000

Agrigentum

Leontini

Syracuse

200–1000

Utica

Gela

0–200

Carthage

Camarina

0   25   50   75   100 miles

0   50   100   150 km

A
B
C

MAP I. ITALY

I

Early Rome and Italy

❧❧

MICHAEL CRAWFORD

THE central theme of this chapter is the Italian element in Roman history. Already under her early kings, before 509 BC, Rome was beginning to expand at the expense of her immediate neighbours. This process continued under the Republic, so that by the early third century Rome had no serious rivals south of the Po valley, where the Gauls remained an active threat. But Rome had not simply conquered Italy, she had also forced its different peoples to fight for her when required. The military manpower thus acquired was used first to defeat an invader from the east, then to win two wars against Carthage, then to conquer the whole of the Mediterranean basin.

The great wars of conquest after 200 BC form one of the themes of Chapter 2. But the relationship of Rome with Italy remained till the age of Augustus one of the determining factors in her history. The conquest of the Mediterranean basin led to changes in the economy of Italy, which from the end of the second century onwards generated a series of political crises, some of which form the theme of Chapter 4, but some of which are considered here, since they concern the relationship between Rome and Italy. At one level, these crises were resolved by the emergence of Augustus as Emperor; at another level, their resolution involved the final stages of the Romanization of Italy and the Italianization of Rome.

The Peoples of Italy

In attempting to write of the early history of Rome, one is confronted at once by the fact that no account written earlier than the late third century ever existed and that no continuous account written earlier than the age of Augustus now survives. (The Roman tradition of historical writing is discussed in Chapter 10.) Perhaps the gravest weakness in the literary tradition on early Rome, however, is its ruthlessly Romanocentric character. Before Polybius, Greek writers such as Aristotle occasionally became conscious of the existence of Rome, and some of this material is preserved, either directly or as used by later writers. But the

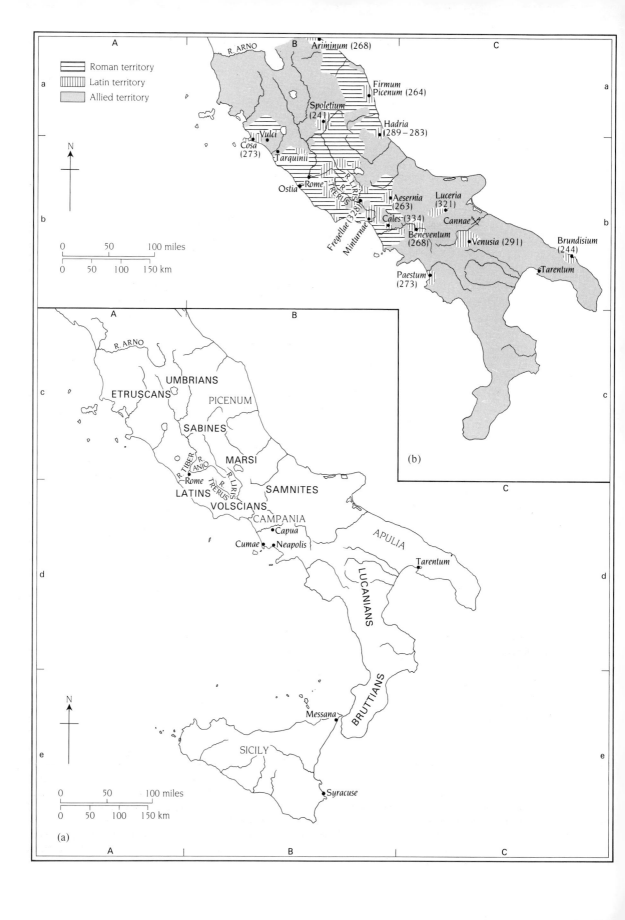

Roman territory
Latin territory
Allied territory

R. ARNO

B Ariminum (268)

A

C

a

Firmum
Picenum (264)

Spoletium
(241)

Hadria
(289–283)

Vulci
Cosa
(273)

Tarquinii

Rome

Ostia

Aesernia
(263)

Luceria
(321)

Cales-(334)

Cannae

Beneventum
(268)

Venusia (291)

Brundisium
(244)

Fregellae (328)

Minturnae

b

Tarentum

Paestum
(273)

c

0   50   100 miles
0   50   100   150 km

N

(b)

A   B   C

R. ARNO

UMBRIANS

ETRUSCANS

PICENUM

SABINES

MARSI

R. TIBER
R. ANIO
Rome
TRERUS
R. LIRIS

SAMNITES

LATINS

VOLSCIANS

CAMPANIA

Capua

Cumae   Neapolis

APULIA

LUCANIANS

Tarentum

c

d

BRUTTIANS

Messana

N

SICILY

e

Syracuse

0   50   100 miles
0   50   100   150 km

(a)

A   B   C

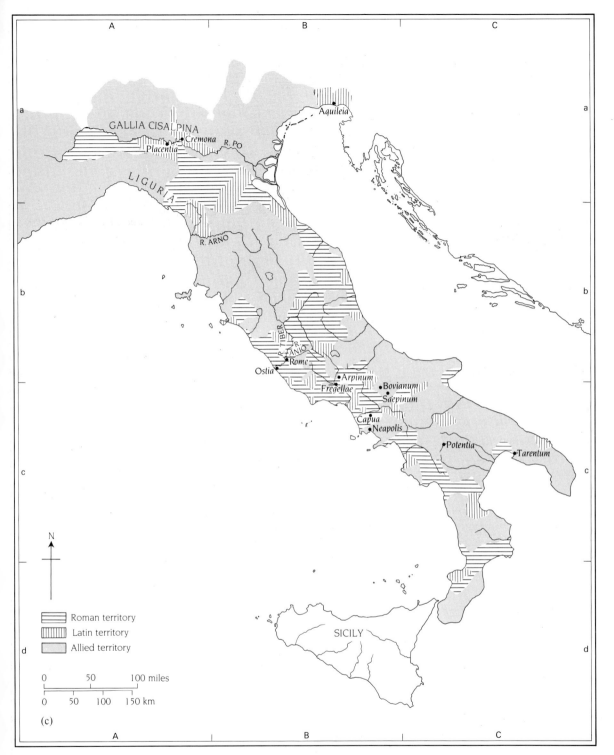

N

```
         Roman territory
         Latin territory
         Allied territory
```

```
0        50        100 miles
0    50   100   150 km
```

(c)

MAP 2. THE GROWTH OF ROME IN ITALY (*Facing bottom*): In the early period of her history, Rome was no more than one city among many in Italy, her territory restricted to the area immediately outside her wall, the Latins one tribe among others competing for mastery. (*Facing top*): By 241 BC not only did Roman territory spread south into Campania and south-east to the Adriatic, but a far-flung network of Latin colonies controlled much of the rest of Italy. (*Above*) By the time of the outbreak of the Social War, Roman and Latin territory had penetrated and isolated allied territory throughout Italy; the rebels of 91 were essentially the inhabitants of the last great block of allied territory in the central and southern Apennines.

ARCHITECTURAL TERRACOTTAS FROM CAPUA. The two antefixes (eaves ornaments) are both datable to the second half of the sixth century BC and illustrate the strong Greek influence at Capua during the period of Etruscan rule. Both the female bust and the gorgon's head with its frame of radiating tongues are related to work in the coastal cities of Cumae and Pithecusae.

histories written by Etruscans and other local traditions have disappeared almost without trace. It is thus extraordinarily hard to grasp the enormous diversity in ethnic formation, social and economic structure, political organization, religion, language, and material culture of the different peoples of Italy. Rome succeeded in conquering and assimilating not only peoples like the neighbouring and related Latins, but peoples who were as like to herself as chalk to cheese.

The most distinctive group within Italy is formed by the Greek colonies of the south, strung out along the coast from Cumae to Tarentum. Founded as self-contained cities from the eighth century onwards, they ensured that territories which they controlled became in every essential respect part of the Greek world. From the fifth century onwards, however, these territories became increasingly subject to attack and conquest by the peoples of the mountainous interior. Bruttians in the toe, Lucanians in the instep, Samnites further north, a variety of small tribes including the Marsi to the east of Rome, were all anxious to control the fertile lands and established wealth of the coast. The consequence, however, was sometimes very far from being a process of take-over and barbarization.

These peoples of the mountainous interior spoke similar languages (labelled as 'Italic' by scholars) and certainly in historical times regarded themselves as related to each other. Further north, the Latins on the coast and the Sabines and Umbrians in the interior spoke languages belonging to the same 'Italic' group, but had a rather different history from the peoples further south. Legend regarded both Sabines and Latins as playing a part in the formation of the Roman state, and the history of the two peoples was always very closely intertwined. But the crucial influence both on Rome and on Umbria was Etruria. Here, from the eighth century onwards, there developed by a combination of internal evolution and outside, largely Greek, influence (the Etruscan language is neither Greek nor Italic) an advanced urban civilization; this civilization was essentially homogeneous, although the different Etruscan cities remained separate political entities.

Umbrian civilization in the early period was on the whole a pale imitation of Etruscan, and the Etruscan script was used to write the Umbrian language; but at Rome something rather different happened. The villages on the hills around what became the Forum linked up into a single city in the course of the sixth century; a similar process probably occurred at about the same time in the case of other Latin communities, such as Gabii or Praeneste. The material culture of archaic Latium has much in common with Etruscan; but Rome never became either culturally or politically a mere Etruscan dependency.

The story of Campania is even more complex. Here the Greek cities of the coast, principally Cumae and Neapolis, coexisted in the late archaic and classical period with an Etruscan principality based at Capua. The arrival of the Samnites in the fifth century did not lead to the destruction of the civilization which had emerged in Campania, although no Etruscan city survived as such and only Neapolis survived as a Greek city. Rather the Samnites became the new ruling class. The incorporation of this area by Rome in the fourth century was probably the most important formative experience in the history of the republic.

The contrast between Latium and Campania on the one hand and Picenum and Apulia on the other hand is instructive. In both areas a population which seems to have had little in common with the group of peoples extending from the Umbrians to the Bruttians underwent a certain development as a result of contact with the Greek world, in the case of Picenum passing Greek traders, in the case of Apulia the Greek city of Tarentum. But Picenum remained materially backward, barely literate, and hardly urbanized; and although Apulia came to possess a number of cities of native origin, the area seems to have run out of steam, culturally and politically, at the same time as did the Greek cities of the south, between the fourth and the third centuries.

Cutting across the ethnic differences there were important differences in economic and social structures. The Greek colonies were of course fully fledged *poleis*, and it is clear that places such as Etruscan Veii or Capua, Latin Rome or Praeneste, were in many respects similar. But much of central Italy remained without cities down to the age of Cicero. Here the pattern was of scattered villages and farmsteads, often within reach of a fortified hill-top, where it was possible to take refuge in time of war, but which was never built up or lived in, indeed which did not even fulfil the political or religious functions of a city. A clear example of this pattern of settlement is provided by Pietrabbondante, where the greatest of the Samnite sanctuaries, which served also as a meeting place, lay on the open hillside below a hill-top fort, both sanctuary and fort being completely detached from any trace of settlement.

One should not suppose, however, that the absence of cities meant the absence of settled agriculture. Naturally, the Greek *poleis* recruited their armies from the free peasant element of their populations, and the same was true of Rome. It must have been true also of the other communities of early Italy. For the Roman conquest of Italy involved a sequence of battles between the Roman heavy-armed infantry and that of their enemies; and the existence of heavy-armed infantry implies the existence of free peasants. This must be true for Etruria, although what our sources talk about is the serf element of the population (one thinks

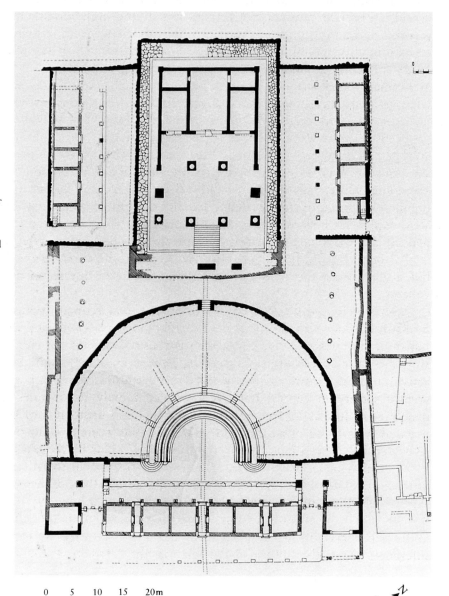

PLAN OF THE SANCTUARY
AT PIETRABBONDANTE
(*c.*100–91 BC). The grandest of
the Samnite religious centres
of the Republican period
testifies to the wealth achieved
by Italian merchants and
bankers shortly before the
Social War. The arrangement
of a temple axially placed
behind and overlooking a
theatre is typical of central-
Italian sanctuaries at this time.

0   5   10   15   20m

of Sparta where the helots supported a hoplite, not an aristocratic society); it must be true of Samnium, although our sources often give the impression that the population consisted of shepherds. And in fact, if one travels in Italy, as opposed to merely looking at a map, one comes time and again on pockets of good land, often at a great height, where arable farming is possible and was certainly practised in antiquity.

That is not to say that there were no shepherds. And the combination of the Italian climate—hot dry summers and cold wet winters—with Italian geography—river and coastal plains and high mountains—meant that sheep farming took on a characteristic form found elsewhere in the Mediterranean. This involved pasture in the lowlands, often on farmland where grain had been harvested, from late summer till spring, and in the high mountains on grassland watered by melting snow for the hot season. Such a system, known as transhumance, might simply involve moving flocks up and down the side of a single valley; or it might involve movement over long distances, from winter pasture in Apulia, for instance, to summer pasture in the central Appennine mountains, when political conditions made this possible.

Early Rome

The city of Rome was formed by the linking of a number of villages; the consequence was that the Forum ceased to be used for burials and became the public open space of the new city. It is interesting that the great Etruscan city of Veii, which was for many years the principal rival of Rome, consisted of a plateau also originally occupied by separate villages. The comparison with Veii is interesting in another respect also; for Rome and Veii were not simply bigger, but orders of magnitude bigger, than any other community in the lower Tiber valley.

Certainly, Rome was a prize worth having, and Roman tradition was unanimous in holding that Rome was originally ruled by kings, and that two of the last three successors of Romulus, eponymous founder of the city and first king, were Etruscan adventurers, Tarquinius Priscus and Tarquinius Superbus. Their arrival in and seizure of power at Rome illustrates an important aspect of archaic society in central Italy as a whole, namely its openness to horizontal penetration. Just as in archaic Greece, tyrants and aristocrats of one *polis* intermarried with those of another, so in archaic Italy there was no rigid conception of citizenship to tie a man to the community of his birth. What is more, openness to horizontal penetration seems to have been true of all social levels; for in the years immediately after the fall of the monarchy at Rome, the Sabine aristocrat Appius Claudius and his retainers were admitted to membership of the community, he at the social level appropriate to his existing standing, they at the level appropriate to theirs. And when from the fourth century we can make reliable inferences about the nature of the relationship between Rome and other Latin communities, we can observe that an essential element of the relationship is freedom of movement between one community and another. It does not much matter whether this element of the relationship is a survival of a period when the Latins were a tribal community or whether it is the product of the diplomatic history of the sixth and fifth centuries. What matters is that it seemed acceptable in the context of archaic central Italian society.

In talking of the social level appropriate to the retainers of Appius Claudius, I have so far left on one side one of the crucial problems of early Roman history. Roman tradition is unanimous in holding that there existed already under the monarchy a group of families known as patricians which succeeded in the early years of the Republic in acquiring both a monopoly of secular and sacred office and almost complete control of the economic resources of the community. Those who were not patricians are presented by our sources as plebeians; this is the system they knew in their own day, but it is likely that the early community of the Romans included social groups which were neither patrician nor plebeian. What is clear is that there emerged with great rapidity a plebeian movement, which created an organization parallel to, and alternative to, that of the patrician state, in the course of what is known to scholars as the struggle of the orders. The plebeian organization set out to break the patrician monopoly of secular and sacred office in the Roman state and to reduce the extent of economic exploitation of the poor by the rich. In the pursuit of its first objective, the plebeian movement was wholly successful; and in the second century Cato could assume that there were no *formal* barriers in the way of any Roman citizen achieving the highest office of the state. We shall see shortly how plebeian economic aspirations were fulfilled.

I have used the term 'Roman citizen'; and the unitary concept of Roman citizenship is the result of the process I have been describing, at the end of which, if one was domiciled at Rome, one was either free and a Roman citizen or a slave. It cannot be too strongly emphasized that the openness of Roman society to plebeian mobility which is the corollary of this fact is *as far as we know* a feature unique to Rome; though it may have applied to other Latin communities, it probably did not apply to Etruscan communities, which continued to display, like some Greek communities, a range of statuses between slave and free.

But there is more. To the astonishment of Greek observers, a slave freed by a Roman citizen became a Roman citizen. And, as we shall see, Roman citizenship came to be available in due course not simply to members of Latin communities, but also to entire Italian peoples. Given the fact that by the time this occurred Rome was the dominant power in central Italy, this too is to be seen as involving the openness of Roman society to penetration from below.

I have talked in general terms of secular and sacred office in early Rome and of the creation of a plebeian organization parallel to that of the Roman state. Under the monarchy, presumably, the kings were in the habit of consulting a body of advisers, the institution which became in due course the Senate of the

Republic. At the end of the sixth century the king holding office for life was replaced by two consuls holding office for one year at a time. There appear in addition in our sources for the early years of the Republic specialist financial officials (quaestors) and a variety of military offices. Probably the sources had no accurate information; but the supposition that there existed already under the monarchy a differentiated administrative structure is entirely reasonable; the method of appointment presumably changed from nomination to election with the arrival of the Republic. There also existed already under the monarchy two different ways in which the Roman people was organized as an assembly, the Comitia Curiata, the people organized in kin groups, and the Comitia Centuriata, the people organized in army units. The growth of the plebeian organization involved the creation of plebeian officials, of whom the most important were the tribunes of the plebs, and of another assembly, the Concilium Plebis or Comitia Tributa, the people organized by *tribus*, areas of domicile.

As the plebs achieved its aim of equality of political and religious rights with the patricians its organization was simply grafted on to that of the Roman state. The tribunes became for all practical purposes officials of the Roman state, the Concilium Plebis became with the name Comitia Tributa one of its assemblies. The plebeian organization, in creating its assembly, also preserved one of the most curious features of existing Roman assemblies, namely voting by groups. No Roman assembly ever reached a decision by a simple majority of those present and voting; each group, however defined, reached a decision in this way and the decision of the assembly was the decision of a majority of the groups.

In the case of the Comitia Centuriata, whose functions included the election of the consuls, the groups were organized in such a way as to facilitate the dominance of the rich. For, at any rate in its developed form in the middle Republic (the fourth and third centuries BC), the Comitia Centuriata contained a number of groups of men who were wealthy enough to serve as cavalrymen, a number of groups with a slightly lower property qualification, and so on. The richer the group, broadly speaking, the fewer men it contained; as a result their influence in the assembly was disproportionately large. Under the monarchy and in the early Republic the system was certainly less complicated, but the underlying principle is likely to have been the same. Of course this principle was not consciously formulated until much later, but its effect was that the wealthy, who paid more in taxes and on whom a greater burden fell in the defence of the community, had a greater say in the making of policy. It must be said, however, that the rich determined the outcome of a vote only if they were united— probably a rare occurrence. Obviously the nature and aims of the plebeian assembly were reflected in the fact that in it no advantage was conferred on the rich in the way in which the groups were formed.

Rome under the monarchy had a relatively differentiated administrative structure, and here too there is continuity of development from the earliest times onwards, as there was in the evolution of the different Roman assemblies.

Throughout their history the Romans showed remarkable willingness to create new offices to take over specific functions from the consuls; thus the praetors came in due course to take over the specialized function of the administration of justice, the censors that of listing roughly every five years the members of the citizen body and the amount of their property liable to taxation, and of renewing the prayers of the Roman people for the favour of the gods. Throughout the Republic, indeed, until the anarchy of its last years, the census was the process whereby men were assigned their place in the community, as soldiers, taxpayers, and voters.

The Roman community did not consist simply of the citizens who belonged to it, together with their female, young, and slave dependents. It also included the gods, and Roman religious structures and history form in a number of very striking ways the mirror image of secular structures and developments.

In the first place, the relative complexity of the administrative structures of the early Republic is paralleled by the diversity of its priesthoods. There were from the start two major colleges, the *pontifices,* with the *pontifex maximus* at their head (and the Vestal Virgins under his general control), and the *augures;* the former were concerned in general terms with sacrifices to the gods (the Vestal Virgins with the sacred hearth of the community), the latter with ascertaining the will of the gods, for instance by observing the flight of birds. And just as the state created new secular offices to meet new needs, so too in the field of religion new priesthoods were created from time to time. Moreover the priesthoods of the Republic were often held by men who also held secular office, with the difference that a priesthood was for life, a consulship for a year at a time. For at Rome religion and politics were not two worlds, but inseparable parts of the same world. One must not suppose that there was something 'wrong' with Roman religion because the world of the gods was involved in the world of political dispute.

Second, the plebeian organization, which developed in parallel to that of the Roman state, created also its own apparatus of cult, centring on the Aventine hill, outside the original boundary of the city of Rome, and involving the cult of Ceres, Liber, and Libera.

Finally, the readiness to innovate in the sphere of religion, which we have observed in the creation of new priesthoods and of a plebeian religious structure, operated also in a much wider context. Perhaps the most conspicuous feature of the religious history of the Republic is the steady importation of new deities, from Etruria, from elsewhere in Italy, or from overseas. The practice is not an indication of dissatisfaction with existing gods, but rather the reverse. Just as her citizens gave Rome her military strength, and Rome sought for most of her history constantly to increase their number, so also, as the gods helped Rome to win battles, the more gods one worshipped the better.

Apart from the creation of the militarily successful patrician-plebeian state, one other consequence of the struggle of the orders requires mention. Among the demands of the lower orders was the demand that the provisions of the Roman civil law be codified and recorded, in order that their interpretation should not be at the fancy of patrician office-holders. The result was the so-called Twelve Tables (traditionally *c*.450 BC), whose provisions still formed the basis of the Roman civil law in the age of Cicero. As a result of citations by writers of this and later periods, we have a fair idea of the original contents of the Twelve Tables; they reveal a society which is still that of a small agricultural community, but one in which the importance of the kin-group is already diminishing and in which there are already substantial numbers of slaves.

The Early Republic

The early years of the Republic were marked by an attempt on the part of the patrician families to achieve a monopoly of secular and sacred office. The fall of the monarchy also meant the partial loss of the superiority which Rome had achieved *vis-à-vis* her immediate neighbours. Furthermore, in the fifth century the Volscians emerged from the upper Liris valley and conquered most of the Trera valley and the coastal plain south of Rome. The first century and a half of the Republic saw first the reassertion of Roman leadership of the other Latin communities and then a long sequence of wars against the southern Etruscan cities, principally Veii (captured and destroyed in 396), and against the Volscians to the south. In the latter struggles Rome and the Latins could usually rely on the Hernicans, who had also suffered from Volscian expansion.

It was undoubtedly a period of economic difficulties which weighed heavily on the lower orders and exacerbated their resentment at patrician exclusiveness. At the same time the fact that some of the lower orders (not the very poor) contributed the manpower on which Roman military success depended conferred bargaining power which they were not slow to use. The erosion of patrician privileges went hand in hand with the steady acquisition of land by conquest, which was used to satisfy the economic aspirations of the lower orders. Such land either formed the territory of a new community, or *colonia*, possessing local self-government, or provided isolated plots of land for settlers not organized as a group. The Gallic sack of Rome in 390, traumatic though it must have been at the time, had little effect either on internal developments at Rome or on the process of conquest. The land acquired as a result of the capture of Veii was distributed to the poor at Rome, resulting in the creation of an enormous new reserve of peasant soldiers. By the middle of the fourth century Rome dominated south Etruria, no longer had anything to fear from incursions by tribes in the upper Anio valley, and was poised on the northern edge of Campania.

The crucial moment in the history of the Roman conquest of Italy came in 338. Most of the Latin communities around Rome, viewing her growing preponderance with alarm, attempted to reassert their independence. They were rapidly defeated and all, except the largest and most distant, incorporated in the

Roman citizen body. From this time on, the original cities of Latium and the *coloniae* founded by them in association with Rome ceased individually or as a group to have any destiny separate from that of Rome. But Rome made the momentous decision to continue to found new communities with the status of Latin cities. Certainly later, and probably by now, Latin status *vis-à-vis* Rome and other Latin communities was defined essentially as involving rights of intermarriage, the enforceability of contractual obligations, and the right to change domicile, with the acquisition of the citizenship appropriate to the new domicile. The first of the Latin *coloniae* founded after 338 was Cales in northern Campania, founded in 334. The primary function of this and later *coloniae* was defensive, to hold down conquered territory or guard Roman territory against invasion. The foundation of a *colonia* was one way in which land acquired by conquest was used to relieve the poverty of the lower orders in Roman (and Latin) society; but *coloniae* of Latin status were also powerful factors making for the Romanization of Italy. They possessed from the outset constitutions modelled on that of Rome, and by their mere presence in an area previously without significant contact with Rome served to spread the Roman model of government. Recent archaeological evidence from Cosa (founded 273) suggests very strongly that Rome exported to the Latin *coloniae* her peculiar practice of voting in groups. But there is an even more important side to the foundation of Latin *coloniae*; it seems that membership was not limited to those who were already citizens of Rome or a Latin community, but that any Italian ally was eligible. The Latin *coloniae* thus served to elevate large numbers of Italians to a status close to that of Roman citizenship. Neither this fact, however, nor the fact that Latin *coloniae* provided a context in which land was assigned to the poor meant that the *coloniae* were egalitarian or democratic foundations. A significant part of the population of Latin *coloniae* was more richly endowed with land than the rest, to provide a social élite and a governing class.

Both before and after 338 Rome also founded a number of *coloniae*, the members of which possessed Roman citizenship. These *coloniae* tended when founded to be smaller than *coloniae* of Latin status and to have guard duties of a very limited and precise nature, for instance at Ostia at the mouth of the Tiber or at Minturnae at the mouth of the Liris. But those possessed of Roman or Latin citizenship were eligible to take part in the settlements and Roman *coloniae* provided an avenue, even if not a very important one, whereby men whose families were of Italian origin could achieve Roman citizenship without moving to Rome.

Far more important as a means of creating new Roman citizens was the incorporation of entire Italian communities as citizens without the vote. Such communities possessed all the other rights of Roman citizens, primarily legal and social, and were also bound to perform all the duties of citizens, to pay taxes, and to fight. We do not know whether the act of conferring citizenship without the vote (perhaps sometimes withheld for reasons of distance or linguistic incompatibility) was intended as a reward or as a means of subjection, and perhaps it does not much matter. Large parts of Italy *became* Roman in this way, however, conspicuously the great Graeco-Etrusco-Samnite city of Capua, and also Arpinum, later the birthplace of C. Marius and of Cicero. The details of the process whereby Capua and indeed much of Campania were in the middle of the fourth century incorporated in the Roman state are obscure and controversial. What matters is that what was by then the richest and most developed area of Italy entered the Roman sphere (below, pp. 24 f.).

The Unification of Italy

We have seen that there were a number of ways in which men belonging to different Italian communities, whether conquered or not, might come to acquire Roman citizenship or Latin status. But there are other aspects of the process whereby Rome succeeded not simply in conquering Italy, but also in moulding it into a single world. In the foundation of Latin *coloniae* Rome exported her own hierarchical pattern for the organization of society. The same general approach was extended to her dealings with the Italian allies. Systematically Rome sought out and privileged their upper classes; she supported them in a crisis, if they were faced with catastrophe from without or revolution from within; in normal times relations between Rome and any Italian community were conducted by means of the personal links between the upper orders of the two cities, based on a close community of interest and involving frequent contact, including intermarriage.

Given this network of personal relationships, it is not surprising that Rome found little difficulty in seeing that the principal demand she made on the communities of Italy was fulfilled. The demand was for troops, a fact which sets Rome apart from most other ancient empires and helps to explain the nature of Roman imperialism.

Most ancient empires demanded tribute from their subjects; superiority was symbolized by the demand, and its fulfilment provided tangible material rewards for having achieved rule over others. Rome, clearly at a very early stage, simply extended to other Italian peoples the demand for manpower which she made on her own citizen body. The result was that the only way in which she could symbolize the power she had over the Volscians or the Etruscans was by demanding troops and the only way in which she could derive any benefit was by using the troops to acquire booty, land, and yet more power. It should not be supposed, however, that the demand for troops necessarily fell on unwilling ears. For although Rome was less generous in distributing booty or land to her allies than she was to her own citizens, she did share some of the ever increasing rewards of victory with them.

The Roman conquest of Italy was also accompanied by a striking physical expression of the fact of a Roman presence. Prior to its distribution, whether as

CENTURIATION IN THE PO VALLEY. The modern road and field system in this air photograph taken in 1945 clearly reveals its origins in the Roman land-divisions of the second century BC. Large squares with sides of 20 *actus* (2,400 Roman feet = 710 metres) and an area of 200 *jugera* are subdivided into narrow strip-fields.

isolated lots or in the territory of a *colonia*, conquered land was at any rate from the late fourth century onwards measured and marked out by an elaborate process eventually known as *centuriatio*. Initially, perhaps from 334 onwards, land was divided into strips 10 *actus* wide (1 actus = *c.* 35.5 m.); the lines of division were known as *decumani*. In due course a full rectangular grid was marked out; the transverse lines of division were known as *kardines*. Just as in the simpler system the *decumani* were sometimes more or less than 10 *actus* apart, so in the developed system a grid of 20 x 20 *actus* was the norm, but not universal. When such a grid was used, the result was 200 *jugera*, or a *centuria*, within each square.

But this elaborate process was not used merely for measuring the land; the lines of the grid were marked out by roads and ditches which left an indelible mark on the countryside; they patterned and structured its use for centuries, if not millennia, and survive in many areas to this day, despite industrial development and mechanized farming.

On one hand, then, there was an almost violent expression of Roman control of the land; but on the other hand, the pattern of Roman-organized colonization in Italy facilitated the acquisition of Latin, or eventually Roman, citizenship by Italians; it also permitted the presence and assimilation of existing ethnic elements. Thus the foundation of the Latin colony of Ariminum (in 268) in what had been Umbrian territory did not have an adverse effect on the major pre-Roman sanctuary of the area, outside the walls of the *colonia*; rather, as the offerings show, the sanctuary continued to be central to the life of the *colonia*, as it had been to that of the area before its foundation. At the other end of Italy, early inscriptions of the colony of Luceria (founded 314), on the borders of Samnite, Lucanian, and Apulian territory, show a mixed Latin-based dialect, which presupposes a mixed population.

A second-century inscription from Aesernia in Samnium (founded 263) shows a group of 'Samnites incolae', resident Samnites, clearly not citizens, but harmoniously established, going about their business and with their own form of corporate organization. And we know from literary sources that a large number of Samnites and Paelignians migrated to Fregellae in the early second century; we have no idea whether they became citizens, but their presence was clearly acceptable.

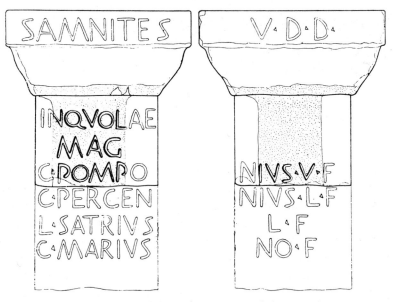

INSCRIPTION FROM AESERNIA (ISERNIA) (second century BC): dedication of a statuette to Venus by the *Samnites inquolae* (resident Samnites), evidently a corporate organization of the native Samnite population within this Latin colony. Four *magistri* (officers) of the body are named. The statuette-base (front at the left, back at the right) has been reconstructed on the basis of a pre-war drawing.

These examples of coexistence and assimilation come from those parts of Italy where the population may be defined as Italic, in general terms ethnically and linguistically close to the Latins. There were two areas of Italy where the story was rather different, Etruria and Gallia Cisalpina. In each case, a distinctive and remarkable culture was eventually submerged without trace, though for rather different reasons. In the case of Gallia Cisalpina, memories of the Gallic sack of Rome in 390 and the role played by his Gallic allies in Hannibal's invasion of Italy largely explain the brutality of the Roman conquest of the area. The first steps were taken already in the third century with the virtual destruction of the Senones, and the policy continued in the second century (below, pp. 30 f.). In Etruria the effect of the early wars in the fifth and fourth centuries had been to create a solid swathe of Roman or Latin territory in the south, leaving a few barely viable Etruscan enclaves, such as Tarquinii or Vulci. In the north, Etruscan territory and culture remained intact, but in an increasingly isolated backwater.

Rome and the Greek Cities

In the sixth century, Greek culture had been mediated to Rome by Etruria. In the fourth century, with the absorption of Campania, Rome entered into close and direct contact with the Greek world, contact that was to increase in intensity and significance over the next three centuries. The Roman link with Campania

STONE SARCOPHAGUS OF L. CORNELIUS SCIPIO BARBATUS (consul in 298 BC). The Scipios, unlike most republican families, favoured inhumation rather than cremation, and a series of inscribed sarcophagi was found in their family tomb on the Via Appia outside Rome. This is the earliest and the best preserved, remarkable for its hellenizing architectural decoration.

DETAIL OF THE ALEXANDER MOSAIC (2nd century BC). The Persian king Darius, in his chariot, looks back in consternation as the onslaught of the Macedonians forces his charioteer to turn in flight.

HELLENISTIC EARRINGS. The smaller example (second or first century BC) is decorated with a cock coated with enamel; the larger one from Cyme (third century BC) carries a series of half-open buds suspended from chains.

INTERIOR OF THE TAZZA FARNESE (first century BC). This dish, carved from sardonyx, and possibly commissioned by Cleopatra, presents an allegory of the fertility of Egypt under the protection of Isis, Horus, and Osiris-Sarapis.

DISH IN GENUCILIA WARE, Rome's answer to Greek-style painted pottery (fourth century BC). Both the female head wearing a diadem and the wave pattern round the rim are favourite motifs of the Genucilia potters.

was both symbolized and strengthened by the building of the Via Appia from Rome to Capua in 312, by Ap. Claudius Caecus as censor. It is likely that it was in this context that the first Roman silver coinage was produced, on the Greek model. The late fourth and early third centuries, indeed, saw the beginning of the rapid Hellenization of Rome. It was in this period that Rome absorbed from the Greek world an interest in the expression of the ideology of victory, a phenomenon which was not the least of the legacies of Alexander the Great. The consequence at Rome was the introduction of new cults of gods of war, gods of victory, Victory herself. It was in this period also that the cult of Hercules, heavily dependent on Greek models, became widespread in the Roman world, evidenced both by the institution by the state of new cults and by the upsurge in humble offerings to the new hero. At the same time a Greek influence on the material culture of the republic became even more apparent. At one level there is the sarcophagus of L. Cornelius Scipio Barbatus, found in the tomb of the Scipios on the Via Appia, which used Greek architectural motifs in its decoration.

At another level, Rome began to produce around 380 her own local pottery, imitated from South-Italian or Etruscan red-figure pottery, known as Genucilia ware, and then in the early third century a fine black-slip pottery, imitative of Greek metal ware.

The late fourth century saw also the development by Rome of increasingly complex administrative structures, going beyond the simple adoption of coinage on the Greek model. It was certainly in this period that there evolved the developed structure of five census classes, each with different fiscal and military responsibilities.

The Defence of Italy and the First War against Carthage

The last serious wars fought by Rome against an Italian people were the wars against the Samnites. These were effectively over by 295, when the Samnites were defeated at Sentinum in northern Italy, along with Umbrian, Etruscan, and Gallic allies; for the Umbrian and Etruscan cities which remained independent had decided to make one last attempt to assert their freedom, while some of the Gallic tribes of the Po valley had decided to attempt to repeat the success of 390.

Fifteen years later the Romans met their first invasion from overseas. We have already seen that the Greek cities of the south were faced from the fifth century onwards by the territorial and political ambitions of their 'barbaric' neighbours (above, pp. 12 f.). Tarentum declined to compromise, as did Cumae or Posidonia, which had accepted the presence of a partially Samnite or Lucanian élite. Instead, she called to her aid a succession of Greek mercenary commanders. The last of

ROMAN SILVER COIN (DIDRACHM) OF THE PYRRHIC WAR (275–270 BC). On the obverse the head of Apollo wearing a laurel-wreath; on the reverse a horse galloping to the right beneath a sixteen-pointed star. By the depiction of Apollo, the Greek god who had lately repulsed the Gauls from Delphi, Rome promotes itself as the champion of civilization against the forces of barbarism.

these was Pyrrhus, king of Epirus, who was summoned in 280 to deal not with Tarentum's Lucanian neighbours, but with the Romans, who were now the principal threat to the independence of Tarentum.

It should be remarked that Tarentine opposition to Rome was by no means typical of the reaction of the Greek *poleis* of the south. Many welcomed the protection and alliance of Rome, both now and later. The obverse type of the issue of silver coins which Rome struck during the war against Pyrrhus should be seen as quite deliberately placing Rome on the side of civilization in the fight against barbarism. The type in question is a head of Apollo, the god who had become in 279 the symbol throughout the Greek world of the victory of the civilized over the barbarous, by reason of his defence of Delphi against a band of marauding Gauls. Rome too, as we have seen, had defeated a similar band, in 295, along with her other enemies.

Pyrrhus succeeded initially in winning a number of costly victories over the armies of Rome (hence the phrase 'Pyrrhic victory'). But he was in due course defeated at Beneventum and returned across the Adriatic. It was undoubtedly his defeat at the hands of Rome that caused the Greek historian, Timaeus of Tauromenium, writing in exile at Athens, to take notice of the new power in the West.

Shortly afterwards, this new power found itself at war with the other power in the West, Carthage, longer established as such and much better known in the Greek world as a result of the long series of bloody wars which she had fought with the Greeks in Sicily.

The earlier relations of Carthage with Rome had been pacific, and the two states had indeed made three treaties with each other, agreeing not to interfere in their respective spheres of interest. The treaties are preserved by Polybius. The earliest, belonging to the first year of the Republic, is the earliest Roman document known in something like its entirety.

In addition to the factors making for Roman expansion which we have already considered, others are evidenced by the outbreak of the First Punic War. Polybius reports that the Senate did not vote for action, but that the assembly did, and there is no doubt that sheer greed played a large part in swaying opinion. The action that led to war was to send an army to protect Messana, in the hands of a band of Italian mercenaries, against Hiero of Syracuse, despite the fact that the protection of Carthage had already been invoked. The action was in character; neither the Roman aristocracy nor the Roman state as a whole could ever resist the temptation to intervene when the chance arose.

The war lasted from 264 to 241 and was in effect a war for the control of Sicily, since Hiero of Syracuse decided at an early stage in the proceedings to throw in his lot with the Romans. Roman persistence won through, and Roman chicanery added Sardinia to the prize. Much is obscure about the way in which Rome set about organizing her new acquisitions, but two points are worth making. In the first place, it is clear that the Italian model of a treaty which imposed on the defeated community the obligation to provide manpower at the behest of Rome was not applied; both Sicily and Sardinia were regarded as territories to be ruled and taxed. In the second place, a group of recently discovered inscriptions from Entella in western Sicily reveal at least one Italian in a semi-official position of influence under Roman auspices during the First Punic War, and probably profiting from the position.

Politics in the Middle Republic

Leadership in the wars that Rome fought in the fourth and third centuries was provided by the mixed patrician–plebeian nobility which had emerged as a result of the resolution of the struggle of the orders. Holders of the consulship or other high office and their descendants came to be regarded as forming the nobility under the new dispensation. It was this group that constituted the Senate in the traditional age of senatorial domination.

It must be said that our ignorance of how politics worked in this society is almost total. The problem arises at at least two levels, within the senatorial élite and between the élite and the population as a whole. Although what our sources tell us about this period, the period of the middle Republic, is no doubt heavily tinged with romanticism, it seems reasonable to suppose that both the élite and society as a whole were united to an extent that was clearly not true in the age of Cicero.

Obviously there was competition within the élite for office, power, and influence. We possess from the third century one early grave monument, that of L. Cornelius Scipio Barbatus (above, p. 24; the inscription is later than the sarcophagus) and part of the *elogium* pronounced at the death of L. Caecilius Metellus, consul in 251. Neither the inscription of Barbatus nor the *elogium* on Metellus makes sense except in the context of a competitive aristocracy. Clearly there were moments of tension, as when an ancestor of Sulla (below, pp. 35 f., 81 ff.) was expelled from the Senate for excessive display of wealth. But it is wildly unlikely that the fourth and third centuries were characterized by the bitterness and the unscrupulousness which marked political conflict in the age of Cicero. The consul of 251 was described as possessing great wealth, honourably acquired. Only the first part of this description could have been applied to Caesar.

When there was disagreement within the élite over policy, we simply do not know how it was resolved. It is, however, worth remarking that one modern theory, according to which entire *gentes* such as the Cornelii or the Caecilii operated as single entities, building stable alliances with other *gentes*, is almost certainly fantasy. The theory does not work for any period where we have first-hand evidence, and it is paradoxical to apply it when there is no such evidence; and men such as Barbatus and Metellus emerge as larger-than-life *individuals*, whose ambitions sometimes actually played a part in pushing Rome into war.

We are even more in the dark when it comes to understanding the nature of the relationship between the élite and the population as a whole. Again, of course, there was controversy, over matters which were to be characteristic causes of controversy in the second and first centuries; thus there was argument in 290 over the relative balance to be achieved in the use of conquered land in Sabinum between its distribution to the poor and its sale to the rich; and Polybius records a controversy aroused in 232 by the proposal to distribute land in Picenum and the south-east of the Po valley. But Roman history in the fourth and third centuries is incomprehensible except on the assumption that the lower orders were largely satisfied with the leadership of the nobility and with the rewards to be won under their command.

Conventionally *clientela*, a traditional, often inherited relationship of dependence of one man on another, is regarded as the principal integrating factor in Roman society of the middle Republic. But other factors were surely at work. Although Rome, as we shall see in a moment, was already in the third century large in comparison with most ancient states, it was probably still a society where contact between different social levels was relatively easy; the number of enterprises, such as war and colonization, in which élite and people shared, ensured that the two remained relatively closely integrated. And now, as later, the élite could and did justify its actions to the population as a whole in terms of shared values; these values involved, among other things, the belief that the approval of the gods was necessary and that with it Rome could not fail.

The third century was not only, as Polybius observed, the high point in the development of the Roman body politic; it also marked the acme of the system of Italian alliances which Rome had built up, before the strains began to show. The last great Gallic invasion which Italy had to face was that of 225, and it is in the context of the preparations against it that Polybius describes the manpower resources available to Rome. To do so he drew on the account given by the first Roman historian, Q. Fabius Pictor, himself a witness of the events of 225. Although the list in Polybius contains some obscurities in detail, it fits with what else is known of Roman citizen numbers in this period and suggests that the Roman and Italian pool of men on which Rome could draw was of the order of 6–7 million.

Hannibal's Invasion: The Second Punic War

The existence of such a reserve enabled Rome to withstand the shock of Hannibal's invasion of Italy in 218. This invasion, the resources for which were provided by the Carthaginian acquisition of an empire in Spain, was a deliberate attempt to reverse the verdict of the First Punic War. Between 218 and 216, Hannibal, a brilliant general, was able to inflict a series of crushing and bloody defeats on the Roman armies sent to face him, culminating in the battle of Cannae in 216, and was able to detach a number of Rome's allies, notably Capua;

at the same time, Carthage attempted to recover Sicily and in due course brought Syracuse over to her side.

But Rome was always able to field new armies to replace those which were lost, and most of her Italian allies never regarded Italy without Rome or Italy under Carthage as serious alternatives to the system with which they had become familiar. Rome first succeeded in confining Hannibal to Bruttium, while simultaneously recovering Sicily, seizing Spain, and fighting against Macedonia, which had allied with Carthage in 215 after the battle of Cannae. In due course the war was carried over to Africa; Hannibal was recalled from Italy in 203, to be defeated at the battle of Zama in 202; Carthage sued for peace and the attempt to dispute Roman hegemony in the western Mediterranean was over.

Hannibal's Legacy

What were the effects on Italy of fifteen years of warfare on Italian soil? It has been argued that the devastation of much of Italy by Hannibal led to the deracination of many Roman and Italian peasant soldiers and a shift to large farming enterprises owned by the élite and run by slave labour; whence the problems which Ti. Gracchus set out to resolve two generations later (below, pp. 33 f.). The argument is hard to maintain. Rome not only continued to field large armies of peasant soldiers throughout the Second Punic War, but undertook after it was over both the final conquest of the Po valley and a series of wars overseas (below, ch. 2).

For those Italian communities that had allied with Hannibal, however, the consequences of his defeat were grave. The Bruttii were deprived of any form of communal institutions and were not even allowed a role in the armies levied by Rome, except as servants. They and many other communities lost land, a fact which lies behind some of the economic developments of the second century. Those communities which continued to provide troops for Rome were forced to provide disproportionately large contingents. In effect, if not in theory, second-century Italy was a single state ruled by Rome, with local government in the hands of its scattered communities, not a mosaic of independent states bound together by a network of alliances.

The principal Roman military effort in Italy after 201 was directed to the definitive conquest of the Po valley. The process had begun after the defeat of the Gallic invasion of Italy in 225, with the foundation in 218 of the *coloniae* of Cremona and Placentia. Rome picked up after the Second Punic War where she had left off, and the next generation saw both the military subjugation of the area and the settlement, either in *coloniae* or in scattered plots, of tens of thousands of Romans and Italians, from Placentia in the west to Aquileia in the east. Of the different Gallic peoples, the Boii simply ceased to exist, as had the Senones earlier. The Cenomani and Insubres survived, albeit with their freedom gone.

Both the nature of the landscape and the unfolding of the Roman conquest help to explain why Gallia Cisalpina is the area characterized more than any other by Roman centuriation (above, p. 22). As they moved across the largest plain in Italy, the Romans felt themselves bound by no existing political, social, economic, or even geographical pattern. A *tabula rasa*, the Po valley was imprinted for ever with the marks of the Roman presence, and absorbed over a whole generation much of the military and colonizing energy of the Roman people, energy which appears undiminished by the experience of the Second Punic War.

Meanwhile, however, the overseas wars which followed the Second Punic War were transforming the social and economic fabric of Italy. These wars had two consequences which concern us here. They led on the one hand to a steady professionalization of the Roman and Italian soldier. Strictly speaking, it is inappropriate to talk of such a thing as the Roman army at this date, quite apart from the fact that an army levied to fight for Rome consisted of a large number of notionally independent contingents. But whereas down to 201 it had been normal for a man to fight in the spare time left over from farming, it became increasingly common after 200 for men to serve abroad for years on end.

At the same time, the wealth of the Mediterranean was pouring into Italy, partly in the form of booty, partly in the form of payments exacted from defeated enemies. Some of this wealth was distributed to the lower orders on the occasion of the triumph celebrated at the conclusion of a successful campaign, but much ended up in the hands of the élite. Further wealth was acquired in the course of the administration of overseas territories or by lending money at exorbitant rates of interest to foreign communities.

What happened to all this money? Some of it, both that which remained under the control of the community and that which had passed into private hands, was expended on the erection of public, as well as private, buildings in Rome and Italy. Rome showed the way, with projects such as the linking of the temples (still visible) in the Largo Argentina into a single monumental complex. Similar projects, on a scale hitherto undreamt of, were carried out elsewhere in Italy. Thus the Latin *colonia* of Fregellae possessed before its revolt and destruction in 125-124 a gigantic sanctuary of Aesculapius—temple, portico on three sides, stone treasure chest, altar, water-supply, monumental access ramp.

Obviously, in so far as free labour was used in the execution of such projects, the lower orders benefited economically. And indeed the emergence of urban markets with considerable spending power is a necessary hypothesis to explain another important second-century development. For it seems clear that much of the new wealth of the Roman and Italian élite was invested in land, in large farming enterprises run by slave labour. These were essentially of two types, market gardens, olive groves, or vineyards on the one hand, transhumant sheep farming on the other. Both types of enterprise created a demand for land in central Italy, to the detriment of the peasant farmer, whose plot might be requested in purchase or sometimes even seized and whose access to common land

REMAINS OF REPUBLICAN TEMPLES IN LARGO ARGENTINA in Rome. Temple C (entrance stairway in the left foreground) is the earliest, probably going back to the early third century BC and dedicated to the Italic deity Feronia. Temple A (standing columns at the rear) is the next oldest, probably dedicated to Juturna in 241 BC. The circular temple B, in the middle, is thought to be that of Fortuna Huiusce Diei (Fortune of the Present Day), inaugurated in 101 BC soon after the unification of the temples into a single monumental complex.

on which he depended might be rendered more difficult. In concentrating central-Italian land in its hands, the Roman and Italian élite was to a certain extent acting against its own interests, since it needed to ensure a steady supply of men for the legions in order to organize its wars of conquest overseas. But men do not always act wholly rationally.

The Age of the Gracchi

A pattern seems to have emerged in the second century whereby peasant soldiers in central Italy surrendered their land and their rights to common land, from which they had in any case become detached in the course of long service overseas, and went to settle in the Po valley; their sons provided the next generation of soldiers. But with the pacification of that area, the great days of colonization came to an end, and there seems to have followed in the generation before 133 a steady build up of men without land of their own and without hope of land to go to. What Ti. Gracchus attempted to do was to reverse the trend in central Italy and increase the number of peasants at the expense of large-scale farming enterprises.

Elected tribune for 133 BC, he introduced a land bill limiting the size of holdings of public land, and redistributing the surplus to the people. The Senate retaliated by putting up another tribune, M. Octavius, to veto the proposal, and Tiberius was finally forced to procure his fellow tribune's deposition from the people. He further antagonized the Senate by seeking to interfere in the arrangements for the kingdom of Pergamum, left by will to the Roman people: the administration of foreign affairs was traditionally a prerogative of the Senate. Finally, in the disturbances caused by his attempt to secure re-election to the tribunate for a second term, he was murdered together with 300 of his supporters.

Perhaps the principal consequence of the attempts at reform in this period was the inextricable entangling of Italian with Roman politics. But there is a further process which must be considered before we can turn to this particular problem, the progressive Romanization of Italy. The golden age of Roman road-building is the generation or so before Ti. Gracchus; as a result the whole of Italy became linked together, both actually and symbolically, to a far greater extent than ever before.

Italy also became in the years after the Second Punic War a monetary and economic unity. Down to the end of that war there circulated in the different areas large numbers of coins produced by Italian communities other than Rome; after the end of the war few communities felt themselves sufficiently independent of Rome to produce coinage for themselves, and earlier issues rapidly disappeared from circulation. It was soldiers returning from service with the armies of Rome who carried Roman coinage into the remote backwaters of the Appennines. And it was the developing market economy of Italy in response to the wealth flowing in from the East that took the monetary and economic unity of Italy a stage further. Down to the middle of the second century there were some inequalities in the pattern of circulation of Roman coins in Italy, both in terms of types and in terms of quantity. These inequalities then disappeared, clearly a sign of the developing process of exchange of money for goods.

The armies of Rome were important in another respect also, as a powerful factor for linguistic unity. During and after the Second Punic War men were away from home for much longer than before, in an essentially Latin-speaking environment. Etruscan survived, as did the languages of Samnium and Lucania, but the rest were in the process of disappearing in the period before Ti. Gracchus.

The principal problem to be faced in dealing with Gracchus' legislation is that we simply do not know whether, let alone to what extent, it was intended to revive peasant farming, not only in Roman, but also in Italian communities in central Italy, although it must be the case that these were suffering from the same developments.

What is clear, however, is that Ti. Gracchus' attempt to resume public land in the hands of the rich in order to distribute it to the poor adversely affected the interests of Italian élites as well as those of the Roman élite. It was not long before the idea was floated of giving Roman citizenship to some or all Italians, partly to compensate them for reduced access to Roman public land, partly to give them a say in the making of policy in this sphere. Once floated, the idea would not go away, though it was not till 91 that the Italian demand for Roman citizenship exploded into war.

Meanwhile politics at Rome between 133 and 91 were marked by a series of attempts, analogous to that of Ti. Gracchus, to win for the Roman poor a larger share in the rewards of the Empire which as soldiers they had helped to win, whether those rewards were in the form of land or subsidized corn. The attempts often ended, as had that of Ti. Gracchus, in the violent death of their authors. Two must be mentioned specifically, the programme devised by Tiberius' brother C. Gracchus, in 123–122, which aimed not simply to improve the material lot of the poor, but also to shift the balance of power within the Roman state; and the career of L. Appuleius Saturninus, who in 103 and 100 set out, in alliance with the conqueror of Jugurtha of Numidia and of the Cimbri and the Teutones, C. Marius, to provide for the need of his veterans for land. The alliance between tribune of the plebs and general was one fraught with danger for the future.

The Division of the Spoils

One reason why the political argument at Rome over the division of the spoils of empire became so bitter in the last generation of the second century was precisely because these were becoming ever richer. In 133 the last king of Pergamum had actually left his kingdom to the Romans; the Roman acquisition of what became the province of Asia falls in the middle of the second great period of Roman acquisition of territory (not to be confused with acquisition of power), between Africa and Achaea in 146 and Provence in 121. The result was a rapid rise in the numbers of Romans and Italians living overseas, as tax-collectors, money-lenders, and slave-traders. Their activities happen to be principally documented in the East, and the greatest wealth was no doubt to be acquired there; but the process clearly went on in the West as well. What is important in this context is that Italians abroad were treated as equals with Romans by the people with whom they dealt; the lack of Roman citizenship was no doubt felt ever more acutely.

Other factors deserve a mention. There certainly took place in this period some genuine urbanization, as opposed to the embellishment of existing centres. For instance, at Bovianum and Saepinum, in central Samnium, where previously there had been scattered villages or farms and hill-forts as places of refuge, urban growth began on the plains below the hill-forts. At Monte Vairano, the hill-fort itself began to be permanently occupied. The Roman urban model of society was spreading. All these developments certainly made Italian communities feel even more acutely their formal inferiority and their lack of control over Roman policy. Romans sometimes behaved high-handedly to members of local élites. And the career of C. Marius—six times consul between 107 and 100, victor over Jugurtha, saviour of Rome from the Cimbri and Teutones—showed what could be achieved by an aristocrat from an Italian community which had been enfranchised.

At the same time, it is certain that the actual grievances of the allies were increasing, as Rome sought to avoid the consequences of her own lack of peasant soldiers by shifting ever more of the military burden on to her Italian allies. It is remarkable in these years how difficult Rome found it to defeat the relatively minor figure of Jugurtha of Numidia and how vulnerable she was to the Cimbri and Teutones. It was luck that brought them no nearer Rome than the Po valley. And one may wonder whether either Jugurtha or they would have been defeated without the skill of C. Marius.

Citizenship for Italy

By 91, it was no longer possible to evade the issue of granting Roman citizenship to the Italians, and when M. Livius Drusus' proposal to do so failed, half of Italy rose in revolt (the so-called Social War). Rome disarmed the revolt by agreeing to grant what she had at first refused and was able with the help of those who remained loyal to subdue the rebels who held out (for what, it is not clear).

The result was that the whole of peninsular Italy together with existing *coloniae* in the Po valley was organized into communities of Roman citizens. We are ignorant of the details of the process, but it was largely complete by 83. For it was in that year that L. Cornelius Sulla, who had in 88 fought a brief civil war in order to secure the command of the Roman armies in the East, returned to

Italy. He was ruthless with particular communities or peoples which opposed him, but made no attempt to undo the enfranchisement or organization of Italy as a whole. In 89 the Po valley had been placed on the road to assimilation with peninsular Italy; Cn. Pompeius Strabo, the father of Magnus, gave the status of a Latin *colonia* to those communities in the Po valley and Liguria which were not already either Roman or Latin. Full Roman citizenship was delayed for more than a generation, but was granted by Caesar.

I have already drawn attention to the spread of the urban model in Italy. But what happened after the enfranchisement of Italy was of a rather different kind. Amidst all our ignorance, it is clear that new Roman communities were equipped with relatively homogeneous constitutions, appropriate to urban societies. Rome in fact found it difficult to think other than in terms of urban centres when dealing with other communities. The enfranchisement of Italy thus provided, with the creation of new Roman communities, a powerful spur to the development of urban centres. This in itself is likely to have been in turn a factor making for the Romanization of Italy.

There are at least two levels at which the phenomenon of Romanization needs to be considered. It is probably easiest to begin with the level of the élite. The Roman system had always been characterized by a relatively high degree of élite mobility. It was naturally rare for a man, none of whose family had ever held office, to reach the consulship, as did C. Marius and Cicero. But the ascent of a family to the consulship over several generations was a common enough phenomenon; and a man who ennobled himself and his descendants by being the first of his family to achieve the consulship or other high office was known as a *novus homo*, new man. Families from newly enfranchised communities, throughout the history of the republic, waited perhaps for a generation and could then begin their ascent to high office. The story was no different with the mass enfranchisement of Italy after 91–89; by the time of Augustus, the Roman Senate was full of members of the élites of recently enfranchised communities, many of whose descendants went on to hold the consulship. The avenues of advancement were those which had always applied, friendship with those already in positions of power, wealth, oratorical skill, military expertise (see Ch. 5 for Italian authors of the late Republic).

Much more difficult to assess is the Romanization of the population of Italy as a whole; we must admit that we can know nothing of the culture of an illiterate farm labourer, too poor even to be drafted into the armies of Rome. All our knowledge relates, if not to the élite, at least to those close to it. Given this limitation, there are four indicators worth considering of the survival or submergence of distinctive local cultures in Italy: language, religious practices, family structures, and funeral rites. The last, if valid, is particularly useful, since there is substantial archaeological evidence.

The evidence of language is striking. Northern Etruria remained substantially untouched by Roman influence down to 91. It is also an area where inscriptions in Latin down to the same date are conspicuous by their absence. In the generation after Sulla, however, bilingual inscriptions make their appearance, and within the lifetime of Cicero Etruscan had virtually disappeared. The case of Samnium is harder to assess, since the destruction wrought by Sulla in 82–81 means that there was little in the way of urban life till Caesar. Inscriptions in the local language, one of the varieties of what is known to modern scholars as Oscan, certainly disappear; but the argument from silence is dangerous. Further south in Lucania, however, the same pattern occurs, without any reason to suppose that Sulla was responsible; and indeed inscriptions in Oscan are here replaced by inscriptions in Latin. It is worth citing the evidence provided by the recent excavations at Rossano di Vaglio; here a rural Lucanian sanctuary was absorbed after Sulla into the administrative structures of the near-by city of Potentia.

The evidence for religious practices and family structures is exiguous; what there is suggests that during the lifetime of Cicero traces of religious diversity, such as different local calendars, disappeared and rules governing marriage and inheritance became steadily more uniform. The evidence relating to funerary practices is substantial, and is spread throughout Italy; it consistently portrays the replacement of distinctive local practices, often of great antiquity, by a relatively uniform set of customs. There remained, of course, enormous variety according to the wealth of the deceased, but that is another matter.

TOMBSTONE FROM S. ANGELO IN FORMIS, near Capua (first half of first century BC), a good example of funerary sculpture in late-Republican Italy. The general type of the commemorative relief has Greek antecedents, but the style of the figures is Italic, and the motif of full-length portraits within a deep-sunk field particularly associated with the Capua region. In the panel below is a scene interpreted as the sale of a slave. The inscription records that the stone was set up by the freedman M. Publilius Satyr for himself and for his own freedman Stepanus.

If it is true that the period between Sulla and Augustus saw an enormous advance in the level of Romanization achieved, it remains to ask why. The principal reason is to be sought in the process of veteran settlement between 59 and the early 20s BC. Beginning in 59 with the veterans from the eastern wars of Cn. Pompeius Magnus, enormous numbers of men, uprooted from their homes, serving together for long periods, were settled in groups far from their place of birth. The consequence for the next generation was the shattering of the existing social fabric both in the places of origin and in the communities where these men were settled. The Italian society of the early Empire which resulted was perhaps the most important and the most lasting consequence of the Roman revolution.

Further Reading

M. Beard and M.H. Crawford, *Rome in the Late Republic* (London, 1984), as well as providing a critical account of the main problems, contains a full account of the available translations of the ancient sources for Republican history as a whole and a full bibliography for the end of the Republic.

T. Cornell and J. Matthews, *Atlas of the Roman World* (Oxford, 1982) contains a good general account of Roman history and an excellent selection of maps and pictures.

Among histories of Rome, note R. M. Ogilvie, *Early Rome and the Etruscans* (London, 1976) and M. H. Crawford, *The Roman Republic* (London, 1978); H. H. Scullard, *History of the Roman World 753-146 BC*, 4th edn. (London, 1981), and *From the Gracchi to Nero,* 4th edn. (London, 1976); P.A. Brunt, *Social Conflicts in the Roman Republic* (London. 1971).

T. R. S. Broughton, *Magistrates of the Roman Republic* (New York, I–II, 1960 III, 1987), provides a year by year list of magistrates, with references to the sources and modern discussions.

For an analysis of recent work in the area, see M.H. Crawford, 'Rome and Italy', in *Journal of Roman Studies* 71 (1981), 153-60. Important books are E. T. Salmon, *Roman Colonisation* (London, 1969); *The Making of Roman Italy* (London, 1983), despite its narrowly political focus; A. N. Sherwin-White, *The Roman Citizenship*, 2nd. edn. (Oxford, 1973); E. Badian, *Foreign Clientelae* (Oxford, 1958); P. A. Brunt, *Italian Manpower* (Oxford, 1971); E. Gabba, *Republican Rome, the Army and the Allies* (Oxford, 1976); T. P. Wiseman, *New Men in the Roman Senate* (Oxford, 1971); E. T. Salmon, *Samnium and the Samnites* (Cambridge, 1967).

For the Roman political system, see H. F. Jolowicz and B. Nicholas, *Historical Introduction to Roman Law* (Cambridge, 1972); E. S. Staveley, *Greek and Roman Voting and Elections* (London, 1972).

For Roman religion, see the seminal article by J. A. North, 'Conservatism and change in Roman religion', in *Papers of the British School at Rome* 44 (1976), 1-12; also J. H. W. G. Liebeschuetz, *Continuity and Change in Roman Religion* (Oxford, 1979).

On the working of Roman politics, see M. Gelzer, *The Roman Nobility* (Oxford, 1969); P. A. Brunt, '*Nobilitas* and *Novitas*', in *Journal of Roman Studies* 72 (1982), 1-17; K. Hopkins, *Death and Renewal* (Cambridge, 1983), ch. 2.

On Rome and the outside world, see K. Hopkins, *Conquerors and Slaves* (Cambridge, 1978), ch. 1; W. V. Harris, *War and Imperialism in Republican Rome, 327-70 B.C.* (Oxford, 1979); J. A. North, 'The Development of Roman Imperialism', in *Journal of Roman Studies* 71 (1981), 1-9; A. D. Momigliano, *Alien Wisdom* (London, 1975); W. V. Harris (ed.), *The Imperialism of the Roman Republic* (Rome, 1984).

For the transformation of Italy in the age of revolution, see L. Keppie, *Colonisation and Veteran Settlement in Italy 47-14 B.C.* (London, 1983).

2

The Expansion of Rome

✻

ELIZABETH RAWSON

The Conquests of Rome

POLYBIUS thought that no one could be so worthless or indolent as not to wish to know how, and under what sort of government, the Romans had succeeded in less than fifty-three years in subjecting almost the whole inhabited world to their rule (below, pp. 229 ff.). We are now to consider Rome's expansion abroad from the beginning of the Punic Wars: but we will carry on the story after Polybius' death to the end of the Republic.

In 264 BC Rome controlled the whole of the Italian peninsula, except the Po valley ('Cisalpine Gaul'), and her defeat of Pyrrhus (above, p. 27) had attracted Greek interest. In that year a Roman army crossed to Sicily, partly to prevent the Carthaginians taking Messana and dominating the straits, and after twenty years' fighting, during which Rome turned herself into a naval power, she expelled the Carthaginians from the island. Part of it was left to friendly Syracuse and other Greek cities; for part Rome seems to have taken responsibility. In 237 she seized (on a poor excuse, but the islands were strategically vital now that Rome and Carthage were foes) Sardinia and Corsica, previously controlled by Carthage. In 227 two new magistrates were elected, for the 'jobs', *prouinciae*, of Sicily and Sardinia. Rome had also just intervened against the newly expansive and piratical Illyrians across the Adriatic, where a protectorate, including some Greek states, was established along the coast. When another and desperate clash with Carthage occurred (the Second Punic War) and Hannibal invaded Italy in 218, Roman forces were sent against his base in Spain, which they were not to leave again, though the peninsula was not wholly pacified till Augustus' day. Finally Hannibal was penned into the toe of Italy, and Scipio, who had fought with success in Spain and won over many tribes, moved the war to Africa itself, to which Hannibal was recalled only to be defeated at Zama in 202. Carthage lost territory to Roman allies in Africa and became another client state. On the other hand, the whole of Sicily became a province, for Syracuse had proved disloyal.

Hannibal's alliance with Philip V of Macedon had also led to Roman troops being deployed across the Adriatic, and finally to the Second Macedonian War, in which the King was defeated by T. Flamininus, though the kingdom was allowed to survive, and Greece proper was declared 'free' in 196; Roman influence in the whole area was, however, now paramount. Thus integrated into the world of the great Hellenistic powers, Rome involved herself in a victorious struggle, led by Scipio and his brother, against Antiochus III of Syria; again, though Rome annexed no territory, she cut down the power of Syria and arranged the affairs of the eastern Mediterranean as she pleased, to the advantage of her friends, the kingdom of Pergamum and the island republic of Rhodes.

The Romans after a time accused King Perseus, Philip's son, of disloyalty; he was crushed in 167 by Aemilius Paullus at the battle of Pydna, and Macedon was split into four tributary republics ('First', 'Second', and so on). There was no war with Egypt, the third of the great kingdoms that had emerged after Alexander's

GOLD COIN (STATER) OF T. QUINCTIUS FLAMININUS, issued after the Roman general had defeated Philip V of Macedon at Cynoscephalae in 197 BC. On the obverse the head of Flamininus, rendered in romantic Hellenistic manner; on the reverse a figure of Victory. The occasion of the issue was probably the famous proclamation of 'freedom' for Greece in 196.

death, but she too almost became a protectorate, as was dramatically shown when a Roman envoy drew a circle with his staff around the person of the invading Antiochus IV and told him to order retreat before he stepped out of it. It is up to this point, from 220 BC, that Polybius' fifty-three years run. The fact that Rome had annexed little territory did not make him doubt that she had an Empire; the Greeks were used to seeing these based on alliances or leagues.

Polybius lived on to recount the anti-Roman movements in Macedon and Greece in 148, which were brutally put down, the city of Corinth being utterly destroyed. Macedon became a province and its governor was made responsible for Greece. Almost simultaneously Carthage, harassed by Rome's ally the King of Numidia, revolted, and was wiped from the face of the earth by the younger Scipio; her territory became the province of Africa. In 133 the last king of Pergamum died without a legitimate heir, leaving his kingdom to Rome (his motives are to some extent disputed), and part of it became the province of Asia. The need to safeguard the route to Spain, and obligations to Rome's old ally Massilia, led to fighting in Transalpine Gaul, and finally the establishment of a province in the area still called Provence.

However, towards the end of the second century Rome met with a number of defeats at the hands of barbarian enemies, notably Jugurtha in Africa and the northern Cimbri and Teutones who had invaded Italy (both wars were in the end successfully concluded by C. Marius). She was also preoccupied by internal problems brought to a head by the brothers Gracchi (above, pp. 33 f.), and from 91 with the 'Social' War against the Italian allies (above, pp. 35 f.). Upon this followed the first real civil war, leading to Sulla's brief dictatorship and his restoration of senatorial government. Understandably only small gains were made abroad in this period. Neglect of the East, which had allowed the rise of Mithridates of Pontus, who seized all Asia Minor, exploiting anti-Roman sentiment, and whose forces even invaded Greece, was ultimately remedied. The Roman general Pompey (below, pp. 85 ff.) decided that more direct rule was needed. He set up provinces in Syria (where the Seleucid kingdom had been in decline since its original defeat by Rome, with resulting disorder) and in Bithynia–Pontus in northern Asia Minor; he enlarged the 'province' of Cilicia, where Rome had for some time been trying to deal with pirates based on the wild coast. The rest of the East was put under selected kings and dynasts, at least some of whom paid tribute to Rome. The Empire had now reached the Euphrates, and Rome was in direct touch with Armenia and Parthia beyond it, kingdoms where the Greek cultural influence predominant in most of the Near East began to wear very thin.

Only a few years later, in 58 BC, C. Julius Caesar (below, pp. 89 f.) became governor of southern Gaul and embarked on a war of conquest in the centre and north which even took him across the Rhine and the English Channel. He failed to make Britain tributary, but Gaul was organized as a province. This was the first of Rome's conquests remote from the Mediterranean or its extension the Black Sea, and led on to the successful Alpine and Balkan, and unsuccessful German, campaigns of Augustus. However the attempt by M. Crassus, the third member of the so-called First Triumvirate (below, pp. 91 ff.), to invade Parthia was a disaster, and the next major annexation completed the circuit of the Mediterranean: Cleopatra was encouraged by her Roman lover, Antony, to rebuild Egypt's power in the eastern Mediterranean, but they were defeated by Antony's rival for supremacy at Rome, the future Emperor Augustus.

The Evidence

No one disputes that the consequences for Rome of these conquests were vast, economically, socially, culturally, and politically. But to particularize raises hotly debated issues. The difficulties are due partly to the shortcomings of our sources. Polybius wrote a full and pretty reliable account of most of Rome's wars from

SHIPWRECK AT LA MADRAGUE DE GIENS, off the south coast of France, near Toulon (first century BC). The wreck is shown in the course of excavation, and most of the cargo of amphorae and Campanian pottery has been removed, exposing the timbers of the hull. The amphorae are of Italian origin, and the majority bear the stamps of a producer based near the Lake of Fondi, home of the famous Caecuban vintage.

264 to 146, but his later books survive only in fragments and for the earlier ones he depended on previous writers whom he knew to be biased. Some of the missing parts of Polybius can be reconstructed from Livy, who sensibly used him for Rome's relations with the East; but Livy, who is again incompletely preserved (only in epitomes and derivatives after 167) also used the so-called annalistic tradition of his Latin-writing predecessors. Its reliability, and the extent to which it draws on documentary evidence, is disputed, but it certainly often distorts events for patriotic or dramatic ends (the desire of most historians to provide moral *exempla*, and their training in rhetoric, must be borne in mind). Of authors later than the Augustan Livy, the Greek historian Appian, who recounts many

of Rome's wars, is notable, as is Plutarch, though the main interest of his *Lives* is in individual character. For Caesar's campaigns we have his own *Commentaries*, often disingenuous; and Cicero's speeches and letters throw much light on his own period, and incidentally on earlier ones. (A fuller account of the Roman historians is given in Ch. 10 below.)

To some extent the literary sources can be supplemented, especially in the Greek world, where there was a tradition of recording documents on stone (in the West bronze was often used for the less common inscriptions, and might be melted down for re-use). In all areas what survives does so by chance, often in fragments; but recent discoveries have changed our ideas in many respects. Archaeology proper shows us how in some parts of Italy in the second century subsistence agriculture gave way to larger slave-run estates producing for a market, and documents the growth of overseas trade with these more developed

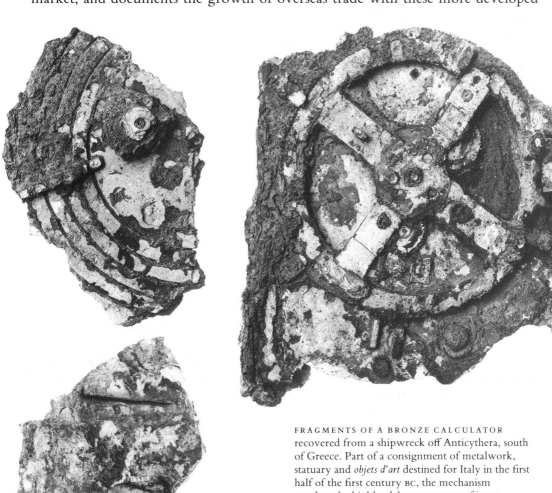

FRAGMENTS OF A BRONZE CALCULATOR recovered from a shipwreck off Anticythera, south of Greece. Part of a consignment of metalwork, statuary and *objets d'art* destined for Italy in the first half of the first century BC, the mechanism employed a highly elaborate system of inter-meshing gears to operate a series of rotating dials which indicated the conjunctions of various calendars and astronomical phenomena. It was probably operated by hand.

areas. But not all Italy has been, or can be, surveyed; and outside it most of the work has been concentrated in, this time, the western Mediterranean. And much trade leaves no trace; pottery and marble may survive, but what of slaves, corn, dried fish, spices? Still, we know that black-glazed table ware was exported from the western coast of central Italy to Gaul and Spain from the earlier second century, with an increasing number of the amphoras or wine-jars, of which it has been estimated that perhaps 40,000,000 were imported into Gaul between 150 BC and the end of the Republic. Wrecks of ships on their way to Rome from the East have also been found; works of art old and new (statues, that is; paintings would perish) have been recovered, with in one case such curiosities as old Greek inscriptions and a complex astronomical device. Finally numismatics, as coin hoards and other discoveries gradually fix the date of Greek and Roman issues, can tell us something of economic changes. But controversy still rages, for example about why, on several crucial occasions, Rome went to war.

Roman Imperialism

The central debate turns on the question: in what sense was Rome imperialist? It was once thought that Rome was not an aggressive power; that she had few contacts with the Greek world in the third century, apart from the old alliance with isolated Massilia, and was uninterested in the East: during the Hannibalic War her treaty with the Aetolians in northern Greece claimed only the movable booty from joint operations, the real estate being left to the Aetolians, and she campaigned without energy, making few, if any, other formal alliances. She was slow to annex, for example setting up in 167 four artificial 'independent' republics in Macedon. She sometimes refused lands bequeathed by will—notably Egypt in the early first century BC—while it took her twenty years to get round to organizing Cyrenaica, left to her in 96. It was further argued that the historians always showed Rome to have declared war for defensive reasons, or to assist allies to whom she had obligations and a reputation for *fides* (good faith) to keep up. For the idea of the *bellum iustum*, 'just war', undertaken in self-defence or to aid allies, obsessed her. Rome perhaps sometimes believed wrongly that she was under threat; there has been argument over whether there was, or Rome thought there was, a secret pact between Philip and Antiochus III in 200, and whether Perseus was really preparing war in the 170s. But if Rome's fears were mistaken, this showed her ignorance of the outside world. Polybius' belief that Rome aimed at world dominion was dismissed as the opinion of a Greek theorist, influenced by Thucydides on Athenian imperialism or by the career of Alexander; his own narrative refuted his general interpretation.

It was also argued that Rome rarely acted from economic motives. Policy was made by senators, and they were forbidden by the Lex Claudia of 218 to own ships over a certain size, and barred from the lucrative public contracts which included supplying the armies and in time collecting provincial taxes. (Anyway such activities were thought low.) There soon came to be tension between the Senate and the contractors, *publicani*, who were mostly of the wealthy class later known as *equites* or knights, whose interests the Senate would oppose; some of the mines of Macedon were shut after 167 to prevent exploitation by the *publicani*. In addition, many of the *negotiatores* ('men of affairs'), engaged in money-lending, banking, trade, and even agriculture, whom we know from literary and epigraphic sources to have settled all over the Mediterranean world in the second century, were mostly, so it was held, until the Social War not citizens, but Italian allies, for whom Rome felt little responsibility. The names indeed of many are not Latin, and point to Oscan-speaking southern Italy, especially Campania (for instance, Stlaccius, found on the island mart of Delos). It has even been argued that most of what trade there was (it is still often minimized) was designed to supply Roman armies and Roman settlers, not to make a profit from the natives, though it had to be admitted that in the first century generals and *publicani* influenced policy, and Roman rule was detested for its greed.

This picture will not altogether do. Rome was in touch with the Greek world from an early date. And Roman society was militaristic. Polybius paints the Romans as above all soldiers of great discipline and ferocity: sacking a city, they even kill the animals. The Senate liked to keep the army in training. Young aristocrats were expected in Polybius' time to serve ten campaigns before standing for office; the top offices were basically military ones. Military prowess was valued above all things—*uirtus* meant primarily valour. The highest ambition was for a triumph, the pompous celebration of a major victory by a grand procession exhibiting the spoils of war, in which the victor was for a day almost equated with a god. (Triumphs proliferated in the second century and had to be regulated.) Only less regarded was the thanksgiving to the gods decreed by the Senate in the name of a victorious commander. Campaigns provoked by generals to earn a triumph undoubtedly occurred, even before the first century when the Senate lost control. A correspondent wished the unwarlike Cicero, then governor of Cilicia, 'enough fighting for a triumph', and he was himself shamefacedly eager for one. Admittedly, generals were often also anxious to end a war and take the troops home to grace the event.

If enough members of the oligarchy were to have a chance of distinction—and there was great pressure on the sons of aristocrats to emulate their ancestors— wars had to be almost continuous. There was resentment against men who, like Scipio, hogged big commands for years, and there was jockeying for appointment if a good war was in prospect. There might be disagreement about where to fight, but not about fighting somewhere. Roman aristocratic tradition was reinforced by Greek influence. Scipio already perhaps modelled himself on Alexander; Pompey notoriously did, adopting his hair-style and letting panegyrists exaggerate his youth at the time of his eastern conquests; Caesar is said to have wept in youth at the thought of the Macedonian, who had conquered the world at an age when he himself had done nothing. But there is public as well as personal glory; first-century Romans were intensely proud of their world Empire and set the globe on their coins.

The Economic Motive

All booty was legally at the general's disposal, though he was expected to give some to the Treasury and use some himself on public works, notably temples vowed in battle. Such buildings, apart from providing employment (to men who would support their employer at elections) kept a man's name, often emblazoned on the façade, before the public. And, as the standard of luxury—and later of electoral bribery—rose, spoil provided the quickest way to the wealth needed by the competitive upper class.

It was also the quickest way to wealth for the troops, to whom the general distributed part of the official booty—there was doubtless unofficial booty too, in spite of the rules. Although the really poor were not eligible for the army till the late second century, the (probably increasingly small) small-holders serving were often in debt to richer neighbours, and doubtless anyway eager to make their fortunes. Later, in a letter of 43 BC, D. Brutus tells Cicero that he has led his men against some Alpine tribes to meet their wishes. During the Italian wars victory had often led to conquered land being parcelled out among poor citizens. This happened much less after wars overseas, though the state acquired some land to rent out, to foreigners or citizens; but a few veterans were placed in the second century in Spain and the Balearics, and there was much settlement in Cisalpine Gaul. Gaius Gracchus, however, who, like his brother Tiberius, had a new vision of how the Empire could be used to support the poor of Rome, proposed colonies abroad; Saturninus, another demagogic tribune at the end of the second century, had a broad plan of transmarine settlement for both veterans, now including many landless, and the urban *plebs*. But in practice Caesar was the first to plant both classes abroad on any large scale.

It has also been suggested that, till the Social War, Rome's only way to profit from her alliances in Italy, since the allies paid no taxes, was to call them out to fight. Most Italian peoples had their own military tradition, and if at times they found Rome's demands oppressive, they took pride in their share in her victories, which many came to feel earned them a right to political equality and Roman citizenship. They did not always get an equal share of booty, but the grand buildings set up at some Italian shrines shortly before the Social War may show its deployment by local magnates; equally, the *negotiatores* hailing from Campania and elsewhere may have sometimes begun operations abroad by investing the profits of war. Pompeii documents the prosperity of Campania, partly the result of such *negotia*.

Booty included slaves—either those already such, or prisoners of war (the Romans perhaps rarely allowed ransom). Marxists, exaggerating the admittedly great importance of slavery in ancient society, have supposed that Roman conquests were fuelled by the need for slaves. No ancient source hints at this, but the sources are coy about the slave trade. Masses of slaves did result from Rome's wars; Aemilius Paullus, the victor of Pydna, is said to have sold 150,000 inhabitants of Epirus in northern Greece, on the Senate's order to deal harshly with the area; it became a virtual desert. Slaves were also acquired by trade; we are told that some Gallic chiefs were so fond of Italian wine they would give a slave for a single jar, and there is literary evidence for Gallic slaves in Italy. The geographer Strabo says that at the height of its prosperity about 100 BC Delos could handle 10,000 slaves a day (some originally kidnapped by pirates or slave-dealers, some foundlings or enslaved for debt, many bought from barbarian tribes in Thrace and elsewhere). It is not strange that servile revolts broke out in Italy and Sicily

REVERSE OF SILVER COIN (DENARIUS) STRUCK BY CN. LENTULUS (76–75 BC). The symbols denote Rome's world power by land and by sea: a sceptre with wreath, a globe, and a rudder. The obverse shows a male bust representing the Spirit of the Roman People (Genius Populi Romani).

in the late second and early first centuries. Though the great expansion in the use of slaves in Italy on the land and on a smaller scale for skilled jobs, including teaching (these were mostly easterners) seems a result, rather than a cause, of the first transmarine conquests, it is likely that later the makers of Roman policy gave some thought to the supply; landowners needed slaves more than anyone, though they were used in every type of enterprise and small men too would profit from low prices.

The growing evidence for commerce after the Hannibalic War also makes it unlikely that senators were totally uninterested in trade. Italian exports were largely in agricultural produce, wine, and to some extent oil; great landowners may have traded in the name of freedmen, who could legally own big ships and were still bound to assist their masters, or sold their produce, sometimes still on the tree, to a merchant, as the elder Cato's agricultural treatise indicates. A gentlemanly distance was thus combined with profit. Even before Sulla enlarged the Senate (below, p. 84) there was intermarriage with rich non-senatorial families; and it has been shown that many of the far-flung *negotiatores* did come from parts of Italy given Roman citizenship well before the Social War. Certainly after Sulla many new senators had close relatives involved in business matters, while some probably refused to drop their own old interests; Cicero tells us in

70 that the Lex Claudia and similar measures were disobeyed, though Caesar may have reasserted them in 59. The rich also depended on luxuries from the East to sustain an increasingly sumptuous way of life; works of fine and applied art, rare foods and wines, skilled slaves, spices transmitted from distant climes.

Senators might lend money at interest; Cato, in the mid second century, did so through a freedman to finance trading voyages, and later senators made a corner in lending to ambassadors at Rome. It seems also that in the first century they could or did take shares in the great companies of *publicani* now farming some provincial taxes. Finally, in spite of friction between the classes, the system of patronage will always have meant that many business men could put pressure on individual senators to support their interests. It is thus hard to maintain that the Senate almost never had an eye to commercial interest, let alone other types of economic advantage.

Cicero indeed claims that Rome often went to war for her merchants. This is partly true, for example, of the First Illyrian War, though at that time and place they will in truth have been mostly Italians (trade in this region is not yet well documented archaeologically); but there was also mistreatment of envoys to avenge and perhaps appeals to answer. In 187 Rome laid down that Romans and Latins (and possibly Italians) should be exempt from harbour dues at Ambracia, and this may not have been the isolated action our sources suggest. The making of Delos a free port in 167 weakened Rhodes and benefited Roman and Italian traders. And Cicero indicates that some time before 129 Rome forbade Transalpine peoples (in southern Gaul; attempts to explain the notice away are perverse) to plant vines and olives, perhaps to protect her own trade in wine and oil. Admittedly this seems a unique measure; and Rome did not, for example, impose a common coinage over her sphere of influence, unlike Athens.

The one form of trade in which the state took a direct interest was that in corn. The urban *plebs* must not starve, the armies must be provisioned. With the increase in population at Rome corn (mainly wheat) from abroad had to be provided regularly, not just in crises (the rest of Italy still fed itself or even sent grain to Rome). Sicily annually gave up a tithe of its harvest as tax (and had from 73 to sell another to Rome at a fixed price if needed). After 146 the corn of Africa became vital. We now know that on one occasion in the second century a Roman magistrate got the Thessalians, in northern Greece, to bring corn to Rome; however, till the city became dependent on Egypt in the imperial age, the East was not often drawn on. Private merchants were responsible for the transfer of corn to Rome, but the Senate must have kept an eye on the situation. Most other basic raw materials, such as wood, were available in Italy, though the mines of Spain were important, and those of Macedon were soon reopened.

The Treasury became increasingly dependent on foreign revenues. At first Rome did not, it seems, always impose taxes, but just demanded reparations, or large sums for which no special justification was claimed; Antiochus III was mulcted of 1,500 talents. In civilized Sicily Rome took over the tax system

AGORA OF THE ITALIANS ON DELOS. Built with endowments from several private benefactors in the late second century BC, this building served as the social and business centre of the Italian community in the Aegean's greatest slave-market. In the foreground, two columns of the portico which surrounded the central court have been reconstructed; behind lies part of an entablature inscribed with the names of the original sponsors.

existing under Syracuse, but it was perhaps gradually that proper taxes were imposed in Spain and the mines let. Contractors' fees, 'indemnities', taxes, and booty became so valuable that direct tax on citizens was abolished after Pydna, even though the armies, now serving all year round, were increasingly expensive to maintain. Taxes were sometimes lowered when an area was reorganized, but new customs dues, for example, were also imposed. Later, particularly after the Social War and Sulla's dictatorship, the state, with heavy wars on hand, faced severe financial problems; it now had to pay for the large part of the army previously financed by the Italian allies, and soon C. Gracchus' corn subsidies in Rome, abolished by Sulla, were reintroduced. Cicero claimed in 66 that the only province to provide a surplus after defence and administration was Asia. But Plutarch says the tax income was doubled by Pompey's new arrangements. Gaul was also to contribute, and Egypt even more.

Finally, many senators made private fortunes from the Empire. Polybius believed that until his time Roman magistrates were remarkable for probity. Cato certainly reiterated that he had not made a sesterce from his service abroad. But Cicero's speeches illustrate the behaviour too common in his day, though we need not think that every governor was a Verres, emulated in rapacity by all his staff. Cicero himself was honest enough, and says in a letter from Cilicia that the other governors then in the East were all decent (though his own predecessor, Ap. Pulcher, was 'not a man, but some sort of wild beast'). The *Verrine Orations* detail every possible abuse, from conniving with pirates to stealing statues on such a scale that the Sicilian tourist trade was ruined. From the second century governors could be prosecuted for extortion, but it was hard for provincials to organize a trial at Rome, or to secure conviction, even at periods when it was the *equites*, not the senators, who formed, or formed a majority on, the jury.

The Reluctance to Annex

If senators and *equites*, private soldiers and the public Treasury, even the urban *plebs*, all profited from Rome's expansion, why was she so slow to annex territories that fell into her lap? Occasionally moral reluctance might be mooted: Flamininus refused to abolish the kingdom of Macedon at the Aetolians' demand, saying that it was unRoman to annihilate an enemy. There was hesitation about the final razing of Carthage, which was felt hard to justify to public, especially Greek, opinion; and the idea that states need an external threat to prevent corruption and decline was perhaps put forward. Not that the Romans doubted the morality of ruling an Empire as such; when the provocative Greek philosopher Carneades, in a lecture at Rome in 155, suggested that justice would demand that they should give up their conquests and return to shepherds' huts, there was outrage. At most, individual wars might be attacked as inspired by one's opponents' greed: thus Cato opposed a project of war with Rhodes in 167, and many objected to Crassus' Parthian campaign.

But it is significant that many people did just as well where annexation had not taken place. 'Kings, nations, and cities', even if technically 'free', were an integral part of the Empire. Some kings already claimed in the second century to be mere agents of Rome. Free states could be expected, or bound by treaty, to send aid in war; an increasing proportion of Rome's forces, especially in ships and cavalry, were 'auxiliary'. Where individuals are concerned, Verres carried off treasures from 'free' as well as from 'stipendiary' cities. Great Romans were patrons of dynasts and communities outside, as well as inside, the provinces, thus gaining power, prestige, and even profit—the line between gift and bribe was fine, as the friends of King Jugurtha of Numidia found. We can see how the Claudii, over two and a half centuries, extended their *clientela* in Greek-speaking lands, or how the Domitii Ahenobarbi, with an ancestor who had fought in southern Gaul and estates on the west coast of Italy, built up influence in the western Mediterranean. (A patron might be able to protect his clients from mistreatment; if he mistreated them himself it was hard for others to intervene.)

Trade and money-lending could be carried on almost better where there was no Roman governor for oppressed natives to appeal to, and where any action against *negotiatores* could be represented as anti-Roman. The wine trade stretched up into central Gaul well before Caesar's time, and when Cicero was in the East the unfortunate young King Ariobarzanes of Cappadocia ('Pious' and 'Pro-Roman' by style) was deep in debt to Roman moneylenders, including M. Brutus, that 'honourable man', and Pompey, a flock of whose agents were dunning him for interest. There is no sign that *negotiatores* wanted annexation; Marius, a friend of the *equites*, did not extend the province of Africa. But Rome's power was there to protect or at least avenge them; Jugurtha's massacre of the hated *Italici* had been one of the causes of the war, and it is significant that if they called themselves *Italici*, the Greeks called them all *Rhōmaioi*, Romans.

Roman conservatism is also relevant. Rome had stretched the idea of the city-state to its limit, but not abandoned it; citizens had to vote in person, and not too many of the upper class at least should be on business abroad. The Senate, until Sulla, consisted of about 300 men, in practice all ex-magistrates; more provinces meant more offices. And the oligarchy, though continually replenished from wealthy outsiders—Marius was one—would not wish the process to be too rapid. It also feared individuals acquiring *regnum*, quasi-monarchic power, for which prolonged absence in a distant province could provide the base—though so might a war not ending in annexation. Sulla attempted to control ambitious governors by a law (flouted by Caesar in Gaul) forbidding among other things leaving one's province with an army without senatorial permission. The Senate set its face against annexing Egypt in the earlier first century partly because the untrustworthy and greedy Crassus wanted to be involved in it.

Furthermore, in the third and second centuries the army was not a standing one, but in theory raised annually, chiefly from the peasantry. Long and hard campaigns were unpopular with the troops, especially in Spain, not an area as rich in booty as the East. Cato said in 167 that Macedonia could not be annexed, because it could not be defended (in part from barbarians on its frontiers). The Romans indeed became anxious at this time about a decline in military quality, partly due to the decline, in some areas, of the peasant class; this was followed by a period, already mentioned, of military disasters, and that, as also noted, by one of financial stringency. No wonder many places were left to defend and police themselves.

Some peoples, too, were attached to their native rulers and better left to them. And where the Greek cities were concerned, Rome discovered that 'liberation' was the best policy—perhaps already in Sicily and on the Adriatic coast, certainly when Flamininus, after defeating Philip of Macedon, declared Greece free at the Isthmian Games of 196, to frantic enthusiasm, and evacuated it completely. Some Greek cities had treaties with Rome (how many is disputed), which left them internal autonomy but bound them to give help in war (only treaties not described as equal bound them to respect the *maiestas* of the Roman People in all ways). Others were simply declared free unilaterally by Rome, a status which, it was in time discovered, she was ready unilaterally to revoke. The desire of Rhodes for a formal alliance in 167 shows this was felt to be some kind of safeguard; but in the end Rome refused to be shackled even by her treaties.

The policy of freedom for Greeks was not inspired by sentimental philhellenism, though Rome had more respect for Greek public opinion than she did for barbarian tribes, against whom her record was undoubtedly worse; rather its purpose was to reduce the power of Macedon and Syria. Rome did not apply it when it did not suit her: for example, she handed over various cities to her friends Pergamum and Rhodes. Under the Roman moral system, by which every *beneficium* had to be repaid by *officium* (act or sense of duty), the 'free' states were expected to conform to Rome's wishes. They did not always grasp this, a fact which contributed to the souring of Rome's relations with the various squabbling Greek states in the first half of the second century, until some of her generals began to behave to the Greeks, shortly before the war with Perseus, with brutality and contempt; this *noua sapientia*, as Livy called it, or new wisdom, was disapproved of by some prominent Romans, in vain.

The Protection of the Propertied Classes

In fact, even where the 'stipendiary' or tribute-paying inhabitants of a province were concerned, much responsibility was left to local communities, especially Greek cities. The Roman governor's duties were chiefly defence (hence the first of the great Roman roads outside Italy) and the administration of justice to Roman citizens; he could take cases between natives, but clearly not all of these, and Cicero says his (not unique) proclamation that he would take none was popular. The Romans made no attempt to impose uniformity; in some provinces a magistrate, the quaestor, was responsible for the collection of direct taxes, but probably only by overseeing local officials. In others both direct and indirect taxes were collected by tax-farmers, sometimes not even Roman, and these might have large staffs; even so, in some cases the cities did the basic work. These cities carried on their political life largely unhampered; when Pompey wanted to annex part of Pontus, he felt it best to found a group of Greek-style cities, if with larger territories than usual. As a result of this system the Romans, in spite of severe friction at times, developed a partnership with the upper classes who did much of the administration for them, and whom they defended against the cry of the poor for the division of land and abolition of debts that was sometimes heard.

Flamininus had left the cities of Greece in the hands of the well-off. Perseus appealed to the poor, though not only to them, for support; and anti-Roman feeling was often based on hostility to the rich—though it would be voiced by well-off leaders, jealous of whatever pro-Roman clique was in power, or genuinely idealistic or nationalistic. It is uncertain how far Rome intervened to make constitutions more oligarchic, as they tended to become; but we have on stone a letter from a governor of Macedon to a Peloponnesian city, of the late second century, which reveals that he has taken steps to crush social unrest there. Polybius, who came of a distinguished political family, thought a newly slavish adherence to Rome deplorable, but realized that dignified independence was only possible

INSCRIPTION RECORDING A LETTER FROM THE ROMAN GOVERNOR OF MACEDONIA. Addressed to the magistrates and council of the Achaean city of Dyme, the letter records measures taken by the proconsul Q. Fabius to deal with the ringleaders of a revolutionary movement: two of them have been condemned to death and a third sent to stand trial in Rome.

within narrow limits. He believed, however, that in spite of recent abuses and the new harshness Rome had given the Greek cities great benefits, and that the revolts of 148 were insane folly (these were again partly inspired by the poor, who would be less aware than the upper classes that Rome was too strong to resist).

Certainly Greek communities, from whatever motives, paid Rome every sort of honour. In early years her *fides*, the good faith to which communities were to entrust themselves, was much celebrated. Fom the early second century cults were founded to the goddess Roma (*Rhōmē* in Greek significantly means power); the poetess Melinno's hymn to Rome perhaps dates from this period. Cults were also set up to individuals, starting with Flamininus; Plutarch describes the cere-monies in his name still carried out in Euboea in his own day. The honour was gradually devalued: even Cicero was voted temples, which he refused in an attempt to keep the cities' expenditure within bounds. No wonder Roman states-men began to feel themselves the equals of Hellenistic kings. Lesser honours—titles, statues—abounded, even for prominent *negotiatores*, such as the Cloatii who lent to and protected—or ran—the little town of Gytheum near Sparta in the early first century.

Even in the dark days of the Mithridatic War, when many places slaughtered the blood-sucking *negotiatores*, a few cities of Greece and Asia stayed loyal, if sometimes from traditional enmity to rebellious neighbours. Thus the Assembly at Aphrodisias in Asia Minor, where Rome honoured the shrine of Aphrodite, voted to go with every available man to help a Roman general, for 'without the protection of the Romans we do not even wish to live'. But the first century was a terrible time for many Greek cities. They suffered in the fighting against Mithridates, and Sulla exacted large sums to punish disloyalty and finance civil war. Piracy got out of hand, till Pompey suppressed it; so it seems did the *publicani*, till Caesar restricted their powers in Asia at least. Communities, like individuals, fell hopelessly in debt to Roman money-lenders. Cicero says in a speech of 66 (of course with an ulterior motive) 'it is hard to express, citizens, how loathed we are by foreign nations.' It was greed he blamed. The poverty of many cities is visible archaeologically; there was little new building. The East had not fully recovered when renewed civil wars broke out. Pompey and Caesar, Brutus and Cassius, Antony and Octavian, all financed their campaigns from Rome's subjects. When Judaea could not pay what Cassius demanded, he sold four towns and many officials into slavery; as Antony observed, this was un-authorised by the laws of war. Cassius also besieged the free city of Rhodes, so long a friend of Rome, and carried off all its wealth except the chariot of its patron god the Sun. An even older friend of Rome's, Massilia, had been taken by Caesar, for supporting Pompey.

And yet, through it all, many members of the upper class saw private and public advantage in—or no alternative to—supporting Rome. They cultivated ties with important Romans, whether in Rome themselves as ambassadors (a second-century inscription thanks a group of these for going round to the morning receptions of great nobles) or when putting up Roman governors on their way to, or on circuit in, the provinces. By the end of the Republic foreign *amici* had even begun to wield power in Rome as advisers to the great dynasts; Theophanes of Mytilene was an intimate of Pompey's, and L. Cornelius Balbus of Gades was Caesar's trusted agent. Though it had for long occasionally been granted as a reward for service in war, citizenship was first given on a larger scale by Caesar, in whose time the rule that Roman citizenship could not be combined with that of another state seems to have lapsed. The way was open for the gradual extension of privilege, ultimately even of senatorial rank, which was to hold the Empire together in succeeding centuries.

Hellenism at Rome

Co-operation between the Greek and Roman élites was possible because the Roman upper class, though loyal to much of its own tradition, became very Hellenized. Indeed, there were attempts to prove that the Romans *were* Greeks, descended not only from Trojan Aeneas, but from Evander the Arcadian (familiar from the *Aeneid*), or from Hercules, and their followers. Some scholars held that Latin was a dialect of Greek. The attitude of many Romans to Greeks and Greek culture was, it is true, ambiguous; they believed in their own superiority in war and statecraft (and Cicero said other systems of civil law were puerile). Many people suspected customs that seemed softening or apt to distract from serious matters. Close and often unhappy experience of second-century Greeks led to these being characterized as effeminate, time-serving, politically inept (a useful justification of Empire), loquacious, and prone to abstract argument at the wrong time. Perhaps they had degenerated; there *are* some men worthy of ancient Greece, concedes Cicero (more philhellene than most), warning his brother to be wary of intimacies in his province. And the inhabitants of the now Greek-speaking cities of the East might be thought inferior to 'real Greeks'. But in Athens itself, which, like Delphi, Rome had treated with respect, Cicero expressed dismay at the arrogant treatment of the locals by his (strictly upright) suite.

Few well-off Romans, however, could resist the attractions of civilized Greek life, and some realized that it was only from the Greeks that they could learn much that the rulers of the world needed to know. Rome had perhaps never been wholly out of touch with the Greek world. Many of her gods had been identified with Greek ones, her art derived from Greek art; some Romans must always have known some Greek, and even perhaps read some Greek books. But a new epoch dawned in the mid third century, with the first plays on the Greek model in Latin (below, pp. 60 ff.), and (it seems) more formal schooling, in both tongues. In the Hannibalic War new Greek cults (and even the Great Mother from Asia) were introduced, to protect the city. The sack of Syracuse in 212 marked for Polybius the start of a taste for Greek art (a pity, he thought; states should stick to their own traditions); certainly innumerable statues and paintings were to be carried off to Rome in the next centuries. The physical face of the city was transformed as it became a great capital, though Polybius shows that its rustic air was mocked by cosmopolitan visitors in his day, and a truly Greek architectural style came a little later; marble was not much used for building purposes till later still.

But the upper classes' way of life was soon transformed. Historians tended to see Roman history in terms of moral decline, especially into avarice and luxury, and liked to mark its stages; some thought the booty brought back from Asia in 190, including handsome furniture, initiated the process. Polybius stressed the defeat of Macedon at Pydna and the wealth it brought: the young went mad for the worst aspects of Greek manners, pederasty, banquets to the sound of music,

ROUND TEMPLE BY THE TIBER, probably to be identified as the temple of Hercules Victor: one of the rare examples of a Greek-style marble building in Rome before Augustan times. Sponsored in the late second century BC by the rich merchant M. Octavius Herrenus, it lacks the emphatic entrance and high podium of Roman Italic temples. The entablature is missing and the present roof is modern.

PAINTING OF A FRIGHTENED GIRL: detail of a mural frieze at Pompeii (*c*.60–50 BC). This famous composition, consisting of twenty-eight or more figures, is the finest surviving specimen of the grand figure-painting of the so-called Second Style.

TABLINUM OF THE HOUSE OF M. LUCRETIUS FRONTO, at Pompeii (*c.*AD 40–50). The rich but delicate wall-decoration marks the break-up of the Third Style of Pompeian painting. In place of restrained elegance and restful colouring we find a more complex colour-scheme, with more elaborate painted detail, and hints of the reappearance of architectural perspective.

and so on. Cato had tried to outlaw, and then to tax prohibitively, various forms of luxury, and continued to inveigh against spending on handsome slaves or imported food, and adorning one's house with statues of the gods 'as though they were furniture'. But even Cato, as his buildings while censor and his own writings show, could not turn the clock back.

The crux of the matter was education, for to the Greeks their *paideia* was their culture. By tradition the upper-class Roman boy absorbed political and legal experience from his father's friends, and spent the campaigning season, from the age of seventeen, with the army. But the Greeks had developed a pattern of formal study, first of literature (primarily Homer), and then rhetoric and, for some, philosophy. Aemilius Paullus provided his sons with a bevy of Greek masters, even in music and hunting, and a philosopher doubling as drawing master. He also brought the royal library of Macedon to Rome, the first great Greek library to reach it. Polybius attests that there were now many Greek teachers there. Distinguished savants began to arrive, at first as envoys; the serious study of *grammatikē* was dated to the embassy of Crates of Pergamum, who broke his leg in an open sewer and lectured while immobilized. And in 155 Athens sent the heads of three philosophical schools, whose lectures caused a sudden rage for philosophy—though Cato, who thought philosophy 'mere gibberish', pressed the Senate to conclude their business quickly so that the young could return to learning from 'the laws and the magistrates'.

One must not exaggerate the depth of Greek influence at this period. There is evidence that Greek medicine was regarded with suspicion still, and in general the Romans were intellectually, as also artistically, clumsy and immature. Poetry was more developed than prose, though even poetry was crude, as Horace complained. Cicero thought that it was only towards the end of the century that orators really profited from the study of rhetoric, which taught one how to organize and argue, as well as ornament, a speech. What we know of prose literature suggests that the Romans, like many primitive peoples, found generalization and abstraction hard. It was only from about 100 BC, too, that they began to use traditional Greek logical structure in treatises, with explicit definitions of the subject and all key concepts, and careful division of the material into parts or aspects, instead of piling up information hugger-mugger like Cato in his agricultural treatise. And it was in the first century that Latin was refined into the splendid vehicle it was to be for prose as well as poetry, and that Latin authors colonized many new prose genres, including the philosophic treatise.

It was only now too that it became common for young gentlemen to study rhetoric or philosophy at Athens or Rhodes (more independent Alexandria seems to have been out of bounds), though sons of *negotiatores* were often educated in the East, and might go through a city's *ephēbeia*, a state-run training course now more cultural than military. The Mithridatic wars swept Greek refugees and captives to Rome, both classes including learned men; also great libraries. And they detained many Romans long years in the East. (The historian Sallust dated

Rome's collapse into luxury from Sulla's campaigns in Asia.) Afterwards, Rome was equal to Alexandria as a magnet for Greek artists and intellectuals; there was patronage to be found almost nowhere else. And the Romans felt that they were, in one field after another, catching up with the Greeks. Cicero and his friend Atticus, admittedly exceptional men, must have met their Greek *amici* on fully equal terms.

In the West Rome felt she had little to learn, though an isolated work on agriculture was translated by official order from Punic. But the very fact that Romans rarely bothered to learn western languages helped to prepare for an extension of privilege here too; for the native élites gradually took on the colours of what seemed a superior, if at first often a hated, civilization. Trade and the influx of settlers helped to Romanize. Rome rarely consciously forwarded the process, though there was some encouragement in Spain of agriculture and urban settlement in the valleys, to replace less controllable pastoral communities. Though there was cultural prejudice against barbarians, there was little racial prejudice. If barbarians gave up their ways (beastly, like the habit of some Spanish tribes of washing their teeth in urine, or less so, like those of the Gauls, whom Caesar found intelligent and courageous, if unsteady), they could rise above the status of barbarians; the geographer Strabo's description of southern Spain in the time of Augustus is illuminating here. In fact, Balbus and his nephew from Gades (admittedly an ancient and civilized Punic city) entered the Senate—though the very idea shocked Cicero—before the son of Pompey's friend Theophanes of Mytilene did so; and the Balbi were soon followed by a few Gallic nobles who, or whose fathers, owed the citizenship to Caesar or Augustus. The lineaments of the Roman Empire in its maturity were taking shape.

Further Reading

A translation of Polybius is most easily available in the Loeb edition; there is a Penguin volume of selections, and F. W. Walbank's *Polybius* (California 1972) provides a good discussion of his work. Books of Livy are also available in the Penguin Classics, and there are Loebs of his entire work and those of the other authors mentioned. For Cicero see pp. 99 f.

The *Cambridge Ancient History* vol. viii (cf. also ix) gives a classic account, in the chapters by M. Holleaux, of the older view of Roman expansion; it is soon to be replaced by a new edition. For a more modern approach, see W. V. Harris, *War and Imperialism in Republican Rome 372–70 B.C.* (Oxford, 1979), with P. A. Brunt's chapter in *Imperialism in the Ancient World*, ed. P. D. A. Garnsey and C. R. Whittaker, (Cambridge, 1978) and J. A. North, 'The Development of Roman Imperialism' in *Journal of Roman Studies*, 1981. There is a good general account in C. Nicolet, *Rome et la conquête du monde méditerranéen*, ii: *Genèse d'un empire* (Paris, 1978); cf. also R. M. Errington, *The Dawn of Empire: Rome's Rise to World Power* (Ithaca, NY, 1972).

E. Badian has followed up his important *Foreign Clientelae* (Oxford, 1958), with *Roman Imperialism in the Late Republic* (Oxford, 1968) and *Publicans and Sinners* (Oxford, 1972). The first two sections of K. Hopkins, *Conquerors and Slaves* (Cambridge, 1978) deal with the transformation of Italian agriculture and economic life as a result of expansion; for *negotiatores* abroad, see A. J. N. Wilson, *Emigration from Italy in the Republican Age of Rome* (Manchester, 1966), less readable than

J. Hatzfeld, *Les Trafiquants italiens dans l'orient hellénique* (Paris, 1919). See also J. H. D'Arms, *Commerce and Social Standing in Ancient Rome*, (Cambridge, Mass. 1981); and M. H. Crawford, 'Rome and the Greek World: Economic Relations', *Econ. Hist. Review*, 1977; for the trade in corn, the first two chapters of G. Rickman, *The Corn Supply of Ancient Rome* (Oxford, 1980).

For study of individual figures, see F. W. Walbank, *Philip V of Macedon* (1940, repr. Hamden, Conn., 1967); R. M. Errington, *Philopoemen* (Oxford, 1969—Philopoemen was a leading figure in the Achaean League, admired by Polybius for his attitude to Rome); A. E. Astin, *Scipio Aemilianus* (Oxford, 1967) and *Cato the Censor*, (Oxford, 1978).

For the East, see A. H. M. Jones, *The Greek City from Alexander to Justinian* (Oxford, 1966) and D. Magie's massive *Roman Rule in Asia Minor* (Princeton, 1950), also D. C. Braund, *Rome and the Friendly King* (London, 1984) and R. Mellor, *Thea Rhômê: The Worship of the Goddess Roma in the Greek World* (1975), also, now A. N. Sherwin-White, *Roman Foreign Policy in the Greek East* (London 1984) and E. S. Gruen, *The Hellenistic World and the Coming of Rome* (California 1984), neither available when this chapter was written.

For Roman attitudes to foreigners, J. P. V. D. Balsdon's *Romans and Aliens* (London, 1979).

3

The First Roman Literature

❧

P. G. McC. BROWN

Plautus

LATIN literature begins with a bang, with a dazzling display of virtuoso verbal fireworks in twenty comedies written by Plautus between about 205 and 184 BC. The start of Latin literature is conventionally dated to the performance of a play by Livius Andronicus at Rome in 240 BC, but these comedies by Plautus are the earliest works to have survived complete. They are modelled on Greek comedies, nearly all of them 'New Comedies' written by Menander and his contemporaries about 100 years before Plautus. Like the Greek comedies, they are written in verse. Greek comedies were written for performance in a permanent theatre at Athens, as central elements in a religious festival. Roman comedies were also performed at religious festivals, but they were one source of entertainment among many, and they were performed on a temporary stage erected for the occasion. Romans of all classes came to watch. We cannot tell to what extent Plautus adapted his style to the taste of his audience and to what extent he helped to form that taste; but he has imported into his plays a boisterousness and a broadness of comic effect which remind us more of Aristophanes (though there is much less obscenity) than of Menander.

The Greek originals of Plautus' plays have not survived, though a tattered papyrus published in 1968 contains the lines on which *Bacchides* ('The Bacchis Sisters') 494–561 are based and enables us to study Plautus' techniques of adaptation at first hand for this stretch of the play. Plautus has preserved the basic plot and sequence of scenes, but he has cut two scenes altogether, and at one point he reverses the order of entry of two characters so as to eliminate a pause in the action where there was an act-break in the original (Roman comedy was usually written for continuous performance, and the act- and scene-divisions found in modern editions do not go back to the authors). The tormented monologue of a young man in love has had some jokes added to it. Passages which would have been spoken without musical accompaniment in the original Greek are turned into passages in longer lines to be accompanied on a reed-pipe. Plautus' play is still set in Athens, and his characters have Greek-sounding names; but he has changed most of them from the original, most significantly that of the scheming slave who dominates the action: Plautus calls him Chrysalus (Goldfinger) and adds some colour to his part by punning on this name (240 'Goldfinger's got to get his fingers on some gold', 361-2 'He'll change my name from Goldfinger to Gallowsbird', etc.). The papyrus shows that this character in the original had the less striking name of Syrus (The Syrian), which adds spice to Chrysalus' boast at 649 that he is superior to run-of-the-mill slaves with names like Parmeno and Syrus—though the joke would doubtless have been lost on most of Plautus' audience.

The plots of the plays show considerable variety. In *Amphitruo*, Jupiter descends to earth disguised as Amphitruo in order to seduce the latter's wife Alcumena; when Amphitruo himself arrives home from a military expedition the next day, he is dismayed to discover from his wife's reception of him that she believes him to have spent the previous night with her. *Mercator* ('The Businessman') shows father and son in love with the same girl, as does *Casina* (named after the girl)

BRONZE BUST OF MENANDER (*c*.342–292 BC), the most famous exponent of the 'New' Comedy which inspired the Latin playwrights Plautus and Terence. In contrast to the rumbustious burlesque of Aristophanes and his contemporaries, Menander wrote situation comedies involving such stock characters as the stern father, profligate son, scheming slave, and good-hearted prostitute.

MOSAIC PANEL FROM POMPEII (second or first century BC) showing a scene from the beginning of Menander's play, the *Synaristosai* ('Breakfasting Women'). Only fragments of the original play survive, but a version by Plautus remains complete (the *Mostellaria*).

MARBLE RELIEF ILLUSTRATING A SCENE FROM NEW COMEDY (first century AD?). The situation is typical of Menander and his Roman imitators: an angry father emerges to chastise his drunken son but is restrained by a neighbour, while the son is egged on by a wily slave. The characters are clearly labelled by the form of the masks worn by the actors.

THEATRE AT POMPEII: Initially constructed during the second century BC, it is the earliest surviving theatre in Italy outside the Greek colonies; auditoria like this might have housed the first performances of plays by Plautus and Terence. Its present form, however, is the result of extensive modernization in the time of Augustus.

in which one of the tricks used to thwart the father is the impersonation of Casina in the bedroom by a male slave. *Rudens* ('The Rope') is set on the coast of north Africa near Cyrene: a slave-dealer is shipwrecked there in a storm, and one of the girls in his possession turns out to be the long-lost daughter of a man living there in exile from Athens. But beneath the surface variety of the plays the basic structure of the plot (preserved from the Greek original) nearly always concerns the removal or overcoming of some apparent obstacle to the course of true love.

But Plautus' main interest was not so much in reproducing dramatic structures as in using them as an opportunity for virtuoso display. We have seen from *Bacchides* that he wrote a creative adaptation rather than a slavish translation of Menander's text. In many respects he can be said to have changed radically the type of comedy which the plays contain. Consistency of characterization and plot development are cheerfully sacrificed for the sake of an immediate effect. The humour resides less in the irony of the situation than in the cracking of jokes and the perpetration of puns. Instead of characters in a dramatic context we sometimes see comedians going through a routine. Three things in particular stand out: the glorification of the scheming slave, the musical element, and the creation of an imaginary world which is set in Greece but includes many Italian features.

Plautus did not invent the scheming slave: the Greek original of *Bacchides* was called *The Double Deceiver*, and the part played in it by Syrus must have been similar at least in outline to the part played by Chrysalus in Plautus' play. But Chrysalus dominates *Bacchides* not simply by his scheming (which is not particularly ingenious) but by his boasting. His plan to trick his master out of money is seen as a military campaign, and his description of it is embroidered at some points with triumph imagery which is peculiarly Roman. Chrysalus has an extended monologue in which he compares his campaign with that of the Greeks in the Trojan War (925 ff.):

They say the two brothers, the sons of Atreus, did a great deed when with their weapons and their horses, with their army and outstanding warriors, and with their thousand ships they overcame after ten years Priam's town of Troy, its fortifications built by the hands of gods. But that was less than a blister on the foot in comparison with the way I'm going to conquer my master without fleet, without army, without that great number of troops

—and so on for fifty lines, with a succession of fantastic and mutually contradictory parallels between the plot of the play and the events of the Trojan War. When he has completed his deception he boasts (1068 ff.):

That's the way to carry out your projects properly. Now I can triumph in style, laden with booty. Safe and sound, the city captured by a trick, I now lead my whole army home intact. But, spectators, don't be surprised that I'm not actually celebrating a triumph: everyone does that, I can't be bothered with it. All the same, my troops will be treated to a tipple. Now I shall take all this booty straight to the quaestor.

ZEUS VISITS ALCMENE: *phlyax* vase painted by Asteas (third quarter of fourth century BC). The *phlyakes* were actors in a popular form of south-Italian farce whose subjects included parodies of Greek myths. This particular subject recurs in Plautus' *Amphitruo*, his only known play with a mythological theme, perhaps based on a 'hilarious tragedy' by the Syracusan playwright Rhinthon (*c.*300 BC). See also Vol. 1, p. 177.

The effect of such passages is to focus our attention on Chrysalus' trickery as an achievement on its own account rather than as a necessary device to secure a sum of money to help a young man in love. The Plautine slave enjoys scheming for the sake of scheming and scarcely requires any further motivation for his actions.

Chrysalus' monologue on the Trojan War was written to be accompanied on a pipe, and we saw earlier that Plautus had increased the musical element in the passage of *Bacchides* which we can compare with its Greek original. In fact substantial portions of his plays would have been accompanied, a considerably larger part of them than of their originals. The effect of the music is entirely lost to us. But we can see that Plautus' language often becomes more colourful for these accompanied passages, and the music perhaps did no more than reinforce the effect of the words. Most striking are the so-called *cantica*, operatic arias and duets written in a variety of metres and displaying many features of high-flown style. They normally do little or nothing to further the action, and we know of nothing like them in Greek New Comedy. Chrysalus' 50-line monologue (his 'Troy-*canticum*') may have been expanded from a far briefer monologue in the original or it may have been spun altogether out of Plautus' head. A favourite type of *canticum* comes in the mouth of a slave who rushes on to the stage in great excitement to deliver an important piece of news. He is in a hurry but takes time to utter a lengthy monologue on entry. Thus the slave Acanthio at *Mercator* III ff.:

Strive with all your strength, struggle with might and main, to save your young master by your efforts. Come on, Acanthio, drive away your tiredness, don't indulge in idleness. I'm plagued by panting, I die for want of wind. What's more, the pavements are packed with people in my way: drive them off, knock them over, push them into the road! What dreadful manners people have here! When a man's in a tearing hurry, not one of them sees fit to make way for him. So you have three things to do at once, when you've begun to do one: dash, bash and brawl in the street!

Plautus is prodigal of his stylistic resources in the *cantica*, and it is presumably no accident that a *canticum* often comes near the beginning of a play where it is important to catch the audience's attention.

We saw that Chrysalus' boasts at *Bacchides* 1068 ff. contained references to the Roman institution of the triumph and to the quaestor, who was a Roman official. There is also a contemporary Roman reference in his remark about the frequency of triumphs (whether this is taken as referring to the celebration of triumphs by generals in real life or by slaves on the stage). There is no attempt to sustain the illusion that we are watching Greek characters in a Greek setting; and the dramatic illusion is further broken by Chrysalus' explicit address of the audience. This is altogether typical of Plautus. Sometimes he goes out of his way to remind the audience that his play is set in Greece, as at *Stichus* 446-8 (where once again the audience is addressed): 'Don't be surprised that mere slaves can drink, make love and accept invitations to dinner: we're allowed to do these things at Athens.' But when his characters talk of a dissolute life-style they speak of 'going Greek' (*pergraecari* or *congraecari*)—a Roman and not a Greek way of putting it. There are many allusions to Roman practices and Roman officials; and when the pimp Ballio addresses the members of his establishment at *Pseudolus* 143 and 172 he speaks as a Roman magistrate issuing an official edict. In the *canticum* at *Menaechmi* 571 ff. Menaechmus of Epidamnus complains that he has wasted his day acting as *patronus* (protector) on behalf of a *cliens* (dependant) in a lawsuit. He begins with a general complaint:

What a completely crazy custom this is of ours, a terribly troublesome one! It's above all the top people who have this habit: everyone wants to have lots of clients; they don't ask whether they're good or bad. They ask more about the reputation of their clients' wealth than of their honesty. If a man's poor and not bad, he's regarded as worthless; if he's rich and bad, he's thought to be a worthy client.

As he proceeds to describe the duties of a patron, he mentions a number of Roman legal technicalities. The entire passage has to do with social practices at Rome in Plautus' day. In effect, the play is set simultaneously in Epidamnus and in Rome.

The element of social comment in this last passage is not typical. Plautus was above all an entertainer and a poet. He uses colloquial speech, but Romans presumably did not often speak in the alliterative style with which this passage opens: 'Ut hoc utimur maxime more moro molestoque multum!' He abounds in wordplay and puns (at *Rudens* 102 a roof whose tiles have been blown off in a storm lets the daylight through 'quam cribrum crebrius': it is 'more perforated than a percolator'), in startling personifications (*Rudens* 626 'twist the neck of wrongdoing'), and in riddling expressions (*Mercator* 361 'My father's a fly: you can't keep anything secret from him, he's always buzzing around'). It is the sheer enjoyment in playing with words that is the hallmark of Plautus' genius.

Terence

The next Latin works to have survived are six comedies written by Terence in the 160s BC. These too are based on Greek New Comedies and written in verse. But there is a world of difference between Terence and Plautus. We do not have any substantial portions of the Greek originals of Terence's plays; but (although we know him to have changed some things) he seems to have preserved far more carefully than Plautus the ethos and general construction of the Greek plays. Roman technical language is occasionally used, but not as obtrusively as by Plautus. There is a considerable musical element, but hardly anything as extensive or as exotic metrically as a Plautine *canticum*. Above all, the comedy remains essentially situation comedy, in which consistency of characterization and clarity of plot construction are of vital importance.

The plots are once again concerned with love affairs and with the misunderstandings which arise from ignorance. In *Andria* ('The Woman from Andros') Simo wants his son Pamphilus to marry the daughter of Chremes, a respectable Athenian citizen; but Pamphilus is in love with a girl from Andros (Glycerium) who appears to be far less respectable. Intrigues and counter-intrigues lead to a number of emotional complications, which are resolved by the discovery that Glycerium is herself a daughter of Chremes. In *Hecyra* ('The Mother-in-Law') a young man (another Pamphilus) has married a woman already pregnant (though he does not know this) as the result of being raped. When she gives birth to a child of which there is every reason to suppose that he is not the father, their marriage appears to be at an end. In the course of the play his wife's attempt to conceal her condition gives rise to various misunderstandings: in particular, we see her mother-in-law being blamed by her father-in-law for the breakdown of the marriage. But all ends happily when it is discovered that it was Pamphilus himself who had raped her one night when drunk in the street. (It seems that the

Greek society portrayed in these plays was prepared to take a tolerant attitude to rape, as being a natural result of youthful drunkenness or high spirits. The girls in question led secluded lives, and young men had few opportunities to strike up acquaintance with them in a more leisurely way. Also, a citizen girl who had succumbed before marriage to a sustained campaign of seduction would have made a less sympathetic heroine than one who had been overcome by force. But the playwrights are not insensitive to the predicament of the victims of rape.) In *Eunuchus* ('The Eunuch') young Chaerea disguises himself as a eunuch in order to gain access to the bedroom of the girl with whom he is infatuated and there rapes her. The girl turns out to be the daughter of respectable Athenian parents, and Chaerea's father agrees to his marrying her. At the centre of the action is the prostitute Thais, who has taken the girl under her wing and is determined to help her find her parents. The picture of Thais is thrown into sharper relief by the fact that other characters in the play entertain quite unjustified suspicions of her behaviour.

These plots are less varied than those of Plautus, but their basic structure is not very different. The main difference between the two playwrights lies in the use which they make of their plots. Terence does not treat them as a springboard for extraneous jokes but preserves from the Greek originals the more elusive and ironic humour which arises out of a carefully constructed dramatic situation. We are told that Greek influence at Rome had increased considerably in the 160s, and Terence's plays have been taken as evidence that Greek refinement was now more widely appreciated than it had been by Plautus' less cultured audience. But there is a danger of exaggerating this difference. Some of the changes which Terence made to his Greek originals suggest that he was still aiming to appeal to a fairly unsophisticated kind of Roman. In adapting Menander's *Eunuchus* Terence has added from another play by Menander the characters of the boastful soldier and his fawning parasite, who bring with them some broad comic effects; and to Menander's *Adelphoe* ('The Brothers') he has added from a play by a different Greek author a scene of movement and violence in which a slave-dealer fails to prevent a young man from abducting one of the prostitutes he owns. Terence tells us of these additions in the prologues which he wrote to be delivered before the start of the plays themselves; and one of his prologues tells us something of the conditions in which his plays were performed. This is the prologue he wrote for the third performance of *Hecyra*, describing how two previous attempts to stage it had been failures:

The first time I began to perform this play, there was talk of a boxing match, and there were also rumours that a tight-rope walker was going to perform. Slaves were arriving, there was a din, women were shouting; and the result was that I had to give up before the end. ... I put it on again: the first act went down well, but then word got around that a gladiatorial show was going to be given. People flew together, there was an uproar, they were shouting and fighting for somewhere to sit. It was impossible for me to hold my own against that.

Hecyra is the only play of Terence which we know to have had difficulties with the public. His more boisterous *Eunuchus* was an unprecedented success.

Terences's prologues are quite unlike anything we know of in New Comedy or in Plautus. He uses them to conduct feuds with his literary rivals and defend himself against criticisms which they have made of him. They give us an exceptional glimpse of the literary world in which he worked, though they do only give his side of the arguments. If we can trust them, he was criticized (among other things) for feebleness of style, for plagiarism, and for combining more than one Greek original to construct a single Latin play ('contamination', as his critics called it). Although more faithful than Plautus to his originals, he seems not to have been faithful enough for some of his contemporaries. We learn of other innovations made by Terence from a commentary on his plays written in the fourth century AD by the famous grammarian Donatus. We can deduce, for instance, from what Donatus tells us, that Terence has spun the first twenty lines of his first play, *Andria*, entirely out of his own head. And one major change which he has made to the openings of his plays is that his prologues do not give the background to the plot (as those of Menander and Plautus do). Perhaps he regarded that as an artificial device, preferring to convey what information he could more naturalistically in the mouths of his characters in the course of the play. The result is that some opportunities for irony are missed, since the audience do not always learn all that there is to learn until a late stage of the play.

Terence is thus a more enigmatic figure than Plautus. He chose to adapt Greek plays whose appreciation often demands some moral and emotional involvement, and he was faithful most of the time in reproducing their essential qualities; but he did not do so slavishly, and he added some scenes with a cruder comic effect. It was no doubt the liveliness of his *Eunuchus* that ensured its success in his lifetime; but it is the quieter elements in Terence's plays that have most impressed his readers in subsequent generations: his sympathetic portrayal of the problems and predicaments of individuals, and his concern for the serious issues underlying the comedy of his plays. These elements ensure that his plays repay thoughtful study more than those of Plautus can ever do. But they are probably reproduced from the original Greek plays; and there is room to doubt whether Terence himself always cared about the refinements he has reproduced, as we shall see in the case of *Adelphoe*.

One thing which was undoubtedly Terence's own achievement was the creation of a Latin literary style quite unlike that of Plautus or of any other previous writer. Although criticized for its feebleness in Terence's own life, it has since then been more generally admired for its elegance and clarity. Terence was the first Latin writer to reproduce the elliptical style of natural conversation. It is not a low colloquial style, but its clipped constructions have a realistic ring which is generally absent from Plautus.

Within a century of his death, Terence's plays had become school texts; and they have continued to be so for as long as we know Latin to have been studied

CIE absquiuis homine cum est opus beneficium accipere gaudeas: uerum enim uero iddemū
iuuat. siquem aequum est bene facere. is benefacit. o frater frater: quid ego te nunc lau
dem. satis certo scio. numquam ita magnifice quicquā dicam. id uirtus quin super et tua.
itaq: unam hanc rem me habere praecipuam arbitror. fratrem homini
neminem esse primarium artium magis principem. SYR o ctesipho CIE o frre aeschi
nus ubiest SYR ellū te exspectat domi. CIE hem SYR quidest CIE quid st illuis
opera frre nunc uiuo festiuum caput quin omnia sibi post putarit esse p meo cō modo.
maledicta famam meum amorē & peccatū in se transtulit. nihil supra potest. quisnā
fores crepuit SYR mane mane ipse & it foras.

AESCHINUS   CTESI   PHO II   SYRUS   SERVUS SAN   NIO II
ADULES
CENS

AES ubiest ille sacrilegus SAN men quaerit nū quidnam effert occidi nihil uideo.
AES ehem opportune te ipsū querito. quid fit ctesipho intuto est omnis res. omitte uero tristi
tiam tuā   CIE ego illa facile uero omitto quiquidem te habeam fratrē omr   aeschine.
omi germane. auereor corā in os te laudare amplius. ne id adsentandi magis quā qd
habeam gratum facere & existimes AES age in epte. quasi nunc non norimus nos inter nos.
ctesipho sed hoc mihi dolet nos paene sero sciisse & paene meū locu rediisse ut si omnes
cuperent tibi nihil possent auxiliarier. CIE pudebat AES aha stultitia est istaec
non pudor tam ob paruolā rem paene & patria turpe dictum. deos quaeso ut istec phibeant.
CIE peccaui. AES quid ait tande nobis sannio SYR iam mitis est. AES ego ad forum ibo
ut hunc absoluam. tu intro ad illa ctesipho. SAN frre infta SYR eamus nāq. hic p
pera in crprum. SAN neta quidem quā uis & ia maneo otiosus hic. SYR reddetur
ne time. SAN at ut omne reddat. SYR omne reddet tace modo. ac sequere hac.
SAN sequor. CIE heus. heus. frre. SYR hem quidest CIE obsecro hercle te hominem istum

in Europe, holding a central place in the school curriculum until the nineteenth century. He has been admired for his style and for his moral sentiments, which can be made to sound more uplifting than Terence intended by being quoted out of context: the most famous of all, 'Homo sum: humani nil a me alienum puto' ('I am a man: I regard all that concerns men as concerning me') comes in the mouth of a tedious old busybody who has been asked why he is poking his nose into his neighbour's affairs. Its effect in context is to make him look pompous and ridiculous. But Terence has not been much praised for his humour, partly no doubt because it depends for its effect on the context created by the plot of the play. In the following passage from *Adelphoe* (413 ff.) the old man Demea boasts to the slave Syrus (who has just returned from buying fish in the market) about the method he has used in bringing up his son to be well behaved. Demea believes his method to have been effective, whereas Syrus and the audience know that the son (now an adolescent) is living a much wilder life than Demea imagines. It is clear that Syrus is mocking Demea in the second half of the passage, but the absurdity of Demea's boasting is much more comic if we bear in mind how wrong he is about the effectiveness of his method of upbringing:

D. I take a lot of trouble over it; I don't let anything slip; I train him. In fact I tell him to look into the lives of others, as into a mirror, and to learn from their example. 'Do this', I say.
S. Quite right!
D. 'Don't do that.'
S. Clever!
D. 'This is praiseworthy.'
S. Just the thing!
D. 'This is blameworthy.'
S. Excellent!
D. Furthermore —
S. Well, look, I really haven't got time to listen now. I've got the fish I wanted; I must make sure nothing goes wrong with them. ... To the best of my ability I give instructions to my fellow slaves just like the instructions you give: 'This is over-salted; this is burnt; this one hasn't been properly washed. That one's right: remember to do it like that next time.' I take a lot of trouble to teach them as well as my wits allow. In fact I tell them to look into the dishes, Demea, as if into a mirror, and I tell them what needs to be done.

Adelphoe is Terence's masterpiece. It was his last play and is the one that provokes most thought about a subject of perennial importance. But there is reason to think that he has distorted the balance of the play by striving for comic effect in its closing scenes. The thought-provoking theme is the question of what the relationship should be between a father and his adolescent son. We have just seen Demea being mocked for his misplaced confidence in a strict, didactic method of upbringing. His views are contrasted with those of his brother Micio, who believes that adolescent sons should be handled with openness and tolerance.

Micio's method seems to be presented for most of the play as the more humane and sympathetic one, and also the more successful. Demea's blind confidence makes him an appropriate comic butt, and Micio seems much more in control of events. But towards the end of the play there is a startling reversal: Demea starts to dominate at the expense of Micio, forcing him to agree to a number of unwelcome proposals (not least that he should marry a 'decrepit old woman'); and it looks as if the final judgement of the play is that Micio's approach was over-indulgent and excessively easy-going. This is very hard to reconcile with the rest of the play. Demea turns the tables on Micio and makes us laugh; but we are left uncertain where our sympathies should lie. Many scholars feel that Menander would not have written an ending so much at odds with the bulk of the play and that it is Terence who has sacrificed consistency to a desire to entertain or satisfy his Roman audience. But *Adelphoe* is not only about tolerance and strictness; it is also concerned with love between father and son and with lack of self-knowledge. Its handling of these themes combines comedy with telling characterization. It is precisely because the play is otherwise so successful that the ending has been found a puzzle; and the merits of the ending have long been hotly debated and will long continue to be so.

Plautus and Terence have survived; and they have influenced the European dramatic tradition. *Ralph Roister Doister* makes use of Plautus' *Miles Gloriosus* and Terence's *Eunuchus; The Comedy of Errors* is based on Plautus' *Menaechmi* and *Amphitruo*. Molière is one of many playwrights to have adapted the latter play, and he also followed Plautus' *Aulularia* (in *L'Avare*) and Terence's *Adelphoe* (in *L'École des maris*) and *Phormio* (in *Les Fourberies de Scapin*). Boastful soldiers, rediscovered foundlings, and scheming servants have long been standard ingredients of comic writing, not only for the stage: although P. G. Wodehouse told me (when I wrote to ask him) that he had not read Plautus or Terence, his Jeeves is clearly heir to the tradition of the scheming servant.

Ennius

One author who has not survived except in fragments must be mentioned because of his importance in the development of Latin literature. This is Ennius (239-169 BC). We have more certain information about his life than about those of Plautus and Terence: born in Calabria, he was brought to Rome in 204 or 203 by M. Porcius Cato and gave lectures on poetry. He accompanied M. Fulvius Nobilior on his Aetolian campaign in 189 and wrote in praise of his patron's achievements. His name is also linked with those of other prominent Romans. One benefit which he derived from such patronage was the Roman citizenship, conferred on him in 184 (by Nobilior's son, according to the traditional but unreliable account).

Ennius was a more versatile writer than Plautus or Terence, composing tragedies, comedies, satires, and a number of minor works in addition to his epic

BRONZE BUST OF A POET, from the Villa of the Papyri at Herculaneum. Long identified as Seneca, it is now generally regarded as an imaginary portrait of Hesiod; but a recent theory sees it as Ennius (239–169 BC), the first great epic poet in Latin. The statue on which it is based evidently belonged to the second century BC.

Annals; but it was this last work that represented his greatest contribution to Latin literature. Covering in eighteen books the history of Rome from Aeneas' flight from Troy down to Ennius' own day, it was written during the last fifteen years or so of his life. We now have about 600 lines, many of them single lines and not all of them complete, from a work which may originally have had 20,000 or more. The lines which have survived have done so because they were quoted by later authors, often to illustrate a linguistic point or an Ennian reminiscence in Virgil. We do not always know their context, and it is often only in the barest outline that we can hope to reconstruct the sequence of events in a book of the *Annals*. But enough survives to make us regret keenly the loss of the rest. Ennius set the tone for Latin hexameter writing in the high style for the next century and a half. Lucretius and Virgil were considerably influenced by him, and if we had more of his work we should understand more of theirs.

Ennius' most important contribution was perhaps the hexameter itself, the traditional metre of Greek epic. He was not the first to write an epic in Latin: Livius Andronicus had written a translation of the *Odyssey*, and Naevius had written an epic about the First Punic War towards the end of the third century. But these authors both wrote in the jerky Saturnian metre. Ennius introduced the more smoothly flowing hexameter into Latin epic, and to go with the new metre he moulded a poetic diction which served as the basis for the style of his successors.

At the beginning of the *Annals* Ennius claimed to be a reincarnation of Homer: the ghost of Homer had revealed this to him in a dream. Many features of his epic were Homeric: a Council of the Gods, battle descriptions, and similes. But there is much which strikes a different note, not least the discussion of his own poetic activity at the beginning of the work. Another autobiographical passage opened Book vii, where Ennius contrasted his own craftsmanship with the crude composition of his predecessors. His self-conscious proclamation of his stylistic skill reminds us more of Callimachus than of Homer. His own style came to seem crude by later canons of taste; but it is clear that he devoted some care to it in full awareness of his rôle as a pioneer. There is also a moralizing streak which must have helped in the establishment of Ennius as a central author in the school curriculum until the time of Virgil. Over half the work was devoted to events of Ennius' lifetime, the Second Punic War and the subsequent remarkable expansion of Roman power. Ennius glorifies the military achievements of the Roman nobility and supports traditional Roman morality. Individual virtue is praised, as in the famous lines about Q. Fabius Maximus Cunctator:

> One man by his delays restored our nation.
> Our weal he put before his reputation.
> Thus now his glory shines more brightly yet
> In later years . . .

('Unus homo nobis cunctando restituit rem . . .'). Such glorification of an individual was perhaps not in the best Roman traditions; but the heroes of the *Annals* displayed virtues which were very much admired by Romans. And other passages combined profound reflection with stylistic vigour in a memorable way, for instance the following on the disruptive effects of war:

> Wisdom is driven out: violence holds sway.
> Sound speakers scorned, rough soldiers have their day.
> No longer with abuse or skilful speech
> Do men express their hatred, each to each.
> But now with weapons, not with writs, they fight;
> They strive to rule, press on with massive might.

Further Reading

There is an excellent survey of Early Latin Literature by A. S. Gratwick in *The Cambridge History of Classical Literature*, II, *Latin Literature* (1982), 60–171 (this survey forms the bulk of the first volume of the paperback edition of the Cambridge History, 'Part I: The Early Republic').

The Loeb Classical Library includes complete texts with translations of Plautus (in five volumes) and Terence (in two volumes); the fragments of Ennius are included in the volume *Remains of Old Latin*, I. In the Penguin Classics series nine plays of Plautus have been translated by E. F. Watling and all the plays of Terence by Betty Radice. There are also lively translations of selected plays of Plautus by Erich Segal (*Miles Gloriosus, Menaechmi, Mostellaria*: London, 1969), Christopher Stace (*Rudens, Curculio, Casina*: Cambridge, 1981) and James Tatum (*Bacchides, Casina, Truculentus*: Baltimore, 1983). John Barsby's edition of *Bacchides* (Warminster, 1986) includes a very successful verse translation and a full commentary based on it; and Frances Muecke has produced a companion to the Penguin translation of *Menaechmi* (Bristol, 1987). The plays of Terence have been translated by Frank O. Copley, The Library of Liberal Arts (Indianapolis, 1967) and by P. Bovie and others (New Brunswick, NJ, 1974).

For Roman Comedy, the best general introduction in English is R. L. Hunter, *The New Comedy of Greece and Rome* (Cambridge, 1985). George E. Duckworth, *The Nature of Roman Comedy* (Princeton, 1952) provides a fuller account, though much of what he says about Greek New Comedy has been rendered obsolete by the discovery of substantial portions of plays by Menander since 1958. Both books are available in paperback.

The most important book on Plautus this century has been the book in German by Eduard Fraenkel, *Plautinisches im Plautus* (Berlin, 1922), which was reissued in an Italian translation with additional notes as *Elementi Plautini in Plauto* (Florence, 1960). Fraenkel was concerned to identify and evaluate the original features in Plautus' adaptations of Greek comedies. Erich Segal's book *Roman Laughter: The Comedy of Plautus* (Harvard, 1968; paperback edn., Oxford, 1987) is an entertaining and enthusiastic account of the 'festival' elements in Plautus' plays, the ways in which they invert everyday Roman values and behaviour.

Gilbert Norwood, *The Art of Terence* (Oxford, 1923; repr. New York, 1965), though outdated in some important respects, provides a very sympathetic appreciation of Terence and is the best book on him in English.

The fragments of Ennius' *Annals* have been edited by O. Skutsch, *The Annals of Q. Ennius* (Oxford, 1985).

4

Cicero and Rome

❦

MIRIAM GRIFFIN

THIS chapter is devoted to the period which opens with the dictatorship of Sulla in 82 BC and closes with that of Caesar in 44 BC. It is concerned with the political life and death of the later Roman Republic.

Cicero

If we know more about these years than about any other period of Roman history, it is due principally to one man, Marcus Tullius Cicero. We have an abundance of speeches and letters written when he was deeply involved in day-to-day politics, either holding the highest offices of state or in contact with the men who were settling the future of the Mediterranean world. But it is not only political history that his works illuminate so brilliantly. When not at the centre of the stage, Cicero turned to literature of a more reflective sort and composed a corpus of theoretical works on philosophy and rhetoric richly adorned with contemporary examples and redolent of contemporary attitudes. Precisely because he was not an original thinker, Cicero helps us to recapture the intellectual habits of his generation.

The voluminous correspondence which Cicero maintained throughout all the vicissitudes of his adult life remains, however, his most valuable legacy to the historian. Some letters were private and not intended for publication; others were clearly written with a wider circulation in mind. Over 900 in number, they concern personal and cultural matters, as well as providing official and unofficial, public and private, views of the most important political events of the day. Of Cicero's most candid letters, those to his intimate friend Atticus, a younger contemporary was to write: 'Whoever reads the eleven books of the correspondence hardly feels the need of an organized history of the time.'

There is a dark side, however, to this picture. Cicero was an intelligent observer, but he was not detached; he was perceptive, but mercurial in mood and outlook; he was interested in other people, but, above all, obsessed with his own reputation. Moreover, his contemporaries have left little to serve as a corrective to his version of things. Their speeches, their works on philosophy and rhetoric

M. TULLIUS CICERO, the great Roman orator and statesman, whose speeches and letters are such a valuable source of information for the high society and politics of his time. Born in a well-to-do family at Arpinum in southern Italy in 106 BC, he rose to be leader of the Roman bar in 70, consul in 63, and a prominent figure in the political intrigues of the 50s; he died in the proscriptions of 43 BC.

have not survived intact, and much of what we know of them comes from Cicero. Over seventy letters from friends and acquaintances are preserved with Cicero's, but as they are mostly letters to him, they throw little light on matters outside his concerns. If it were not for Caesar's account of the Gallic and Civil Wars, Varro's antiquarian and agricultural writings, and some Roman legal documents preserved on stone or bronze, we might almost believe that the life of late-republican Rome, as we conceive it, was a creation of Cicero's fertile imagination.

We need, therefore, to ascertain how great is the distortion which the inevitable prominence of Cicero lends to our conception of the last and greatest phase of the Roman Republic. As regards Latin prose, we can rest easy. However regrettable the loss of works by other authors, either for their intrinsic merits or their value as evidence, Cicero rightly dominates the scene. There is copious testimony to the fact that the survival of so many of his works corresponds to their superiority in the eyes of the Romans themselves. After Cicero, no one could compose a speech in Latin, or a letter of any literary pretensions, or a work on philosophy or rhetoric, without author and audience being acutely conscious of the great exemplar. His works survived as textbooks in the grammar schools and models in the rhetorical schools. He was savagely criticized and passionately defended. Only his poetry was consistently and, as the remains show, justly ignored.

For the Quintilian (below, p. 247), Cicero was 'the name, not of a man, but of eloquence itself'. In what did the literary significance of Cicero consist? In oratory first of all, the indispensable accomplishment of an ancient politician. Cicero excelled in all three branches, deliberative, epideictic (display speeches), and forensic. His speeches before the Senate and people show us how he could present issues differently to different audiences, almost always with success. As consul he could turn the Roman populace against measures of debt relief and land distribution, though there were genuine shortages of currency and corn. At the end of his life he was able to persuade the Senate to vote official powers to Octavian, a revolutionary with a private army, in the name of the Republic. Epideictic oratory was less important as a genre at Rome, but it contributed vital ingredients, invective and eulogy, to different kinds of speech: if Cicero's praise of Pompey's achievements and Caesar's conquests moves us less than it did his contemporaries, we still find his absurd portrait of the ex-consul Piso in the speech *In Pisonem*, with his tame Epicurean philosopher and his mobile eyebrows, or his caricatures of the stern Stoic Cato and the pedantic jurist Sulpicius Rufus in the *Pro Murena*, hard to resist.

The most taxing and the most esteemed type of oratory at Rome was forensic. For at least twenty years, until his death in 43 BC, Cicero dominated the Roman courts, where arguments derived from law and fact counted for less than appeals to passion and prejudice. Though he boasted of being able to 'throw dust in the eyes of the jury', alleging in one case that there had been bribery in a *cause célèbre* and denying it in another four years later (and winning both cases), he was particularly famed for his ability to arouse and calm the emotions of jurors and spectators. He was for that reason regularly asked to give the concluding speech in defence.

The periodic style that Cicero developed, with its elaborately balanced clauses and careful rhythmic cadences, was less florid than that of Hortensius, the great rival of his youth, but by the end of his career it was becoming too ornate for the taste of the younger generation. Hence there is an apologetic element in his major works on rhetoric, which draw on Greek theory and on his own experience in order to present a picture of the perfect orator. In the *Brutus*, a history of Roman oratory written in 46 BC and ostensibly inspired by the death of Hortensius four years earlier, Cicero's own achievement is coyly represented as the climax of Roman eloquence. Here, as in the earlier *De Oratore* and the later *Orator*, Cicero lays great stress on the proper training for an orator, which he believed should not be just a matter of mastering techniques but of acquiring a broad education based on Greek culture. Cicero's hero, L. Licinius Crassus, to whom he had attached himself as an 'apprentice', had, as censor in 92, opposed the opening of schools to give rhetorical instruction in Latin alone: Greek was a richer language with an established tradition of great oratory that had to be mastered.

Though he regarded history and law as essential parts of the orator's education, it is Greek philosophy that Cicero recommends most strongly in these works: first because it imparts wisdom which the statesman needs to combine with eloquence, but also because it offers training in argument. These motives for interest in philosophy help to explain Cicero's choice of philosophical sect. Though he exposed himself to all the major schools, Epicureanism, which preached abstention from public life and had little interest in fine words, he gladly left to his friend Atticus. A Stoic philosopher named Diodotus lived in his house while he was still a boy and eventually died there: with him Cicero studied dialectic. His preference went to the teachers of the New Academy, the name given to a sceptical phase in the history of Plato's school, who taught that certain knowledge was not to be had, but that probability was an intellectually respectable basis for practical life. They were naturally committed to the Academic tradition of arguing both sides of a question, which gave excellent practice in speaking. Their beliefs also gave Cicero the freedom to choose what philosophical view he found most convincing on particular issues. For example, he was able without inconsistency to favour Stoic views on divine providence and on fundamental morality, while rejecting their view that oratory should be unemotional.

Though Cicero always maintained that public service should take precedence over study and writing, philosophy remained his favourite leisure activity. But it really came into its own when the political scene ceased to be hospitable to his talents. Given his priorities, it is not surprising that the first theoretical works he produced were the treatises on rhetoric we have mentioned and two works of political philosophy, *De re publica* and *De Legibus* ('On the State' and 'On the Laws'). But already in 46, two minor works gave the sign of things to come. *The Paradoxes of the Stoics* is a rhetorical *tour de force* in which Cicero defends these extreme formulations of Stoic doctrine, for instance, that virtue is the only good, and that all bad deeds are equally wicked. The work is dedicated to Cato's nephew Brutus and opens with praise of Cato for his ability to make his philosophy acceptable to the general public. Cato was then leading the Republican forces in Africa, which no doubt explains why Cicero wished to make amends for the ridicule he had heaped on his Stoicism some seventeen years earlier. Later in the year, after Cato's suicide, Cicero was to produce a moving eulogy of him.

By the next year he had embarked on a grand plan 'to provide for my fellow citizens a path through the noblest form of learning'. In the next two years he produced a dozen works, mostly in the dialogue form that Plato and Aristotle had invented, covering the three branches of ancient philosophy. The series began with the *Hortensius*, an exhortation to the study of philosophy now lost but whose impact can be judged from the words of St Augustine: 'That book changed my character and directed my prayers to you, Lord.' To the logical branch of philosophy, he devoted only one work, the *Academica*, which presented the sceptical standpoint of the New Academy. In the other two branches, he started with an 'academic' exposition of the views of the different schools on the most basic and general philosophical questions and then proceeded to defend his preferred doctrine on the more specific and practical questions. Thus in natural philosophy, the dialogue *On the Nature of the Gods* was followed by works *On Divination* and *On Fate*, and in moral philosophy the dialogue *On Ends*, discussing the goal of life as advocated by the different dogmatic schools, was followed by the *Tusculan Disputations* and *On Moral Obligations*, which defend the Stoic view of happiness and of duty.

Yet Cicero's purpose was not to preach particular philosophical doctrines. Indeed, even in his more dogmatic works, he asserts that there is no certain truth and defends his right to find different views more convincing according to the argumentation used on each occasion. His desire was to do the state some service and, in the process, to earn glory for himself when other avenues were closed. He made no claim to original philosophical ideas. What he had to contribute was his ability to reproduce Greek philosophy in eloquent Latin, to create a philosophical literature for Rome that could rival that of Greece, as Roman oratory already did. The eloquent orator would repay his debt to his education. Serious philosophical discourse had up to now been written in Greek: even Lucretius seems to have been regarded as a poet rather than as a philosopher. Cicero did not altogether reverse the pattern; but he had a firm follower in Seneca (below, pp. 253 f) and his ultimate heirs were the Latin Church Fathers. 'Latin philosophy, which before him was rough and ready, he polished by his eloquence', wrote a contemporary. He himself, in explaining how he could write so many books so quickly, says to Atticus: 'They are only copies and involve little effort; only the words are mine, of which I have a copious store.' There were Epicureans and Stoics who wrote in Latin before him, but they themselves, he says, made no pretension to stylistic elegance or even definition and arrangement. Though Cicero here exaggerates his role as a mere translator, which he elsewhere denies, there is no doubt that most of the evidence for his taking pains concerns not the meaning of the Greek doctrines but the choice of interlocutors and the problems of vocabulary. It was Cicero who fixed the correlation between Greek technical terms and the Latin word or words used to render them, because he was more interested in instructing all educated readers than in preaching to the converted. Not only does he often give the Greek original: he often discusses alternative translations and changes his mind in later works.

Before and after Cicero, it was common to complain of the deficiencies of Latin as a philosophical language. Cicero protested, with some justice, that new subjects in any language require the creation of new words, and that Greek philosophers too had resorted to neologisms. He himself introduced, for example, *qualitas, moralis,* and *beatitudo,* for 'quality', 'moral', and 'happiness' (it is suggestive that Rome, left to herself, needed no word for happiness). But though he patriotically maintained that Latin was potentially richer than Greek, it had certain fundamental limitations that were particularly serious for philosophical exposition: Latin was inhospitable to compound words, and it lacked the definite article. As Seneca was to complain, '"Quod est" is a feeble substitute for Plato's *to on*,' ('that which exists'). Cicero often resorted to periphrasis, especially as he was aiming for eloquence, which meant respecting the genius of the language. 'We do not need to translate word for word, as unstylish translators do', he writes. The same consideration lead to the more irritating habit of translating Greek technical terms differently in different places, or by pairs of words, in accordance with his normal style. Nonetheless, his achievement was immense. His greatest pagan successor, Seneca, though he added many new terms of his own to the Latin philosophical vocabulary, almost never rejected one of Cicero's translations: they permanently enlarged the resources of Latin.

That such a self-conscious stylist should also leave behind the most spontaneous personal letters may at first seem paradoxical. But it was part of Cicero's consummate talent for finding the right style for each occasion. The letters include official dispatches to the Senate on military affairs in his province which are quite different, in their formal simplicity, from the witty and entertaining picture of his duties that he gives his young friend Caelius, or the irritable coldness with which he addresses his inconsiderate predecessor Appius Claudius, or the bitter and anxious confidences he makes to his friend Atticus. The letters not only show us Cicero's literary versatility and the intricacies of Roman politics: they give us a glimpse of cultivated and sophisticated society—marriages and dowries, divorce and bereavement, property and investment, patronage and promotion, declamation and dinner parties. Above all, they furnish us with a more candid and intimate picture of an individual than we shall meet again until Marcus Aurelius and St Augustine.

Cicero's place in the political, military, and social history of Rome is not as secure as his place in cultural history. It is true that he held the major magistracies, that he suppressed a serious social revolt in his consulship, and that he governed a distant province for a year and might even have attained a triumph for his military achievements in the Taurus mountains, had the civil war not intervened. On the other hand, he can claim no part in the constitutional reforms or extensive conquests of his generation.

Sulla and his Legacy

The closest approximation to a historical account of Cicero's time written by a contemporary was eventually provided by Sallust (below, pp. 232 ff.). His monograph on the conspiracy of Catiline, the chief episode of Cicero's consulship, demonstrates to the full how difficult it was even for a contemporary witness of events to escape from Cicero's interpretation of them. Yet at the same time, the work exposes the misleading character of Cicero's version. For Sallust affords glimpses of the economic and social problems that afflicted the Italian peninsula and led to the unrest represented by Cicero as the work of a few aristocratic reprobates.

Sallust is valuable in another respect: he furnishes us with a starting point for the period of the late Republic, namely, the dictatorship of L. Cornelius Sulla. He singled out the return of Sulla's booty-laden legions from the East, their seizure of the city by force, and the vindictiveness of Sulla's victory as the final turning-point in Roman conduct. Decline, he held, had set in when the destruction of Rome's mighty enemy Carthage left her without an incentive to self-discipline. Now personal greed and ambition came to dominate Roman political life. The historical perspective of Sallust, if not his diagnosis of the Republic's demise, can stand: it is not difficult to show that the age of Cicero was, in many respects, the legacy of Sulla.

Not only Catiline, whom Sallust specifically described as the product of the corrupt Sullan era, not only Crassus and Pompey, who were active partisans of Sulla, but Cicero, born in 106, Caesar, born in 100, and the younger Cato, born in 94, could remember the first armed conquest of Rome by a Roman, the proscriptions in which men all over Italy lost their property and their lives, and finally the astonishing abdication in 80 BC.

Though related by marriage to Sulla's enemy Marius, Cicero and his family, like many others, kept a low profile during the fighting and stayed in Rome when Sulla was away fighting Mithridates. Until 84, when Sulla's return was imminent, things were peaceful under the regime of Cinna and Marius; but the state was, as Cicero later described it, 'without law, without any semblance of authority'. As a result of the 'total dearth of orators', the young Hortensius Hortalus, only eight years older than Cicero, gained the limelight, and it was he whom Cicero opposed when he pleaded his first case after Sulla's return to Rome. Cicero's next two cases brought him face to face with the hardship inflicted on Italy by Sulla. The speech in defence of Roscius of Ameria in Umbria, delivered in 80, revealed the corrupt way in which Sulla's minions exploited the proscriptions and local feuds in the Italian towns for their own profit. In the second, delivered after Sulla had retired into private life, Cicero defended the rights of a woman of Arretium, one of the towns in Etruria from which Sulla had attempted to remove the rights of citizenship.

Cicero's attitude was not out of tune with the times. Many of Sulla's own allies had soon realized that the ruthlessness with which he destroyed his enemies and rewarded his friends could, in the long run, jeopardize his constitutional arrangements. To deflect the antagonism generated by his methods from the nobility that Sulla had left in charge, stories were circulated to the effect that this or that prominent supporter had queried the extent of the proscriptions, asking 'With whom shall we conquer?' The Metelli, the family of Sulla's wife, turned out in force to demonstrate sympathy with Roscius. Pompey, always adept at seeing how the wind was blowing, made a marriage alliance with them and

REMAINS OF THE
TABULARIUM IN ROME, the
building which housed the
state archives. It was
commissioned by one of
Sulla's lieutenants, Q. Lutatius
Catulus, and designed by the
architect L. Cornelius in 78 BC.
Only the high podium and a
gallery at first-floor level
survive; the upper storey has
been replaced by the medieval
Senatorial Palace.

successfully supported for the consulship of 78 a man no longer favoured by
Sulla. This was Marcus Aemilius Lepidus, who was eventually to side with the
dispossessed of Etruria when they attacked the Sullan colonists planted like garrisons on their land.

If Sulla had hoped that his confiscations would make his veterans prosperous
and Italy secure, he was mistaken. The land allotted was often not of the best,
while the forces that had been driving the small farmer off the land for a
century—extended military service and capitalist farming by the rich—continued
to operate. Some of the confiscated land had not actually been allocated and was
held either by the original Marian partisans or by Sullan squatters. Threatened
by every agrarian proposal, these men remained insecure in their tenure and
hence ripe for revolution for the duration of the Republic.

Sulla's methods also left moral scars. The richest prizes had been used to keep
and buy the loyalty of the upper orders. Leading men of the late Republic were
known to be enjoying ill-gotten gains, and few consciences were absolutely clear.
It is not surprising that in the seventies and sixties there were repeated attempts

to revoke Sulla's exemptions and reclaim for the state treasury the price of proscribed property and the rewards given to agents of the proscriptions. One of Caesar's early claims to political notoriety was his willingness, as president of the murder court in 64, to accept charges against those who had killed for Sulla. Cicero was only too willing to exploit in his campaign for the consulship that year the threat this posed to his competitor L. Sergius Catilina whom men could still remember carrying the head of one of Marius' kinsmen through the streets of Rome to present it, still 'full of life and breath', to the dictator himself. Once elected, however, Cicero opposed a move to restore political rights to the sons of the proscribed, for, he argued, 'nothing could be crueller than to exclude men of such excellent families from political life, but the cohesion of the state is so dependent on Sulla's laws that it cannot survive their dissolution'.

Public Life at Rome

Most of Sulla's constitutional and legal arrangements survived to determine the character of political life throughout the late Republic. The dictator had laid down rules for the senatorial career, the *cursus honorum*, which were designed to ensure that men who finally found themselves, after holding the top magistracies, in command of armies and provinces would already have sat in the Senate for twenty years, absorbing its traditions and learning to set a high value on oligarchic cohesiveness. Holders of the quaestorship, the lowest office to carry senatorial rank, were now to number twenty a year, instead of eight, in order to maintain a Senate of 600. For the old council of 300 was inadequate to provide juries for all of Sulla's reorganized statutory courts where senators, as before C. Gracchus, were to be tried for public crimes by their peers. The number of officials required to administer Rome and its ten provinces was ensured, without damage to the prestige of the highest offices, by retaining two as the number of annual consuls and increasing the number of praetors from six to eight. Savage competition was built into the system, for every year saw twenty men spurred by initial success to hope for high office, fewer than half of whom would ever be elected praetor. It is therefore not surprising to find an increased emphasis on legislation against electoral corruption in the late Republic. Sulla's *lex de ambitu* carried the penalty of ten years' disqualification from public office; Cicero's *lex Tullia*, passed in his consulship, imposed ten years of exile.

Cicero's speeches give a vivid picture of a highly organized system for distributing largesse to the voters in various forms, from free seats at the games to outright bribes. In his indictment of C. Verres, who was on trial in 70 for extortionate practices as governor of Sicily, Cicero recounts how Verres tried to use his illicit gains to prevent Cicero's election to the aedileship in that year. One effect of the increased competition resulting from Sulla's measures was to make it even more difficult than before for a man of non-senatorial background to reach the higher offices, and Cicero wanted the aedileship, an optional office between quaestorship and praetorship, because it offered an opportunity to give games and win popularity. Despite Verres he was successful, but in that very year the electoral situation was made still more complex by the activity of the censors.

The year 70 was altogether momentous. For it was then, in the consulship of Cn. Pompeius Magnus and M. Licinius Crassus, outstanding partisans of Sulla, that the dictator's restrictions on the legislative and judicial powers of the tribunes of the *plebs* were removed, after nearly a decade of popular agitation. After his election, Pompey had made a speech combining this promise with an attack on the corruption of provincial governors and the senatorial juries who failed to punish them. A decade of expensive and prolonged war with accompanying food shortages had made the senatorial government vulnerable to criticism. Scandals involving marked ballots and lavish bribery had rendered the senatorial courts, despite the conviction of Verres, indefensible. If Sulla's senators were, as he probably hoped, less liable than their predecessors to acquit their peers, since most of them would never enjoy the same opportunities, they were more vulnerable to bribes, since the new men among them found maintaining a senatorial life-style a strain and could not borrow easily in the expectation of later provincial profits. Though Pompey does not seem to have specified how the judiciary was to be straightened out, he did not oppose the passage of the *lex Aurelia* which gave the *equites* two-thirds of the seats on the juries.

The censors of the year, friends of Pompey, ejected from the Senate sixty-four members, mostly men who had proved themselves corrupt in the provinces or the courts. Their struggles to recover senatorial rank by being elected to office again compounded electoral competition in the sixties, while other action by the censors introduced a further element of uncertainty into the electoral game. The Italians, who had gained the franchise at the end of the Social War (above, pp. 35 f.) were at last enrolled in the thirty-five Roman tribes. Henceforth candidates for office had to consider a wider electorate, of whom at least the more prosperous members might actually find it worth while to come to Rome and vote. Thus when Cicero was planning his consular campaign, he included in his schedule a visit to the governor of Cisalpine Gaul (the Po valley) for 'the district is likely to count heavily in the voting'.

Optimates and Populares

Sulla's legislation and the struggles that led to its modification also had a profound effect on terminology and habits of thought.

It was in this period that the ideology or, on a cynical view, the propaganda familiar to us from the works of Cicero and Caesar became defined. The habit of mapping out the political scene in terms of a Right and a Left by the words 'Optimates' and 'Populares' could in fact be older than the days of Sulla, for the programmes and methods of the Gracchi gave shape to such a division. But it was Sulla's legislation that made explicit the dominance of the Senate that had developed in the third and second centuries BC and started to be seriously challenged in the middle of the second. It was, in essence, Sulla's view of the proper balance of the constitution that became the bulwark of the Optimates. And it was the struggle over the modification of his laws, principally in 70, that gave definition to the *popularis ratio*.

In speaking of Optimates and Populares we are speaking of ideological labels, not of organized political parties. Indeed 'popularis', as applied to people, normally refers to leading politicians with a certain political style, not to leaders and followers, and usually to a succession of such leaders, not a group working together. A *popularis* was a politician who used and defended the powers of the popular assemblies and the popular office of tribune as a counterweight to senatorial authority and/or championed such economic measures as land distribution, debt cancellation, and subsidized corn.

In the years immediately following the resurrection of the tribunate some ambitious men held the office and sponsored legislation that the establishment regarded as a threat. Gabinius even threatened to re-enact the most notorious act of Tiberius Gracchus (above, pp. 33 f.) and depose his colleague from office rather than accept his veto. The kind of left-wing image affected by the tribune Rullus in 63 who, according to Cicero, grew his hair long and took to wearing dirty old clothes and a farouche expression; the self-advertisement of his colleague Labienus who put a statue of his uncle, the martyred tribune Saturninus, on the rostra—these were only to be expected of young men on the make; they might yet end as stalwart supporters of the Senate. For there is no warrant to assume sincerity, or even consistency, in the conduct of Roman politicians. Indeed the prime example of ambiguity and opportunism was the restorer of the tribunate himself.

Pompey

Though he had inherited from his father some connection with Marius' ally Cinna, Pompey raised an army of his father's clients in Picenum and joined Sulla on his return from the East. For his ruthlessness in destroying Sulla's enemies in Sicily and Africa he acquired the nickname 'teenage butcher'; for his selfish ambition he earned the distrust of his own side. From the dictator, who had treated him as an exception to his own rules and allowed him to command legions when he had not held public office, Pompey extorted a triumph. After being cut out of Sulla's will for supporting Lepidus, he then suppressed Lepidus' rebellion and used his troops to extort the Spanish command from the Senate. In Spain he managed to steal the limelight from Metellus Pius, who was already making headway against the rebel general Sertorius, and then returned to Italy to do the same to Crassus. After dealing with some fugitives from the rising led by the gladiator Spartacus, Pompey wrote to the Senate that Crassus had conquered the slaves, but that he himself had extirpated the war.

Pompey had nothing to lose by a shake-up of the Sullan system. He had made too many enemies to fit comfortably into Optimate politics: only the presence of his army in Italy had secured him senatorial dispensation to stand for the consulship without having held the lower offices. Now, after the popular measures of his consulship, enthusiastic tribunes secured for him from the people first, in 67, sweeping powers to clear the Mediterranean of pirates and then, in the next year, the command of the war against Mithridates, in which, true to form, he replaced Sulla's trusty officer L. Licinius Lucullus, who had been appointed some years ago by the Senate.

In Pompey's absence, Rome speculated on the manner of his return. Would the great man come home in a conservative or a radical mood? In the end he tried to manoeuvre a return in the company of his troops as in the past, but a

HEAD OF POMPEY (CN. POMPEIUS MAGNUS), the most powerful Roman general of the 70s and 60s BC and chief architect of the downfall of Sulla's political system. During the 50s he lost ground to his fellow triumvir, Julius Caesar, and was assassinated in the course of the civil wars of 49–45. The romantic Alexander-inspired hairstyle sits oddly on the realistic facial features— furrowed brow, large nose, small piggy eyes, double chin.

move to recall him to suppress Catiline's forces was thwarted by the consul's decisiveness and the Optimates' determination. Eventually, towards the close of 62, Pompey dismissed his army at Brundisium and returned to confront the Senate of Sulla making its last stand.

Cicero, Pompey's exact contemporary, presents a similarly complex, if less sinister, political image. By conviction he was a conservative, by temperament a moderate, while his municipal equestrian background gave him a certain perspective on the Roman scene. To enhance the favour his forensic work could bring him, Cicero identified himself with the rising star, prosecuting in 70 the man who had mistreated Pompey's Sicilian clients and going on to support the proposal to give Pompey the Mithridatic command. In the first he castigated the corruption of senatorial juries; in the second he lamented the sufferings of the Asian *publicani*. These were themes to attract the *equites*, but in 65 he defended Pompey's ex-quaestor Cornelius and the radical activities of his tribunate, with moving appeals to the ancient struggles of the *plebs*. His famous doctrine of the *concordia ordinum* (harmony of the orders) was more in line with Sulla, who had himself broadened the composition of the Senate: the upper orders, senators and *equites*, were to fulfil their different public obligations and co-operate against revolutionary movements. But when Cicero opposed a whole series of tribunician proposals which appealed to the rural and urban poor, he said, and no doubt partly believed, that he was a *popularis consul* safeguarding the true interests of the people.

Cicero believed that in 63 he had actually achieved the *concordia ordinum* and indeed a wider 'consensus of right-thinking men' against the subversive movement of Catiline. The Senate, too, was in elated mood and, led by a young man who succeeded by force of personality in persuading his peers that he embodied old republican morality, faced the demands of the triumphant Pompey in an uncompromising spirit. Pompey wanted a marriage alliance with Cato, but, to the disappointment of the women of his family, Cato said 'No'. Pompey wanted the Senate to ratify his eastern arrangements, which reversed many decisions of Lucullus, immediately and *en bloc*; Cato, a relative of Lucullus, and others said 'No'. Pompey wanted to distribute to his veterans and needy citizens Italian land, including the *ager Campanus* which even the Gracchi had spared; here even Cicero said 'No', for the rents from the Campanian land provided the closest, and hence the most reliable, source of public revenue.

Cato had the bit between his teeth. One of the effects of the civil wars of Sulla and Marius had been to deprive Rome of the men who should have been her senior statesmen. Those that were left were often too inclined, Cicero thought, to withdraw to their luxurious villas and fishponds and lead a life of cultured ease. Hence there was room for a strong character such as M. Porcius Cato to become a leader of the Senate before he had held the praetorship. Pompey was not his only target. Cato offended the *equites* by threatening the long-standing immunity from prosecution for bribery that equestrian jurors enjoyed. In addition he opposed making any concession to the *publicani* who had overbid for the tax-contract in Asia in the expectation that the province would quickly return to normal after the Mithridatic War. Here Cicero parted company with him. Cato was destroying the *concordia ordinum*: he behaved 'as if he were living in Plato's Republic and not in the cesspool of Romulus'.

Crassus

In the course of his crusade, Cato alienated not only Pompey but Crassus who had urged the tax-farmers to ask for a remission of their contract. The importance of Marcus Crassus is easier to demonstrate than to explain. He was a decent orator, but easily surpassed by Cicero; he was a talented general, but outclassed by Pompey and Caesar; he was rich, but hardly more so than Pompey when he returned home with his eastern booty. Like Pompey, Crassus had raised an army and joined Sulla on his return to Italy; unlike Pompey, he was a notorious profiteer in the proscriptions. What ancient writers liked to emphasize was his avarice and the political ambition he made it serve. He was said to have augmented his property by taking advantage of the frequent fires in Rome and the lack of a regular fire brigade: owners of burning buildings would sell them for a song, and Crassus, with his team of trained slaves, would repair and rebuild them for profit. A much quoted remark of his was, 'No man is rich who cannot support an army': the fact that Crassus could may help to explain how he obtained the command against Spartacus at a time of financial stress.

Less dramatic uses of his wealth included lending money to political associates free of interest, and providing lavish hospitality. The result, we are told, is that Crassus had considerable influence with the Senate. It is likely that he was one of the first to take the measure of the changed political conditions brought about by Sulla's doubling of the Senate's membership. The new men often needed money to maintain their new station, and they would relish invitations to dine with a noble of ancient family. But Crassus was not content to be a conservative politician. Shady and unorthodox himself, he liked to support black sheep and sponsor radical causes. Though resentful of Pompey's successes, he joined him as consul in 70 in restoring the rights of tribunes, and in successive years he supported several tribunes on trial. He also lent money to young aristocrats such as Caesar, or funded their electoral campaigns, as in the case of Catiline. Some of his more daring political initiatives were often unsuccessful: both of his projects as censor, to enfranchise the communities of Cisalpine Gaul and to exploit the will of the Egyptian king who left his country to Rome, were baulked by his colleague.

Caesar

While Cato preached and Pompey and Crassus fumed, an abler politician than any of them was planning how to exploit the situation. 'Caesar, from the outset

C. JULIUS CAESAR, the conqueror of Gaul and dictator of 48–44 BC. He rose to power as a politician 'of the left', but achieved his ultimate triumph through brilliant generalship. Subsequently, however, his accumulation of powers and honours alarmed even his own supporters, and he was assassinated in the famous Ides of March conspiracy.

and as it were by hereditary right the head of the popular party, had for thirty years borne aloft its banner without ever changing or even so much as concealing its colours.' So Mommsen wrote of the murdered dictator, 'the sole creative genius ever produced by Rome'. C. Iulius Caesar has been appreciably cut down to size in the past century, but it remains hard to deny that he was the most consistent politician of the late Republic.

Related by marriage to Marius and Cinna, he had escaped the proscriptions because of family connections on the other side. But tradition credited Sulla with the prediction that he would eventually destroy the Optimates for 'he harbours in him many a Marius.' In 70 he supported the restoration of the tribunes' powers and the amnesty granted to the followers of Lepidus, one of whom was his wife's brother. In youth Caesar had refused Sulla's request to divorce Cornelia, who was Cinna's daughter; when she died in 67 he delivered a public eulogy of her In the same year, at the funeral of his aunt Julia, he displayed the images of her husband Marius, not seen since the days of Sulla. Then, as aedile in 65, Caesar restored to public view the trophies that Marius had brought back from his victories, and in 64 he countenanced the prosecution of Sulla's agents.

To the development of his *popularis* image Caesar brought all his considerable talent for publicity. In 63 he prosecuted Rabirius, first by an obsolete procedure dating from the time of the kings, then by trial before the popular assembly. Through this attempted vindication of the murdered tribune Saturninus, Caesar demonstrated not only his belief in the Gracchan principle that no citizen could be put to death without a trial authorized by the people, but also his grasp of ancient tradition and religious lore. For Caesar was aiming to be elected *pontifex maximus*, the head of the state religion. A similar combination of political principle and personal ambition had led him to support the bills granting Pompey his great commands. Then, in the last phase of the Catilinarian affair, he nearly succeeded in swaying senatorial opinion against the execution of the captured conspirators without trial, and he made clear his support for the recall of Pompey to deal with the rebel forces.

Caesar had become a much hated man in some quarters. When he returned from governing Spain early in 60, Cato led the Senate in blocking his request to be allowed to stand for the consulship in absence. Caesar wished to remain outside the sacred boundary of the city which he would then cross as part of his triumph, a privilege which the Senate had already granted him. The Senate further showed its reluctance to have him as consul by allocating as the consular provinces for that year the task of clearing out the woods and cattle-runs of Italy: there lurked the remnants of the bands of Spartacus and Catiline, the latter, as some alleged, Caesar's own supporters.

The 'First Triumvirate'

Caesar gave up his triumph and retaliated by soliciting the support of those other victims of Cato's righteousness, Pompey and Crassus. Once elected consul for 59 BC, he reconciled the two rivals and set out to fulfil the promises he had made to them. Cato was therefore largely responsible for the formation of the so-called 'first triumvirate', and that moment, he later said, was the real beginning of the end for the Republic.

It is tempting to conjecture what might have happened had Caesar not been denied his triumph and the expectation of an important province after his consulship. Caesar was no radical fanatic: he had performed the requisite military service under two Sullan generals and not felt tempted to join the Marians under Lepidus and Sertorius. He was ultimately to say that his honour had always come before anything else; he held it dearer than his life. If he had not felt humiliated by the Senate, might he have proved a decorous consul, a rebel who had 'come round', as Cicero always hoped he would? Perhaps the answer does not matter so very much. Perhaps the same can be said even of that more obvious, but related, question: might civil war have been averted in 49? The interesting question for the historian is not whether any particular event is inevitable, but whether it is explicable. Why the fall of the Republic occurred exactly when and how it did is, after all, secondary to the main question: why did leading members of the Roman governing class, who themselves had most to gain from the existence of the Republic, destroy it, thereby committing political suicide?

The Romans, as we have said, thought of the issue in terms of moral degeneration. They believed that, whereas their ancestors had aspired to glory through service to the state, their contemporaries had come to put their own ambitions above the public welfare. The catalyst in the decline of traditional morality they felt to be the increase in Rome's power and wealth. The enormous opportunities for ruthless self-aggrandizement by individuals threatened the state in two directions. If her subjects were exploited, Rome might lose her Empire, for she had not the men or money to control such a vast area by brute force: an element of consensus in her rule was essential. Again, if some members of the governing class became a great deal more powerful than others, the essentially oligarchic system of the Republic would be replaced by one less beneficial to the governing class as a whole. Roman thinking ran on patriotic self-control where we might stress the need for institutional checks on the power of individuals. In fact some of the legislation they traditionally saw as encouraging the first can be interpreted as steps towards the second: sumptuary laws to limit conspicuous consumption and largesse, extortion laws to check greed and related abuses by Roman officials, canvassing laws to prevent men from buying their way into office on the profits of Empire. But certain changes, such as making generals strictly accountable for their booty, or taxing citizens enough so that the state could itself provide for discharged veterans, or creating a police force that could control political violence, were not in keeping with the closely guarded tradition of aristocratic independence. It was easier for the Senate to forgo a rich and strategic province such as Egypt, which might give excessive scope to one of its members, than to make the great generals, who behaved like kings abroad, toe the line when they returned home.

The standards for success were rising as the Empire grew. After the military triumphs of Marius in the West and Sulla in the East, Pompey would not have been satisfied with the normal one-year governorship after his consulship. Caesar, too, would be thinking of prolonged and extraordinary commands. Eventually Pompey could not bear an equal nor Caesar a superior. But the Republic was incompatible with the ascendancy of one or two. It was also incompatible with the notion that great deeds exempt one from the legal restraints placed on one's peers, an idea Caesar is said to have voiced as he surveyed the enemy dead after Pompey's defeat: 'They would have it so. Even I, Gaius Caesar, *after my great achievements*, would have been convicted in the courts, had I not sought help from my army.' Socrates knew that the laws must be obeyed even when they led to an unjust decision. By the start of the Civil War in 49 the laws of Rome had been bent and ignored by powerful individuals too often to seem worthy of obedience.

The expediency of conciliating Rome's subjects, however, had been grasped by intelligent men of differing political complexion, such as the Gracchi, Sulla, Pompey, Cicero, and Cato. Even Caesar, who was to treat the conquered Gauls with great brutality, tightened up the extortion law. A more difficult issue was how far to share the profits of empire with the whole citizen body, for there was no conception of an impersonal 'government' that bestowed specific benefits. The established tradition of aristocratic largesse made it easy for men who legislated for the distribution of land or money to gain the same credit and popularity as those whose generosity came from their own pockets. Thus *popularis* moves to increase the welfare or power of the *equites* or the *plebs* looked like threatening bids for individual power. It was bad enough when a tribune of the *plebs* made himself a nuisance in this way; still worse when the tribune was in league with a senior magistrate. The year 59 presented the spectacle of a consul who himself behaved like a tribune and had the support, not only of a tribune, but of a general whose veterans were on the scene. It is not surprising that on the brink of civil war there were Optimates who feared nothing so much as the thought of Caesar holding that office again.

Caesar's First Consulship

Caesar began, however, by attempting to secure a smooth passage for his legislation through tact and diplomacy. The settlement of Pompey's veterans had top priority, and in December of 60 Caesar solicited the support, or at least the silence, of the best orator in Rome, who had already sabotaged two previous attempts. Cicero was flattered, but decided to remain independent: he valued the opinion of Cato and others who had called him 'Father of his Country' after his consulship. In March Cicero confirmed Caesar's worst fears by indulging in critical remarks about the state of public affairs. Caesar, with the co-operation of Pompey (both in their priestly capacities), retaliated by carrying out a highly questionable adoption of Cicero's personal enemy, Clodius, into a plebeian family so that he could be elected tribune that summer. They no doubt hoped to lure Cicero, this time by fear, into collaboration, but, if that failed, Clodius would remove the nuisance. Cicero refused invitations from Caesar to serve on his agrarian commission or accompany him to his province (where he would have provided excellent company in the long evenings). Cicero paid for his refusal by being sent into exile in 58 for his execution of the conspirators five years earlier. When he was recalled through Pompey's good offices over a year later, he was easy to divert from further moves towards independence.

It is important to realize that our best informant was not only hostile to the coalition, but did not enjoy the confidence of its members. Though Caesar's invitations amply demonstrate that Cicero's political importance was not a figment of his own vanity, he can offer us only his own intelligent speculations on the motives and plans of those who came to control the destiny of Rome.

Casesar's other attempt to employ diplomatic methods was also unsuccessful. He carefully omitted from the agrarian proposal itself all the most controversial features of the earlier bills, excluding the Campanian land from distribution, using only Pompey's new revenues for purchase of land, and relying on voluntary sale. He brought the proposal to the Senate and, only after meeting with total and unreasoned opposition, put it to the Assembly without senatorial sanction. Caesar's colleague in office was Cato's son-in-law, M. Calpurnius Bibulus, whose obstruction Caesar no doubt hoped to avert by impressing the body of the Senate with his sweet reasonableness. From now on, however, he showed how little he could be deflected from his course by shame or the pressure of public opinion. He affixed to the bill a clause, associated with Saturninus, that required the senators to swear individually to uphold it. Pompey and Crassus were induced to speak openly in its support and to promise to meet force with force. Against Optimate tribunes and his consular colleague, Caesar invoked the violence of the mob and Pompey's veterans. After the bill was passed, Caesar took all of his subsequent proposals directly to the people. His other bills ratifying Pompey's eastern settlement, granting a concession to the tax-farmers, recognizing the Egyptian king (who paid handsomely for the privilege), were passed without regard to opposition. Bibulus had resort to religious obstruction of an unorthodox kind and on an unprecedented scale: from his house he observed bad omens every day.

The intense opposition Caesar faced in passing measures that were addressed to real problems arose from fear of the political power he would thereby acquire with the *plebs*, with the veterans, with the *equites*, and with foreign potentates. Worse was still to come. The tribune Vatinius secured for him from the people a five-year command in Cisalpine Gaul and Illyricum: the first would enable him to keep a threatening eye on Rome when not on campaign, while the second offered him the opportunity for glory in forging the land route through the Balkans that Pompey's expansion of the eastern Empire now made imperative. In the end, politics interfered with the rational expansion of Rome, and Caesar extended the Empire north to the Channel and beyond. For his legislation, including the *lex Vatinia*, was vulnerable to subsequent attack because of the way it had been passed, and Caesar was therefore eager to gain the additional province of Gaul from the Senate. This he achieved through Pompey, whose continued loyalty he had secured through a marriage alliance.

Caesar was well aware, however, that Pompey was an unreliable ally. Dependence on a junior, though it had achieved its end, seemed to Pompey a humiliating position, which the scurrilous edicts of Bibulus and the growing unpopularity of the three only aggravated. As time rendered less vulnerable what he had gained from Caesar, his hankering for respectability, already demonstrated in 62, would reassert itself. But for a while the malice of his enemies made him cling to the alliance which was, in fact, renewed in 56, just as Cato's brother-in-law was about to stand for the consulship. The presence of Caesar's troops on leave in Rome ensured the election of Pompey and Crassus instead, and they promptly renewed Caesar's command in both Gauls and secured for themselves the control of Spain and Syria for five years.

Crassus left for Syria and was killed a year later fighting the Parthians. Caesar was tied up in Gaul and unable to cross the Alps until the winter of 53/2. But Pompey, who chose to govern Spain through legates and remain in the vicinity of Rome, was in a position to exploit political developments. Electoral chaos and gang violence eventually played into his hands since, as proconsul with the power

MODEL OF THEATRE AND PORTICOES OF POMPEY IN ROME. Pompey inaugurated the first permanent stone theatre in Rome in 55 BC, perpetuating a time-honoured tradition of self-advertising munificence on the part of leading politicians during the Republic. The adjacent Porticoes of Pompey contained trees and fountains, and acted as a kind of public art-gallery for paintings and sculptures.

to command and levy troops, he was the obvious person to restore order. When Clodius was murdered at the start of 52, the Senate had him elected sole consul. The death of Caesar's daughter Julia in 54 had already ended Caesar's family connection with him, and Pompey now seemed within reach of recognition as leader of the traditional government. But, to keep his options open, he supported a tribunician bill which granted Caesar the right to stand for a second consulship in absence: he would be eligible for election in 49 after the requisite ten-year interval had elapsed.

Civil War

Meanwhile a change in the method of appointing provincial governors not only resulted in the dispatch of the reluctant Cicero to govern Cilicia, but introduced complications into Caesar's length of tenure in Gaul. Behind the legal question, however, lay constitutional questions, and behind them lay a struggle for power more complex than the rivalry of Pompey and Caesar.

Cato's antagonism had removed any temptation Caesar may have felt to sacrifice his *popularis* image to his ambition. Instead, he remained true to the first as long as there was any risk to the second. Caesar now took his stand on the fact that the people had granted his command and the right to stand for the consulship in absence, which, he claimed, implied that he would still be in his province in the summer of 49. The Optimates had always disapproved of provincial commands granted by the people: they believed that the Senate should retain over foreign affairs the control it had acquired *de facto* as the only organ of government with a continuous existence and membership. Though sovereignty lay with the people, they did not agree with those Populares who held that the people could properly legislate on any matter, even without senatorial guidance. Had not the Republic long been thought of as 'the Senate and People of Rome'?

Marcus Marcellus, the consul of 51, tried to force the issue and recall Caesar a year early. Pompey tried to arrange a compromise, while nevertheless agreeing that the Senate ought to be obeyed. In 50 and early 49 Caesar had recourse to conciliatory offers, reinforced by the vetoes of friendly tribunes: when the diehards ignored them, he crossed the Rubicon, the river that marked the boundary of his province, in defence of their sacred rights—and of his honour.

Pompey went east to gather his forces, saying 'Sulla did it: why not I?' But the only resemblance lay in his threat of reprisals against his enemies. Speed and organization belonged to Caesar, and his policy of clemency captured public opinion.

Cicero, an honourable man trying to choose the side of the Republic, lamented that neither Pompey nor Caesar had any aim but *dominatio*. He could not do other than attribute blame to the protagonists, including the enemies of peace in the Senate, because he believed that the political system itself was blameless. If Cato spoke as if living in Plato's Republic, Cicero had written that the Roman

Republic surpassed even that utopia. In the late fifties, when chaos and violence had become the order of the day, he was moved to write two works of political philosophy based, in title and in content, on Plato's *Republic* and *Laws*. In the first he explained that Roman tradition had evolved a mixed constitution, which was the most balanced and stable kind. The laws he presented in the second work were designed for a future citizen body trained to virtue and resembled closely existing law and practice. What innovations there are in the part of the treatise that survives are designed to increase the power and authority of the Senate and senior magistrates.

Both *De re publica* and the roughly contemporary *De oratore* are set in the past when public affairs were in the hands of Scipio and Laelius or Lucius Crassus and Marcus Antonius. Cicero's answer to the problems of the Republic was the existence of statesmen or a statesman of their calibre who could serve as a model of conduct to others. He had never entertained such hopes of Pompey and Caesar, though he had once offered to play Laelius to Pompey's Scipio and was to offer advice to Caesar as dictator.

The Dictatorship

Caesar's victory destroyed the system within which he had wanted primacy. There is little sign that he enjoyed the task of reconstruction. Perhaps the only thing that rings true in Cicero's fawning speech *Pro Marcello*, delivered in 46, is his picture of the arbiter of men's destinies as weary of life. Until the spring of 45 Caesar could turn his attention to Rome's problems only in the intervals of fighting the civil war all over the Mediterranean. By March of 44, when he was killed, he was planning to leave Rome to fight the Parthians. Cicero was baffled. What of the programme he had outlined for him: the reorganization of the courts, the restoration of financial credit, the passing of moral legislation, the reform of political life? Caesar had in fact taken steps to ease the burden of debt. He had legislated against luxury and in favour of increasing the birth-rate. But Cicero could not grasp the difficulty of reforming Roman politics any more than he could appreciate Caesar's concern for Italy and the provinces.

In the short time he had, Caesar achieved enough to show how widely his mind ranged. The settlement of his veterans was to contribute to the restoration of Italian agriculture and manpower, for they were to be scattered up and down the peninsula, not planted like garrisons in the Sullan mode. Some of the administrative anomalies neglected since Italian towns became Roman *municipia* after the Social War were sorted out. The number of magistrates was increased to allow for the expanding number of provinces, and the unsatisfactory system of tax-collection by *publicani* based in Rome was discontinued, at least in Asia. Most important of all was the enfranchisement of Cisalpine Gaul and the settlement of veterans and poor citizens in colonies abroad. The immediate effect of the colonies would be to cut down the urban population and, with it, public disorder and the

SHOPS IN THE FORUM JULIUM, Caesar's answer to Pompey's theatre and porticoes. Begun in 51 BC to provide a much-needed enlargement to the old Roman Forum, this complex introduced the formula adopted by the subsequent imperial *fora*, i.e. a colonnaded piazza dominated at the rear, directly opposite the main entrance, by a grand temple (here that of Venus Genetrix, the alleged ancestress of the Julian family).

cost of the corn dole. But in the long run the colonial policy, combined with Caesar's generosity in granting citizenship to individuals and communities, was to rejuvenate both the Roman legions and the Roman governing class. Caesar, who included some provincial aristocrats in his enlarged Senate, was perfectly aware of what he was doing.

The reform of Roman government was a different story. It was hard for a man of fifty to think afresh about the system that had so far determined his life: Caesar applied some traditional remedies, such as the abolition of certain urban clubs, the revision of criminal statutes, the restriction of the tenure of provincial commands. Accustomed to working at top speed in Gaul—he dictated letters to two secretaries while on horseback—Caesar had lost patience with the niceties of political life: Cicero complained that his own name was attached to senatorial decrees passed in his absence. Worse still, Caesar was about to leave for an indefinite period, having been made *dictator perpetuus* ('dictator without term'): perhaps he wanted to preclude any wrangles this time over his tenure of command, but it looked as if he had lost the will to restore the Republic. As dictator, he had shown no sign of relinquishing his stranglehold on the political machinery, designating governors, appointing many of the magistrates, and exercising personal jurisdiction. Hence the Ides of March.

After Caesar's death one of his intimates, Gaius Matius, was to lament: 'If he, for all his genius, could not find a way out, who is going to find one now?' Caesar knew that his peers disliked being kept waiting in his antechamber while he monopolized affairs. Yet what solution would they accept to the political chaos and armed conflicts he had brought to an end? Augustus was to avoid many of Caesar's mistakes, including the celebrated clemency which left his most determined opponents alive. Yet Augustus' solution was not so different, though he was more creative in adapting traditional language to describe his paralysis of the constitution. The greatest difference lay in the attitude of others. Another round of civil war had by then made peace in any form seem acceptable to those who survived. Augustus was young and had time to evolve a solution. The Catos and the Ciceros were gone. Who was there left who had seen the Republic?

Further Reading

PRINCIPAL ANCIENT SOURCES

The works of Cicero are readily available in translation. The Loeb Classical Library offers the complete works translated by different hands with facing Latin text. The Penguin Classical Series includes volumes of selected speeches in translation and, particularly worthy of note, a rendering of the letters by D. R. Shackleton-Bailey. This is a byproduct of his great edition and commentary, published by the Cambridge University Press, of which only the volumes of the *Letters to Atticus* contain a translation.

Other ancient works which contribute to our knowledge of the period can also be consulted in English. Sallust's monograph on the Conspiracy of Catiline appears in the Loeb and in the Penguin *Sallust*. One volume in each of these series is devoted to Caesar's accounts of his campaigns in Gaul and in the Civil War. The *Life* of Atticus by Cornelius Nepos can be found in the Loeb volume containing Florus. Plutarch's *Lives* of Sulla, Crassus, Pompey, Caesar, and Cicero feature in the Penguin *Plutarch: Fall of the Roman Republic*. They can also be found, with other relevant biographies, in the eleven Loeb volumes containing all of Plutarch's *Lives*. Suetonius' biography of Caesar is available in the Penguin volume *Suetonius: the Twelve Caesars* and in the first volume of the Loeb *Suetonius*.

MODERN WORKS

There are many modern accounts of this, the most richly documented period of the Roman Republic. They vary greatly in scope, emphasis, and level of detail.

Brief accounts in a long perspective can be found in the works of H. H. Scullard, P. A. Brunt, and M. Crawford, mentioned on p. 38.

For more detailed narrative, older works such as volume iv of the Everyman Edition of T. Mommsen's *History of Rome* (Engl. trans. 1880) and T. Rice Holmes, *The Roman Republic*, 3 vols. (Oxford, 1923), are still worth reading. The relevant chapters of the *Cambridge Ancient History*, vol. ix (1932), are still useful, though soon to be superseded by a new edition.

The great modern work on the fall of the Republic is Sir Ronald Syme's *The Roman Revolution* (Oxford, 1939), which concentrates especially on the later part of this period. A more recent analysis of political activity in the late Republic, combined with a penetrating, but controversial, diagnosis of the fall of the Republic, is contained in E. S. Gruen's *The Last Generation of the Roman Republic* (Berkeley, 1974). For a lively account of the working of Roman politics and of the mechanics and setting, see Lily Ross Taylor's *Party Politics in the Age of Caesar* (Berkeley, 1949) and *Roman Voting Assemblies* (Ann Arbor, 1966).

Much of the up-to-date and detailed analysis of the politics of the period is, however, contained in biographies of the leading figures. Most notable are those by M. Gelzer, of which only *Caesar, Politician and Statesman* (Oxford, 1968) is available in English. J. P. V. D. Balsdon's *Julius Caesar and Rome* (Harmondsworth, 1967) is brief and readable; Z. Yavetz, *Julius Caesar and his Public Image* (London, 1983), concentrates on his dictatorship. Several biographies of Pompey have appeared recently, by J. Leach (1978), R. Seager (1979), and P. Greenhalgh (1980–1), of which Seager's is the most detailed on politics at Rome. The unrewarding task of constructing a biography of Crassus has been attempted by B. Marshall (1976) and A. Ward (1977).

Cicero, the most feasible subject for a biography, has been well served in English. D. L. Stockton's *Cicero, a Political Biography* (Oxford, 1971) provides a useful account of his work as a statesman; D. R. Shackleton Bailey in *Cicero* (London, 1971) makes good use of his work on the letters in evoking Cicero the man; E. D. Rawson offers a sympathetic and well-rounded study in *Cicero, a Portrait* (London, 1975; repr. Bristol, 1983). Different aspects of Cicero's life and work are illuminated in a collection of essays edited by T. A. Dorey (London, 1965).

Finally, it may be useful to list a few books that help to put the political life of the late Republic in a broader social context: C. Nicolet, *The World of the Citizen in Republican Rome* (London, 1980); J. Crook, *Law and Life in Rome* (London, 1977); W. Liebeschuetz, *Continuity and Change in Roman Religion* (Oxford, 1979); K. Hopkins, *Conquerors and Slaves* (Cambridge, 1978); *Death and Renewal* (Cambridge, 1983); C. Wirszubski, *Libertas as a Political Idea at Rome* (Cambridge, 1960).

5

The Poets of the Late Republic

❧❧

ROBIN NISBET

Lucretius

EARLY in 54 BC Cicero ended a letter to his brother with a note on his recent reading. 'Lucretius' poetry is just as you say; many brilliances of natural genius, all the same much technique; but more anon. If you read Sallustius' *Empedoclea* I'll think you a man, but I'll not think you a human being' (*QF* 2. 10. 3). Here we glimpse a society where some public men find time for new literature, and comment on it without affectation. Both the works mentioned are philosophical and scientific, reflecting the intellectual curiosity of a small Hellenized élite, an enlightenment that Cicero was to transmit but did not originate. The didactic poem was a familiar form that continued the Alexandrian tradition of versified scholarship; Cicero himself in his youth had produced a translation, innovating for its day, of the astronomical *Phaenomena* of Aratus. Such works were more noted for technique than genius, but Lucretius in his six books *De rerum natura* found a theme to engage both the reason and the imagination, the now fashionable Epicurean explanation of the universe. The poet himself is a shadowy figure, no doubt comfortably born, certainly well educated, perhaps recently dead; his poem will speak for him.

'Aeneadum genetrix, hominum diuumque uoluptas,/alma Venus', 'Mother of Aeneas' race, pleasure of men and gods, life-giving Venus' (1. 1 f.): already in the resounding invocation we find the complexity of reference that was thereafter to characterize much of the greatest Roman poetry. Venus is the mythical and literary goddess of Love, the ancestress of the Roman People, the protecting deity of Memmius, the ambitious politician for whom the work is nominally written, but at a deeper level she personifies the creative forces in the world, and in particular *uoluptas* or pleasure, the prime impulse and supreme good of the Epicurean moral system. The poet tells how at the goddess's epiphany the inventive earth sends up fragrant flowers, and beasts bound through the lush pastures: the universality of the divine influence is described in conventional religious patterns, but the comprehensive sympathy suits a philosophy that sees man as part of nature. Then, as is appropriate in prayer, the suppliant relates Venus' powers to his own needs: 'forasmuch as without thee nothing rises to the radiant shores of light, nor does anything joyful or lovable begin ... grant, goddess, to my precepts a charm everlasting' (28 'aeternum da dictis, diua, leporem'); the archaic alliteration suits the solemnities of old Roman poetry, but 'charm' (here paradoxically combined with 'everlasting') suggests a more up-to-date awareness of beauty. Finally Lucretius prays that Venus may bring peace on earth by making love to the war-god Mars; once again he astonishes us by blending traditional religious diction with a sensuousness of description associated with the poetic movements of his own day (35 f. 'leaning back his shapely neck, and gasping at thee, goddess, he feeds his greedy gaze with love'). He conflates scandalous Homeric story-telling with a more sophisticated hint of Harmonia, the daughter of Mars and Venus; at the same time he includes a reference to the political anxieties of 60–55 BC, when Caesar was already subverting the Republic.

Lucretius next turns to a panegyric of Epicurus, who like Hercules ridding the world of monsters liberated oppressed mankind from the lowering menace of religion. In a typically Roman metaphor we are told how the philosopher's mind sallied forth through the walls of the world, and after scouring the universe like a reconnoitring raiding party, brought back 'a knowledge of what can be and what cannot': 'quare religio pedibus subiecta uicissim/obteritur, nos exaequat uictoria caelo' (78 f. 'and so religion in turn is crushed underfoot and victory raises *us* to heaven'). These fighting words are at odds with the mild piety of Epicurus, who recommended the observance of one's local form of worship, and Lucretius recognizes that his line of argument may be thought wicked; but he reflects that the true impiety is religion's. With suitably epic, or rather tragic, diction he pictures the fate of Iphigeneia, whose significance is of course symbolic rather than literally relevant to Roman cult: 95 ff. 'lifted by the hands of men she was escorted trembling to the altar, so that pure impurely, at the very time for her to marry, she might fall a sorrowing victim, slaughtered by her sire.' And so to the scathing summing up, not easily paralleled in antiquity, 'tantum religio potuit suadere malorum' (101 'so much evil could religion recommend').

The first two books are devoted to the atomic theory of Epicurus (Vol. 1, pp. 368 f.), which was itself derived from Leucippus and Democritus (Vol. 1, p. 115). Lucretius copes skilfully with his technical problems, the poverty of his ancestral tongue ('patrii sermonis egestas') at least before Cicero standardized an abstract vocabulary, the clumsiness of Latin compared with Greek as a vehicle for subtle disputation, the constraints of the metre (for the hexameter was not indigenous in Rome and still could prove a recalcitrant medium). The theme required argumentation of a kind unusual in poetry, at least since the fifth-century Empedocles, and as suits a rationalist, there is an abundance of prosaic, logical words like 'for', 'whereas', 'nevertheless', 'moreover', 'finally', 'therefore'. Each book is ordered into self-contained sections, which ram home a point by repetition as well as deduction, often ending with a triumphant restatement of the propositions with which they began (for the procedures are more polemical than those of a technical philosopher); and as in the physical system that is being described, these sections interlock in larger structures. It would be quite wrong to suppose that the work consists of purple passages of eloquence stitched to a monotonous scientific fabric: when Lucretius talks of 'smearing honey on the medicine cup' (1.936 ff.), he is referring not to the set-pieces, but to the poetic form itself, which must have startled more professional Epicureans (their founder had rejected the arts as not conducive to happiness). But while some of the poet's qualities can be demonstrated, the grasp of reality, the passionate faith in reason, the actuality of the supporting illustration, no anthology can do justice to the interdependence and cumulative persuasiveness of the system as a whole.

The second book opens with an exposition of Epicurean ethics, for which the physical theory was simply the foundation. 'suaue, mari magno turbantibus aequora uentis, / e terra magnum alterius spectare laborem' (2.1 f. "tis sweet, when the winds disturb the calm of the great sea, to look from land at the great tribulation of another'): here we have the Epicurean ideal of *ataraxia* (freedom from turmoil) expressed with the self-centredness of ancient moral philosophy. 'Sweet' is not just a conventional poeticism, but alludes to Epicurus' theory of pleasure, not the excited pleasure that he disapproved of, but the static sort which arises from the absence of pain and anxiety. To know the true pleasures of the body, men do not need a house shimmering with gold and silver, or panelled ceilings echoing to the lute, as they can enjoy themselves by lying on the soft grass, beside a stream of water, under the branches of a tall tree (29 f. 'prostrati in gramine molli / propter aquae riuum sub ramis arboris altae'); such passages show how far Epicurus was from the popular misconception of the epicure (Vol. 1, p. 366). Fame and riches do no more for the mind than for the body: you may see your legions swarming over the plain, and still be obsessed by religious scruples and the terror of death (40 ff). Men are like children fearing phantoms in the dark: 'hunc igitur terrorem animi tenebrasque necessest / non radii solis neque lucida tela diei / discutiant, sed naturae species ratioque' (59 ff. 'this terror and darkness of the mind must be dispelled not by the rays of the sun or the shining shafts of day but by the outward appearance and inner rationale of nature').

Lucretius then reverts to his atoms, whose unseen collisions and reboundings he illustrates by characteristically memorable analogies: they manœuvre and fight like specks of dust seen in a sunbeam in a darkened room (114 ff.), but their motion is no more visible to the senses than that of sheep crawling on a far-off hill (317 ff.). They move in the first place because they have weight and fall; but if they fall in parallel lines, that does not explain the collisions that produce aggregations of matter (the poet is unaware of the possibilities of attraction). They cannot catch up with one another by falling at different speeds, for as they fall in a void they must all fall at the same speed (225 ff.). Lucretius is thus led to the theory of the *clinamen* or swerve which was Epicurus' most important contribution to atomic physics: 'at times quite undetermined and undetermined places they veer a little from their track, with the smallest possible change of course' (218 ff.). Cicero thought that nothing was as disgraceful for a scientist as to say that something happens without a cause, but modern physicists can understand an appeal to indeterminacy; they will be more shocked by Epicurus' ethical intention, a desire to exempt human volition from the shackles of determinism (Vol. 1, pp. 370 ff.).

The third book expounds the structure of the soul, and its mortality. Lucretius tells how Epicurus banished the fear of death: it is this that muddies the waters of life, clouding them with darkness, and leaving no pleasure clear and unpolluted. Men profess a disbelief in survival, but in adversity the mask is torn off, and they revert to their old superstitions (55 f.). Such remarks reflect a traditional preoccupation of the Epicureans, and Philodemus himself, the most distinguished contemporary member of the school, wrote a treatise *On Death*. Nor should one underestimate the credulity about an after-life in the poet's own society; it is true that Cicero mocks the Epicurean obsession ('what old woman is crazy enough to be afraid of such things?'), but he confines the issue to the fables of mythology, and his rational scepticism was untypical even of the governing class. Some have thought that Lucretius protests too much, but for a poet he seems remarkably clear-headed: St Jerome's story of his madness can be explained by the incomprehension of the Church.

Lucretius naturally rejects the mind–body dualism that has haunted the history of thought for so long; as Epicurus had uncompromisingly put it, 'soul is body'. He also opposes the more plausible view that the soul is simply a condition of the body, or *harmonia* as it was called ('attunement' gives the idea); he derisively comments that the *organici* or instrumentalists are welcome to keep the word (131 f.). Following the psychology of his master he distinguishes the *anima*, the vital principle that is common to all living creatures, from the governing *animus* or mind, that is found only in man; but as both are equally mortal, he does not always use his terms precisely. The soul can influence the body, and the body the soul; this can only be effected by physical contact, and touch is a property of body (161 ff.). The atoms of the mind are exceptionally small and smooth, as is shown by the speed with which volition can be translated into action; in the same way a puff of breath can scatter a heap of poppy seeds, while corn-ears are too big and spiky (196 ff.).

Lucretius now accumulates some thirty arguments to show that the soul cannot survive the body. As it consists of small atoms of exceptional mobility, when its vessel is shattered it must dissipate like smoke (425 ff.). The mind keeps in step with the body in its birth, development, and decay, as can be seen from children and old men; therefore it dies with the body (445 ff.). The body and mind are affected together by drunkenness (476 ff.) and epilepsy (487 ff.); the fact that the mind can be cured, i.e. changed, by medicine is itself an indication of its mortality (510 ff.). Sufferers from creeping paralysis lose sensation first in the toes and the feet, 'and then through the other limbs go haltingly the steps of cold death'

(529 f.); as the soul cannot be concentrated in the sound part of the body (which does not acquire extra sensation), it must be mortal. The mind cannot originate in the head or the feet (Lucretius put it in the breast), but has a fixed place appointed for it where alone it can exist (615 ff.). If the soul is to have sensation when separated from the body it must be endowed with five senses, as poets and painters have portrayed the dead in the Underworld; but in isolation from the body it cannot have eyes or nostrils or hand or tongue or ears (624 ff.). When you cut through a snake, the severed part twitches, and similar things can be seen in chariot battles (a very Roman illustration); but if the soul can be severed it cannot be immortal (634 ff.). Plato and others had argued that the soul had a previous existence, but if it has forgotten its past, that is virtually equivalent to death (670 ff.); for the ancients the notions of pre-existence and after-life were closely connected, as they reasonably thought it implausible that what is born should be eternal. The different species of animals inherit temperamental as well as physical characteristics (741 ff.); this shows that the soul and body grow up together. It is ridiculous to suppose that at the moment of conception immortal souls are queueing up for a body to occupy (776 ff.).

Lucretius sums up the conclusion of his argument with an aphorism of Epicurus, 'nil igitur mors est ad nos' (830, 'therefore death is nothing to us'). If anyone takes it amiss that his body will rot in the grave or be consumed in the pyre, he must have some lingering belief in survival after death. And so to the mourners' memorable lament, which is meant to sound over-emotional and cliché ridden, even if humanity seems to break in:

> Iam iam non domus accipiet te laeta neque uxor
> optima, nec dulces occurrent oscula nati
> praeripere et tacita pectus dulcedine tangent . . .
> (894 ff.)

Now no more will your household greet you joyfully, nor your best of wives, nor will your dear children race to snatch first kiss and touch your heart with a silent sweetness . . .

Epicurus had urged a serious and rational enjoyment of the present ('life is whittled away in thinking of the morrow, and each of us dies before he has time to relax'). His sentiments are here echoed in a remonstrance from a personified Nature, who speaks with the derisive vigour of popular philosophy (931 ff.):

Away with your tears, you rascal, and muzzle your moans . . . Because you always long for what you don't have and disregard what you have, your life has slipped away from you unfulfilled and unenjoyed . . . Now give up things unsuited to your years and make way for younger men; for there is no escape.

(Lucretius emphasizes, as elsewhere, the natural cycles of growth and decay.) Then with a characteristic rationalization of myth he explains that the fabled punishments of the underworld represent the self-inflicted torments of life (978 ff.): the overhanging rock of Tantalus stands for the oppressive terrors of religion, the vultures that tear at Tityos are the desires of the flesh, Sisyphus pushing the stone up hill is the ambitious politician (what did Memmius make of that?). The sermon then turns to the staple of consolation through the ages, 'You are not the first'. Good King Ancus died, and Scipio, the terror of Carthage, and Epicurus himself, who dimmed the light of all men as the sun blots out the stars (1042 ff.). We spend our lives running away from ourselves, without understanding the cause of our discontent; peace of mind can only be attained when we accept that death is eternal.

The fourth book first defends the Epicurean theory of perception, by which objects give off a thin film of atoms, (Vol. 1, pp. 373 f.), like heat from the sun or exhalations from the sea. Lucretius is at his vivid best in describing distortions of perception, the motion of hills when seen from a passing ship (389 f.), the continued rotation of hall pillars when children have stopped spinning (400 ff.), the bending of oars as they pass beneath the surface of the sea (440 'refracta uidentur'). 'A gathering of water no deeper than a finger's breadth, standing between the stones on the paved street, provides a view beneath the earth with a reach as far as the chasm of the sky stretches on high above the earth' (414 ff.): the image shows the child-like clarity of the poet's vision, and his ability to use minute observation to achieve immense perspectives. Yet in spite of strange cases Lucretius insists that knowledge depends on the senses, which are irrefutable. In yet another section he denies that the eyes were created to give us sight, a teleological explanation that is literally preposterous, as it confuses cause and effect: 'nothing grew in the body in order that we could use it, but what has grown generates a use' (834 f.). Here he is reacting against Aristotle and the Stoics, with an approach that went back to Empedocles and Democritus: Bacon and Darwin understood.

The latter part of the book provides a mechanical explanation of sex that is extended to the emotional concomitants; here Epicurean non-involvement is expressed with a cynicism that counters the growing romanticism of the poets.

Fathers' hard-won earnings turn into ribbons and head-scarves, ... yet from the very fountain of enchantment a bitterness wells up ('surgit amari aliquid'), to bring anguish amid the blossoms, when the lover's mind is gnawed by the awareness that he is passing his life in idleness and going to ruin in brothels, or because she has left unclarified a word she has let fly that sticks fast in his passionate heart and ignites like a flame, or because he thinks she flaunts her eyes too freely or gazes at another, and he sees in her face the traces of a smile. (1129 ff.)

This leads to a satirical account of lovers' euphemistic endearments, which are expressed in the affected Greek of the girls concerned: 'the black is "honey-gold", the filthy and smelly "unadorned"' (1160 'nigra melichrus est, immunda et fetida acosmos'). Yet the poet concedes that even an unattractive woman may persuade you to live with her by her trimness and obliging ways; even without divine assistance habit can make you love her, like water dripping on a stone (1278 ff.). This cool conclusion may have encouraged the story, familiar from Tennyson's poem, that Lucretius was driven mad by an aphrodisiac administered by his wife.

The fifth book turns to the cosmos, which originated from the concourse of atoms and will one day disintegrate. The gods had no part in creating it, and no reason to think of such a thing (165 ff.): serene and immortal beings could not be dissatisfied with their previous condition. (Epicureans were not atheists, but their gods were indifferent to the world of men.) The natural order was not made for us: there is too much wrong with it (199). Much of the earth has been denied to man by mountains, forests, and the sea, as well as the extremes of cold and heat; and hard-won cultivation may be blighted by sun, frost, or wind.

Furthermore a baby, like a seafarer cast up by the cruel waves, lies naked on the ground, speechless and lacking all vital support, when once nature has ejected him on the shores of light by travail from his mother's womb, and he fills the place with woeful wailing, as is right for one who is destined in life to pass through so many troubles. But the different flocks and herds and wild beasts thrive without need of rattles, and none has to be treated to soothing lisps by a cherishing foster-mother (222 ff.)

Though Lucretius is far from idealizing the animals, he sees like others before him the particular helplessness of the human child.

The latter part of the book gives a non-theological explanation of the origin of life and the development of civilization. Grass and shrubs came first (783 ff.), and then animals, which grew up in wombs rooted in the soil (a curiosity derived from Epicurus himself). The poet more plausibly emphasizes the warmth, moisture, and fertility of the primeval world, which nowadays is like a woman past the age of child-bearing. Many individual monstrosities were produced (837 ff.), but if they could not find food or reproduce, they died out; Lucretius is using an idea of Empedocles, but rejects his fantastic belief in hybrids of men and beasts. The species that have survived have been preserved by cunning, courage, or speed (857 ff.), or, like dogs and sheep, by the protection of man. But in spite of the notion of natural selection, Lucretius has no idea of evolution: though the species were originally produced by chance, they remain for him distinct and immutable.

Primitive men had no agriculture or navigation, but lived in woods and caves off acorns and berries. They must often have been mangled horribly by wild animals (a good instance of the poet's constructive imagination), but thousands were never slaughtered in a single day's battle (999 ff.): Lucretius has no illusions that our first ancestors can have been anything but brutish, but he is also aware that technical innovation need not be accompanied by moral development. In due course men acquired huts and skins and fire, which was produced in the forest by lightning or friction. They were softened by family life (in his grim chronicle Lucretius finds a place for the Epicurean virtues of friendship and affection), and formal compacts for mutual support; these must have been kept for the most part (1025 ff.), otherwise the human race would not have been preserved (a sometimes forgotten aspect of the 'survival of the fittest'). Language was not arbitrarily invented but grew out of natural cries, as can be seen from the variety of sounds made by dogs:

when they set about licking their puppies fondly with their tongues or throw them about with their paws and as they go for them with bites put on a show of soft gobbling without using their teeth, they nuzzle up to them with eager moans that are very different from their baying when left alone in the house or their whimpers when with cringing body they shrink from a beating. (1067 ff.)

Here we have a poet who loves words and dogs and ideas all at once.

Towns were built and lands distributed, and men competed for wealth in a self-defeating search for security (1120 ff.). Kings rose, and were toppled by envy, and violence gave way to law. Men saw gods in visions and dreams, and falsely assumed that natural phenomena were devised by them (1183 ff.); that is why they still spatter altars with blood, and shiver at thunder, and pray in storms at sea. Metals were discovered in forest fires (1241 ff.), and then mined in the earth (first bronze, then iron). Horses were tamed for war (1297 ff.), and less successfully bulls and lions. Plaiting came before weaving, as looms need metal parts (1350 ff.); men worked wool before women, as they are the more ingenious sex. Then as things became easier, music was made in imitation of birds and the wind (1379 ff.); by Epicurean doctrine the inventiveness that was first prompted by necessity was extended to add the graces of life. Lucretius has no nineteenth-century belief in ever-continuing improvement, but following ideas current in the Hellenistic world he recognizes that progress has historically occurred: 'usus et impigrae simul experientia mentis / paulatim docuit pedetemptim progredientis' (1452 f. 'practice and with it the experimentation of the active mind taught men gradually as they felt their way forward').

After a eulogy of Epicurus and Athenian civilization, which serves as a climax to what has preceded, the sixth book expounds irregular natural phenomena, thunder and lightning, waterspouts and rain, earthquakes and volcanoes. Lucretius wishes to show that his system can provide rational explanations for these traditional puzzles, some of which were responsible for the terror and superstition that the Epicureans were so concerned to avert; if some of his details were now out of date, that simply underlines that he was a moralist and a poet rather than a scientist. Finally he turns to epidemics with a description of the plague at Athens four centuries before (1138 ff.); his treatment is less objective than that of Thucydides, on whom he depends, but he is not so concerned with a clinical scrutiny of the physical symptoms as with a rhetorical presentation of human nature under stress. The end of the work is gruesome and abrupt, with mourners fighting to lay their dead on other people's pyres, and some have suspected that the poet was interrupted by terminal illness; yet the passage implies a plan, as it sets off not only the panegyric of Athens at the beginning of the book but the joyous hymn to Venus at the beginning of the poem. Familiar themes recur, the mechanical causation of the calamity, man's social and self-seeking propensities, the terror of death, the uselessness of religion. If we are not explicitly offered the consolations of philosophy, that is not just because the plague came before Epicurus. Better simply to describe things as they are, and the limits of human capacity.

Catullus

There is much about humanity in Lucretius, but no people. The balance is redressed by his young contemporary Catullus, the second-greatest poet of the Republic.

> Marrucine Asini, manu sinistra
> non belle uteris: in ioco atque uino
> tollis lintea neglegentiorum.
> hoc salsum esse putas? fugit te, inepte:
> quamuis sordida res et inuenusta est . . .
>
> (12. 1 ff.)

Asinius from the Abruzzi, that's not a nice thing to do with your left hand: in the middle of fun and wine you nick the napkins of the inattentive. So you think it's smart? You're making a big mistake, you clown: it's as nasty and unattractive a thing as you can think of.

Asinius has gone off with a table-napkin belonging to Catullus, who pretends to believe that he has stolen it deliberately. Episodes as personal and particular are uncharacteristic of Hellenistic epigram, but a new generation of Roman poets had the individuality to make everyday occurrences a subject for verse. Such poems were too slight to be categorized as lyrics; for the graceful metre with its eleven syllables ('hendecasyllables') one may refer to Tennyson's imitation, 'Oh you chorus of indolent reviewers'. The sometimes mannered vogue-words commend an informal elegance and wit, both in life and in poetry, and show a corresponding distaste for rusticity and ineptitude. Friends are treated as unique and precious individuals: the shift from teasing mockery of Asinius to over-exquisite affection for others is typical of this self-regarding coterie. The poem catches a society in transition as well as a literature: we are meeting here for the most part not the old Roman aristocracy but rich young men from Italy who are very conscious of their newly acquired metropolitan sophistication. Catullus himself, like other poets of the 'Neoteric' movement, (below, pp. 183 f.) came from beyond the Po (Cisalpine Gaul, as it was then called); his father was a leading citizen of Verona, with an estate at Sirmione on the Lago di Garda. Asinius may be derided as a countrified boor (1, 'Marrucine'), but his grandfather had led Italy against Rome in the Social War; his smart young brother Pollio was to become a tragedian, patron of Virgil, consul, *triumphator*, and historian.

Catullus provides a sketch-book of incidents and people that can be paralleled in antiquity only in Cicero. Among many vivid characters we meet the polished

Suffenus, who yet writes poetry like a *caprimulgus* or goat-milker (22), Egnatius with the silly grin, who cleans his teeth in the Spanish manner (39), Sestius whose frigid oratory gave the poet a bad cold (44), Arrius who has trouble with his aspirates, and says 'hinsidiae' or 'hambushes' (84). Catullus tells how he boasted to a girl that he had acquired eight litter-bearers in Bithynia, only to be found out when she asked for a lift (10. 33 f. 'you're a tactless, tiresome creature, not to let a fellow be careless'). He recalls to his brother-poet Calvus a competition of the previous evening (50. 4 ff. 'the two of us played at writing verselets, now in one metre, now in another, tit for tat amid laughing and drinking'); the very fact that he explains the details shows that he is building up the occasion for a wider public. With the verbal and political licence of his day he directs ribald fantasies at his enemies, even Julius Caesar and his chief-of-staff: 57. 6 ff. 'morbosi pariter gemelli utrique, / uno in lecticulo erudituli ambo, / non hic quam ille magis uorax adulter, / riuales socii puellularum' ('a couple of queers, both identical, two *cognoscenti* in one snug sofa, each an equally avid adulterer, partners in competing with the girlies of the town'). Caesar was not amused but knew the rules of the genre, and on receiving an apology asked the poet to dinner.

Catullus did not address all his poems to men. Of the dozen pieces on the lady he called Lesbia we may begin with one that is written without disillusionment:

> Quaeris, quot mihi basiationes
> tuae, Lesbia, sint satis superque.
> quam magnus numerus Libyssae harenae
> lasarpiciferis iacet Cyrenis
> oraclum Iouis inter aestuosi
> et Batti ueteris sacrum sepulcrum;
> aut quam sidera multa, cum tacet nox,
> furtiuos hominum uident amores:
> tam te basia multa basiare
> uesano satis et super Catullo est,
> quae nec pernumerare curiosi
> possint nec mala fascinare lingua. (7)

You ask, Lesbia, how many kissings of you are for me enough and to spare. As many as the grains of the Libyan sand that stretch in silphium-bearing Cyrenaica between the oracle of sweltering Jove and the hallowed tomb of old Battus, or as many as the stars that when night is hushed look on the stealthy loves of mortals: so many kisses are enough and to spare for crazed Catullus to kiss you with, so that busybodies cannot count them up or an evil tongue cast a spell on them.

At a formal level this belongs to the same category as the poem to Asinius: *basia* is a colloquial word for kisses, unsuited to serious literature; the repeated 'enough and to spare' keeps up the informal tone; the pedantic formation *basiationes* and the mock-conventional 'silphium-bearing' or 'asafoetidiferous' are humorously pretentious; though the poet claims to be crazed, he has not lost his sense of proportion. But there is also a more serious note that raises the poem far above the level it professes. Sand and stars are the tritest of models for the innumerable, but here they evoke an atmosphere that is more important than the literal comparison: the ancient shrine in the desert heat and the dispassionate witnesses in the silent night suggest the tranquillity that envelops the lover's passion. The last couplet adds a typically wry assertion of self-sufficiency: if the kisses are too many to count, the gossiping tongue, like the evil eye, will lose its power to blight. The poem has an emotional range that belies its informal manner, but unlike the critics who write about him Catullus is content with fifty-seven words.

Love-poetry of this sort has no precedent in Greek literature, and was conditioned by a novel combination of social circumstances. The Lesbia of Catullus was really Clodia, one of the spectacular sisters of the aristocratic demagogue Clodius, and probably the wife of Metellus Celer, the consul of 60 BC. Upper-class women had achieved greater emancipation than at any time in the ancient world, and Clodia had not only the style to inspire sophisticated poetry but the education to understand it. If she showed a conspicuous disregard for the ancestral proprieties, her lover could woo her with a sense of adventure and write about her with a lack of reticence impossible within the context of marriage. It is true that some Greek courtesans had been cultured and intelligent, but new elements were the Roman interest in the individual (witness Lucilius and Cicero's letters) and the outspoken independence of a privileged class. When Meleager writes elegant epigrams to his Zenophila or Heliodora, nobody cares whether they ever existed, but Catullus can build up a convincing series of poems about a real relationship in all its vicissitudes. Nothing like that had ever been done before.

Most of the Lesbia cycle is in fact poetry of disillusionment. What gives it its characteristic tone is not just the piquant blend of apparently incompatible emotions but the persistence of the rational voice: here we find subsisting together rueful self-examination, resolute self-exhortation, reasoned reproaches, and virulent hate. Catullus may start at the traditional level of epigram, but he ends by adding a new element to literature.

What a woman says to her eager lover should be written in wind and in swirling water (70. 3 f.)

I hate and yet love. You may wonder how I manage it. I don't know, but feel it happen, and am in torment. (85)

I loved you then not just as the world loves its girl but as a father his sons and sons-in-law (72. 3 f.)

Poor Catullus, you must stop being silly and cut your losses (8. 1 f.)

It's hard suddenly to put aside a long love; it's hard, but somehow you must accomplish it. This is the only way out, this fight you've got to win, this you must do whether it's possible or impossible (76. 13 ff.)

Let her go and get on with it with those lechers of hers whom she clasps in her embrace, three hundred at once, loving none really but repeatedly bursting the loins of all of them, and let her not this time count on my love which has collapsed through her fault like a flower on the field's edge when touched by a passing ploughshare (11. 17 ff.)

The modern world tends to regard such personal pieces as the poet's most significant achievement, but ancient critics would have set a higher value on his more elaborate artefacts. Catullus was a member of the so-called 'Neoteric' movement, which with its precision and preciosity suddenly made traditional narrative poetry seem old-fashioned; though there was an overlap with the writers of occasional short poems, the two trends were distinct in origin. The new movement, which had its roots in Callimachus, was stimulated by the Greek poet and mythographer Parthenius, who was brought to Rome as a prize of war about 65 BC; his captor Cinna has been identified with the Cisalpine poet of that name, who will be familiar to readers of Shakespeare's *Julius Caesar* ('tear him for his bad verses'). The young officer found Parthenian poetics so seductive that he spent nine years composing a short and obscure mythological poem on Zmyrna's passion for her father, and an admiring epigram by Catullus brings to life what the Neoterics were about (95):

My Cinna's *Zmyrna* has been published at last nine summers and nine winters after it was begun, when meanwhile Hortensius(?) has written half a million lines in a single month. *Zmyrna* will be sent as far as her waters of Satrachus [a river of Cyprus which figured in the poem], *Zmyrna* will long be read through by the white-haired centuries. But the *Annals* of Volusius [a conventional narrative poet] will expire at the mouth of the Po [where their author belonged], and will provide lots of loose wrappers for mackerel [i.e. to fry them in]. Dear to me be the small-scale memorials of *my* favourite writer, but the vulgar can rejoice in their bloated Antimachus [a verbose poet derided by Callimachus].

The Neoteric influence on Catullus may be seen at its simplest in a harmonious wedding-poem whose symbolism goes back to Sappho: 'ut flos in saeptis secretus nascitur hortis / ignotus pecori, nullo conuolsus aratro, / quem mulcent aurae, firmat sol, educat imber' (62. 39 ff. 'as a bloom grows secluded in a walled garden, unfamiliar to the herd, plucked by no ploughshare, that the breezes fondle, the sunshine builds up, the shower brings on'). A more fantastic specimen of the movement's tastes is a bizarre *tour de force* on the self-castration of Attis, which with its syncopated rhythms and accumulation of short syllables evokes the orgiastic music of Cybele's eunuch-priests:

> Where the cymbals' voice is sounding, and the tambourines re-echoing,
> And the Phrygian piper blaring with a curved pipe's cacophony,
> Where the ivy-wearing Maenads toss heads energetically
> And with shrilling ululations celebrate rites inviolable,
> Where is wont to come cavorting Cybele's vagrant retinue,
> It befits us there to hasten with accelerated three-step.   (63.21-6)

In a more profound poem that was to become the prototype of Roman elegy Catullus relates the sorrows of his life to the paradigms of myth. Just as Laodamia's passionate marriage was unhallowed from the beginning, so Lesbia came to him with an omen of doom: 'my radiant goddess entered with dainty steps, and planting her gleaming foot on the worn threshold, halted there with a click of her slipper' (68. 70 ff.). In the same way an anguished couplet on his brother's death near Troy recalls the sufferings of the *Iliad*: 'Troia—nefas—commune sepulcrum Asiae Europaeque / Troia uirum et uirtutum omnium acerba cinis' (68. 89 f. 'Troy, oh horror, the common burial-ground of Asia and Europe, Troy the untimely dust of all true men and manhood'). Greek elegiac poetry was never as personal or as deeply felt.

Catullus' most ambitious work is the 'Wedding of Peleus and Thetis' (64), a poem in the hexameters of epic, but in accordance with neoteric principles lasting only for 400 lines. He begins with the wondrous voyage of the first ship Argo 'Phasidos ad fluctus et fines Aeeteos' (2 'to the floods of Phasis and the realm of Aeetes'); the exotic proper names and the slow quadrisyllabic line-ending already suggest the poem's languorous beauty. 'As soon as the ship ploughed the windy plain with her beak and churned by the oars the wave whitened with spume, there emerged strange faces from the shining deep, the Nereids of Ocean marvelling at the apparition. In that and no other dawn mortals saw with their own eyes nymphs with bared bodies protruding to their breasts from the white deep' (64. 12 ff.). Such was the first encounter of the mortal Argonaut Peleus with the divine sea-nymph Thetis, and the rest of the poem depicts the celebration of their wedding. Pindar says that Peleus then achieved the highest happiness known to mortals, but even he was doomed to sorrow: the child of the marriage, Achilles, was to die young at Troy. Catullus' poem cannot be understood unless we remember both the supreme felicity of the occasion and the implicit undercurrent of sadness.

After recording the arrival of the guests, Catullus turns to the splendours of the scene, in particular a tapestry on the bed that depicted the story of Theseus and Ariadne (50ff.). First we see a windswept heroine on the shore of Naxos as she gazes out to sea at her departing lover. Then a flashback describes how she had first met Theseus and how he had slain the Minotaur. Then we return to Naxos and hear an emotional soliloquy from Ariadne on her lover's forgetfulness. Next comes a projection of Theseus' return to Athens: he had forgotten to signal his victory by hoisting white sails, an arrangement expounded in another flashback, so his father Aegeus jumped over a cliff. Then back to Naxos again, where Bacchus approaches Ariadne with his outlandish revellers. The happy ending is hinted at rather than stated: every literate person knew that the god would marry the heroine and translate her to the sky.

The presentation of this digression illustrates important characteristics of the Neoteric poets and their Hellenistic predecessors. The dislocations of chronological order show a lack of interest in story-telling for its own sake: organic unity of action now matters less than the effects of diversity and surprise, and the aesthetic balance of the composition as a whole. The significant moments are caught in a series of colourful tableaux which suggest the influence of a pictorial art that was romantic in conception and ultra-realistic in execution. The love interest is neither Homeric nor traditionally Roman but derives from the psychologizing of some Hellenistic poets, especially Apollonius in his *Argonautica*: so too the attempt of a male-dominated world to enter into a rejected woman's feelings, an approach that went back to the *Medea* of Euripides and was to influence Virgil's portrayal of Dido. The sheer length of the episode may seem curious (it takes up more than half the piece), but such digressions were regular in poems of this type. Nor need we speak of irrelevance unless we apply inappropriate criteria: in ancient poetry descriptions of works of art often include elements that foreshadow something in the main action, and Ariadne's change from misery to happiness, while it reverses the movement of the poem as a whole, underlines the vicissitudes of human experience.

The action resumes with the departure of the wedding guests, which is described in a simile which no earlier Roman poet could have written:

> hic, qualis flatu placidum mare matutino
> horrificans Zephyrus procliuas incitat undas,
> Aurora exoriente, uagi sub limina Solis,
> quae tarde primum clementi flamine pulsae
> procedunt, leuiterque sonant plangore cachinni,
> post uento crescente magis magis increbescunt,
> purpureaque procul nantes ab luce refulgent.
>
> (269–75)

Then just as the West Wind ruffles the calm sea with morning breath, and sets the waves rolling, as dawn rises, towards the portals of the roving sun, and driven by the gentle breeze they proceed slowly at first, and their ripples sound with a soft plash; then, as the wind freshens, they crowd thicker and faster, and as they float along, shimmer afar with the purple light.

The comparison primarily illustrates how a trickle of departing guests develops into a flood, and nobody who has taken in the poet's words will forget them on such occasions. But there are other points of correspondence: 'cachinni' suggests the guests' merry babble, 'purpurea' their fine clothes, 'nantes' their undulating movement. The luminosity of the passage is typical of the poem as a whole: Catullus has imitated the more glittering aspect of Hellenistic poetry and given it a delightfully new colour and freshness.

As the poem draws towards its close it appropriately includes an epithalamium, which is sung not by a choir of young girls (the usual practice), or by the Muses (as in Pindar's account of this particular wedding), but by those grisly spinsters, the Fates. Their chant begins normally enough with a mention of the Evening Star, a commendation of wedded bliss, and an annunciation of the child of the marriage. But the prophecy of Achilles gradually assumes a sinister note: 'his surpassing merits and glorious deeds mothers will often acknowledge at the funerals of their sons, when they let fall dishevelled hair from grey heads and bruise withered breasts with palsied palms. Run, drawing the threads, run, spindles' (348 ff.). And to remove all doubt about the poet's stance, they predict that Achilles' tomb will be honoured by the sacrifice of a girl. The poet's revulsion at these barbaric deeds is all the more effective for the matter-of-fact way in which they are presented. The poem's limpid beauty, which suited so well the lost age of innocence, now takes on a characteristically ironic note: just as in some of the love poems, the subject-matter and the style have begun to pull in opposite directions.

In spite of their very different subjects, Lucretius and Catullus have much in common. Both are recognizably poets of the Republic, and can describe intellectual or emotional adventures with a candour difficult in later periods. Both write Latin with an elegant propriety that is sometimes lost in the subtleties of the Augustans. Both observe the world with an uncluttered directness that had been unknown for centuries, and was never quite recovered in antiquity. Lucretius' awareness of beauty shows the influence of the new poetry, and some of Catullus' descriptions are modelled on Lucretius. But though the Neoteric movement refined techniques and enlarged sensibilities, its effect on literature was not all good. When art is pursued for art's sake, there is a danger of forgetting the nature of things.

Further Reading

LUCRETIUS

The best way of finding what Lucretius was like is to buy M. F. Smith's revision (Cambridge, Mass., 1975), including text and translation, of W. H. D. Rouse's Loeb edition. The standard commentary is by C. Bailey (3 vols., Oxford, 1947, including text and translation); this is particularly informative on the Epicurean background, but is long for non-specialists. There is a good short commentary on Book III by E. J. Kenney (Cambridge, 1971).

E. J. Kenney has summarized the issues in a very useful pamphlet (*Lucretius.* Greece & Rome New Surveys in the Classics, no. 11, Oxford, 1977). D. West, *The Imagery and Poetry of Lucretius* (Edinburgh, 1969) encourages the reader to look closely at the Latin, and should be compulsory reading for all who wish to understand any Roman poetry. D. R. Dudley, *Lucretius* (London, 1965), includes articles of varying interest by different hands. P. Boyancé, *Lucrèce et l'épicurisme* (Paris, 1963), is a specialized account of the philosophy of the poem.

CATULLUS

The best introduction is G. P. Goold, *Catullus* (London, 1983); this contains a text that is more radical than most, and a facing translation that is both literal and literary. The best English commentary is by C. J. Fordyce (Oxford, 1961, revised 1973); this includes Mynors's Oxford text except for a number of poems that have been expurgated. The commentary by K. Quinn (London, 1970), which contains all the poems, is better on bibliography but less good on Latin.

A. L. Wheeler, *Catullus and the Traditions of Ancient Poetry* (Berkeley and Los Angeles, 1934) is full and informative, but old-fashioned in manner and some of its matter. K. Quinn, *The Catullan Revolution* (Melbourne, 1959; Cambridge, 1969) covers less ground but will appeal more to the literary reader. Perceptive criticism may be found in the relevant chapters of R. O. A. M. Lyne, *The Latin Love Poets from Catullus to Horace* (Oxford, 1980) and R. Jenkyns, *Three Classical Poets/Sappho, Catullus and Juvenal* (London, 1983); the latter helps the reader to appreciate the beauty of the poet's words. T. P. Wiseman, *Catullus and his World* (Cambridge, 1985) gives an expert and very readable account of the social and political background.

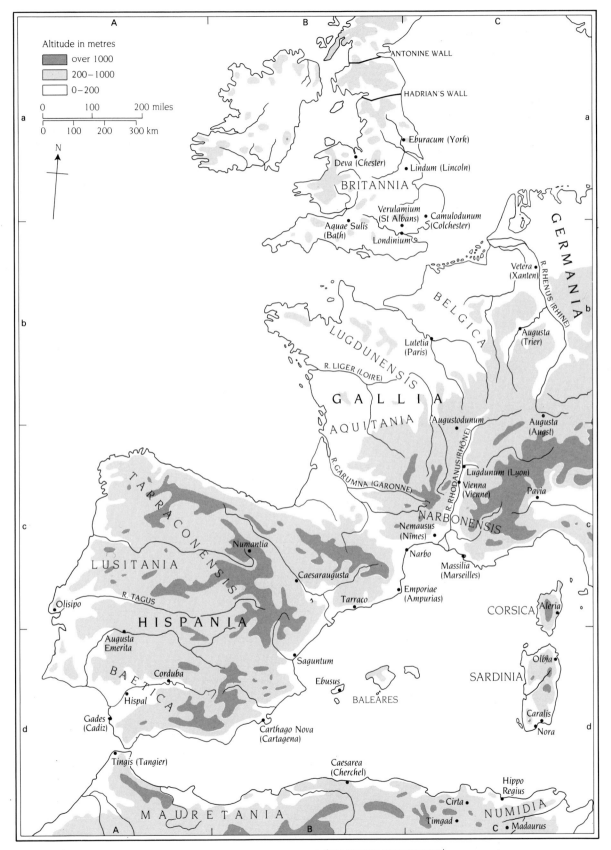

Altitude in metres
over 1000
200–1000
0–200

0   100   200 miles
0   100   200   300 km

N

ANTONINE WALL

HADRIAN'S WALL

Eburacum (York)

Deva (Chester)
Lindum (Lincoln)

BRITANNIA

Verulamium
(St Albans)
Camulodunum
(Colchester)
Aquae Sulis
(Bath)
Londinium

GERMANIA

Vetera
(Xanten)
R. RHENUS (RHINE)

BELGICA

Augusta
(Trier)

LUGDUNENSIS

Lutetia
(Paris)

R. LIGER (LOIRE)

GALLIA

AQUITANIA

Augustodunum

Augusta
(Augst)

R. GARUMNA (GARONNE)

R. RHODANUS (RHÔNE)

Lugdunum (Lyon)

Vienna
(Vienne)

Pavia

NARBONENSIS

TARRACONENSIS

Numantia

Nemausus
(Nîmes)

Narbo

Massilia
(Marseilles)

CORSICA   Aleria

LUSITANIA

Caesaraugusta

Emporiae
(Ampurias)

R. TAGUS

Olisipo

Tarraco

HISPANIA

Augusta
Emerita

Corduba

Saguntum

Ebusus

SARDINIA

Olbia

BAETICA

Hispal

BALEARES

Gades
(Cadiz)

Carthago Nova
(Cartagena)

Caralis

Nora

Tingis (Tangier)

Caesarea
(Cherchel)

Hippo
Regius

Cirta

MAURETANIA

Timgad

NUMIDIA

Madaurus

MAP 3. THE ROMAN EMPIRE (WESTERN PROVINCES)

RAETIA

Augusta
(Augsburg)

Carnuntum

NORICUM

Aquincum
(Budapest)

Pavia

Aquileia

P A N N O N I A

I L L Y R I C U M

D A C I A

Drobeta

Arretium

Ancona

Salonae
(Split)

R. DANUBE

Adamkli

Perusia

I T A L I A

DALMATIA

M O E S I

Rome

MACEDONIA

THRAC

Capua

Thessalonica

Doriscus

Brundisium

Tarentum

EPIRUS

LESBOS

Messana

Thebes

CHIOS

SICILIA

Corinth

SA

Catana

ACHAEA

Athens

Agrigentum

Syracuse

Sparta

Carthage

Hadrumetum

CRETE

Thapsus

MELITA (MALTA)

BYZACENA

N

Sabratha

Oea

Leptis Magna

Ptolemais

Apollonia

Berenice
(Benghazi)

Cyrene

AFRICA

Barca

TRIPOLITANIA

CYRENAICA

L I B Y A

Altitude in metres

over 1000

200–1000

0–200

0   100   200   300 miles

0   100   200   300   400   500 km

MAP 3. THE ROMAN EMPIRE (CENTRAL AND EASTERN PROVINCES)

6

The Founding of the Empire

DAVID STOCKTON

THE future Emperor Augustus was born at Rome in September 63 BC. His father, Gaius Octavius, held a praetorship two years later, but any hopes there may have been of a consulship died with him in 58 BC. The Octavii of Velitrae were well-to-do, but hitherto of only equestrian standing, and Octavius' wife Atia came of no higher than modest senatorial stock on her father's side; it is not surprising that a story later spread that the destined ruler of the world had been fathered on her by the god Apollo. Yet the boy's 'bourgeois' pedigree was singularly appropriate for one who was to engineer and secure the victory of the non-political classes of Italy. And Atia's mother was sister to Gaius Julius Caesar, who himself had no son and whose only daughter Julia died without surviving issue in 54. Julius early discerned his great-nephew's precocious promise, and after his death in 44 BC his will disclosed that the young Octavius was to be his adopted son and so keep alive the name of the noble and patrician Julii Caesares. Marcus Antonius sneered that his challenger was 'a mere boy, owing everything to a name', but he was only half right: the magic of the name of Caesar was a necessary, but not a sufficient, cause of the success of Gaius Julius Caesar Octavianus, who at the tender age of eighteen at once plunged head first into the maelstrom of intrigue and war that swirled all over the Mediterranean world.

By 30 BC, still little over thirty years old, Octavian had eliminated the last and most formidable of his rivals and, like his adoptive father before him, bestrode that world 'like a Colossus'. But this new Colossus did not have feet of clay. Julius had survived barely six months after his return to Rome from his final victory in Spain before he lay murdered beneath the statue of his great opponent Pompey. His assassins (they preferred the name of 'liberators') were an ill-assorted collection of ex-Pompeians, 'Republicans', and prominent adherents of the dictator himself, united by a shared fear or abhorrence of Julius' openly despotic authority. The new Caesar, in stark contrast, survived his own final victory at Actium by nearly half a century, and when he died in his bed in his seventy-sixth year he bequeathed to Rome and Italy and the Empire not civil war and insecurity, but that stable and durable system of government that we call the 'Principate'.

The Second Triumvirate

'If Caesar, for all his genius, could not find a way out, who is going to find one now?' The bleak pessimism of Julius Caesar's old friend Gaius Matius proved amply justified, for it was to be over thirteen years before the Roman world was delivered from disruption and uncertainty, pillage and slaughter, near-anarchy and the ever-present threat of disintegration, years in which the rule of law was set aside and justice was merely 'the interest of the stronger'.

Caesar's assassins, as Cicero saw at once, had been ingenuous in their hope that with his death 'normality' would return. Marcus Antonius soon gained control of the situation in Italy. Cicero's own cynically clever attempt to use Octavian against Antony and so divide the Caesarians against themselves back-fired, and by the autumn of 43 Antony and Octavian and Marcus Aemilius Lepidus with his Gallic legions had reached the sensible conclusion that they must all hang together or all hang separately. The 'Second Triumvirate' which resulted was a three-man legal dictatorship for five years; and Cicero's head was one of the earliest to roll when the first proscription since Sulla's day issued the death-warrants of some 300 senators and 2,000 knights, as the new masters of Rome sought security and a war-chest. Leaving Lepidus to hold Italy, Antony and Octavian moved to crush the only challenge to their dominance, and in October 42 the last 'republican' leaders, Brutus and Cassius, perished in defeat at Philippi in Macedonia.

While Antony left to set the East to rights, Octavian was saddled with the unenviable task of finding land in Italy on which to settle about 100,000 discharged triumviral soldiers. Virgil's First *Eclogue* (below, pp. 207 f.) affords a glimpse of the misery of the dispossessed, driven from their holdings to penury and bitter exile. Antony's wife Fulvia and his brother Lucius (consul 41 BC) tried to exploit Octavian's unpopularity, but were briskly driven from Rome and starved into surrender at Perugia. When Antony himself returned, a fresh civil war threatened, but the legions had had enough of fighting each other, and the diplomacy of Maecenas and Asinius Pollio patched together the so-called 'Treaty of Brundisium' in October 40 BC. Lepidus was fobbed off with Africa, and Antony, before returning to the East, was married to Octavian's sister Octavia. The feeling of relief produced by this reconciliation of the dynasts and the widespread longing for a settled peace are perhaps mirrored in Virgil's Fourth *Eclogue* (below, pp. 209 f.) with its vision of the new Age of Gold that seemed about to dawn.

Such hopes quickly died. Pompey's son Sextus won naval dominance in the western and central Mediterranean, and his threat to the corn-routes compelled concessions—a five-year proconsular command in Corsica, Sardinia, Sicily, and Greece. But once Marcus Agrippa had secured Gaul for Octavian, Sextus' days were numbered. After yet another open clash between Antony and Octavian had been narrowly averted, Octavian and Agrippa (who had built and trained a fleet out of nothing) and Lepidus from Africa regained Sicily and destroyed Sextus and his huge navy off Naulochus in north-west Sicily (September 36 BC). A year earlier the tenure of the triumvirs had been retrospectively renewed for a further five years, but the three were now quickly reduced to two: Lepidus, with twenty-two legions at his back in Sicily, threw down the gauntlet in a bid for a larger share of the spoils, but his troops were not ready to shed more blood for him and preferred Octavian. Though his life was spared, Lepidus was stripped of his triumviral powers. The stage was now set for the final and decisive clash between the master of the West and the master of the East.

From 41 BC onwards Antony had had plenty of work to do. The northern marches of Macedonia had first to be secured against invaders; thereafter the Parthians never ceased to threaten Asia Minor and the Levant, where Rome's subjects were bled white by his heavy financial demands. He became increasingly dependent on the wealth of Egypt and on its Queen Cleopatra. In 37 he packed a pregnant Octavia off back to Italy, and shortly afterwards publicly acknowledged his twin children by Cleopatra, who was herself dreaming of recreating the great empire of her Ptolemaic ancestors. In the autumn of 34 he provocatively proclaimed Cleopatra's son Caesarion to be the legitimate issue of Julius Caesar, and much of the East was parcelled out to Caesarion and his mother, 'King of Kings' and 'Queen of Kings', and to his own two children by Cleopatra.

That gave Octavian a chance too good to miss: Antony could now be caricatured as a renegade apostate from the great traditions of Rome, the creature of an Egyptian she-devil. The Triumvirate was not renewed when it expired at the

GOLD COIN (*AUREUS*) ISSUED BY MARK ANTONY JUST BEFORE THE BATTLE OF ACTIUM (32–31 BC). The so-called 'legionary issue' stresses Antony's naval and military might, with a galley on the obverse, and a legionary 'eagle' (*aquila*) between two standards on the reverse. Different dies name the different military units for which the coins were intended. Note Antony's claim to possess triumviral authority: *IIIVIR R(ei) P(ublicae) C(onstituendae)*.

end of 33; Antony retained the title and claimed the powers, but Octavian eschewed both, posing as no more than the universally desiderated champion of the ordered West. Antony was enormously powerful in ships and men and money, for he 'held the East in fee': his splendid general Ventidius Bassus had driven the Parthians back over the Euphrates in 39, and in 34 Armenia briefly became a province of Rome. But he could not invade Italy as the consort and champion of the 'scarlet woman'. He planned to lure Octavian to defeat in north-west Greece, but, outguessed and outmanoeuvred by Agrippa, he was beaten at sea off Actium in September 31, and escaped to Egypt with Cleopatra, leaving his massive, but leaderless, forces to surrender. By the summer of 30 Octavian was in Egypt, closing in for the kill. Antony took his own life, falsely believing Cleopatra to be dead, and died in her arms: she herself was taken prisoner, but preferred the deifying bite of an asp to the humiliation of being led in a Roman triumph. Two decades of civil war had at last come to an end. It remained to be seen if the new Caesar could find that way out which had eluded the old.

The Augustan Constitution

For three years or so after Actium Octavian's rule was essentially of a personal and irregular nature. He took care not to formalize his ascendancy and used this breathing space to tidy up loose ends in readiness for his first constitutional settlement in 28/7 BC, when he surrendered his supremacy and formally restored the government to Senate and People. As he himself expressed it later in his *Res Gestae* (34), the autobiographical inscription which he directed to be erected outside his mausoleum in the Campus Martius where the citizens could read and admire what their great leader had done for the Roman commons:

In my sixth and seventh consulships [28/7 BC], after I had stamped out the civil wars, and at a time when by universal consent I was in absolute control of everything, I transferred the *res publica* from my own charge ('ex mea potestate') to the discretion of the Senate and People of Rome. For this service I was given the name 'Augustus' by a decree of the Senate.

The Augustan Age had begun, and the quintessential character of the Augustan Principate was determined. The *princeps*, the 'first man' of the Roman Commonwealth, was to have no institutionalized authoritarian power, no perpetual dictatorship such as Julius Caesar had had himself voted early in 44, or anything like it. From Senate and People he accepted the charge of Gaul, Spain, Syria, and Egypt, where the great bulk of the legions was stationed and which he could govern in absence through successive deputies chosen by, and immediately subordinate to, himself. At Rome his overt authority rested on his repeated tenure of one of the two annual consulships, while his enormous personal wealth, patronage, influence, prestige, and diplomatic and political skills could be counted

WALL OF THE TEMPLE OF ROME AND AUGUSTUS AT ANKARA, showing the *Res Gestae*. Augustus' propagandist account of his achievements was inscribed on bronze tablets and set up outside his Mausoleum in Rome after his death. The original is lost, but the text was replicated on public monuments in the provinces; the copy at Ankara is the best preserved.

on to plug any gaps and to oil the wheels of government, and friends and confidants—most notably Agrippa and Maecenas—shared the burden of administration and policy-making.

Some four years later, in 23, after recovering from a near-fatal illness, Augustus resigned his consulship. (He was consul twice later, in 5 and in 2 BC, but on both occasions for only part of the year.) In its place he was voted tribunician power for life, and his command (*imperium*) as proconsul and governor of the 'imperial' provinces was specifically declared superior (*maius*) to that of any governor of a non-imperial or 'public' province. These changes and the reasons behind them have occasioned much argument: they were probably influenced both by the

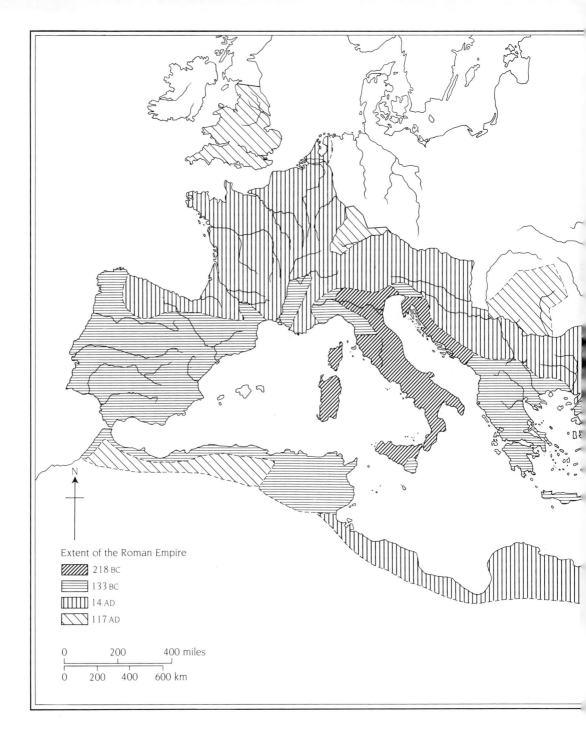

Extent of the Roman Empire

218 BC
133 BC
14 AD
117 AD

```
0        200      400 miles
|----|----|----|----|
0    200   400   600 km
```

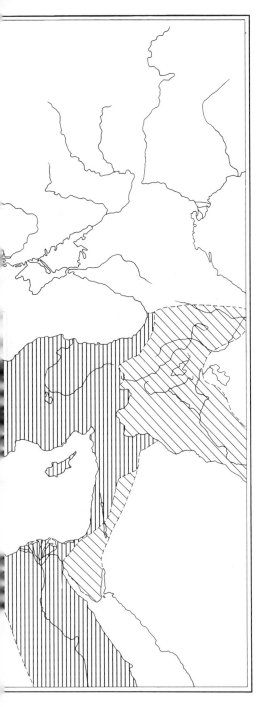

MAP 4. THE GROWTH OF
ROMAN RULE

practical experience of the working of the earlier settlement and by certain dimly detectable, but elusive, stirrings in a section of the ruling aristocracy and even among his own leading supporters. Some have judged the revisions of 23 as constituting a tactical withdrawal by Augustus, to be balanced by a new advance in 19 with the grant to him in that year of the consular power for life. (His provinces were always voted him for set periods and renewed at ten- or five-year intervals.) Others see the grant in 19 as one merely of outward trappings and appearances rather than of any substance of power. In the long-term perspective it hardly matters which view one takes. Augustus had consular *imperium* from 28/7 BC until the day he died, either as consul or as proconsul. After 23 his *imperium* was not only explicitly superior to that of any other pro-magistrate, but also exercisable within Rome itself; and in that year he had received, not only a life tenure of the tribunician power with its wide discretion to veto the administrative and legislative acts of others, succour aggrieved and injured citizens, and initiate legislation in the tribal assembly, but also a consular priority in convening the Senate and ordering its agenda. Moreover, we later find him conducting censuses and revising the Senate-roll and appointing commissioners and superintendents of several new metropolitan departments. Given all that, his pre-eminent and wide-ranging powers at and in, as well as outside, Rome were and are plain for all to see, whether we choose to attribute them to a general 'consular power' for life or alternatively to piecemeal enactments empowering Augustus to use his *imperium* in particular areas and to the gradual establishment of accepted conventions.

It is plain that the *ciuilis princeps* Augustus understood the great importance of preserving and respecting outward forms, whether we regard this as evidence of craft and duplicity or of tact and diplomacy. To have 'restored the Republic' in any literal sense would have been misguided, if not impossible, and as damaging to the loyalties and interests of the mass of the inhabitants of Italy and the Empire as to any personal ambition of Augustus himself. To have established an overt autocracy would have been to fly in the face of five centuries of history and discard much that was of immense psychological significance and solid practical value. Augustus chose a middle way, preferring (one of his own favourite maxims) 'to make haste slowly'. He appreciated, consciously or instinctively, that to close the wide rift which had opened up between loyalty to the state and loyalty to the government must call not just for skill, but for a great deal of patience.

'Res publica' connoted constitutional government, the operation of recognized rules, as opposed to what the Romans called 'regnum', absolute and arbitrary domination. In that sense, the claim that Augustus 'restored the *res publica*' was not altogether hollow. By defining his formal powers, he necessarily delimited them, making it clear in which areas he would exercise direct and open authority and in virtue of what precedents and conventions; simultaneously, he advertised in which areas he did not seek to exercise open authority. There were going to be rules, and the rules themselves were not new. Stable government and long-

term policies demanded that he free himself effectively from those two fetters
with which the Republican nobility had sought to restrain overgreat ambition:
collegiality and limitation of tenure of powers. In practice, Augustus had no
colleagues with equal power save for Agrippa and Tiberius, whom he himself
chose to be his destined successors; and all his formal powers were his for life,
although some—his provinces, for example—were renewed periodically, while
others—like his influence over elections and his control of public finance—
burgeoned gradually with the development of convention and interpretation.
Augustus had come to power young, and time was on his side. Even in 23 BC,
nobody much under sixty had been even a freshman member of the pre-Caesarian
Senate; by AD 14 a man had to be over sixty even to have been born before
Caesar crossed the Rubicon.

None of the foregoing is to be taken to imply that the sheer power of
Augustus—his immense patronage, his 'party' following, his stupendous wealth,
his control of the army—was not the ultimate guarantee of the stability of his
new order. Had any rival been able to use the army against him, his formal
prerogatives would have been of little or no avail. But in civilized societies rule
is more than the possession of the biggest club to hit people on the head with.
We do not take it amiss that modern governments can count on the loyalty and
obedience of their military and police forces: it would be a sorry state of affairs
if they could not. What worries us is the spectacle of a government which uses
army and police to dominate a populace which otherwise would not tolerate it.
There is no evidence at all that that was true of Augustus' government; quite the
contrary, since we have good reason to believe that, apart from a very few
ambitious men whose notions of what constituted 'liberty' were anything but
egalitarian or democratic, the mass of the inhabitants of Italy and the Empire
welcomed the peace and stability, material prosperity, and increased administrative efficiency which came with the Principate. Augustus took the army out of
politics; but we may legitimately question whether his security and that of his
regime would have been very long lived had he not also done much to remedy
actual or potential social and economic distress and disaffection. For all its ambi-
guities, Augustus devised a system far more acceptable than the autocracies and
anarchies which were the only practical alternatives. It was his achievement that
what the Elder Pliny was to call 'the immense majesty of the Roman peace' gave
to the Roman world a freedom from war and the fear of war unmatched in its
duration, and that freedom under the law, one of the ideals of classical Greece
and republican Rome, was still an ideal of the Principate; it grew gradually more
remote, but survived to be transmitted to modern Europe. Thus, when the
Emperor Claudius wanted to marry his own niece, he did not assume that he
was above the law, but had the law changed so that any man could do the same:
the distinction may appear slight, but on reflection can be seen to be of profound
significance.

It was once accepted that one could talk of a 'dyarchy', a system in which power and executive responsibility were shared between two parties, *princeps* and Senate. That is now frowned upon, but it was certainly long accepted as the principle behind Augustus' new order. In his 'programme speech' to the Senate on his accession in AD 54, the young Nero declared his intention of abandoning the centralizing practices of his predecessor Claudius and returning to the true Augustan pattern:

he would not set himself up to be the judge in every case or issue, for a powerful few to grow fat behind the closed doors of one man's home at the expense of prosecutors and defendants alike; nothing in his household would be bought by money or open to intrigue; his private self and his public self would be kept quite separate from each other. The Senate would keep its traditional prerogatives, Italy and the public provinces should take their stand before the tribunals of the consuls, who would bring their business before the Senate for a hearing; he, the Emperor, would answer for the armies entrusted to his care. (Tacitus, *Annals* 13.4)

And earlier Augustus' immediate successor, Tiberius, had been quite explicit about the Senate's role:

I say now what I have said often before on other occasions, conscript fathers: a good and healthful *princeps*, whom you have invested with such great discretionary power, ought to be the servant of the Senate, and often of the whole citizen body, sometimes even of individuals. Nor do I regret having said this; I have found you, and I still find you, good and fair and kind masters. (Suetonius, *Tiberius* 29)

It is indicative of a very important change in attitude that, while both Augustus and Tiberius are on record as having steadfastly refused to allow themselves to be addressed as 'dominus' ('master'), by Trajan's day at latest 'dominus' had become the customary form of addressing the *princeps*, as can be seen from Pliny's letters to that Emperor.

Between appearance and reality there was, however, a great gulf set. Although Augustus owed his formal powers to the granting of Senate and People, powers theoretically and constitutionally revocable by their grantors, Senate and People had in fact simply 'rubber-stamped' Augustus' own wishes, public opposition to which would have been, to say the least, ill-advised. It was only in the most trivial sense that Senate or People had invested Tiberius with 'such great discretionary power': his adoptive father had ensured that there could be no genuine alternative. Gaius (Caligula), Claudius, and Nero—all three total strangers to the long and distinguished record of public service and high responsibilities of which Tiberius could be proud on his accession—owed their elevation to factors over which the Senate had no control, and were duly voted *en bloc* the ever-growing powers and prerogatives which went with the office of *princeps*. Thus it is no surprise to find the Senate, during the confused power struggle that followed Nero's demise, tamely decreeing 'all the customary prerogatives of the *princeps*' to each usurper in turn, nor Vespasian preferring to date his reign from the day six months earlier when he had been saluted as 'imperator' by the legions at Alexandria.

The Emperor and the Senate

The organization of Rome's military forces under the Principate and their deployment, the growth and structure of an 'imperial secretariat' of equestrian officials and slave and freedman servants of the imperial household, the administration of the provinces and the consolidation and extension of Rome's imperial domains, and the spread of the rights and opportunities of Roman citizenship beyond the limits of Italy itself, all fall to be treated in Chapter 22. Here it must suffice to stress that in all these areas Augustus laid the solid foundations on which his successors were to build. But in the end all roads led to Rome, where by the time of Augustus' death new attitudes and expectations had become established. Ever since 5 BC, when Augustus was again consul after a gap of almost twenty years, with the names of a Caesar and a Sulla adding lustre to the date, there had been four consuls in nearly every year, holding office as successive pairs, a scheme regularly followed thereafter. This can be taken to mark the definitive 'arrival', a generation after Actium, of the 'new Italians' and the steepening decline of the old republican nobility. By now the overriding influence of the *princeps* on the choice of the highest magistrates was accepted, and in practice inevitable. It was from among ex-praetors and ex-consuls that he was constrained to select his provincial governors and legionary legates, senatorial curators and prefects, so that no *princeps* could fail to be vitally concerned about the stocking of the pool in which he must fish. Direct appointment to public magistracies was neither politic nor necessary: lip-service could be paid to constitutional forms while indirect methods and the *princeps*'s public and private support did their work— though in the less deftly sure hands of a Tiberius the legerdemain lacked conviction. Tiberius indeed effectively transferred elections to the Senate in AD 15, leaving to the popular assemblies a mere ceremonial role. But those assemblies had by then lost any effective role even in legislation, which became in practice the field of senatorial decrees and imperial edicts, rescripts, and constitutions. The free inhabitants of Rome and its immediate environs had long ceased to constitute a representative cross-section of Rome's widely scattered citizens; and among the consequences of this eclipse was a diminution of extravagant electoral expenditure and a decline in the influence of the political element among the *equites*. The latter also suffered from judicial changes, for before Augustus died cases of political importance had come regularly to be heard by the Senate sitting as a high court, instead of by the mixed courts of the late Republic and of the first part of his reign, while by Claudius' time the supreme and independent jurisdiction of the *princeps* had come to be exercised frequently.

The *de facto* subordination of the Senate itself was exposed in its helpless nakedness when an ageing Tiberius removed himself from Rome to Campania and then to Capri for the second half of his reign and ruled the world through his letters and the agents of his will. In the early books of his *Annals* Tacitus often underlines and castigates the servility, and even sycophancy, of the members of the Senate. Lacking as they did the hereditary self-contained power-bases of later European nobles or any formidable 'constituencies', hopelessly outgunned by the power and patronage of the Emperors themselves, and acutely aware that any 'dyarchy' was no more than a convenient fiction, they chose the line of least resistance. Yet what other possible counterweight could men see to the potential or actual misuse or abuse of the imperial prerogatives? The Senate enjoyed an important place in the constitution, and had gained a new role as a high court of justice; it handled much business of a routine nature from Italy and the public provinces; it numbered in its ranks nearly all the highest officers of state, as well as their recent predecessors and expected successors, not to speak of the great 'friends' (*amici principis*) who had the ear and the confidence of the Emperor; it had behind it half a millennium of independent history as Rome's great council of state and of imperial success. It is then not hard to appreciate that it remained a focus of opposition dreams, even when criticism of a *princeps* had to be whispered 'at private parties and in intimate gatherings' (Tacitus, *Annals* 3. 54), or the repository of the hopes of independents like Thrasea Paetus in the early years of Nero, until men finally reconciled themselves to the 'futility of long speeches in the Senate, when the best men were quick to reach agreement elsewhere, and of endless haranguing of public meetings, when the final decisions were taken not by the ignorant multitude but by one man' (Tacitus, *Dialogus* 41). For all that, the Empire relied chiefly on senators to run it, and so no Emperor could be really secure unless his rule was founded on their consent or acquiescence. The Senate never lost its *esprit de corps*, and there was hostility to Emperors who were thought to abuse their great powers. As Tacitus expressed what was surely his own philosophy,

There can be great men even under bad emperors, and duty and discretion, if coupled with energy of character and a career of action, will bring a man to no less glorious summits than are attained by perilous paths and ostentatious deaths, with no advantage to the Commonwealth. (*Agricola* 42)

It may be that the weakness of the Senate went beyond what Augustus had desired. On more than one occasion, he tried to reduce its size to a really effective level, but in the end retired baffled from the task. He was probably well aware of the danger of distancing himself too far from average upper-class opinion. In the late Republic, the leading politicians had relied on informal 'cabinets' of friends and associates for discussion of policy and practicalities, and thus the constantly changing mosaic of politics had ensured a variety of experience and involvement not automatically guaranteed by the Augustan system. At some time before 4 BC Augustus had instituted a committee (*consilium semenstre*) made up of the consuls in office plus one each of the other magistrates and fifteen other senators selected by lot, serving for periods of six months, to help the *princeps* to prepare business for the Senate. Its random membership and relative informality should have made it a useful sounding-board; but its nature and composition changed significantly in the last year of his life, and it came to an end with Tiberius' withdrawal from Rome in AD 26. Of course, Augustus had always had an intimate circle of 'friends' and supporters (most of them senators, but including also *equites* such as Maecenas and Sallustius Crispus) whose advice and judgement and experience he valued—and needed, for 'no man is an island, entire of itself'— and with whom he could discuss in confidence the most sensitive and important issues and options; and this less institutionalized body continued under his successors. Outside Italy Tiberius was ready to devolve wide areas of delegated discretion and initiative for very long periods: the outstanding example was Poppaeus Sabinus who was left as virtual viceroy of the Balkans from AD 11 until his death in 35. But Tiberius was exceptional, and Poppaeus surely sometimes came back to Italy for leave and consultations.

The Emperor and the Gods

When M. Aemilius Lepidus, the erstwhile triumviral colleague of Octavian and Antony, long retired from public life, finally died in 12 BC, Augustus was elected to succeed him as Rome's Chief Pontiff (*pontifex maximus*), an office which now took its place among the imperial prerogatives. His election was the occasion for a massive demonstration of popular support, and this formal position as 'head of the national church' sat well with his programme of regeneration of traditional religion and morality. Already the very name 'Augustus' with its 'by the grace of God' overtones had marked him out as somewhat larger than life-size; and in 2 BC he was formally accorded the title of 'Father of the Fatherland' (*pater patriae*). Official deification had to await his death, but from very early days he had advertised that he was 'divi filius', the son of the deified Julius Caesar. For Virgil's Tityrus (*Eclogues* 1. 7–8), 'He will always be a god, often will a tender lamb from my flock be sacrificed at his altar'; and for Horace (*Odes* 3. 5. 2–4), 'Augustus will be held to be a god here on earth with the addition to the empire of Britain and Persia.' The cult of his guardian spirit, his *genius* or *numen,* became established in many western municipalities, temples were set up in most provinces to 'Rome and Augustus', and oaths were regularly taken in his name. At Rome itself the splendid Altar of Augustan Peace (well worth seeing in its modern reconstructed form) portrayed the 'royal family' in simple and awesome majesty (below, pp. 134, 370 f.). Nevertheless, there was a line which could not be overstepped, and the living Augustus was never formally and explicitly a god in Italy and the West. Things were different elsewhere: in Egypt he was as divine as the Pharaohs had been, and an inscription (*ILS* 8781) from Gangra in Paphlagonia preserves an oath of total and unreflecting devotion and loyalty to Augustus and his descendants which was taken in 3 BC 'at the altars of Augustus in the temples of Augustus' by all the inhabitants of the region (including resident Roman citizens), an oath in which Augustus is named along with 'all the gods and goddesses' as a guarantor of the oath and of the dreadful penalties for betraying it.

RELIEF OF THE IMPERIAL FAMILY on the Ara Pacis Augustae (Altar of Augustan Peace), Rome (13–9 BC). This detail is thought to show Agrippa (with head veiled in the customary Roman manner for the priest about to sacrifice), his son L. Caesar and his wife Julia, Iullus Antonius (the son of Mark Antony), and Augustus' nieces, the two Antonias, with their respective families. (Cf. below, pp. 370 f.)

By and large, Augustus' policy was followed by his Julio-Claudian successors, although neither Tiberius nor Gaius nor Nero was posthumously deified. Tiberius indeed seems to have entertained a sceptic's distaste for such matters; but a temple to the living god Claudius was early established at Camulodunum in the new province of Britain (he had to wait for Vespasian's accession for a temple at Rome itself), and Gaius notoriously came to have exaggerated notions of personal divinity. Vespasian could take it all in his common-sense stride: as he lay dying, he blandly observed, 'My goodness, I think I am turning into a god!' He was right, as usual, and like subsequent Emperors whose memory was not officially damned he duly became 'divus'.

Augustus took pains to restore the gods, and especially the old deities of Rome and Italy, to their pre-eminent place in public life. Many decayed or dilapidated temples and shrines were rebuilt, many traditional rites and ceremonies renewed or reinvigorated. He aimed to restore public confidence in divine providence, duty to fatherland, and a secure sense of continuity and order and permanence. Yet here too the might and majesty of the *princeps* and his family were kept well in evidence. New temples of the Deified Julius, Mars the Avenger, Venus the Progenitress of the Julian line, and his own special patron Apollo enriched the capital; a temple and altar of Vesta, goddess of the sacred hearth of the

TEMPLE OF MARS ULTOR, vowed after the defeat of Brutus and Cassius at Philippi in 42 BC, but constructed mainly in the last decade of the century as the dominant feature in the new Augustan Forum (dedicated in 2 BC). The temple and forum are strongly influenced by the architecture of classical Athens.

commonwealth, actually formed part of his home on the Palatine; on his return to Rome from Greece and Asia in 19 BC an altar was dedicated to Fortune the Home-Bringer; vows were regularly offered to heaven for his safety, each new year and the various anniversaries of his birth and achievements were marked by solemn public prayers for his well-being and that of his family; throughout Rome his personal household tutelary spirit (*Lar*) was venerated in the various 'parish chapels' alongside the public *Lares Compitales*. The pomp and circumstance of the great priestly colleges (of all of which he was himself a member) were refurbished, and comparable institutions created and consolidated at lower levels of society. The glittering high-point was the magnificent celebration of the Secular Games in the summer of 17 BC, the tenth anniversary of the new order, a massive public thanksgiving for the past and present grandeur of Rome.

Domestic Policy

Hand in hand with this religious renaissance went a determination to restore that high moral seriousness and restraint which had, in pious memory or myth, assured the greatness of the old *res publica*. Sallust had not been the only man to incriminate and castigate, albeit over-ingeniously, the sad and steep decline from such sober standards as the root cause of the many and grave ills that had beset Rome in the febrile brilliance of the last generations of the Republic. However much we must allow for some measure of hypocrisy in this area, Augustus set a public example in the simplicity of his personal life-style, the modesty of his house on the Palatine and its furnishings (the austerity of which later astonished Suetonius) in contrast with the splendour of the public buildings with which he beautified Rome (below, pp. 365 f.), and in his dress and table—a legacy, perhaps, of his paternal ancestors and their solid municipal tradition at Velitrae. Legislation was passed to visit severe penalties on adultery, agents and accessories as well as the guilty parties themselves. Marriage and the procreation of children to restock the human wealth of Italy were encouraged by a blend of 'stick and carrot',

THE 'TABLINUM' IN THE SO-CALLED HOUSE OF LIVIA on the Palatine in Rome. Painted about 30 BC in the late Second Style, this house almost certainly formed part of the properties owned by Augustus, properties whose modesty (by the standards of later Emperors) was commented upon by Suetonius.

penalties for the celibate and rewards for the philoprogenitive. Measures were taken to restrict ostentatious private extravagance and to check licence at public shows. Historic noble names, some half-buried in the mists of time, adorned the consulship (though the consulship was not itself normally a preliminary to a great military command, for Augustus prudently reserved such appointments in the provinces under his direct command to close relatives or 'new men' in whose competence and loyalty he could trust). The public dignity and display of the senatorial and equestrian orders were actively promoted. The older and more respectable guilds were encouraged, and Rome itself was organized in fourteen 'regions', subdivided in turn into 'districts' (*uici*) with their own local officers (*uicomagistri*). The realization and exaltation of a united Italy was nurtured with an ever-increasing number of Italians entering the Senate and other levels of government service, civil and military, and a continuing move towards a greater uniformity in municipal institutions. New building and traffic regulations, a new Board of Public Works, the creation of a Metropolitan Police Force and Fire Brigade, a Water Board to ensure the needs of a city now approaching a million inhabitants, a Tiber Conservancy Board to dredge and embank the river, and proper provision and supervision of the corn supply are only the most noticeable of the benefits which could come from a stable and effective government. Much of this spirit and achievement of regeneration and progress is reflected in the poetry of the period as well as in public architecture, statuary, and inscriptions. Cicero had ruefully observed how most men at all levels of society cared little about fighting despotism and valued above all else peace and stability in their lives; it is not surprising then to read in Tacitus (*Annals* 1. 2) how Augustus contrived to seduce all and sundry with the sweet lure of tranquil security, and lead them to prefer the present and visible prosperity and security to the uncertain dangers of the old Republic, while the provinces too, where the power-struggle of the great at Rome and the greed of governors had destroyed any confidence in the institutions of the Republic, were no less ready to accept the tangible benefits of the new order.

The Problem of the Succession

A major question for Augustus to answer was how to provide for the continuity of his new order; for, as the event showed, he was concerned to do so, whether from altruistic motives or out of a sense of pride in his achievement or following the instinctive dynastic principles of a Roman noble. A formal hereditary succession was impossible, but it was not hard to associate a destined successor as a virtual vice-gerent and 'heir-presumptive' by having him voted the requisite offices and appointments, powers and dignities. His earliest choice seems to have lighted on M. Claudius Marcellus, only son of his sister Octavia, who was married in 25 BC to his only child, his daughter Julia, and in 24 marked out for more rapid acceleration up the ladder of office than Augustus' stepson Tiberius, who had been born in the same year (42 BC) as Marcellus. The obvious favour shown to his nephew/son-in-law may have occasioned some serious reactions, especially from his old and indispensable friend and general, M. Vipsanius Agrippa; but Marcellus' premature death in 23 removed that piece from the board. The immensely capable Agrippa now emerged as the obvious candidate; Augustus had handed him his personal signet-ring during his own grave illness in 23, and two years later he was married to the widowed Julia, who bore him three sons (Gaius and Lucius Caesar and Agrippa Postumus) and two daughters (Julia and Agrippina). Entrusted in the same year with overall control of the eastern half of the Empire, he moved subsequently to Gaul and then to Spain, where he finally subdued the Cantabri. In 18 BC came the grant of tribunician power for five years, followed by a renewal for a further five years in 13, and his *imperium* was made either superior (*maius*) like that of Augustus himself or at least equipotent (*aequum*) with that of all other provincial governors in whichever part of the Empire his public duties might require him to be.

Agrippa's death in 12 BC came as a surprise: he was only fifty, and had been expected to outlive his exact coeval Augustus by some years, for his robust health contrasted with Augustus' somewhat delicate physique. His sons by Julia, Gaius and Lucius, born in 20 and 17, had been adopted by their grandfather in the latter year, but were still only children. So Augustus had to turn to his thirty-year-old stepson Tiberius, requiring him to put away his wife Vipsania (daughter of Agrippa by an earlier marriage) and marry the widowed Julia. In 6 BC Tiberius in turn was granted tribunician power. But his marriage to the wayward and imperious Julia was singularly loveless, and the one child of their union, a boy, died in infancy; on top of that, it was clear that Tiberius was cast as a stop-gap until Gaius and Lucius Caesar should reach maturity. Whether through pride or apprehension or calculation, Tiberius withdrew from public life to Rhodes— a potentially risky move, but he probably counted on his formidable mother Livia, Augustus' wife, to keep him from serious harm. Ill luck continued to dog Augustus: Lucius died at Marseilles in AD 2; and Gaius, consul for the whole year in AD 1 at the age of nineteen and then sent on an important mission to the East with experienced advisers to guide his early steps in high responsibility, fell fatally ill in Lycia on his way home in February AD 4. Two years before that, Tiberius had returned to Italy, though not to public life. Now Augustus had to turn to him again: there was no alternative, and he was himself already in his middle sixties. Tiberius became Augustus' adopted son, and received the tribunician power for ten years and an *imperium* matching that of the *princeps* himself, both grants being subsequently renewed in AD 13.

Julia meanwhile had finally tried her father's patience too far and too often with her scandalous liaisons, and probably constituted a focus of attention for men with aspirations to become the ward and guardian of her young sons: expelled to the tiny island of Pandateria in 2 BC, she was allowed to return five years later only to the very tip of Italy at Rhegium, where she remained until her death in the early months of Tiberius' principate in an exile voluntarily shared by her mother, Augustus' first wife Scribonia. Still Augustus refused to relax his determination to secure the eventual succession of his own blood-line. Tiberius, who had a sixteen-year-old son, Drusus, by his first marriage, was required to adopt his eighteen-year-old nephew. Germanicus was the elder son of Tiberius' dead brother Drusus and Antonia Minor, younger daughter of Augustus' sister Octavia; and Germanicus' children by his wife Agrippina were Augustus' great-grandchildren, since Agrippina was the daughter of Julia.

Tiberius

Some ancient writers were apparently puzzled by a certain vagueness about the precise moment of Tiberius' assumption of the office of *princeps* in AD 14. In part that was due to the uniqueness of the occasion: no precedents existed, there was no time-honoured sequence of a 'The King is dead—long live the King' kind. Further, unlike his successors in the purple, Tiberius already shared the central powers of his adoptive father: ever since AD 4 he had been his 'partner in the *imperium* and the tribunician power'; these prerogatives were his by law and in his own right and not held by delegation, so that there could be no question of their lapsing with Augustus' death, though in theory they could have been revoked by Senate and People—but not in the teeth of a veto from Tiberius himself.

The next *princeps*, Gaius, came naked to empire, so that, as Dio (59. 3) observed, 'he had to be voted in a single day all the prerogatives which Augustus over so long a span of time had been voted gradually and piecemeal, some of which indeed Tiberius had declined to accept at all'; such too was the position of Claudius, Nero, and the four Emperors of 68/9. Hence later writers, puzzled by the absence of such an enabling grant for Tiberius, may have been left floundering or guessing, ascribing delay to a supposed concern about disaffection in the Rhine and Danube legions or wariness about what Germanicus might do—although such threats, had they been real, should have called for speed rather than indecision. Apart from that, the 'accession debate' (Tacitus, *Annals* 1. 11–13) was badly mismanaged, with Tiberius clumsily or deviously rehearsing or inviting other options (when in practice all that was needed was an expression of his readiness to take over the role of Augustus), and in the end not so much saying 'yes' as ceasing to say 'no'.

Tiberius had had an outstandingly successful military and administrative career from his early twenties, in the East, Germany, and the Balkans, interrupted only during the years of his retirement. He thus came to the task of government in his mid-fifties with excellent and unrivalled credentials. But his character was dour and introspective, poisoned by unhappy private experience, with more than a touch of melancholia and insecurity. Above all, he lacked the consummate political adroitness of Augustus, his self-confidence and prestige as the restorer of

RECONSTRUCTION OF THE VILLA JOVIS ON CAPRI, viewed from the north-east. According to Tacitus, Tiberius owned twelve villas on the island; the so-called Villa Jovis, perched on the cliffs of the eastern promontory, over

1,000 feet (334 m) above sea-level, is the best preserved. The remote situation suited Tiberius's need for security and privacy and led to the growth of scurrilous reports of his activities there.

peace and security to a world shattered by civil war, his genial tact which had moved him to ask on his death-bed 'if everybody had enjoyed the play'. Men could never be quite sure what was going on in Tiberius' mind. This led to the view, particularly prevalent in Tacitus' *Annals* (below, p. 238), that he was a hypocrite, a master of dissimulation, a view sometimes ludicrous in its strained invention or innuendo. In fact, the true dissimulation stemmed not from the man, but from the system which he inherited, the product of the great illusionist Augustus; it was only underlined by his successor's maladroitness. Criticism, flinching from finding fatal flaws in the system itself, or seeing no practical alternative to it, turned instead on the failings of individual emperors once they were safely dead and adulation must be transferred to the new from the old master. Tacitus gave grudgingly good marks to the early years of Tiberius' rule; but the curse of premature mortality fell heavy on him as it had on Augustus, and by AD 23 first his adopted son Germanicus and then his true son Drusus were in their graves, leaving him with no younger shoulders to lean on as he approached old age. He came to rely heavily on his praetorian prefect L. Aelius Sejanus, especially after his withdrawal from Rome in 26. Sejanus used his chance and the vague, but deadly, charge of treason (*maiestas*) to pick off enemies and rivals, mostly adherents of Germanicus' strong-minded and ambitious widow Agrippina, sister of the dead Gaius and Lucius Caesar and grand-daughter of Augustus himself: she and the sons whom she fought to protect and advance were deported or imprisoned. Sejanus himself aspired to the hand of Claudia Livilla, Germanicus' sister and widow of Tiberius' son Drusus, in the hope no doubt of ruling as regent and guardian of Drusus' son Tiberius Gemellus (born AD 19) once the boy's grandfather was gone. Tiberius was too wary to allow that; but by AD 31 Sejanus had reached the consulship and had thoughts of the tribunician power, which Drusus had held for the year before his death. With the *princeps* now in his seventies and no 'heir apparent' in sight, more and more men must have looked to his great minister as the star to steer by. Then came swift and utter ruin: Antonia, the widow of Tiberius' brother Drusus, penetrated the fence which Sejanus had woven around the Emperor on his remote island retreat and alerted him to much of which he had been ignorant; Sejanus was out-guiled, arrested, and executed, and there followed a blood-bath of his supporters and associates, including his children.

The final years were years of gloom, intrigue, and uncertainty, over which loomed the cynical and suspicious shadow of a lonely old man encompassed by astrologers (and, so scabrous gossip would have it, the instruments of nameless sexual perversions) on the island of Capri. If we shift our sights from Rome, it is true, the Empire seems to have been well governed, prosperous, and (apart from a quickly suppressed revolt in Gaul occasioned by the greed of Roman financiers) secure; the Treasury was healthy, and Italy flourishing. But that something went wrong under Tiberius there is no doubt. The Augustan pattern was marred, above all, by Tiberius' neglect or refusal to imitate his predecessor in persisting in the search for a tried and trusted successor who could be trained for empire and give a secure sense of continuity and direction to men with longer horizons than the failing *princeps*. To have died leaving it virtually certain that Gaius must succeed is the blackest of all indictments, whether we seek an explanation in embittered cynicism, suspicious insecurity, or a lingering and misjudged 'constitutionalism' which saw it as the Senate's part to decide what must follow.

Gaius (Caligula)

Gaius was the son of Germanicus, and the great-grandson of both Augustus and Mark Antony: his nickname 'Caligula' he owed to the little soldiers' boots he wore as a child with his parents in the cantonments of the Rhine, 'Bootikins', an ironically innocent name. Just under twenty-five on his accession in AD 37, he lost little time in making away with the young Tiberius Gemellus, voiding the will in which Tiberius had named Gemellus as his coheir, and executing Macro, Sejanus' supplanter as praetorian prefect, who had been prompt in supporting Gaius' own accession. His brief reign has an air of melodramatic unreality: mental and emotional instability, vicious cruelty, incest, ridiculous indecision and waywardness as exemplified in the farce of his projected invasion of Britain, fantasies of divinity which *inter alia* bred unrest among the Jews. Within less than four years it was all over, and he and his fourth wife and his young daughter all lay dead in his palace. The murder was not part of a plan to seize power for a successor, and the Senate seemed to have a fleeting chance to reassert its authority. 'But while they deliberated, the praetorian guards had resolved.' In January 41 Tiberius Claudius Nero Germanicus, Gaius' uncle and the brother of Germanicus, became the penultimate Julio-Claudian Emperor.

Claudius

Modern assessments of Claudius' principate vary widely. For some he was a strong ruler with a clear sense of direction, who had spent his long years of obscurity studying Roman history and reaching his own conclusions about the correct blending of tradition and innovation, concealing behind his unprepossessing physical exterior and manners an incisive and inventive intelligence; for them, his chief freedman secretaries, Pallas, Callistus, Narcissus, and the rest were the servants of the policies of a *princeps* who saw that the time was ripe for a forward development. But other scholars see him as a weak-willed, absent-minded, erratic, and malleable man, suddenly and quite unexpectedly bundled on to the throne at the age of fifty, totally devoid of any experience of the corridors of power and hence swiftly becoming the pliant tool of far more adroit and experienced manoeuverers within the imperial household—in Dio's classic formulation, 'dominated by his slaves and his wives' (60-2); for them the increased centralization which marked his reign was the consequence not of his deliberate decision, but of his own ineffectual weakness and the ambitions of his ministers. It is impossible to be sure how much truth there is in these two contrasting pictures (and neither is likely to be completely false) since the overt facts can often be interpreted to suit either. But there is probably more truth in the less favourable portrait, which was certainly that recognized by many contemporaries, criticized in Nero's accession speech to the Senate, and caricatured by Seneca (below, pp. 253 f.) in his *Apocolocyntosis*. There can be no doubt that his freedmen achieved a far greater public prominence and influence than those of his predecessors and successors (there is, incidentally, no sound basis for the view that Claudius 'created' or even first organized an imperial bureaucracy), or that his wives exerted a potent influence; Messallina's public 'wedding' to the consul-designate Silius while her husband Claudius was out of Rome was so bizarre an affair that Tacitus felt compelled to reassure his readers twice in a single paragraph (*Annals* 11. 27) that his account was history and not a farcical fairy-tale; and Augustus' private correspondence shows that that shrewd and close observer, while recognizing some faint redeeming qualities in his young kinsman, had seen him as generally incoherent, absent-minded, easily influenced, and far from circumspect in his choice of models (Suetonius, *Claudius*, 4).

Not that Claudius' reign was a failure: whatever view we take, his chief advisers were clever and able men who had risen high in the imperial household by their own talents and energies. The invasion and conquest of southern Britain was a copy-book exercise, superbly well executed, commanded by generals of ability and dash; although the conquest made little economic or strategic sense, it was a resounding and valuable political success. Something was done to repair the damage Gaius had done to the susceptibilities of the Jews; the barbaric and potentially dangerous cult of Druidism was firmly repressed; citizenship was conceded widely, if not always wisely, with the Emperor's personal advocacy of the importance of this large-minded approach, though in a speech remarkable for its banality and irrelevance; public finances were buoyant; and Mauretania and Thrace were brought from indirect to direct rule. But the judicial carnage among senators and *equites* was heavy (quite a number of them had been implicated in Scribonianus' abortive revolt in Dalmatia a few months after Claudius' accession); and for all his good intentions, which need not be denied, it seems that only too often Claudius' left hand did not know what his right hand was doing. Thus it was all very well for him to adjure senators not to behave like 'yes-men'; but Tacitus (*Annals* 11. 23-5) makes it clear, for instance, that the possible admission of some leading men from Gaul to the senatorial order had been discussed and already decided on in the Palace before Claudius brought it to the Senate, where the *princeps*'s somewhat incoherent speech was promptly followed by the automatic assent of his docile audience.

Nero

Claudius' death in October 54 was quite possibly due to poisoning by his second consort, his niece the younger Agrippina, whose son by her earlier marriage to Domitius Ahenobarbus (consul AD 32) now came to the Principate one month short of his seventeenth birthday. Like Gaius before him, Nero (or his mother—some of the imperial females were more ruthless than their kinsmen) lost no time in dispatching Britannicus (four years younger and Claudius' son by his earlier marriage to Messallina). For some time, however, all seemed fair. Nero's old tutor Seneca, and Agrippina's sometime favourite Burrus, sole praetorian prefect since 51, got the better of the Empress Dowager in the struggle to dominate the adolescent *princeps*, and presided over a period of stability and sound administration—although Thrasea Paetus, as already noted, stoutly deplored their neglect to exploit the chance to recruit the Senate's influence and authority. The first serious storm signal was hoisted when in 59 Nero grew impatient of his mother's insistent meddling and had her murdered. Three years later Burrus died, and was replaced by a pair of praetorian prefects, one of them the infamous Tigellinus, who secured a maleficent influence over the Emperor he was in the end to abandon. At this point Seneca retired, and soon Octavia, Claudius' daughter and Nero's wife, was ousted by the scheming Poppaea and later murdered. Nero was free to indulge his artistic and aesthetic pretensions, surrounded by a claque of corrupt and greedy advisers and toadies, some base-born, like the Sicilian Tigellinus, many others Greek or Levantine freedmen. His extravagance and their unscrupulous venality—not to mention the expense of warfare in Britain, where Boudicca's uprising was sparked off by Roman avarice and greed, and later in Asia Minor, where an ill-thought-out and mismanaged forward move in Armenia ended in a thinly disguised surrender of actual Roman sovereignty and the collapse of Augustus' 'diplomatic solution'—led to depreciation of the coinage and the quasi-judicial fleecing of rich victims. The Great Fire of AD 64 gave Nero the opportunity to start building his grotesquely expensive 'Golden House' (below, pp. 378 ff.) on the ruins of much of the capital: rumours that he had started the fire himself 'to clear the site' and had celebrated the occasion with poetry and song induced him to make the newly spreading Christian community of Rome, no longer seen as merely a dissident sect within Judaism, the innocent scapegoats.

Understandably, men steeled themselves to the perils of conspiring to remove a ruler who had strayed so far from the Augustan path. But in 65 a plot to replace him with the noble and popular Calpurnius Piso was uncovered, and Piso and the others involved or implicated (they included Seneca himself and his nephew, the poet Lucan) were executed. A legacy of suspicion and apprehension led to further deaths, most notably those of Gaius Petronius, 'the arbiter of elegance', and the prominent Stoics, Thrasea Paetus and Barea Soranus. When in the next year the great general Corbulo, mirror of Rome's ancient military virtues and victories, was ordered to take his own life, who could feel safe? An increasingly insecure Nero had committed the cardinal sin of unsettling his own ruling class and army commanders.

The Year of the Four Emperors

It was a descendant of an enfranchised princely house of Aquitania, Julius Vindex, the legate of Gallia Lugdunensis, whose inhabitants had, like those of Spain, suffered heavily from Nero's recent exactions, who raised the standard of rebellion in March 68 against an Emperor who had suddenly and sulkily to be summoned back to Rome from an 'artistic tour' of Greece. Vindex had appealed for support to other legates, without much response; but in Spain the seventy-one-year-old Servius Sulpicius Galba, the sole direct descendant of a Republican noble house—apart from Nero himself—holding high office, agreed to accept the headship of the movement and styled himself 'Legate of the Senate and People'. In Africa Clodius Macer threw off his allegiance. Even so, had the legions and their commanders been firmly and competently handled, Vindex and Galba must have been overwhelmed. A mysterious collision, perhaps unintended by their commanders, at Besançon between Vindex's ill-trained Gallic levies and the crack legions from Upper Germany saw the insurgents scattered like chaff: Vindex took his own life, and Galba meditated imitating him when he heard the appalling news. But Nero's house of cards was tumbling down, and few retained any confidence in him. Verginius Rufus marched his legions back to Germany, waiting on events; Tigellinus turned his coat and suborned the praetorian guard. Before other help could arrive, Nero panicked and ran, and committed suicide. On 9 June 68 the Julio-Claudian line died with him.

Against all the odds, Galba had succeeded. But his power-base was perilously narrow: he had not won a war, he had marched through an open and undefended gate. His urgent need was to consolidate his position; but a combination of short-sighted ineptness and stiff-necked disciplinarianism and parsimony served him ill. His choice of a lightweight young noble, Piso, as his successor added nothing but the empty lustre of an historic name, and antagonized the energetic and ambitious Marcus Salvius Otho. The victorious German legions were neglected and unrewarded, the Gallic tribes opposed to Vindex alienated, the praetorians denied their expected donative. Throughout the Empire those who had remained loyal to Nero urgently needed a reassurance which they did not receive. Aulus Vitellius, sent by Galba to take command in Lower Germany, was saluted as Emperor by his troops on 2 January 69, and the legions of Upper Germany promptly followed suit. At Rome and on the Danube, Otho's intrigues bore fruit, and he was himself hailed as Emperor a fortnight later. Galba and Piso were murdered, and with them died the last pretensions of the old nobility. The advance elements of Vitellius' forces under Caecina and Valens won a bloody victory over Otho's army at Bedriacum near Cremona, and Otho took his own life on 16 April. But 'the long year' was far from over.

Over a century earlier, the refugees from Pompey's beaten army at Pharsalus had included a centurion or re-enlisted veteran called Titus Flavius Petro, who made his way back home to Sabine Reate where he spent the rest of his life in the humble calling of a collector of moneys due to bankers and auctioneers. His son spent most of his life as an agent of the customs-farmers of the province of Asia, and later became a money-lender in a small way in Switzerland. Of his two sons, the elder, Flavius Sabinus, reached the consulship and the command in Moesia before becoming Prefect of the City in the latter years of Nero; the younger, Flavius Vespasianus, after brilliantly commanding the left wing of the Claudian invasion of Britain, was also a consul and a governor of Africa before Nero appointed him in 67 to a special command to suppress the Jewish rebellion. Both brothers may stand as exceptional examples of the sort of opportunities which were opened to able, ambitious, but sensible 'new men' under the new system. Cut off by space and time from the rapidly changing pattern of events to their west, Vespasian and Gaius Licinius Mucianus, the legate of Syria, composed earlier disagreements and along with Tiberius Julius Alexander, an apostate Jew who was currently Prefect of Egypt, put together a powerful coalition of military, logistic, and financial strength and high experience, which also offered a second chance to all those who had 'backed a wrong horse' previously. Mucianus set off through Asia Minor and the Balkans, while Vespasian headed for Alexandria, where he was saluted as Emperor on 1 July.

Events now moved far more quickly than anyone could have expected. The southward march of the Vitellian army from Germany to north Italy had savagely scarred the regions which it traversed, and Vitellius himself behaved more like a conqueror than a saviour. He also made the mistake of humiliating Otho's troops, but not disbanding them. The bulk of the powerful Danubian armies had not arrived in time to make their weight felt decisively at Bedriacum. The meteoric Marcus Antonius Primus now took a hand, and what an Aquitanian Roman had begun a Roman from Toulouse finished. Something of a rapscallion, he had been exiled under Nero for his part in a scandalous testamentary fraud, but recalled by Galba and given the command of one of the Pannonian legions. War, confusion, and intrigue were his true *métier*; he had little difficulty in getting the disgruntled Danubian troops to declare for Vespasian, and he used them with a speed and *élan* worthy of Julius Caesar himself. Scorning caution and delay, which could also have strengthened the enemy, he declined to await the arrival of the eastern armies and drove at full speed into Italy, catching his opponents off guard and crushing Vitellius' army, itself demoralized by the recent dismissal of its general Caecina on suspicion of treachery, in a second battle at Bedriacum in October. Vitellius fell back on Rome, where Vespasian's brother Sabinus all but persuaded him to abdicate, but was himself killed when rampaging German auxiliaries overran the Capitol. After a furious resistance and some murderous street-fighting, Primus stormed to victory. Vitellius was hunted down and butchered, and a few days later Mucianus at last reached Rome, cut Primus down to

VESPASIAN (AD 69–79), the first Roman Emperor not to have emerged from the old urban aristocracy. Born in AD 9 to an equestrian family in the central Italian town of Reate, he enjoyed a distinguished military career before his victory in the civil wars of 68–9. His portraits stress qualities of hard-headedness and experience in place of the hellenizing idealism of the Julio-Claudians.

size, and established a provisional government for the sixty-year-old Vespasian, whose two grown sons Titus and Domitian offered a prospect of continuity which the childless Mucianus could not match. 'The long year' ended at last in December 69. The task of rebuilding the shattered Empire was now in the hands of a hard-headed, down-to-earth, experienced, and immensely capable man who was to prove himself the first truly worthy successor to Augustus and who was, like Augustus, *princeps* by his own making and on his own merits.

Further Reading

I

Tacitus (*Annals* and *Histories*) and Suetonius (*Lives* of the individual Emperors) provide the most complete coverage, see ch. 25. The standard edition and commentary on Tacitus' *Annals* is that of H. Furneaux in two volumes (second editions respectively 1896 and 1907); *Histories* 1 and 2, and 4 and 5 are equipped with a *Historical Commentary* by G. E. F. Chilver (Oxford, 1979, 1985);

book 3 with one by K. Wellesley (Sydney, 1973). Other important sources are Cassius Dio's *Roman History* and the works of Velleius Paterculus and Seneca, Strabo and Pliny the Elder. All of these are available in the Loeb Classical Library. Augustus' own *Res Gestae Divi Augusti* can be consulted in the excellent edition, with translation and commentary, by P. A. Brunt and J. M. Moore (1967). A selection of the most important epigraphical evidence is to be found (untranslated) in Ehrenberg and Jones, *Documents Illustrating the Reigns of Augustus and Tiberius* (2nd edn. repr. with addenda, Oxford, 1976) and E. M. Smallwood, *Documents Illustrating the Principates of Gaius, Claudius and Nero* (Cambridge, 1967).

II

Pre-eminent place must be given to the two great works of Sir Ronald Syme: *The Roman Revolution* (Oxford, 1939) and *Tacitus* (2 vols., Oxford 1958); and mention should also be made of his *History in Ovid* (Oxford, 1978). The *Cambridge Ancient History* devotes the whole of its tenth volume (1934) to this period (44 BC–AD 70). The later chapters of H. H. Scullard, *From the Gracchi to Nero* (5th edn., 1982) constitute the best and most reliable concise treatment of the years down to AD 68. On a slightly larger scale, A. Garzetti, *From Tiberius to the Antonines* trans. J. R. Foster (London, 1974), is to be commended. T. Rice Holmes, *The Architect of the Roman Empire* (vol. I, Oxford, 1928; vol. II, 1931) covers the reign of Augustus in detail and with full citation of evidence; more recent studies in *Caesar Augustus* (Oxford, 1984) ed. F. Millar and E. Segal. For Tiberius, see R. Seager, *Tiberius* (London, 1972) and B. M. Levick, *Tiberius the Politician* (London, 1976); for Gaius, J. P. V. D. Balsdon, *The Emperor Gaius (Caligula)* (Oxford, 1934); for Claudius, A. Momigliano, *Claudius, The Emperor and His Achievement*, tr. W. D. Hogarth (repr. Cambridge, 1961) and V. M. Scramuzza, *The Emperor Claudius* (Cambridge, Mass., 1940); for Nero, B. W. Henderson, *The Life and Principate of the Emperor Nero* (London, 1903), B. H. Warmington, *Nero, Reality and Legend* (London, 1969), and Miriam Griffin *Nero: the End of a Dynasty* (London, 1984). Finally, K. Wellesley, *The Long Year A.D. 69* (London, 1975) takes us through to the accession of Vespasian.

H. M. Pelham, *Essays on Roman History* (1911), remains excellent reading, especially his chapter on 'The Domestic Policy of Augustus'; so too do chapters x and xi by H. M. Last in vol. XI of *The Cambridge Ancient History*. On public and private law, see H. F. Jolowicz and B. Nicholas, *Historical Introduction to the Study of Roman Law* (3rd edn. Cambridge, 1972); on emperor-worship, L. R. Taylor, *The Divinity of the Roman Emperor* (Middletown, 1931); on the Greek cities, A. H. M. Jones, *The Cities of the Eastern Roman Provinces* (Oxford, 1937, revd. 1971) and *The Greek City* (Oxford, 1940); on the municipalization of Italy and the spread of citizenship outside Italy, A. N. Sherwin White, *The Roman Citizenship* (2nd edn., Oxford, 1973); on economic matters in general, vols. ii–v of Tenney Frank, *An Economic Survey of Ancient Rome* (Baltimore, 1933–40).

The modern scholarly literature is enormous in its extent, and archaeology keeps uncovering new material, including inscriptions. References to such specialized work can be found in most of the books that have been mentioned. In particular, the detailed bibliographies for each chapter in H. H. Scullard's latest (paperback) edition of *From the Gracchi to Nero* (London, 1982) are comprehensive.

7

The Arts of Government

❧❧❧

NICHOLAS PURCELL

The Principate from Nero to Gallienus

IN AD 193 the military and political crisis of AD 69 was repeated; the commanders of provincial armies contended for the position of *princeps*. The balance of power of the armies had shifted east from the Rhine, but in almost every respect the conflicts were very similar. The crisis of 193 exchanged Commodus, the last of the Antonines in a succession of adoption and blood which had been continuous since the accession of Nerva in 96, for Septimius Severus, nominal heir to that tradition and founder of a similar sequence of succession which lasted until 235. Many have seen this disturbance as the harbinger of the chaos of the middle of the third century. Nothing could be further from the truth. In its resemblance to the turmoil of 69 the war of 193 is one of our most striking indications of the stability of the high principate.

In this period, to a large extent an 'age without history' in the normal sense, the narrative of events (accessions, usurpations, battles, deaths) actually obscures the tendencies and evolutions on which the historian, whose job it is to explain, must concentrate. And stability and peace challenge explanation much more than destruction and disaster. This stability had been created above all by the Flavian Emperors Vespasian and Domitian (69-79 and 81-96). Three achievements in particular may be emphasized, though we should be wary of asserting that they were brought about by design or policy rather than by accidental development. First, the revenues of Empire were organized to a high enough specification for expenditure over several years to be planned ahead; this had never before been the case. In the process some degree of administrative organization had to be fostered (but it is argued in this chapter that this should not be mistaken for a bureaucracy). Second, the last client kingdoms were subjected to the process of provincialization which had been emerging for sixty years, and at last the Empire became a tessellation of provincial units within clearly demarcated boundaries. The armies were now permanently fixed on similarly clear frontiers which divided an increasingly self-conscious empire from the non-provinces beyond. Third, the Flavian Emperors, largely disembarrassed of the remnants of the republican high aristocracy by the political chaos of Nero's reign, and of municipal Italian origins themselves, regularized the recruitment and replacement of the upper classes at Rome and advanced the process by which, through an ever more refined set of public positions in the gift of the Emperor, the élites of the cities of the Empire increasingly came to feel part of the establishment. This was the process, recognized by Tacitus in its early stages in one of the most perceptive and sophisticated historical discussions in Latin (*Annals* 3.55), that completed the transformation of the conqueror of the world into its capital. The Flavian Emperors came from the municipal élites of rural Italy. While they lacked the luxurious sophistication and amoral superiority of the ancient aristocracy which supplied and continued to flourish under the Julii and Claudii, they failed also to maintain the ceremonious constitutionalism which had characterized the wiser of their predecessors. Their impatience with the forms of Roman political life rapidly led them into autocratic manners which in the end brought down their dynasty with the assassination of Domitian.

But it was too late to return to before the Civil War. The safely respectable senator Nerva was replaced, perhaps not wholly voluntarily, by Trajan, a second-generation senator whose origin was from the Italian diaspora in the provinces. Recruitment to the Roman governing class was becoming wider all the time. Men like Trajan, native Latin speakers of Italian stock who spent all their formative years in Roman public life, were less surprising newcomers than the increasingly numerous magnates from the cities of the Hellenic East, often the descendants of the client kings through whom that area had been ruled a century before. Greek and Latin mixed on more equal terms than ever before; the new cosmopolitanism was expressed by Trajan's successor Hadrian in the style of his personal appearance and the assiduity with which he travelled in every part of the Empire. The new cultural homogeneity found one of its most splendid expressions in the lavish beautification, from Vespasian to Antoninus Pius, of the world's capital in a cosmopolitan architectural style, though the advancement of so many provincials gave a boost to competitive display in cities all over the Empire. The result—'the glitter of our age' (*nitor saeculi*), as Pliny calls it—was the imperial architecture which forms such an important part of our picture of the ancient world (below, pp. 380 ff.) The political life of the time involved the intrigues of the court and the struggle for personal advancement among the Emperor's entourage more than it had done before, for the Augustan ideal of the Principate had finally ended, and with it had come the age in which we may first legitimately call the *princeps* Emperor. Paradoxically it was now that relations between *princeps* and Senate became most amicable; even the fluctuation in popularity of Emperors, the variations in their adherence to the increasingly clear rules for respecting senatorial autonomy, became an endlessly repeated pattern. With the concerns of the Emperor increasingly related to the provinces, it mattered much less whether he was 'good' like Pius (138-61) or 'bad' like Commodus

HADRIAN (AD 117–38). Great nephew and adopted successor of Trajan, he hailed, like his predecessor, from Spain and brought a new cosmopolitan outlook to his office: more than half his reign was spent on tours of the provinces. His revival of the fashion for wearing a beard broke with a tradition of clean-shaven chins stretching back to Hellenistic times.

(180–93): except, perhaps, that Commodus' murder precipitated the crisis referred to at the beginning of this account.

The concern of the Emperors for the provinces is a reflection of the new homogeneity of the Empire, not a sign of crisis. Disorders there were, Jewish revolt under Hadrian, and plague under Marcus Aurelius, but these did not do serious damage to the inert and enormously stable fabric of Empire. The imperial élites had the prosperity which comes from peace and an ever more sophisticated economy, and opportunities of upward social mobility to invest their wealth in. In foreign affairs, too, despite the hardening of the frontiers with the great defence works of Domitian and Hadrian, the Empire was not really more defensive in the second century than in the first. The clashes were all in similar places, victories came no less easily, defeats were no more common. We see a repeating pattern of warfare, against Parthia under Trajan, Verus, and Severus; on the Danube under Nero, Domitian, Trajan, and Marcus; on the margin of the Sahara under

Tiberius, Claudius, Domitian, and Pius. Of real extensions of Empire there was only the conquest of gold-rich and fertile Dacia beyond the Danube under Trajan. The conquest of Parthia directly afterwards proved unassimilable—a significant fact. The task which Severus won for himself in 193 was no harder than that of Vespasian. Severus died at York in 211. That his family was of African background only makes it typical of the homogeneous world of that age. His power passed to men of Syrian connections, no more exotic than he, despite the colourful anecdotes attached to the name of Heliogabalus. If the emperor's power during the succession of these individuals seems less effective and his position less secure, that is not the decadence of personalities or the feebleness of characters. At last the Roman world was reaping the whirlwind which sprang from the never resolved impracticalities of the fortuitous system by which it held together.

The disasters of the third century were the product of a set of coincidences.

BUST OF COMMODUS IN THE GUISE OF HERCULES. The foppish face of the last Antonine Emperor (AD 180-92) contrasts bizarrely with the muscular torso, knotted club, and lion's head helmet of the great Greek hero; but Commodus was merely reviving a Hellenistic tradition of equating rulers with Heracles.

The homogeneous Empire was an ephemeral creation. The provinces, having been raised to a similar high level of importance and prosperity, began to drift apart and to behave independently. Their armies, recruited locally to an ever greater extent, became loyal to the regions, not to Rome. The soldiers became distanced socially and culturally from the new élite of the Graeco-Roman Empire. Chronic political instability cut short the reign of Emperor after Emperor. And all this at a time when the pressures of available manpower beyond the Empire, prevented by hard frontiers from entering the Empire unobtrusively to fill the vacancies of its perpetually falling population, posed a military threat which had not been seen for generations, and when the weak Parthian state had evolved into the ferociously effective Sassanian power in the East. The cumbersome and inefficient system of the high Empire could not cope. In the crisis economic disaster overtook most of the Empire (though many areas, including most of Italy, escaped physical devastation). But it is essential to realize that this catastrophe was sudden. The first and second centuries with their many problems and lackadaisical amateur government had been no golden age; but it was not the troubles of that age which multiplied into the chaos of the third century. The disasters were new.

The Arts of Government

'And it came to pass in those days, that there went out a decree from Caesar Augustus, that all the world should be enrolled to be taxed' (Luke 2:1). The evangelist wants to emphasize the centrality in world history of the coming of the Messiah, and accordingly links the birth of Christ to the moment when the power of Rome seemed at its most universal. For him, as often for us, the power of Rome is most potently expressed by reference to its administrative activity. St Luke, however, was wrong. We know now that no such decree commanded a universal registration of the Roman world, at this time or any other; he exaggerated Roman omnipotence on the basis of the experience of a single province. It remains extremely easy for us too to misunderstand the scope, practice, and effects of Rome's governmental procedures. We mistake patterns of decision-making for policies and take hierarchical sequences of posts for career-structures. When we find the taking of minutes or the accumulation of archives, we immediately see a bureaucracy. Virtuosity in the public service is confused with professionalism. Recent work has been able to show well how far Rome's administration failed, or could be corrupted or subverted, or simply had no effect but oppression on thousands of provincials. There have been fewer examinations of the way in which the arts of government at which the Romans thought themselves that they excelled actually worked—imposing civilization and peace, leniency to the defeated, and war to the last with the proud (Virgil, *Aeneid* 6. 852-3). The analogies which spring most readily to our minds often mislead. Either, beguiled by the delightful portrayal of Roman administration in

Evelyn Waugh's *Helena*, we see Imperium as Raj, or we transpose to Rome with W.H. Auden the perpetual movement of memos in the offices of White-hall:

> Caesar's double-bed is warm
> As an unimportant clerk
> Writes 'I do not like my work'
> On a pink official form.

These images of government will fit neither the headquarters of the governor nor the imperial Palatine. What follows is an outline alternative.

Roman theories of government were not elaborate; the practice too was simple. Two broad categories cover almost all the activities of Roman rule: settling disputes between communities or individuals, and assembling men, goods, or money—jurisdiction and exaction. Antiquity recognized three main types of authority: magistrate, soldier, and master of a household; and all governmental activity in the Roman Empire can be linked with one of these. The first, deriving from the Greek city, covers both the immemorial officers of the city-state which Rome had been and the magistrates of the hundreds of essentially self-governing cities which made up nearly all the Roman Empire. In a *polis* magistrates ran the military; at Rome the usual citizen militia became under the Empire a permanent, institutionally separate army, whose officers played an ever greater part in government culminating in the militarization of the third century. Finally, in a slave-owning society the type of authority exercised within the household was naturally recognizably different, and also came to be of considerable importance in government. These three administrative approaches will be examined individually. But it was always through activities which we would hesitate to call governmental that Roman rule was most effectively maintained: through the involvement of the upper classes in public religion, spectacles, impressive patronage of architecture, philosophy, literature, painting; and in civil benefactions all over the Empire. The civilizing and beneficial effects of this should be remembered as we move on to find the actual administrative and executive structure of the Empire erratic and illiberal.

The City Magistrate at Home and Abroad

Rome had from the earliest times enjoyed very close contacts with the Greek world, and had, like most ancient cities, a tripartite political structure of magistrates, council (the Senate), and popular assembly. The importance of the last for our purpose is that its early power produced the uniquely Roman and constitutionally vital concept of *imperium*. The Roman people conferred upon its chosen magistrates the right to command it and the sanctions against disobedience—ever more strictly circumscribed—of corporal and capital punishment of its members. On this depended the powers of the magistrates, and therefore of the Emperor and of provincial governors under the principate. *Provinciae*, which were at first simply the military spheres of command of consuls or praetors, changed greatly towards the late Republic. Not only had access to, and tenure of, the commands been progressively regularized, but proconsuls and propraetors, encouraged no doubt by the opportunities for reasonable or unreasonable profit, found themselves deeply involved in diplomacy, in the settling of disputes, the managing of their province's finances, and the giving of justice. They often spent more time on what came to be a regular assize-tour of their province than on military matters. When Augustus, needing to take over practically all the armies of the Empire, left the provinces of senatorial governors almost without legions, there was no governmental difficulty. Some provinces came to be governed not by men who might command Roman soldiers, but by freedmen and by equestrians whose title, *procurator*, was drawn not from public law, but from the language of the household. Finally, from the Flavian period, governors who found themselves overburdened by military duties began to be assisted by special deputies who would see to the jurisdiction of the governor and were called *iuridici*. The subordination of the governors of the provinces to the Emperor—although in the case of the proconsular provinces some still showed signs of their old independence in the Julio-Claudian period—eventually also brought about the establishment of a fixed hierarchy of provinces and exact definition of their boundaries, so that the Antonines ruled an Empire which was a tessellation of exactly fitting administrative units which, it is interesting to note, showed a tendency to divide and subdivide in the second and third centuries. This exactly bounded Empire was, however, a recent creation, and until the Flavian period much remained vague about the boundaries of Empire and provinces alike. But despite the changes of the early Empire, in the second century there was still much in the government of the provinces that would have been familiar in the age of Scipio Aemilianus: proconsuls and propraetors, assisted by quaestors and assistants such as scribes and messengers drawn from public panels, and delegating their *imperium* to deputies called, if senators, *legati*, and if equestrians, *praefecti*, still ruled much of the Empire. And this includes the legates and prefects appointed by the Emperor as proconsul of his enormous province. To that extent the Roman Empire was run by the magistrates of a city-state.

This is why Rome long retained the habit of dealing with her subjects with the respect deserved by the free, and why Roman rule so long remained indirect. To the end of antiquity most of the cities of the Empire and their territories were ruled by local magistrates many of whose domestic executive actions were taken as if they were independent; indeed they often needed to be reminded that there were limits to the licence they were allowed. Similarly Rome also long tolerated local kings and dynasts, and the survival of these dependent kingdoms and free cities contributed much to the fuzzy informality of the power structure of the Empire before the age of the Antonines. Even in the third century, tens of thousands of Rome's subjects would have contact with superior executive autho-

INSCRIPTION IN HONOUR OF C. MINICIUS ITALUS at Aquileia (AD 105), the record of a distinguished equestrian career in the imperial service. From prefect of various cohorts of cavalry, Italus advanced to the rank of military tribune with the Sixth Legion, then served as a procurator in various provinces, as the Prefect of the corn supply, and ultimately as the Prefect of Egypt.

rity only through whatever magistrates had authority in their own city. It was in Italy that the autonomy of the cities was first seriously weakened; there, already before the end of the Republic, regulations define the limits of city magistrates' competence. More significant is the interference in the financial affairs of cities which becomes widespread during the second century AD. Governors in the provinces or the Senate or the Emperor had always been able to intervene in some such matters, but their competence was of course severely restricted by their limited time and knowledge. In the appointment from Rome from the end of the first century AD of senatorial or equestrian state guardians (*curatores rei publicae*) or accountants (*logistai*) in the cities we find a momentous departure from the traditional *laissez-faire* attitude to government which had hitherto prevailed. In Italy the change can be linked with other administrative policies, such as the setting up of charitable foundations for poor children or the centralizing of many local administrative functions on regions based on the great Italian highways, developments which confirm that a new attitude to government was being born. Because of the crisis of the third century and the different direction taken by the administration of the late Empire as a result of the reforms of the age of Diocletian (284–305), this attitude never evolved fully; but combined

HELP FOR NEEDY CHILDREN. This relief
on Trajan's Arch at Beneventum (AD 114)
commemorates the Emperor's scheme for
the upkeep of the children of the poor.
Trajan stands to the left of the dispensing
table at the centre; parents and children
queue up or depart at the right;
Beneventum and three other city-goddesses
who have benefited from the scheme
attend in the background.

THE VIA APPIA ANTICA, near Albano
Laziale, south of Rome: the first of the
great highways by which the Romans
secured their military and administrative
grip on Italy, and the precursor of the
network which was later built throughout
the Empire. Initiated by Appius Claudius
Caecus in 312 BC, it linked Rome with the
port of Brundisium (Brindisi) in south-
eastern Italy.

with the final stage in the evolution of the provinces and the maturing of the office of provincial governor, it forms one of the hallmarks of the Antonine Empire. Of this world of diminishing autonomy and growing governmental solicitude the experience of the Younger Pliny in Bithynia is not untypical. But a reading of his correspondence with Trajan, which forms our best evidence for this acme of Roman administrative excellence, leaves an abiding impression of how arbitrary, haphazard, and superficial Roman government was even then.

Without direct rule, how did Rome maintain order? The answers are social and cultural rather than administrative. It was, for example, by her open policies of corporate status and individual citizenship that she succeeded where imperial Athens had failed. The Romans remembered without shame how the nucleus of Romulus' city had been collected from nationless vagabonds and runaways who had seized their womenfolk by main force. Historically, the Romans' power in Italy had been consolidated through the slow evolution of a sophisticated hierarchy of partly citizen status which they had been prepared to extend to whole communities. From the last century of the Republic this policy was followed elsewhere too, and with the enfranchisement of non-Roman troops, the personal gift of Roman citizenship to Rome's supporters in foreign cities, the founding of Roman towns in the provinces, and the grant of privileges or citizenship to foreign communities, a highly successful means of incorporating the most influential members of the subject peoples in the Roman system was evolved. The citizenship carried various privileges, often, as St Paul found, of considerable personal use; but most importantly it gave provincials access to public appointments. The subject was involved in government, and stability resulted. The wooing of the provincial élites was one of Rome's most successful tools.

At Rome itself, the growth of the Empire had brought about indirectly an ever growing population of slaves, freedmen, foreigners, and Italians, the ambitious, the curious, the needy, and the desperate. Quite apart from the very serious problem of keeping the peace, the nourishment of scores of thousands of people and the keeping of the city wholesome and habitable posed very serious difficulties. Fortunately proceeds of empire could be devoted to the building projects, above all the aqueducts, which alone made it possible for so large a population to survive. But such projects needed organization as well as capital. In the (usual) absence of the consuls and often of the praetors, the management of Rome, the *cura Urbis*, devolved on other magistrates. Their principal resource for the job was a distinctive Roman procedure for the letting of contracts, *locatio*. This needs some stressing because it always remained one of the main governmental activities of Roman administrators, and because it was through this that so much of the civil engineering which is so eloquent a testimony of Roman rule was carried on. It was also for a very long period the principal mode, through tax-farming, of collecting public revenues, that basic activity of ancient governments. Moreover it was unique to Rome in its developed form, and appeared to Polybius (6. 117) one of the most striking and effective aspects of Roman state activity,

ARCHES OF THE AQUA JULIA IN ROME, one of the aqueducts on which the city's water-supply depended. Built by Agrippa in 33 BC to supplement the Aqua Claudia (312 BC), the Anio Vetus (272 BC), the Aqua Marcia (144-140 BC), and the Aqua Tepula (125 BC), it brought water from the Alban Hills south-east of Rome and was part of a major enlargement and modernization of water services under Augustus.

embracing all activities from the contract for feeding the sacred geese of Juno (always let first) to the taxes of the provinces or the resurfacing of main roads. Polybius saw this practice as a democratic aspect of Roman public life, no doubt because it involved in state business some prominent plebeians. For our purposes it is doubly important. First it encouraged the formation of semi-public corporate organizations, *collegia* and *societates*, the spirit of which contributed to Roman notions of how to form administrative institutions—and indeed it is from this world that the important late-Roman official title *magister* derives. Second, and even more importantly, we see again here the unwillingness of Roman magistrates to undertake themselves the direct overseeing of the activities which they sponsored. The wish to limit the public sphere and privatize official actions is again apparent.

There were occasional administrative improvements at Rome during the

Republic; but simple coercion by their attendants, and jurisdiction thus enforced, remained the magistrates' only executive agencies. By contrast, under Augustus and his immediate successors a still further worsening of the city's problems prompted a connected series of institutional innovations. Some of the new expedients were of the highest importance to the government of the Principate; moreover, the exercise of institutional change itself acted as a precedent for the later proliferation of new posts and offices. The Augustan administrative revolution consisted in the creation of boards of senior magistrates in departments (*curae*) responsible for the management of the aqueducts, the roads of the city, the banks of the Tiber, and so on; in the systematization of responsibility by means of artificial compartments, such as the fourteen regions of Rome or the eleven of Italy; and in the appointment of senior assistants responsible to the *princeps* who would control military or paramilitary bodies permanently stationed in Rome or very near by, for political and civil security. The creation of the *curae* did away with the ancient principle of annual tenure, and provided something of a permanent staff in place of sole reliance on contract labour. The formal systems of administrative units diminished competitiveness between patrons and helped ensure uniformity, stability, and comparison of results of administrative activity. And in the creation of the much more powerful posts of prefect of the praetorian guard, prefect of the city, and prefect of the fire-brigade, Augustus equipped future *principes* with three great ministers, as well as judges whose courts would acquire an importance which helped to centralize large areas of Italy on Rome and relieve other magistrates of much of their jurisdiction. We happen to know that already by the reign of Nero the prefect of the city had acquired jurisdiction comparable to that of the urban praetor. This centralization of Italian administration in turn provided an example for the management of the provinces; it is significant that the *curatores* of Rome lent their name to the functionaries described above whose financial supervision came to infringe the cities' autonomy.

This Augustan administrative revolution, for which Greek theoretical and practical precedents are perhaps to be sought, was, however, unique. Moreover, the senatorial *curae* were in part created not for administrative excellence but to subordinate these potentially prestigious activities of great senators to Augustus' regime, and they flourished as status symbols for the successful senator, to be held often by corrupt, lazy, or incompetent men. Above all, despite all the innovation, and all the extra posts and increase in personnel, the main activities remained the letting of contracts, the giving of permissions, and the business of arbitration—new posts, more subtle hierarchies, but the same old jobs.

The Army

The second general group of associations which political authority had for the governed is connected with war. Even when mercenary troops had been

CAMP-BUILDING: relief on Trajan's Column in Rome (dedicated in AD 113). The sculptured narrative of the emperor's Dacian campaigns shows the army in all its varied activities, including not only actual engagements with the enemy but also marching, sacrificing, entrenching, and listening to imperial addresses.

important, fighting had, in the classical *polis* and its heirs, remained to a large extent the preserve of a citizen militia. Until the second century BC this had been true of Rome too. It followed that a city's magistracies were often very closely associated with military command, from which derived the vital Roman concept of *imperium*, which underlay the whole governmental activity of the Empire and actually gave it its very name.

As the Hellenistic cities came increasingly to group themselves in leagues or to submit to the control of their foreign affairs by the kings and eventually by Rome, military titles such as *stratēgos*, 'army-leader', often lost their military connotations. So at Rome the praetors first, and with the Empire the consuls, came to acquire what we would call civilian functions. From the middle Republic the praetors were mainly concerned with jurisdiction, though it is interesting to observe that the regular Greek term for praetor (the Greek equivalents of Latin constitutional terms are often very revealing) is in fact *stratēgos*. Lower down the social scale the post of superintendent of engineers (*praefectus fabrum*) was practically non-military by the Julio-Claudian age, and even some types of military tribune were military only in name. It is only in the third century that the process is reversed, and military titles spread in areas of government with no necessary connection with war; the eventual militarization of the Empire brings to an end the processes described here (though, significantly, military titles such as *praepositus* and *optio* spread earlier among the servants of the Emperor). But throughout the Emperor was called by the honorific military title *imperator*, first as an informal description, then as a name, finally as a formal title, and took on himself many of the military functions once carried out by the republican magistrates. Although we usually refer to him by his senatorial style of *princeps*, it was as *imperator* (*autocrator*, 'the ruler answerable to none' in Greek) that he was perceived by the Empire. And the Emperor's military power pervaded the government of the Empire.

In the ancient world, to question the rightness of a standing army was unthinkable; and peace was the product of victory won by the soldier. But there is no easy way to translate 'civilian' into Greek or Latin, and this is because the legacy of the citizen army ensured an intermingling of the apparatus of warfare with the activities of peace. The distinction between soldier and civilian, so clear to our minds, and in our times possessing a moral as well as a practical flavour, did not exist before the triumph of the military, which began in the Severan period.

Augustus established the military system which lasted until the third century. The army was composed of two parts (and there was also a considerable fleet). The senior part was a citizen army of some thirty legions (about 165,000 men), each commanded by a senator of middling status, and subject to the more senior senatorial governors of the imperial and senatorial provinces. Gradually these legions became a permanent feature of the frontier areas in which they were established. They recruited mostly from those areas. Although some legions changed their bases, such moves were not overall very frequent. Rather more numerous were the auxiliary troops who from the reign of Claudius regularly received the citizenship on discharge. Rome had always relied on the military help of non-Romans, and the employment and incorporation of the auxiliaries became one of the most important ways in which the Empire acquired a cultural homogeneity. The regiments of auxiliaries, much smaller than legions, were commanded by citizens of equestrian rank, usually from the élites of Italy or the provinces and using these jobs to win further status and opportunities for themselves. The whole system was financed from a military treasury established by Augustus, one of the first and most fundamental steps towards financial planning taken by the Romans.

It follows that before the third century the military commanders provided from the Empire's élites were not what we would call professionals. The effectiveness and expertise of the army rested with the senior and junior centurions who often rose from the ranks and would serve as long as any ordinary soldier. It was, as far as we know, very unusual for such an officer to receive equestrian rank, and still rarer to proceed to equestrian military office. And equestrian commands, although important in the promotion game of the upper classes, were usually short and variegated, including horse and foot and in a whole range of different places. So too even with senators, whose military service as junior officer, legionary legate, or governor of a garrisoned province would usually occupy only a short period of their whole career, take place in many different areas, and give them little opportunity to become professional. This is true of almost all the military commanders we know, and it is clear that it became standard practice for the Emperor to ensure that no senator acquired too much familiarity with armies and warfare. This practice of drawing the high military command from essentially unmilitary personnel helped integrate the army into the more peaceful activities of the Empire.

The legionary army always remained part of the citizen body of Rome. Its communities, especially in non-citizen areas, enjoyed privileges like other citizen settlements, and expected the facilities—aqueducts, amphitheatres, baths and so on—of any classical city. The *castellum* (fort) was originally an ordinary member of the sequence of possible settlement-institutions which ranged from village to city. The *colonia*, originally in the late Republic a town of discharged citizen veterans which was autonomous but expected to defend itself and the interests of Rome in case of trouble, and which came to be the coveted highest status

LEGIONARY AMPHITHEATRE AT VINDONISSA (Windisch, in Switzerland). Vindonissa was the fortress of the Thirteenth Legion from about AD 16, and was subsequently occupied by the Twenty-first and Eleventh Legions before being evacuated about 100. The amphitheatre was used both for military drill and to provide the entertainments to which the legionary soldiers were accustomed at home.

attainable by a provincial city, helped to blur the distinction between camp and town still further. Outside fortresses, moreover, people congregated to form whole settlements dependent on the presence of the army, which often became independent. When not on active duty—which was more often than not, as in all armies—soldiers cultivated the land, engaged in trade, and generally lived their lives like ordinary citizens. This close contact between soldiers and other citizens and non-citizens was still further fostered by the direct involvement of soldiers in the day-to-day administration of the Empire.

A study of a system of government must not only concern itself with top level decision-making and the bureaucracy which may give it stability and effectiveness; it must also give some account of the actual execution of the directives which emanate from these two sources. Who, we must ask, actually put into effect the decisions of the Roman government? The Roman magistrates had immediate agents in their staff of strong-arm men, errand-runners, and announcers. But these were few, and it is only in the command of real soldiers, given to him by his *imperium*, that the executive power of the Roman official eventually lay.

The army was not exclusively deployed in the remoter or more barbarous provinces. True, in the mid second century Britain had three, the Rhine four, and the Danube ten of Rome's twenty-eight legions; but most of these were placed, even in this period when the frontiers were hardening, so that they commanded large areas of province as well as foreign soil; and before the Flavian period even more legionary bases were within the Empire. Detachments from these legions or auxiliary troops were anyway widely dispersed through the provinces, especially in their capitals. In the East the nine legions (above all in Egypt) were positioned even more clearly with control of the local populace in mind; and settled Africa and Spain both retained a legion each. Besides these, in coastal or riverine cities there were large naval bases. Rome had its own huge, complex garrison. Wherever the Emperor was there was a large body of troops. There were always soldiers moving from one detachment to another, above all on the great roads connecting frontier areas—living off the land by permission, by the generosity of local magnates, or by extortion, with their privileges (only military courts tried soldiers) and the needs of imperial security to justify even their crimes. 'Your teeth are shattered?', asks Juvenal, 'Face hectically inflamed, with great black welts? You know the doctor wasn't too optimistic about the eye that was left. But it's not a bit of good your running to the courts about it. If you've been beaten up by a soldier, better keep it to yourself' (16. 10 ff.). The government of the Roman Empire was what we would call military rule.

It would have been hard, indeed, for the Roman Empire to be run on any other system. Even the civil services of modern states, like the British, have often developed from military models, retaining, for example, the concept of leave. There were few possible structures of authority available that could cope with the scale involved in Roman administration: the city-state had already proved an inadequate institution for world government, and the authority of the patriarchal family was too limited. Participatory institutions there were, like the cartels which undertook the public contracts described above or collegiate organizations of city populations, worshippers, artisans, and so on; and all these bodies played a part in imperial rule, since through representatives they could deal with the rulers of the state, make petitions, and receive replies; through their privileges and corporate influence security might be maintained in sensitive areas like the larger cities of the Empire. But none of these offered the convenient, disciplined, extensive structure of the army, and so the army came to have the public image we have just seen in Juvenal. Using its own courts, answerable only to itself, privileged and greedy, it became a tyrannical force because it was omnipresent in government.

Soldiers were involved in public building; they surveyed land; they manned the customs posts at provincial boundaries; and their value to the collection of other taxes is sufficiently demonstrated by the fact that they were from time to time forbidden to take part in it. During the second century a secret service of government spies, the so-called 'grain militia' (*frumentarii*) came into being, the predecessors of the sinisterly bland *agentes in rebus* of the later Empire. Examples could easily be multiplied, but it is enough to end by referring to the vivid testimony of two papyrus lists of soldiers' duties, in one happy case referring not to atypical Egypt, but to the Danube. From Moesia we hear of soldiers with corn-shipments, on mine duty, requisitioning horses, running prisons; and from Egypt of harbour-dredging work, duty at the mint, at the paper factory (so essential to Egyptian administration), and on general river-guard duty, a police activity further illuminated by the countryside surveillance attested in a new document of this kind. Altogether there were few places in the Empire where it will have been odd to meet a soldier. 'To the soldier, at his demand—500 drachmae' is a typical note in the pathetic list of protection payments made by a wretched Egyptian subject of this government. In this at least the Egyptians were by no means unusual.

Administration Household-Style

Most governmental actions were undertaken by a very few people in every ancient state. Ancient government was top-heavy, in that a great deal of what seems to us mundane work was done by the men with most authority; there was relatively little delegation or selection of business. In the Roman Empire in the second century AD only some hundred or so men actually held *imperium* by direct grant or delegation at any one time: on them in thory fell the whole burden of government. Indeed some senators did feel that their dignity should be reflected in their agenda, and that they should not debate trivial or demeaning subjects, but others considered that an exhaustive concern for every corner of the *res publica* had been the great ideal of the statesmen of old. 'How every single thing mattered to our ancestors!', exclaims the Elder Pliny admiringly of a censorial regulation about laundrymen passed in 220 BC (*NH* 35. 197). The evidence suggests that the opinion of Pliny prevailed: even if an issue came to the attention of the authorities, it was only at the top that any consideration of it could take place. Hence the hours that the Emperors, their high officials, and the provincial governors spent in routine jurisdiction; the inscriptions recording minor local administrative decisions often taken at a very high, even at an imperial level; the small issues discussed in the surviving letters between the relatively few executives of the Roman Empire; hence too, no doubt, the hundreds, thousands of matters as important as those that did receive attention, that simply went by default. There was a great reluctance to multiply positions of authority or to complicate the business of government. There was little forward planning; new administrative measures (sometimes) followed only on acute crisis. So it was naturally to dependents that over-pressed office-holders looked for their assistants; some of these might be equestrians or free plebeian clients, but the total obedience of the unfree offered much more extensive possibilities in a slave-owning society. It is with the role of authority conferred within the household, but applied to public life, that we are here concerned.

The Emperor was the most hard-pressed administrator of all; Fergus Millar has demonstrated conclusively how his detailed concern for specific matters and his virtually undivided responsibility for all the business for which he could find time left no time for the creation of what we would call policy. His it was to begin to deal, rather, with all the appeals, petitions, embassies which reached him from below. Because it was only as judge that he was expected to act, whole areas of government—education, the economy, welfare, administration—only impinged on him accidentally, and were treated unsystematically. Nevertheless the volume of material reaching him required some management, and so it was that in the imperial household we have our clearest example of an administrator's personal dependents gaining responsibility for public affairs and enormous political power.

So great were the fortunes of some late-republican senators that the slaves or freedmen on whom they relied might find themselves in control of sums of money or tracts of land comparable in size to objects of the state's administration. This was naturally most true of Augustus, whose personal property and wealth was truly imperial in scale. The private estate of the Julio-Claudians was settled by the falling in of the shares allotted by Augustus to his family, above all to Livia and Antonia the younger, and by the policy of accumulating goods by inheritance and confiscation. Thanks to the ravages in the Roman upper class of Caligula, Nero, Domitian, Commodus, and Septimius Severus, this imperial *patrimonium* gave the Emperor control over a substantial proportion of the real estate of the Empire by means of direct ownership, not simply constitutionally sanctioned political control. Ownership entailed a different style of administration, and one which evolved very fast.

There were other ingredients as well. In Egypt royal land was a phenomenon which survived from the time of the Pharaohs. As their successors, the Emperors enjoyed in this province at least the experience of the direct management of a large proportion of the soil. Although Egypt was a very special case in this, as in so many ways, it provided a precedent, if not a model, for the running on behalf of the Emperors of other formerly royal lands, especially in the eastern part of the Empire, where royal lands had previously become public land of the Roman People. It would be very interesting to know how such tracts had been administered in the last years of the Republic. A good example is Galatia, where the extensive estates of the last king, Amyntas, became under Augustus an imperial property of a sufficient scale to make an impact on the organization of the province. The potential power of the supervisors of these estates is clearest in the case of geographically circumscribed areas like the Gallipoli peninsula (the Thracian Chersonese) which formed a single imperial property. In places like this the agent of the emperor had to exercise functions not unlike those of a provincial governor, and we hear of the punishment of one such in Judaea in the reign of Tiberius who took it on himself to give orders to Roman soldiers as if he held *imperium* (Tacitus, *Annals* 4.15). As we shall see, such licence was soon to be regularized. It was in Africa that the imperial estates reached their greatest extent, and epigraphic evidence from the second century, especially the *Lex Manciana*, reveals a good deal about their scale and management. But every province had them; they included mines, quarries, forests, as well as agricultural land; and Emperors were not slow to add to them. Septimius Severus, in particular, vastly increased the imperial holdings in the provinces, and the substitution of imperial for private markings on oil-jars from southern Spain eloquently reveals how sudden, complete, and economically important such a step could be. The inhabitants of these estates, through the hierarchy of procurators and bailiffs which separated them from the Emperor, had very much the same opportunities—or lack of them—for appeal and petition as ordinary provincials did through the governor.

It was natural that the administrators of imperial property should derive their titles from republican practice. But *procurator* remained a term of private law, and it will have sounded very strange to Roman ears to call the governors of public provinces by it. This practice, introduced for small equestrian provinces by Claudius, is a striking departure from the scrupulously traditionalistic tact of the Augustan constitutional changes. These governors had previously quite correctly been called *praefecti*. At times, too, other officials with the innovative title appear in other departments of the government as assistants to senators in their public capacities—in the various concerns of the urban administration of Rome, for example, and as financial assistants of the legates of the provinces to which the *princeps* as proconsul had to delegate governors (the 'imperial' provinces).

The change is of great importance because it made it possible for there to grow up from these domestic origins over the following two centuries what we may call a procuratorial service, in which there was available to men of equestrian rank a series of important governmental posts in the provinces and in the city of Rome, in charge of a great variety of imperial concerns, from the control of whole provinces to the running of mines, and as the assistants of senatorial functionaries. In the end there were, at any one time, some 170 of these posts, and it is here that Rome's administrative excellence, that elusive beast, used to be located. It is clear, however, that these posts did not constitute a hierarchical sequence linked by a regular promotion pattern, and that the holders of them needed no more expertise, knowledge, devotion, professionalism, or talent than their senatorial colleagues. Jurisdiction and financial watchfulness was what was expected of them too, not a serious businesslike approach different in kind from what was expected of a noble magistrate. A procurator of an Alpine district describes his job as 'the supervision of the law and the carrying out of the interests of the emperors' (*CIL* XII. 103). These posts were much less important as means of increasing the efficiency of imperial rule than as a way of incorporating in the life of government the upper classes of the provinces. Through these posts social advancement was obtained, and this secured the loyalty of the powerful men of the Empire. This cannot be overstressed: it was the ability to incorporate, not administrative excellence, that was Rome's greatest Art of Government.

Who the equestrian procurators were, and where they came from, therefore mattered. What they did mattered less. Recognition of this has sent the hunt for the supposed Roman bureaucracy into other fields. 'The description "imperial civil service" better fits the freedmen and slaves of Caesar', says a recent scholar. Here again the republican senator's dependence on his slaves and freedmen sets the precedent. The *familia* of Augustus and his successors acquired enormous power. Under Claudius and Nero in particular their influence with the *princeps* became notorious. The principal freedmen used titles derived from their principal occupations—secretary for letters, or for accounts, and the like—which became so closely associated with the Emperor that it was considered treasonable for others to use them in their households. In reaction to the hostility shown to these men, the posts they had held gradually became the preserve of men of equestrian status; but the household—the *familia Caesaris*—remained highly influential. Two flattering poems of Statius (*Silvae* 3.3 and 5.1) give us an idea of their possible concerns, and we get further information from some 4,000 inscriptions, mostly recording simply the title of the slave or freedmen. These titles, intricate, technical, and specific, seem to give support to the bureaucratic view. But the hostility to the freedmen raises a doubt; it seems that the Emperor was not free to delegate important matters to his freedmen without infringing public opinion. It therefore seems appropriate to look more critically at what the *familia Caesaris* actually did. It is clear that they acquired a mastery of technical information. Augustus left a list of 'names of freedmen and slaves from whom accounts could be obtained'. Some freedmen are praised by courtiers like Statius for this. Another is described on his epitaph as 'occupied throughout his life with the utmost attention to the interests of the imperial palace' (at Formiae: *ILS* 1583). But this devotion to duty does not entail administrative professionalism, and the importance and quantity and nature of business handled by a freedman administrator need have been no different from that dealt with by a senator or equestrian in public office. The administrative jobs which they did were, however mundane, like those of their superiors, generally to be described under the heading *litterae*. Their copying, writing, recording, and transmitting of information was important: as an expert on the subject says, 'the *tabellarii* (secretaries) were without doubt a necessary cog in the administrative machine, but most of the others in the jungle that was the Palace service seem to have been somewhat less than indispensable to the efficient running of the Roman Empire.' But in that case we are entitled to ask where the machine of which the *tabellarii* were a cog actually was. The freedmen did not constitute an administrative cadre; they were not dogsbodies doing the 'real' work of running the Empire. The specific titles that they enjoyed, great and humble alike, mislead; they reflect only the aspect of household life which gave them status, proximity to the Emperor. Hence, for example, the moral indigna- tion of Epictetus (1.17. 18–19) at the high authority of the man who empties the Emperor's chamber-pot. Epictetus, freedman of a freedman of the Emperor and famous—if unconventional—philosopher (below, pp. 298 ff.), embodies an im- portant truth about this milieu. The successful retinue of the Emperor were, or aspired to be, part of the ordinary upper-class world of Rome, taking part in its literary and intellectual culture. The inscriptions show us imperial freedmen in all sorts of activities quite unconnected with the Palace. Like any influential Roman, they devoted themselves to government only in an amateur and part- time way, and when they reached, like Pallas and Narcissus, the councils of state, it was as the friends, advisers, and confidants of the Emperor, not as expert bureaucrats. It is because of their *personal* power that by the late Empire the imperial domestics like the Grand Chamberlain have acquired the legitimate public functions which make the court of that period begin to seem medieval.

Government and Litterae

The search for bureaucracy in the Roman world is vain. We should now look a little more closely at the concern with jurisdiction and exaction which Roman administrators really did have. Then, in conclusion, we can consider in general terms the nature of the governmental process and attempt to discover what really held the empire together.

Because Roman officials spent so much time in jurisdiction it was natural that Roman law should become more complicated and more sophisticated. The natural rule that jurisdiction gravitates to the highest available authority operated to increase the workload of governors, the great prefects at Rome, and the Emperor himself, and to hasten the adoption of Roman law. Even in the reign of Augustus, Strabo can already write that Crete, despite its own venerable legal

THE BASILICA JULIA IN ROME, begun by Caesar in 54 BC and completed by Augustus. One of the great judicial buildings of the capital, it housed the civil court of the *centumviri* and was divided by wooden screens so that four cases could be heard simultaneously; but for cases of exceptional importance the whole hall was employed. Only the foundations remain.

tradition, had come, like all the provinces, to use the laws of Rome (10. 4. 22). And the bitterest realism about conditions in the Roman Empire cannot overlook the advantages of the existence of a legal framework to imperial rule, which the Hellenistic kingdoms had lacked, and which offered the Empire's subjects at least the theoretical possibility of redress and restrained the arbitrariness of Rome's rule. Law too grew at Rome with the problems first of city and then of Empire, and legal expertise came to provide an entry to the governing class. Professional legal practice was eventually one of the activities which gave many provincials a place in government, and Roman law was one of the most tenacious legacies of imperial rule—its greatest codification was the product of the eastern Empire under Justinian. There is not space here to recount the gradual evolution of Roman law, but the long accumulation of legal interpretations and precedents in the annual edicts of the praetors, which, when codified by Hadrian, formed the foundation of the legal system, and the role of the Emperor as a source of law and patron of the great jurists of the late second and early third centuries need stressing. For our purposes, however, two connected things are important. First, at Rome there was no question of the separation of judiciary and legislature which is so important a liberal principle to modern political thinkers. The law at Rome was on the whole the creation of judges, not lawgivers. The second point follows from this: legal measures show the same variety, casualness, and lack of generality which we find in Roman administrative decisions, and indeed it is difficult to separate the two. There is no proper ancient equivalent of statute law. The result was that the law was not always sufficiently universal, and the under-privileged might well not reap its benefits. Jewish nationalist writers, for example, compare the hypocrisy of Rome to the ambiguous associations of the unclean pig: 'Just as a pig lies down and sticks out its trotters as though to say "I am clean" [because they are cloven], so the evil empire robs and oppresses while pretending to execute justice.'

For the burdens of Roman rule on the Empire were heavy and hated, and much of Roman government was devoted to ensuring their efficacy. The collection of tribute, direct and indirect tax, rents, levies in kind, recruits, protection money, requisitioning, and so on in total amounted to a very heavy oppression, even if the amount of tax formally due was not by comparative standards very high. Roman officials from the highest to the most menial were involved with these matters, and finance was a serious administrative concern. Augustus' great catalogue of his achievements is called in full *Res Gestae et Impensae* ('His Deeds and Expenditure'). And this is undoubtedly the view that most provincials had of the way the Empire worked. A prophecy of Rome's fall concentrated on both the exactions of the ruling power and the—less often discussed but equally odi-ous—drain of manpower to Italy via the slave trade: 'the wealth that Rome has received from tributary Asia threefold shall Asia receive again from Rome, which will pay in full the price of its insolent pride. And for each of those who labour in the land of the Italians twenty Italians shall toil in Asia as needy slaves', (*Oracula Sibyllina* 3. 350 f.). Given this hostility to the harsh realities of the Empire, and given the amateur nature of Roman government, how was stability achieved?

Communications have been described as the nervous system of the body politic. Compared with what had gone before and what followed the rule of Rome, the frequency of movement and the security of roads and harbours was most impressive (though banditry never completely disappeared even from Italy). The imperial posting system, a creation of Augustus refined over the following centuries, became so huge, authoritative, and elaborate that it represented one of the heaviest burdens on the provincials whose food, animals, and dwellings were constantly being requisitioned for passing officials, as inscriptions from a wide range of places and times bear eloquent witness. But there can be no doubt that the roads and harbours of the Empire were one of the most necessary organs of Roman rule.

The transmission, retrieval, and storage of information is a still more basic

c. 1000 FEET (300 M.)

AERIAL VIEW OF THE PORT AT CARTHAGE, one of the major harbours of the Roman Mediterranean. The two artificial basins visible in the photograph go back to the Punic period; the rectangular one was designed for commercial shipping and the circular one for warships. At the centre of the circular port is an island on which recent excavations have revealed Punic ship-sheds. These were replaced by a monumental precinct in Roman times.

ingredient of the stability, durability, and effectiveness of government. Max Weber called documents the bureaucrat's tools of production. The Roman Empire has won a reputation for bureaucratic sophistication. So what of its documents? Before the nineteenth century, it is interesting to note, this aspect of Roman imperial rule did not strike students of the period. It was the discovery of the *papyri* of Egypt which contributed to the view that Rome too had been a bureaucracy like those burgeoning in the excavators' homelands. Since then the spectacular complexity of the administration of Egypt has been further revealed, and evidence from other dry regions—Dura Europus on the Euphrates is a notable example—has shown that the volume of administrative paperwork in other eastern provinces was likewise very great. The figures can be astonishing. A third-century regional administrator's office in Egypt consumed 434 rolls of papyrus in a particular period of about a month. The archives of the fortress at Dura Europus occupied more than ten rooms. It is easy incautiously to assert that this society can truly be called bureaucratic'. But two problems must be faced. First, is the

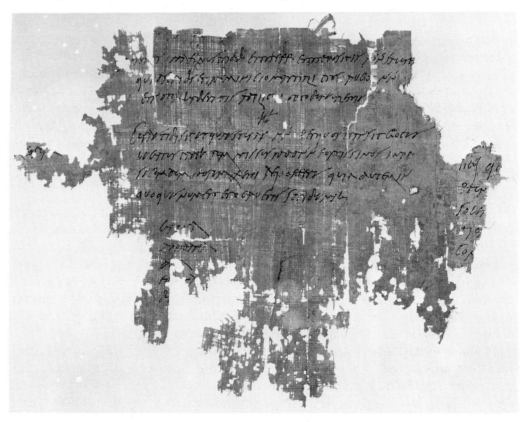

DOCUMENT FROM THE ARCHIVE AT DURA-EUROPUS (first half of third century AD). The numerous papyri from the archive include legal documents and contracts, a calendar of military festivals, records of the purchase of horses, lists of soldiers, and so forth. This particular document is a letter of one Marius Maximus concerning the reception and entertainment of a Parthian envoy.

practice of either Egypt or Mesopotamia, where the accumulation of documents was an extremely ancient aspect of government, typical of the eastern Empire in general, and is the East typical of the Empire as a whole? Papyrus archives naturally would not survive elsewhere, but the absence of the potsherds which were also extensively used at the lowest level of the Egyptian administration, is a better testimony to the singularity of the Egyptian system, since pottery is virtually indestructible. But the second question is more important: how far is this accumulation of mounds of paper by dozens of officials evidence for a bureaucratic administration of the kind found in modern states? To answer that question it will be necessary to discover why records were accumulated and how they were then deployed. Are our ancient administrative documents from working bureaux, lumber rooms, or something in between?

Even the ability to write documents such as the papyri which survive was not common in antiquity. We even hear in Egypt of illiterate scribes. Not so absurd: to be a scribe was a significant status, worth aspiring to through fraud. Of Pharaonic Egypt we know that scribes were men of very great importance in the state, and the pairing of Scribe with Pharisee is a still more familiar example of the way in which the skills conferred status. In China the skills of scholar and scribe, regulated by an amazing system of public examinations, defined the governmental class. In neither Greece nor Rome does the scribe have this status. At Rome the scribes played a role of their own in the political and social life of the city. The Emperor's service employed numerous clerks and secretaries. But it was not the handlers of documents, the men with the skills, who rose high. It was much more the *cubicularii*, the personal servants, the confidants of the Emperor or of powerful men. And they rose not through skill, dedication, or inside information, but through the patronage which came from social contacts. None of this speaks of a bureaucracy.

The scribe of ancient Egypt is portrayed cross-legged, his writing equipment on his lap, ready to move wherever he may be required. The classical scribe likewise was always mobile: there were clerks, but no offices. No ancient office building and no ancient desk will ever be discovered. Strikingly, when ancient administrative departments acquired a metaphorical name, it was not that of an unportable item of furniture, but the scribe's portable roll-satchel, the *scrinium*. Administration revolved around people, not around places or buildings, and not, despite those mountains of papyrus, around documents.

The documents were stored in archive rooms, some of which are known archaeologically. But although papers were kept, there were no filing cabinets, card indexes, reference numbers, registration forms. Collections of documents were made by pasting them together in chronological or—by no means as often as convenience would dictate—in alphabetical order. The codex, the presentation of documents as a book, was occasionally used, but the cartulary, a choice of really important documents for frequent reference, was unknown. Papers were preserved in archives, but it was well known that in most conditions papyrus did not keep well. Why did these things not matter? Because retrieval of documents from the archive was not a particularly urgent consideration in its formation. The tax assessment notice, the letter from the commanding officer, the tax receipt, the birth registration were used only once, in the process of checking a particular tax collection, or implementing a decision. Access to the document *might* be required a second time, but probably only a tiny fraction of all documents was ever looked at twice. The consultation of a document was a serious matter: 'for which reason, pious and benevolent Caesar, order that I be given a copy from your *commentarii* as your father intended' says a petitioner to Hadrian (*ILS* 338). Administrative processes were a favour, a privilege, a wonder, which is why on documents like this, where only what does credit to the purchaser of the inscription appears, what seem to us to be banal details of this kind are recorded in full. So this one actually preserves Hadrian's orders to his secretaries: 'Stasimus, Dapenis, publish the decision or opinion from the recorded version (*edite ex forma*)'. Authentication was a serious problem, never entirely solved, which helped prevent reliance on documentary authority. The *sardonychus* or imperial signet-ring gave its name to a Palatine department (see, e.g., *ILS* 1677), but there were often rumours that it had fallen into unauthorized hands. The Emperors used codes, but only rather simple ones. One of the principal reasons for the abuse of the public post system was that there was no reliable way of ensuring that only a limited number of people possessed authentic licences to demand hospitality and service. Distribution was another problem. It is very hard for us to imagine how difficult, despite the efficiency of communications, the systematic exchange of documentary information was. A letter of Trajan to Pliny making an important administrative point need never have been known in next door Asia, let alone Germania Inferior. This is perhaps one reason why Pliny's heirs

DOCUMENTS AND WRITING EQUIPMENT. From left to right an eraser, a four-leaved tablet, a double inkwell with a pen leaning against it, and a scroll. Wooden tablets coated with wax, in which writing was inscribed with a metal stylus, were used for a variety of documents, from official and business records to private letters; scrolls of parchment or papyrus, with writing in ink in the modern manner, were the standard vehicles for longer texts.

actually published his correspondence. This difficulty no doubt helped to discourage the formation of any monolithic imperial administrative structure.

Documents, once stored, were of surprisingly little use. Governmental acts could not afford to depend on such an unreliable basis. The archives represented continuity and stability, and were not for regular use. The truth appears well from the story of the disastrous fire of AD 192 at Rome, when the central imperial archives of the Palatine were completely destroyed (Dio 73. 24). There is no hint that Roman government was disrupted; but the event was taken as a token that the authority of Rome, embodied in these documents, would weaken. The omen is not so far removed from the association of Rome's universal rule with a census registration at the beginning of the Gospel of St Luke.

Another famous fire, this time not accidental, destroyed 3,000 inscribed tablets on the Capitoline during the Civil War of AD 69. Vespasian, by contrast with the events just described, saw to it that new texts were inscribed whenever another version of one of the perished documents could be discovered. State documents, we must not forget, included texts on stone and bronze and wood, and in the arts of government these were perhaps more important than the ones which were stacked in dusty muniment rooms. The ancient world was a uniquely epigraphic culture—otherwise our view of it, and especially of its institutions, would be very different. In classical Greece Athens had been exceptional in the extent to which it encouraged the publication on stone of official texts. During the Hellenistic period this important governmental act became a universal practice which was naturally enough adopted by Rome. The inscribing of a decision made it seem more permanent; it gained from the association of other venerable and welcome enactments inscribed nearby, and from the religious, political or sentimental tone of the place in which it was set up. To give only one example: the patents of citizenship of discharged auxiliary soldiers were at first tacked in hundreds to the Temple of the Good Faith of the Roman People to its Friends, high on the Capitol in the very heart of the Empire, powerfully expressing the relationship of Rome to its loyal subjects. A collection of privileges, honours, even historical or—in at least one case—philosophical texts could be a source of pride even to those who could not read them. For although there are pieces of evidence that the inscription was a source of information to the public—it was a tyrant's trick to hang savage edicts out of clear sight—it is revealing that published Roman laws sometimes contained the provision that the text was to be read aloud at regular intervals. Similarly we may assume that it was the moment when herald, ambassador, or magistrate first read the Emperor's letter to the city that it had its effect: the inscribing was a symbol of the city's gratitude and appreciation, and of the measure's permanence.

Depositing a document in an archive was not so different an act. The record depository might be in a significant temple (at Rome death registrations were kept in the grove of the goddess of funerals). The main Roman archive was part of a prestigious complex of buildings on the sacred Capitoline hill, high above

CITIZENSHIP DIPLOMA OF GEMELLUS. Dated 17 July 122, the two bronze tablets, wired together through holes at the adjacent corners, are a personal certificate of the privileges granted to a veteran on his discharge. The front (left) concludes with the words 'certified copy taken from the bronze plaque posted at Rome on the wall behind the temple of the Deified Augustus near (the statue of) Minerva'.

the Forum. The close connection between the perishable documents and the public inscription, and the purpose of preserving the text, is excellently shown by an epigraphic version from an Italian town, page by page with chapter headings, of a section of the town-council minutes relevant to the honorific purpose at hand (*ILS* 5918ᵃ). It emerges that the minutes themselves were less practical in purpose than a part itself of civic ceremony; it seems that a new roll would be formally started each year on Augustus' official birthday. The keeping of such records had very little to do with future practical utility.

If record keeping in antiquity is understood in this way, it begins to become clear that we should not be surprised at finding no serious bureaucracy and no administrative art as such in the ancient world. Those involved in government needed no special training. It is true that, for example, shorthands were developed, but it is revealing that they are associated at Rome with the names of two men of high culture, Cicero's amanuensis Tiro and Horace's patron Maecenas. But importantly, although so many papyri concern counting and taxation, the ancient world had no systematic knowledge of accounting, and no concept of numeracy. Book-keeping, hindered by the number systems of Greek and Latin, always remained primitive. It is very strange, when the marginal subsistence of the ancient poor is considered, how low a standard of accuracy is found in papyrus and epigraphical calculations. What was required of an administrator was (after loyalty and probity) *litterae*, the whole world of ancient literary culture. The Younger Pliny (*Ep.* 1. 10. 9) is most revealing on the subject. As prefect of the Roman treasury he has to spend his time at the most banal and routine administrative business; his work is 'extremely uncultured'—but the word he uses to describe it is *litterae*, none the less.

That administration was *litterae* is an observation which will enable us to end on a rather more positive note: up to now we have been necessarily preoccupied, sadly, with abandoning Auden's image of the bored clerk's 'pink official form'. It has been stressed that ancient government was concerned with warfare, jurisdiction, and the management of private property. What kept alive this ideology was the aristocratic literary culture for which ancient civilization has always been most famous. The leader of men, the just judge, and the fair master had been ideals since Homer. For Herodotus the origin of the power of the Median—and hence the Persian—kingship was simply the impartiality and importance to society of the judgements of Deioces. There was no distinction between the Arts of Government and the other *technai, artes,* with which ancient élites concerned themselves. The art of rhetoric above all united what we see as these two distinct worlds. Eloquence is one of the main requirements of the ancient administrator. The Roman Emperor himself always expressed himself in the literary forms of letters or speeches, and spent most of his day listening to similar products of ancient literary culture. The generalizations and principles expressed in Roman governmental pronouncements are not a coherent ideology, and still less an indication of imperial policies, but simply commonplaces of moral or political thought deployed appropriately in a literary composition. It was not easy to aspire to participation in this sort of exercise. In fact, in its formal intellectual demands, membership of the Roman administrative élite was not after all so very different from the system which evolved in China.

Vitruvius, the architect in the public service, expressly praises his parents for the general philological and technical/artistic education which has made him what he is (6, pr. 4). Philostratus sneers at the lack of success of an imperial freedman whose inadequate literary attainments let him down, 'Celer, a writer of technical works and a good enough secretary of the emperor, but lacking in polish' (*VS* 1. 22). For slaves and freedmen, equestrians and senators alike, culture was the sign of and often the way to social success, and at no level of the Roman administration do we find functionaries who are carrying out some sort of 'serious' administrative activity while their seniors indulge in cultural pursuits.

I have also emphasized the importance of Rome's inclusion of the élites of the Empire, above all of Greece, in her government. This too would not have been possible had Greek and Latin speakers not already come to share a common cultural heritage. It is therefore no coincidence that the age of the greatest governmental complexity of the ancient world and that flowering of culture which we call the Second Sophistic came together. The aristocratic ideals which underlay ancient government also required conspicuous expenditure on the part of rulers. Much that is familiar about the Roman world from Gibbon's portrait of the Antonine golden age derives from this. The enormous tomb which Claudius' freedman Pallas built for himself, the vast scale of the military engineering of Hadrian's Wall, and the great building projects of the Emperor at Rome and the urban upper classes in the hundreds of cities of the Empire are all themselves part of the great Art by which the Empire was maintained. The reciprocal relations of benefaction, competition, and prestige among those who controlled the resources of the ancient world are found throughout antiquity, from the aristocracies of the archaic Greek cities to the Roman Emperors. In these relations were included the whole range of ancient cultural activities, from architecture and utilitarian building to the patronage of literature, music, and painting—and also to the entertainments of the circus and the amphitheatre and the religious festivals which were the setting of almost all these forms of display. This characteristic aspect of ancient society produced a type of bond between the élite and the peoples of the cities which was unique—a major source of the stability and continuity which we associate with the Greek and Roman world.

Unfortunately ancient culture had never rid itself of its uneasy companion, warfare. In the end this aspect came to be dominant. There came a time when scribes were soldiers, bishops were soldiers, local governors were soldiers, the

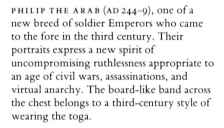

PHILIP THE ARAB (AD 244-9), one of a new breed of soldier Emperors who came to the fore in the third century. Their portraits express a new spirit of uncompromising ruthlessness appropriate to an age of civil wars, assassinations, and virtual anarchy. The board-like band across the chest belongs to a third-century style of wearing the toga.

Emperor was a soldier. At that point the end of the ancient world was in sight. It is therefore again no coincidence that the first great crisis of Roman rule and the cultural desert of the third century came together, even if it would be too simple to say that either brought about the other.

Further Reading

Fundamental is F. Millar, *The Emperor in the Roman World* (London, 1977), not only for the role of the Emperor but for very many aspects of Roman government. For the city-state M. I. Finley, *Politics in the Ancient World* (Cambridge, 1983) is suggestive and interesting though unreliable on Rome itself; on citizenship A. N. Sherwin-White, *The Roman Citizenship*[2] (Oxford, 1973) remains basic. For the Greek world A. H. M. Jones, *The Greek City* (Oxford 1940), and for Italy W. Eck, *Die staatliche Organisation Italiens* (Munich, 1979). On town statuses F. Abbott and A. C. Johnson, *Municipal Administration in the Roman Empire* (Princeton, 1926) is still very useful. On the definition of provinces and *imperium*, A. Lintott, *Greece & Rome* 28 (1981), 53 f. For governors' assizes, G. Burton, *JRS* 65 (1975), 926. An account of how the Empire worked which complements what is said here will be found in P. Garnsey and R. P. Saller, *The Roman Empire, Economy, Society, and Culture* (London, 1987), ch. 2, 'Government without bureaucracy'.

For the military angle R. MacMullen, *Soldier and Civilian in the later Roman Empire* (Harvard, 1963), is crucial; and see now L. Keppie, *The Making of the Roman Army* (London, 1984), and J. B. Campbell, *The Emperor and the Roman Army* (Oxford, 1984); on the Emperor's military planning F. Millar, *Britannia* 13 (1982), 1 f. For *praefecti fabrum* B. Dobson, *Britain and Rome* ed. B. Dobson and M. G. Jarrett (Kendal, 1966) pp. 61 f. Amateur commanders: J. B. Campbell, *JRS* 65 (1975), 11 f.

For slaves in the public service L. Halkin, *Les ésclaves publics chez les romains* (Liége, 1897); for the *apparitores* N. Purcell, *PBSR* 51 (1983), 125 f. On the imperial household A. M. Duff, *Freedmen in the Early Roman Empire* (Oxford, 1926); P. R. C. Weaver, *Familia Caesaris* (Cambridge, 1972). The quotation about the imperial civil service is from P. A. Brunt, *JRS* 65 (1975), 124 f., which establishes that the administrators of Roman Egypt had no particular qualifications for the job. On equestrian procurators H. G. Pflaum, *Les procurateurs équestres* (Paris, 1972) presents the results of a monumental survey. For reasons for promotion see R. P. Saller, *Personal Patronage under the Early Empire* (Cambridge, 1982), chs. 2–3, making a very strong case against promotion for merit. For status, not administrative function, as the way to understand the *familia Caesaris* G. Burton, *JRS* 67 (1977), 162 f. The quotation about the *tabellarii* is from Weaver, cit.

On law, J. Crook, *Law and Life of Rome* (London, 1967); A. N. Sherwin-White, *Roman Society and Law in the New Testament* (Oxford, 1963). For a detailed survey of imperial finance, P. A. Brunt, *JRS* 71 (1981), 161 f. The remark about the pig is quoted from N. de Lange, 'Jewish Attitudes to the Roman Empire', in P. Garnsey and C. Whittaker, edd. *Imperialism in the Ancient World* (Cambridge, 1978), p. 255. For the miseries of ancient provincial subjects R. MacMullen, *Roman Social Relations* (Yale, 1974). On benefaction and dependence, P. Veyne, *Bread and Games* (English edn. of *Le Pain et le cirque* (Paris, 1976), in preparation).

Roman Egypt: a useful survey is A. K. Bowman, *Egypt after the Pharaohs* (London, 1986). On documents and records E. Posner, *Archives in the Ancient World* (Cambridge, Mass., 1972). For Rome's fostering of the élites of the empire G. E. M. de Ste. Croix, *The Class Struggle in the Ancient Greek World* (London, 1981), who (p. 503) likens the behaviour of the rulers of the Empire to that of vampire bats.

8

Augustan Poetry and Society

❦

R. O. A. M. LYNE

THIS is perhaps the most eventful period of Roman history, witness to civil wars, revolution, and, eventually, an imposed peace: Republic becomes Empire. Meanwhile, Latin literature produces its greatest works; Italy produces poets destined to achieve immortality. The present chapter offers a sketch of this extraordinary time. First, three divisions within the period must be identified.

Dates and Divisions

The triumviral period begins in 43 BC, when the Roman world was put into the hands of Octavian, Antony, and Lepidus 'for the purposes of setting the state in order'. Antony was defeated at the battle of Actium in 31 BC, but the first Augustan period may be said to begin in the year 27 BC when Octavian's imperial role is effectively, but discreetly, defined and he himself assumes the name Augustus. Another change is then discernible about 20 BC: Augustus exercises his monarchical power more assertively, and this has a large effect upon literature.

The works that will be considered below may now be assigned to these three divisions, though some of the assignations are approximate and some insecure. Into the first, the triumviral period, fall the *Eclogues* and most of the *Georgics* of Virgil, the *Epodes* and *Satires* of Horace; Propertius' Book 1 is published at the beginning of the first Augustan period, but much of it may have been composed earlier. Propertius' Book 2, Tibullus' Books 1 and 2, Horace's *Odes* 1–3, and Virgil's *Aeneid* are all substantially works of this first Augustan period (though the *Aeneid* is unfinished at Virgil's death in 19 BC); at the end of it we can place Horace's *Epistles* 1 and 2.1, and Propertius 3, and we can detect signs of the atmosphere of the second Augustan period in those works. To this second Augustan period we may then assign Propertius 4, and Horace's *Odes* 4, *Epistle* 2.2 (the *Epistle to Augustus*), and *Ars Poetica*. Ovid's *Amores* straddle the two Augustan periods, while the remainder of his works all belong to the second.

The Role of Poets

Our period sees the culmination of a process of change in the status of poets and poetry, a change of fundamental importance. Traditionally—let us say in the second century BC—poets, unlike historians, had been of low social status (foreigners or freedmen for example) and their works and profession were positively revered only in one particular respect, their power to confer lasting fame. Drama was of course valued as entertainment, and dramatists unlike other poets were directly paid; but in general philistinism towards poetry was endemic. Aristocrats with aesthetic taste and education like Scipio Aemilianus were exceptions. Even by the time of Cicero things have not much changed: Cicero has to tread cautiously in his defence of the poet Archias, presupposing philistinism in his audience. Nor is Cicero himself boundlessly aesthetic. Given a second life, he said, he would still not bother to read the Greek lyric poets.

When upper-class Romans do start to turn their hands to poetry, one gets the impression of amateurs, more or less condescending. Q. Lutatius Catulus and others toss off epigrams at the end of the second century, showing an acquaintance with Greek precedents, probably from anthologies; but Catulus at least, consul in 102 BC with C. Marius, had better things to do with his serious time. The satirist Lucilius is a much more significant figure (his literary *floruit* can be put in the 130s BC). He is rich and of high rank, great enough to be friend and foe of the greatest men of his generation—great enough also to utter his sometimes scarifying opinions on these great men, as well as on more humble figures, in his able and fluent verse. His development of the genre of satire is important in the history of Latin literature; so is his assertively autobiographical standpoint; so in particular is the importance he accords to the business of writing. Nevertheless I do not think we have in Lucilius an instance of an aristocrat seriously adopting the profession of poet. It was what he said that mattered to him; and, clothing his thoughts in a racy patchwork of Greek tags and often colloquial Latin and disposing all that in a range of metres, he found an eye-catching and ear-catching way of saying what he wanted to say. It was the message that mattered for him; he was a commentator on the contemporary scene rather than an artist—although as an artist he was, incidentally, pretty good.

In the shift in attitude towards poets and poetry it is the so-called Neoteric movement in the late Republic that is crucial: the group of poets comprising Catullus, Calvus, Cinna, and others. These are men of the provincial or Roman upper classes who take the profession of poetry with utmost seriousness. They at least think that it well befits an upper-class Roman simply to be a poet. Catullus, of course, we know most about. After a brief brush with active life he devoted his whole energies to poetry—and love. Symptomatic of his poetical professionalism is his interest in and knowledge of the professional poet and scholar of Alexandria, Callimachus (Vol. 1, pp. 355 ff.). Catullus is probably best known for his love poetry and for his lampoons and invectives; but arguably most indicative of him as an artist and certainly as a Neoteric are his intricate and highly wrought longer poems, such as 64 (the *Peleus and Thetis*), 68, and his translation of Callimachus, 66. But these poems are also indicative of something which went hand in glove, perhaps inevitably, with this new interest in the business of poetry: aestheticism, an interest in technique for technique's sake. This tendency was probably more pronounced in Cinna. His 'miniature epic' *Zmyrna* took nine years to write and attracted a scholarly commentary in the next generation.

Our period sees the final shift in attitude towards poetry and poets. Not only can poetry now appear a reputable full-time occupation for Romans of good class. Poets relinquish aestheticism, engage themselves with society, discover or profess commitment—or have to defend non-commitment. In short, the classical Greek view of poetry is again in play: it is the work of important people and may serve the citizens of the state in a moral and educative fashion. Virgil and his poetry will be glanced at below and discussed in another chapter. Of the elegiac poets (the term refers to their metre, cf. Vol. 1, p. 94, and does not have the mournful overtones of the English 'elegy'), Tibullus is a knight, well off in Horace's eyes, though less so in his own; Ovid and Propertius were knights (*equites*), and Propertius had relations of senatorial rank and friends of consular standing. The attitude of these poets towards society will be discussed below. Horace is less grand than Propertius or Tibullus: he is the son of a freedman, but a freedman with enough cash to put him through the equivalent of a university education at Athens. Eventually Horace gained the status of a kind of poet laureate. He not only performs, with some intermission, the function of moral and educative poet; he expresses it in theory.

Given that poets were traditionally of low social status, and given that no system of royalties or the like existed in the Roman world (except for dramatists), how did poets live? The answer basically is: patronage. Poets attached themselves to, or were collected by, wealthy Roman aristocrats. The great epic poet Ennius, for example (above, pp. 72 ff.), was patronized by, among others, M. Fulvius Nobilior, and a catalogue of other poets could be adduced who wrote epics celebrating aristocratic generals and thereby gained their sustenance. Poets fitted into the general Roman client–patron system whereby great men were attended, cultivated, and in humble matters assisted by the humble, and in return bestowed their bounty and their protection. But even in early days there was a difference between poet-clients and ordinary clients. For what the patron got from the poet was something that was rather more estimable than that which other clients could offer: the perpetuation of their fame and glory. More than that: *memoria sempiterna*, 'being remembered for ever', was the way in which many Romans, including Cicero, viewed how they might 'live' after death; so what a poet might offer was in effect a chance of immortality. This is the keynote of Cicero's defence of Archias, mentioned above: Archias had provided immortality for

Marius and Lucullus and, through them, for the Roman People. This aspect of the poet's function in Rome is a vital one, continuing into our period.

As the status of poet changes, so does the nature of patronage. Catullus, whose family is friendly with Julius Caesar and soon to become senatorial, has no economic need of a patron and does not have one. His circle is a coterie, a grouping of equals, and his address to Cornelius Nepos in his first poem is to be construed as a friendly or polite gesture, no more. Similarly Propertius, in his first book. But patronage does persist, even among the socially enhanced poets of the Augustan period.

The circle of the great orator, soldier, and statesman, M. Valerius Messalla, consul with Octavian in 31 BC, is indicative, exhibiting both continuity and change. There are in fact points of resemblance between his circle and a coterie such as that of Catullus. Pliny tells us that Messalla interested himself in the writing of erotic versicles, and we can observe him surrounded by other love poets and poetasters (coterie fashion), who include his aristocratic niece Sulpicia. On the other hand, if the author of the *Panegyricus Messallae* in the Tibullan corpus belongs to the circle and is talking of our Messalla (as is likely), then here is continuity in the role of poet as client: the client-poet immortalizes the great man. But it is the relation of the elegist Tibullus to Messalla that is most interesting.

Although Tibullus is vastly the social inferior of the noble Messalla, he is a knight, he does reflect the change in status of poets—and yet his relationship to Messalla resembles the old one of client and patron. He writes poems that, while not being technically panegyrics, devote themselves to the celebration of Messalla and his family (1.7 and 2.5), and scatters his other poems with laudatory allusions. Patronage survives the changes in status of poets and poetry. The phenomenon is of course observable in the circle of Maecenas, and elsewhere. So we ask ourselves: To what extent is this literary patronage like the old kind? What are both parties now getting out of it?

Some basic points can be inferred—Ovid, who was patronized early in his career by Messalla, is informative. These upper-class poets were not dependent economically in the way that their predecessors had been (though more on this anon). What they obtained was the encouragement of a great man usually himself a littérateur, the cachet of being associated with a well-known group of poets, access to such like-minded people (they would meet and some would even live in the great man's house), and perhaps above all publicity. Although at this time literature is intensely literate, written ultimately to be read and propagated in texts, an initial and important mode of communication is oral: various kinds of readings—private readings among the poets, semi-public and public recitations (formal public *recitationes* were instituted in Rome by Asinius Pollio). This was the scene in which a poet might make his name, and the chance to recite to an audience organized by a great patron was crucially important to a rising poet. Horace deplored both the institution of recitation and the fact that fame accrued thereby; but deploring it did not remove it, and even Horace himself recited. As for the patron, he had the natural satisfactions that such patronage brings, and he had, too, his chance of a piece of immortality. And in the circle of Maecenas something else was happening.

In the first Augustan period, Maecenas is the Augustan patron, mediating between poets and *princeps*. We can identify very important points of difference between his circle and, say, Messalla's. First, Augustus naturally wanted his heroic deeds enshrined in an epic—his piece of immortality. The trouble was that Maecenas' poets—Virgil, Horace, and subsequently Propertius—had to a varying extent scruples, moral and literary. The accommodating Tibullus could include celebrations of Messalla and his military exploits amongst his elegies in praise of love and peace. Not so Propertius. Besides, he was not an epic poet. Nor was Horace. Neither, to begin with, was Virgil. This presented a problem. These men were not old-style client-poets to be booted into an uncongenial genre. But Augustus was, to put it mildly, powerful. How does one deal with, on the one hand, upper-class poets with scruples and, on the other, an Emperor who wants an epic? The answer is that one is diplomatic, one mediates, one explains; and it is greatly to Maecenas' credit that his poets had the freedom, for a time, to decline impositions or fulfil them in their own individual way (as will be illustrated below).

Besides the moral and artistic sensitivity of his poets, Maecenas' circle was different from others in other and crucial respects. First and simply, the scale of what was on offer. These poets were not humble paupers, but Horace at least needed a living, and all had lost property in the land confiscations of the triumviral period. What Maecenas and Augustus bestowed on Horace and Virgil was vast (particularly, it seems, in Virgil's case), enabling them to live in very comfortable leisure in town or country. A certain moral pressure must therefore have been felt by these morally sensitive artists. Secondly, the task towards which they were being pressured was not just to immortalize the heroic deeds of the greatest general. It was something unique to the circle of Maecenas, reflecting the unique nature of his and later Augustus' patronage. Augustus and the state were effectively synonymous. To be in his patronage, directly or indirectly, was to be in the patronage of government, and there was a pressure to publicize the government's policies and to burnish its image. This task could be seen as invidious, but it could also be seen as a challenging responsibility; and with varying degrees of enthusiasm and directness, these scrupulous poets tackled it.

The nature of patronage in the imperial circle changes with the second Augustan period. Indeed this change may be seen to be part-cause of the second period arising. The sophisticated Maecenas, for reasons that cannot be defined with certainty, fades in importance, and the poets come under the direct patronage of the emperor. His hand was heavier, and it was becoming increasingly so. Political life around 20 BC reveals a more confidently autocratic ruler (witness, for instance, the marriage laws of 18 BC), and poetry, lacking the mediation of Maecenas, must also respond to his touch. A fourth book of *Odes* is elicited

AGRICULTURAL SCENES, mosaic at Cherchel (Algeria). Early third century AD. The upper scenes show ploughing and sowing; the lower the tending of vineyards in the winter. Such operations are referred to in Virgil's *Georgics*, the first in Book 1 (on the cultivation of crops), the second in Book 2 (on fruit-growing).

from an unwilling Horace, for example, containing what he had largely avoided in recent years: panegyric. The 'educator of citizens' becomes the court poet—but he has ways of striking back.

Virgil

Against this background I shall now outline the careers of the individual poets. Virgil's place in the picture must be adumbrated, but with all brevity since a separate chapter (Ch. 9) is devoted to him. His *Eclogues*, written in the triumviral period, show him ambivalent between the aestheticism of the Neoterics and an emerging sense of commitment. Elegant imitations of Theocritean pastoral glance at the miseries caused by land confiscations. While writing the *Eclogues* Virgil is not in the patronage of Maecenas. While writing the *Georgics* he is; and the *Georgics*, instigated or at least encouraged by Maecenas, show that Maecenas was not immediately concerned to elicit material that directly or crudely served Octavian. But the poem is to a great degree a moral didactic, hence of potential if rather indefinite use to a ruler; and it shows Virgil's strengthening sense of his committed poetic role.

It also demonstrates an attitude towards country life, an attitude which can be paralleled. Unlike Catullus and, say, Propertius, Virgil loves and esteems rustic life. But whereas the dominating reality of contemporary agriculture was large slave-run estates, Virgil esteems the small independent farmer—and exploits his way of life as a metaphor for morality. The simple point I want to stress is that in spite of the prevalence of great ranches, such small farmers were still around. Evidence testifies to their minority existence; and the policy of settling soldiers on confiscated property might, if it was successful (as it probably was not), have increased their numbers. So Virgil's affectionate view of the country is we might say old-fashioned, blinkered, even slightly romantic; but it is not a mere fiction or poetic convention.

I said above that no immediate pressure was being exerted by Maecenas for a poem directly to serve Octavian. But both he and Virgil would know that the great man would want his exploits celebrated in epic, and that is what Virgil seems to promise at the beginning of *Georgics* III. In fact, in the sophisticated atmosphere of the first Augustan period, he developed an indirect, mythical mode whose fruit was the *Aeneid*—and the Emperor was, perhaps rather surprisingly, well pleased.

Horace

In the triumviral period Horace writes his *Epodes*, in Archilochian *iambi*, and his *Satires*, his development of Lucilius' genre. We can still discern vestiges of republican libertarianism and non-alignment in them. *Epodes* 7 and 16 consider with neutral despair the imminence of civil war. Other *Epodes* are vicious attacks, in Archilochian vein. Some *Satires* too attack personages, but in general Horace's *Satires* are more general and genial than those of Lucilius, and neither *Epodes* nor *Satires* assail men of eminence. Horace had not the protection of rank; and besides, the triumviral period was a despotic one, with the added complication that one could not be sure which despot would come out on top.

This is, however, also the period in which Maecenas gathers Horace into his circle, and Horace is induced to commit himself enthusiastically to Octavian. *Epode* 9 is a celebration of the victory of Actium, and *Epode* 1, addressed to

REMAINS OF HORACE'S VILLA AT LICENZA in the hills 40 km east of Rome. The identification of the site as the Sabine farm bestowed on the poet by Maecenas in 33 BC was made as early as the eighteenth century and is supported not only by topographical indications in Horace's own writings but also by the styles of construction and decoration, characteristic of the early Augustan period.

Maecenas, is the effusive poem of a man who definitely sees himself in a patron-ized position; it reminds one of Tibullus talking to Messalla. *Satire* 2.6 records with gratitude the gift of the famous Sabine estate, and *Satire* 1.1 is also addressed to Maecenas.

On the other hand, Horace is careful about himself and his image in his patronized position. In *Satire* 1.9, and in 1.6, the poem in which he describes his acceptance into Maecenas' circle, he is careful to define that acceptance as an honourable process, based on merit, and the circle as one of like-minded men free from the debasing procedures which characterized many client-patron groupings. Indeed he terms himself the 'friend' (*amicus*) of Maecenas. Although the language of *amicitia* was conventionally used between clients and patrons, and it would be quite clear who was the grand *amicus* and who was not, there is much evidence that Horace genuinely was friendly in the full sense of the word with Maecenas and even with Augustus. Indeed, he was familiar enough with Maecenas to allude in *Epode* 14 to an erotic liaison on the great man's part with an actor, Bathyllus.

In *Odes* 1–3, belonging to the first Augustan period, Horace assumes the role of a Roman Alcaeus. It was the usefulness of the image rather than the material of Alcaeus' texts that suggested this choice. Horace presents the image of Alcaeus, with discreet distortion, as follows (*Odes* 1.32). Alcaeus was an intensely committed citizen-poet, *engagé*, patriotically writing about the burning issues of his time; he also knew, however, that there was a place on the margins of life for leisure, for love and wine, and for poetry of leisure, poetry of love and wine; and he wrote such leisure poetry, as well as *engagé* poetry, knowing it to be leisure poetry, marginal poetry. Thus the image, and it was indeed useful to Horace. Committed at this time to his belief in the social and educative role of the poet and yet at the same time a delighted and delightful poet of love and wine, he could thus, as a Roman Alcaeus, justify his production. Like Alcaeus, he was the committed public poet, but he knew nevertheless that it could be appropriate to relax and not unseemly to write poetry for such occasions. It was vital, simply, to keep a sense of proportion, and not to let the life and literature of leisure usurp the position of the serious business of life. That was the mistake of the Elegists. Tibullus is read a lesson in this connection in the *Ode* immediately following the presentation of the Alcaean image.

Horace makes a couple of false starts in his public poetry: *Odes* 1.2 and 12 border on unpalatable panegyric, and 1.2 imputes divinity to an Augustus anxious to avoid such adoration. But during this period he evolved a satisfying and sophisticated method of public poetry, an 'indirect' method which bears comparison with Virgil's procedure in the *Aeneid*. Horace's method is a process of *association* and *substitution*. A good example is *Odes* 3.5, in which the sequence of thought is this: Augustus will be considered analogous to a god (that sort of expression was seemly) when he has conquered Britain and Parthia; mention of Parthia brings to mind Crassus' defeat at the hands of the Parthians in 53 BC and the shocking fact that Roman prisoners were now living among the Parthians as Parthians; this disgrace is, Horace implies, what Augustus will avenge. Then Horace is prompted to recall an event, almost a myth, from Roman history, the story of Regulus, a story which also involved a hated enemy, Roman prisoners, and a great Roman general; and the telling of this story occupies the rest of the *Ode*.

Now in fact the parallels between the two episodes are slight, extending not much beyond the broad features just mentioned. But by means of a glossing formula of transition and by the mere fact of juxtaposition, Horace manages to associate the two generals (Augustus and Regulus), to assimilate Augustus' imminent honourable action in the matter of Parthians and prisoners to Regulus' action in the matter of prisoners and Carthaginians. Indirectly, therefore, he presents Augustus as a new Regulus: Stoic, honourable—and republican, a useful suggestion. By this process of association he avoids the invidiousness of direct and implausible praise. By the process of substitution—eleven of the fourteen stanzas of the *Ode* are devoted to the associated figure of Regulus, who is thus substituted for the contemporary figure Augustus—he gives himself artistic and indeed moral liberty. In both artistic and moral terms it is hard to sing stirringly about the impending expedition of a contemporary general; much easier to evoke the heroic action of a quasi-mythical figure. Similarly in 3.4 Horace discreetly associates Augustus' victory at Actium with Jupiter's victory over the Giants, a traditional paradigm of the victory of civilized force over barbarism; and he then devotes his lyrical attention to this, the substituted story. What poet could not write epically about such a story? What poet, on the other hand, would not find difficulties in lauding a contemporary battle like Actium? Horace himself had, back in *Odes* 1.37.

That is Horace in public vein. Here is a taste of Horace as poet of love. The first three stanzas of the famous Pyrrha *Ode* (1.5) run thus:

> quis multa gracilis te puer in rosa
> perfusus liquidis urget odoribus,
>   grato, Pyrrha, sub antro?
>   cui flauam religas comam,
>
> simplex munditiis? heu quotiens fidem
> mutatosque deos flebit et aspera
>   nigris aequora uentis
>   emirabitur insolens,
>
> qui nunc te fruitur credulus aurea,
> qui semper uacuam semper amabilem
>   sperat nescius aurae
>   fallacis. miseri, quibus
>
> intemptata nites! . . .

What slim boy, Pyrrha, drenched in liquid scents presses you in an abundance of roses under some pleasing grotto? For whom are you binding back your blonde hair in simple elegance? Alas, how often will he bewail fidelity and the gods changed, and wonder amazed at the sea made harsh by dark winds, he who now trustfully enjoys golden you, he who expects you always available, always lovable—ignorant of the deceiving breeze. Wretched are they for whom you shine untried . . .!

That carries a typical Horatian message which Horace, unlike the gullible youth in the poem, knows only too well. Love, the occupation of leisure, is a fleeting, evanescent, untrustworthy thing, though it can be none the less painful for that.

Odes 3.28 gives a taste of Horace as poet of wine as well as love. It too carries a typical Horatian message: Horace announces that it is a holiday, the *Neptunalia*, and therefore leisure time. What is he to do? Answer: drink good wine, make music—and love. So, in Horace's view, leisure pursuits, love and wine, should not usurp the position of serious business; but it is equally his view, embodied in this *Ode*, that leisure is not leisure without them.

It will be noted that the girls in Horace's poetry of love and wine have Greek names. If we investigate these names, if we investigate other details in the poems, we find that this leisure poetry reflects—with discretion, stylization, romance—a real society: the Roman *demi-monde*, the *symposion* scene, where girls of probably slave or freedwoman class entertained with music and sex. This fact is important in two respects. It shows that Horace's erotic and sympotic poetry is not mere fancy and convention. And it also shows that Horace as a rule enjoyed, or liked to be seen to be enjoying, his erotic pleasures with women, or boys, of the lower classes employed for that purpose. That was considered correct at Rome. To attempt an erotic liaison with an upper-class *uirgo* was or should be an impossibility, and to have affairs with married ladies was in the Augustan age to become literally criminal. That point was not always well taken.

Many of Horace's *Odes* in Books 1–3 are concerned neither with affairs of state nor merely with leisure and pleasure, but with ethics on a private scale: how a man in his private capacity should conduct his life. After the production of *Odes* 1–3 Horace returns to the hexameter metre of his *Satires* and, in the late twenties BC, writes *Epistles* (Book 1) which are devoted to such ethical exploration and instruction. In his introductory *Epistle* to Maecenas he explains that, for this new production, he is giving up verse 'and other such frivolities'. The statement lacks neither ambiguity nor disingenuousness: for a start, Horace is at that very moment technically writing verse. It is nevertheless true that he does temporarily relinquish his role as public poet and the more overtly poetical mode of lyric.

BREASTPLATE OF THE STATUE OF AUGUSTUS FROM PRIMA PORTA (early first century AD). The imagery of the reliefs is closely related to that of Horace's *Carmen saeculare*, composed for the Secular Games of 17 BC. At the centre is depicted the recovery of the standards captured by the Parthians at the battle of Carrhae, and at the lower left and right are Apollo and Diana, the deities addressed by Horace in his hymn.

Why? Some reasons are stated, some may be inferred. Horace's dislike of the business of being a professional poet (recitations and so on) is affirmed in *Epistle* 1.19 and reaffirmed in the *Epistle to Florus* (2.2) of 19 BC. He also attests lack of public acclaim for *Odes* 1-3, due to his unwillingness to participate in such business; that too may have been discouraging. Then again, the question of private ethics had always been a preoccupation of his, in *Satires* as well as in *Odes*. There is perhaps one more factor: something to do with the role of public poet, the poet as immortalizer, the poet as educator. Horace may have experienced lack of confidence in the role, or perhaps disenchantment with it, as the Maecenas era drew to its close; whatever it was, the cap was no longer fitting. In Book 3 Horace had been the 'priest of the Muses', addressing future generations in public and edifying tones. In the *Epistle to Florus*, this same man turns to discuss the various reasons for writing poetry—the reasons that might induce him to turn professional again—and does not mention poetry's grand functions, its functions to immortalize and in particular to edify. The silence seems to me significant: for some reason, Horace was unhappy about the poet in this sort of role.

Not for long, or he was not allowed to be for long. The second Augustan period is upon us. For the Secular Games of the year 17 BC, the games to mark the New Age, Horace writes the public hymn, the *Carmen saeculare*. Next he is induced under the direct patronage of Augustus to compose a fourth book of *Odes* containing, as I have said, courtly poems directly panegyrical of the Emperor and his family. On the other hand—a gesture of conscious or unconscious self-assertion—the book contains some of Horace's finest poetry of love and wine. The very first poem movingly evokes Horace in love, in love again at fifty, in love with a boy called Ligurinus. Note that name. For once the love-object in a Horatian homosexual love poem does not have a Greek name; so he is neither cloaked in disguise nor assigned to an acceptably lowly class. Ligurinus is a real Roman *cognomen*. The poem is assertively personal—and very beautiful. Another beautiful poem of love and wine, also affectingly personal, is poem 11; and, satisfyingly, it is built round the birthday of the once great figure of Maecenas.

I do not think that Horace took up his public pen again totally willingly in this second Augustan period; but perhaps he was not totally unwilling. The reasons for his retirement are not, as I have said, perspicuous, and his description of poetry as frivolity was disingenuous. Certainly he came to be proud of the *Carmen saeculare*. And his *Epistle to Augustus* (2.1, of 12 BC) asserts once more the educative function of the poet and the power of poetry to immortalize. An interesting, incidental fact: in this epistle Horace implicitly argues for classic status to be accorded the Augustan poets: Virgil, the now lost Varius, and presumably himself. Over the love elegists a significant veil of silence is drawn: Ovid was, for example, by now the rage, but there is not a word on him. Finally, the *Ars Poetica* of the last years of his life shows him seriously occupied with poetry as a serious business, both entertaining and educative.

Propertius

Propertius is socially grander than Virgil and Horace and strikes a provocatively unconventional stance in life and literature (these two facts will not be unconnected). He seems never to have been so devoted or complete a member of Maecenas' circle as Virgil and Horace were.

Pragmatic Roman attitudes held that a man should do something serious with his life: conventionally, in the upper classes, he should advance it either in political or in economic terms. That was one position that Propertius confronted. But our period also sees, as I have said, poets regaining their classical status as civically committed, useful to the state, estimable creatures. Propertius confronts that idea too. He professes himself unemployed and unemployable in any conventional sense outside poetry, and 'useful' as a poet in ways which the conventional would regard as worse than useless. Whereas, therefore, Catullus the man had been prepared simply to *be* at leisure, Propertius declares it assertively, makes a manifesto of it; whereas Catullus the poet had occupied a position of unconcerned aestheticism, Propertius, in the new climate of artistic commitment, makes an aggressive statement of what in effect was non-commitment. I look at these points separately.

In a sequence of poems in Book 1 (1, 6, 14), Propertius declares his position on life and love. In contradistinction to Tullus, his addressee, Propertius cannot, he says, engage upon an active career. He must devote himself to love, and neither military/political nor economic advancement can distract him. He represents his love as something without sense, mad even; a disease, degradation. He takes upon himself all the condemnatory terms that Roman society customarily assigned to a hopelessly lost romantic lover. He even accepts for himself a title that society was not accustomed to fling around; he is the slave of his mistress. And yet he insists: this is for me. His position remains much the same in Book 2, and in some poems of Book 3. The commitment to love may be taken seriously; the self-condemnation less so. Later Romantics were to find that a willing espousal of wrong could be satisfyingly provocative. Propertius presents a programme of life designed to provoke—and to provoke not only stern moralists, but discreet proponents of acceptable *amour* such as Horace. Here was exactly what Horace decried: love, which should be the occupation of leisure, usurping the serious business of life, indeed becoming coterminous with life.

Before we consider Propertius' views on poetry we must consider the woman of whom he writes. Who is Cynthia? She is quite fully sketched: among other things she is described as a woman of fine artistic accomplishments, but fond too of the lower sympotic pleasures. Her exact social status is hard to pin down: she sounds like a high-class courtesan, but she may have been perhaps a divorcée or a widow of dubious morals. The point to be stressed about her is that she is sexually independent, or relatively so. Unlike the bought objects of Horace's erotic world she can and does dominate; she can dominate the besotted Propertius simply by the power of being able to say 'No'. She is an important figure. Without such a figure, the Propertian type of 'life of love' could not exist.

How does Propertius view his role as poet? In Book 1 (poems 7–9) he phrases it with a provocativeness to match the provocativeness of his programme for life. He bases himself on his premiss that love equals life. That allows him to describe the traditionally grand genre of epic as useless. Meanwhile, he claims, his elegy can perform the vital task of winning round a recalcitrant or errant mistress; and, because of the knowledge and experience it contains, it can benefit others. In other words, within the 'life of love' (the only life for Propertius), elegy is useful and indeed educational, in contrast to epic's uselessness. We should mark what Propertius is doing here. He is managing to assign to his poetry the traditionally esteemed functions of usefulness and edification, while denying them to their traditional recipient, epic. It is a neat turnabout; non-commitment is nicely phrased as commitment. In Book 3 we find him similarly misassigning, misusing (some would say) a grand view of poetry's function, the grand idea that poetry can immortalize. Poem 2 boasts the power of Propertian elegy to immortalize a *girl*. Horace would certainly be among those who would call this a misuse; and, a nice touch, Horace's own language of immortality is imported to phrase that misuse.

Such statements as these are designed to provoke rather than to offer serious information on the nature of Propertius' poetry. His love poems tend, particularly in Book 1, to be either dramatic, a 'staged' interaction between himself and Cynthia or another character, or rhetorical, speeches of indignation, pain, joy, and so on, to various addressees. They all frequently exploit mythological comparisons, the resonance of the mythical world. And their achievement is to offer insight into the personalities of Cynthia and Propertius, insight into their feelings and relationship, insight into love.

For example, poem 2 of Book 1 is a speech to Cynthia dissuading her from meretricious behaviour, in particular the use of cosmetics, and Propertius' mode of tackling the topic reveals much about his own personality, about Cynthia's personality, and about how the two interrelate. Poem 16 shrilly enquires of Cynthia why she cannot display the devotion of Calypso, Hypsipyle, and other romantic figures from myth—and exposes thereby a tension that pervades Propertius' life and fuels much of his love poetry. For Cynthia of course is not a romantic figure from myth. But that is something that the romantic Propertius finds so hard to accept. For a sample of a rhetorical poem the reader is referred to 2.8. There Propertius justifies the grief he is exhibiting at the loss of Cynthia by an appeal to the vast grief displayed by Achilles on the loss of Briseis.

In Book 1, much of which may have been composed in the triumviral period, Propertius is non-aligned and non-attached. He includes a bitter poem (21) on the Perusine war of 41 BC, bitter at the expense of the victor Octavian. This sort of independence of spirit is something he never loses.

Independence of spirit notwithstanding, the quality and popularity of Book 1 attracted the attention of Maecenas; and Maecenas suggested, inevitably, that Propertius might be well employed in putting Augustus' deeds into epic. The opening poem of Book 2 (first Augustan period) is a response to Maecenas' approach. It contains several interesting features. First, to decline the proposition of epic, Propertius employs a device which had been invented by Virgil and was used by other poets, including Horace. It is basically to say 'I would if I could', and to explain the inability by appeal to poetic powers or lack of them, or to poetic alignment. Propertius, like Virgil, claims an alignment with Callimachus and, as everyone knew, Callimachean aesthetics excluded epic. It is, however, clear that Propertius neither phrases his Callimacheanism seriously nor indeed (unlike Virgil) was seriously Callimachean; nor did he intend to be taken very seriously. He is simply declining a suggested imposition with grace and wit. And a bit of sting. When Propertius lists the heroic deeds of Augustus that he would have celebrated, had he been able, Maecenas must have felt relief that he did not. The list contains the ugliest episodes of the Civil War, including Perusia; and these, in the Augustan age, were best forgotten or reinterpreted.

Propertius declines the task of epic; but we must hereafter regard him as associated with the imperial circle—although this does not mean that his independence is snuffed. Poem 2.1 ends with the sort of praise for Maecenas that suggests the patronized: 'you whose favour all our young men covet and who are my true glory in life and will be when I die'; but the conclusion of the poem also insists on Propertius' role as a love poet—until he dies. Poem 2.7 rejoices in the abandonment of Augustus' first attempt at legislation to coerce Romans into marriage; and in 2.16, while making his characteristic noises about how shocking and degraded he is, Propertius associates himself with the shocking, degraded, romantic and magnetic figure of Mark Antony. Poem 2.34 celebrates the imminence of Virgil's *Aeneid* and, in the last couplet, celebrates Propertius himself as poet of Cynthia.

Book 3, written in the late twenties BC, opens with poems (1 and 3) that are a flamboyant assertion of Propertius' role as love poet and Callimachean. Not only flamboyant, pretentious: but one of the things Propertius is doing here is parodying Horace's just published and pretentious claims to be a Roman Alcaeus. Yet the book exhibits less interest in love poetry and, on the face of it, more concern with public issues. One scents the approach of the second Augustan period. But what Propertius gives with one hand, he takes with another—by irony and other methods. For example, poem 4 celebrates Augustus' expected Parthian victory. Propertius represents himself as the loyal observer of the triumph, reproducing an idea used by Horace and Cornelius Gallus. But he adds the slightly insolent touch that he will observe from the vantage point of his mistress's bosom; and he pairs the poem with one reminding us that Love is a god of peace.

In Book 4, which dates from the second Augustan period, we see the signs of Augustus' direct patronage. While Horace was induced to write a fourth book

ACHILLES SURRENDERS
BRISEIS to the emissaries of
Agamemnon: Pompeian
painting (between AD 62 and
79) from the House of the
Tragic Poet, probably based
on a Greek masterpiece of the
late fourth century BC.
Achilles' loss of his favourite
mistress provoked the bitter
quarrel which is the subject of
Homer's *Iliad* and provided
Propertius with a model for
an elegy on his loss of
Cynthia.

of *Odes*, the 'Callimachean' Propertius felt it prudent or compulsory to produce
something rather more genuinely Callimachean—and patriotic. Poems on the
causes or origins of institutions had absorbed Callimachus, and Propertius in his
fourth book produces poems on the causes and origins of Roman institutions: he
now styles himself the 'Roman Callimachus' explicitly, and with some justification. The time was of course no longer propitious for oppositional tactics of the
type seen in Book 3; yet Propertius still preserves his integrity and sense of
humour. For example, one 'origin' leads into a narrative of the battle of Actium,
and it is told, not parodically (as some think), but exactly as a Roman Callimachus should tell it; the exotic, rococo result would have caused Propertius much
pleasure and the Emperor no pain. It is perhaps one of his best compositions. In
another fine poem the moral story of Tarpeia is given an erotic motive—again
pleasure for Propertius and not much pain for the emperor. In fact Book 4
contains much very good writing. Pressure, if it is not completely totalitarian,
can inspire artists to creative ingenuity.

The final poem of the book is notable. It is a funeral elegy for a Roman lady, celebrating indirectly many of the moral virtues that Augustus was trying to inculcate. It should, we might think, bore, cloy, or irritate. It does not. In fact it is moving, and, for the reader of the entire Propertian collection, moving in a particular way. The dead lady speaks in the poem, and affirms how faithful, loving, and loyal she had been to her husband throughout her life—precisely the devotion that Propertius had sought and failed to find in Cynthia. Propertius' monument to an impeccable Roman lady is also therefore, by contrast, a monument to his own failure and sorrow: a pathetic irony. The poem provides a suggestive and moving end to the Propertian corpus.

Tibullus

I have touched upon Tibullus as the quasi-panegyrist of Messalla and his family. Beyond this, he hardly interests himself in national affairs, nor feels the need to explain his non-attention—a fact interesting in itself: imperial influence need not extend beyond the imperial circle. Nor is Tibullus interested in describing his role as poet, or his place in literary history. In discursive, associative elegies addressed mostly to the reader he writes of the country and his life of love.

Tibullus displays the same blinkered and slightly romantic love of the country as Virgil. But the feeling is none the less genuine, and a poem such as 2. 1, a celebration of an annual rural festival, largely depends upon it. So indeed does much of Tibullus' poetry. Tibullus would in fact like to live in the country—so he says.

The first forty-four lines of the first poem of the first book are devoted to an expression of this wish. Exactly what the wish comprised should be identified. To begin with it sounds as if Tibullus actually wants to be a small-holding and labouring farmer ('Let me as a farmer set vines in the early season'). This is revealed to be a humorously intended feint. What he actually wants to do is to dabble with work, to be a dilettante, to live a life of, in fact, leisure in rural simplicity on his own estate. He sketches this estate for us in the first poem and subsequently. It has been reduced in size, perhaps in confiscations, but it is still sufficient, with slaves to run it. Tibullus therefore, like Propertius, wants—shocking fact—a life committed to leisure, a 'life of inaction', *uita iners*, as he actually terms it; and, like Propertius, he scorns military and mercantile activity. But unlike the urban and urbane Propertius he wants to spend his life of leisure in the country. This dissimilarity between them is one among many that Tibullus wishes us to discern.

Forty-four lines express this Tibullan wish. What, we might ask, of love? Where is its place? And why, we might also ask, does Tibullus not just up and go to his estate, instead of moaning elegiacally in Rome? The basic reason is—love.

Here is how the expression of Tibullus' rural dream continues:

parua seges satis est, satis est requiescere lecto
    si licet et solito membra leuare toro.
quam iuuat immites uentos audire cubantem
    et dominam tenero continuisse sinu

(I. 1. 43-6)

A small crop is enough, it is enough if it is possible to rest in a bed and lighten the limbs on a familiar couch. How pleasant it is lying there to listen to wild winds, and *to hold my mistress in tender embrace.*

By 'mistress', *domina*, Tibullus means the woman to whom he as lover is slave (as Propertius was to Cynthia), and he has in mind the one he calls Delia. The exact social status of Delia can, like Cynthia's, be argued about. But she is not dissimilar to Cynthia, probably a freedwoman, and presented to us as highly materialistic and of course essentially urban. And yet we now learn that she is part of Tibullus' vision of rural life, indeed as poem 2 reveals to us, an essential part of his vision of rural life: he would wish to rough it in the country, he says, *provided* that Delia is there. Here is the reason why the rural wish cannot be realized: it proves to contain an incompatible element—Delia: 'But I am held a prisoner . . . and take my post as keeper at her door' (cf. 1. 55-6). In the first place this fact is offered as a reason why Tibullus cannot go on campaign with Messalla. But clearly a man bound to an urban mistress's door cannot simultaneously be a man of country pursuits on his rural estate.

Delia precludes Tibullus' wish being realized. So we have discovered. We have also discovered a source of tension that pervades Tibullus's life and fuels his poetry, and makes him a romantic visionary to be compared (and contrasted) with Propertius. Propertius tried to see in Cynthia a mythical figure, an attempt doomed to fail in the face of reality. Tibullus tried to see in Delia a figure compatible with his rural aspirations, an attempt also doomed to fail in the face of reality. And he, like Propertius, had moments when he knew the truth only too well. Poem 5 provides the fullest description of Tibullus' rural and erotic vision: life in the country, with Delia taking a wifely part in the harvest, and so on. But the description concludes: 'haec mihi fingebam'—it was all a dream. Tibullus has been quoting his former vision with bitter irony, in a present mood of cruel self-knowledge.

Tibullus, we have sensed, is concerned to be different from Propertius in the way he provokes conventional sensibility. He is also concerned to be even more provoking. Take the question of 'servility': Propertius professes his slavery as an unwilling burden, and has in mind psychological bondage. Tibullus talks actually of the physical humiliations meted out to slaves, and seems masochistically willing to accept them at the hands of his mistress. Tibullus, too, moves on to a different and worse mistress: Nemesis, harder, more rapacious, and more mercenary than Delia.

We might have thought that esteem for the country and love of his own estate were constants in Tibullus' life. Not so. Through Nemesis Tibullus shows us that love can make the romantic abjure not only society's values but his own. In 2.3 a rival has taken Nemesis off to a country villa, at harvest time. Tibullus' response is to curse the country's fruitfulness, to curse what he has hitherto supremely valued. There are other instances like this—and Nemesis causes Tibullus to perform abrupt about-turns on other cherished points as well: for example, he will reverse his declared views on mercenariness in love, if that is what she wants. The most poignant reversal, however, comes in 2.4. Should Nemesis want it, he would even sell off the beloved family estate. Delia had rendered the rural aspiration unrealizable, by being part of it. Nemesis can make him simply and completely abandon it. Such can be the destructive power of romantic love. So Tibullus suggests.

Tibullus produces yet a third lover to whom he is exclusively devoted, a boy, Marathus; and for this boy he demonstrates as intense and abject a love as he and Propertius had for their mistresses. This is a remarkable fact. Of course, homosexual love is often enough professed, by Horace and Catullus among others. But among the love poets it is normally considered a slight business, a sideline, not a thing to engage emotions and passions. What we are observing is Tibullus once more upping the stakes in the game of provocation. Not only does he profess devoted love for three lovers. He exhibits himself as the abject romantic lover of a mere boy.

In fact the affair with Marathus presents Tibullus at perhaps his most abject—and amusing. The relationship is triangular: Tibullus loves Marathus, while Marathus loves a girl, Pholoe; and, to ingratiate himself, Tibullus gives the boy servile and humiliating assistance in his affair with the girl.

We need not doubt the real base of Tibullan poetry in Tibullan experience. But it is also clear that this experience is organized and orchestrated to interest and provoke, in particular in comparison with Propertius (Propertius, similarly, had presented his experience with an eye on Catullus): to interest and provoke—and, sometimes, to amuse. The word crept into the previous paragraph, and humour is perhaps quite pervasive in Tibullus. The kind and degree of Tibullus' humiliations, of his masochistic assertions, all neatly narrated, preclude total earnestness. There is hyperbole here, consideration for humorous effect. And it is all 'neatly narrated': Tibullus' grovelling words to his lovers, and indeed his prayers to be a rustic, are dressed in the urbanest of styles. That suggests a certain Tibullan distance from the Tibullan story, a wink in our direction.

Ovid

It has often been said that Ovid was anti-Augustan. The label is not exactly appropriate. Ovid was indeed irreverent towards Augustus' state, laws, image. But he was irreverent towards any solemn and sitting target.

Ovid came from an old equestrian family, and began a public career, but he soon abandoned it for poetry. He was assisted in his youth by Messalla, and his later books bow in the direction of Augustus and his house. But the evidence suggests that he never maintained a position with a literary circle, even to the extent that Propertius did. He had no need to: his work was instantly popular, and he had no economic problems. And his exuberant spirit was probably best served by such non-involvement.

His first poems, the elegiac *Amores*, were published in two editions: the first was begun about 25 BC and issued over the next ten years or so; the second and smaller edition (the one which we possess) was published about the turn of the millennium.

Ovid's irreverence is instantly visible in these poems, its potential catholicity already guessable. The most obvious targets here are, not conventional moralists, but the romantic elegists, the old protesters themselves. Ovid presents himself in the first book as a lover and poet in the tradition of Propertius and Tibullus, in devoted thraldom to one mistress, whom he calls Corinna. But what he actually gives us is parody. For example, Propertius and Tibullus had expressed their dissociation from public life, from war and the life of action ('soldiering'), by projecting themselves as 'soldiers' of love. Ovid gets hold of this expressive idea and probes it for ingenious and funny effects. How can a lover be represented as a soldier in detail? Poem 1.9, comparing lover and soldier, shows us. A sample:

> Tacticians recommend the night attack,
> use of the spearhead, catching the foe asleep . . .
> Lovers use them too—to exploit a sleeping husband,
> thrusting hard while the enemy snores.

This is a ludicrous, parodic exploitation of an elegiac motif. Other elegiac motifs (the slavery of the lover, the divinity of the beloved, and so on) are similarly treated. So is the Propertian use of myth: Propertius had evoked a romantic ideal of devotion by means of resonating myths; Ovid deploys resonating myths to depict beautiful legs.

In Books 2 and 3 of the *Amores* Ovid drops his mask and displays himself as a cheerfully promiscuous lover. Love is, or should be, simply fun—a game; and the books contain racy lectures and dramatic episodes illustrating it. In this we must observe, besides his dissimilarity to the romantic elegists, his similarity to Horace. Horace considered that love should be a game, even if it could turn out bitter-sweet. So Ovid is similar to Horace—but dissimilar too. Ovid took the game so to speak earnestly, committed time and trouble to it. He did not have things in perspective, Alcaeus-fashion. He even devoted a didactic treatise to the game of love, purporting to teach one how to play it—indulging an interest in the incongruous mixture of solemn didactic form and frivolous content that he displays in other works. This treatise was the 'Art of Love' (*Ars Amatoria*), first published about 9 BC and reissued about the time of the second edition of the *Amores*, not an auspicious time.

Such a didactic obviously affronts Horatian standards. And consistently and obviously, it affronts (once more) elegiac romanticism. And Ovid turns the knife. The cynical instructions of the *Ars* are repeatedly couched in terms that recall agonized elegiac devotion. For instance, the powerless elegist was forced to utter 'you are my only love'; Ovid instructs his pupils on how to *choose* someone to whom to say 'you are my only love'. But, in affronting the old protesters, the *Ars* also affronted Augustus, a very solemn target. So, probably, had the *Amores*.

The social status of Corinna and the other women in the *Amores* is as usual hard to pin down, but what seems clear is that she, and others, are described in a way that suggests they are legally married. The *Amores* therefore explicitly suggests adultery. Adultery, too, is obviously in mind in the *Ars*, despite an unconvincing statement to the contrary at the beginning of the poem and plangent protestations from exile. For exiled is what Ovid eventually was, and the *Ars* was adduced as part cause. His exile is hardly surprising. He writes in explicitly adulterous terms, in the second Augustan period, after Augustus' laws had made adultery criminal; he produces a second edition of *Ars*, and *Amores*, at about the time when Augustus' own daughter was banished for adultery (2 BC), and when the inefficacy of the laws was only too apparent. We can see that Ovid's adulterous line fits into a pattern of catholic and non-malicious irreverence—it is not 'anti-Augustan'. But to a gloomy and disappointed Augustus it might have appeared otherwise. It is perhaps a wonder that he took so long to react, but finally he did. In AD 8 Augustus' grand-daughter was also banished for

EROTIC SCENE on a Roman pottery lamp from the Naples area. Cheerful eroticism of a type which Ovid would have approved was a favourite theme of the Roman decorative arts in imperial times, appearing in media as different as relief-decorated ceramics and domestic wall-painting.

PHAEDRA AND HIPPOLYTUS: detail of a carved sarcophagus (late second century AD). The youthful Hippolytus (centre) is shunning the advances of his stepmother, conveyed by the old nurse beside him. At the left sits the love-struck Phaedra herself, with two Erotes (Cupids) in attendance; at the right a groom or companion holds Hippolytus' horse. The fourth of Ovid's *Heroides* is an imaginary love-letter in which Phaedra declares her passion.

adultery, and Ovid, guilty of perpetrating some 'mistake' as well as his poem ('carmen et error'), was banished too, to Tomis, from whence he dispatched bookloads of not wholly laudable laments.

In between the *Amores* and the *Ars* come the *Heroides*, Ovid's first experiment with mythical narrative. This is safer fare, nevertheless congenial to read. Ovid's basic idea was to invent letters (in elegiacs) from mythical heroines to their lovers: Ariadne to Theseus, Phaedra to Hippolytus, Dido to Aeneas, Penelope to Odysseus, and so on. The examples cited show the wide range of situations that he dealt with, providing himself with wide scope for his rhetorical ingenuity and facile emotive ability. Nor is the irreverent spirit suppressed. Ovid takes pains to translate Virgil's Dido into a much more easily sympathetic figure, and one indeed who spots that Aeneas is vulnerable in the matter of his first wife's death.

At approximately this time Ovid composed his now lost tragedy *Medea*. His first extant attempt to compose on a larger and more ambitious scale is the *Fasti*. This work can reasonably be dated to the years AD 1–4; it is also reasonable to see in it an effort to balance the recently republished erotic works with something less *risqué*. The *Fasti*, also in elegiacs, aimed to go through the Roman calendar offering 'causes' for events and nomenclature in the Roman year. Thus Ovid, who had light-heartedly adopted a Callimachean stance in the *Amores*, felt as Propertius had done before him that it might be prudent to attempt something at once seriously Callimachean and patriotic: the calendar offered ample pegs on which to hang praise of Rome and praise of Augustus. Irrepressible irreverence periodically mars or improves the poem, depending on one's point of view. It was never finished. Disinclination seems to have moved Ovid to abandon it, after six, instead of twelve, books. There were external factors to support or cause disinclination. The year AD 4 saw the adoption of Tiberius and therefore another set of laudatory allusions to include; and, on the calendar, the month of August loomed, a daunting prospect for a subject of Augustus. Ovid gave up.

But he did not give up poetry, nor even Callimachean poetry. Subsequent to the *Fasti* is the *Metamorphoses*, Ovid's great hexameter poem in fifteen books. Here he assembles dozens of attractive stories from myth, stories which end in the metamorphosis of characters into animals, plants, and other forms. The stories are linked together with ingenious transitions, so ingenious that progress can seem bewildering. The opening of the poem seems sequential (from the creation of the world, through Jupiter's punishment of sinful man, to Deucalion and Pyrrha), but soon we find ourselves conducted through the stories of Daphne, Io, Phaethon, and so on—all the way through to the metamorphosis of Julius Caesar into a god in Book 15.

What is this poem? By a judicious choice of words at the beginning Ovid surprisingly advertises it as something that Callimachus eschewed: a traditional epic. We expect, therefore, an epic in which the plot is serious and a single, unified, action unfolds objectively, an epic in which the consequences of actions follow; hence, a moral poem. It very soon transpires that the *Metamorphoses* is nothing of the sort. The advertisement was a spoof. The action of the poem is neither single nor serious, but a mass of disparate stories ingeniously, artificially linked and subjectively told—told with Ovidian wit, humour, and grotesqueness. And the consequences of actions do not follow. They end in the fantasy of metamorphosis. The poem is a gloriously amoral Callimachean collection got up in epic dress, an affront to the traditional epic genre.

As always, Ovid affronts. Here, in particular, there is irreverence towards Virgil's genre—and Virgil's material: in various ways the material of the *Aeneid* gets mauled. Another sitting and solemn target. There is, too, irreverence towards the house of Augustus, despite overt but unconvincing flattery. Jupiter compared to Augustus in one context is, within a few hundred lines, chasing a girl in another. Nor does the company in which Julius Caesar's 'metamorphosis' finds itself dignify it. And there is irreverence, in a sense, towards life: it is simply the material for amusing, amoral literature.

There is a great risk of assessing Ovid too negatively: he is, we say, parodic, irreverent, unserious, unAugustan, amoral, even immoral, merely rhetorical or ingenious. This can, and should be, rephrased. Ovid is funny. His immorality serves humour, and his parodies are the sort which direct laughter on to themselves, not the parodied original (see the example quoted above, p. 201). Ovid is a poet of 'art for art's sake': Ovid reveres technique, reveres art; and amorality is indispensable to the construction of a self-contained artistic experience. Un-Augustan? In a sense Ovid is the Augustan poet *par excellence*, particularly of the second period. Augustus' actions and legislations were designed to stem a tide, to combat a prevailing spirit. Ovid represents that spirit, pleasure-loving, sophisticated, and, it must be admitted, cynical. Horace, twenty-two years older than Ovid and belonging to a different generation, may draw a veil of silence over him. But Ovid's contemporaries did not. They praised him to the skies. For them he was the true Augustan poet.

Further Reading

The Loeb Classical Library provides texts with facing translations of all the poets discussed in this chapter. The following translations may also be recommended: Niall Rudd, *Horace, Satires and Epistles* (revd. edn. 1979); W. G. Shepherd, *Horace's Odes and Epodes* (1983); Guy Lee, *Tibullus: Elegies* (2nd edn. 1982), and *Ovid's Amores* (2nd edn. 1968); Rolfe Humphries, *Ovid, The Art of Love* (1957), *The Metamorphoses* (1955).

Indispensable to a full understanding of Horace is E. Fraenkel's *Horace* (Oxford, 1957), but David West's *Reading Horace* (Edinburgh, 1967) is perhaps the best introduction; comparably useful are Margaret Hubbard's *Propertius* (London, 1974) and L. P. Wilkinson's *Ovid Recalled* (Cambridge, 1955), abridged as *Ovid Surveyed* (Cambridge, 1962). Tibullus lacks any balanced introductory book; there is Francis Cairns' *Tibullus* (Cambridge, 1979) and David F. Bright's *Haec Mihi Fingebam, Tibullus in his World* (Leiden, 1978), but both these are idiosyncratic and the initiate is better served by the introduction to Guy Lee's translation.

The following books treat the period and its poetry (or aspects thereof) more generally: R. O. A. M. Lyne, *The Latin Love Poets from Catullus to Horace* (Oxford, 1980); K. Quinn, *Latin Explorations* (2nd edn. London, 1969); L. P. Wilkinson, *Golden Latin Artistry* (Cambridge, 1963); G. Williams, *Tradition and Originality in Roman Poetry* (Oxford, 1968), abridged as *The Nature of Roman Poetry* (Oxford, 1970). C. O. Brink, *Horace on Poetry*, vol. iii (Cambridge, 1982), pp. 523 ff., offers a masterly overview of the period, and vital illumination of the social background is provided by Jasper Griffin's *Latin Poetry and Roman Life* (London, 1985)

9
Virgil

JASPER GRIFFIN

Preamble

PUBLIUS VERGILIUS MARO, in English normally called Virgil, was a celebrated figure in his own lifetime, and soon after his death a number of writers
tried to satisfy the popular curiosity about the life of the greatest of Roman
poets. We are consequently much better informed about him than about most
poets in antiquity. Like most Roman writers, he was not born in Rome. He came
into the world in 70 BC, near Mantua, in what was still called Cisalpine Gaul.
Although thoroughly Romanized—we recall that Catullus came from Verona,
and Livy from Padua (Patavium)—the area did not receive the Roman citizenship
till 49, and it became officially part of Italy only in 42. Virgil's family seems to
have been respectable though by no means prominent. The ultimate origin of
the names 'Vergilius' and 'Maro' was probably Etruscan, but only the credulous
will try to explain the poet's art or his character by invoking Etruscan ancestry.

It is worth looking at the period through which Virgil lived. Born in the year
in which Pompey and Crassus forced their way into the consulship, he was seven
when Catiline fell fighting at the head of a revolutionary army opposing the
Roman legions. The gathering disorder of the 50s led to civil war; the assassination of Caesar to another, followed by proscriptions, by wars in Italy, and the
eventual victory of Octavian, after a third civil war, in 31. As late as 19, the year
of Virgil's death, there were serious riots in Rome. Of the fifty-one years of the
poet's life, sixteen were years of civil war; the proscriptions which followed the
battle of Philippi are said to have caused the deaths of at least 150 senators and
2,000 *equites*; considerable areas of Italy were devastated by fighting, by famine,
and by the forcible expropriation of land. It was a terrible period, in which even
the survival of Rome seemed to be in doubt, and that fact is of central importance
for Virgil's poetry.

The Eclogues

His first published work was a collection of ten bucolic *Eclogues*, which pro-
claim themselves as in the tradition of Theocritus (Vol. 1, pp. 350 ff.), but which

also echo and evoke many other poets, both Greek and Latin. The influence of Callimachus, for instance, is clear at the opening of the Sixth *Eclogue*, that of Lucretius in the middle of the same poem, that of Catullus in the Fourth. There were allusions to the work of other poets, contemporary or in the last generation, which we are not now in a position to recognize. Virgil is thus, at his first appearance, a learned poet. That was always to be his manner, and in antiquity some critics made names for themselves by sniping at the poet for his 'thefts', meaning plagiarism.

It is quite wrong to imagine that Virgil lacked originality, or that his poems are no more than imitations or distillations of the work of his predecessors. If we read the first five lines of the First *Eclogue* we find a good example of the creative reworking of a model. The countryman Meliboeus speaks to a friend who is singing of love, stretched out in the shade of a tree:

> Tityre, tu patulae recubans sub tegmine fagi
> siluestrem tenui Musam meditaris auena;
> nos patriae finis et dulcia linquimus arua:
> nos patriam fugimus; tu, Tityre, lentus in umbra
> formosam resonare doces Amaryllida siluas.

> Beneath a shady beech you may rehearse
> At ease, my Tityrus, your simple verse;
> I'm forced to leave my country and to roam,
> My Tityrus, from country and from home:
> You here can fill, at leisure in the shade,
> With Amaryllis' name the wooded glade.

At once we see that we both are, and are not, in the world of Theocritus. The Greek poet is the source of the names, and of the pastoral world of love and song; the languorously beautiful hexameters, with their melodious vowels and artfully simple repetitions, also owe a lot to Theocritus' inspiration. But the world of reality, of politics and suffering, has invaded the pastoral Arcadia in which nothing but love and song could happen. Why is Meliboeus not able to stretch out and sing? Because, it soon emerges, Rome has burst into his world. After the defeat of Brutus and Cassius in 42, the Caesarian party had to take care of the soldiers in the enormous armies which now looked to them for their reward. What the soldiers wanted was land, and that could only be found by ejecting its present owners. A recent calculation estimates that a quarter of the land of Italy changed hands in the proscriptions and evictions. Meliboeus, despite his pretty Greek name, is sufficiently Italian and contemporary to be among the ejected victims:

> A godless soldier has my cherished fields,
> A savage has my land: such profit yields
> Our civil war. For them we worked our land!
> Ay, plant your pears—to fill another's hand.

Tityrus has miraculously escaped the general disaster, thanks to a 'wonderful young man' in Rome, who secured him his land. For that, Tityrus had to go to Rome:

> Urbem quam dicunt Romam, Meliboee, putaui
> stultus ego huic nostrae similem, quo saepe solemus
> pastores ouium teneros depellere fetus . . .

> I used to think the city men call Rome
> Was like our market-town, to which we come
> On market days, and drive our kids to sell.
> O foolishness . . .

The lines, standing on the very first page of Virgil's published work, have a prophetic ring. The poet, like his rustic speaker, will discover Rome; and will find that Rome is something very different from the innocent joys and sorrows of country life. The imperial city, with its fabulous wealth and power, can at will reward or destroy. That will be a central problem for the *Aeneid*.

The *Eclogues* form a unified work of art, with a structure of its own. The number of poems is itself not a random one: the first book of Tibullus contains ten poems, so does the first book of *Satires* of Horace. A poet was expected to organize his work into a pleasing shape. The First *Eclogue*, as we have seen, is in the form of a dialogue: so are all the odd-numbered *Eclogues*. The even-numbered ones, on the other hand, are monologues. The fifth poem ends with a little recapitulation, the speaker presenting his friend with the pipes on which, he says, he played the second and third poems. That marks the half-way point, and a little break, comparable to that after the third of Horace's six Roman odes (*Odes* 3.1–6); as in that cycle of poems, the second half begins with a fresh scene of invocation, in this case not of the Muse but of Apollo. Another structure, also meant to be felt, centres on the Fifth *Eclogue* (allusion to the death and deification of Caesar), which is immediately framed by the two most ambitious and least simply pastoral poems, (iv and vi), and at furthest remove framed by two poems on the evictions (i and ix). The last poem, in this structure, stands rather outside the rest; it is explicitly introduced as 'my last pastoral song'.

As we have seen, the Ninth *Eclogue* returns to the theme of the evictions. Menalcas, a singer and translator of Theocritus, has been turned out of his property near Mantua. So far from saving his land by means of his song, he was lucky to escape with his life. Ever since antiquity people have tried to make the two *Eclogues* on the evictions into an autobiographical account by the poet of his own ejection and restoration to his Mantuan property. But it is surely clear that Virgil did not mean to produce such an account. Tityrus, restored by a super-human young man (who in real life could only be the nineteen- or twenty-year old Octavian) is elderly and a slave, in neither respect like Virgil; and he is balanced by Meliboeus, for whom no providential saviour averts disaster. And in the Ninth *Eclogue* Menalcas too, it seems, finds no remedy. The two poems would add up to a very odd way of saying 'Thank you' to Octavian. What Virgil has done, rather, is to show us scenes from the evictions, what is going on in the Italian countryside, filtered through the poetic medium provided by Theocritus. If we are to guess what happened to Virgil himself, it may seem likely that he lost his family land near Mantua, and was given by his patrons a property near Naples. That is where we find him living later on, one of a group of friends of the Epicurean philosopher Siro.

One point is a vital one for understanding Virgil. Already in the *Eclogues* he is working towards the special way of writing, which in the *Aeneid* he has perfected: a manner which allows the reader to see through the poetical surface to events and personalities of a different kind, which are never made fully explicit. So in the Fifth *Eclogue* two herdsmen sing of the death and deification of Daphnis, another name from Theocritus. Cruelly cut off and lamented by his mother, Daphnis becomes a god, a patron of peace, hailed as a divinity by all nature and by the country people. Daphnis was young, beautiful, a herdsman—a far cry from the middle-aged dictator Caesar. But so soon after the assassination and elevation to godhood of the most celebrated man in the world—descended from the goddess Venus—those spectacular events could not have been wholly out of the mind of Virgil's readers.

The Fourth *Eclogue* prophesies the return of the Golden Age. The poem is addressed to Asinius Pollio, an early patron of the poet, as a compliment to his entry on the consulship in 40 BC. Its exalted language draws on a wide variety of sources: oracles, Greek versions of Jewish prophecies, Etruscan techniques of divination, Platonic myths, Homer, Catullus. In Pollio's consulship the 'mighty months' will begin to roll: a child will be born, whose birth will be marked by miraculous signs, and whose growing up will be accompanied by the gradual blossoming of the age of Apollo. The earth shall produce all good things everywhere, without the need of agriculture; lions shall be harmless; venomous serpents shall cease to exist. War, too, shall cease, and the divine child shall rule the world. Many modern scholars think that this poem was written to celebrate the pact agreed at Brundisium in October 40 (above, p. 122), which included a marriage between Antony and Octavian's sister Octavia, and which averted the danger of war between the two men: the child of the poem will be the expected son of the new marriage. But a poem to honour a man's consulship should be ready for presentation on 1 January, not ten months later; and the striking parallels with Isaiah and other similar works show that this really is a Messianic poem. Such works are produced, not when successful political arrangements seem to have secured peace on earth, but when the earthly scene is so dark and hopeless that the mind turns away in despair to another order of thought. The Fourth *Eclogue* was for centuries believed to be a prophecy of the coming of Christ. The modern mind is unhappy with such notions; but perhaps that view comes closer to the real nature of the poem than it does to pin it to a specific political happening. Again Virgil is being deliberately evasive as to his exact meaning, and the sugges-

RELIEF OF MOTHER EARTH ON THE ARA PACIS (13–9 BC). The fruitfulness of the earth, portrayed in typical Hellenistic style with children in her arms, and fruit, flowers, and livestock all about her, is symbolic of the new Golden Age which Augustus sought to inaugurate and which recalls passages in the Augustan poets, such as the fourth *Eclogue* of Virgil. (Cf. below, pp. 369 f.)

tiveness of the poem is more effective than clarity would have been. And after all the treaty of Brundisium did not in the end mean lasting peace; while Octavia bore Antony two daughters, but no son. Virgil would have been surprisingly credulous if he had not thought of such possibilities.

The *Eclogues* can be ranged between two poles: some are fairly close to Theocritus (2, 3, and 7) others are further distanced but still Theocritean (8 and 9); at the other extreme some have very little contact with Theocritus at all (4 and 6). They all have in common a highly polished technique, in which Virgil shows that he has learnt everything that Theocritus, Callimachus, and Catullus had to teach him. The choice of words is punctilious, the sound of the verse is melodious, and there is a pervasive atmosphere of an exquisite and faintly melancholy beauty. The paintings of Claude Lorraine are perhaps the best analogy in another art; and he of course was much influenced by Virgil. It is a small but significant part of this that the first and last poems of the collections, and others in between, end with the coming of evening and the shadows lengthening from the hills.

Despite much scholarly endeavour, agreement is not possible on the order in which the *Eclogues* were composed. Their style does not enable us to extract many dates from the poems, which no doubt were polished to fit the positions they occupy in the final published collection. It is likely that the book of ten *Eclogues* was published about 38 BC; recent attempts to put the completion as late as 35 are not convincing. The poems seem to have been an immediate success. We are told that they were acted on the stage, and that the shy and evasive poet, on his rare appearances in Rome, was pointed at in the street. In the spring of 38, already an established writer, he introduced Horace to Maecenas, whose name does not appear in the *Eclogues*, but to whom Virgil was to dedicate his next work, the *Georgics*.

In the *Eclogues* Virgil addressed several great men: Asinius Pollio chiefly, but also Alfenus Varus. They both seem to be in the position of actual or potential patrons. In this respect Virgil resembles Horace rather than Catullus and (in his First Book) Propertius, who have no patrons but only friends. The poet Cornelius Gallus, who is praised in the Sixth *Eclogue*, also receives the supreme compliment of being the subject of the Tenth. In that poem Virgil presents the elegiac love poet as a pastoral lover in Arcadia, his amorous complaints transposed into Virgil's own metre, and the lover himself recalling Theocritus' Daphnis. The

PASTORAL LANDSCAPE BY CLAUDE LORRAINE (1645). The great seventeenth-century landscape painter was much influenced by Virgil, and this scene, with its group of shepherds (one playing the flute) and its grazing cattle and goats, perfectly catches the mood of the *Eclogues*.

procedure seems strange to us in poetry, but it would surprise us less in music: Virgil has written a variation in his own style on a theme by Gallus.

The Georgics

All that is in the past, once we turn to the *Georgics*. Lesser patrons must give way to Maecenas, friends are no longer named, and Octavian—never named and barely hinted at in the *Eclogues*—is now in the centre of the poet's view. Ancient scholars claimed to know the contents of Virgil's will, and they report that he left the very large sum of 10,000,000 sesterces, with substantial legacies to Maecenas and Augustus. No doubt they were the source of the poet's wealth. But it would be wrong to think of the relationship as primarily a financial one. In the second half of the 30s the relative position of Octavian and Antony gradually changed. The ruthless young heir of Caesar, who 'kills and keeps his temper' (a phrase which Dryden put into the mouth of Antony in *All for Love*), was cleverly transforming himself into the defender of western values against an Antony dead to decent feeling and going native in the East. The war of propaganda was lost by Antony before the battle of Actium. Maecenas, personally a luxurious, even a decadent figure, wrote verse himself, as such men usually do, in the manner of the poets of his own youth; he was of great value as an intermediary between Octavian and the poets. An artist must be flattered when the holders of power express interest in his work, and much more when the master of the world (as Octavian was after 31) is anxious to recruit his support for a programme of reform and restoration, which is to replace civil wars and disasters with peace and the good life. In their different ways Virgil, Horace, and Propertius all responded, more or less, to that most seductive appeal.

Virgil refers to the *Georgics* as 'your exacting command, Maecenas' ('tua, Maecenas, haud mollia iussa', 3.41). The phrase is hard to interpret. Obviously Maecenas did not 'command' the poet to write a poem in four books on agriculture, and Virgil also says of his writing:

> Sed me Parnasi deserta per ardua dulcis
> raptat amor; iuuat ire iugis, qua nulla priorum
> Castaliam molli deuertitur orbita cliuo. (3.291)

> But over high Parnassus' lonely crest
> Poetic rapture bears me: sweet to pass
> Where never wheel has marked the tender grass.

He wanted to produce the poem, and he felt confident that Maecenas would welcome it. For the poet it offered the challenge of a work on a large scale, some 2,000 lines in four roughly equal books, far exceeding the length not only of the *Eclogues* but also of anything ever attempted by Horace, Propertius, or Tibullus. In a period deeply marked by the Callimachean rejection of the long poem (Vol. 1, p. 355), that was a striking departure. The subject-matter was challenging, too. For Catullus and his friends, the word 'rustic' had stood for all that was uncouth, ill bred, boring—both in manners and in poetry. Could the homespun rustic verse of Hesiod (Vol. 1, pp. 82 ff.) be transformed into a Latin poem which would satisfy the aesthetic demands of Virgil and his audience? He was not aiming to translate Hesiod, nor simply to paraphrase him and dress him up in more elegant poetic form. Hesiod had made his practical instructions on sowing and reaping part of a moral picture of life, with hard work and traditional piety. Virgil, too, will produce a vision of a way of life, based on work, and embodying the old virtues which made Rome great: piety, tenacity, patriotism, genuineness. It must combine exact vision and description of detail, without the golden haze of beautiful generality which so often marks the *Eclogues*, and also a grand style, elevated but not hollow, for moral and poetical set-pieces. As for Maecenas and Octavian, they would have preferred an epic on Octavian's war-like feats: in the prologue to *Georgic* 3 Virgil promises that 'soon' he will write it. But the *Georgics* not only praised Octavian in glittering eulogy, but also endorsed a view of Italian and Roman life which was, in general terms, highly acceptable to him. The age of civil war must be over, and Octavian must heal a world turned upside down (1. 500). Then the vices of ambition and greed must be rooted out in favour of modesty and hard work (2. 165 ff., 458 ff.). On all that, Virgil's poem and Octavian's policy were agreed. Of course, neither of them will have expected that educated readers of the *Georgics* would rush out to buy small farms and start ploughing with their own hands.

The *Georgics* were completed in 29 BC, and some passages were clearly written after the Battle of Actium. Virgil had been at work on the poem for seven years or so, a length of time which implies constant revision and slow progress. For facts he had prose works on agriculture at his disposal. Especially valuable was Varro's *De re rustica*, a systematic treatise packed with information, far more exhaustive and practically useful than the *Georgics*. Varro's work could also give the poet other hints, as the First Book opens with the characters looking at a map of Italy (cf. *Georg.* 2. 135 ff.), and ends with the random murder of one of them in the street, a vivid instance of the violence and lawlessness which Virgil laments in his poem.

The first book of the *Georgics* has some close echoes of Hesiod, to establish the colouring of the whole. 'Nudus ara, sere nudus' ('Strip to plough and strip to sow', 1. 299) which was found very comical in antiquity, is an exact translation of a quaint Hesiodic line. Hesiod told how Zeus made life hard for men as a piece of vengeance, and laughed aloud as he did so (Vol. 1, p. 90); Virgil prefers to tell how Jupiter made life hard for man's ultimate good, 'ut uarias usus meditando extunderet artes' ('that need and thought should useful arts devise', 1. 133). Virgil's Jupiter is more benevolent than Hesiod's Zeus. But even in this book there is far less of Hesiod than there is of Theocritus in the *Eclogues*. Lucretius, the great Latin poet of the last generation, is far more pervasive.

Virgil is careful to be selective. What appears to start out as a list of the necessary equipment (1. 160 ff.) actually includes only half a dozen tools, and those are mostly chosen for having a connection in Greek poetry which ennobles them: not 'a cart', but 'the slow rolling waggon of the Mother of Eleusis' (because in the great Eleusinian procession (Vol. 1, pp. 262 f.) waggons were used); not 'a winnowing fan', but 'the mystic fan of Iacchus' (a minor Eleusinian deity). Virgil is anxious to avoid being dragged down from the high style by his humble subject matter. He also embellishes his material by many stylistic devices. When, for example, he is explaining that it is important to rotate crops, as some plants exhaust the soil, he creates out of this unpromising idea an exquisitely shaped couplet:

> urit enim campum lini seges, urit auenae,
> urunt Lethaeo perfusa papauera somno.
> (1. 77–8)

> Flax burns, and oats will burn, the fertile ground:
> No less burn heavy poppies, slumber-drowned.

The repetition of the verb, the shaping of the sentence, the unusual rhythm of the last line which goes with the drowsy poppies, all work together to impose a formal unity and beauty.

He also varies the work with great skill. The passages on actual rustic work alternate with all kinds of more obviously 'poetical' passages—on the zones of the globe, on storms, on winter in the Scythian snows, on the glories of Italy. Some of them are both lengthy and highly ambitious in style, the poet trying his wings for his future epic. The most spectacular come at crucial points in the structure of the whole. Book 1 opens with an elaborate invocation of the gods, including a startlingly fulsome address to Octavian. Book 3 opens with a long passage on the epic which Virgil will write in the future. By designed contrast, the second and fourth books have very short introductions, and each has a long poetic excursus at the end. Book 2 closes with an emotional passage extolling the life of the farmer ('O all too happy, if they knew their luck!'), contrasting rustic innocence with the vicious luxury of the city, and extolling the lot of the poet who (like Virgil) knows the rustic gods. Book 4 ends with the epyllion of Aristaeus, to which we shall return. Other set pieces are darker in tone. At the end of Book 1, an account of the weather signs which the farmer needs to know runs into an emotional treatment of the fearsome portents which marked the divine anger at the assassination of Julius Caesar, the guilt of Rome which is punished by civil war, and a fervent prayer for the survival and success of Octavian, the only hope of the world. Book 3 closes with a grisly account of the ravages of plague among cattle, arising from some apparently simple instructions for preserving the health of one's animals. The four books thus end with alternating passages of gloom and hope, a structure which has often been compared to that of a great work of music.

It would be wrong, though, to think of the *Georgics* as consisting of unpoetical instruction, enlivened by purple patches of poetry. Virgil has shot through the instructions with all sorts of devices of variety. The tone is constantly changing, from mock-solemnity and humour to pathos and indignation. Vivid pictures—of clouds, snakes, birds, horses—are enlivened by echoes of military language, or Ennius, or Hellenistic verse. The poet constantly looks at events from the standpoint of the animals he describes. An example in Book 3: Virgil follows his sources in advising that bulls and stallions should be kept from dissipating their energies by sexual indulgence:

> The female saps their vigour as they gaze;
> The bulls look on her and forget to graze,
> So sweet are her enticements: in her sight
> The haughty rivals for her favour fight.
>
> (3. 215–18)

The passage goes on to develop the battle of the bulls, the chagrin of the loser 'in distant exile, groaning for the shame of defeat and the loss of his love', his practising, and his eventual thunderous return.

In the fourth book the bees are handled in much the same way. Varro's work shows that bee-keeping was only one branch of specialized farming, listing it along with the raising of chickens, pigeons, peacocks, dormice, hares, deer, edible snails, and fancy fish. Virgil ignores all but the bees: for they are an image of human life, orderly and public-spirited. They are treated with a mixture of sympathy, admiration, and irony. The book ends with a great surprise, the epyllion of Aristaeus. The poet tells that, if one's bees die, a new swarm will be forthcoming from the correct treatment of the corpse of an ox. This fantastic procedure was discovered by the legendary hero Aristaeus, whose bees all died to punish him (as he discovers) for causing the death of Orpheus' wife Eurydice. The story of Orpheus' descent to the Underworld to fetch her back, his fatal turning to look at her, his second and final loss, and his death, is told in Virgil's most magical verse. It seems to have been Virgil who first said that Orpheus failed to revive his wife. Why he ended the *Georgics* with this tale, narrated at a length of nearly 250 verses, is not easy to say. A possible reason is that he wanted to give another side of the vision of the virtuous, patriotic bees, 'little Romans' ('paruos Quirites') as he calls them: these impersonal creatures, sexless and free from passion, who kill themselves with work and gladly die for the community, can be brought back from death: 'the race is immortal', as the poet says. But something is irreparably lost: the beautiful Eurydice and her lover, the musician Orpheus. Irreplaceable individuals, passionate and creative, they are the prey of death. Such an interpretation would be in line with an important strand in the *Aeneid*, with its bitter awareness of the conflict between fate's impersonal purposes and the passions of the human heart.

The Aeneid

Virgil was still working on his epic when in 19 BC he died. We are credibly told that at the last he asked his friends to burn his unfinished poem. Antiquity did not share our romantic interest in fragmentary and suggestive works of art, and ancient writers, like ancient artists, aimed to offer the public works as perfect as they could make them. An obvious mark of its unfinished state is the presence, unevenly distributed through the poem, of metrically incomplete lines: lines, that is, to which the poet intended to return. Some of them are very effective, and romantic readers have been tempted to think that Virgil would have left them; but that is an idea which would not have occurred to him, any more than it occurred to any of his imitators in antiquity to include incomplete lines in their poems. He did not, however, intend to carry the story further forward than the point it reaches at the end of Book 12.

Maecenas tried to induce each of the poets to produce an epic on Augustus: none of them complied. That fact alone shows that the pressure was civilized. We are not in the world of Stalin and the Writers' Union. Virgil was unlike Horace and Propertius in that from the beginning he did talk in terms of writing a martial epic 'one day' (*Eclogues* 4. 54; 8. 6-10), whereas they always made it clear that they could not, or would not. In the introduction to the third book of the *Georgics* he seemed to undertake that he would write it 'soon'. But in the event he produced something quite different: a mythical epic on the ultimate origins of Rome. Augustus, we know, followed its progress with impatience, begging to be shown portions of it. He accepted, that is, that the *Aeneid* really was the fulfilment of his own wish; and he was right.

Virgil had come to see that it was not possible to write an epic of which Augustus should be the central figure, and which should satisfy the highest artistic demands. The framework of an epic must be the Homeric poems, and that entailed both the constant presence of the gods as characters, and also hand-to-hand fighting among heroic warriors. But to intrude divine councils and interventions into very recent history would be a jarring fault of taste, constantly risking bathos and absurdity; so, too, would the representation of Augustus mowing down thousands with his own strong right arm. Again, the plain fact was that the battle of Actium was unsatisfactory as a theme for verse. Not only did Augustan propaganda insist that it be represented not as a civil war but as a war with the Queen of Egypt, which was universally known to be untrue; there also apparently was hardly any fighting, some contingents changing sides at the last moment, and Cleopatra suddenly sailing away in flight. Nor, finally, could Virgil have found a central role for his great talent for pathos. If Augustus were the hero, there could be little sympathy for the defeated, and no ambiguity about his triumph. Cleopatra could not be treated as sympathetically as Dido. And Virgil was to succeed in making a natural flair for the pathos of loss and defeat into a central feature, not only of the decoration of the *Aeneid*, but also of its interpretation of imperialism and of history.

The chief difficulty about the creation of the *Aeneid* was that of writing a poem which at one level should be a mythical epic about the distant past, yet which should also be about the present and the future. The difficulty was so great that Virgil said in a letter that he must have been mad to attempt it. The poem was to be all-embracing, drawing upon both *Iliad* and *Odyssey*, Attic tragedy, Hellenistic poetry, and Latin predecessors, especially Naevius and Ennius; it was to be permeated by philosophical ideas from the Greek thinkers; it must be strongly marked by Roman history and characteristically Roman values; and Virgil was anxious also to include not only Rome but also Italy, with its geography, its peoples, and its virtues. Roman history must be presented as a crescendo leading up to Augustus, a thousand years in the future. Finally, the whole poem must be written in a style grand yet flexible, showing its author's familiarity with all preceding literature.

Romans believed that their city was founded in the eighth century BC, Romulus being the actual founder, but some places in Latium had for centuries believed that their origins went back to Troy: after the sack of the city, fleeing Trojans came to the West. Such beliefs were indeed widespread all over the Mediterranean, as non-Greek peoples became sophisticated enough to wish to attach themselves somehow to the great cycles of Greek legend. (In the Middle Ages this continued to be true: Britons descended from the Trojan Brut, for example.) Some aristocratic families at Rome claimed to have migrated there from other Latin cities, and to trace their ancestry back to Troy, among them the Julii. Now, the story of Romulus was not very suitable for an epic, and it had no direct link with Augustus. Aeneas, who actually is a character in the *Iliad*, was a much better hero; and through the Julii he was Augustus' ancestor. A great drawback, however, was that Aeneas could not found Rome, as scholars put the fall of Troy 400 years earlier, in the twelfth century BC. Aeneas can only found Lavinium, from which in time Rome will derive. Virgil turns this difficulty to account brilliantly in Book 8, when Aeneas is entertained by an ally on the very site which will be that of Rome. The hero is shown the Capitol and all the places which will become opulent and celebrated, now green hills and trees. The touching scene is programmatic: Aeneas must live for a future he will not live to see.

The epic starts with Aeneas and his Trojans on their sea-journey to the West. The poet opens with a weighty introduction:

> Arms and the man I sing, who, forced by Fate
> And haughty Juno's unrelenting hate,
> Expelled and exiled, left the Trojan shore.
> Long labours, both on land and sea, he bore . . .
> (trans. Dryden).

THE BUILDING OF LAVINIUM, depicted in a painted frieze from a Roman tomb on the Esquiline (mid first century BC). The frieze showed episodes from the foundation legend of Rome and is of exceptional interest as testimony of the stock of stories available when Virgil came to compose his *Aeneid*. The city goddess is seated at the centre.

A mighty warrior with a destined mission, the hero is persecuted by a hostile goddess: and more than that, he is 'famous for his *pietas*', and even that quality—in English 'sense of duty', 'devotion'—does not protect him. Virgil goes on to remonstrate, shocked by the theology of his own story:

> O Muse! tell why the queen of heaven began
> To persecute so brave, so just a man:
> What grievance must his suffering assuage?
> Can heavenly spirits feel such human rage?

The hostility of Juno arises, we learn, from personal pique: Ganymede, Jupiter's paramour, and Paris, who judged the beauty contest of the goddesses and gave the prize to Venus over Juno, were Trojans. But also she favours Carthage and hopes to frustrate the plan of Jupiter and Fate to confer dominion on Rome.

Aeneas had long been famous for his 'piety', and he was often depicted in the act of carrying his old father on his shoulders out of burning Troy. Virgil makes him also carry the Trojan *penates*, resident gods who are to take up their new home in Italy. *Pius* is his regular epithet in the poem (Virgil suggests but does not copy the Homeric use of 'formulaic' epithets: Vol. I, pp. 60 ff.), meaning that he above all men identifies his will with the plans of Fate. His sufferings in the poem, in which he is ship-wrecked, forced to fight a hateful war with the people of Italy, and to abandon the woman he loves, are thus clearly unjust. We hear him complain to his mother, the goddess Venus, when she has appeared to him in disguise: the episode will illustrate the way in which Virgil uses and transforms Homeric material. Asked who he is, Aeneas replies bitterly 'Sum pius Aeneas' ('I am the dutiful Aeneas') and goes on to complain that in obedient pursuit of his destiny he has seen his ships wrecked and himself cast up on an unknown African shore. His mother sharply rebukes him for his complaints. As she turns away and leaves him she allows him to recognize her, too late, and he pursues her with reproaches: why will she never stay with him? The scene, occurring in Book 1, is programmatic. It is based on several Homeric motifs: the scene in *Odyssey* 9 when Odysseus identifies himself to the listening Phaeacians ('I am Odysseus, famous everywhere for my clever tricks'); the relationship between Achilles and his goddess mother Thetis; and several scenes where gods

AENEAS AND ANCHISES: carved gemstone of the Roman imperial period. The motif of the Trojan hero carrying his father on his shoulder and leading his son Ascanius (Iulus) by the hand became a popular subject in art after the publication of Virgil's *Aeneid*, in which the dramatic episode of Aeneas' escape from Troy is described in Book 2. The composition seems to have been used for a famous statue-group in Augustus' Forum.

allow their identity to be realized only as they turn away. But Odysseus' boast is a proud and justifiably confident one, and Thetis is a different sort of mother from Venus—she truly understands her son, comes when he calls, and never deceives him. Virgil has created from these Homeric hints a scene of great poignancy, which shows us the whole position of Aeneas. He is struggling to carry out the apparently arbitrary orders of heaven; and he is lonely. That combination is an explosive one, and we are meant to understand how it follows that the next thing that happens to Aeneas is that he falls in love.

He has been driven ashore at Carthage, were Dido, a glamorous and heroic widowed queen, is founding her new city. Aeneas' wife disappeared in the confusion at the fall of Troy. Humanly, the two seem made for each other, even without the interference of the meddling goddesses. Juno hopes that Aeneas will

THE STORY OF DIDO AND AENEAS:
fourth-century AD mosaic found at Low Ham
in Somerset. The events are related counter-
clockwise from the bottom right, beginning
with the arrival of Aeneas' ships on the
African coast. At the top Venus supervises the
meeting of Aeneas and the Carthaginian
queen, at the left they go hunting, and at the
bottom they embrace while sheltering from
the storm described in Virgil's *Aeneid* 4. In the
central octagon Venus is flanked by Cupids
with lowered and raised torches, symbolizing
respectively the death of Dido and the
continuing life of Aeneas.

DIDO AND AENEAS IN THE CAVE:
illustration from a manuscript of Virgil in the
Vatican Library (*c.*AD 500). The immense
importance and popularity of the *Aeneid* in
imperial times is attested by the flourishing
manuscript tradition as well as by the frequent
echoes in the visual arts. The cave, which had
to be omitted in the Low Ham mosaic, can be
portrayed without difficulty in the
polychrome painting.

stay in Carthage and not found Rome; Venus, that Dido will be nice to her son. Together they push Dido to fall in love with Aeneas. Like Odysseus (*Odyssey* 9–12) he tells the story of his adventures, starting with Troy's fall (*Aen.* 2–3). Odysseus' audience listened with pleasure to the narration of exciting tales; Virgil adds the emotional point that, like Desdemona, Dido comes to love Aeneas as he tells her of the dangers he has passed. Juno is an unscrupulous enemy of the Trojans and anxious to frustrate the will of Jupiter and Fate, and we now see that Venus is essentially no different. She is on the right side because it happens that Aeneas is her son, but not for the right reason; and at Carthage she gets him into a terrible difficulty.

The fourth book of the *Aeneid* is the tragedy of Dido. Virgil is here strongly influenced by Euripides' Medea and by other unhappy heroines, including the Medea of Apollonius of Rhodes (Vol. 1, p. 353). Dido is overwhelmed by her love, and Aeneas (we infer) drifts into a passionate affair with her. He is seen by disapproving neighbours and gods dressed up in Carthaginian crimson and gold, Dido's gift, actually helping to found Carthage (4.259). Dido, indeed, claims that they are married; though Aeneas is able to say, when the gods push him into leaving, that he never went through a regular marriage ceremony with her. Virgil was in a tight corner here. Aeneas cannot abandon a wife, but Dido cannot be allowed to carry on light-heartedly with a lover. The poet has dealt with the difficulty by constructing a situation which both is and is not a marriage. Out on a boar-hunt, Dido and Aeneas are driven by a storm to take shelter together in a cave. Juno, goddess of marriage, is present as *pronuba* (matron of honour); the nymphs raise a cry; lightning flashes, and the sky was 'conscious witness to their union' ('conscius aether conubiis'). In a sense, that is a marriage; in another important sense it is not. But we are meant to think, when Aeneas advances that plea to her, that he has sailed very close to the wind. The book is dominated by a series of passionate speeches by Dido, of reproach, entreaty, bitterness, curses. The hero speaks only once, pleading the imperative instructions of Jupiter. There is nothing else he can say. He is right to go, but he does not cut a good figure. As he sails hastily away, Dido invokes eternal enmity between Carthage and Rome, and kills herself.

Aeneas finally lands in Italy in Book 6, and is immediately told to visit the Underworld. The sombre splendours of this book lead him through the stages of his past life, meeting his own dead, as well as the traditional inhabitants of the lower world. He is not spared a terrible encounter with Dido, who in death refuses to forgive him or to speak to him, and at last turns away to the company of her first husband, 'who answered her cares and matched her love'. A last bitter twist of the knife: even Dido is better off than the isolated Aeneas. This is the only happy marriage we ever see in the *Aeneid*; and it is among the dead. Aeneas is left in no doubt that he destroyed Dido, and he can only say that he did not intend it.

In the second half of the poem he will find himself destroying other things, too. Juno stirs up a fearful war with a coalition of Italian peoples, and Books 9 to 12 are full of epic fighting. Aeneas finds an unexpected ally, an aged Greek king named Euander, who entrusts his son Pallas to the hero, to learn from him to be a warrior. Pallas is killed, and Aeneas feels bitterly responsible. He himself is forced to kill the attractive young Etruscan prince Lausus, who persists in attacking him to rescue his own father: Aeneas weeps over Lausus' body. He tries repeatedly to make peace with King Latinus and his recalcitrant people, but they break the truce and force him into battle. His fighting rage is at last aroused, and he slaughters great numbers of the Italians; yet these are peoples who are to live together in peace, and the war is horrible, a kind of civil war. The poem ends with another masterly transformation of a Homeric scene. The Italian champion Turnus finally comes face to face with Aeneas, in a duel deliberately reminiscent of the duel between Achilles and Hector. Turnus is wounded, he falls; he admits defeat and begs for his life. Aeneas is about to spare him, his fighting rage is subsiding—and then he sees round Turnus' waist the belt which he stripped from the body of Pallas when he slew him. Inflamed with anger, Aeneas avenges the death of his young friend by killing Turnus, and the epic ends with the lines

> A deadly chill his loosening limbs invades:
> His soul lamenting passes to the shades.

Such an ending reminds us that in the *Iliad* Hector was killed in Book 22, and that two books followed in which Achilles came to terms, first with the other Achaeans, and then with his enemy Priam. Here there is no such healing process of reconciliation, and the work ends with the act of killing—an act which could easily have been made less disturbing. Turnus is a killer, and his death is just; but Aeneas would have liked to spare him, if he could. That is Virgil's deepest reflection on the nature of imperialism: that it is a hard and lonely destiny, in which the conqueror repeatedly finds himself destroying what he would prefer to spare. By his victory Aeneas wins the hand of the young princess Lavinia, an *ingénue* who had been betrothed to Turnus, and who never speaks in the poem. Unlike Odysseus' wife Penelope, and unlike the Dido he has been forced to leave and to destroy, this young girl will not be a wife to console the loneliness of the battered hero—who in any case will live for only three years.

It would be superficial to regard the *Aeneid* as anti-imperialist or anti-Augustan. The message of the poem is that the domination of Rome over the world is willed by heaven, and that it will impose peace and civilization (*mos, ius*). Virgil devises a series of forward perspectives through history, to make this vision real. In Book 1 Jupiter reveals to Venus the plans of Fate: a Roman Empire without limits in time or space, and Augustus as its climax, a future god. In Book 6 Aeneas' dead father shows him the spirits of the unborn Romans of the future, who will conquer the world and, renouncing to the Greeks the fine arts, practise the arts of rule, putting down the proud and sparing the conquered. At the end of Book 8 Aeneas is brought a marvellous shield, the work of Vulcan, on which

WOUNDED AENEAS: painting from the House of Siricus at Pompeii (between AD 62 and 79), closely based on a passage in Latin poetry (Virgil, *Aeneid*, 12. 383–416). All the main motifs (Aeneas leaning on a tall spear, his son weeping beside him, the doctor trying to operate with a forceps, Venus descending with a sprig of healing dittany) occur in Virgil's description of this episode in the final battle between Aeneas and Turnus.

are depicted the wars of Rome, with the battle of Actium in the centre (brilliantly represented as a tableau, not a narrative). And in Book 12 Juno at last abandons her hostility to Rome, and she and Jupiter agree that the Italians, far from being simply defeated by the Trojans, shall contribute the native Italian toughness and valour to form the unique essence of Rome—'Italian hardihood shall make Rome great':

Sit Romana potens Itala uirtute propago.

Other poets might have produced fine poetry on the greatness of conquest and dominion. The supremacy of the *Aeneid*, and its continuing importance when the Roman Empire has turned out after all to be less than eternal, depends on two things. One is the haunting beauty of Virgil's verse, never equalled in Latin literature; the other is his ability to present at the same time, with justice but also with passion, both the achievement of Empire and also its inevitable human cost. The exquisite balance comes out clearly when Aeneas is brought the shield, glittering with the representation of Rome's martial history, culminating in the figure of Augustus receiving tribute from a conquered world. Aeneas marvels at the wonderful work, but of course he cannot really understand it, as these events have not yet happened; but he must bear the weight of them:

> These figures, on the shield divinely wrought,
> By Vulcan laboured, and by Venus brought,
> With joy and wonder fill the hero's thought.
> Unknown the names, he yet admires the grace;
> His shoulder bears the fame and fortune of his race.
>
> > (trans. Dryden, adapted).

Such was Virgil's fame that a number of spurious poems were ascribed to him. At least one, the *Culex*, was a deliberate fake, widely accepted as Virgilian within eighty years of the poet's death. Others make no pretence of Virgilian authorship,

DETAIL OF A MOSAIC PAVEMENT (fourth century AD) in the villa at Lullingstone, Kent. The scene of Europa and the bull is accompanied by an inscription in faultless Latin elegiacs which presupposes a knowledge, even here in the remote province of Britain, of Virgil's *Aeneid*: 'If jealous Juno had seen the swimming of the bull, more justly would she have repaired to the halls of Aeolus.' This alludes to Juno's mission to the god of the winds in *Aeneid* 1.

and it seems that the attribution was simply the result of an insatiable desire in the reading public for more poems by Rome's greatest writer. Several are quite interesting in their own right, notably the *Copa*, a short hedonistic piece about the charms of a dancer at a country inn, and the *Ciris*, a self-consciously decadent epyllion about a girl betraying her country for love. The only members of the collection with any chance of being by Virgil are one or two of the very short pieces collectively known as the *Catalepton* ('In the Slender Style'). Certainty about them will never be reached.

Further Reading

The standard text of Virgil is the Oxford Classical Text of R. A. B. Mynors. Dryden's translation is splendid in rhetoric and verse, though it is often rather far from the Latin, and his rhyming couplets inevitably impose a different movement on Virgil's hexameters. C. Day Lewis translated all of Virgil into readable modern verse: *Eclogues* and *Georgics*, with an Introduction by R. O. A. M. Lyne (Oxford, 1983); *Aeneid*, with an Introduction by J. Griffin (Oxford, 1986). There are good versions of the *Eclogues* by Guy Lee (Liverpool, 1980); of the *Georgics* by L. P. Wilkinson (Harmondsworth, 1982) and Robert Wells (Manchester, 1982); and of the *Aeneid* by Robert Fitzgerald (London, 1984).

Virgil is the subject of an immense modern literature, much of it speculative and idiosyncratic. J. Griffin's *Virgil* (Oxford 1986, in the Past Masters series) deals particularly with the poet's ideas. The *Cambridge History of Classical Literature* ii (1982), 297-369 gives a generally reliable account of the poet and his works (but it is not, as is there stated, certain that the *Eclogues* were published in 35 BC). The poet's early life is well treated in the second chapter of L. P. Wilkinson, *The Georgics of Virgil* (Cambridge, 1969: paperback); the historical and political background in R. Syme's classic *The Roman Revolution* (Oxford, 1939: paperback).

The Introduction to Robert Coleman's edition of the *Eclogues* (Cambridge, 1977) is very helpful. L. P. Wilkinson's book on the *Georgics* is the best on that poem. A useful approach to the *Aeneid*: W. A. Camps, *An Introduction to Virgil's Aeneid* (Oxford, 1969: paperback). W. Y. Sellar, *Virgil* (Oxford, 1877) is a good example of solid Victorian criticism; Brooks Otis, *Virgil: A Study in Civilized Poetry* (Oxford, 1963) is more subjective. A good collection of papers: *Virgil, a Collection of Critical Essays*, edited by S. Commager (Eaglewood Cliffs, NJ, 1966; paperback). T. S. Eliot's essay 'What is a Classic?' appears in his book *On Poets and Poetry* (London, 1951). Gordon Williams, *Tradition and Originality in Roman Poetry* (Oxford, 1968) illuminates many passages in Virgil, and in other authors. See also R. O. A. M. Lyne, *Further Voices in Virgil's Aeneid* (Oxford, 1987).

Important commentaries have appeared recently: on *Aeneid* 1, 2, 4, and 6 by R. G. Austin; on 3 and 5 by R. D. Williams; on 7 and 8 by C. J. Fordyce (all Oxford University Press); also on 8 by K. W. Gransden (Cambridge, 1976). R. D. Williams has published a shorter commentary on the whole of the *Aeneid* (London, 2 vols., 1972).

Two classic works of German scholarship: R. Heinze, *Virgils epische Technik* (3rd edn., 1914), repr. 1957), and E. Norden's Commentary on *Aeneid* 6 (Stuttgart, 1927, repr. 1957).

IO

Roman Historians

ANDREW LINTOTT

Origins

A small proportion of the works of the Roman historians has survived the hiatus in culture and learning that followed the decline of the western half of the Roman Empire. We have only about a half of Tacitus' major works, for example, thanks to precisely two manuscripts, and only thirty-five of the 142 books of Livy. Such is the fate of the acknowledged masters; our information about the pioneers and many other later historians is confined to brief comments and quotations. Greek historians by contrast fared much better as a result of Byzantine scholarship.

Generalization from this limited evidence is made easier by the homogeneity of what survives. A Roman historian was first and foremost a historian of Rome, 'rerum Romanarum auctor'. Like Thucydides or Xenophon, he dealt primarily with public affairs at home and abroad: 'vast wars, the sack of cities, the defeat and capture of kings, or in domestic history conflicts between consuls and tribunes, legislation about land and grain-distribution, the struggles of the aristocracy and plebs'—such in Tacitus' view was the subject-matter of the historians of the Republic. The basic aims of the historians were simple: to preserve the memory of Rome itself and to transmit to future generations the exploits and characters of her famous men. To quote Tacitus again, 'I think it a particular function of annals, that virtues should not be passed over in silence, while those responsible for wrong actions and words should be threatened with disgrace in the eyes of posterity.' This history was not purely secular, however; it also concerned Rome's relations with the gods who watched over her growth and prosperity, as revealed in the portents by which the gods communicated with mortals, and the cult practices which were the human response to them. Ideally the historian of public affairs was a man who had participated in them. With the occasional exception, notably Livy, Roman historians were senators or had held important positions in public life. Sallust claims that he was diverted from historiography by political ambitions but, when these failed and he was no longer committed to a particular faction, he readily devoted his retirement to history rather than to a life of leisure or the 'servile activities of agriculture and hunting'.

The most inspiring topic for a Roman historian was Rome's phenomenal rise to dominance over the Mediterranean during the Republican period. Yet it was only when they were approaching the zenith of this achievement that the Romans developed both the will and the ability to chronicle it properly. The first Roman historians, Q. Fabius Pictor and L. Cincius Alimentus, held public office during the second Punic War (Cincius was captured by Hannibal) and probably wrote their histories immediately afterwards, in the first decade of the second century BC. They wrote in Greek—Fabius has recently been discovered among a group of Greek historians commemorated by texts painted on wall-plaster at Taormina in Sicily. Fabius and Cincius did not merely write about their own lifetime, but tried to reconstruct Roman history from its origins. We must therefore briefly consider what sort of historical material survived from the past and how it affected the subsequent composition of histories.

The Romans maintained records of the consuls of every year (*fasti consulares*), which, as transmitted to us, stretched back to the founding of the Republic about 500 BC. These probably derive from the yearly registers said to have been kept by the chief priests, *pontifices maximi*, containing the magistrates and notable events of each year. Questions, which cannot be discussed here, inevitably arise about the genuineness of these early records and the extent to which, even if basically genuine, they were corrupted later; what is certain is that at best they were a bare factual account of wars, triumphs, portents (e.g. eclipses), and food-shortages. There was also a great stock of stories about Rome from its mythical origins onwards, some written down by Greeks like Timaeus (below, p. 229), others deriving from native traditions. By far the most significant of these were the family traditions preserved by the noble families. These had their particular origin in funerals, whose contribution to Roman self-consciousness of their military prowess was noted by the Greek historian Polybius. The dead noble was carried to the rostra in the forum amid mourners wearing the clothes and death-masks of his ancestors, and there his son or a close relative pronounced an encomium (*laudatio funebris*), which began with the dead man himself and then embraced the exploits of the other dead ancestors included in the gathering. These orations were preserved for future exploitation, but both Cicero and Livy complain of their corruption of history by the invention of achievements and improper genealogical claims.

As far as we can judge, the earliest histories were far from a mere chronicle. Their writers probably had two major purposes, corresponding to their two different readerships. Now that Rome had become the dominant power in the Mediterranean, the Roman version of recent conflicts was a useful adjunct to foreign policy. So was publicity about the nature and antiquity of the city. About this time a friend of Rome in Chios set up an inscription showing the genealogy of Romulus and Remus—interestingly, it was Fabius Pictor who first seems to

STATUE OF A ROMAN WITH THE
BUSTS OF HIS ANCESTORS (late first
century BC). The practice of mourners in
funeral processions wearing masks to
personate dead ancestors, as recorded by
Polybius, tended to give way during the
late Republic to the carrying of portrait-
busts, presumably in a light material such
as wax or terracotta.

have reconciled the Greek view that Aeneas had founded Rome with the Roman
view that it was Romulus. At home the historians not only followed the poets
in glorifying Roman virtues, but educated in another way by establishing the
'truth' about the Roman constitution and mores, so as to preserve these from
erosion in a time of increasing foreign influence and one when many new families
were reaching high office. Roman historiography was thus at the start essentially
conservative in outlook.

Other senators followed Fabius and Cincius, the most noteworthy among

them being the ex-consul and censor M. Porcius Cato from the town of Tusculum in Latium. Cato wrote his *Origines* in Latin. As the work's title suggests, he
was concerned with the early history, not only of Rome, but of other Italian
cities; but he then moved swiftly on to discuss the Punic Wars and his own
lifetime (234-149 BC), enlivening the narrative with digressions on marvels, as
Herodotus had done, and also versions of his own speeches. From Cato's time
onwards Romans usually wrote their history in Latin, but they were still subject
to Greek influences, of which three may be distinguished.

Polybius

The first of these, antiquarianism, was apparent in Roman historiography from
the beginning. The obvious Greek example for the Romans was Timaeus of
Tauromenium (Taormina), a Sicilian writer of the early third century BC, who
in the course of his histories of Sicily and the western Mediterranean had become
in effect the first historian of Rome. Secondly there was the 'tragic' approach
associated with certain Hellenistic writers, whose chief features were pathos,
sensationalism, and the cult of the bizarre. The third influence was Polybius of
Megalopolis, a Greek taken to Italy as a political detainee in 168 BC, who became
a close friend of Roman aristocrats there and set himself to describe how 'almost
the whole inhabited world had come under the sole rule of the Romans within
fifty-three years'. He aimed to write 'pragmatic' history, a political and military
history, which would be of practical value for the serious reader, both because it
explained the links of cause and motivation between events and because it judged
critically the behaviour of men under stress as examples for future conduct.
Because the whole history of the Mediterranean had become united through
Roman power, he believed it was possible to write a universal history which was
at the same time coherent and had explanatory value. Polybius' work was thus
the culmination of Hellenistic historiography, in that politico-military history,
traditionally focused on the city-state, was given the breadth of a universal
chronicle. His narrative, chronologically based on Olympiads and their consti-
tuent years, dealt successively with the different regions of the world known to
the Greeks, cross-cutting in order to keep parallel stories in step with one another
and stressing their interrelation and convergence. At the same time he transformed Greek historiography because his central theme was the rise of an alien
empire.

Like Thucydides (Vol. 1, pp. 187 f.), he is a historian's historian, self-conscious
about the principles and methodology of his craft, but more ready to discuss
openly problems such as the selection of material, composition of speeches, portrayal of character, and explanation of causes. His approach is in essence a re-
affirmation of Thucydides' first priority, the search for the truth from the most
authentic evidence possible—autopsy, the questioning of eyewitnesses, and the
sifting of their accounts. However, he extended his researches to the past,

especially the generation before his own, and he made critical use of other men's writings. Yet he also stresses the historian's personal contribution to history and, while in abhorring the fabulous and over-emotional he distances himself from both the antiquarians and the 'tragic' writers, he shares the latter's preoccupation with making an impression on his readers. He reconciles these beliefs by a theory centring on the Greek term *emphasis*, which covers the authoritative impression given by a writer, the vivid significance of the events he recounts, and the powerful impression left in the reader's mind. He believes that it is the truth of events which influences a reader more than rhetorical devices. Yet this requires the historian as a medium, selecting and presenting events with appropriate comment on motive, cause, and outcome. On the other hand, the historian's ability derives from his own political and military experience either in the events themselves or other events like them. So the good historian is writing out of his own experience, whatever he relates, and the resulting authenticity and explanatory power makes the impact on the reader, without which history is useless for the man seeking instruction.

The instruction Polybius gives is often explicit. He discusses technicalities such as the computation of the size of cities and the use of fire-signals; he moralizes on the fortitude of Regulus in disaster, the foolish presumption of the Aetolians, the arrogance of Philip V of Macedon; he illustrates the dangers of using mercenaries. One book is devoted to the relative merits of the Roman, Carthaginian, and Spartan constitutions. Individual political decisions are analysed directly: he claims to have avoided fiction in speeches, but to have selected from the available material the central arguments, on whose background and outcome he adds his own comments. His treatment of the causes of war is perhaps not quite sophisticated enough. Although he carefully distinguishes the preliminary acts of a war and the pretexts alleged by the combatants from the causes proper, he finds the latter only in the mental disposition of the aggressor and the circumstances which had so disposed him. No allowance is made for occasions when there is no long-term resolve to fight, but the diplomatic interaction of the two parties drives one or both of them over the brink, nor is enough weight given to complicity in the state attacked, for example Rome in the Second Punic War, when it acquiesces in, and plans for, the attack threatening it. Like Thucydides, Polybius refused to attribute to chance what can be rationally explained. However, he shared the fascination of his Hellenistic and classical predecessors with the paradoxes of fortune (*tychē*), that is, rapid changes in human circumstances, whose particular components can be rationally explained, but whose cumulative effect is unpredictable and awe-inspiring. Most strikingly, he states that the rise of Rome to world-domination was directed by *tychē*, though he argues elsewhere that chance played no part in Roman success, but it was to be expected in the light of their power, political stability, and enterprise. This apparent inconsistency can be explained. Polybius seems to have regarded Rome as the worthy victor in a contest which had, as it were, been promoted by *tychē* through the coincidence in time of several great and ambitious powers. But it was chance that the conflict in the West between Rome and Carthage, which had a causal nexus of its own, coincided in time with the expansion of Philip V and Antiochus III, and so political processes throughout the Mediterranean became enmeshed with each other.

The Late Republic

Roman historians did not share Polybius' interest in theory, nor did they match his universality in treating events. Nevertheless, he had put Rome firmly in the centre of world history, and the practical educational aim he ascribed to history would have ensured its respectability in Roman eyes. Furthermore, his desire that politicians and generals should write history, not men sitting in libraries, was in accordance with existing Roman tradition. How did Roman writing develop under these Hellenistic influences? In the late second century a distinction was drawn between *annales*, in the strict sense of a chronicle of events year by year, and *historiae*, which involved causal analysis. In due course the term 'historiae' was to be used by Sallust and Tacitus for works about their own lifetime, while 'annales' tended to mean ancient history. Cato had been the pioneer in turning history into a political weapon; by 100 BC politicians were writing memoirs to set the record right about themselves. This trend led in time to Caesar's commentaries and Augustus' autobiography and *Res Gestae*. Biography developed also: C. Gracchus wrote about his elder brother and in the late Republic great men—Caesar, Pompey, Cato, and Cicero, for example—were commemorated by their admirers. However, side by side with contemporary history antiquarian history flourished as never before. The material in the earlier annals was expanded by material culled from a variety of documents, whether genuine or forged, and supplemented by frequently stereotyped inventions, such as led Livy to wonder how the Volscians and Aequians had enough men to be slaughtered so often by the Romans.

No one could now complain of a shortage of Roman history, but in the view of Cicero's contemporaries what existed was not readable. Cicero's friends pestered him for a history—'a work in itself most suited to an orator'—and when he died, Cornelius Nepos (himself a writer of chronicles and short biographies) lamented that the chance of casting the rough and shapeless mass of material into a worthy literary form was lost. Cicero himself argued that Roman histories could not be compared with Greek because they lacked *ornatus*, attractive presentation. This comprised variations in colour and tone, good word-order, and an easy flowing style, in which ideally the rhythm of the sentences reproduced the rhythm of events. However, more than language was involved in Cicero's view: histories required proper chronological disposition and geographical descriptions, interpretations of policy and motive, and judgements on the execution of these policies. Although the fragments known to us of early annalists show spectacular language and a vigorous narrative skill, they lack the smoothness to beguile a reader over long periods. More important, they may not have given enough space to interpretation.

Julius Caesar

Caesar's commentaries on his Gallic and Civil Wars are the first good evidence we have of the progress of Roman historiography. Although they are memoirs with a political purpose, they share many of the characteristics of less committed histories: indeed tendentiousness and self-glorification are not vices unique to autobiography. Stylistically, Caesar seems to have improved on his predecessors. The narrative flows clearly and smoothly, but there is little variety of tone nor a great range of vocabulary, and the style generally resembles that of the official letters we find in Cicero's correspondence. Cicero praised their naked and austere beauty, precisely because they were stripped of verbal ornament. In organization and interpretation of his material Caesar meets Cicero's requirements more closely. Indeed the themes of Caesar's *Gallic War* are typical of mature Roman history. Caesar tells us of the expansion of Roman power in a successful war, enlivening the story with digressions on geography and the characteristics of foreign races, and explains its significance by comments in the first person and by speeches in which both he and his opponents justify their conduct. The whole work is a testimony to Roman virtue, not only that of Caesar himself, but of his troops, whose abilities are rarely portrayed so effectively elsewhere. There is a political message too. Although Caesar was radical and violent in his own political career, when discussing the Gallic communities he exalts established power and conservatism. Danger comes from ambitious men who solicit help from the plebs by largesse and aim at revolution. In spite of the irony which the reader can find in these remarks, Caesar would have written them quite sincerely: Rome had traditionally sought aid from the 'establishments' among her allies when securing her empire. The *Civil War* could not so easily be given a Roman interpretation. Yet once again Caesar's soldiers are heroes, and Caesar defends his own conduct according to traditional values: when his dignity was threatened and he was deserted by former friends, he took up arms in defence of the liberty of the Roman people against the machinations of a few powerful men.

Sallust

C. Sallustius Crispus (born 86 BC), a partisan of Caesar's who took to history about the time of the latter's murder, was more innovative stylistically and developed a terse epigrammatic style, which owed much to the short simple sentences and ponderous vocabulary of the early annalists, in particular Cato, but had greater variety of language and tone. Unfortunately his major work, the *Histories*, which dealt with late Republican history down to 67 BC, only survives

VICTORIES WITH A SHIELD: relief from a triumphal monument in Rome (early first century BC). This and other reliefs in the same hard grey stone, all showing trophies and armour, have been attributed to the base of a statue-group of 91 BC depicting Sulla's capture of Jugurtha, the North African king whose conflict with Rome forms the subject of Sallust's *Jugurthine War*.

in fragments, and we have to base our judgement of him mainly on the monographs *Catiline* and *Jugurtha*. In these Sallust makes plain his preoccupation with the portrayal of virtue; in fact he alludes to the importance of the death-masks of the nobility as inspiration for later generations, thus recalling the influence of Roman funerals on historical writing. However, to throw virtue into relief he gives as much emphasis to vice, and he does not limit himself to the character of individuals but portrays the *mores* of whole sections of society. Patriotically he gives Roman military glory its due, but contrasts this with the moral corruption which in his view attended the expansion of the Roman Empire. It was above all the aristocracy itself which through greed and ambition was not only self-destructive, but created injustice for the poor or encouraged corruption in them also. Rome was only saved by the outstanding virtue of a few of her leaders. Sallust also highlights conflicts between the nobility and the plebs, which had begun in the early Republic before corruption had set in, but returned in earnest in the late Republic after a brief period of harmony during Rome's most critical wars. He shows sympathy with plebeian sufferings (he had himself been tribune of the plebs and taken a popular stance at that time). Yet when writing of the late Republic, in a passage influenced by Thucydides, he denounces both those who claimed to defend the status quo of senatorial dominance and those who championed plebeian rights, for seeking in reality their own power. For Sallust vice and decadence were as important subjects as virtues and victories, and it was vice which gave him the greatest opportunities for extended portrayal of character, for example those of Catiline and Jugurtha themselves, and minor characters like Sempronia, the educated society woman in Sallust's *Catiline*. However, the analysis of the causes of decadence is comparatively superficial. Roman political organization and the Roman economy are but briefly mentioned. For Sallust the fundamental causes were prosperity and the lack of foreign enemies: these gave rein to a sort of original sin, which only the hardships of foreign wars could hold in check. This notion was not discovered by Sallust: it goes back to the politics and historiography of the second century BC. But Sallust transmitted it in a most memorable form.

Livy

T. Livius is the first annalistic writer whose work survives in any quantity, and it is through him and the elements of earlier writings discernible in his history that we are able to form judgements on the annals of the Republic. Moreover, his history was the last great annalistic history of the Republic written in Latin. Livy was born at Patavium (Padua) in 59 BC and wrote from about the age of thirty onwards after twenty years of civil war and the conversion of the Republic into a form of monarchy. A man of industry and learning rather than political or intellectual distinction, he came nearest to fulfilling the expectation which Cicero's friends had of Cicero—the production of a readable history of Rome. His resources in language and deployment of his material were everything

THE BATTLE OF PYDNA: detail of the sculptured frieze on the monument set up by Aemilius Paullus at Delphi in honour of his victory in 167 BC (above, p. 40). Besides accurately reproducing the army of the combatants (note the characteristic Macedonian round shield with embossed ornament) the artist corroborates Livy's account of the part played by a runaway pack horse in precipitating an engagement.

that Cicero himself could have wished. Avoiding Sallustian abruptness, he yet contrived a swift and varied narrative built from a rich vocabulary and an immense flexibility of construction. His approach to his subject was conservative, as had probably been traditional among annalists: in wars he was patriotic, in politics he supported senatorial authority against the demagoguery of tribunes. Although he shows some sympathy with the *plebs* in his account of their struggle with the patricians, he shows an immense fascination with aristocratic hardliners who resisted inflexibly any concession to the *plebs* or deviation from tradition. It is likely that he retained this attitude in his lost books on the fall of the Republic and saw a reason for that fall in the failure of such men. One supreme example would have been Cato Uticensis, who opposed Caesar and had already been highlighted for selfless devotion to the Republic in Sallust's *Catiline*. Although Livy wrote in the aftermath of political failure and civil conflict, it was also a period when Roman imperial power was at its height. Faced by this discrepancy and by the coincidence of prosperity with the moral turpitude exemplified by the shedding of Roman blood, Livy, like Sallust, argued that Rome had succumbed to the weight of her own success.

As an interpreter of history in detail, Livy was unoriginal or simply defective in his treatment of causes. However, he substituted for explanation a vivid human sympathy shown in his portrayal of emotions both in the speeches he composed and in the narrative. This is essentially an imaginative skill. There was no evidence about the feelings of the people of Veii, when the Romans drove them from their city and razed it to the ground, or about what the Roman soldiers felt when sent under the yoke by the Samnites (both these episodes took place in the fourth century BC); there was probably little more about the Romans' reaction to their defeat by Hannibal at Trasimene in 217. Yet these are some of the most memorable passages in what survives of Livy. It was the 'tragic' approach to history that influenced him much more than the 'pragmatic' approach of Polybius. Livy carried his history down to 9 BC—a mammoth work never to be emulated, not least because in the meantime the Republic became a dead subject.

The Early Empire

The Principate of Augustus and his successors brought changes in political life and in literary style. Both the People and the Senate gradually lost the power to make effective political decisions on matters of importance: policies were formed by the Emperor and his intimates *in camera*; promotions ultimately depended on imperial favour. So secrecy led to ignorance of the *arcana* of the Empire among contemporaries and later historians and, to compensate, fed rumour and suspicion, while the court atmosphere encouraged intrigue and backbiting. Meanwhile the luxuriant oratory of men such as Cicero was abandoned in favour of a style pointed and abrupt, like Sallust's, but more striking in its phraseology, especially apt for lampoon and denunciation.

Some historians who chronicled the transition from republic to monarchy maintained their independence from the new regime. One, Cremutius Cordus, had his books burnt under Tiberius and later reproduced under Gaius in a censored edition. In general, however, history, as Tacitus pointed out, was corrupted in two ways, by flattery of the present emperor and detraction of his predecessors. The former was stimulated by the requirement to deliver formal panegyrics of the Emperor in the consul's oration of thanks, instituted in Augustus' time (Pliny's *Panegyric* of AD 100 is the first surviving example). By contrast, Seneca's *Ludus* or *Apocolocyntosis* about the death and deification of the Emperor Claudius is a remarkable specimen of licensed defamation. Equally detrimental to the historian was the lack of traditional material. After Augustus' time most emperors did not seek major new conquests; at home there was no room for the great political conflicts of the Republic. The rivalries of the aristocracy centred on trials for treason, as they jockeyed for position in the Emperor's favour or the esteem of their equals. Important developments in the early Principate—changes in administration at home and abroad, the spread of citizenship and Graeco-Roman culture, the growth of cities—were not the stuff which had interested historians in the past and did not lend themselves to pathos or sensationalism. Yet Rome's greatest historian worked in what he himself believed was a narrow and inglorious field.

Tacitus

C. Cornelius Tacitus was born in the middle of the first century AD and reached senatorial rank and high office under the Flavian dynasty. He wrote mainly under the Emperor Trajan, in what was held to be an unexampled era of security and prosperity after the murder of the last Flavian Emperor, the 'tyrannical' Domitian. One early work was a written version of a funeral panegyric about his father-in-law Agricola. Both here and in his two major historical works—the *Historiae*, dealing with the Flavian period (AD 69-96), and the *Annales* on the Julio-Claudian dynasty from AD 14 to AD 68—he proclaims his traditional concern with virtue and vice. 'The age was not so barren of virtues that it did not produce some fine examples of conduct.' These were not quite those of republican annals. 'Mothers accompanied their children into exile, wives followed their husbands ... loyal slaves even gave insulting answers to their torturers.' Nevertheless,

INSCRIBED LEAD WATER-PIPE FROM THE FORTRESS AT CHESTER, one of the only two documents from Britain which name Agricola. The longest-serving and most successful of Britain's governors (AD 78-84), Cn. Julius Agricola was also the father-in-law of the historian Tacitus, who commemorated him in a famous, if somewhat rose-tinted, biography. The imperial titulature dates the pipe to 79.

Tacitus' work is full of miniatures of the *Agricola* type—obituary notices of those who prospered under the regime or fell foul of it through treason trials. 'Let us make this concession to the reputation of famous men that, just as in their funeral rites they are kept apart from mass burials, so they may each have their own notice in the records of deaths.'

He aimed not only to give moral edification by parading virtue and vice, but to give practical instruction. This justified his attention to intrigue and treason trials. Under the Republic, he explains, when power was at one time with the *plebs*, at another with the Senate, one had to discover how to manage the masses and equally how to influence the nobles who dominated the Senate. By the same token under an autocracy it was helpful to understand how an Emperor's mind worked. It was for success in this respect that Tacitus was so admired by men like Machiavelli and Guicciardini in the Renaissance. Although he gave their due to those who were destroyed by Emperors, he reserved his greatest admiration for those like himself and his father-in-law Agricola, who survived. 'Let all those, whose habit is to admire acts of civil disobedience, realize that great men can exist under bad emperors, and that compliance and an unassuming demeanour, if backed by energy and hard work, can attain a pitch of glory, which the majority reach through an ostentatious and untimely death.' He had no illusions about the leading victims of the Julio-Claudians, pointing out how they tried to maintain status by self-display and extravagant spending, and contrasting them with the modest and parsimonious new men brought into the senate.

As a historian of the Empire he is most interesting for his ability to put the case for the opposition, not only denouncing the corruption of Roman rule (part of a Roman orator's stock-in-trade in so far as he had to appear for Rome's subjects in extortion cases), but also highlighting courageous independence and resistance to the blandishments of Roman civilization. 'If you wish to rule everyone, does it follow that everyone should accept slavery?', asks the captured British leader Caratacus. A feature of that slavery was 'the amenities that make vice agreeable—porticoes, baths, and sumptuous banquets'. On the other hand he could contrast the peace and justice that Roman rule brought with the insecurity of tribal rivalries. Most revealing, however, is the comment attributed to a Roman commander rejecting a plea from a German tribe to be allowed to settle in Roman territory. 'Men must obey their betters: the gods they invoked had empowered the Romans to decide what to give and what to take away, and to tolerate no judges but themselves.'

Tacitus lamented the lack of military material available to him. Yet, though he can give an exciting and not inaccurate account of a campaign (like Livy, he is especially effective in portraying the feelings of the men involved), his style leads to an irritating vagueness about detail. This style, however, was admirably suited to the portrayal of imperial politics. Two chief features were irony, used to contrast the appearances of public life with the underlying realities of power, and a deliberate cultivation of ambiguity. Tacitus delights in the deflating post-

ROMAN BATHS AT WROXETER (ancient Viriconium) near Shrewsbury (second century AD). Thermal baths were one of the amenities that, according to Tacitus, made 'vice agreeable' to the natives of Britain. Here the pillars of the underfloor heating of the warm room (*tepidarium*) have been partially restored in the foreground.

script. He also has an elaborate technique of providing alternative explanations—some his own, some ascribed to others—which do not clarify but increase the uncertainty over the motivation of those he describes. His classic achievement was his portrayal of Tiberius. His sources reported an Emperor who, in spite of great talents and a concern for the well-being of the Empire, ended his life with an intermittent grasp over his administration and abominated by his people. Tacitus seized on Tiberius' well-known hypocrisy as the answer to the enigma, and saw his life as the gradual peeling of skins of plausibility from a bitter and malevolent inner self. Tiberius was presented as a man of acute intelligence warped by his early life and love of domination. Guicciardini wrote, 'Cornelius Tacitus teaches very well every man who lives under a tyrant the way to live and manage his affairs prudently, just as he equally teaches tyrants the ways to found their tyranny.'

In spite of the supposedly happy era in which he wrote, Tacitus' attitude to history was pessimistic. The doom of the Republic was inevitable; the miseries under Tiberius were ascribed to divine wrath. Tacitus seems to have had genuine doubts about the free will of men, which should have subverted his endeavours to give them advice. Did the friendship or enmity of the Emperor depend on predestination and one's lot at birth or was policy of some avail? For Tacitus the world was either a realm of pure chance unmitigated by divine providence or else determined in its destiny, whether by rational chains of cause and effect, as the Stoics believed, or by the planets. Though not always complimentary to individual astrologers, Tacitus was respectful to the science itself, as were many of his contemporaries, including the Flavian Emperors. As for the old gods of Rome, Tacitus said little of religious ceremonies and his treatment of portents was equivocal. The disasters which befell the Roman people were proof that the gods had no care for their tranquillity, only for their punishment. In AD 69 there

HEAD OF TIBERIUS, second of the Roman Emperors (AD 14–37). The portrait conveys something of the character painted by Tacitus in his *Annals*: a man of ability but of an underlying viciousness whose true nature was only revealed as the layers of hypocrisy were gradually cast off. Modern historians take a more charitable view, attributing Tiberius' failure to indecisiveness, reserve, and mistrust.

were 'monstrous animal births and numerous other signs and wonders of the kind that in primitive centuries were noted in peacetime, but now are only heard of when men are afraid.' It is hard to deduce a consistent religious or philosophical view from his work. However, this did not affect his moral purpose. Destiny might provide an explanation for human conduct, but not an excuse.

Suetonius

Tacitus' achievement was to adapt traditional principles to the history of the early principate and create a historical style which reflected the period. For over two centuries no one writing in Latin tried to match his achievement. Already in his lifetime literary fashion was turning from history to biography, where special attention could be given to psychology and personal relations, the subjects that had fascinated Tacitus himself. Moreover, from the point of view of the Roman upper class the lives of the Emperors were the main thread of history. Monographs might be written on their achievements, especially their campaigns. Fuller biographies would spice their official career with succulent details of their private life and judgements on their character. Tacitus' younger contemporary, C. Suetonius Tranquillus, is the most effective exponent of this literary genre known to us and he was followed by other writers, whose work was the basis for the creation in the late empire of the *Historia Augusta*, a collection of imperial biographies whose authorship and reliability are much disputed.

The core of Suetonius' work is the raw material of a Roman epitaph or funeral oration—the public record of an Emperor, his exploits at home and abroad, and the moral qualities revealed by these. Set against the official career is his private life. The domestic virtues of an Emperor had become a topic for panegyric by the time of the Younger Pliny. But there was much more scope there for detraction. Certainly, an Emperor was criticized for military failure, the waste of public money, and brutality towards the rest of the upper class (Suetonius did not on the whole judge the administrative reforms he recorded). Yet public faults could best be exploited as the result of the personal inadequacies of the Emperor, and his vices were revealed in his home, especially in his dining-room and bedroom. So we find in Suetonius catalogues of achievements placed side by side with scandalous descriptions of the Emperor's more intimate life, both copiously illustrated by anecdotes. In spite of the fact that these two elements are rarely well fused, an effective, though not necessarily accurate, character portrait often results.

Suetonius may be compared with a Greek contemporary of Tacitus, Plutarch of Chaeronea, the greatest biographer of antiquity (below, pp. 257 ff.) Most of Plutarch's biographies took the form of parallel lives, in which an eminent Greek was compared with an eminent Roman of the Republic. These were intended as character portraits (Plutarch specifically compares his work to both sculpture and painting), in which small faults were to be toned down without being completely omitted, in order that the requirements of truth should be fulfilled but the reader should not be distracted from the general outline of the man. To this end Plutarch did not simply recount the lives of his subjects from birth to death, but included general descriptions of their behaviour in certain contexts (it is here especially that, like Suetonius, he introduces anecdotes). The men are described and compared in terms of ethical concepts derived from Platonic and Aristotelian philosophy. Men should be brave, but not rash; modest, and not insolent in success; moderate and scrupulous in their use of wealth; and they should control the passions of their subordinates while not being themselves swept away by passion. The biographies seek to show the relative success or failure of great men in living up to such precepts. Compared with this, Roman biography is ethically crude. The values of the Roman historians had arisen not so much from a view of the good man, but from a view of the success of Rome, and utility to Rome was a narrow foundation on which to base judgements on personality.

Why did the flow of Roman history dry up after Tacitus? It is significant that the next great history of Rome was written in Greek by a Roman senator of Greek origins, Cassius Dio from Bithynia. This was a universal history of Rome up to the time of writing (the early third century AD), which was intended to emulate Thucydides' work in its explanations and political generalizations. By contrast, Roman explanations of their political history (in spite of Polybius' example) had rarely gone beyond the simplistic in political terms. Thus, once the history of a period had been eloquently written by a Livy or Tacitus there was little call to rewrite it. Since the Empire and the Principate were consolidated and apparently unlikely to change, the lives of the Emperors might be written as a series of appendices to a story already well told. Later, in the fourth century, a Syrian from Antioch, Ammianus Marcellinus, tried to make a new start by writing in Latin on the period from the end of Tacitus' work to his own day. The usual material is to be found there—wars, geographic and ethnographic descriptions, trials, seditions in Rome and other cities, and, not least, digressions on morals. Yet, in spite of the vivid and sensational presentation, little is said to explain the crises of the fourth century and the changes in society. This is perhaps one reason why the Roman upper class had abandoned writing history in the traditional fashion. They could find nothing new to say within the old framework.

Further Reading

English translations exist of most surviving historical works mentioned in this chapter; there is, however, no translation of the fragments of Roman historians. Apart from the translations facing texts in the Loeb Classical Library, the most complete range is now in the Penguin Classics. Especially good are those of Tacitus' *Annals* (M. Grant) and *Histories* (K. Wellesley), Sallust, Caesar (S. A. Handford), and Polybius (I. Scott-Kilvert), although this contains little of Polybius dealing with events after the Second Punic War. The best translation of Polybius is by E. S. Shuckburgh (2 vols., 1889/1962). Major translations of Tacitus include those of A. J. Church and J. Brodribb (London, 1882) and W. Fyfe (Oxford, 1912).

A general survey is provided by M. L. W. Laistner, *The Greater Roman Historians* (California, 1963). There are also useful collections of essays, *Latin Historians* and *Latin Biography* (ed. T. A. Dorey, London, 1966 and 1967), which contain chapters on Polybius and Plutarch respectively as well as on writers in Latin. A. Momigliano, *Essays in Ancient and Modern Historiography* (Oxford, 1977), especially chs. 4, 5, and 7, is important for both the historians themselves and their place in the development of historiography.

On *Early Historians* see E. Badian's chapter in *Latin Historians* (above) and Momigliano (above); for a more controversial study of early Roman records B. W. Frier, *Libri Annales Pontificum Maximorum. The Origins of the Annalistic Tradition* (Rome, 1979).

Polybius has been studied above all by F. W. Walbank. See his *Polybius* (California, 1972); also the introduction to *A Historical Commentary on Polybius*, vol. i. (Oxford, 1957). For Polybius' views of the historian's function see K. Sacks, *Polybius and the Writing of History* (California, 1981).

The best introduction to *Sallust* is D. C. Earl, *The Political Thought of Sallust* (Cambridge, 1961; Amsterdam, 1966). R. Syme, *Sallust* (Oxford, 1964), is a more detailed and wide-ranging investigation.

Caesar has been treated by F. E. Adcock, *Caesar as a Man of Letters* (Cambridge, 1956). P. G. Walsh, *Livy* (Cambridge, 1961), provides a concise and valuable general study of that author. Also useful is the introduction in R. M. Ogilvie, *A Commentary on Livy I–V* (Oxford, 1965).

R. Syme, *Tacitus* (2 vols., Oxford, 1958), is the major work in English on that historian. R. Martin, *Tacitus* (London, 1981), is a simpler work full of good sense. The introduction in H. Furneaux, *The Annals of Tacitus*, vol. i (Oxford, 1884), is also useful. B. Walker, *The Annals of Tacitus* (Cambridge, 1952, 1960), seeks to distinguish the factual and non-factual elements in the work. See also the collection of essays in *Tacitus*, ed. T. A. Dorey (London, 1969), and K. C. Schellhase, *Tacitus in Renaissance Political Thought* (Chicago, 1976).

On biography see A. Wallace-Hadrill, *Suetonius* (London, 1983); D. A. Russell, *Plutarch* (London, 1972); C. P. Jones, *Plutarch and Rome* (Oxford, 1971).

Other developments in imperial history and biography are most easily appreciated from reading *Latin Historians* and *Latin Biography* (above).

I I

The Arts of Prose
The Early Empire

❧❧❧

DONALD RUSSELL

Two Languages, One Literature

THE first two centuries of the Christian era produced an extensive and important prose literature, both in Greek and in Latin. Though the greatest genius, Tacitus, was a Roman whose ways of thinking seem peculiarly difficult to express in Greek, the two languages were in many respects vehicles of a single literature, and the Greek contribution is arguably the more significant of the two.

Not that Greek and Latin were at all on an equal footing. Native Greek speakers seldom troubled to learn Latin, except for the purposes of official life, and they seem to have found its nuances hard to grasp. 'Longinus' (*On Sublimity* 12.4) wisely asks indulgence for trying to judge Cicero; Plutarch (*Demosthenes* 3) disclaims the ability to do so, and clearly had a struggle with his Latin. It was natural that there should be a steady demand for Greek books giving information on Roman subjects: Dionysius of Halicarnassus' *Roman Antiquities*, Plutarch's Roman *Lives*, Appian's *Wars of the Romans* catered for the need, which increased as the period advanced and more and more Greek speakers sought positions of influence in imperial administration and politics. Thus by the end of the second century Latin historiography has dried up, but Herodian and the much more competent Cassius Dio attest the vigour of Greek. Latin speakers, on the other hand, if they were destined for official position or literary education (and the two were always closely linked), learned Greek from childhood, and often preferred it, especially for philosophical or scientific purposes, to their native tongue. It is in no way surprising that the Emperor Marcus Aurelius wrote *To Himself* in Greek, nor that Pliny's friend Corellius Rufus announced his resolution to take his own life with the Greek word *Kekrika*, 'I have decided'. At the same time, there is an extensive literature conveying Greek learning and philosophy to a Latin public, pursuing the Ciceronian and Augustan ideal of making Latin literature a complete and self-contained expression of Graeco-Roman culture. Celsus' encyclopedia, Quintus Curtius' *Alexander*, Pliny's *Natural History* are examples of this.

But what was common to the two languages is more important than this difference. Both were self-consciously literary languages, diverging considerably from the spoken tongue. The difference was sharper in Greek. From the Augustan period onwards—indeed earlier—teachers of Greek grammar and rhetoric inculcated an ever closer approach to the precise linguistic and grammatical forms attested by the Attic classics of the fifth and fourth centuries BC, especially Thucydides, Xenophon, and the orators. This movement reached a high point in the middle of the second century, when the marvellous archaizing pastiches produced by great 'sophists' won the applause of packed theatres and the admiring patronage of Emperors. In Latin, the chronological perspectives were different. Latin literature had only recently reached what was quickly recognized as its classical maturity. Prose style had continued to develop naturally after Cicero, partly in reaction against the norms of sentence structure and decorum which he had tried to establish. This reaction lasted about a century, until Quintilian tried to reverse it. It was not till the Antonine period (AD 97-180) that the trickle of prose archaizers (*antiquarii*) became a flood, and something rather like Greek 'Atticism' developed. Before this happened, there had been much enrichment and experimentation; but the sources of this, it is important to notice, lay much more in poetry and in the devices of older Greek rhetoric than in the resources of everyday Latin speech. These remained largely untapped, though educated speech is clearly echoed in parts of Seneca, and Petronius (below, pp. 279 ff.) went so far as to make some of the characters in his comic novel speak the incorrect language of the uneducated: a unique experiment, so far as we know, whether in Latin or in Greek.

The salient point is that almost all the works of significance, in both languages, are written in what Eduard Norden, the scholar who has contributed most to our understanding of these matters, called *Kunstprosa*, 'prose of art' or 'formal prose', the product of assiduous teaching and imitation. The main mark of *Kunstprosa*, both in Greek and in Latin, is its dependence on deliberate choice made in advance by the writer for the particular task before him. He has to determine what is the appropriate stylistic level (*genus dicendi* or—in Greek—*charaktēr*) for the job; a common classification distinguished 'grand', 'middle', and 'delicate' styles, but this was by no means the only categorization that was possible. In any case, there was a choice to be made in vocabulary, and this was very much determined by literary precedent and association; there was also a choice of sentence-structure, between the long and elaborately organized 'periodic' sentence and a more simple pattern; and, most striking to the modern reader, there was the choice of rhythm. Some regularity in the quantitative pattern of sentence endings (*clausulae* in Latin) is to be seen in classical Greek prose; but it seems to have been the Hellenistic rhetors and their Roman pupils who systematized and enforced practices which had become second nature to writers of our period. Most Roman historians and

VITRUVIUS AND BUILDING TECHNIQUES: Vitruvius' prose treatise on architecture (*c*.28–23 BC) has proved an important manual for modern students. He describes one of the favourite techniques for good-quality domestic architecture (opus reticulatum) as 'charming' but he comments also on the danger of cracks along the joints. The technique, illustrated here at Pompeii, is essentially a wall of mortared rubble, but with an attractive surface provided by a network of little pyramidal blocks set point inwards. On Vitruvius see also p. 365.

some Greek sophists do, it is true, break all known rules; but this is itself an act of choice, dictated by the genre. Tacitus has regular Ciceronian 'clausulation' in his *Dialogue*, but not in his historical works. Quintilian (9. 15. 18) rationalizes this traditional preference—probably based on observation of Thucydides—by alleging that the speed of historical narrative makes the pauses marked by rhythmical *clausulae* inappropriate, because they slow the whole movement down.

Kunstprosa had already had a long history. Developed by the fifth- and fourth-century Greek sophists and orators, partly to give prose something of the dignity and affective power of poetry, but partly also to provide an unambiguous and elegant written language (*graphikē lexis*: Aristotle was the most important theorist who discussed this), it existed, in our period, in many different forms, and was a versatile and many-sided instrument. It was the vehicle, not only of the higher ranges of literature—history, oratory, *belles-lettres*—but of a great deal of technical and didactic writing. Dionysius' *The Arrangement of Words*, 'Longinus' *On Sublimity*, and Onasander's *The General*, are good Greek examples, all of the first century; Celsus' encyclopedia (of which the medical books alone survive), Columella's treatise on farming, and Quintilian's manual of oratory are Latin ones of the same epoch. There are, however, works from which the signs of formality are absent, and which seem much less 'literary': Vitruvius' *Architecture* in Latin and Arrian's *Discourses of Epictetus* in Greek are notable instances.

This lack of formality was itself often deliberate. Arrian wrote his *Expedition of Alexander* in Xenophon's Attic dialect, and his book on India in Herodotus' Ionic; so it was with the same deliberate selection of medium that he set down the discussions of the slave-philosopher Epictetus in the first-century technical language in which such things were actually expressed.

Critics and Rhetoric: The Sense of Decline

A literature with such exacting formal standards and so closely linked with education was bound to be self-conscious and self-critical. It is no wonder that this was the great age of literary criticism, though not, strictly speaking, of literary theory. In particular, the progress and decline of letters were anxiously monitored. Some saw improvement, more saw decline. This was a conventional pessimism, a literary application of the idea, which is as old as Homer and Hesiod, that men are 'not what they were'. Often a convenient mode of polemic, it is not therefore necessarily insincere.

Dionysius of Halicarnassus arrived in Rome very soon after Octavian's victory at Actium (31 BC). He settled there for a career which included rhetorical teaching, literary criticism, and the composition of an elaborate history of early Rome. In the preface to his series of studies on the Attic orators, he sets out the achievement of his age as he sees it. There have been great changes. The 'old philosophic rhetoric'—which embraces the Attic orators down to Demosthenes—was displaced 'after the death of Alexander the Macedonian' by an 'ill-bred' substitute, a new immigrant from some Asiatic hell-hole; but this vulgar and abandoned upstart has miraculously been put in her place by a revival of classical standards, the result of the good taste of the educated Roman governing class. This is a polemical picture, but it makes important points. The new mandarin prose is the expression of a rhetoric which is not just a bag of tricks, a technique of fallacious advocacy and intellectual blackmail, but 'philosophical rhetoric' (*philosophos rhētorikē*), a proper moral and social formation for an age of good government. Essentially, this was the ideal of Isocrates, 350 years earlier, restated for a larger world.

The three stages of development presupposed by Dionysius' account—acme of perfection, degeneration, and revival—are a familiar pattern in Greek theoretical accounts of literary and artistic history. It was at first not easy for the Romans to adapt this scheme to the circumstances of their own development. When Horace, Dionysius' contemporary, glories in the Augustan poetic achievement, his pride is in the techniques that have superseded the immaturity and imperfections of the past, not in the displacement of a corrupt or degenerate fashion. But it is not long before the pattern appears. In oratory, the Ciceronian age was seen to be the acme, corresponding to the period of Demosthenes. Everything that followed was a decline. The Elder Seneca, writing under Tiberius or Caligula, is an early witness to the discussion of corruption and decline which is prominent in first-century speculation. He gave weight to three causes of deterioration: a political cause, the loss of republican liberty; a moral cause, the idleness and indiscipline of sensation-seeking youth; and finally the mere malevolence of the natural order which lets nothing stay at the peak of its development. His son, the philosopher Seneca, urged the moralists' view. Style, he thought, reflects a way of life, both in the individual and in the society: 'Where you see *oratio corrupta* give pleasure, you may be sure that morals also have strayed from the right path' (*Epistles* 114. 11). He wrote this in AD 62. A generation later, he himself is pilloried in the Roman replay of a sort of Dionysian classicism, initiated by the great teacher Quintilian (*c.*AD 35–100), in whose eyes the very charm of Seneca's faults makes him a particularly pernicious model. From Quintilian's point of view, this is not unjust. Seneca's short sentences, unselective vocabulary, and jaunty fluency make him the type of a Latinity radically opposed to Ciceronian dignity and decorum. But Seneca too, we must not forget, writes *Kunstprosa*; in no writer is the beat of the *clausulae* more insistent.

Quintilian's important *Institutio Oratoria*, in twelve books, describes the education and training of the orator in greater detail than any other ancient work. It insists on morality as the basis of oratory, and it is especially interesting on education. He also wrote a book, now lost, on the causes of 'corruption' in style, doubtless a statement of his programme. Tacitus' *Dialogue on Orators*, the dramatic date of which is AD 73 though it was probably written nearly thirty years later, is concerned to state both 'conservative' and 'modernist' points of view. Another statement of the problem is in Greek, in the last chapter of 'Longinus', *On Sublimity* (*Peri hypsous*). This little book is a detailed discussion of the means by which grand, solemn, and emotionally powerful effects may be obtained in literature. It is the most stimulating of ancient critical works, as well as one of the most influential. Some uncertainty about its date must be admitted. It is transmitted as the work of a famous third-century scholar and statesman; but this attribution is widely disbelieved, and with reason, for the links with first-century speculation and interests are unmistakable. 'Longinus' represents 'a philosopher' as advocating the view that the inferiority of contemporary oratory is due to loss of liberty and of 'democracy', but he himself, though rhetorician by trade and not philosopher, very pointedly takes the more moral line: it is the war of the passions and the corruption of the heart that inhibit the creation of great thoughts. It is difficult to cash these statements in terms of a specific historical situation. In a Greek context, *On Sublimity*, taken as a whole, makes sense as a reaction against Hellenistic extravagance and frivolity. Indeed, it seems a more sophisticated and profound reaction than Dionysius' frigid classical revival, because 'Longinus' puts the primary emphasis on the importance of emotional impact in oratory and in literature generally, and the thrust of his argument is to show how this is involved with high thinking and moral ideals. He thus makes a contrast between classical Greek literature, in which all the worth-while models are to be found, and the rhetors and sophists of his own degenerate day, whose only chance of salvation lies in a supreme moral and imaginative effort.

In the closing chapter, however, the perspective seems rather to be Roman. The 'philosopher's ' view that high oratory has been destroyed by loss of freedom seems to reflect the transition from Republic to Principate. The author's 'reply' to this then takes the debate away from political revolutions to personal ethics, but makes the point, clearly directed against his imagined opponent, that 'people like us' are perhaps better under control, lest our greed ruin the world. The combination of Greek and Roman perspectives is confusing, but typical of this bilingual culture.

The Uses of Formal Prose

The carefully fostered, and minutely monitored, arts of prose were used in this period for a wide range of purposes.

First, and most importantly, for history, as the preceding chapter has explained.

Secondly, for oratory. This was of course the original primary function; but critics such as 'Longinus' were clearly right in their perception that the age no longer offered political rewards for the orator. The great trials and debates in which Cicero's contemporaries had re-enacted the dramas of the Demosthenic age were in the past; imperial *causes célèbres* were less earth-shaking. First-century Roman oratory anyway is lost to us; we do not know how significant or innovative it was, and the classicizing revival at the end of the century caused a change of taste which consigned it to oblivion. We do, however, have two important dated works from the second century: Pliny's *Panegyricus* (102) and Apuleius' *Apologia* (157/8: below, pp. 282 ff.) The 'panegyric', spoken by Pliny as consul in the Senate before Trajan, shows what Quintilian's Ciceronianism, with a strong element of 'silver' ingenuity and point, could achieve in the 'epideictic' or ceremonial mode. The 'apology', in which Apuleius defends himself on a charge of using magic to secure the affections of a wealthy widow, shows forensic oratory turning into pure literature, a vehicle for verbal virtuosity, frivolous erudition, and emotive rhetoric. Pliny is of course inspired by the values of Roman public life, and Apuleius is steeped in old Latin learning; but they both exemplify here a Greek phenomenon, the use of rhetoric for entertainment, the typical activity of the 'sophists' of the age.

The history of oratory throughout this period is in fact much more a Greek than a Latin theme. Dio Chrysostom—that is, 'the golden-mouthed'—a leading citizen of Prusa in Bithynia, orator and moralist, harangued the citizens of Rhodes and Alexandria, calming passions and rebuking folly, around the end of the first century AD. Polemo of Laodicea, Favorinus of Arles, Herodes Atticus, and many others went on embassies, pleaded cases, taught pupils, and entertained multitudes with their ingenious historical or grimly comic fantasies, all in the Greek of Demosthenes or some other early classic. This period, with its celebrated travelling virtuoso orators, is often called the 'Second Sophistic': the great speakers

PONT DU GARD, near Nîmes (late first century BC). This gigantic aqueduct bridge bears witness to the engineering skills of the Romans and to their ability to endow functional architecture with nobility of form.

DETAIL OF THE CANOPUS in Hadriah's Villa at Tivoli (between AD 124 and 133). As often with Roman villas, parts of the emperor's country retreat were named after famous sites and monuments of the East, in this case a suburb of Alexandria.

HEAD OF AUTUMN: detail of a mosaic at Cirencester, Gloucestershire (late second century AD). The Four Seasons were a popular subject in mosaic pavements and painted ceilings, since one could be placed at each corner. Here Autumn is characterized by the grapes in her hair and a pruning knife above her shoulder.

were idolized like pop-stars. In the sight of posterity it has often seemed a vanity; in its time, it was a literary and social movement of great influence and significance.

A third use of *Kunstprosa* breaks new ground. This is the age in which what may be called the 'essay' flourished as a recognizable, though unnamed, literary form. Very many of the works of Seneca, Dio, Lucian, and Plutarch are best so described. They are short discourses, often dealing with ethical questions, but sometimes with literature or education or some antiquarian matter. They are, as a rule, very personal in tone, in the sense that the *persona* of the writer is prominent, though they admit also much allusive learning and literary elaboration. In style, they tend to the less periodic. Several traditions went to the making of this class of writing. One was that of the philosophical dialogue, not in the form Plato generally preferred, but in that used by Aristotle, with long speeches instead of sharp question and answer. The dialogue continued to be written throughout our period—Cicero, Tacitus, and Plutarch were notable practitioners—but its techniques and even its name (*dialogus*) were also applied to works in which the element of conversation was not present. Another ancestor was the less polished popular sermon or moral address—'diatribe' is the modern scholars' word—which seems to have flourished in Hellenistic times, and is especially associated with the Cynics. Bion of Borysthenes, acknowledged by Horace as an exemplar for his satire, certainly contributed to the technique of imagery and anecdote which Seneca and Plutarch deployed with such lavishness and enthusiasm. Though these urbane essays were, for the most part, philosophical in tone and content, this does not mean that they did not sometimes come within the province of the rhetorician. Philosophical *theses*—'on providence', 'on marriage', and the like—were an established part of the elementary rhetorical curriculum. Moreover, the popularity of the casual-sounding address led the teachers of rhetoric to lay down precepts for it much as they did for formal speeches; they called it *lalia*, 'chat', and prescribed simple style, an anecdote or simile to capture attention at the start, and studied concealment of rhetorical and logical structure.

Barely separable from the 'essay' is the letter (the fourth use), for the 'essay' is often cast in epistolary form. The letter was, however, a recognized genre, for which we have intelligent and careful instructions in the treatise of Demetrius *On Style*, probably to be dated around the beginning of our period. Artemon, who had published the letters of Aristotle, had said that the letter was 'one side of a dialogue'. Demetrius (223 ff.) disagrees: the dialogue-writer imitates an extempore speech, the letter is 'sent as a gift' and one must pay the recipient the compliment of care and art. The central consideration is that a letter is 'the image of one's mind'; more than any other kind of writing, it presents its author's personality. So it must not be too technical—'a treatise with an address at the top'—nor periodic in style like a forensic speech. In a word, it is 'a brief expression of affection, an exposition of a simple theme in simple words'.

RECONSTRUCTION MODEL OF PLINY THE YOUNGER'S LAURENTINE VILLA, based upon the detailed description in one of his letters. C. Plinius Caecilius Secundus (*c.*AD 61–*c.*112) was one of the most important prose-writers of the Trajanic period, being a master both of the literary epistle and of the art of rhetoric. Like his uncle and adoptive father (the Elder Pliny), he enjoyed a distinguished career in public service.

The letter is a particularly important form in our period. Seneca used it for what is by common consent his best work, the *Epistulae morales*, written in retirement to his friend Lucilius. Epicurus' letters were an influence here; so were Cicero's letters to Atticus. Roman gentlemen recognized the letter as a form ideally suited to the amateur, an apt expression of the friendships and common interests of their class. Statius (*Silvae* 1.3. 104) imagines his friend Vopiscus, in his country retreat at Tibur, writing epic or lyric or satire—or else a letter, as highly polished as any of these. He does not make it clear whether the letter is prose or verse; it may, we must remember, be the latter, in the model of Horace's or Ovid's 'epistles'. The Younger Pliny's stylish collection of letters is one of the most elegant and informative witnesses to the culture and education of the time. It is interesting, and perhaps surprising, that we have so little comparable Greek material. We have, it is true, a mass of Greek letters dating from this period; but these are fictions, purporting to be written by imaginary characters or historical figures. They are little more than rhetorical exercises, though occasionally (as in the *Letters of Crates* and *Chion of Heraclea*) we find sets of letters composed to form something like epistolary romance.

This may remind us that the last of the areas in which *Kunstprosa* was employed is pure fiction. This was a late development, despite the partial classical model of Xenophon's *Cyropaedia*. Origins and influences are hotly debated; whether the characteristic content is of 'oriental' origin and whether the stories were used as a vehicle for religious teaching, specifically that of the mystery religions, are questions which have been repeatedly raised and variously answered over the past century. What seems certain is that the novel, not being a part of the high classical tradition, originally had a different audience in view from history or philosophy. It gradually makes its way into more sophisticated circles, sometimes viewed patronizingly and parodied, sometimes taking its place as a serious successor to epic and drama. The surviving Greek novels are surprisingly similar in plot, and it is a plot which has the suggestiveness of myth. Two lovers undergo long travels, dangers, and separations, their chastity is sorely tried, but they are ultimately united and live happily ever after. Such is the framework of the novels of Chariton, Longus, Achilles Tatius, Xenophon of Ephesus, and Heliodorus. Their tones and settings of course differ: love, magic, violence, humour, the curiosities of distant countries and remote historical times, the rhetoric of trials and debates, are standard ingredients, present in varied degree. Most charming to modern readers is the pastoral romance of Longus, *Daphnis and Chloe*; most divergent from the common pattern are the two Latin examples, Petronius' *Satyrica* and Apuleius' *Metamorphoses*. The novel is, in many ways, the most intriguing literary achievement of the period; it looks forward to mediaeval romance, and it is one of the roots of modern prose fiction. But it is an escapist form; set in the past or at the ends of the earth, its fictions generally portray the human condition with the minimum of reference to the social and political structures within which its readers lived.

Seneca: Father and Son

The remains of this literature fill many volumes. Many of the Greek authors— Plutarch, Lucian, Aristides—were morally and stylistically ideal texts for Byzantine education, and their survival was assured. The Latins were less lucky. Though Pliny's *Natural History* and Seneca were much read in the medieval West, Tacitus survived by a singular accident, and much important historical writing has been lost. But, in both languages, there is a lot to read; and we must confine ourselves here to a brief indication of the qualities of some of the principal figures.

Given the association between education and power, literary success and political activity, it is no wonder that families figure largely in the story. A good example is the family of the Annaei, from Corduba in Spain, who held a high place in both literary and public life for three generations. L. Annaeus Seneca, 'the Elder', was born around the middle of the first century BC, studied at Rome in the triumviral and early Augustan period, and then divided his time between Rome and his native place. Like many writers of the time (Livy, Caecilius of

Caleacte, Dionysius) he was both historian and rhetorician, though he was not a professional teacher of rhetoric. Late in life, he compiled for his three sons a collection of the brilliant rhetorical strokes he remembered from the 'declaimers' of his youth. His enthusiastic anthology has much charm. The prefaces and character sketches especially display an attractive shrewdness. I cite as a specimen a piece from the 'deliberative exercises' (*Suasoriae* 2. 17), in which he speaks of a connection of his own who made a fool of himself by his handling of the hackneyed theme of the Three Hundred Spartans at Thermopylae:

There was a person called Seneca—his name may have reached your ears—of a confused and disorderly cast of mind, who wanted to speak in the big style. In the end, this weakness obsessed him and made him ridiculous. He wouldn't have slaves unless they were big, or silver vessels unless they were big. Believe me, I'm not joking. His madness led him ultimately to wear shoes that were too big for him, to eat no figs except *mariscae* [these had a poor flavour, despite their size], and to have a mistress of vast proportions. He was nicknamed Seneca Grandio. Well, when I was a young man, he gave a version of this exercise. He posed the objection: 'All who had been sent from Greece ran away.' To answer it, he raised his hands, and stood on tip-toe (he used to do this, to seem bigger) and cried: 'I rejoice, I rejoice!' We wondered what piece of luck had come his way. 'Xerxes will be entirely mine', he cried.

L. ANNAEUS SENECA the Younger (*c.*4 BC–AD 65). Born at Corduba in Spain, he uneasily combined the roles of a wealthy money-lender, imperial tutor and minister, and Stoic philosopher. His fame as a philosopher accounts for this portrait-bust being set back to back with one of Socrates.

That is to say, speaking in the role of a Spartan at Thermopylae, he welcomed the absence of reinforcements, on the ground that he would be able to fight Xerxes and his million men single-handed. Of the three sons to whom Seneca's anthology is addressed, one (Mela) was the father of the poet Lucan, one (Novatus) was adopted by Junius Gallio and appears in history as the proconsul of Achaea at the time of St Paul's stay in Corinth (Acts 18: 12), and the middle son, another L. Annaeus Seneca, became without question the leading literary figure of his generation, as well as a man of great wealth and influence, especially in the early years of Nero, whose tutor he was.

Growing up in the early years of Tiberius (*Epist.* 108. 22), the younger Seneca was much attracted by philosophy, especially the more ascetic kind. He became a vegetarian, influenced by Pythagorean ideas, and only desisted in deference to his father, who feared that such eccentricity would earn a black mark from people who mattered: it was one of the times when 'foreign superstitions' were under governmental attack. Seneca was in any case no rebel. His ambitions soared high. He was prominent enough to be exiled for a court intrigue under Claudius, but was recalled, and was continuously in a position of influence from about AD 49 to AD 62. He then fell from grace, and spent the last three years of his life in study and writing: a retirement not unlike Cicero's, and perhaps modelled on it. His tragedies are discussed in Chapter 28. His surviving prose works (some interesting pieces are only known indirectly) include 'consolations'—notably that to his mother Helvia on his own exile—and a number of 'essays' on moral themes, some short, some (*On Anger, On Benefits, On Clemency*) elaborate treatises in several books. In his retirement he embarked on grander schemes: *Natural Questions*, a rhetorically elaborate account of current theories about winds, earthquakes, lightning, and similar phenomena; and a comprehensive study of ethics from the Stoic point of view, never executed, but reflected in many of the *Moral Letters*, which he addressed to his friend Lucilius and which are his most popular and readable work. When Macaulay said that reading Seneca was like dining on nothing but anchovy sauce, he expressed something of the pleasure in witty detail and the dissatisfaction with the whole that most readers experience; it is the smaller scale and more intimate tone of the *Letters* that saves them from the worst effects of Seneca's incontinent ingenuity. So repetitive a writer seems made for the anthologist; and I cite two passages from which his manner may perhaps be judged.

In the first (*Tranquillity of Mind* 12–13) he adapts a theme from the end of the third book of Lucretius, on restlessness of soul; Stoic though he is, he has no compunction about using the common stock of philosophic moralizing, even if it is of Epicurean origin. What he implies about taste in scenery in this passage is of interest; so is his incidental attack at the end on the cruel fashion for gladiatorial shows.

Some things give the body pleasure and pain at once, like turning over before one side is tired, or tossing in one position after another. Thus Achilles in Homer, now on his face, now on his back, makes himself comfortable in different ways. This is what sick people do, who cannot endure anything long and use change as medicine. Hence futile travels and coastal excursions. The inconsistency that hates whatever is at hand experiments with the sea one moment, with the country the next. 'Let's go to Campania.' Pretty scenery is a bore. 'Let's go to a wild place, let's head for the mountains of Bruttium (the Abruzzi) and Lucania.' But in the wilderness some softer charms are wanted, something to relieve an eye sated with the grimness of a savage land. 'Let's make for Tarentum, the harbour everyone admires, the mild winter resort, the countryside that kept even its ancient population in affluence.' 'Now back to town!' It is too long since he heard the applause and the uproar. Now he wants the pleasure of human blood!

Secondly, one of the shorter *Letters* (60). The theme is the vanity of human desire and the narrowness of our real needs. The technique is very characteristic: exclamations, rhetorical questions, allusion to a classic (here Sallust), examples from the animal kingdom, personification of Nature, and a striking epigram at the end.

I've a grievance, I'm taking you to court, I'm angry. Do you still wish for what your nurse and your tutor and your mother wished for on your behalf? Don't you understand how much harm they wished for? How true it is that our friends' prayers are our enemies! All the more so if they have been fulfilled. I no longer find it surprising if all our troubles stay with us from childhood; we grew up amid our parents' curses. Perhaps one day the gods may hear a disinterested prayer from us! How long shall we go on asking them for something, as though we could not yet feed ourselves? How long shall we go on filling the territories of vast cities with our crops? How long shall a whole nation harvest them for us? How long will all those ships from many a sea supply the service of one man's table? The bull contents himself with a few acres' pasture; a single forest feeds many elephants; does one man need earth and sea to nourish him? Has Nature, having given us so modest a physique, then endowed us with a belly so insatiable that we surpass the greed of the hugest and hungriest of beasts? Indeed not. How small a quantity it is that is given to Nature! She is cheaply dismissed; it is not our belly's hunger that costs dear, but our pride. So let us count 'the belly's obedient servants', as Sallust calls them, as beasts, not men—and some not even live beasts, but dead creatures! A man who is of use to many is alive. A man who uses himself is alive. But for those who hide away in torpor, home is no better than a tomb. You might as well inscribe on marble at their door 'They predeceased their death.'

Pliny: Uncle and Nephew

The Annaei suggest a comparison with a rather later literary family, the Plinii. The earlier man of note is C. Plinius Secundus, 'the Elder Pliny', born about AD 23. He had a distinguished military and administrative career as an *eques*, serving in Germany under Claudius and Nero, but then retiring to a more private life until his friendship with Titus and Mucianus assured a succession of procuratorships under Vespasian. He died, as commander of the fleet at Misenum, in the eruption of Vesuvius in AD 79. He was curious to observe it, and went too far.

Pliny was not only an active official but a tireless student and writer. He wrote a history of the German wars in which he had served, a narrative history of Rome from AD 47 to AD 70, and a life of one of his commanding officers, the literary man Pomponius Secundus. All this is lost. What survives is a *Natural History*, in thirty-seven books, an encyclopedia of knowledge of the universe, the earth, man, animals, and plants, with large sections also on medicines and on the visual arts. It was a prime source of belief about the universe in the Latin Middle Ages and later, 'an immense register', as Edward Gibbon put it, of 'the discoveries, the arts, and the errors of mankind'.

Pliny's stylistic ambitions were not matched by competence or taste. He does not appear to have mastered either the periodic elegance in which, for example, Columella and Celsus wrote successfully on technical themes, or the staccato Senecan lucidity, which Seneca himself had used impressively for science. But he aims high; and, though a torment to translators, he has often tempted them, not only for his content but for a certain richness of language, especially in his many moralizing digressions and exclamations. His summary of Augustus' career (7.147 ff.) reveals a talent for satire, and the syntax of Mr. Jingle:

In Divine Augustus ... if all things were judged carefully many volumes of human destiny might be found; defeat in his uncle's time for the Mastership of the Horse; preference given to Lepidus over his candidature; unpopularity from the proscriptions; participation in the triumvirate with the most evil men—and in no equal share at that, but dominated by Antony; illness at Philippi, flight, three days' hiding in the marsh, ill and (according to Agrippa and Maecenas) swollen with subcutaneous water; Sicilian shipwreck; another concealment, this time in a cave; plea for death made to Proculeius in the rout at sea, with the enemy fleet hard upon him; anxiety in the Perugian war; mutinies; dangerous illnesses; suspicion of Marcellus' intentions; shocking exile of Agrippa; all the plots against his life; accusations about his children's deaths; mourning whose sadness was not due simply to bereavement; daughter's adultery and the disclosure of her plans for parricide; his stepson Nero's rude withdrawal from court; adultery again, in his granddaughter; then a combination of evils—lack of revenue, rebellion in Illyricum, call-up of slaves, shortage of recruits, plague in Rome, famine in Italy, determination to die, four days without food, when much of death entered his body; on top of this, disaster of Varus, foul insults to dignity, Postumus Agrippa adopted, rejected, and then missed, suspicion of Fabius and his betrayal of secrets, apprehensions concerning his wife and Tiberius. This was his last anxiety. In short, this god who perhaps not only achieved heaven, but deserved it, died leaving his enemy's son as his heir.

Pliny's nephew, 'the Younger Pliny', could never have written this. A studious youth, who wrote a Greek tragedy at fourteen, he describes himself, at the age of about eighteen, quietly reading Livy during the great eruption that killed his uncle. The boy was a pupil of Quintilian and of a noted Greek rhetor Nicetes Sacerdos. He went on to have a distinguished senatorial career, culminating in a consulship under Trajan in AD 100, the honorific and important *cura* of the Tiber river-works and urban drainage system, and finally the governorship of Bithynia. His most famous work, his *Letters*, to some extent reflects his public life, especially

STATUE-GROUP OF LAOCÖON AND HIS SONS (*c.* AD 10–30), one of the few works of art described in Pliny the Elder's *Natural History* to have survived. It was discovered in 1506 near the Golden House of Nero, where Pliny appears to have seen it. He describes it as 'a work superior to all paintings and sculptures.'

his and others' advocacy in the courts. But it is more a demonstration of what should be a cultured man's interests and values than an image of an individual achievement or personality. The letters have great elegance and finish. There are certain links with Greek rhetoric. In the formal descriptions (*ecphrases*), the reports of wonders of nature, and the technique of anecdote, we recognize the skills of Greek sophists such as Lucian. The general effect however is essentially Roman. Pliny depicts, no doubt in an idealized form, the style of public duty and literary taste that his generation felt to be its own. Literary prestige is important to him. He writes to Tacitus (7.20) that he has read and commented on his book—it is probably a part of the *Histories*, just possibly the *Dialogue*—and hopes for the like service in return, such being the traditional function of Roman 'friendship' (*amicitia*) when the parties are men of letters. He is pleased with the thought:

How it delights me that, if posterity cares at all, it will always be told in what harmony, sincerity and loyalty you and I lived! It will be a rare and notable thing that two men, near equals in age and position, and of some repute in letters—for I must needs speak sparingly of you when I am also speaking of myself!—encouraged each other's studies.

Plutarch

Among Pliny's contemporaries, and sharing some of his acquaintance, was the most important Greek writer of the age. L. Mestrius Plutarchus—to give him his names as a Roman citizen (he was in fact of equestrian status)—was from mainland Greece. His was the leading family of the historic, but decayed, town of Chaeronea in Boeotia. The past of his native district was particularly real to him: he defends the ancient Thebans against Herodotus' innuendos and accusations, and he sets up Epaminondas as an ideal of the philosopher statesman. But it was not enough to record the past, for there was a present revival to be fostered. Plutarch chose to teach his pupils philosophy at Chaeronea, he served the city whenever he could, and he worked hard for the restoration of the oracle and shrine at neighbouring Delphi, which enjoyed imperial patronage under Domitian and his successors. But for books and learned conversation—other than what he could gather around him at home—Plutarch had to visit Athens, where he learned his Platonist philosophy and enjoyed the company of the wise and the rich. Towards the end of his life, under Trajan and Hadrian, a happy age for many literary men, he received signal honours, notably the insignia of a consul (*ornamenta consularia*, a great distinction for an *eques*) and a post as procurator of Greece, nominally in charge of all imperial properties in the province. In later times it was well if a philosopher or scholar could claim descent from him; some did so even in the fourth century. This reputation was built on two foundations: personal charm and wisdom, and an immense activity of writing. Plutarch was not the man to command audiences like the great histrionic sophists of the age, nor did he wield any real political influence. His massive but superficial learning and his generous and unpedantic style served to project a conspicuously—some would say self-righteously—humane personality. We possess about half of what he wrote. He was popular in Byzantine times, but this was all that the thirteenth-century scholars managed to collect. All the same, it fills a dozen volumes. It falls into two parts: the great unified effort of the *Parallel Lives* and the seventy or so surviving miscellaneous works—mainly 'essays' and dialogues—which are usually called the *Moralia*.

The *Parallel Lives* were dedicated to Q. Sosius Senecio, an acquaintance of Pliny, and a great man—four times consul—of Trajan's reign. The plan was open-ended. Each book contained the lives of a Greek and a Roman whose careers had something in common: wisdom as lawgivers, courage, perseverance, eloquence, a period of exile, or a great fortune. Formal comparisons usually followed. The result was a presentation of classical history that, more than any other, created the Renaissance image of antiquity. Plutarch's purposes were confessedly moral. He sought to expound the virtues and vices of his great men and show how they responded to the challenges of fortune. He was not concerned with them as historical forces, only as men of certain qualities who were placed under the stress of great events and decisions. Whether it is Theseus or Pericles, Coriolanus or Caesar, the problem is seen in the same light, and (sources allowing) the biography follows more or less the same pattern: origin and childhood, introduction into public life, the career and its points of crisis, the death and posthumous reputation. It has often been pointed out that this partly echoes a well-attested rhetorical scheme for 'encomium'—origin, nature, character, actions and virtues, accomplishments, comparison with others—and this is of course true. But the distance between Plutarch's attitudes and that of a rhetorical encomiast can hardly be exaggerated. 'Rhetors', said Cicero, 'are allowed to tell lies in history, so as to be in a position to say something clever.' This is what Plutarch never does. His respect for evidence should not be questioned, though his interpretation of it, and his view of what biographical evidence is, may excite surprise. We should not expect in him any recognition of the difference between a primary and a secondary source; and we must be willing to accept 'probability'—meaning accord with what one expects of a certain kind of person in certain kinds of circumstances—as a criterion for judging between alternative accounts of the facts. What makes the *Lives* live, however, is not their moral preoccupations, nor yet their evident concern to demonstrate the political as well as the intellectual greatness of classical Greece; it is above all Plutarch's narrative gift, his willingness to listen to his sources and his skill in choosing the telling detail. No one forgets the death of Cato at Utica, or the love of Antony and Cleopatra; and it is from Plutarch that these episodes came into the consciousness of the modern world.

Some of the *Moralia* provoke comparison with Seneca. Both men wrote on Tranquillity and on Anger, though with different philosophical outlooks and with different expectations of their readership: Plutarch is far richer in learned allusion

PAINTING OF ANTONY AND CLEOPATRA by Sir Lawrence Alma-Tadema (1885): a late-Victorian romantic view of the affair which Plutarch immortalized in his *Life* of Antony. Plutarch's influence on the Renaissance was considerable, and North's translation of the *Parallel Lives* (1579) inspired Shakespeare's play, which set the tone for the modern conception of the fatal lovers.

and quotation, and is naturally critical of Stoic views. 'Essays' such as these, and the pieces on Curiosity, Talkativeness, and False Shame have been to many the most attractive of Plutarch's works. Through the translations of Amyot and Philemon Holland they have made a strong impact on the French and English essayists, from Montaigne to Emerson. But Plutarch himself would presumably have laid the weight elsewhere, on his more substantial philosophical exegesis (below, pp. 294 f.) and controversy, and especially on a group of dialogues which he wrote, it seems, towards the end of his life. Four of these have their setting in contemporary Delphi, and explore the antiquities of the oracle and the theory of prophecy. The most elaborate of them—'On those whom God is slow to punish'—rehearses views on the nature of evil, and concludes with a myth in the Platonic manner on the fate of the soul after death. Plutarch's revival of this theme—he used it twice besides in the works we have, and notably also in the lost *On the Soul*—is remarkable. His 'Underworld' has a stellar setting, and his descriptions are full of colour, light, and vividly imagined horror.

   Philosophy and myth are not, however, the only elements in his dialogues:

there is also a dramatic dimension. Thus he wrote *The Divine Sign of Socrates* with the liberation of Thebes from Spartan occupation in 379 BC as background (Vol. 1, p. 142). The adventure story, told again in the life of Pelopidas, is punctuated by discussions on prophecy and the most splendid of the myths. In the *Eroticus*, again, he weaves a contemporary intrigue—a widow has enticed a younger man to marry her—into a discourse on homosexual and heterosexual love, Platonic in detail but very un-Platonic in conclusions. For all their dependence on tradition—not only Plato's *Symposium*, *Critias*, and *Phaedrus*, but a Hellenistic inheritance, now only dimly discernible—Plutarch's dialogues are works of powerful originality. More than any of the other authors we have here selected for consideration, he is a witness to the deepening religious and theological consciousness of the age. In *The Decline of the Oracles*, he portrays a Spartan called Cleombrotus, freshly arrived in Delphi from the desert shores of the Red Sea. This personage advances views on 'demons' which there is good reason to think Plutarch does not take seriously; but the description of Cleombrotus' mission in life passes well for Plutarch's own:

Fond of seeing and learning, having adequate means and not thinking it worth while to acquire more, he employed his leisure for such travels, and assembled information (*historia*) to be the material of what he himself called 'philosophy with theology as its goal'.

Not that Plutarch would wish to seek out holy men in the desert. He stayed at home, and they came to him.

Lucian

The second great Greek writer of the period was born in Plutarch's latter years, around the beginning of the reign of Hadrian.

Lucian is in many ways Plutarch's antithesis. He came, not from the old heartland of Greece, but—much more typically of the period—from the more recently Hellenized East. His home was Samosata on the Euphrates, capital of the defunct kingdom of Commagene, one of whose princes—Philopappus—had been a friend of Plutarch's at Athens. His education would be quite different from Plutarch's, and this indeed is evident from their writing. Plutarch's Greek, allusive and classicizing as it is, is a link in a continuous tradition, passing through Hellenistic writing back to classical times. Lucian's—he claims it was his second language, Syriac being the first—is pure imitation (*mimēsis*) of the classical models, fascinatingly flexible, but clearly an artificial creation. There are other contrasts too. Plutarch takes religious belief, especially men's hopes and fears for what follows death, with great and humane seriousness. For Lucian all this is mockery. The judgement of the dead, the ferryman of the souls, 'and all the Vain, Infernal Trumpery', are for him simply the setting for a rather simple form of satire; visions, ghosts, magic are the contemptible inventions of charlatans whom it is the honest man's business to expose. Again: what Plutarch tells us of his life is evidently true. We believe in his regard for his father and his grandfather, his affectionate marriage, and his sorrow at his little daughter's death. Lucian, by contrast, gives us a stylized picture which it is foolish to treat as autobiography. We are not bound to believe in the family council that apprenticed him to his sculptor uncle, or his vision of Education (*Paideia*), or his abandonment of Rhetoric for Dialogue at the age of forty. We recall that Socrates too started as a sculptor, and Ovid's vision of Elegy and Tragedy (*Amores* 3. 1) is all too similar to Lucian's. A good deal of what Lucian says about himself is no more to be trusted than the voyage to the moon that he recounts so persuasively in the first person in *True Stories*.

Even his claim to have been the first to adapt the philosophical dialogue to comic purposes is hard to sustain. To go no further back, there is something of this in Plutarch—notably in *Gryllus*, where one of Circe's new pigs converses with Odysseus—and the evidence of Varro and Horace suggests the Hellenistic model of an earlier Syrian Greek, Menippus of Gadara, held by some to be a main source of Lucian's ideas. That Menippus' writings were a significant model is doubtful. More important than any such borrowing is Lucian's relentless exploitation of the limited range of classical texts that everybody knew, and his ingenuity in using the same motifs again and again. He does indeed have his originality, and it may well be that the 'miniature dialogue', in which he excelled, is one place where we should look for it. It was in this form that he composed his dialogues of the dead, of the gods, of the nymphs and deities of the sea, and of the educated prostitutes (*hetairai*) of comedy. Like the epigram, the letter, and the apophthegm—all of which flourished in this period—the miniature dialogue is directed at a readership which finds long texts trying. It has a clear connection with the elementary rhetorical exercises of narrative, anecdote, and description, and indeed with the even more elementary game of paraphrase. Yet in Lucian's hands it has real charm. We enjoy Doris' suggestion that Polyphemus really only likes Galatea because her complexion reminds him of the milk and cream cheese in which his riches lie. We admire the *ecphrasis* of Europa and the bull as seen with the eyes of Zephyrus, the West Wind, or Zeus' pleased revelation to Ganymede of who he really is. We relish the mild salaciousness of the conversations between the innocent young prostitute and her hopeful and ambitious mother— so long, that is, as we suspend any social feelings towards the widow whose only resource is to employ her daughter in this way. Lucian is sometimes regarded almost as a socialist before his time. This is to take him much too seriously. To see virtue in the poor and wickedness in the wealthy is a standard rhetorical pose of the age. And Lucian's consistent aim is to entertain.

Many of Lucian's dialogues are enlargements of the techniques of the 'miniatures'; but we also have—among nearly eighty books which seem to be genuine— not only purely rhetorical pieces ('talks', declamations, pastiches of Herodotus), but some works with a more serious link with the intellectual life of the time. These last include a 'life' of the Cynic Demonax, and devastating, though largely

fictitious, accounts of two famous religious charlatans, Alexander of Abonuteichus, an inventor of Mystery Rites, and the cynic Peregrinus Proteus, who
spectacularly burnt himself to death at Olympia in 167. But it is perhaps *True
Stories*, an ancestor of science fiction, that best conveys the elegance of his
imagination, the Lucianic blend of satire and fantasy that appeals to educated
children of all ages. The following episode needs no explanation; its techniques
of surprise are easily seen (1. 30-1).

Often, it seems, a change for the better heralds trouble. We had just two days' fair
weather sailing. As the third day broke, we suddenly glimpsed against the sunrise a
multitude of monsters and whales, the biggest of all being about 200 miles long. It was
approaching with its mouth open, stirring up the sea, the foam breaking around it. It
was displaying teeth taller than a human penis, sharp as rocks and white as ivory. We
embraced one another and spoke our last farewells. Then we waited. It was upon us
now, and it swallowed us up, ship and all. However, it failed to break the ship in pieces;
she slid down through the gaps in the teeth into the interior. When we were inside, all
was dark at first, and we could see nothing. After a while, however, the monster opened
its mouth and we had sight of a high, broad area, large enough to accommodate a city
of 10,000 people. In the middle, there were little fishes and many other animals, all
chopped up, with ships' sails, anchors, human bones, cargoes, and, among all this, land
and hills—formed, I imagine, out of the silt that had settled down. There was a wood
and trees of all kinds, with vegetables growing, and they had the look of being cultivated.
The circuit of the land area was 30 miles. Sea birds—gulls and halcyons—could be seen
nesting in the trees.

Aelius Aristides

Neither Plutarch nor Lucian figures among the second-century 'sophists' whose
lives Philostratus wrote, though both were on the fringe of the grand 'sophistic'
world—Lucian indeed more closely involved. Aelius Aristides, Lucian's near contemporary, may stand as the typical Antonine sophist, wealthy, much travelled,
flamboyant, egocentric. He has had little favour in modern times. Unravel his
complexities—his style aimed especially at the density of thought of his models,
Demosthenes and the speeches in Thucydides—and the labour seems wasted, so
little is there left to grip the mind. We admire, but hardly wish to read twice,
the subtle reconstructions of the political situations of 413 and 370 BC which
underlie his 'Sicilian' and 'Leuctrian' declamations. It is no wonder that no complete translation of Aristides in any modern language has been attempted till
recently; the magnificent scholarship of Willem Canter's Latin (1566) lay long
unstudied and unappreciated. But it is all a little unjust. There are at least three
claims that Aristides has on our attention. One—perhaps the best known—arises
from his encomium of Rome, delivered in the summer of 144, a fine, flattering
statement of the achievement of the Antonine Empire, from a grateful subject's
point of view. A second rests on his achievement in extending the range of prose

COSMOLOGICAL MOSAIC AT MERIDA (EMERITA) IN SPAIN (mid second century AD). The imagery of the pavement has been compared with that of Aelius Aristides' encomium of Rome, delivered in 144, in which Rome is likened to a sea into which all rivers flow and the Roman Empire is equated with the inhabited world. In the mosaic personifications of the winds, seasons, rivers etc. frame a symbolic representation of the Mediterranean, and the central position was perhaps occupied by a seated figure (now missing) of Rome.

oratory to include the hymn, hitherto the prerogative of poets. He is proud of this, and not unjustly. His prose hymns to Sarapis, Athena, and Dionysus have many splendours; the hymn 'to the Aegean Sea', with its colourful vision of sea and islands, is perhaps the most attractive of all. Thirdly, Aristides is the author of a singular spiritual autobiography (*Hieroi Logoi*), the day-by-day record of the interventions of the god Asclepius in his life, as adviser and healer. Hypochondriacs are not attractive people; but the completeness of Aristides' record, his naïve vanity and credulity, and the vividness of his language (for once not elaborate, indeed hardly *Kunstprosa* at all) combine to produce a text which has claimed deserved attention from historians, psychologists, and students of the religious mind. Asclepius guided him in strange ways; here he is on a short, but stormy, voyage from Clazomenae to Phocaea, along the coast of Asia Minor (2. 12–14):

An easterly breeze got up, and, as we proceeded, a brisk east wind, which broke out in the end into a fearful gale. Up went the ship at the prow, and down at the stern. She nearly foundered. She was awash everywhere. Then she headed out to sea. Sweating and shouting from the sailors, screams from all on board—some of my friends were with me—but all I said was 'O Asclepius!' After many hazards, driven out to sea time and again when we were on the point of making port, and causing the people watching great anxiety, we finally reached land—safe and happy, but only just! When night came, the god commanded me to purge myself, and told me how. The purging was as complete as if I had taken hellebore, as those who had had experience of that drug told me. *Everything* was moved by the waves! The god now told me the whole truth, namely that I was destined to be shipwrecked and this was why these things had happened, and now, both for safety and to fulfil my destiny, I must get into a boat in the harbour and contrive that it should capsize and sink; someone would then rescue me and bring me ashore. I was of course happy to do this. Everyone was amazed at the ingenious fake shipwreck, coming on top of the real danger. We knew that it was Asclepius who had saved us from the sea. The purging was an additional blessing.

Conclusion

We began this survey by emphasizing that the prose literature of the period was one of highly professional art. Both in Latin and in Greek, the reading public expected accuracy, elegance, and virtuosity in a very elaborate verbal game. We conclude by making the complementary observation, to which the intimate detail of our last extract from Aristides particularly lends colour, that it was also a literature of personal statement. The letter, the essay, the speech that confesses a personality are, for the first time, leading literary forms. What unites these two features—which may at first sight seem ill matched—is the nature of the society on which the literature is based. This was a governing class of diverse origins but homogeneous education, for whom distinction in their studies both lent respectability to worldly success and often led to it. The members of this élite, whether in Syria or in Spain, were of personal interest to themselves and to one another. Their feelings, their moral problems, even their illnesses were fit matter for writing. They shared a common range of cultural reference, and a common interest in the classical past.

It is hard to point to a prose genius, though common consent would except Tacitus. The Christian writers to come have a better claim. But the high level of skill, the charm and interest of the persons concerned, and the massive information they communicate about so many aspects of ancient life, in their own and earlier days, deserve appreciative readers and careful students. Seneca and Pliny,

Plutarch and Lucian, and many others, are articulate witnesses to a state of civilization which has many affinities with our own. They look inwards upon themselves and backwards to the past, and in their two literary languages they have a superb instrument to express these two great concerns.

Further Reading

GENERAL

Besides the standard histories of literature etc. the following works are particularly useful for the whole period: E. Norden, *Die antike Kunstprosa* (3rd edn. Leipzig, 1915, repr. 1958); A. D. Leeman, *Orationis Ratio* (Amsterdam, 1963), on Latin prose; B. P. Reardon, *Courants Littéraires grecs des IIe et IIIe siècles* (Paris, 1971); G. Kennedy, *The Art of Rhetoric in the Roman World* (Princeton, 1972). Two older books may be added: J. P. Mahaffy, *The Silver Age of the Greek World* (Chicago-London, 1906); S. Dill, *Roman Society from Nero to M. Aurelius* (London, 1904). Both are still worth reading.

AUTHORS

Texts and translations of most of the works mentioned are available in the Loeb Classical Library (LCL). This, like the bilingual French Budé series, is of varying quality, but is particularly useful for late Greek authors, and contains some recent editions of great value, e.g. Seneca the Elder (M. Winterbottom), Pliny's Letters (B. Radice), Herodian (C. R. Whittaker). Authors *not* available in Loeb are asterisked in the following list. When an author is not mentioned, it may be assumed (i) that there is a Loeb; (ii) that there is no outstanding special study in English.

*Aristides: A. Boulanger, *Aelius Aristide* (Paris, 1923). Good discussions of the 'diary' of his illnesses in E. R. Dodds, *Pagan and Christian in an Age of Anxiety* (Cambridge, 1965); and in A. J. Festugière, *Personal Religion among the Greeks* (Berkeley and Los Angeles, 1954), LCL has a selection only; the most recent translation of the 'diary' is C. A. Behr, *Aelius Aristides and The Sacred Tales* (Amsterdam, 1968), which also contains a discussion of Aristides' career. A complete translation of Aristides by C. A. Behr is now available (Amsterdam, 1981).

Arrian: P. A. Stadter, *Arrian of Nicomedeia* (Chapel Hill, 1980).

M. Aurelius: Good study by A. S. L. Farquharson, whose text, translation, and commentary are standard: *The Meditations of the Emperor Marcus Antoninus* (Oxford, 1944; reissued 1968).

Demetrius: Tr. G. M. A. Grube, *A Greek Critic* (Toronto, 1961). Also (part) by D. C. Innes in *Ancient Literary Criticism*, ed. D. A. Russell and M. Winterbottom (Oxford, 1972), where translations of other critical texts of the period (e.g. 'Longinus', Tacitus, extracts from Dionysius and Plutarch) may be found.

Dio Chrysostom: C. P. Jones, *The Roman World of Dio Chrysostom* (Cambridge, Mass., 1978).

Dio Cassius: F. Millar, *A Study of Cassius Dio* (Oxford, 1974).

Dionysius of Halicarnassus: S. F. Bonner, *The Literary Treatises of Dionysius of Halicarnassus* (Cambridge, 1939). LCL edn. of critical works not yet complete; Budé (G. Aujac) supplies the gap, also edns. of some treatises by W. Rhys Roberts (Cambridge, 1901; London-Edinburgh, 1910).

*Greek novelists: A collected volume of translations (ed. B. P. Reardon) is promised. Meanwhile, Xenophon of Ephesus, Chariton, and Heliodorus are *not* in LCL, but Budé has a good edn. of the last. General study: B. E. Perry, *The Ancient Romances* (Berkeley, 1967); but E. Rohde, *Der griechische Roman* Leipzig, 1876 3rd. edn. 1914) remains a classic. See also G. Anderson, *Eros Sophistes* (*American Classical Studies* 9, 1982).

Greek letter-writing: Few of the 'epistolographi' are available in English: R. Hercher's edn. (Paris,

1873) remains standard. But note esp. I. Düring, *Chion of Heraclea* (Göteborg, 1951) which has a translation of this 'epistolary romance' and a useful introduction.

'Longinus': Ed. with commentary, D. A. Russell (Oxford, 1964; repr. 1982). For translation see under Demetrius.

Lucian: J. Bompaire, *Lucien écrivain* (Paris, 1958); G. Anderson, *Lucian: Theme and Variation*, and *Studies in Lucian's Comic Fiction*, *Mnemosyne*, suppls. 41 and 43 (1976); Penguin selection, tr. P. Turner. Complete Eng. tr. by H. W. and F. G. Fowler.

Philostratus: Abridged translation of *Life of Apollonius*—part novel, part pagan hagiography—by G. W. Bowersock (Penguin).

Pliny (the Younger): Comm. A. N. Sherwin White (2nd edn. London, 1969).

Plutarch: C. P. Jones, *Plutarch and Rome* (Oxford, 1971); D. A. Russell, *Plutarch* (London, 1972); A. G. Wardman, *Plutarch's Lives* (London, 1974). Penguin translation of many Lives. Elizabethan translation of Lives (Sir T. North) and 'Morals' (Philemon Holland), both important for English literature.

Quintilian: G. Kennedy, *Quintilian* (New York, 1969).

Seneca (the Elder): Recent studies by L. A. Sussman: *The Elder Seneca*, *Mnemosyne*, suppl. 51 (1978) and J. Fairweather (Cambridge, 1981).

Seneca (the Younger): M. T. Griffin, *Seneca: A Philosopher in Politics* (Oxford, 1976); A. L. Motto, *Seneca* (New York, 1973); also a collection of essays in *Seneca*, ed. C. D. N. Costa (London-Boston, 1974).

12

Silver Latin Poetry and the Latin Novel

❦

RICHARD JENKYNS

The Silver Age: Problems and Solutions

THE word 'silver', applied to those Latin poets who wrote after the death of Augustus, is a modern label. Like all such labels, it can easily be misleading; time flows on continuously, and any attempt to divide the past into ages or periods is bound to be a more or less artificial attempt to impose simple patterns upon a complex and unceasing flux. None the less, the phrase 'silver age' has its uses. We customarily think of the Augustan age as a time of dazzling poetic achievement, but it is often forgotten that this achievement belongs largely to the first half of Augustus' long reign. During his last twenty-five years and more there was no major poet still active except Ovid; and there is evidence in his later work that Ovid saw himself as a lone survivor, the last of a line. The quarter century following Ovid's death is one of the most barren for poetry in Latin literary history; it is not unrealistic to think in terms of one chapter closing and another beginning.

The term 'silver age' is of course designed to contrast with the 'golden age' which preceded it. This implied contrast contains, once again, a truth and a danger. We should not let ourselves be trapped by a mechanical view of the rise and fall of cultures into supposing that the silver age was a second-rate period which necessarily produced second-rate literature; it includes, at the lowest estimate, at least one poet of genius and several distinctive talents of a lesser order, and it also gave birth to a great historian and by far the best prose fiction to come out of the ancient world. On the other hand, it is indeed true that the poets who came after the Augustans were faced with a peculiar difficulty and a peculiar challenge; and to understand what these were we must first recall the situation of their predecessors.

From the start the Latin poets wrote in the consciousness that the Greek achievement loomed large behind them; the shadow of a mighty past falls dark across their verses. The Greeks seemed to have mastered every field of literature; how could Latin poets hope to produce anything that would not seem a pale and lifeless imitation? That was their dilemma, and a number rose to the challenge by openly acknowledging their debt to Greece, sometimes boldly, sometimes with a studied modesty. The aim was to point the reader's attention to the Greek models, in order to draw out the no less significant divergences from those models; imitation could thus become a kind of originality. The supreme example of this technique is the *Aeneid*.

The silver poets inherited this situation, but with a new difficulty. There was now a mighty body of Latin classics as well. Virgil, Horace, and Ovid, in their different ways, had brought the various genres which they had attempted to such a pitch of perfection that it must have seemed impossible for their successors to develop them further. How could one now write an epic poem which would not read like a pastiche of Virgil, or lyric poetry which would not seem a mere shadow of Horace? It is interesting to find Velleius Paterculus, who wrote second-rate history during the reign of Augustus' successor Tiberius, observing that the highest achievements in any particular genre of literature all occur within a relatively brief period of time; he concludes that genius, despairing of surpassing what has already been perfected or seeking for new territory to conquer, passes on to new fields of endeavour. These remarks are significant precisely because Velleius was himself no genius: he reflects the attitudes of a more or less conventional literary gentleman. We find much talk of decline in the writers of the first century AD. Some of them assert that there has indeed been a decline, others indignantly deny it. Naturally there was no general agreement; what matters is that the state of contemporary literature was an issue that was in the air as never before.

It is intriguing, too, to find Statius, near the end of the century, concluding his epic *Thebaid* by insisting that his work is far inferior to the immortal *Aeneid*. What Statius is doing is dramatizing his dilemma and at the same time playing an elegant literary game by adapting a traditional motif to new circumstances. The theme of self-deprecating homage to a great predecessor had been heard often—Horace, for example, with nicely calculated humility contrasts himself with the torrential genius of Pindar—but never before in epic, where a pose of confidence was expected. Statius, however, who begins his poem by asking what story he shall take for his subject, concludes it on a note of self-doubt. More than ever, poetry has become reflective upon its own nature; the Augustan self-consciousness has been given a new twist.

Manilius' *Astronomica*, begun in the last years of Augustus and continued under Tiberius, illustrates the possibilities and the pitfalls. This is a didactic poem on the theory of astrology, conceived on a heroic scale. Lucretius' *De rerum natura* is the obvious exemplar, and its influence is patent throughout. Like Lucretius, Manilius speaks of struggling with the intractability of his subject-matter; the difficulty of putting arithmetic into verse is at once his problem and his delight.

HYLAS SEIZED BY WATER-NYMPHS: painting by William Etty (1833). This romantic episode from the voyage of the Argonauts was described by several Hellenistic and Roman poets, including Valerius Flaccus, who introduced one or two new elements into the story (e.g. the idea that Hylas came to the spring in pursuit of a deer, not in search of water).

But whereas Lucretius' wrestle with the complexities of Epicurean physics is inspired by deep moral seriousness and driven forward by a formidable intellectual energy, the *Astronomica* seems to be at heart a literary exercise. The game of putting sums into polished hexameters is essentially pointless and quickly becomes tedious. In other parts of the work Manilius reveals himself as a poet of considerable talent, with a gift for the sonorous line and the piquant phrase; but his gifts have not found an adequate object.

The epic poet had two types of model before him, the mythological (such as the *Aeneid*) and the historical, such as Ennius' *Annales*. Silius Italicus (*c.* 26–101) got the worst of both worlds by trying to combine the two: his *Punica*, which is (alas) the longest of classical Latin poems, relates Hannibal's invasion of Italy, but with the full mythological apparatus of divine interventions, a descent to the underworld, and so on. The result is painfully incongruous. The *Argonautica* of Valerius Flaccus (died *c.* 92) and the *Thebaid* of Statius (*c.* 45–96), both mythological epics, are better; but though both poets had talent, neither found a way of imparting genuine freshness and life to his subject. Few are those who have read to the end of either work for pleasure. Of Statius' other verse there survives the *Achilleid*, a fragment of an uncompleted epic, and the *Silvae*, a collection of mostly occasional poems, of which the shortest (5.4), nineteen lines addressed by the insomniac poet to the god of sleep, is deservedly well known.

But, as Martial unkindly observed (10.4), there was not much life left in the old mythology now: 'You who read of Oedipus and of Thyestes in the dark, of Colchian women and Scyllas, of what are you reading but monsters? ... Why does the empty nonsense of a wretched sheet please you? Read this, of which life can say, "It is mine." You will not find Centaurs, Gorgons, or Harpies here; my page smells of man.' (Oedipus appears in Statius' *Thebaid*; Seneca had composed a *Thyestes*.) The one man who found a way to reinvigorate the epic genre was Lucan. He went to history for his theme, but to history told in a wholly new way.

SILVER DISH FROM KAISERAUGST (fourth century AD) depicting scenes from the early life of Achilles, the subject of Statius' *Achilleid*. On the rim (anti-clockwise) the dipping of the child Achilles in the River Styx to confer immortality on him, his education by the centaur Chiron, and his concealment, disguised as a woman, among the daughters of King Lycomedes on Skyros. In the central tondo his exposure by the ruses of Greek warriors.

Lucan

Lucan (39-65) is one of the most remarkable figures in Latin literature. He was compelled by Nero to take his own life at the age of twenty-six; by this time he had already composed numerous works, all of which have perished except for the ten books of his uncompleted epic on the civil war between Caesar and Pompey, known as the *Bellum civile* or *Pharsalia*.

Conventionally, the epic poet announces the heroic character of his theme in the first line, and even with the first word. Thus Virgil opens the *Aeneid* with the word 'arma' ('arms'), and Lucan, in apparently similar vein, begins 'bella', ('wars'). But then immediately he twists the theme in a new direction:

> Bella per Emathios plus quam ciuilia campos
> iusque datum sceleri canimus . . .

Of wars more than civil on the plains of Thessaly I sing, of legality granted to crime . . .

This will prove to be a heroic poem without a hero, for Caesar is portrayed as a villain, and though Pompey is more sympathetic, he is, as Cato is made to say, far inferior to earlier Romans in his respect for the bounds of law. (Cato himself, though the pattern of republican propriety, is of secondary importance only.) The staple of epic warfare had been the *aristeia*, in which an individual hero showed his prowess in a series of duels, each vividly described. Lucan allows none of his characters so much honour. There is not a single *aristeia* in his account of the battle of Pharsalus, and only one individual death is described; the rest is a senseless welter of mass slaughter. The gods, too, hitherto essential in epic, are given no place at all in the poem, but instead we see a world plunging to disaster, and at the climax of the action Lucan shouts out (7. 446 f.), 'The world is swept along by blind chance; we lie when we say that Jupiter reigns.'

In the same spirit, there is not the usual appeal to the Muse for aid and inspiration at the beginning of the work. After announcing his theme, Lucan turns instead to address the citizens of Rome with sorrow and indignation (1.8): 'Quis furor, o ciues, quae tanta licentia ferri?' ('What was this madness, citizens, what was this great orgy of slaughter?') For this is to be not just a historical, but also a political, poem. Homer and Virgil had been remarkable for the breadth of their sympathies: both Greeks and Trojans in the *Iliad*, both Trojans and Italians in the *Aeneid* excite our admiration and compassion. Lucan deliberately does away with this, admitting that his approach is partisan and his purpose to get his readers to favour one side against the other (7.207-13).

In keeping with this outlook is the poet's declamatory method. The epic poet had traditionally kept his own personality out of his work, preserving an Olympian objectivity, but Lucan constantly involves himself with his characters, haranguing and mocking them, For example, Book 7 begins with one of Lucan's most moving passages: Pompey on the night before his defeat dreams of the triumphs of his earlier life. At first the scene is described without the author intruding his presence, but at line 24 he addresses the guards of the camp, urging them not to sound the reveille and disturb their general's slumbers. At line 29 he speaks to Pompey himself and continues addressing him until line 42. In line 43 he addresses the whole Roman nation; in line 44 he is back with Pompey again. He is like an advocate in court, turning to the gentlemen of the jury and then back to the witness in the box. Constantly we are aware of the poet's personal voice, harsh, passionate, and sarcastic.

On every page of the *Bellum civile* we find epigram, paradox, and bitter wit. Lucan carried to its extreme the fondness of the silver age for what Romans called the 'sententia', the pithy or pointed saying. The first line of the poem, besides asserting the work's epic character, announces this other element also, for it contains the poem's first epigram. The war is 'more than civil' because it is a conflict not just between fellow citizens but between members of the same family, Pompey having previously been Caesar's son-in-law. Lucan remodels epic to give it a sardonic and even a satiric tone.

The blend of political passion and rhetorical conceits is the essence of the *Pharsalia*. In the first book the character of Caesar is sketched in sharp terse phrases which recall Sallust. Cato's summing up of Pompey's career shows a historical sense, setting the great man in the context of his time and balancing virtues against faults with a dignified restraint:

> 'ciuis obit', inquit, 'multum maioribus impar
> nosse modum iuris, sed in hoc tamen utilis aeuo,
> cui non ulla fuit iusti reuerentia; salua
> libertate potens, et solus plebe parata
> priuatus seruire sibi, rectorque senatus,
> sed regnantis, erat.'
>
> (9. 190-5)

'A citizen has died', he said, 'far inferior to our ancestors in recognizing the limits of legality, but valuable in this present age, which has had no reverence for justice. He was powerful, and yet preserved liberty; he alone stayed a private citizen when the people were ready to be his slaves; he was ruler of the Senate, but of a Senate which kept the sovereignty.'

The last five words show how the *sententia* could be directed to the service of a political and historical theme: the difference between autocracy and dictatorship is put with admirable concision. Sometimes, too, the *sententia* displays a psychological acuity, as when the boy king of Egypt takes a child's delight at 'being grown up' and ordering the death of Pompey:

> adsensere omnes sceleri. laetatur honore
> rex puer insueto, quod iam sibi tanta iubere
> permittant famuli.
>
> (8. 536-8)

All voted for the crime. The boy king delights in the unaccustomed honour—that now his slaves should allow him to issue such important orders.

Unfortunately, though, an account of Lucan that dwelt only upon his virtues would be seriously misleading, for his faults are very gross. The promise of historical and political seriousness which the poem appears to make is for the most part unfulfilled; Caesar soon turns into a mere pantomime villain, a preposterous ranter hardly worth the compliment of our hatred. The rhetoric is often absurd, and the ceaseless search for paradox produces results that are often tedious and far-fetched; worst of all, the poem lacks variety of style and theme, and the unchanging note of sardonic bleakness becomes wearisome. The way in which Lucan allowed a taste for rhetorical smartness to run away with him can be seen (for example) in the speech of Pothinus at the court of Ptolemy (8. 484-535): for a line or two it looks as though this may be a powerful if cynical defence of expediency against absolute morality, but Pothinus quickly becomes a cardboard monster mouthing clever epigrams of the kind that would persuade nobody. Lucan is, apart from Ovid, the one major Latin poet surviving who composed with speed and fluency, and he has all the faults of the man who never blots a line. His early death leaves us with one of the most intriguing 'ifs' of Latin literary history: had he survived, would he have developed into a great master, or was he by nature one of those highly talented men who are for ever revealing unexpected shallows?

Tragedy

Quintilian (above, p. 247), while admiring Lucan's passion and epigrammatic brilliance, judged him more suitable for orators than poets to imitate. The influence of rhetoric has been commonly blamed for the vices of silver Latin poetry, and the charge has force; but it is wrong to regard rhetoric as the necessary enemy of poetry, and it should be clear that Lucan's virtues are as much the product of his rhetorical cast of thought as are his faults. In Juvenal rhetoric becomes an essential element of great poetry—as it does in the *Aeneid*, for that matter. If, on the other hand, we want to see what happens when the rhetorical manner is used in the absence of imagination, we may turn to the tragedies of Seneca. Ten plays have come down to us under his name, of which one is certainly and another probably spurious. The loss of all other Roman tragedies and the influence which Seneca's are supposed to have had on renaissance drama— an influence, however, which was probably much smaller than has usually been thought—have ensured for them a greater attention than their literary quality alone would deserve.

Like other Latin poets, Seneca develops a Greek genre in a new direction: he turns Attic tragedy towards the gruesome, the sensational, and the extreme. The Hippolytus of Euripides is chaste, pure, puritan; Seneca's Hippolytus is a neurotic with an exaggerated aversion from city life. Euripides' *Medea* ends sensationally enough, but Seneca has a still more sensational, though much coarser, *coup de théâtre* in store for us: Medea, aloft, prepares to ascend into the skies in her chariot,

THE DEATH OF ASTYANAX: terracotta relief of the late first century BC or the early first century AD. In front of a typical theatrical backdrop (*scaenae frons*) tragic actors perform a scene from a Roman drama, probably the *Astyanax* of Accius (second century BC). The same scene, in which Odysseus demands the surrender of the child Astyanax from its mother Andromache, recurs in the *Troades* of Seneca (lines 707–813).

and tosses down to Jason the bodies of their dead children; he closes the play by railing at her, 'Go through the lofty regions of high heaven, and bear witness where you ride that there are no gods' (testare nullos esse, qua veheris, deos'—there is a savage punch in the very last word of all). Euripides' Theseus beholds the mangled body of his dying son Hippolytus; Seneca's Theseus tries to re-assemble the corpse's scattered pieces, while the chorus add helpful advice, as though he were doing a jigsaw puzzle. In more talented hands such bizarreries might have a grotesque kind of power, and some critics have claimed to find unappreciated merits in these plays; but when we contemplate the amount of feeble rant that fills play after play, we may conclude that they have let faith triumph over plausibility.

Epigram and Satire

'I have not drenched my lips in the nag's spring,' declared Persius (34–62), in disrespectful allusion to the fountain Hippocrene, that classic symbol of poetic inspiration. Vitality came more easily to those poets who did not burden themselves with the pretensions of the more exalted genres. Persius himself, who wrote six satires before his early death, is a curious and intriguing figure. He describes himself as 'iunctura callidus acri' (5. 14 'clever at the pungent combining of words'): his blend of a compressed, clotted style, thick with literary allusion, and a contorted moral seriousness makes difficult reading. He was much admired and imitated by the satirists of the English renaissance, and the reader of Donne's satires may catch something of his odd, pungent flavour.

Martial (*c.* 40–101), as we have seen (above, p. 270), also took trouble to set himself at a distance from the grander poets; but he is, by contrast, easy and undemanding. Active mainly in the reign of Domitian, he is the father of the epigram in the modern sense of the term: the short poem, sometimes very short, with a witty point or a twist in the tail. For example:

> Hesterno fetere mero qui credit Acerram,
> fallitur: in lucem semper Acerra bibit.
> (1. 28)

He who thinks Acerra reeks of yesterday's wine is wrong: Acerra always drinks till dawn.

Sometimes the wit has a touch of Ovid's or (to look forward) of Herrick's charm:

> Intactas quare mittis mihi, Polla, coronas?
> a te uexatas malo tenere rosas.
> (11. 89)

Why, Polla, do you send me chaplets that you have not touched? I had rather hold roses that your hands had disturbed.

And sometimes he achieves pathos, still without losing his epigrammatic pointedness, as in his poem on the death of Erotion in childhood, which ends thus:

> mollia non rigidus caespes tegat ossa nec illi,
> terra, grauis fueris: non fuit illa tibi.
> (5. 34. 9 f.)

Let the turf be not hard that covers her soft bones; earth, be not heavy upon her; she was not heavy upon you.

On the other hand, a high proportion of his epigrams is obscene; and he cheerfully allows that his object is to titillate his readers.

We have seen that silver epic was most successful when, with Lucan, it shaded into satire; the finest fusion of rhetorical magnificence and epigrammatic harshness comes, however, in Juvenal, the greatest poet of the silver age. Little is known about his life: a fair hypothesis is that he was born around 65 or a little later and died around 130. His style is dense, muscular, declamatory. He seems to have composed slowly and laboriously, since he has left us just fifteen satires and a fragment of a sixteenth, probably unfinished.

Since Juvenal's is the Latin poetry most like satire in the modern sense, it should be stressed that he departed decisively from the traditions of Roman *satura*. Lucilius and Horace had adopted a rapid, discursive, informal manner; they offered, or purported to offer, a view of the poet off duty, with the quirks of his personality freely on display. Juvenal, by contrast, reveals very little of himself. His voice is exceedingly distinctive, but we learn next to nothing of the man behind it. The combination of impersonality and distinctive timbre recalls Lucretius; and it is again Lucretius whom of all Roman poets he most resembles in his blend of satiric sharpness with the grand manner. Many details of style and allusion show that the poet who most influenced him, surprising as it may at first seem, was Virgil, echoes of whom he sometimes uses to point an ironic contrast between the imaginary worlds of heroic or pastoral poetry and the ugly realities of the present time. Though he pays lip-service to the memories of Lucilius and Horace in his first satire, they seem to have made no substantial impression on his verse.

Much ink has been spilled on the question whether Juvenal was a genuine moralist or an opportunist who did not care what his target was, provided he could make a poem out of it; but the whole debate is to some extent misconceived. Though in a few of his later (and generally weaker) satires he assumes a high moral tone, he is for the most part concerned to excoriate human behaviour not for being wicked but for being sordid, vulgar, or disgusting. He is above all a social observer, who combines exactness of observation with imagination. We do not turn to him for wisdom, and he did not intend that we should.

In his first satire Juvenal presents himself as almost overwhelmed by the chaos of his own impressions; and the sixth, a diatribe against the female sex almost 700 lines long, is (by design, we may suppose) a vast ramshackle edifice in which women are assailed for every vice from promiscuity to artiness, and even for being tediously virtuous. But he also liked to organize his satires along a particular line of argument illustrated by a mass of examples, a technique borrowed from the declaimers. Thus Satire 8 opens with the words 'What is the use of family trees?', and the entire poem argues the vanity of noble birth. Even the sixth satire is strung along a thread of this kind, however loosely: the poet purports to be giving an acquaintance the reasons for not marrying. This technique is seen at its most impressive in the tenth satire. 'What should a man pray for?' is the theme, and Juvenal passes one by one over the traditional objects of human aspiration—power, fame, conquest, long life, beauty—exposing the vanity of each by a succession of illustrations from history, mythology, and Roman life: Sejanus, Cicero, Hannibal, Alexander, Priam are all paraded before the reader's eyes.

Juvenal's favourite line of attack is to display things exactly as they are: to refuse to be deceived, as he sees it, by ideas and abstractions. What is military glory, with its processions of captured weaponry and triumphal arches, if you simply *look* at it? Juvenal gives us the answer (10. 133-6): 'The spoils of war, a corslet fastened to a stump as a trophy, a cheek-piece hanging from a broken helmet, a yoke shorn of its pole, the flagstaff of a captured trireme and a sad prisoner at the top of an arch ...' Broken objects and wretched humanity—that is all there is to see, if one looks with Juvenal's dispassion.

In similar spirit, the first question that he asks about Hannibal is how much does his dust now weigh; the solid, physical world is what concerns him. And Hannibal's ambition—to ride in triumph through Rome—is viewed with the same harsh literalism: he wanted to plant his standard in the Subura, a shabby and crowded part of the city. The Carthaginian general had lost an eye, and he rode upon an elephant (a 'Gaetulian beast'). Juvenal puts these facts together, considers the picture that they make (notice the words 'facies' and 'tabella') and ends up with a vision both strange and ludicrous:

> o qualis facies et quali digna tabella
> cum Gaetula ducem portaret belua luscum.
> $\qquad$ (157 f.)

What a sight it was, what a picture it would make, when the Gaetulian monster carried the one-eyed commander.

And the great man is finally dispatched in some famous lines:

> finem animae, quae res humanas miscuit olim,
> non gladii, non saxa dabunt nec tela, sed ille
> Cannarum uindex et tanti sanguinis ultor
> anulus. i, demens, et saeuas curre per Alpes
> ut pueris placeas et declamatio fias.
> $\qquad$ (163–7)

Not swords, not stones or spears shall put an end to the life of this man who once threw human affairs into confusion, but that punisher for Cannae and avenger for so much blood, a little ring. Go, madman, run over the savage Alps, to become the schoolboys' favourite and become a subject for declamation.

This is magnificent rhetoric. The epigrammatic *sententia* which concludes the passage has an irony that embraces not just the boys in school but, more subtly, the poet as well: for what is he doing himself with Hannibal if not declaiming about him? The little word 'anulus', thin and scornful in its isolation at the beginning of a new line, contrasts admirably with the slow massive rhythm of the line before. But characteristically, the metrical technique serves a visual purpose as well: it is a *little* ring in which Hannibal kept poison ('anulus' is a diminutive, a fact which in the context is felt), and we are made to see how small an object has put an end to so great a life.

Juvenal is, indeed, a masterly observer, with a brilliant eye for the telling detail: a woman's ear-lobes pulled downwards by the weight of the pearls worn on them (6.458 f.), the wife whose infidelity is betrayed to her husband by her glowing ears (11.189), the soldiers' 'brawny calves drawn up to big benches' when their civilian victim appears before the military court (16.14). Often this vividness is enhanced by a touch of fantasy, and inanimate things are 'brought to life'. The windows seem to be watching the man rash enough to walk through Rome by night (3.275); roast boar, piping hot, seems to be foaming like the living boar of Meleager (5.115 f.); the figure on an equestrian statue seems to be in the act of aiming his lance (7.128); a purse crammed with money 'swells with

PORTRAIT OF A WOMAN from Roman Egypt (first half of second century AD). Juvenal's denunciation of women in his sixth satire includes scathing references to female self-adornment, such as the wearing of emerald necklaces, heavy pearl ear-rings, and make-up.

its mouth stuffed full' just like a greedy human being (14. 138). Some of his grimmest inventions are poetically suggestive, as in this picture of one of the emperor Domitian's councillors (4. 109 f.): 'saevior illo/Pompeius tenui iugulos aperire susurro' ('Pompeius, more savage than he [Crispinus] at slitting throats with his thin whisper'). The sinister sound of the verse matches the sinister compression of phrase which assimilates the thin sound of the informer's whisper to the thin edge of the razor cutting through flesh. Juvenal has often enough been praised as a satirist; he deserves to be more widely known for his powers of poetic imagination.

His contemporary Tacitus remarks (*Ann.* 4. 32), 'nobis in arto et inglorius labor' ('Mine is a narrow and inglorious task'). We catch a similarly self-contemptuous note in the poet; we are often reminded of Juvenal's claim that 'indignatio' inspired his verse, less often of the context in which that claim was made:

> si natura negat, facit indignatio uersum
> qualemcumque potest, quales ego uel Cluuienus.
>
> (1. 79 f.)

If nature denies, scorn makes such verses as it can—such as I write or Cluvienus.

In other words, the kind of verse that scorn produces is poor stuff. Yet both the poet and the historian, we may feel, protest too much. Tacitus would not really prefer, as he pretends, to be relating the glorious deeds of the Roman republic: the very bleakness and narrowness of his subject have a poetic grandeur of a novel kind. The same moral may be applied to Juvenal: his bitter, grating voice and narrowness of theme are not at odds with the splendour of his rhetoric but are the very essence of that splendour. The kind of sardonic grandeur that was achieved fitfully by Lucan was attained with full assurance by Juvenal. Political circumstances made men sour; literary circumstances demanded a new kind of poetry. Juvenal was the one poet, as Tacitus was the one historian, who found a theme and tone which answered to both the social and literary conditions of his age.

The Novel

Prose fiction was conventionally regarded as a very low form of art. Not one of the literary critics of antiquity thought it worth his consideration. Tacitus treated the life and death of Petronius in his *Annals* without deigning to mention that the man had written a novel; such things were below the dignity of history. We have seen that the poets who continued to work in the traditional or 'classic' genres were always liable to fall under the curse of academic art and become competent but lifeless. Perhaps we should not be surprised to find in the novel, the most despised of all genres, unfettered by literary convention, unencumbered by the legacy of great predecessors, a new sparkle and vitality. An ancestry can, it is true, be found for the Roman novel; in 'Milesian tales', stories of erotic or supernatural adventure; in Menippean satire, a genre which mixed prose and verse, as does Petronius; and, in the case of Apuleius at least, the Greek love romance. But all that we know about these often obscure ancestors suggests that our two surviving specimens of Roman novel-writing went far beyond them; they are gloriously original and uninhibited works, as unlike anything else in antiquity as they are unlike each other.

Petronius' date and identity have been disputed. Most scholars, though not all, believe him to be identical with Nero's 'arbiter elegantiae', compelled by the Emperor to take his own life in AD 66, and that is the assumption made here. Only one episode of the *Satyrica* (to give what is commonly called the *Satyricon* its correct title) has come down to us entire: this is what has become known as the *Cena Trimalchionis*, 'Trimalchio's dinner-party'. The rest of the *Satyrica* survives in very patchy fragments only. If it was written on the same scale as the *Cena*, it must have been an enormous work, far longer than any other novel of antiquity; but it is possible that the dinner party was a centre-piece, like the tale of Cupid and Psyche in Apuleius' *Golden Ass*, developed in far more detail than any other part of the story.

Since so much is lost, any account of the work as a whole has to be somewhat vague. The story is narrated by one Encolpius, thief, pervert, parasite, and man of the world. The novel charts his wanderings, along with his faithless catamite, the boy Giton, and his rival Ascyltus (all three names have sexual connotations): we find them by the Bay of Naples, on shipboard, and at Croton in the far south of Italy. A recurrent theme appears to be the hero's persecution at the hands of Priapus, the god of sexual potency. It has been suggested that the whole work is a kind of burlesque epic, with Encolpius as a disreputable Ulysses or Aeneas, and the ithyphallic Priapus taking the role of the more dignified gods Neptune or Juno.

Encolpius himself, cultivated and depraved, is scarcely a character in the modern sense but a pair of hard clever eyes through which we view an extraordinary comic world. Part of the *Satyrica*'s fascination lies in its combination of low life with literary wit and social satire, all set out with a cold brilliant detachment. Some of the scenes are obscene, even monstrously obscene. There are grotesque inventions, as when Eumolpus, turning metaphor into actuality, decrees that his legatees must first eat the flesh of his corpse; but we also meet the rhetorician Agamemnon, who elicits from Encolpius a fruity declamation against declamation, while Eumolpus, for his part, is depicted as an obsessed versifier. Several times incidents are compared to scenes from mime, and there is something of the quality of pantomime, too, when members of the cast step out of character for the better entertainment of the audience. Encolpius, by turns rogue and literary gentleman, cynical and soft-hearted, is a protean figure who adapts to whatever role is suggested by the convenience of the moment; the blundering Eumolpus is allowed to tell the story of the widow of Ephesus in dashing style; Trimalchio's foolish astrology has a sharp edge to it (39): anyone born under the sign of the ram, he remarks, has a 'a hard head, a brazen forehead, sharp horns. Many professors are born under this sign . . .'

In the conversation of the guests at Trimalchio's dinner, Petronius deploys a racy colloquial Latin to brilliant effect. The talk is fast and varied: dour, gossipy, and sentimental. We even catch a foretaste of Sam Weller. '"Oro te," inquit Echion centonarius, "melius loquere. 'Modo sic, modo sic' inquit rusticus; uarium porcum perdiderat"' (45) ('"Please, please," said Echion the rag-merchant, "don't talk so gloomily. 'There's light patches and there's dark patches', as the yokel said when he'd lost his spotted pig"').

Trimalchio himself is one of those characters, like Shylock, who ought to be a monster but turns out oddly endearing; whether Petronius designed this effect

NILE BOAT-TRIP: mosaic panel from Tivoli (second century AD). General Nilotic subjects were popular in the Roman decorative arts. Here some unusual features, such as the water pouring from a hole in the boat, suggest that a specific story was being illustrated, perhaps an episode from romantic fiction.

ARRETINE BOWL MADE BY
M. PERENNIUS TIGRANUS
(late first century BC). Relief-
moulded pottery superseded
painted ceramics as the favourite
fine tableware of the
Mediterranean from the third
century BC onwards. This fine
example, from Arretium
(Arezzo), is decorated with
scenes of lovemaking in an
elegant classical style.

DECORATED GLASSWARE
FROM THE RHINELAND (third
century AD). The so-called
'snake-thread' glass, pioneered in
the eastern Mediterranean
during the late second century
AD, later became a popular line
in the Rhenish workshops. The
jug is decorated with swan-like
forms, the cup (in the shape of a
gladiator's helmet) with a bird
pecking cherries.

is perhaps an open question. His behaviour is self-contradictory, in this case not because the author has no consistent view of his character but because it is in the nature of that character to be a mass of inconsistencies. A former slave who has attained enormous, even preposterous riches (he contemplates buying property in Sicily so that he will be able to travel all the way to Africa on his own land (48)), he is anxious to play a part, but unable to decide what part to choose. At one moment he tyrannizes over his slaves, at another he apes the philosophers, declaring that slaves are human beings and have drunk the same milk as other men. He observes sagely that one should talk culture at dinner, and treats his guests to an outrageously confused account of the Trojan War; but he cannot forgo the rival pleasures of inverted snobbery: the epitaph he has composed for himself declares (71), 'Virtuous, brave and true, he began humbly, left 30,000,000 sesterces, and never listened to a philosopher.' He has a skeleton brought in to remind him of his mortality (34)—a gesture which would be more impressive were the skeleton not made of silver. He is superstitious and sentimental, his puns are childishly awful, and his attempts to be stylish are disastrously vulgar (he uses

SILVER BEAKER WITH SKELETONS of Greek p and philosophers (first h first century AD). Severa works of art in late Hell and Roman times betra morbid fascination with foretokening the medie 'dances of death'. Comp Trimalchio's silver skele 'So shall we all be, whei Underworld has claimeᵢ then let us live while all well.'

a silver chamber-pot in public, and then wipes his hands on a slave's head). Some of his remarks are what Englishmen call Irish: he has cups depicting 'Cassandra's dead children' so skilfully engraved 'that you would think they were alive' (52); he has told his slaves that he means to free them in his will 'so that my household may love me now just as though I were dead' (71). Constantly he craves affection: 'No one in my house loves me more,' he says, as he feeds his dog (64). At the end of the feast, now thoroughly drunk, he decides to rehearse his funeral. Trumpeters are summoned, his shroud fetched, and lying on a heap of cushions he announces (78), 'Pretend I'm dead. Say something nice.' This is childish behaviour, certainly; perhaps childlike also. The scene seems an extravagant flourish on Petronius' part to mark the climax of Trimalchio's feast, so it is sobering to learn from Seneca's letters of a certain Pacuvius who behaved in just such a fashion. It is Petronius' strength that he is a fantasist who does not lose touch with reality.

Apuleius was born at Madaurus in the province of Africa around 123 and was active in the second half of the century. Several works from his hand survive, including the *Apologia*, his self-defence on a charge of gaining his wife's love by the use of magic (below, p. 357); but his fame rests above all on his novel the *Metamorphoses*, also known as *The Golden Ass*. This is based on a Greek tale, *Lucius, or The Ass*, possibly written by Lucian, of which an abridged version is still extant. Comparison with the Greek story serves to demonstrate how brilliantly Apuleius enlarged and adapted his model. *The Golden Ass* is in eleven books and is told in the first person. After nearly three books of amorous and humorous incidents the narrator, as a consequence of an experiment with magic which goes wrong, finds himself transformed into a donkey; and the rest of the work consists of a series of picaresque adventures which befall the hero in his animal form, interrupted by a large number of other tales recounted by various of the characters who figure in the main narrative. The longest of these, the tale of Cupid and Psyche, occupies about a fifth of the entire work.

Finally, after a vision of the goddess Isis, the narrator Lucius is restored to his human shape. The last scenes of the novel provide one of the most remarkable accounts of religious experience to come down from classical paganism. It has often been thought that we see here the influence of Christian spirituality; on this supposition Apuleius was fighting Christianity but doing his best to steal the rival religion's clothes. The last book also presents the interpreter of Apuleius with his most teasing problem; no entirely satisfactory explanation has yet been given, and perhaps none is possible. How are we to reconcile the tone of the conclusion, with Lucius as an adept of the goddess, vowed to celibacy and simplicity of life, with the huge gusto with which the rest of the story is told? Lucius repeatedly tells us that he is 'curiosus' ('inquisitive'), or 'sititor . . . nouitatis', ('a thirster after novelty'); for this inquisitiveness he is punished and ultimately redeemed, but until the last book the whole atmosphere and style of the narrative encourages us to rejoice and share in this thirst for adventure and experience. The work begins,

THE WORSHIP OF ISIS: painting from Herculaneum (mid first century AD). Lucius' conversion to the Egyptian religion which enjoyed such success in late-Hellenistic and early-imperial times forms a rather uneasy conclusion to Apuleius's rumbustious novel *The Golden Ass*.

indeed, with an explosion of zest and hilarity: the narrator presents himself in ingratiating and persistent tones, almost as though he were a huckster pressing dirty postcards on a passer-by:

At ego tibi sermone isto Milesio uarias fabulas conseram auresque tuas beniuolas lepido susurro permulceam—modo si papyrum Aegyptiam argutia Nilotici calami inscriptam non spreueris inspicere—figuras fortunasque hominum in alias imagines conuersas in se rursum mutuo nexu refectas ut mireris.

Now then, I would like to stitch together a variety of stories in this Milesian tale and soothe your kindly ears with an elegant whisper—so long as you do not scorn to examine this Egyptian manuscript written with the neatness of a pen of the Nile—so that you may marvel at men's forms and fortunes changed into new shapes and then one with the other restored to themselves again.

Suddenly there is an interruption from the audience: 'exordior. "quis ille?" paucis accipe' ('I'll begin. "Who's this fellow?" I'll tell you briefly'). In elaborate and eccentric language the narrator explains that he is a Greek who learnt Latin at Rome in his adolescence. 'Lector intende; laetaberis', he concludes ('Reader, attend; you will be entertained'). All this passes in a very few sentences; everything speaks of briskness, energy, entertainment. And entertainment indeed is what we get, though often of a grotesque sort. Sex and magic, comedy and horror, elegant romance and coarse bawdy are blended into an intoxicating mixture: men are soused in urine or spattered with excrement; cuckoldry, castration, copulation are recurrent themes; the entire work is drenched in blood, torture, and hideous death.

The cement that holds this strange diversity together is provided by Apuleius' idiosyncratic style; it is his style, again, which prevents the work turning, as the Greek romances sometimes do, into mere vulgar titillation, by giving to the whole the gloss of an elaborate sophistication. The vocabulary is a weird blend of archaism, poeticisms, colloquialism, and neologism, elements which are curiously reminiscent of the babu English spoken in the last century by Indians who had educated themselved from a mixture of Shakespeare, newspapers, and modern slang imperfectly understood. That analogy is not as far-fetched as it may at first appear, for the narrator reveals that he is a Greek and apologizes for his imperfect command of the Latin language. 'Fabulam Graecanicam incipimus,' he explains ('I am beginning a Grecian tale'); characteristically he replaces the ordinary word for Greek, 'Graecus', with an uncommon form.

But of course the claim to imperfect Latin is all a feint; he is a stylistic virtuoso, a 'circus rider' by his own confession. With much adroitness he arranges his bizarre vocabulary into lilting mesmeric rhythms which sometimes have an almost incantatory effect. He loves assonances like 'sauia suauia' ('sweet kisses' 6. 8) or, more elaborately, 'sordis infimae infamis homo' ('a notorious fellow of extreme squalor', 1. 21). In place of the periodic structures and careful variations traditional in Latin art prose, he favours loose series of echoing phrases which on occasion even fall into the pattern of rhyming verse. Psyche's prayer to Ceres, for example, is a kind of coloratura aria (part of it is arranged here so as to bring out the rhyming effect):

Per ego te frugiferam tuam dexteram istam deprecor, per laetificas messium caeremonias, per tacita secreta cistarum et per famulorum tuorum draconum pinnata curricula et glebae Siculae sulcamina

    et currum rapacem
    et terram tenacem
    et inluminarum Proserpinae nuptiarum demeacula
    et luminosarum filiae inuentionum remeacula

et cetera quae silentio tegit Eleusinis Atticae sacrarium, miserandae Psyches animae supplicis tuae subsiste.   (6.2)

I beseech you, by your right hand that bears the fruits of the earth, by your joyful ceremonies of harvest, by the unspoken secrets of your baskets, by the winged cars of the dragons your servants, by the furrows of the Sicilian soil, by the chariot that seized your daughter and the earth that held her, by the descent of Proserpine to a wedding unlighted by torches, by her ascent when she was found by the light of torches, by all else that the shrine of Eleusis in the land of Athens shrouds in silence, help the pitiable soul of Psyche, your suppliant.

Apuleius' rococo glitter is at its most dazzling in the story of Cupid and Psyche. On one level this is a fairy story, rich in folk-tale motifs, and opening with a disarming simplicity (4.28): 'In a certain country there lived a king and queen' (it comes as small surprise that Psyche is the youngest and fairest of their three daughters, more lovely than Venus herself). On another level the tale hints at quasi-Platonic allegory: the marriage of Psyche, the soul, with Cupido, fleshly desire. On a third level the story is a comedy in the Ovidian manner, with Olympian goddesses constrained by the laws and etiquette of contemporary Rome; and on yet a fourth level it is the *ne plus ultra* of bejewelled preciosity. One of the virtues of Apuleius' high fantastical style is that it enables him to drift among these different levels of discourse.

Outside the story of Psyche, too, it enables him to create an atmosphere of his own, and to produce effects unlike anything else in Latin literature. His is a fantasy world, and yet it gives a curiously convincing picture of life under the Roman empire. The scene in which Lucius falls for the slave-girl Fotis when he sees her stirring the porridge in a seductive manner is at once erotic and absurd (2.7). Lucius asks a cackling crone for directions to Milo's house; she answers with a terrible joke, but Lucius continues straight-faced with an elaborate gravity (1.21): '"Remoto" inquam "ioco, parens optima, dic oro et cuiatis sit et quibus deuersetur aedibus"' ('"Jesting aside, my good woman," I answered, "tell me, pray, what manner of man he is and in what abode he lodges"'). Set against the comedy are glossy set-piece descriptions: the statues in Byrrhaena's house, so lifelike that they seem to be in motion (2.4); the beauty of a head of hair,

CUPID AND PSYCHE: marble statue-group from the House of Cupid and Psyche at Ostia, copied from a second-century BC original. The fairy tale of Cupid and Psyche is the most famous of the stories embedded in *The Golden Ass*. The two lovers are eventually united after various trials and tribulations occasioned by the jealousy of Venus and Psyche's sisters.

glittering gold in the light, with shadows the colour of honey (2.9); the sheen of Cupid's dewy wings, with tender little downy feathers dancing tremulously at their edges as he sleeps (5.22). Many of Apuleius' stories are told with an outrageous insouciance, with loose ends left hanging all over the place. One might expect the result to be a disordered ragbag, but the combination of mannerism and panache holds the work together. Apuleius is a curious figure with whom to end the account of a period; but it is stimulating to know that in the second half of the second century AD Latin literature could still throw up a writer so full of vitality and imagination.

Further Reading

Petronius has been translated by W. Arrowsmith (Ann Arbor, 1962); there are translations in the Penguin Classics series of Persius (together with Horace's *Satires* and *Epistles*) by N. Rudd; Petronius (together with Seneca's satire *Apocolocyntosis*) by J. P. Sullivan; selected epigrams of Martial by J. Michie; Juvenal by P. Green; and Apuleius, *The Golden Ass* by R. Graves. Marlowe translated Lucan's first book. Dryden's rendering of Persius and five satires of Juvenal (*The Poems of John Dryden*, ed. J. Kinsley (Oxford, 1958), vol. 2) are a part of English literature; his version of Juvenal gives a better idea of the grand declamatory manner than is possible in a modern idiom. Compare too Samuel Johnson's 'imitations' of *Satires* 3 and 10, 'London' and 'The Vanity of Human Wishes'. Walter Pater incorporated a translation of Apuleius' story of Cupid and Psyche into ch. 5 of his *Marius the Epicurean*; it conveys something of Apuleius' elegance, though not of his verve. The Loeb Classical Library contains none of Apuleius' works except *The Golden Ass*, but otherwise includes all the works discussed in this chapter.

G. Williams, *Change and decline: Roman literature in the early empire* (Berkeley, 1978) surveys the whole period. On individual poets see M. P. O. Morford, *The Poet Lucan: Studies in Rhetorical Epic* (Oxford, 1967); F. M. Ahl, *Lucan: An Introduction* (Ithaca, 1976); J. C. Bramble, *Persius and the Programmatic Satire: A Study in Form and Imagery* (Cambridge, 1974); D. Vessey, *Statius and the Thebaid* (Cambridge, 1973); G. Highet, *Juvenal the Satirist* (Oxford, 1954); R. G. M. Nisbet, 'Persius' and H. A. Mason, 'Is Juvenal a classic?', in *Critical Essays on Roman Literature: Satire*, ed. J. P. Sullivan (London, 1963); R. Jenkyns, *Three Classical Poets: Sappho, Catullus and Juvenal* (London, 1982), part 3 'Juvenal the poet'. On satire generally see M. Coffey, *Roman Satire* (London, 1982), part 3 'Juvenal the poet'. W. Anderson, *Essays on Roman Satire* (Princeton, 1982), which contains several pieces on Juvenal. On satire generally see M. Coffey, *Roman Satire* (London, 1976).

On the Latin novel: B. E. Perry, *The Ancient Romances: A Literary-Historical Account of their Origins* (Berkeley, 1967); P. G. Walsh, *The Roman Novel* (Cambridge, 1970); J. P. Sullivan, *The Satyricon of Petronius: A Literary Study* (London, 1968); J. Tatum, *Apuleius and The Golden Ass* (Ithaca, 1979). J. Winkler, *Auctor and Actor: a narratological reading of Apuleius's Golden Ass* (Berkeley, 1985).

I3

Later Philosophy

❧❦

ANTHONY MEREDITH

General Tendencies

THE period with which this section is concerned is bracketed by the lives of the two most interesting and important figures of later philosophy, Posidonius of Apamea in Syria (d. 51 BC) and Plotinus, an Egyptian by birth, who died in Rome in 270 AD. The former of these two was one of the most widely travelled and deeply learned men of his age, who interested himself in a whole range of subjects including rhetoric, geography, and recent history, taking over in the latter field where Polybius had left off. He was also a philosopher and represents a tendency present in a good deal of the philosophy of the period, to harmonize the apparently conflicting views held by the main schools of the age. So, though he was himself a Stoic, he seems to have been willing to depart from the traditional views of his school in two important matters, theology and anthropology. Unlike such Stoics as Zeno and Chrysippus, he seems to have admitted the existence of a god who was in some sense transcendent, and also to have accepted the existence in man of the irrational appetites as being truly human. In both of these areas he departs from the monism and the intellectualism of the Stoic school as it is represented both in the founders of the fourth century and the later Stoics, Epictetus and Marcus Aurelius in the second century AD. Plotinus, too, though an immeasurably greater philosopher, indeed arguably the greatest since Aristotle and for a long time to come, was also prepared, as his biographer and pupil Porphyry tells us in his *Life*, to use the teachings of both Aristotle and the Stoics in addition to his master Plato.

In between these two towering figures crowd a host of lesser men whose main claim to fame is that they help to explain the genesis of Plotinus, but who also shed light both on the history of their respective schools and on the early growth of Christian reflection and doctrine. There are, however, certain overall features which can be found to a greater or lesser extent in all the writers of the period.

(a) The first two centuries after Christ were intensely conservative and traditional in their interests, and although it is doubtless true that under cover of a devotion to the past they intruded their own particular concerns, it cannot be

POSIDONIUS OF APAMEA (*c*.135–50 BC), the last of the great polymaths of the Hellenistic age; he wrote on geography, astronomy, and history, as well as philosophy. His ideas influenced several Roman writers, including Sallust, Caesar, Tacitus, and especially Cicero, who studied under Posidonius in Rhodes in 78.

denied that in all branches of their literary activity the writers of the age looked back to the great masterpieces of the golden age of Athens for their inspiration both in point of content and of style. It was their preoccupation with style that led many of the writers of the Second Sophistic to devote a good deal of attention to Plato, and it was perhaps for that reason that the philosophical renaissance of the age owes more to him than to Aristotle. As to content, most of the writers of the age can in general be classed as Platonists. The interest in the more dogmatic side of Plato can be dated to the earlier part of the first century BC and is connected with the figure of Antiochus of Ascalon, the first systematically to break away from the scepticism which had dominated the school since the days of Carneades (d. *c*.129/8 BC). The devotion to Plato shows itself in a number of ways, but above all in the constant use of quotation from him and in the general adherence to the main lines of his philosophy, the belief in the transcendence of God and in the immortality of the soul. So often were some of the commonplaces of Plato repeated by the writers of the period, above all by Plutarch, Maximus, and Albinus, that it has been thought by some scholars that they possessed a Platonic anthology, now lost, from which these excerpts were taken. It does not seem necessary to postulate such a book, but it still remains true that certain phrases, such as that from Plato's *Timaeus* 28 b 'To discover the maker and father of the universe is indeed a hard task, and having found him it would be impossible to tell everyone about him', recur with remarkable frequency in all the writers of the period, whether pagan or Christian.

(b) Alongside the intense traditionalism of the period may be found a strong tendency to amalgamate the central tenets of differing philosophical schemes, with the result of forming a united philosophical front. All the main schools must have had substantial followings over the period. Mention has already been made of Platonists and Stoics. But there was also a flowering of Pythagoreanism, again beginning at the opening of the first century BC with the figure of Nigidius Figulus (praetor in 58 BC). He was followed by men like the wandering preacher Apollonius of Tyana, whose biography, written by Philostratus for the Empress Julia Domna at the opening of the third century AD, came to be thought of as a rival to the Gospels. Another interesting Pythagorean of a slightly later date and more immediately philosophical interests was Numenius of Apamea, who made the interesting claim that Plato derived his doctrines from Pythagoras. He is therefore a witness to the belief that not only were Plato's doctrines derived, but also that underneath certain verbal differences all philosophers were saying the same thing. This mixture of appeal to antiquity, together with a desire to water down important divergences in favour of a common front, is characteristic of nearly all the writers of the age and is a mark of their learning, sterility, and general timidity.

(c) Most of the authors with whom we shall be concerned exemplify the revival in classical Greek style, known as the Second Sophistic Movement, of which Philostratus writes in his *Lives of the Sophists*. Marcus Aurelius wrote in Greek, and the 'cultured commonplaces' of Maximus were intended to help young men to develop the power of speaking elegantly in public on general themes. Again the interest of all the writers of the age, with the solitary exception of Plotinus, was practical. In Plutarch the moral and practical interest predominates, and in one of his *Discourses* Epictetus asks: 'But what is philosophy? Does it not mean making preparation to meet the things that come upon us?' It was for their lack of interest in giving practical help to the state that the Platonist philosopher Celsus was critical of Christians. Such a criticism would have sounded oddly from Plotinus, with his resolute and consistent exaltation of contemplation over action and his lack of interest in either the theory or the practice of politics. Finally, Plotinus differs from all his immediate predecessors in the systematic rigour that he brings to philosophy. Neither Plutarch nor Epictetus has

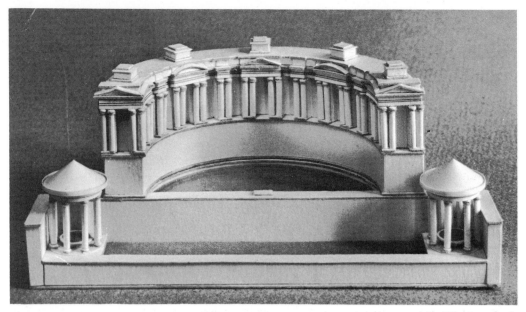

THE NYMPHAEUM OF HERODES ATTICUS AT OLYMPIA (reconstruction model). The immensely wealthy Athenian sophist (*c.*AD 101–77) was not only a much admired literary stylist but also a Roman senator and consul, a friend and tutor of Emperors, and a liberal patron of the arts. Among the buildings which he sponsored were concert halls in Athens and Corinth and fountain-buildings in Corinth and (here) Olympia.

any interest in speculation as such; for them philosophy subserves the life of action.

(d) The second-century sceptical writer Lucian (above, pp. 260 ff.), makes it clear that there was a good deal of religiosity in evidence in these years, and several of his essays are designed to poke fun at the various quacks and charlatans who thrived on some such atmosphere. *Essay* 42 deals with the false prophet Alexander of Abonuteichus who played grossly on the credulity of the period, and no. 55, 'On the death of Peregrinus', is an amusing account of a man who passed through Cynicism and Christianity to end up an Indian mystic. Lucian is hardly more merciful on grammatical pedants (*Essay* 41) or on philosophers (*Essay* 70, 'Hermotimus', a sustained attack on all philosophical schools). It was an era in which there appears to have been an abnormal flowering of many forms of occult piety, philosophical syncretism, and genuine religion. This sort of evidence has led E.R. Dodds to label it 'an age of anxiety', and to suggest that what led men and women to seek peace and revelation in all manner of mysteries was a sense of misery, a *fin de siècle* feeling, which encouraged such strange and unwonted outbursts. It is an attractive hypothesis, though it is hard to see why the age of the Antonines (97–180 AD) should be thought of as especially wretched. The historian Gibbon would hardly have subscribed to such a view. It is certainly true that many of the writers of the period seem to be very self-obsessed; some of them indeed like Herodes Atticus seem to have been pathological cases. It is also true that the age saw the rapid expansion of Christianity, but it would be hardly fair to label all Christians as either pathological introverts or seekers after secret and mystical revelation.

Platonism

It is possible to discern at least two widely different strands in the writings of Plato, the dogmatic and the critical: the Plato, in other words, who is responsible both for the theory of forms and the immortality of the soul on the one hand, and on the other the Plato who, in the tradition of his master Socrates, subjected all propositions to the sharpest criticism. Not long after his death in 347 the Academy which he had founded came under the influence of those who belonged for one reason or another to the second, sceptical stream. Partly in opposi-

PLATO'S ACADEMY: mosaic panel found near Pompeii (late second or first century BC). According to a recent theory, the figure at the left is Heraclides Ponticus; the figure pointing to the globe would be Plato himself; and the whole scene would represent a discussion on astronomy. Platonic philosophy continued to exercise influence, in modified form, on the thinkers of Roman times.

tion to Stoic dogmatism, partly under the influence of Pyrrho, the leaders of the school, above all Arcesilaus (316/15-242/1) and Carneades, denied the possibility of any formal knowledge of anything. The last undisputed head of the Academy was Philo of Larissa (160/59-80), after whom, under the influence of his pupil Antiochus of Ascalon, the school lost its nerve and lapsed into dogmatism—a characteristic which it retained throughout the rest of its history right down to the closing of the Athenian Academy in 529 AD by order of the Emperor Justinian.

Of Antiochus we know very little, and that little is derived almost wholly from Cicero. He was born somewhere between 130 and 120 BC, and his death is put in 68. Our sources clearly regard him as a breakaway from the true Academy, largely if not entirely because he rejected the sceptical attitude to truth, which had been received 'doctrine' since the days of Arcesilaus, if not before. In another respect also he heralds a new age. He believed that there was fundamental agreement between the Old Academy of Plato and the Lyceum of Aristotle. Again this was a revolutionary step; and as we shall see, some Platonists, who might have been happy to admit the possibility of knowledge, regarded the proposed alliance between Plato and Aristotle with some distaste. The best known of the 'opposition' were Plutarch and Atticus. But beyond the fact that in these two respects Antiochus betrayed his immediate predecessors it is hard to be at all clear precisely what he taught.

Ironically enough, the clearest and most copious witness to the views of the Middle Platonists, as they are now called, is the Alexandrian Jewish writer Philo (*c*.25 BC–*c*.45 AD). From his lengthy allegorical commentary on the first five books of the Bible it is possible to extract a system which closely resembles the sort of picture which emerges from Plutarch and Albinus. It must, however, be remembered that, useful though he is for our purposes, Philo was a Jew and was thoroughly influenced by biblical ideas and images. Even so, in the first book of his commentary he provides us with a structured hierarchy of reality, beginning with the supreme God and ending with matter, like that which characterizes Middle Platonism. The question which the structure seeks to answer is 'How is it possible to derive the multiplicity which we see from the absolute unity which we believe to lie at the summit of the world?' The Bible, in common with all the great transcendental philosophers of classical antiquity, had assumed that above all there was a single indivisible self-sufficient principle; and although they might call it (him) sometimes God, sometimes Monad (Pythagorean), sometimes Absolute Beauty or the Idea of the Good (Plato's *Phaedrus* and *Republic*), sometimes the Unmoved Mover or Self-thinking Thought (Aristotle's *Metaphysics*), they were all agreed that it was single. The derivation of or relation to the One of the All was the problem. The theory of forms and the account of the making of the world in the *Timaeus* represent attempts at a solution. But Plato, Aristotle, and arguably the account of creation in the first chapter of Genesis, all tend to assume the eternity of matter as the condition of the possibility of the making of the world. Philo was perhaps the first to take the bold and interesting step of trying to present a picture of the making of the world which took into account all these insights. For him the maker of the world is the only one who is eternal in both senses of the word. That is, he held that God is both without beginning and without end (=durationally eternal) and also absolutely timeless. 'For God is the maker of time also, for he is the father of time's father. ... Thus time stands to God in the relation of a grandson. ... To the elder son, the intelligible universe, He assigned the place of the first-born.' This passage gives us in a nutshell the Philonic system. Beneath the first God and Father of all, who is incomprehensible and eternal, there comes a second God or Logos, who is described sometimes as the mind of God, sometimes as the place of the ideas or the intelligible world, sometimes as the first-born, sometimes as the agent in creation. Beneath him is the world of sense, created through the agency and on the model of the Logos. This last is less perfect and more multiple than is the world of forms.

It is clear what Philo is aiming at:

(a) He has replaced the confusing picture of three independent principles in the *Timaeus* with a neatly ordered pattern.
(b) He has achieved this by welding together rather disparate elements which he assumes enjoy a basic coherence.

Above all, the second principle draws together into one the creative word of Psalm 33:6, the Stoic Logos (though it is raised above and not identical with the material universe), the Platonic world of forms, and the Aristotelian self-thinking thought. On occasion he even calls the Logos 'God' and distinguishes him from the first God by the simple device of dropping the definite article. This distinction within the realms of the divine, which suggests the possibility of introducing degrees within the concept of God, was subsequently employed with considerable fruit and frequency by most of the later Middle Platonists and some of the Neoplatonist writers, notably by Albinus, Numenius, Plotinus, and the Christian Origen.

Plutarch was by birth a Greek and came from Chaeronea in Boeotia. He studied philosophy in Athens and at a later date went to Rome, where he taught for a period, and then returned home. He spent the last thirty years of his life a priest at Delphi. He died *c.*120 AD at about the age of seventy-five. Opinions about his philosophical seriousness vary from the declared and consistent, if not always orthodox Platonism attributed to him by Donald Russell, to the dismissive 'tea-table transcendentalist' of E.R. Dodds. A good example of this alleged incoherence is in his attitude to Stoicism. On the one hand he was sharply critical of much that the Stoics stood for. This is clear from two books of his *Moralia*, *Stoic Self-contradictions* and *On Common Conceptions*. So, for example, in the former book he argues that the Stoics believed that 'whatever is, is right', while believing at the same time that God chastises the wicked. On the other hand

Plutarch owes a good deal of his belief in a benign providence to the Stoics, and to them also he, indirectly, owes his conviction that it is possible to know.

Plutarch's own attitude to the possibility of accounting for the existence of evil in a divinely ordered universe is not without its difficulties. His explanation of the origin of evil is not quite the same as Plato's, though he adduces passages in *The Laws* and *Timaeus* in defence of his own account. In his treatise *On Isis and Osiris*, an allegorical discussion of the Egyptian pantheon, he argues that there are two independent and eternal principles: Osiris, the principle of good, and Typhon, the principle of evil. This assertion of the existence of an eternal evil principle may be attributed to the influence of Xenocrates and could owe something to Iranian dualism, the eternal struggle between good (Ahura-Mazda), and evil (Ahriman); but it is at variance with the general tendency of Plato to deny to evil any place among the forms, and it is in clear conflict with the optimism of the Stoics and of Plotinus. In another treatise, *On the Obsolescence of Oracles*, Plutarch produces a slightly different explanation, attributing evil to the demons that exist between the divine world and that of the visible universe. Here we can see clear echoes of Plato's *Symposium*, with again the significant difference that Plato's demons are good or neutral, Plutarch's are evil.

In one final respect Plutarch's Platonism was modified by his Pythagorean teacher Ammonius, whose interpretation of the mysterious E at Delphi is related for us by Plutarch in his treatise of that name. According to Ammonius the purpose of the inscription is to identify the supreme principle of the universe with the utter simplicity of oneness that stands at the summit of the Pythagorean system. He concludes as follows: 'Under these conditions, therefore, we ought, as we pay Him reverence, to greet him and to address Him with the words, "Thou art"; or even . . . as did some of the men of old "Thou art One".' This Pythagorean influence enables Plutarch to go beyond the other Middle Platonists; and in his insistence on the unity and simplicity of the supreme principle he closely approximates to the One of Plotinus.

Of all the Middle Platonist writers known to us the most characteristic and the most easily available is Albinus, sometimes called Alcinous. Of his life next to nothing is known, except that he lived in the middle of the second century AD and that he wrote two *Introductions* to the philosophy of Plato, both of which survive. His particular interest for us is that, unlike Philo and Plutarch, he seems to have been untouched by non-Hellenic influences. His work is decidedly eclectic in tone and marks a deliberate attempt to schematize his inherited Platonism on hierarchical principles. At the summit of the pyramid is the first God or Mind, ineffable, perfect, eternal, father of all. He fills the whole universe with himself because of his will. Beneath him comes second Mind: Mind, that is, in its active and passive side. After him comes the third principle, Soul. It should be noted that for Albinus the supreme God is both ineffable and personal and shares certain features in common with the first Mind of Aristotle, though differing from Aristotle in attributing to him both ineffability and personal involvement in the universe. Again, exalted though the God of Albinus is, he is not so utterly simple as the Pythagorean Monad of Philo and Plutarch, or the One of Plotinus. It is not surprising, therefore, to to discover that he makes no use in his writings of the passage in *Republic* 509 b, on the source and nature of Being, of which later Platonists made so much.

From what has been said it is clear that Albinus, in common with Celsus and Maximus of Tyre, but unlike Plutarch and Atticus, believed in the fundamental harmony between Plato and Aristotle. This is clear not only from the willingness to treat the ideas of Plato as thoughts in the mind of Aristotle's god, but also from the extensive use made of Aristotle's logical works. On one further point of major importance the Aristotelianizing Platonists were at one. They all thought that the account of creation contained in Plato's *Timaeus* demanded an allegorical rather than a literal interpretation. The natural sense of Plato is that the making of the world took place in time. For Albinus such a suggestion implied some sort of change in God and must therefore be ruled out. It is of interest to note that on the three occasions when Plotinus discusses the problem of the making of the visible world he sides with Albinus. The same may also be said for the great Christian theologian Origen (185–254), who perhaps owed his views to Aristotelian influence.

The Middle Platonists hardly form a clear, organized body of thought. There is very little evidence that they exercised any influence on each other. It has indeed been suggested that Plotinus read Philo, but that is hardly likely. What unites them, rather, is the possession of certain common concerns and a general, if ill-defined, allegiance to Plato. The Bible, Pythagoras, and Aristotle were all thought of in their differing ways as being somehow in accord with Plato. The common concern that unites them is the desire on the part of all to interpret Plato in such a way as to overcome the crucial difficulty in his system; that of bridging the gulf created by the theory of forms between ultimate, static, reality and the changing unstable world of matter and sense. Connected with this is the effort towards transcendence manifested in differing ways by all the main authors: the incomprehensible God of Philo, the simple/complex Mind of Albinus, and the Monad of Plutarch.

Plotinus (204/5–270), the founder of Neoplatonism, is known to us both from the biography written by his devoted, but possibly not altogether comprehending pupil, Porphyry, and from the collections of his writings, organized topically into six volumes, *Enneads*, by the same pupil. He was by birth and early training an Egyptian and claimed to have learnt most of his philosophy from Ammonius Saccas. The content of this teaching is beyond recovery, since Ammonius left no writings behind him and speculation about him has yielded no certain results. In 244 Plotinus left Egypt for Rome, where he spent the rest of his life. His teaching was conducted by means of seminars, to which he attracted some of the influential men of his day. An index of the power of his views and personality is the fact that one of his auditors, a senator, Rogatianus, was persuaded to abandon his life of public service. This incident highlights the fact that politics was the only branch of ancient philosophy in which Plotinus showed no interest. Indeed at times he displays a positive antipathy towards it.

Plotinus thought of himself as a Platonist, and in much of his teaching Platonic influence is evident. Like Plato he believed in the superiority of intellect to sense and of the spiritual world to the material. In this area he consciously rejected precisely those philosophies which he thought undermined the basis of Platonic intellectualism, above all Scepticism, Stoicism, and Gnosticism, (a body of esoteric doctrines which denied the reality of the flesh and the physical world). Against the first of these he insisted that we can know, and that our knowledge is neither derived from nor reducible to sense impressions, but comes on the contrary from a direct, ever present awareness of spiritual reality, which is always available to us if only we concentrate our minds upon it. Against the Stoics Plotinus argued that 'reality' is not primarily material but spiritual, and that the existence of matter results from the absence of form and spirit; in other words, that it is a negative rather than a positive thing. However, we are not to suppose that his critique of Stoicism made Plotinus into a despiser of the visible order. His third main opponents were the Gnostics, whose devaluation of matter made it necessary for them to believe in the need to escape from this world. He also objected to their tendency to underrate the importance of choice and mind in their effort towards salvation. One of his grandest *Enneads*, 2. 9, is directed against the Gnostics and has been described as a 'noble apology for Hellenism' in its insistence on the goodness and beauty of the visible order and its vindication of the centrality of freedom and reason in the good life. In his reactions to Stoicism and Gnosticism we can see Plotinus delicately or precariously balanced between two conflicting world views, tending respectively to the deification and vilification of the world we see.

Apart from the evident Platonism of the *Enneads* and the no less evident willingness to incorporate into this general system elements drawn from Aristotle and the Stoa, two other features need mention. The most widely known and distinctive of these is the One, the supreme principle which stands at the climax of the ladder of reality. The One is impersonal and beyond the reach of predication and of any direct knowledge, yet it is at the same time the source of all reality and all value. It combines the One of Plato's *Parmenides* and the Good of the *Republic*. It is from the One as the infinite and generous source of life and value that all else comes. In making this step Plotinus goes beyond both Plato and his own immediate predecessors. For them, absolute reality is both limited and static. For Plotinus, on the other hand, the One, and even more the second substance, the Mind, is boiling with life. On one occasion he writes that being is 'not a corpse, and not not-life and not not-thinking.'

The second feature of importance in Plotinus' system is that it is experienced rather than argued for. It was his own acute awareness of the One gained as the fruit of intense concentration that helped him to formulate the system above outlined. His biographer tells us two important things about him. He was strongly opposed to all forms of ritualistic religion and observed on one occasion that 'the gods must come to me, not I to the gods'. Towards the end of his biography Porphyry also says that during the time during which he knew him Plotinus experienced ecstasy. This state, which is described in great detail at the end of the last *Ennead*, entailed for him 'a simplification and surrender of the self, an aspiration towards contact, which is at once a stillness and a mental effort of adaptation'. Union of this type is experienced only briefly and is the climax of a process of moral purification, introversion and contemplation of 'the vision that makes happy'. The culminating state of union, in which any awareness of distinction is for the time abolished, seems to have led Plotinus to postulate the One at the summit of the hierarchy of reality, as the only possible explanation for the variety we normally experience and for the state of exalted unification which he underwent on at least four occasions.

It is hard to exaggerate the importance of Plotinus. His system was the outcome both of the philosophical syncretism that preceded him and of his own personal mystical experience. He is also significant because of his attempt to break down the layered vision of his immediate predecessors in favour of a dynamic, spiritual monism, in which as Dean Inge notes 'there are no straight lines drawn across the map of the universe'. The tensions in his own vision result almost entirely from his effort to break through the more static, dualistic presuppositions of his ancestors. Finally, it would be unfitting not to mention the extraordinary influence he exercised directly or indirectly on later Platonists, like Porphyry and Proclus, and on Christian writers of the stature of Denis the Areopagite and St Augustine.

Stoicism

Epictetus (*c.*55–135 AD) was a rough contemporary of Plutarch, but whereas Plutarch was a Boeotian aristocrat, Epictetus was by birth a slave. He belonged to Epaphroditus, the freedman and secretary of Nero, who later served Domitian until his murder in 95 AD. Epictetus was allowed to attend the lectures of the celebrated Stoic Musonius Rufus, and in 89, together with all other philosophers, he was banished from Rome and took up residence at Nicopolis in Epirus. There he spent the rest of his life expounding the precepts of Chrysippus (above, Ch. 15) and making his own comments on them. These comments were collected and organized by one of his hearers, Flavius Arrian, consul for 130, into eight books, four of which still survive. His work has a wider appeal than that of his predecessors; it was addressed to the humble and the poor rather than to the few and the self-reliant, and the main tenet of his teaching was the need to cultivate inner peace as the way to true freedom.

'With Posidonius the Stoa opened itself to Platonic influence.' The principal question to be asked about the philosophy of Epictetus is whether he continued in the direction mapped out by Posidonius, or whether he reverted to the pure doctrine of Zeno, Cleanthes, and Chrysippus, the founders of the school. On this central point opinions differ. Some scholars believe that in Seneca, Epictetus, and Marcus Aurelius, the Platonizing of the Stoa continues. Others, however, take the opposite line, at least for the central figure, and see in him a reversion to origins.

It cannot be doubted that a good deal of the language of Epictetus' *Discourses*, if taken literally, suggests a departure from the monistic position of Chrysippus. In some places, for example, God is described, not as a world process, as nature, but rather as the Other or Another. On the same point it is worth noting also that on many occasions reference is made to 'the God', 'the gods', and to 'Zeus'. It is not clear how far the use of such religious language implies belief in a god, or gods, existing separately from nature. Another arguably Platonizing element is the treatment of the soul. In *Discourse* 1.9.11 Epictetus speaks about our natural kinship to the gods, which we will be able to realize once we have dispensed with the fetters that bind us; that is, the body and its possessions. Such language is more akin to the 'body a prison' idea of Plato's *Phaedo* than to the doctrines of most of the Stoics, who denied such an opposition of soul and body. Again, therefore, the question must be asked: does such language express a profound metaphysical dualism, or has it some other function? In making a decision about the best method of understanding Epictetus' position three points should be noticed. First of all he was not primarily interested in the construction of an ontology but rather had an ethical concern, to which his metaphysical beliefs, if he had any, were not of the first importance. Then also, despite the appearance of transcendental, dualist language, such talk accounts for only a relatively small part of the actual usage of the *Discourses*. The old Stoic identification of 'God' and 'Nature' continues to be used (cf. fr. 1). Finally, it would be unfair to suggest that the existence of dualist language is restricted to Epictetus and the later Stoics. It also occurs in the *Hymn to Zeus* written by the unquestionably 'orthodox' Cleanthes somewhere towards the beginning of the third century BC. As Bonhoeffer notes, the Stoic school from its beginning had employed a dualist language alongside its basic monism. It seems therefore on the whole preferable to see in Epictetus, though arguably not in Seneca and Marcus Aurelius, a return to pure Stoicism, after the brief flirtation with Platonism evident in the Middle Stoicism of writers like Posidonius, Panaetius, the Pseudo-Aristotle, and the Book of Wisdom. If the above analysis is correct, it means that we see in Epictetus, and perhaps also in Cleanthes before him, a very interesting juxtaposition of two ways of talking, a metaphysical monism alongside a religious dualism.

The main concern of Epictetus is ethical. Like all the great moral philosophers of classical antiquity, he is concerned to ensure the happiness of those whom he addresses. But, unlike Aristotle, and to some extent unlike Plato, he subordinates philosophy to the cure of the soul. 'Men,' he writes, 'the lecture room of the philosopher is a hospital' (*Diss.* 3.23.30). Happiness is made to consist in peace of mind, a quality which is always within our power, and therefore must in no sense be made to depend upon things outside our control. Dependence upon external things, whether they be material possessions, the affection and esteem of others, even good health, necessarily impedes our own peace, because any of these things may be taken from us. Such a system, if it is to succeed, clearly relies on the power to make the fundamental distinction between what does and what does not lie within our power. In the first chapter of his *Encheiridion* or *Handbook* he writes as follows: 'Some things are under our control, while others are not under our control. Under our control are conception, choice, desire, aversion, and in a word, everything that is our doing; not under our control are our body, our property, reputation, office, and, in a word, everything that is not our doing.' This is all clear enough, though it might be objected that the clarity with which the distinction is made is a little deceptive. It is an often expressed corollary of this that the way to happiness is not straining after the impossible, but cutting down desires, not allowing yourself to be disturbed at all by the things that you cannot remedy, and even when you can remedy evil, not impairing your own peace of mind in the process. At *Diss.* 4. 4. 33 he writes:

And how shall I free myself?—Have you not heard many times that you ought to eradicate desire utterly; direct your aversion to things that lie within the sphere of the moral purpose, and these only; that you ought to give up everything, your body, your property, your reputation, your books, turmoil, office, freedom from office? For if once you swerve aside from your course, you are a slave, you are a subject.

It follows from all this that the root of our malaise is failure to make the correct judgements about what is and what is not in our power, and that the remedy for such errors is the formation of correct judgements and the control of the impressions that come into the mind. The aim of life and the way to happiness is for me to adapt myself to the particular expression of nature that is to be found in me. Once I have discovered that, I shall be in a position to live my life and adapt my moral purpose accordingly.

The system as outlined above clearly aims to offer the maximum of happiness, and at the same time it is highly intellectualist, in the best traditions of the primitive Stoa. Unlike Aristotle, and also unlike the Middle Stoics, Epictetus is not prepared to allow the emotions any part to play in the picture of man or in the end of the moral life. Again, an ethical system that consists largely in discovering where nature calls and following there, can hardly be prescriptive. In other words if 'whatever is, is right', there is little if any room left for any attempts to bring about the improvement of the world. By concentrating his efforts on the purification of the moral purpose—a central and new idea in him—Epictetus hardly preached a revolutionary system. Epictetus' ethics can be summed up not unfairly in the celebrated life formula 'Endure and Renounce'. Their restraint may echo his early life as a slave, where freedom of movement would have been greatly restricted; and it may be true that, as his translator

BRONZE STATUE OF MARCUS AURELIUS ON HORSEBACK. The Roman Emperor (AD 161–80) was inspired by Stoic philosophy and wrote the *Meditations*, a collection of personal thoughts which has achieved great success since the sixteenth century; it was his tragedy to have been committed, during his reign, to a career of almost continuous warfare.

observes, 'they hardly provide a sufficient programme for a highly organized society making towards a goal of general improvement.' Nevertheless there is something inexpressibly noble in the character they reveal and the programme they outline. In an age where the little man must have been made increasingly aware of his impotence in the face of a crushing imperial machine, Epictetus' invitation to win peace of soul, and with it happiness, by adapting oneself to one's circumstances and restricting one's desires within the bounds of the possible, must have sounded both wise and attractive. Conformity of such a sort reaches religious proportions when 'nature' becomes the same as 'God'.

Marcus Aurelius, born in 121 AD, was adopted by the Emperor Antoninus Pius in 138 and himself became Emperor in 161. A good deal of his time in power was spent pacifying the northern and eastern frontiers of the Empire, and the twelve books of *Meditations* are almost certainly the result of his private self-communing during his campaigns. Book 2 was probably written 'among the Quadi on the Gran' and Book 3 at Carnuntum, now Haimburg, in Austria. This will give a date of somewhere between 171 and 173. Unlike the *Discourses* of Epictetus, they were not intended for an audience; but like them they are not composed in an orderly, schematic fashion. There seems to have been no idea in the mind of Marcus of future publication, and in that respect they differ from the *Letters* of Pliny or of Gregory of Nazianzus, which though perhaps initially meant for the immediate addressee, seem almost always, perhaps as a result of later revision, to have a wider audience in view. Marcus' *Meditations*, however, passed unnoticed until 350, and then they drop out of notice for 550 years. It was, in fact, only with their printing in 1558 that their popularity as a work of comfort and instruction began.

He presents the same sort of problems of classification as did his master Epictetus. He too uses from time to time dualistic language about the relation of body and soul, and personal transcendent language about the divine. *Meditation* 5. 27 is a good example of this practice. 'Walk with the Gods. And he does walk with the Gods who lets them see his soul invariably satisfied with his lot and carrying out the will of that "genius", a particle of himself, which Zeus has given to every man as his captain and guide.' On the other hand *Med.* 4. 23 seems to hold up as an ideal conformity with the Universe, which is taken as the equivalent of Nature and the city of Zeus. Such language is more monist in tone. In another traditionally Stoic passage Marcus writes 'For there is but one Universe, made up of all things and one God immanent in all things, and one substance and one law, one Reason common to all created intelligences, and one Truth.' There is also an unresolved ambiguity in his mind on the question of personal survival, an ambiguity which seems to distinguish him from Epictetus. Thus he can write 'What then remains [*sc.* of us] after death? To wait with a good grace for the end, whether it be extinction or translation.' One point, particularly connected with his moral advice, seems to distinguish him from his master, and to argue at the same time in favour of a slightly greater influence of Platonism. Marcus was

AERIAL VIEW OF CARNUNTUM, where Marcus Aurelius wrote part of his *Meditations*. Occupying an important strategic position on the Danube frontier, Carnuntum was permanently garrisoned from the time of Tiberius, and was Marcus' headquarters from AD 172 to 174 during the Marcomannic wars. In the left foreground the excavations of part of the civil settlement near the modern town of Petronell; the site of the legionary fortress is in the distance (under the light-coloured field next to the modern highway).

a great advocate of introversion. 'Look within. Within is the fountain of Good, ready always to well forth if you are prepared to dig deep enough.' Introversion of this sort, and the reflexion it implies, would appear to rule out a purely materialistic concept of the soul, and this point, together with the distinct possibility of the existence of life after death, seems to tip the scales in favour of seeing in Marcus a Platonizing Stoic.

Despite the tendency to adopt certain Platonic ways of thinking on occasion, it remains true that in the basic drive of his system Marcus keeps to the fundamental Stoic tenet that the way to well-being in this life is through obedience to nature and the suppression or mastery of passion. We ought to follow the god or the gods and live in agreement with nature. He uses the classic Stoic formula of 'life in accord with nature' only once; but the idea is always there in the background. On the whole Marcus prefers the more to the less personal expressions. He has less to say about curbing desire than does Epictetus, but being a person in supreme authority he had less obvious need to free himself from unsatisfiable wishes than his master. Among the precepts which he records there is one which expresses in a paradoxical way the ideal of the Stoic sage: 'At the same time to be utterly impervious to all passions and full of natural affection.' Noble though such an ideal undoubtedly is, it may be doubted whether it is at all attainable.

Stoicism, much more than Platonism, was devoted to helping men to live at peace with themselves and with the world, and was always in danger of toppling over into conformity, comfortable or otherwise. In accepting nature, or what happens, as the ultimate criterion of right and wrong, the Stoics were incapable on their own principles of criticizing society, and found some measure of peace in adapting themselves to its vagaries. This inevitably led them to pursue a sort of inner tranquillity through introversion, which represents at the same time a withdrawal from the external world and the assumption of an inner reality that lay beyond the reach of external tyranny. But in seeking such a peace it may be doubted if they remained true to the very principles of anti-dualism from which they began.

Scepticism

Despite Antiochus' abandonment of the sceptical position of the New Academy in favour of a Stoic belief in the possibility of certainty in perception and knowledge, it must not be supposed that the anti-dogmatic habit died at once to be resurrected only with the sixteenth century. Almost at the same time as the Academy abandoned the scepticism common to it since the days of Arcesilaus and Carneades, there arose at some time between 100 and 40 BC a champion of the ancient and true sceptic tradition—Aenesidemus of Alexandria. Little is known about his life except that he denounced, not surprisingly, Antiochus and, surprisingly, Arcesilaus and Carneades, because, he argued, they taught that scepticism was a dogma, whereas they should have said that it was a possibility, not a certainty.

The final flowering of Scepticism as a system took place in the second century and is available to us through the writings of Sextus Empiricus (d. *c.*200 AD). In the course of fourteen books he expounded the principles of Scepticism, and then took issue with all brands of dogmatists and instructors. His work and that of those he represents has been described somewhat eulogistically as the 'antecedent of freedom of conscience, rational criticism, and the absolute right of scientific thought'.

As in the other systems here described, the central aim was one of offering the maximum of happiness. It must be admitted at the outset that their conception of happiness is decidedly negative and owes a good deal to Epicureanism—a philosophy by no means dead, at least to judge from the massive inscription put up at the close of the second century AD by Diogenes of Oenoanda in his native city to instruct his fellow citizens in the Epicurean system. The aim of life is *ataraxia* or freedom from disturbance. The way to this state of mind is through

PART OF THE INSCRIPTION OF DIOGENES OF OENOANDA (second century AD). Over 200 fragments of this amazing philosophical text have now been discovered. It is thought originally to have been about 100 m long. This particular fragment sheds interesting light on Epicurean attitudes to the gods: they should not be portrayed as forbidding or vengeful, and should not be feared, but should be reverenced and accorded the traditional cult-practices.

suspension of judgement, which is arrived at by a realization that certainty is impossible and no argument incontrovertible. The main interest of the whole system is the way in which they thought this state of realization was to be achieved. It was supposed to happen through the ten celebrated 'tropes' of Aenesidemus. The aim of the tropes is to challenge the value, and even more the bare possibility, of going beyond the appearances and arriving at what Stoics and Platonists alike would have termed knowledge. Antisceptic though he was, Plotinus thought it necessary to refute their objections to the possibility of knowledge. In fact *Ennead* 5. 5. 1 can be read as accepting their critique of Stoic sensualism, before he propounds his own theory. The principal type of argument proposed by Aenesidemus and Sextus is that, because the way in which objects appear to us differs from person to person, it is impossible to make absolute claims about the nature of the thing in itself. The first trope argues that, as the same object produces differing impressions on different living creatures, no valid inference about the actual object may be drawn from the report of our senses, and therefore that the only proper and possible attitude towards them is one of suspension of judgement, *epochē*. In his treatise *On the Drunkenness of Noah* Philo writes: 'These and similar phenomena are clear proofs of the impossibility of apprehension'. There is a certain rigour evident in the arguments of the Sceptics, which is in striking contrast to the somewhat incoherent dogmatism of the founders of Middle Platonism, notably Antiochus of Ascalon. As far as we know, no refutation was provided of the arguments of Sextus and Aenesidemus; nevertheless the school did not last. Perhaps it was thought of as too uncompromisingly destructive for an age which needed the support of a metaphysical or religious vision.

Further Reading

One of the best introductions to the thought and atmosphere of the whole period is *Conversion* by A. D. Nock (Oxford, 1933), a study in the Old and the New in Religion from Alexander the Great to Augustine of Hippo. To this should be added *Pagan and Christian in an Age of Anxiety* by E. R. Dodds (Cambridge, 1965), which offers an explanation of the success of Christianity in psychological categories. The chapters on philosophy by Nock and F. H. Sandbach in Vols. x and xi of the *Cambridge Ancient History* are also useful.

   For more specifically philosophical treatment the last volume of Zeller's *History of Philosophy*, entitled *Stoics, Epicureans and Sceptics* (London, 1892), is still probably the most thorough and helpful treatment, though he does not deal with Plotinus. A good, though rather general, survey of the whole classical period of philosophy is also to be found in Vol. i of *A History of Philosophy, Greece and Rome* (London, 1946) by F. C. Copleston. The most easily accessible account of Plotinus and of his immediate predecessors and followers, and also of Philo and of the main Christian philosophers of the first three centuries AD, is to be found in *The Cambridge History of Late Greek and Early Medieval Philosophy* (Cambridge, 1967) ed. A. H. Armstrong. More detailed accounts of imperial philosophy can be had in *Stoic Philosophy* by R. M. Rist (Cambridge, 1969) and in *The Middle Platonists, a Study in Platonism, 80 BC–AD 220* by J. Dillon (London, 1977), and *Neoplatonism* by R. T. Wallis (London, 1972).

Most of the authors of the period can be read in the Loeb Classical Library, which are often furnished with useful introductions and, in the case of Plutarch and Plotinus, with helpful analyses of the contents of the various treatises. The Stoics are represented by the *Discourses* of Epictetus (London, 1925) with an introduction and translation by W. A. Oldfather, and by the *Meditations* of Marcus Aurelius Antoninus (London, 1916), edited, translated, and introduced by C. R. Haines. The appendix contains the speeches and sayings of Marcus and a useful note on his attitude to Christians, in which Haines challenges the popular view that Marcus was hostile to them. Later Platonism is best illustrated by the *Moralia* of Plutarch, especially in Vol. v (London, 1936), translated by F. C. Babbit, which contains *Isis and Osiris* and *The E at Delphi*. Neoplatonism is represented by the *Enneads* of Plotinus (1966), not yet all available, with translation and useful synopses of the complex argument by A. H. Armstrong. A good impression of the mind of Plotinus is available from *Ennead* 1. 6 On Beauty and 2. 9 Against the Gnostics.

14

The Arts of Living

❧❧

ROGER LING

Introduction

THE object of the present chapter is to review those aspects of Roman art and architecture which impinge upon life, and conversely those aspects of life which encroach upon the realms of art. Thus, while Chapter 16 will deal with High Art and 'art for art's sake', we shall here concentrate on topics such as houses and gardens in so far as they affect and reflect life-style, on fittings, furnishings, and interior decoration as documents of contemporary taste and attitudes, on eating and drinking, on personal effects and ornaments, and on household implements and utensils. The field is vast and varied, and generalization is inevitable. It is inevitable, above all, that much of the material discussed will relate to Roman Italy and to the first and early second centuries AD, for which we have an unparalleled abundance of evidence, both literary and archaeological. The literary evidence is provided by social poets such as Persius, Statius, Martial, and Juvenal, by novelists (Petronius), by encyclopedists (the Elder Pliny), and by letter-writers (Pliny the Younger and, for an earlier period, Cicero). The archaeological evidence comes chiefly from the remarkable remains of two 'provincial' towns, Pompeii and Herculaneum, buried by the eruption of Mount Vesuvius in AD 79. There is, of course, much evidence from other archaeological sites, for example second- and third-century Ostia; but none of these supplies the same *embarras de richesse* as Pompeii, still less the same precision of dating.

Houses and Villas

The traditional middle- and upper-class town-house of republican and early-imperial Italy was the *domus*, a spreading mansion focused on two inner light-sources, the *atrium* at the front and a colonnaded garden or peristyle at the rear. The *atrium*, the social and religious centre of the house, was the first open space to confront the visitor as he entered from the street, and it was fittingly endowed in most cases with majestic height, and sometimes with lofty columns framing the shallow rectangular catchwater basin (*impluuium*) in the centre of the floor.

Light flooded through a central opening in the roof (*compluuium*) and was diffused to the chambers round the *atrium*—bedrooms, offices, store-rooms, small dining-rooms, often a pair of broad and deep recesses (*alae*) used to display masks or busts of the family's ancestors. At the back, separable from the *atrium* by a curtain or wooden partition, was the main reception room, the *tablinum*. The second light-source, the peristyle, generally lay behind this. Often of great size, it was surrounded by further rooms, including open-fronted *exedrae* and banqueting-halls (*oeci*).

The first important characteristic to observe in this kind of house is its privacy. The ground floor at least was entirely inward-looking; apart from a few slit

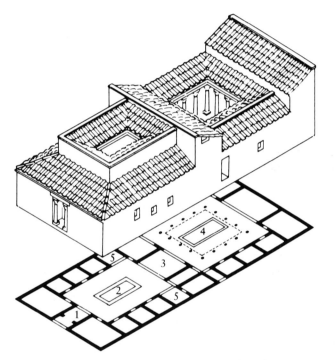

ISOMETRIC DIAGRAM OF A POMPEIAN HOUSE. The tendency to an axial layout with a sequence of roofed and unroofed elements is clearly emphasised: the entrance passage (1) leads to the front hall or *atrium* (2), behind which the reception room or *tablinum* (3) opens on to the colonnaded garden or peristyle (4). The recesses (*alae*) for the display of family portraits are at the back corners of the *atrium* (5).

windows at a high level, its exterior walls presented a blind face to the surrounding world—as much to insure against burglary, one imagines, as to shut out the noise and bustle of the streets. Another characteristic is a tendency to axial planning. Even if it could not always be achieved in practice, the implicit ideal of the *domus* was a vista running from the front door through the centre of the *atrium* and the *tablinum* into the peristyle, often focusing on an architectural feature of some form at the rear. In the House of the Faun, a grand double-*atrium* survivor of Pompeii's palmiest days, larger even than the royal palace at Pergamum, the main vista through the western *atrium* culminated in the columnar *exedra* paved with the Alexander mosaic (plate facing p. 24). In other Pompeian houses a more ostentatious later generation installed a brightly coloured mosaic

THE INTERIOR OF THE HOUSE OF THE TRAGIC POET AT POMPEII: imaginative reconstruction drawing by William Gell (1832), looking from the *atrium* through to the peristyle. At the rear a mosaic
fountain-niche forms the focus of an axial vista from the street door. Gell's drawing, together with the other
illustrations in his *Pompeiana*, helped to inspire Lytton's description of the house of Glaucus in *The Last Days
of Pompeii* (1834).

fountain-niche at the back of the garden, strategically placed to catch the eye of
callers at the street-door. A further notable feature of the house was its strong
contrasts of light and shade. In the bright Mediterranean summer the aesthetic
effect of the vista would have been conditioned by the alternation of deep shadow
and dazzling sunlight, and even in the darker days of winter the rhythm of light
and shade would have been a potent visual factor.

This last point leads naturally to the consideration of lighting, heating, and
related amenities. In summer the cool, lofty rooms and the shady garden porticoes
of the *domus* provided welcome relief from the heat and glare; but in winter the
same rooms could be uncomfortably cold and dark. Although the chill of mosaic
and mortar pavements could doubtless be alleviated with the aid of woven rugs,
there was no entirely satisfactory way of heating living-rooms and bedrooms in
early-imperial times. The underfloor heating systems which were employed in
bath-suites were rarely introduced for other kinds of room, except (later) in the
colder climes of the northern provinces. Generally householders had to rely on
charcoal braziers, a source of heat which would have been unpleasantly smoky,
especially in those chambers which were less well ventilated. At the same time
the rarity of window glass, not widely available before the first century AD,
created a lighting problem, since openings created to admit light would let out
the heat. This is one reason why the older parts of houses had few and small

windows. By the time of Seneca the darkness of old-style bathrooms was a matter for comment, but even now the problem of lighting must have remained in many rooms, whether in baths or elsewhere, if the owner could not afford the luxury of window glass and was obliged to employ shutters or hangings to retain the heat. The candelabra and oil lamps used in antiquity would have provided, at best, an inefficient light and would have contributed to the fumes emitted by braziers. Under the circumstances it was often felt appropriate to decorate the walls of badly illuminated rooms with light colour schemes; but there are just as many examples where the heavy polychromy of the murals increased the gloom.

Generally speaking, however, amenities improved as time went on. The increasing use of window glass led to a better lit and more efficiently heated style of housing; the gradual introduction of more durable and fire-resistant building materials, notably (from Augustan times onwards) brick-faced concrete, brought new standards of stability and safety; and the steady expansion of aqueduct schemes provided running water to cities which had previously relied on wells and rainwater cisterns. Even now, however, running water reached very few private houses. In Pompeii, while well-to-do proprietors such as the Vettii and D. Octavius Quartio could service elaborate garden fountains and water-plays which looked forward across the centuries to the aquatic showpieces of Renaissance Italy, the vast majority of householders, including even the family which lived in the imposing House of the Menander, had to use rainwater or fill their pitchers at the streetside fountains.

The improvements in amenities were accompanied by general changes in the style of urban housing. The *domus*, laid out chiefly on one floor, was prodigal of space and belonged primarily to those periods and those cities in which there was plenty of room for expansion. But right from the first it was not the only, or even the predominant, mode of dwelling. In second-century BC Pompeii, a remarkably prosperous town, there were innumerable small 'lower-class' houses and shops, many of which consisted of only a couple of rooms or a single room containing a mezzanine storey; and in contemporary Rome population pressures were already promoting the development of 'high-rise' apartment blocks. We have a fascinating report in Livy of an ox which, as early as 218, climbed to the third storey of a house near the Roman cattle-market, whence it fell to its death; and in 191 two oxen in another quarter of Rome went up the stairs right to the roof (they survived the climb but were immolated for their efforts). By the late first century BC the architectural writer Vitruvius was able to refer to tower blocks with fine views, and Augustus was obliged, for safety reasons, to limit their height to 70 feet. An echo of this development is discernible at Pompeii, where upper storeys were added piecemeal to many of the older houses, and new blocks such as the Forum Baths, built soon after 80 BC, were provided from the start with upstairs flats accessible directly from the street. By AD 79 Herculaneum had at least two new-style shop-and-apartment blocks, one of which has survived to a height of three storeys. Pressure on space and the growth of the small

THE HOUSE OF DIANA AT OSTIA, a fine example of brick-faced tenement architecture of the mid second century AD. It rose at least four floors, with separate small apartments grouped round a central light-well. The broad shop-openings, the small windows lighting mezzanine floors above them, and the shallow balcony carried on arched corbels, are all characteristic of this building type.

commercial classes also led to the break-up of the old mansions, many of which, like the Victorian houses of modern Britain, came to be divided into independent rented units.

The housing of a major commercial city of the high imperial age is best studied at Ostia, largely rebuilt according to new building standards during the second and early third centuries AD. Here, although some single-storey *domus* still survived and new kinds of courtyard houses, complete with resplendent marble veneer, were added at a later date, the characteristic type of accommodation was the *insula*, or apartment block, three, four, or five storeys high. Unlike the *domus*, this faced outwards, with large windows often opening on to shallow balconies (not always accessible, however, and designed more to shelter the windows beneath than to provide extra space for the tenants). Its great virtue was its flexibility, both in plan and, as a consequence, in the life-style that it offered. It could take the form of a long narrow block, one living-unit in depth; of a rather deeper block, with two sets of living-units arranged back to back; or, where a building plot was particularly deep or neighbouring buildings obstructed the light, of a four-sided block round a central court. Within these basic formulae the variations were legion. A favourite treatment of the street front, foreshadowing the architecture of medieval and Renaissance Italy, was a succession of barrel-vaulted shops interspersed with stairways leading straight from the street

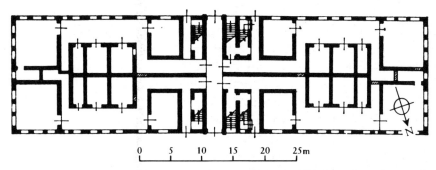

GARDEN HOUSES AT OSTIA (AD 117–38): one of a pair of identical blocks at least three, and probably four, storeys high. These symmetrically planned groups of maisonettes surrounded by open space must have presented a remarkably modern appearance.

to the upper storeys. The ground floor of the *insula* might, alternatively, be divided into two or four more or less identical self-contained flats, entered either directly from the exterior or from an internal dividing corridor. Sometimes, as in the House of the Muses and the House of the Painted Vaults, the whole, or a large part, of the ground floor constituted a single living-unit. In such cases the occupant was perhaps also the owner of the block, and the other occupants his tenants; at the very least he was himself a superior tenant, able to afford space and amenities denied to his upstairs neighbours, many of whom may have had very small apartments and even single rooms.

We know less about the quality of life in the Ostian *insulae* than we do for the houses of Pompeii, because so few of the furnishings and fittings survive. Doubtless standards of comfort were a great deal higher than in Late-Republican Rome; and doubtless Juvenal's accounts of tumbling tenements and the constant danger of incineration in the Rome of his own day were somewhat exaggerated. But conditions in these multiple dwellings could not have been ideal. Even if water could be piped to the ground floor, upstairs tenants would still have been obliged to draw water from the public fountains or cisterns. Very few flats would have had private lavatories: the cry of 'gardyloo' was perhaps as familiar in the streets of Ostia as it was in eighteenth-century Edinburgh. Moreover there was enough timber in the upper floors and internal fittings to make the risk of fire a real one, especially since no truly safe means of heating and cooking were available. Lighting also remained a problem, as at Pompeii, for those tenants who could not afford window glass; many windows were filled with barely translucent panes of selenite or simply had wooden shutters.

Country residences, like town dwellings, ranged over the whole gamut of possibilities, from simple huts and cottages through small working farms to grand villas in which the management of an estate, though generally an important factor, was strictly segregated from a luxurious quarter in which the owner could maintain a life-style appropriate to his taste and station. This last type is well represented in the archaeological record, both in the countryside devastated by the eruption of Vesuvius, and in other parts of Italy and the Empire. We also see it portrayed in Pompeian paintings and read about it in the letters of Cicero and Pliny. Generalizations are difficult, but recurrent features included peristyle gardens, grand colonnaded façades, and (on sloping ground) a podium which Vitruvius calls the *basis uillae*, often containing an underground corridor (*cryptoporticus*). In the grandest examples, including the Villa of the Papyri at Herculaneum and the recently excavated villa at Oplontis, west of Pompeii, both of which have been attractively ascribed to leading families of the Roman nobility, no check was imposed upon the spatial extent of the buildings. At the same time such

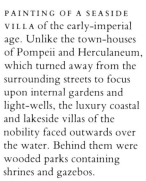

PAINTING OF A SEASIDE VILLA of the early-imperial age. Unlike the town-houses of Pompeii and Herculaneum, which turned away from the surrounding streets to focus upon internal gardens and light-wells, the luxury coastal and lakeside villas of the nobility faced outwards over the water. Behind them were wooded parks containing shrines and gazebos.

villas, unlike the aristocratic town-houses, were outward-looking; their colonnaded façades and terraces addressed themselves to a landscape or overlooked a garden. In the coolness and shelter of the portico the owner could stroll and philosophize, like the Younger Pliny, about the delights of nature, far from the toils of the city. A favourite form, especially renowned in the Bay of Naples and reflected in numerous murals, was the maritime villa, built along the sea-front or even terraced out into the sea; Pliny, for example, could dine in his Laurentine villa with 'a view from the front and sides, as it were, of three different seas' (above, p. 250). In vain did Horace inveigh against the villa-builders of fashionable Baiae, whose concrete piers seemed almost to remodel the coast-line.

Interior Decoration

Interior decoration was an essential ingredient of the Roman life-style and can hardly be considered apart from domestic architecture. Its strictly art-historical aspects are dealt with elsewhere (Chapter 16); here we must examine its function and its meaning to the householder.

At the most mundane level a fine mosaic pavement or a set of painted murals were designed to beautify a room. The finest decorations were generally reserved for the main dining- and reception-rooms, but other areas of the house which were likely to be seen by visitors—the *atrium*, the peristyle, the baths, certain bedrooms—could also receive special treatment. Only in the more prosperous houses, however, was the majority of rooms elaborately decorated. Even in Pompeii the painted walls which conform to the four well-known styles were outnumbered by those with simple striped and panelled schemes and by walls with plain plaster, and the mosaic pavements were concentrated in a few particularly opulent dwellings, while the majority of floors were of mortar with perhaps at the most a sprinkling of inset tesserae or marble fragments. In less prosperous cities or societies, for instance in certain parts of Roman Britain, the house- or villa-owner concentrated most of his resources upon adorning one room: the central dining-room of the Lullingstone villa, with its Bellerophon and Europa mosaics, is a case in point (above, p. 250).

At a more ambitious level the proprietor used decorations to transform and enhance his environment. This is particularly true of the Pompeian styles of wall-painting, in which the imitation veneering of the First Style echoed the real veneers of Hellenistic palaces. The porphyry columns and exotic architecture of the Second Style (Vol. I, p. 407; above, 136) also evoked the grandeur of a court, though probably transmitted through the medium of stage-painting, and the baroque extravagances of the Fourth Style (below, p. 378) may have owed something to the theatre but were probably more a form of escapism into a world of pure imagination. The perspectival forms of both styles also, of course, seemed to enlarge the physical space within a room; and in some instances, by offering a glimpse of sky above the painted architecture, or by opening a window through it on to a mythical world, the decoration seemed to break right through the bounds of the wall. The ultimate expression of this is provided by those paintings, such as the garden murals from Primaporta, which turned the room into an open-sided pavilion set in a magic forest. The aesthetic value of such paintings in rooms which were often cramped and badly lit is easily appreciated.

Another role of interior decoration was to turn parts of the house into picture-galleries (*pinacothecae*). In Hellenistic times, copies of well-known paintings were carried out in mosaic to embellish the central fields of pavements, and the same tradition continued in certain cities of the east, such as Syrian Antioch, through the imperial age. But in the Roman west these copies were incorporated as painted panels within wall-decorations. Well-off Pompeians, such as the brothers Vettii and the owner of the House of the Tragic Poet, collected reproductions of Greek old masters in much the same way as more recent generations have collected copies of the Laughing Cavalier or the Mona Lisa. This was one means whereby the *nouveaux riches* could make a display of their culture. Truly cultured householders, like the owners of the villa at Boscotrecase just north of

THE PENTHEUS ROOM IN THE HOUSE OF THE VETTII at Pompeii (between AD 62 and 79): one of the finest surviving examples of a domestic 'picture-gallery', with copies of well-known Greek paintings set at the centre of each wall-decoration: the Punishment of Dirce, the Death of Pentheus, and the infant Heracles strangling the snakes sent by Hera, perhaps the famous work by Zeuxis of Heraclea (c.400 BC).

Pompeii, preferred original paintings in which the stories of Alexandrian and Ovidian elegy and the bucolic world of Theocritus' *Idylls* could be evoked in an altogether more subtle and mysterious manner (Vol. 1, p. 351).

Whether there are deeper meanings to be discerned in ancient wall-decorations is a question which has recently roused controversy. The Swiss scholar Karl Schefold argues from the Pompeian evidence, not only that painters or their patrons chose subjects which were relevant to the type of room being decorated, but also that the subjects within a decoration were normally linked in a consistent programme embodying deeply-felt moral or religious ideas. Thus one decoration will present a hymn to the great deities of love and fertility, Aphrodite and Dionysus; another will contrast the exploits of a divinely favoured hero with the sufferings of an offender against the gods. Landscape paintings are invariably sacred, still lifes are offerings to the gods, and so forth. The same idea is explored by Mary Lee Thompson, though with a more pragmatic approach: for her most of the programmes are on a relatively superficial plane, dealing with a particular hero such as Achilles, a particular locale such as Thebes, and particular conceptual combinations such as love and water. There is doubtless some truth in all this, for a strong religious element appears in many Roman murals (compare the cult-objects and sacrificants lurking in the painted architecture), and in some cases a thematic link between balancing paintings is unmistakable. The left *ala* of the House of the Menander at Pompeii contains a Trojan cycle in which paintings of the wooden horse and of the death of Laocoon, both allusions to warnings unheeded by the Trojans, are combined, as in a Greek tragedy, with the ruinous sequel: Priam watching griefstricken while Menelaus seizes Helen and Ajax assaults Cassandra. That the Romans often looked for thematic associations is illustrated by a picture gallery described by Petronius, fictional but perhaps based on fact, in which the story of Ganymede is grouped with those of Hylas and Hyacinthus, all three illustrating the love of immortals for beautiful youths and the resulting 'apotheosis' of the loved ones. But to try to apply such rules universally, and above all to look for recondite religious and ethical interpretations, is to expect too grave and profound an outlook in the ancient householder, whereas Pompeian painting contains much that is clearly humorous and much that appeals directly to the senses. It also leads very quickly to inconsistencies: to fit his theories Schefold has to argue that Medea is now contrasted with Penelope as a paradigm of false love, now compared with her as a beatified heroine.

The other main art form found in private houses is sculpture. Here we must distinguish between the religious statuettes of the household shrine (the *Lares*, the *genius* of the paterfamilias, and the protecting deities of the household) and works which were more purely decorative or ostentatious. The latter can again be divided. On the one hand there were small figurines designed to be kept on shelves or sideboards in private parts of the house, for example the terracottas including a gladiator, a porter, Venus arranging her hair, and two slaves carrying a litter, all less than 16 cm. high, found in the family quarters of the House of M.

Lucretius at Pompeii, or the even smaller bronze figurines (a seated philosopher, an old man milking a goat, and an ape brandishing arms) from the ruins of the upper storey of the House of the Marbles, also at Pompeii. On the other hand there were the statues, statuettes, and reliefs which were displayed in gardens and other open parts of the house. These raise the same programmatic questions as wall-paintings and merit closer attention.

In most cases domestic sculptural displays were somewhat arbitrarily compiled and arranged. The need to 'shop around' for available pieces presented a totally different situation from that involved in commissioning a mural decoration and naturally led to heterogeneous collections. The great and wealthy imported works from Greece, but not always with great discrimination, as we can judge from Cicero's requests to Atticus to supply him with sculptures for his villa at Tusculum: 'anything you consider suitable for the palaestra and gymnasium ... reliefs to be set in the plaster of the *atriolum* and a couple of figured well-heads'. Apparently almost any pieces would do so long as they were Greek. Even the sculptures of Hadrian's Villa at Tivoli seem to have been employed in a rather haphazard way. The statues round the Canopus ('Egyptian pool') included a splendid crocodile and much other appropriately Egyptian or egyptianizing material, but there were also very different items, for example copies of Classical Greek wounded Amazons, figures of Hermes and Ares, a statue group showing Scylla and her victims, and replicas of the Erechtheum caryatids. Since Hadrian and his successors were presumably better able than most patrons to get what they wanted, this heterogeneous assortment could hardly have been dictated solely by market forces.

The private collection about whose arrangement we know most is that of the Villa of the Papyri at Herculaneum, from which no fewer than eighty-seven sculptures were recovered and all their find-spots recorded. The late-republican or early-Augustan aristocrat who formed the collection, perhaps L. Calpurnius Piso Pontifex, the consul of 15 BC, was clearly a man of culture rather than of great artistic sensibility: his penchant for busts of Attic orators, Stoic and Epicurean philosophers, and early-Hellenistic dynasts evinces an interest in humanistic studies, but the artistic quality of the collection was variable, ranging from excellent copies of Greek masterpieces to second-rate pastiches and decorative hackwork. Such programmatic arrangements as can be discerned were superficial and not consistently carried through (despite the efforts of modern commentators to argue otherwise). For example, in the large peristyle two figures of runners, a statuette of the seated Hermes, and busts of various philosophers evoked the idea of a gymnasium, but interspersed with them were Hellenistic *condottieri*, animal figures, and drunken satyrs—strange bedfellows indeed. Hermes actually sat back to back with one of the inebriates. Indeed this latter grouping illustrates the point that compositional balance, well exemplified by the favourite Roman device of pairing statues in mirror image, was more important to the householder than thematic correspondence.

THE GARDEN OF THE HOUSE OF M. LUCRETIUS at Pompeii, an excellent example of the use made by the early-imperial *bourgeoisie* of decorative statuary. At the rear, standing in a niche, a Silenus poured water from a wine-skin down the steps into the central pool; all around, scattered in the shrubbery, were animals, birds, and satyrs; in the foreground a young satyr inspected the foot of a Pan, and cupids rode dolphins.

The average Pompeian householder of the years before 79 did not lay claim to the literary culture of Piso: he preferred to concentrate on decorative subjects. Admittedly he might display a portrait herm of an ancestor in his *atrium* as a kind of guarantee of a respectable pedigree, but the bulk of his collection consisted of Bacchic figures, *putti*, herms, and animals, with perhaps the odd decorative statuette of a divinity such as Venus, Apollo, or Diana thrown in for good measure. Some of the items were inherited or bought from older collections, where no doubt they had been used in different roles; many, especially the marbles, were churned out by contemporary local workshops. A large number of them were designed or adapted to serve as fountain-pourers, in which capacity they could be set along the margins of the *impluuium* in the *atrium*, between the columns of the peristyle, or actually in the garden, where they discharged their water into ponds or marble basins. A good example is the satyr squeezing water from a wine-skin down the steps of a *nymphaeum* in the House of M. Lucretius. In addition to figures in the round, many collectors had reliefs, whether set in walls, displayed on top of pillars, or hanging in the form of shields between the columns of porticoes. Whatever the theme or function of the individual works, the householder's chief goals were to accumulate as many exhibits as possible and to place them so as to be visible from certain crucial vantage-points: thus the

IMPLUVIUM AND CARTIBULUM in the House of the Wooden Partition at Herculaneum. The *impluvium* in the foreground is the basin which collected rainwater from the opening in the roof of the *atrium* and channelled it into an underground cistern. Behind it, the *cartibulum* was a marble table for the display of utensils and serving-ware.

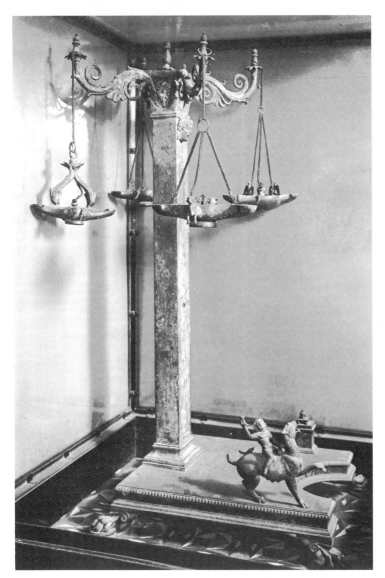

BRONZE LAMP-STAND from the Villa of Diomedes at Pompeii (before AD 79): a particularly ornate example in which the lamps are suspended from spiralling branches and the base is decorated with a figurine of a satyr riding a panther. As so frequently in Roman furnishings, the feet are in the form of animal paws.

garden statuary of M. Lucretius is disposed for the benefit of visitors in the *tablinum* and the adjacent dining-room. Bronzes in particular, being more expensive and more highly prized, were flaunted in prominent positions.

If we combine the Pompeian material with evidence from elsewhere, we get a reasonable idea of decorative furnishings in use in imperial times. Tables in both bronze and marble, round or rectangular, were regularly supported by elaborate legs compounded of lions' paws, volutes, griffins' foreparts, and the like. Small bronze tripod stands, complete with raised rims to prevent things from rolling off, had deers' legs or (less tastefully) legs formed by ithyphallic satyrs. Couches were mainly of wood, which with one or two exceptions has perished, leaving only the bronze fittings: elegant lathe-turned legs, headboard ornaments with cast appliqués in the form of busts or horses' heads, and railings

WOODEN CUPBOARD-SHRINE in the House of the Wooden Shrine at Herculaneum. The shrine, in the form of a little temple with finely carved Corinthian colonnettes at the corners, contains statuettes of the household gods, the Lares and Penates. Below is a cupboard containing glassware and ornaments. The lighter coloured parts of the woodwork are modern restorations.

with silver inlay. Sometimes such fittings were in other materials, such as silver, tortoise-shell, or ivory, and a couch with reliefs of bone has recently been partially restored with the aid of remnants in the Fitzwilliam Museum, Cambridge. Bronze lamp-standards came in many more or less ornate types, among which the simplest consisted of a slender fluted column resting on three animal-paws and surmounted by some form of calyx, while more complicated versions had four or more arms, either in the form of volutes or shaped like tree branches, from which lamps were suspended. An especially ornate example from the Villa of Diomedes at Pompeii had a platform at the base, decorated with a figurine of a satyr on a prancing panther. Household chairs and stools, which were mainly of wood, have not survived, but interesting representations of armchairs in basket-work are known from later imperial times. Also of wood were cupboards and cabinets: examples from Pompeii and Herculaneum reveal that they were usually simple affairs divided by shelves into compartments and closed at the front by twin doors; but occasionally an architectural touch was bestowed by the addition of a gabled top or of flanking colonnettes. Even the family strongbox, a stout chest of wood or iron (or both) kept in the *atrium*, could be decorated with bronze plaques carrying figural and vegetal ornament.

Gardens

Ornamental gardening was not invented by the Romans: shrubs and trees had been used by the Greeks to beautify temple precincts and *gymnasia*, and a late-Hellenistic landscaped park has recently been identified outside Rhodes. But it was only in the Roman period that pleasure gardens became a major facet of the arts of living.

The term used by the Elder Pliny for ornamental gardening is *opus topiarium*, whose derivation from the Greek word *topia* (landscapes) reveals both the Greek origins of the art and one of its main themes. The original aim of the gardener was, in fact, to create attractive natural settings: in a famous passage Pliny seems to list varieties of landscape gardens as 'groves, woods, hills, fish-pools, canals, rivers, coasts'. But the artificial element soon came to play a predominant role, and we find increasing evidence for the use of statuary and garden furniture, the introduction of formal layouts and the shaping of trees, and the combination of plants with water displays.

The association of statuary and landscape began with works such as the Victory of Samothrace (Vol. 1, p. 389), set on a ship in a rock-filled pool, and continued with the sculpture-grottoes of the Rhodian park, a theme later carried to extremes of grandiloquence by Rhodian artists working in the service of the emperor Tiberius at Sperlonga and on Capri. But the combination of statues with foliage soon became equally fashionable. When the word *topiaria* first appears in Latin literature, in a letter of Cicero dated to 54 BC, it is in connection with the growing of ornamental ivy as a backdrop to Greek statuary in one of his brother's villas at Arpinum. Such effects were doubtless employed by many of Cicero's illustrious contemporaries in the parks which they created in the area of Rome itself and round their luxury villas in the country; it was for Italian garden settings that the sculptured marble bowls and candelabra produced in Neo-Attic workshops were primarily designed.

Formal planning and topiary in the modern sense probably began in the time of Augustus. This is when, according to Pliny, one C. Matius invented *nemora tonsilia* ('barbered groves'). As the desire to impose formal shapes almost certainly went hand in hand with the desire to create formal plans, we can assume that the same period saw the first symmetrically planned gardens, especially as the improvements in the water-supply of Rome and other parts of Italy undertaken by Agrippa and his successors would have favoured the cultivation of low, ornamental plants. The first formal gardens in wall-painting belong to the first half of the first century AD, laid out in plots framed by hedges or trellis fences: an example in the *tablinum* of the House of M. Lucretius Fronto at Pompeii shows an enclosed flower-bed on either side of a focal tree, reflecting the symmetry of the villa-façade which overlooks it (plate facing p. 57). Little archaeological evidence of formal gardens is known, though one fine specimen has been reconstructed in the villa at Fishbourne, with a central path bordered by hedges fashioned into a series of alternating rectangular and semicircular recesses. But that such gardens existed on a grander scale in Rome and its surroundings is demonstrated by examples represented on the Severan marble plan of the city (for example, in Vespasian's Temple of Peace) and by parts of a plaque now in Urbino preserving the plan of a funerary park. The further development of

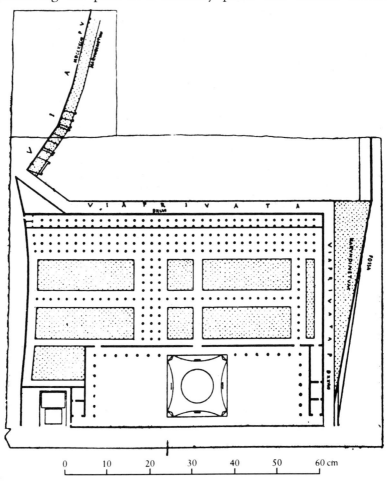

```
0      10      20      30      40      50      60 cm
```

PLAN OF A FUNERARY GARDEN IN ROME: engraving on marble (third or fourth century AD). The actual mausoleum, evidently a three-storeyed affair with a square podium supporting a concave-sided structure crowned by a small rotunda, is shown at the bottom; behind it lies the garden, a formal arrangement of lines of trees (indicated by small circles) and rectangular parterres.

topiary, as distinct from formal plans, apparently knew no bounds. By the time that the *Natural History* was published Pliny could report not only that cypresses were clipped to form hedges but also that they were shaped into elaborate tableaux portraying 'hunt scenes, fleets of ships, and other images'; and in his nephew's villa at Tifernum in Tuscany there were box trees cut into the shapes of wild animals and into numerous other forms, including the letters of Pliny's and his gardeners' names. It was the description of the gardens at Tifernum that inspired the box parterres and labyrinths of the sixteenth and seventeenth centuries.

The same improvements in water-supply which favoured diversification in types of planting also ushered in the age of the garden fountain. Already in the wall-paintings from Boscoreale, dated around 40–30 BC, we see a depiction of a piano-shaped marble fountain at the mouth of a vine-draped grotto; while Propertius, writing in the 20s, reveals that a fountain decorated with a sleeping

CANAL IN THE GARDEN OF D. OCTAVIUS QUARTIO at Pompeii (between AD 62 and 79). In imitation of the canals of villa-parks, this wealthy householder laid out a series of elaborate waterways and fountains, spanned by pavilions and pergolas. In the middle pavilion is a statue of the sleeping Ariadne, derived from a well-known Hellenistic type.

Silenus played among the plane trees of Pompey's porticoes in Rome. The importance of water displays in Pompeian house-gardens has already been mentioned. In addition to statuettes pouring water into basins, many peristyles enclosed large ornamental pools fed by jets of water or fountain-niches at the rear, while other gardens, foreshadowing a vogue of the third and fourth centuries AD, had whole walls enlivened by a façade of niches and pavilions (*aediculae*) from which water flowed. Two large gardens in the east of the city, those of D. Octavius Quartio and Julia Felix, contained central canals with bridges at intervals, sculptures along the edges, and open pergolas bestriding them. On either side ran pathways overhung by climbing plants. A generation later the Younger Pliny took great pride in a fountain which played within a vine-arbour in his Tuscan villa and whose marble basin he and his guests used as a kind of supper table, resting larger dishes on the rim and allowing small dishes of hors d'oeuvres to float in the water.

The trees and plants cultivated in ornamental gardens put the accent on greenery rather than floral displays. Besides the box and cypress trees favoured by topiarists, the ancient sources mention plane trees, laurel, myrtle, hound's tongue, acanthus, maidenhair, butcher's broom (whose evergreen foliage, we are told, was sometimes used in wreaths to make up for a lack of flowers), and a shrub called 'Jupiter's beard' which had silvery leaves and could be trimmed into a round shape. Our picture is supplemented by the shrubberies represented in garden paintings; among the items identified by modern botanists are such flowering plants as poppies, oleanders, lilies, and viburnum. Roses, one of the few flowers attested in Pliny's garden at Tifernum, are shown next to fountain-basins in a mural in the House of the Floral Chambers at Pompeii.

An idea of the overall appearance of small private gardens in the early Imperial age is obtainable at Pompeii, where the recent work of Wilhelmina Jashemski, involving excavation, the study of carbonized plant-material, and pollen analysis, has opened a whole new perspective on the subject. A surprisingly large proportion of peristyle-gardens has turned out to contain fruit- and nut-trees, not to mention vines, all grown for food rather than for fancy; but purely ornamental gardens laid out to formal designs certainly existed in the better appointed houses. The more pretentious examples, combining shrubs, fountains, decorative statuettes, and often frescoes on the enclosing walls, reflect the aspiration of the wealthy middle class to import the villa life of Roman aristocrats into their urban homes. Thus the huge wall-paintings of wild animals which overlook many late-Pompeian gardens evoke the game- or safari-parks (*paradeisoi*) of the nobility, a theme which is also echoed by statuettes of dogs attacking wild boar amid the actual plants and fountains. Some details, such as marble ducks and ibises at the waterside, a bronze fisherman dangling his rod in a fountain, and a sleeping marble pixie amazingly akin to a modern garden gnome, are almost kitsch. The palm for vulgarity should perhaps be awarded to L. Ceius Secundus for commissioning a painting of a nymph who appears to empty her bowl of water into a real gutter in the pavement.

Eating and Drinking

Closely linked with the garden were the delights of dining. The U-shaped masonry dining areas (*triclinia*) found in Pompeian gardens, often accompanied by clam or snail shells and the bones of meat-animals, confirm that the modern Mediterranean practice of eating out of doors on hot summer evenings goes back

WILD ANIMALS PAINTED IN THE GARDEN OF THE HOUSE OF THE CEII AT POMPEII (between AD 62 and 79). Such paintings were inspired by the safari parks of Hellenistic monarchs and of the republican nobles who imitated them; they introduced an incongruous element of grandeur and exoticism to the cramped internal garden of a small town-house.

SLEEPING PIXIE: marble statuette of a small boy wearing a hooded cloak, from the House of the Small Fountain at Pompeii (before AD 79). Round him lie three baskets, one of which serves as his pillow; they have been identified as the apparatus of a fisherman. Such genre subjects were much in fashion as garden-ornaments in the imperial age.

to antiquity. Sheltered by an awning or by a vine-arbour and cushioned by mattresses and pillows, the diners would recline on their elbows in the Greek manner, picking titbits from a central table or, like Pliny's guests, from floating dishes in the form of little boats and water-birds; as night drew on, lamps would be lit in surrounding candelabra, some of them, as in the House of the Ephebe, suspended from the hands of bronze statues.

The banquets described by Martial, Pliny, Petronius, and others should not mislead us; the diet of the vast mass of the people was always frugal, and even the great men of affairs ate little before evening. But when occasion demanded meals could be splendid and cooking carried to the realms of fine art. A cookery book ascribed to the early-imperial gastronome M. Gavius Apicius gives some fascinating glimpses of Roman haute cuisine: for example, 'Sucking pig à la Frontinus: fillet, brown, and dress; put in a casserole of fish-sauce and wine, wrap in a bouquet of leeks and dill, pour off the juice when half-cooked. When cooked, remove and dry, sprinkle with pepper and serve.' Apicius was famous for his sauces and dressings, and gave his name to various cakes; he is also said by

GARDEN DINING AREA IN THE HOUSE OF THE EPHEBE AT POMPEII (between AD 62 and 79). The masonry couches formed a ∏-shaped *triclinium*, on which diners reclined round a low central table, shaded by a vine-covered pergola. In the background water played from a small fountain shrine; in the foreground a cylindrical pedestal supported the bronze statue of a youth who held candelabra to light the evening banquets.

Pliny to have invented dishes of flamingos' tongues and mullets' livers, and to have pioneered a form of pâté de foie gras. It was one of the arts of the Roman chef to disguise dishes so that no one could divine their ingredients. This was taken to extremes at the feast described by Petronius, where a dish of pork was dressed up by Trimalchio's cook to look like a fattened goose garnished with fish and different kinds of birds ('If you want it, he'll make you a fish out of a sow's womb, a wood-pigeon out of bacon, and a turtle-dove out of a ham', brags the host), and the guests were treated to a whole sequence of unnerving surprises: peahens' eggs containing beccaficos rolled in spiced egg-yolk, a wild boar containing live thrushes, a pig full of sausages and black puddings, cakes and fruit filled with liquid saffron, thrushes made of pastry and stuffed with raisins and nuts, quinces decorated with thorns to look like sea-urchins. Each dish emerged in artistic form or with some histrionic display; the wild boar, for example, arrived with an escort of hunting dogs, and a boiled calf was sliced with a sword by a slave impersonating the frenzied Ajax. Such excesses, though inflated by the writer's fertile imagination, were certainly based upon the pageantry of real banquets. So too were some of the entertainments devised for Trimalchio's guests. The gold hoop laden with gifts which was let down from the ceiling recalls the revolving dome of Nero's Golden House which showered flowers on the diners below. The musicians, singers, acrobats, and dancing girls echo the performances provided at banquets such as the one that seduced a potential guest of Pliny: invited to a homely supper with a poetry recitation and a performance on the lyre, this philistine preferred the gourmet dishes and Spanish dancing-girls of another host.

The delights of more modest dinner-tables are celebrated by the succulent fruits, game-birds, and sea foods represented in Pompeian still-life paintings. These *xenia* ('guest-gifts'), named, according to Vitruvius, after the provisions Greek hosts supplied to visitors on self-catering holidays, call to mind menus described by Martial and Juvenal. Martial, for instance, offers a dinner in which the hors d'oeuvres are listed as mallows, lettuces, leeks, mint, rocket, sliced eggs and anchovies, and sows' udders in tunny sauce; the main course was a kid and cutlets with haricot beans and tender green-sprouts, with the addition of a chicken and the residue of a ham which had already served three suppers; and the dessert consisted of ripe fruit and a vintage Nomentan wine. Wine was, of course, the essential concomitant of good eating, and no meal was complete without a jar of a fine vintage—preferably the 'immortal Falernian', the Château Lafite of Roman Italy.

To serve a sumptuous repast the host needed the best silver and tableware. Discoveries of silver hoards hidden by their owners in Pompeii and nearby Boscoreale at the time of the eruption of Vesuvius reveal both the quality of the plate in domestic use during the early imperial period and also the zeal with which it was prized and protected. The superb beakers, cups, bowls, and dishes decorated with repoussé reliefs of plant arabesques or mythological scenes, together with the simpler, but still elegant, spoons and ladles, lend significance to Petron-

STILL-LIFE PAINTINGS OF
FOOD, from Herculaneum.
According to Vitruvius, such
paintings were called *xenia*
('guest-gifts') after the gifts of
poultry, eggs, vegetables, fruit,
and the like, provided by hosts
for their guests. One panel shows
a hare and a plucked game-bird;
the other a brace of partridges
and a pair of eels.

ius' gibes at the extravagance and tastelessness of his millionaire freedman Tri-malchio, who used a chamber-pot of silver and gave orders for a silver dish which had been dropped during his banquet to be swept away like broken pottery. The quality of silverware was maintained during the later Empire. It is to this period that we must ascribe such masterpieces as the octagonal dish from Kaiseraugst in Switzerland, adorned with scenes from the life of Achilles.

If an owner could not afford silverware, the next-best thing was bronze or glass. Both these materials were in much wider use in the home than is generally realized, since the process of recycling has militated against the survival of speci-mens in domestic contexts. The excavations at Pompeii and Herculaneum have again done much to set the record straight; among the finds are numerous graceful bronze jugs and wine-jars with appliqué reliefs at the base of the handles, and a rich, but barely known, series of glass vessels of all types: bottles, phials, cups, beakers, plates, jugs and the like, translucent or coloured, blown or cast, plain or decorated. Deluxe items of glassware are the so-called 'cameo-glass' vessels, of which the most famous are the Blue Vase from Pompeii and the mysterious Portland Vase, decorated with figures in white relief on a blue-black ground. During the second, third, and fourth centuries the use of glass became more widespread, largely replacing bronzeware (the snobbish Trimalchio makes excuses for using glassware rather than antique Corinthian bronze), and the later imperial period saw the production of further expensive lines, such as various

EMBOSSED SILVER WINE-CUP from the Hildesheim hoard (first century AD). The finely worked Bacchic reliefs, including theatrical masks, Bacchic wands (*thyrsi*) and masks of Silenus, are wholly appropriate to the function of the vessel. Roman silver plate frequently found its way, through trade or plunder, to sites such as Hildesheim which lay beyond the imperial frontiers.

kinds of figured cut glass and the cage-cups with openwork decoration manufactured probably in Italy and the Rhineland.

Lack of space precludes a full examination of the domestic equipment of Roman times. Fine pottery, notably the red-gloss ware from Arretium (Arezzo) and (later) Gaul, imitated the embossed reliefs and even some of the subjects of figured metalware; but the careful moulded decoration of the first and second centuries tended to die away in many areas, to be replaced by simpler techniques including rouletting and relief motifs in applied clay. By the fourth century pottery was to a large extent overtaken by glass as the usual form of fine tableware. Other artistic products in domestic use included carved bone or ivory handles for knives and the ubiquitous bronze or terracotta lamps, with their simple figure-reliefs and distinctive wick-holding nozzles. Less artistic, but unambiguously geared to the pleasures of the table, was the extraordinary series of objects known as *gliraria*—large terracotta jars used to rear dormice, a delicacy which particularly appealed to the Roman palate. Surviving examples from Pompeii are provided with regular holes to admit air and with a spiral ramp round the interior wall to enable the animals to reach a pair of feeding trays near the rim.

Dress and Personal Effects

Dress is the aspect of the arts of living about which we are perhaps least well informed. We know from Roman writers that the ceremonial toga, a semicircular white woollen wrap between 5 and 6 m. in diameter, had to be donned with great art and no little difficulty, a circumstance which encouraged many men to view with relief those 'off-duty' occasions when they could wear the simple *tunica*. Portrait statues give us some idea of what the toga looked like, with its distinctive curving hem; and from the same source we get representations of the long dress, or *stola*, of the Roman matron. Other works of art illustrate further garments, such as the *pallium*, a version of the heavy Greek cloak; the *lacerna*, a short cape fastened at the neck with a brooch; and the *paenula*, a kind of hooded poncho. To the late-imperial period belong depictions of the long-sleeved tunic or dalmatic. But for all this comparative wealth of illustrative material there is little to convey the rich colours and embroideries, still less the fine fabrics (muslins and silks), worn especially by society ladies. The fragments of surviving textiles from Egypt, though instructive on the range of possible weaves, patterns, and colours, are mostly late in date (fourth or fifth centuries), while the pieces from other parts of the Roman world are rarely well preserved or of any artistic pretensions. Nor is there much information in the Latin authors beyond vague indications of cut or colour, for example the green tunic and red belt of Trimalchio's flunkey, the red tunic, yellow belt, and gilded slippers of his wife, and the close-fitting *lacerna* and well-tailored red, green, and purple cloaks given by Statius' friend Atedius Melior to his young favourite Glaucias.

FEMALE HAIR-STYLE OF THE TRAJANIC PERIOD (AD 98–117). The honeycomb quiff of the preceding (Flavian) period now gave way to superposed rows of tightly spiralling curls, with a great interwoven chignon like a bird's nest at the back. The most prominent patron of the new fashion was Trajan's sister Marciana.

We may know little of fine clothing, but fashionable hairstyles are well known from the sculptured portraits of Emperors and their womenfolk. These varied considerably over the years. In the first century the studied disorder of Augustus' hair gave way to the carefully styled waves and sideburns of Nero; and in the second century Trajan's 'Beatle' cut was replaced by the neat Hellenic beard and carefully cultivated coiffure of Hadrian, a fashion carried to extremes in the full beards and tightly crisped locks of his Antonine successors. The imperial ladies were not surprisingly even more fashion-conscious. Although Livia and the Julio-Claudian princesses favoured classicizing styles with gently waving hair running from a central parting to loose ringlets over the ears and a chignon at the nape of the neck, the *grandes dames* of Flavian and Trajanic times piled up elaborate edifices of spiral curls or interwoven plaits on wire frames. In the most extravagant examples these scaffoldings, like the *onkoi* of heroines in Greek tragedy, doubled the height of the head, and it must have been a great relief to all and sundry when the trend-setters of the second century reverted to simpler styles reminiscent of the Julio-Claudian period, albeit with a more deliberate crimping of the waves.

Beautification of the female did not, of course, stop with the hair. References in the Latin poets to tooth polish, painted cheeks, pencilled eyebrows, and eyeshadow have a familiar ring; and the wearing of excessive jewellery was a practice which legislators had long since given up trying to curb, though moralists still condemned it. Pliny rails against women who wore pearls on their fingers, on their ear-rings, and on their slippers, and reports with disapproval how Caligula's first Empress, Lollia Paulina, turned up to a feast wearing emeralds and pearls on her head, hair, ears, neck, and fingers. Similarly in Petronius' novel it is a mark of Trimalchio's lack of decorum that he flaunts his wife's gold jewellery—anklets, bracelets, and a gold hairnet. 'She must have six and a half pounds weight on her', he declares.

Numerous items of personal gold jewellery have survived. At Pompeii some of the objects, such as rings and bracelets in the form of snakes, continue the Hellenistic tradition, but new types also appear—ear-rings decorated with pendant clubs, hemispheres, or clusters of plasmas, and necklaces with crescent or wheel-shaped pendants. Generally speaking the use of inset stones remained popular in Roman times, but in place of a single species we find a profusion of colours and materials combined, for example sapphires, garnets, and crystals alternating in a single necklace. At the same time the fine techniques of filigree and granulation declined in favour, giving way to plain surfaces of gold or to a new openwork (*interrasile*) style of ornament. Finger rings were widely worn, both by women, as tokens of engagement, and by men, as signets. A popular device was an engraved portrait of the Emperor, and imperial gold coins or medallions were frequently set as bezels in rings; they also appeared as pendants on necklaces and as ornaments on brooches. Among the various types of brooches the most successful was the crossbow, widely worn in the fourth century. All this jewellery retains the technical quality of its Greek forerunners, but there is a certain reduction in artistic sensitivity in favour of bolder and showier effects.

This last comment, applicable also to other personal ornaments and effects, from combs and hairpins to toilet-boxes and mirrors, sums up what is a general characteristic of many of the arts of living discussed above. There is in them a certain lack of restraint, even a certain vulgarity—a love of immediate and over-elaborate effects which places imperial taste in the same bracket as that of the Victorian period. Like Victorian taste, it was the product of the fruits of world empire, for example of the free availability of exotic materials and commodities, from precious stones and metals to coloured marbles, tropical beasts,

CARVED-IVORY TOILET BOX (third century AD). The wall is carved with Dionysiac reliefs: a reclining maenad (one of Dionysus' female followers) and two running Cupids, one of whom (here) carries a purse. The knob on the lid is in the form of a pine-cone.

and (in the case of nineteenth-century England) American and oriental timbers. And, like Victorian taste, it was the prelude to an age of chaos and uncertainty, an age in which life and art suffered an almost total divorce.

Further Reading

For the ancient authors who give us information on this subject (Cicero in his letters, Petronius, Statius, Ovid, Martial, Juvenal, the Younger Pliny) see the translations etc. cited in the bibliographies of Chapters 4, 8, 11, and 12.

Pompeii and Herculaneum. The best book is T. Kraus and L. von Matt, *Pompeii and Herculaneum: the Living Cities of the Dead* (New York, 1975). Also valuable, though difficult to obtain, are the various editions of the exhibition catalogue *Pompeii 79* (London, 1976; Boston, 1978) edited by J. B. Ward-Perkins and A. Claridge. Brief popular surveys are M. Grant, *Cities of Vesuvius: Pompeii and Herculaneum* (London, 1971); A. De Franciscis, *The Buried Cities: Pompeii and Herculaneum* (London, 1978); R. Seaford, *Pompeii* (London, 1978); and J. J. Deiss, *Herculaneum: A City Returns to the Sun* (London, 1968). Still an important synopsis, though excluding the twentieth-century discoveries, is A. Mau, *Pompeii, its Life and Art* (transl. F. W. Kelsey, 2nd edn., New York, 1902).

Ostia. R. Meiggs, *Roman Ostia*, 2nd edn. (Oxford, 1973) includes much relevant material on housing. See further A. Boethius, *The Golden House of Nero* (Ann Arbor, 1955).

Many of the aspects covered in the present chapter are dealt with in the stimulating, but somewhat too gloomy, survey of J. Carcopino, *Daily Life in Ancient Rome* (New Haven, 1940). On domestic architecture the only general book is A. G. McKay, *Houses, Villas and Palaces in the Roman World* (London, 1975), which is confused and frequently at fault; much better are the relevant sections in J. B. Ward-Perkins, *Roman Imperial Architecture* (Harmondsworth, 1981). On gardens the fundamental work is now W. F. Jashemski, *The Gardens of Pompeii, Herculaneum and the Villas Destroyed by Vesuvius* (New York, 1979).

Decorative and luxury arts. See the general works cited in the bibliography of Chapter 16, especially M. Henig (ed.), *A Handbook of Roman Art* (Oxford, 1983). On specific themes the following are all useful studies: R. J. Charleston, *Roman Pottery* (London, 1955); R. A. Higgins, *Greek and Roman Jewellery* (London, 1966); G. M. A. Richter, *The Furniture of the Greeks, Etruscans and Romans* (London, 1966); D. E. Strong, *Greek and Roman Gold and Silver Plate* (London, 1966). The techniques of artists and craftsmen are examined in D. Strong and D. Brown (eds.), *Roman Crafts* (London, 1976).

15

Roman Life and Society

✤

JOHN MATTHEWS

Distances and Diversity

IN the year AD 333 a Christian pilgrim set out from his home city of Bordeaux for the Holy Land. Measuring the early stages of his journey by the 'leagues' still at this late date in use in south-western Gaul, he travelled by land across the Alps and north Italy, through the Balkans to Constantinople, and from there through Anatolia and Syria until, 170 days and 3,300 Roman miles (about 3,100 modern miles) after his departure, he came to Jerusalem. The pilgrim's journey is not merely testimony to the long-distance travel possible, and frequently undertaken, in all periods of the Roman Empire; it is also a challenge to the imagination. How did the pilgrim react to the different landscapes through which he travelled, the languages he heard spoken, the cities, towns, and way-stations in which he lodged as he passed from Bordeaux, penetrated by the Atlantic tides, to the edge of the Judaean wilderness? The modern historian, influenced perhaps by the Mediterranean perspective of his ancient informants and by his own knowledge of the future, tends to see the history of the Roman Empire in terms of the relationship between East and West, Greek and Latin; but a journey not much shorter than that of the Bordeaux pilgrim could be made from north to south, beginning at the militarized frontier region of Hadrian's Wall and passing through Celtic Britain and Gaul through Romanized north Africa to the edge of the Sahara. Such a journey might take in the capital of the Empire and, in southern Italy and Sicily, enclaves of Greek speech in the west surviving from the colonial period. The traveller would find diversities of dress no less striking than those of climate and geography, from the wool-clad, hooded countrymen of the cool northern provinces, as we see them on grave reliefs and wall-paintings, to the bright oriental silks of a family from Edessa, shown with its Syriac names on a mosaic pavement from that city. The jurist Ulpian pronounced that it did not matter in what language certain legal documents were framed, citing Punic and Celtic as examples of languages that might be used, and in another he considered the legal status of statements made in Punic or Syriac 'or any other language' in reply to questions asked in Latin. If modern scholars are hesitant as

TRAVELLERS: detail c
funerary relief from A
(Orolaunum) in Belgi
(third century AD). Th
figures, well wrapped
woollen cloaks against
cool northern climes, ;
seated in a wagon. Th
Roman peace (and the
system) facilitated lon;
distance journeys, but
communications were
painfully slow by moc
standards.

to the actual extent of the franchise of Celtic and Punic by the time of these pronouncements in the early third century, no such uncertainty attends Syriac (better called Aramaic), a language spoken in its various dialects by Levantine easterners for centuries before its rise to become a great literary language. The same is true of Egyptian demotic, a spoken language for long before it acquired a script and, as Coptic, became a language of the written word. Celtic leaves no indigenous literature from ancient (as opposed to medieval) times, nor at any time does the language which modern scholars sometimes, though misleadingly, call 'Berber'—an indigenous African language commemorated on hundreds of inscriptions from one end of Roman north Africa to the other, and by a distinctive nomenclature attested as late as the fourth century.

A single city could present an extraordinary cultural diversity between the town and the surrounding country, and even within the town itself. Paul and Barnabas, performing a cure at Lystra in Lycaonia (Asia Minor), were hailed as Zeus and Hermes by the local people shouting 'in the Lycaonian language' (Acts 14: 8 ff.). The priest of Zeus was all for making a sacrifice, as he brought oxen and garlands to the gates of the town from his temple outside the walls, but was dissuaded, and the evangelists' visit was terminated when hostile Jews from the cities of Pisidian Antioch and Iconium provoked the evidently volatile crowd into pelting them with stones. Despite this misadventure, the journeys of St Paul generally show him exploiting the modest social prestige of a man who had inherited the Roman citizenship from his father in the days when, as Tacitus remarked of a Gallic Roman citizen of the same period, that honour was given only rarely and in recognition of merit. A Jew from Tarsus, he no doubt belonged at Jerusalem to that community of Jews from Greek cities who stirred up hostility to Stephen (Acts 6: 9 ff.). Then, after his conversion and decision to turn to the Gentiles—that is, to the non-Jewish Greek communities of the East—he travelled from city to city, attracted particularly to centres where Greek culture, philosophical learning, and Roman officials were to be found; finally using his status as a citizen to appeal to the Roman Emperor, he went to Rome and for a time lived there, among many thousands of Graeco-Orientals who had settled there before him. Jesus of Nazareth, in contrast with this picture of physical and cultural mobility, pursued his mission in the villages and townships of local communities, eventually meeting his death during his single known visit to Jerusalem as an adult, exchanged by an indifferent Pilate for a popular bandit chief and executed by a penalty reserved for slaves, brigands, and aliens of the lowest social status. The contrast between the social milieux of Acts and of the Gospels leaps to the eye at every turn.

It was precisely the achievement of the Roman Empire to have assimilated in one political and administrative system the immense diversities of the Mediterranean, and much of the northern European, worlds. The Bordeaux pilgrim undertook his journey to the Holy Land to see for himself the historical location of a religion that was within a few years of the conversion of Constantine (AD 312) to provide a coherent ideology for the entire Roman Empire. His near-contemporary, Eusebius of Caesarea, saw in the *pax Augusta* the providential dispensation of God to facilitate the expansion of Christianity through the Roman world.

For the power of the Romans [he wrote] came to its zenith at precisely the moment of Jesus' unexpected sojourn among men, at the time when Augustus first acquired power over all nations, defeating Cleopatra and putting an end to the succession of the Ptolemies. ... From then also the Jewish nation has been subject to the Romans, that of the Syrians likewise, the Cappadocians and Macedonians, Bithynians and Greeks; to put it briefly, all the nations which now fall under the Roman Empire. (*Demonstratio Evangelica* 3. 7. 30 ff.)

With what difficulty, remarked Eusebius, would the disciples otherwise have travelled to foreign lands, 'the various nations being at war with one another, their diversities of government preventing relations between them'.

Eusebius' conception, for all its grandeur, fails even to mention the western and northern regions of the Roman Empire. It is not just that, by his time, the

Empire was divided into largely self-contained administrative and political units. The reserved attitude of Greeks towards the West, the Latin language, and its literature, though modified when, in the fourth century, a Latin-speaking imperial court governed from Constantinople, is a fundamental aspect of ancient cultural history. Not that they otherwise allowed themselves to be inhibited, for in the republican and early-imperial age the intellectual and human current from east to west massively exceeded that in the reverse direction. In the three centuries before Eusebius' time, Greeks by the myriad had gone to the west to seek their fortune as artists, writers, teachers, and exponents of the other diverse skills mentioned by Juvenal: 'grammarian, orator, geometer, painter, wrestling-master, prophet, tightrope walker, medical man, wizard—he can do anything, your penniless Greek . . .' (*Satires* 3.76–8). It was of course precisely his 'penniless' state that the humble Greek wished to remedy in going to Rome, and he had many examples, at the highest levels of distinction, to spur him on; Tiberius' astrologer, the famous mathematician Thrasyllus, Claudius' doctor Xenophon of Cos and his librarian Ti. Claudius Balbillus of Alexandria, not to mention the cohorts of literary men and scientists found at Rome under Augustus. In these professions, as Virgil had conceded in a famous passage (*Aeneid* 6.847 ff.), Greeks were allowed the supremacy.

Juvenal's attitude to Greeks is usually linked with his notorious allusion to the Orontes pouring into the Tiber, bringing its hordes of Greco-Syrian rhetoricians, musicians, religious fanatics, and prostitutes, but he goes on in later lines to mention also towns and islands of old Greece and Asia Minor, his examples (Sicyon, Amydon, Andros, Samos, Tralles, Alabanda) being chosen, no doubt, for their adaptability to hexameter verse and their ability to suggest the sound of Greek speech, but truly identifying the ancient homelands and colonial area as well as the Hellenized Orient as the origins of the Greeks who made their presence felt in imperial Rome. From the greater cities of Asia Minor, notably metropolitan centres such as Ephesus, Sardis, and Mytilene, had come ambitious dynasts (hardly 'penniless' Greeks) of the first and second centuries, to hold senatorial office, the consulship and provincial governorships (thereby refuting the second part of Virgil's prophecy, reserving for Romans the arts of government and administration). The historian Cassius Dio came from Nicaea in Bithynia. The son of a senator who had himself become consul and governed the province of Lycia-Pamphylia, Dio was twice consul and in the later 220s, as an old man, rather surprisingly made governor of Pannonia, a Danubian military province for whose inhabitants and culture he had little understanding or sympathy. A barbarous race, he thought them, their life enhanced by no liberal arts or any of the things that make an honourable life worth while. They produced only a little poor wine, drank beer, and lived in extreme cold. Dio wrote this (he claims) from personal observation of conditions among them, having been their governor, but his attitude is in reality as prejudiced as that of Juvenal towards Greeks, and with as little excuse. It betrays the depth of a Mediterranean man's, and a Greek civilian's, incomprehension of those non-Mediterranean military provinces of the Empire which, as events would quickly show, were crucial to its survival.

The limits to the cultural unity achieved, or attempted, by the Roman government in its diverse regions and between its social classes, were then palpable—no less so, perhaps, than those between the Empire at its fringes and the barbarian world beyond; for the frontiers, generally based on rivers, which promote cultural exchange, rather than on mountain ranges, which prevent it, were far from impervious to the influence of foreign cultures. Yet the degree of uniformity of language and culture achieved within the empire, and the physical resources which made this uniformity possible, were extraordinarily impressive. Tacitus wrote of the Roman Empire as encircled by rivers and seas, every part—armies, provinces, navies—joined together as one system, and he was right. It was a rhetorical theme, sustained to the end of the Roman Empire, that Rome the city (*urbs*) had made the world (*orbis*) its own; conversely, that in Rome the city the entire world possessed a symbol of its identity. A commonplace sentiment perhaps, but a real one, and one with practical (if sometimes unexpected) consequences. It was not permissible, for example, for a man exiled from his own city to reside in Rome, for this was the 'common homeland' of all citizens. It is conventional to point to the sheer distances that were involved in travel between provinces, and between Rome and the frontiers, to the constant dangers of sea journeys and the inevitable slowness (given the nature of the available technology) of transport by land. But this is a relative matter; journeys like that of the Bordeaux pilgrim were undertaken, made possible by roads driven through provinces, over passes, across wide rivers. The bridge built by Trajan across the Danube at Drobeta was dismantled by Hadrian to prevent easy access to the Empire for hostile intruders; its piles were left in place and seemed to Dio, who had seen them, to show that there was nothing that could not be accomplished by human ingenuity. Its designer, Apollodorus of Damascus (below, pp. 385 f.) who was responsible also for the Forum of Trajan, with its column and library, was an architect of genius who would have been perfectly at ease in the company of Leonardo or Brunelleschi. He was certainly aware of his own abilities; indeed, his contemptuous opinion of the architectural efforts of Hadrian, a gifted amateur, was believed to have led to his exile and execution by that jealous man when he became Emperor.

The roads built by the Romans, originally for military purposes but in the nature of things quickly acquiring economic uses, linked together distant regions by direct routes that were not matched until modern times, for it is not every society that has a frequent use for long-distance travel. Aerial views of the Roman roads of Britain often show vividly the contrast between their direct, purposeful routes, professionally surveyed for long-distance communications, and the local lanes and field-boundaries of medieval and early modern England which adjoin them, betraying the lines of an altogether more local economy. The maintenance

BRIDGE ACROSS THE DANUBE, shown in a detail of the reliefs from Trajan's column (AD 113). Constructed by the greatest engineer and architect of the day, Apollodorus of Damascus, the bridge consisted of a timber superstructure carried on stone piers; the roadway is shown in bird's eye view at the top between a pair of railings. In the foreground the emperor conducts a sacrifice.

of the roads, once built, fell as a corvée on the local communities through whose territories they passed, and these communities naturally undertook the construction of subsidiary roads, way-stations, and bridges. Of the latter, the most 'stupendous' (Gibbon's word), and certainly from a historical point of view one of the most interesting, is the bridge over the river Tagus at Alcantara in western Spain, standing high over the river to accommodate winter spate and built, as an inscription shows, by the co-operative efforts of eleven Lusitanian communities. The name of its builder, C. Julius Lacer, appears in another inscription attached to the shrine of Trajan at the bridge; his achievement, he there declared with a totally justified pride, would 'last for ever through the ages'.

Along the roads of the Empire and across the pacified seas, the Emperor sent his emissaries, confident that, whatever diversities of culture and language they traversed, they would be understood by those to whom they were sent. In turn, and perhaps still more to the point, provincial communities could dispatch envoys to the Roman government with a similar confidence that, within the normal limits of human will and energy and with only a small allowance for misadventure, they would reach their destination; knowing too that within the mode of communication established by Greco-Roman culture and maintained by the educated élite, their petitions would be understood. Such embassies, undertaken by leading citizens on behalf of their communities, are among the best-attested civic functions of Roman society. They reveal vividly the sheer physical movement required of subject as well as of Emperor in the administration of the Empire and show how this too was, from the point of view of the communities themselves, an expression of their social structure; for the ambassadors, filling their role as a social duty and deploying in its service the classical education which marked them out as members of the élite of their cities, returned (if successful) as the benefactors and patrons of their cities, leaving an enhanced prestige for their sons to inherit and, in their turn, surpass.

As all this implies, the comprehension of the Roman Empire as a rational social organization involves a marked simplification of its actual nature—a simplification in which the emperors themselves and the leaders of local communities concurred, for it reinforced their power over outsiders and the less favoured classes. Celtic might still be spoken in Gaul and Britain, Aramaic in the Levant, demotic in Egypt, Libyan in large areas of north Africa, and who knows what in the remoter parts of Asia Minor; but all could be reached in one of two major languages. However diverse the physical nature of the communities of the Empire, they could be defined in terms of one civic status or another (*colonia, municipium, uicus, castellum*) and their inhabitants' status described in terms of Roman law, even if the actual law to which they were subject in minor matters was based on local practice and custom, administered by local magistrates. On major matters and before the Roman governor, no such concessions were envisaged. Pliny the Younger, encountering Christians in a town of Pontus, consulted Trajan on certain matters of legal procedure and social status, and on the question of anonymous denunciations posted in public places. In cases of admitted Christians of low social status, he had no hesitation in ordering immediate execution and was apparently prepared to treat 'pertinacious obstinacy' as a punishable offence. Pliny noted to Trajan that before his intervention the 'contagion' of Christianity had attacked not only the cities, but also the villages and the countryside of the province (it is the only reference to the countryside in his whole correspondence from Bithynia-Pontus); now, however, the temples were full of pious worshippers and sacrificial meat was again on sale in the markets. One wonders for how long *that* revival lasted, once Pliny had departed.

Town and Country

It is a natural instinct, encouraged somewhat by our sources, the products of city men, to see the Roman Empire as a vast confederation of city-states. If there is an over-simplification here it relates to the degree of uniformity to be found in the cities and in their economic functions, and in the different rates at which cities in fact developed. Tacitus in one passage shows himself aware of a process of urbanization which had in his own day become established in Numidia but had not yet begun in the time of Tiberius. The process is documented for just that region by the archaeology and epigraphy of cities such as Madaurus, Cuicul (Djemila), Milevis, and Sitifis, native settlements which progressed from municipal to colonial status at the turn of the first and second centuries. In Britain the governor Agricola encouraged the use of the toga, the building of houses and public amenities, and the use of the Latin language, and put his name to the forum building at Verulamium (St Albans) at a time when the settlement, though already a *municipium*, still consisted largely of wooden-framed structures and generally lacked properly made-up streets. Again according to Tacitus, the tribe of the Frisii in the Low Countries, having rebelled under Tiberius because of oppression in respect of their taxes, paid in elk-skins, were in the time of Claudius settled by the military governor and given 'senate, magistrates, and laws'. Presumably what is meant is some sort of civic foundation with a charter; but we are left to imagine for ourselves what this new civic community actually looked like.

Everywhere in the West arose new cities. In central Gaul the Celtic *oppidum* of Bibracte (Mont Beuvray), inconveniently located in the hills of the Morvan, gave way to Augustodunum (Autun), a city of immense circuit built on an accessible site by the river Arroux. By the time of Tiberius the sons of the Gallic nobility were already receiving there an education in liberal studies—to pave their way (which, for reasons too complex to describe here, they never really took) into the high aristocracy of the empire. Bibracte declined, not through coercion—for archaeology shows that the site was still inhabited after the foundation of Autun, and declined progressively—but through sheer inconvenience and the attractions of the new city. In similar fashion, the native settlement of the Magdalensberg in Noricum gave way to the new town and provincial capital of Virunum (just to the north of Klagenfurt). In the East little new city foundation was called for, nor did the activities of Hellenistic kings leave much room for it. With certain exceptions such as colonial foundations in areas of uncertain tranquillity like southern Asia Minor, the main influence in the East was the steadily increasing prosperity made possible by the *pax Augusta* rather than any particular intervention of the Roman power. The caravan cities of Palmyra, Gerasa, Bostra, and Damascus gained new prosperity as more settled Roman relations with the East encouraged economic activity and Roman control of the area became more definite. The spectacular urbanization of Palmyra, though its origins were in the Hellenistic period, was essentially a product of the Roman Empire, beginning in

AERIAL VIEW OF CUICUL (Djemila, in Algeria): a fine example of urbanisation in Numidia during the first and second centuries AD. In this photograph, taken from the west, the initial colony of AD 96–7 is in the foreground, occupying a rocky spur between two wadis; the more irregular second-century suburb lies outside the south gate, at the right.

the time of Tiberius and ending only with the collapse of the Palmyrene empire in the later third century.

It was above all in the West that living conditions were transformed, by the growth of cities and the development of those resources most conducive to public health, economic development, and organized leisure. Rome itself saw an immense change, achieved by huge capital outlay on the part of Augustus and his successors, which not only altered the appearance of the city, as Augustus rightly claimed for his own achievement, from one of brick to one of marble, but raised the quality and reliability of its food and water supplies to unheard-of levels. The gang of slave maintenance-workers assembled by Agrippa for the upkeep of the aqueducts was on his death inherited by Augustus and transferred by him to public ownership (that is, to the domain of the *curator aquarum*). We should not forget that in the cities of the Empire most men lived, not in palaces or the town houses of Pompeii and Herculaneum, with their gardens, fountains, statuary, and frescoed rooms, but in the plain tenement blocks best known to us from the remains of Ostia (above, pp. 312 f.). After the fire of Rome in 64, remedies were undertaken which have much to say about the general conditions of life in first-century Rome and, no doubt, in other large cities also. Limits were fixed to the permitted height of residential buildings, which must possess their own walls and not adjoin others directly; a proportion of the construction must be of fireproof stone, without timber frames; financial incentives were offered for early completion of building works; unauthorized tapping of the water system was prevented by government inspectors, to ensure an adequate flow to the public supply, and householders were required to keep fire-fighting equipment in an easily accessible place. All agreed that the new city was more gracious than the old; some claimed (it being impossible to please everyone) that it was less healthy than the old city, whose narrow streets and high buildings had provided shade and coolness which the new open spaces did not allow. A more pertinent complaint might have concerned the area of the city taken up by Nero's dream, the 'Golden House' (below, pp. 378 ff.), with lawns, lakes, and rustic landscapes devised by its builders, as Tacitus said, to make good by art the deficiencies of nature.

Although the city was the fundamental unit of ancient social and administrative life, many were those who lived outside its range, in different ways; in tribal reservations which, at least in certain parts of north Africa, persisted to the late Empire and beyond; in townships (*uici*) and the great villas which in the northern provinces were quite as important a facet of the economic and social process of Romanization as were the cities. In mountain areas, such as exist in north Africa

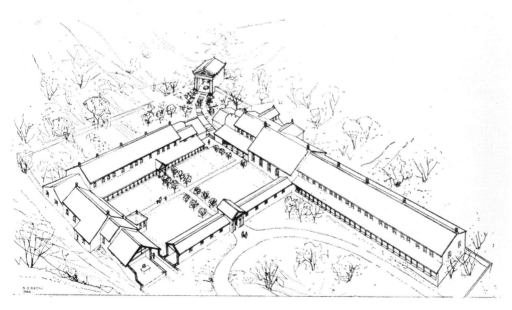

VILLA AT CHEDWORTH (Gloucestershire): reconstruction drawing of the buildings about AD 300. This well-preserved example of a comfortable farm-house in the northernmost of Rome's provinces has a secluded inner courtyard surrounded by the best-appointed domestic accommodation and an outer yard opening to the estate. The owner's wealth was probably based upon stock-breeding and wool-production.

(the Kabylie and Aurès) and Isauria in southern Asia Minor, lived enclaves of mountain folk hardly touched by Roman civilization but a threat to it if economic conditions turned against them, for then they would descend on the agricultural territories of Roman cities. On the desert fringes to the south and to the east transhumant peoples, and in the north barbarians, moved in and out of Roman territory in a way that paid little regard to the formal barriers of the frontier systems.

In taking the cities and their articulate classes (and therefore most of the surviving evidence) as the basis for the analysis of Roman society, we risk ignoring the great majority of the population on whose labours the prosperity of the cities depended but who do not make a proportionate impact on the surviving source material: the rural peasantry. That the cities in fact depended on the economic exploitation of the peasantry is axiomatic. But it would be a mistake to assume from this that the cities and the countryside were in consequence divided by an overt mutual enmity. The city, as a market, centre of distribution, source of occasional delights and pleasures and, not least, home of the major gods, was a real and active presence in the life of the peasantry, even if a relatively small part of their physical existence was spent there. In the fourth century John Chrysostom remarked on the Syriac peasantry flooding into Antioch on Christian feast days, 'divided from us in language but at one in faith'; it is one of the few literary acknowledgments we possess of the peasantry or, as in this case, of its non-classical language, but the situation it evokes is evidently common and immemorial. By the same token the local aristocracies, in whose hands lay the conduct of civic politics and the provision of public services, were the owners of the land and spent much time on their farms and country estates—a pattern of life illustrated by Apuleius for second-century Oea (in Tripolitania) as much as by the historian Ammianus Marcellinus for fourth-century Leptis Magna and Nisibis (in Mesopotamia). Among true 'city-dwellers' we should count professional men such as teachers and doctors, craftsmen, fortune-tellers and magicians, traders, merchants, and so on. For the activities of many of these professions, the value system of Greek and Roman society, rooted in the attitudes of landed amateurism, was reluctant to assign proper respect. At all levels of society, provincial and metropolitan, it was the landed interest that was most closely connected with the tenure of political office. The senatorial class of the early Empire was composed of landed magnates who came to politics with a census qualification that ensured they were men of substantial private means, and they embarked on careers that did not in general (though exceptions could always be made) require a specifically military, financial, or other expertise so much as all-round literary culture and general experience. In the domain of local politics trade secured no foothold even at Arles or Lyon, where it was a prominent and profitable activity; only at Ostia, an exceptional case because of its restricted territory and the overwhelming dominance of trade in the economy, did the trading interest make much impact on the conduct of its civic and political life.

APPLE SELLERS: funerary relief from Arlon (second century AD). The produce of the farms and smallholdings would be brought, as in medieval and modern times, to the market-towns for sale; here we see a fruit-stall with a customer (or the farmer himself?) standing at the right.

SHOP-KEEPER AND LADY WITH A DOG: reconstructed funerary monument from Lillebonne (second century AD). The shopkeeper is shown standing behind his counter with glass flagons and boxes on the shelves above him and tools hanging on the wall behind him. The lady (his wife?) holds her pet dog in her left hand and offers it a titbit with her right.

A man who turned his back on politics to pursue commercial interests might be spoken of as following a life of *quies*, that is, the freedom to make money without the constraints and inhibitions imposed by the political life and its values. The two brothers, Seneca and Mela, were prominent respectively in the senatorial and equestrian orders of later Julio-Claudian Rome, the latter expressing what Tacitus called a 'perverse ambition' in choosing to enrich himself by holding imperial procuratorships. Possibly the brothers were even cleverer than Tacitus acknowledged, in vesting their interests equally in the two great enterprises, politics and commerce. Cassius Dio alleged that among the causes of the revolt of Boudicca was Seneca's calling-in of loans of 40,000,000 sesterces he had made to the Britons, with an eye to the high interest rates he might extract. If true, or even plausible, it is an intriguing suggestion, not only of a senator indulging in speculative finance, but also, we may suspect, of the high costs to the leading men of the new province of their own Romanization. Buildings to construct and furnish, mosaicists to commission, statuary and luxury goods to import from all over (the early palace at Fishbourne gives an indication); there was a lot to pay for and not much money yet in the province.

The importance of trade, manufacture, and commerce in the actual conditions of life in the Roman provinces is as obvious as that of agriculture, which provided their economic base and of which they were very often the direct expression. So much is clear from many sources: from one of the most important inscriptions of any period of Roman history, the Edict of Maximum Prices by Diocletian in AD 301; from the patterns of ostentatious expenditure manifest in the great consuming cities of the Empire; from the incidence of discovered shipwrecks, rising to a peak in the late-republican and early-imperial periods; not least, from the illustration on large numbers of grave reliefs, especially from the western provinces, of a wide variety of trading, commercial, and generally professional enterprises, in which those commemorated evidently took pride and found respect (they would not otherwise have been shown on their tombstones). Viewed in another perspective, there are the various trades and occupations, more than a hundred of them, named on the inscriptions of a small town in south-east Asia Minor; and no less than 250 in the slice of life represented by a fourth-century manual of astrology. Why should we ever wish to apply to such modestly successful *petits bourgeois* a social attitude to trade, commerce, and manual labour formulated by the philosophers, and repeated by the rhetoricians, of a different social class—men freed by position, unearned income, and the labour of others from the need to contemplate the normal facts of economic life?

Yet it remains true that it was in the hands of the traditional aristocratic, rather than of the trading or commercial, interest that the physical maintenance and political conduct of the cities of the Roman Empire rested and also, therefore, much of what appears to us as its achievement. By generosity and munificence, these local aristocracies built their cities, sustained their physical amenities, patronized their literary culture by supporting municipal chairs of grammar and rhetoric, and provided their entertainments. They constructed aqueducts, porticoes, temples, theatres, built and provided the heating for public baths, kept the streets clean and lit at night. They maintained peace in the surrounding countryside, provided distributions of oil, grain, and cash and, at a personal expense recorded on many a commemorative inscription, employed professional gladiators and charioteers, acrobats and jugglers, singers and musicians, and imported exotic beasts to be hunted down in public shows for the general enjoyment. In return they were acclaimed by grateful multitudes as 'benefactors', 'providers', and 'patrons' of their cities in demonstrations of goodwill which ensured the continued influence of their families.

There was also the pressing need to channel into legitimate forms of expression the social tensions which, left unchannelled, could have destroyed civic life. Life in the ancient world did not possess the measured regularities of modern times—office hours and working weeks, factory shifts and teaching days, time-tabled

INTERIOR OF THE *FRIGIDARIUM* (COLD ROOM) IN THE NORTH BATHS IN PARIS (last quarter of second or first quarter of third century AD). This well-preserved example of a public bath-building now forms part of the Cluny Museum. The original fabric, courses of small blocks punctuated by bands of brickwork, is clearly distinguishable from later alterations.

SCENES OF BEAST HUNTS (*VENATIONES*) IN THE AMPHITHEATRE: mosaic from Smirat in Tunisia (mid third century AD). Four huntsmen named Spittara, Bullarius, Hilarinus, and Mamertinus have been pitted against four leopards named Victor, Crispinus, Romanus, and Luxurius; in the centre a herald holds a tray with four money-bags, and a pair of inscriptions record the munificence of one Magerius who has put up the money to pay the performers.

transport, deep-frozen food stocks, and regulated prices; not to mention the instant communication of verbal and visual information (what did the Emperor even look like?), and a mode of political organization designed to promote class and economic interests by systematic process of election, discussion, and legislation. Ancient social life was more discontinuous, the role of government more passive and intermittent. Through provincial councils focused on the imperial cult, cities could periodically exchange views and explore their common interests, if necessary send an embassy to press their case before the Emperor; but for most of the time they lived separate lives, as often inclined to seize advantage over their neighbours as to co-operate with them. Disputes about provincial primacy, as between Ephesus and Smyrna, Nicaea and Nicomedia, or local economic rivalries, as between Lyon and Vienne, could impinge on the imperial administration because they led to disorder. They might occasionally affect the course of a civil war or campaign for the imperial throne by a pretender, a situation in which a mistaken judgement might lead a city into the need to make an expensive apology (or worse), but in which a correct one could enhance the status of a community and enrich those leading members who had guided its choice.

Even the financial situation of the landowning politicians contributed to the

AERIAL VIEW OF THE AMPHITHEATRE AT ARLES (last quarter of first century AD). The elliptical auditorium was developed in central Italy about 100 BC as the home *par excellence* of the immensely popular beast-hunts and gladiatorial games; and the Colosseum in Rome (inaugurated in AD 80) inspired a rash of stone versions in northern Italy and the western provinces. That at Arles is still used for bull-fights, the modern equivalents of *venationes*.

relative abruptness of civic life. It was in fact the fundamental cause of it, as the landowners drew incomes in cash rentals and the sale of market produce, in a society with few banking facilities, low liquidity ('I am totally involved in farming', said the Younger Pliny in explanation of his inability at short notice to raise 3,000,000 sesterces to purchase another estate), few possibilities for alternative investment, and a consequent need to dispose of their surpluses in whatever ways would give them satisfaction, add lustre to their material wealth, and increase their prestige.

The explosions of colour, pageantry, and popular demonstrations that mark ancient games and entertainments, not to mention their ritualized violence, reflect this discontinuous pattern of life, much as the disorder and rioting in the cities often reflect the abruptness of the economic conditions that framed it. It was not easy to be a recluse in an ancient town. Public life was conducted in specific locations, much of it out of doors in a particular area of the city (the *agora*, flanked by public buildings, temples, and the senate-house), and the leaders of the society would be known by personal appearance to the population; if things went wrong it would be known who was to blame. Famine, which could be sudden and extremely local in its incidence, could turn the affection of the people for its leaders into aggression, when mobs demonstrated in the streets and the landowning politicians fled for safety to their well-provided country estates. At such moments the upper classes show themselves in one of the more self-interested of their many roles, as they hoard grain supplies to secure high prices in times of shortage, by physical obstruction and specious argument resisting governors' attempts to bring down the price. For the historian of the city of Rome above all, social unrest and violence are to the end a central theme, their causes impressively consistent; partisanship over performers and factions in the public games and races provided by the Emperors and (in the late Empire) the resident aristocracy of Rome, and food shortages, especially of corn and wine. A new factor may be mentioned here, though it is beyond the scope of this survey; rioting and

CIRCUS GAMES, shown on a funerary relief of the second century AD. At the left are portraits of the deceased couple, while in the centre a charioteer drives his team past the triple turning-posts (*metae*) and the central obelisk of the Circus Maximus. Rivalry between the four colours of the circus (red, white, blue, and green) frequently led to violent disturbances, which increasingly took a political form.

violence (on one notorious occasion resulting in 137 dead on the floor of a Christian basilica) over rival claims for the bishopric of the city. We might take these as the remote descendants of the late-republican battles between Clodius and Milo and the demonstrations in favour of rival triumvirs—just as the ritualized acclamations of the late Empire in circus and theatre descend from the political demonstrations so frequently mentioned in the *Lives* of Suetonius and described, with dubious political theory but fascinating examples, in the later chapters of the *Pro Sestio* of Cicero. At Alexandria, a city well known for its civic disturbances, riots in the fourth century between Christians and pagans, and between rivals for the bishopric, appear as the natural successors to the rioting of the early Empire between the Greek and Jewish communities.

Social Organization

The inequalities of wealth, social standing, and privilege between what a modern government might have called the 'socio-economic categories' of the Roman world were immense. They embraced not only the physical conditions of life and the opportunities open to individuals for their self-betterment, but areas in which modern citizens, in theory at least, are equal: as in the differing legal penalties thought appropriate for different classes of men. Those described as 'more honourable' (*honestiores*) were in the course of the second century made exempt from such punishments as flogging, burning alive, exposure to wild beasts, and condemnation to the mines and quarries, penalties regularly imposed, by the most summary of legal procedures, on members of the lower classes. *Honestiores*, to be broadly identified with the order of local councillors of the cities of the Empire, might legally be executed only by the sword, and were able to claim rights of appeal to the jurisdiction of higher courts; in these respects they had inherited some of the privileges enjoyed by Roman citizens in the first century, before that class had become too extensive to make them worth while.

Had a programme of social reform ever been devised by the Roman government (which in fact never saw any need for such a thing), it would no doubt have identified a free urban citizenry consisting of the craftsmen, traders, and professional men whose activities were indicated earlier. Since it was usual for a craftsman to market his own products in a shop attached to the premises, there would be no need to separate sharply the means of production and of exchange, though it might be necessary to distinguish those people who, like porters, teachers, entertainers, and prostitutes, provided a service for a fee, and whose only asset might lie in physical strength or adroitness, intelligence, and the possession of an acquired skill. There were also the free labourers, whose numbers, for long underestimated, are in more recent study attaining their correct proportions; builders and manual workers, who ignored the contempt of Cicero for such occupations and worked for hire for any employer who would pay them. 'You must let me feed my people', said the Emperor Vespasian to an inventor who offered him a labour-saving device for the transport of building materials. We should no doubt consider separately the skilled workers, such as bakers, whose services to the community merited, and attracted, special attention. They and analogous workers, such as masons, silversmiths, wool-workers, undertakers (to select just four examples) belonged to trade associations, or *collegia*, which possessed social, religious, and sometimes quasi-political functions, as well as providing an organization for the businesses with which they were concerned. The city of Ephesus offers cases of silversmiths organizing demonstrations in the theatre against the preachings of St Paul in order not to lose their trade in the manufacture and sale of images of Ephesian Artemis and, in the second century, of the guild of bakers withholding their labour in pursuit of some aim of their own and being called to order by the proconsul. Considerations of public order prevented Trajan from agreeing to the formation of a fire brigade at Nicomedia, against the clearly implied advice of Pliny as governor of the province. Apart from the active political role implied by such episodes, the trade guilds were active in the ceremonial and pageantry of their cities. When Constantine entered Autun in 311, he was received by the usual crowds, and by the 'statues of the gods, music, and the emblems of the collegia'; the emblems were evidently not devised for this particular occasion, but indicate the regular part played by the trade guilds in their cities' public lives.

The countryside would be seen (from the socio-economic point of view here imagined) in far simpler terms, the more so because some of its most prominent figures, the local gentry, would already have been classified as urban dwellers, with the consequent over-simplification of their actual way of life mentioned earlier, and because the cities, the economic focus of the surrounding countryside, were also the centres for its administration. Yet here again we should not underestimate the diversity in the conditions of life found in the countryside. The peasants themselves might own their land or rent it from local or absentee landlords; in the fourth century Libanius (an influential professor of rhetoric at Antioch) draws the distinction for Syria between villages under 'one master' and those owned by 'many masters', that is by free peasant proprietors. Some were lessees of public land taken under long leases with preferential terms to encourage the planting of uncultivated or unsurveyed land, some were tenants of temple lands or of the Emperor. Such farmers, like the tenants of absentee landlords other than the Emperor, would normally be supervised (in some cases, which are documented for this reason, oppressed) by a land agent or bailiff or, in the case of imperial estates, the procurator of the province. As in the towns, so too in the country there would be a numerous free labour force, sometimes recruited as need arose from the surplus labour of nearby towns or from those local peasants who happened at a given time to be underemployed, sometimes migrant from region to region; and there were pastoralists following the seasons between upland and valley, desert and steppe. This is the context of a famous episode of republican history, the *calles siluaeque*, the 'tracks and forests' offered as a prospective command to the consuls of 59 in order to curb the ambitions of Julius Caesar. *Calles* are the droveways, in Italian *tratturi*, of transhumant shepherds, as described in an informative inscription of the time of Marcus Aurelius, from Saepinum in old Samnite country.

The women of the community would generally be seen in terms of the socio-economic categories assigned to the men. Their rights at law were however much more extensive than one might have expected, the institution of 'guardianship' of adult women, though it was not abolished, having by the late second century become a formality. It is already clear in the late Republic that women of senatorial status could in practice manage their own business and financial affairs, and with the early and almost universal acceptance of a form of marriage in which the woman retained her own legal identity rather than passing into the control of her husband, women had rights to own, inherit, and dispose of property which in modern Britain were not matched until the Married Women's Property Act of 1870. The marriage of Pudentilla of Tripolitanian Oea to the young philosopher Apuleius (above, pp. 282 ff.) in the mid second century was the occasion of a provincial *cause célèbre* from which Apuleius, accused before the proconsul by her first husband's relatives of having bewitched her by magic arts, was no doubt glad to escape. Pudentilla had for her part gone against their expressed wishes in choosing to marry Apuleius, which she was perfectly able to do. The real issue was that of the property, and Pudentilla's 'guardian' had to certify in court that a farm whose purchase he had formally authorized had been acquired not for Apuleius but for herself.

At less opulent social levels women are found frequently, in evidence that seriously under-represents their actual numbers, sharing in their husbands' work and its organization, particularly in the finer crafts and luxury trades such as silver-working and perfumery; and there were of course those service occupations in which opportunities to make a living, and even to achieve a certain scandalous distinction, conflicted with a social disapproval that was itself, as we should expect, shaped by that essential tool of a dominant class, moral hypocrisy. An early-fourth-century law on adultery took it for granted that the mistress of a tavern need not have sexual relations with the male clientele, while the serving-maids would normally be expected to, and so, unlike their mistress, were exempt from accusation as being 'unworthy of the cognizance of the laws'; and the same assumption was applied to women of the stage, whose immorality was held, again in Christian legislation of the fourth century, to preclude their returning to their profession after baptism. The social role of the woman was dominant, above all, in the home and in the day-to-day upbringing of children. The most intimate, if not the most endearing portrayal of this relationship, as of many other aspects of provincial family life, is Augustine's description of his mother Monica in the *Confessions*. It was not exclusively as an expression of personal affection, but of the normal patterns of family life in ancient cities, that Augustine's relations with his mother were so intense, and with his father so formal and distant by comparison.

A distinction in Roman society instantly recognizable through fundamental legal and social distinctions was that between slave and free. It is a truism hardly worth asserting, that Roman society was in some sense dependent on slave labour. But in what sense? One of the most important facets of the social and economic history of the Empire as opposed to the Republic is the declining rate of slave importation, the servile population being now to a far greater extent (one would not say entirely, in view of the evidence for the continuance of the slave trade under the Empire) maintained by reproduction among those who were already of this status, through what were in effect recognized as slave marriages. The effect of this is that the function of slavery in the Empire evolved within a wider social and economic pattern and was not imposed upon it. In whatever occupational milieu we find ourselves—among shopkeepers, building workers, members of *collegia*—we encounter a mixed population of slave, freedman, and free citizen. By a *senatusconsultum* of AD 52—introduced to the Senate by Claudius as the idea of his freedman Pallas—free women who entered into permanent relationships with slaves were themselves reduced to that status *if the master was unaware of the relationship*, or to that of freedwoman if he was aware and had given his consent. Though sometimes viewed as a socially oppressive measure, the *senatusconsultum* is more interesting to the historian for the situations it entitles him to visualize, of stable marital relationships freely undertaken between men and women of different legal status, but similar occupational groups, living (no doubt) in similar social conditions and in situations where the master might not know what was going on. The woman might find her legal status affected, but her marriage took her into the social network and protection afforded by the house to which her husband belonged; and in those frequent cases where the slave husband worked independently of his master, or under only indirect supervision, she might find her way of life little changed. Tacitus wrote of the disorder arising in Rome during the Civil War of AD 68 as affecting in opposite ways the stable part of the people connected with the great houses, and the spectacle-loving mob and the worst of the slave population. The first group, including by implication the 'better sort' of the slave population, welcomed the end of the reign of Nero and the prospect of better things to come; the second, used to Nero's extravagances, regretted his end, and, fearing the worst and fed on rumour, aggravated the general instability.

The social relations, expressed through various forms of munificence, between the great houses of Rome (and so, on a lesser scale, in all cities of the Empire) and their dependants, and between the Emperor and his special clients, the people of Rome, provided a common interest for sectors of society that ought, on any rational calculation of economic advantage and disadvantage, to have been irrevocably opposed to each other. Yet this was only the tangible expression of the more extensive moral and legal relations between 'client' and 'patron' upon which ancient society was built. The failure of societies in which such inequalities are rampant, extreme, and blatant to the eye, to articulate their differences in terms of class conflict is a tribute (if that is the word) to the strength and flexibility of the relations between classes which can be summed up in the word 'paternalism': the art of extending social benefits and alleviating the effects of misfortune while enhancing the prestige and moral worth of the giver of the benefits, and thereby reinforcing rather than undermining the existing social structure. There were of course other means of 'alleviating the effects of misfortune', and it would be hard in conclusion to imagine a more vivid expression of the sheer variety of social relations and vicissitudes of human experience of which the historian must take account, than some questions envisaged on a late-third- or early-fourth-century papyrus as appropriate for putting to an oracle (the numbers are given on the papyrus):

72. Shall I get my pay? ... 74. Shall I be sold up? ... 78. Am I to get leave? 79. Shall I get the money? ... 82. Is my property to be proscribed? ... 85. Am I to be sold as a slave? 86. Shall I go into exile? 87. Shall I go on an embassy? 88. Am I to become a town councillor? 89. Is my escape cut off? 90. Shall I be separated from my wife? 91. Am I under a spell? ... (*Oxyrhynchus Papyri*, No. 1477)

Further Reading

The literary sources mentioned are available in the Loeb Classical Library, and in most cases also in Penguin Classics, especially Tacitus, *Annals* (by Michael Grant, 1956) and *Histories* (by Kenneth Wellesley, 1964; all dates are those of first publication); Suetonius, *Lives of the Caesars* (by Robert Graves, 1957); Pliny the Younger, *Letters* (by Betty Radice, 1963). See also Lucian, *Satirical Sketches* (by Paul Turner, 1961) and Apuleius, *The Golden Ass* (by Robert Graves, 1950); the last two are extremely rewarding from a historical point of view, though their literary complexity makes them difficult to use. Particularly recommended is the splendid collection of source-materials, documentary and epigraphic as well as literary, by Naphtali Lewis and Meyer Reinhold, *Roman Civilization, Sourcebook II; the Empire* (paperback, New York, 1966). This collection contains hundreds of well-chosen passages, and responds equally well to browsing or to systematic reading; a real education in Roman history.

Fundamental both to the interpretation of Roman society and to the appreciation of the actual conditions of life in it is M. I. Rostovtzeff's *Social and Economic History of the Roman Empire* (2nd edn. by P. M. Fraser, Oxford, 1957); to be read (for it is a controversial work) with Arnaldo Momigliano's appreciation in his *Studies in Historiography* (London, 1966), pp. 91–104. Fergus Millar, *The Roman Empire and its Neighbours* (2nd edn., London, 1981) shares some of Rostovtzeff's emphasis on the provincial diversities of the Empire. G. E. M. de Ste. Croix's marvellously fertile *The Class Struggle in the Ancient Greek World* (London, 1981) in fact contains much directly on and relevant to the Roman imperial period. In Tim Cornell and John Matthews' *Atlas of the Roman World* (Oxford 1982) are brief illustrated accounts of some of the issues mentioned above (for instance public shows, manufacture and trade, technology) and of the provinces of the Empire and the city of Rome. There is still much of interest in Ludwig Friedlander's old *Roman Life and Manners under the Early Empire*, especially in the Supplementary Volume with various excursuses (English tr. London, 1910).

On the conditions of travel in the Roman empire, see Lionel Casson's two books, *Ships and Seamanship in the Ancient World* (Princeton, 1971) and *Travel in the Ancient World* (London, 1974), with E. D. Hunt's fine *Holy Land Pilgrimage in the Later Roman Empire* (Oxford, 1982). On the role of Greeks in Roman Society, G. W. Bowersock, *Augustus and the Greek World* (Oxford,

1965) and *Greek Sophists in the Roman Empire* (Oxford, 1969) are both excellent books, concise, lively and well documented.

The economic functioning of the cities of the Empire is much discussed; see especially Chapters I and II of A. H. M. Jones, *The Roman Economy: Studies in Ancient Economic and Administrative History* (ed. P. A. Brunt, Oxford, 1974); R. Duncan-Jones, *The Economy of the Roman Empire: Quantitative Studies* (Cambridge, 1974) includes particularly full discussions of levels of civic munificence, and Philip Abrams and E. A. Wrigley (edd.), *Towns in Societies: Essays in Economic History and Historical Sociology* (Cambridge, 1978) contains a particularly good discussion by Keith Hopkins on the roles of trade and agriculture in the economic development of classical cities. The subject of Bruce W. Frier, *Landlords and Tenants in Imperial Rome* (Princeton, 1980) is urban leasehold law but he has much to say about the physical conditions of life, especially at Ostia; on which see Russell Meiggs, *Roman Ostia* (2nd edn., Oxford, 1973). Among the many interesting articles reprinted from the journal *Past and Present* in M. I. Finley (ed.) *Studies in Ancient Society* (London and Boston, 1974) is P. A. Brunt's splendid 'The Roman Mob' (pp. 74–102).

The debate about trade and labour and social attitudes towards them, reopened by Finley in *The Ancient Economy* (London, 1973), has been vigorously pursued; see, for instance, the collections of studies edited by Peter Garnsey, Keith Hopkins and C. R. Whittaker, *Trade in the Ancient Economy* (London, 1983), by Garnsey and Whittaker, *Trade and Famine in Classical Antiquity* (Cambridge, Philological Society, Suppl. Vol. 8, 1983) and by Garnsey, *Non-slave Labour in the Greco-Roman World* (ibid. 6, 1980); and John d'Arms, *Commerce and Social Standing in Ancient Rome* (Cambridge, Mass., and London, 1981). On the techniques of farming, K. D. White, *Roman Farming* (London, 1970).

On the role of law in social life, see J. A. Crook, *Law and Life of Rome* (London, 1967), and on the penal system of the Empire Peter Garnsey, *Social Status and Legal Privilege in the Roman Empire* (Oxford, 1970) and more generally A. N. Sherwin-White, *The Roman Citizenship* (2nd edn., Oxford, 1973). On slavery and social relations there are articles of interest in M. I. Finley (ed.) *Slavery in Classical Antiquity* (Cambridge, 1960); and see from a very different historical tradition Joseph Vogt, *Ancient Slavery and the Ideal of Man* (transl. Thomas Wiedemann, Oxford, 1974).

Social relations in general are discussed in two most illuminating books, written with characteristic zest and an eye for detail, by Ramsay MacMullen, *Enemies of the Roman Order; Treason, Unrest and Alienation in the Empire* (Cambridge, Mass., and London, 1967) and *Roman Social Relations, 56 B.C. to A.D. 284* (New Haven, Conn., and London 1974). Zvi Yavetz, *Plebs and Princeps* (Oxford, 1969) discusses the relations between the Emperor and People of Rome in the context of developments from the late Republic, and has most interesting material on modes of popular expression. Keith Hopkins, *Sociological Studies in Roman History*, I: *Conquerors and Slaves*, and II: *Death and Renewal* (Cambridge, 1978 and 1983) offers a radical approach to the evidential problems inherent in the writing of ancient social and economic history. Still more intractable are those relating to religious history, on which a stimulating introduction for the imperial age is E. R. Dodds, *Pagan and Christian in an Age of Anxiety* (Cambridge, 1965).

16

Roman Art and Architecture

❧

R. J. A. WILSON

Republican Prolegomena

WHEN the chaos and civil war which marked the collapse of the Roman Republic erupted in the third quarter of the first century BC, there had already been sown some of the seeds of architectural and artistic innovation which were to bear such remarkably productive fruit during the early years of Empire. Yet, architecture apart, the period of the Republic in central Italy down to the middle and later years of the second century BC was not marked by any brilliant outpouring of artistic creativity, or by many works which display striking originality: little that is genuinely and independently 'Roman' can be identified in the art of early and middle Republican Rome. Rather it was the twin cultural influences of Etruria and the Greek world that were dominant, the latter being by far the more significant. When, sometime around 300 BC, a Latin-speaking artist called Novios Plautios made in Rome a splendid bronze circular box (known as the 'Ficoroni cist'), his total dependence on the Greek artistic repertoire (the mythological scene on the body of the box, for example, or its fine lotus and palmette border), as well as his familiarity with the masterly Etruscan techniques of metal engraving, are abundantly clear. Etrusco-Hellenic influence was similarly at work in the Roman ('Italic') style temple as it emerged in the course of the third and second centuries BC after a long period of experimentation. The frontal emphasis and the lofty platform (*podium*), both features foreign to full-dress Greek temples, are derived from Etruscan architecture, but the ornamental details, such as the use of engaged columns or pilasters to decorate the sides and back of the *cella*, as well as the architectural order itself, are almost invariably of Greek derivation and inspiration. A good surviving early example of the type is the second-century-BC 'temple of Fortuna' (probably dedicated to Portunus) near the Tiber in Rome.

By the time that this temple was built, Greek influence on the artistic life of the capital was all-pervasive. It had first made an impact in Italy in the sixth century BC, when it began to affect the development of Etruscan art, and some Greek artists are known from scattered literary references to have lived and worked in Rome from the fifth century BC onwards; but it was only in the third century BC, when Rome's political expansion brought her into direct contact with the Greek cities of southern Italy and Sicily (Tarentum's fall in 272 and Syracuse's in 212 being notable landmarks), that the steady trickle of Greek culture flowing into Rome became a constant stream; and that in turn reached flood proportions in the second century B C, when first Greece and then Asia Minor came within the orbit of Rome. Not only were Greek artists migrating westwards in increasing numbers in response to the demands of a new, large, and wealthy clientele; in addition, the craze for collecting Greek originals to adorn town and country houses grew to fever pitch, and led to the wholesale looting of masterpieces from their original settings. When originals were not to hand, copies could be manufactured, ever more faithful to their models thanks to continuing improvements in the pointing technique; and major workshops were already established in Athens, Rome, and elsewhere to meet this huge demand, which continued well on into the Empire. There were, of course, some commissions for new types, and the school of Pasiteles enjoyed modest success in producing pastiches of classical figures in novel arrangements, but free-standing sculpture in general at this period broke little fresh ground. Portraiture is quite another matter. Early in the first century B C there appear the first examples in a long and impressive series of marble portrait busts, in which the sitter is represented with striking fidelity, double chins, wrinkles, warts, and all. This was a far cry from the bland, impersonal idealism of most (but not all) late classical and Hellenistic Greek portraits; the new type reflects, perhaps, a pragmatism, a rugged determination, and a certain ruthlessness in the Roman character, as well as a taste for unvarnished truth. The busts are generally of imported Greek marble, a material with which Italian sculptors were unfamiliar, and there can be little doubt that it was Greek sculptors working in Rome who were responsible for their execution; but although the strikingly uncompromising realism of this portrait-type has been seen as a reflection of the Greek artist's disgust for his sitter, the patron must have liked what he saw—otherwise the portrait sculptor would soon have been out of business, and the fashion would never have caught on.

One or two pieces of Roman relief sculpture in the last century of the Republic also show hints of a fresh approach, one that was to be fully developed only under the Principate. A pair of crisp but lifeless limestone reliefs depicting victory trophies, from the Capitoline hill in Rome, perhaps executed early in the first century B C in commemoration of African campaigns against Jugurtha, stand at the beginning of a long series of commemorative relief sculptures designed to leave a permanent, tangible record in stone of actual historical events. The approximately contemporary marble relief known misleadingly as the Altar of Domitius Ahenobarbus shows the hand of a Greek sculptor working none too confidently for a Roman patron. While three of the sides depict a playful marine scene wholly in the Hellenistic tradition, carved with confidence, even gusto, the fourth has the hitherto unfamiliar (and very Roman) scene of the sacrifice of pig, sheep, and bull (*suovetaurtilia*), probably on the occasion of a military census-taking: the rather awkward arrangement of the figures and the disparity of scale between animals, humans, and 'props' such as the altar, betray the sculptor's unfamiliarity with his subject.

Wall painting, too, embarks on a dramatically different and more adventurous course from the beginning of the first century B C, again the fruit of successful co-operation between Roman patrons and (for the most part at least) Greek artists. Private houses up until *c.* 100 had their walls rather monotonously decorated in imitation marbled blocks, sometimes simply painted, sometimes executed in moulded stucco as well (the so-called First Style of Roman painting). That gives way to an ambitious scheme of wall decoration which depends for its effect on a series of architectural frameworks and vistas in different planes, giving the illusion of space as the viewer looks out on a succession of often fantastic architectural creations receding into the distance. There can be little doubt that some of the features of this elaborate style came from the painted stage sets of the Hellenistic theatre, witnessed by such recurring features as the central door, the broken pediment, the circular pavilion, and above all the theatrical masks; indeed, a room in the villa at Boscoreale near Pompeii has paintings which correspond exactly with Vitruvius' description of the tragic, comic, and satyric sets of the Greek theatre. The originality of this style of painting (the so-called Second Style) lies not so much in its subject matter as such, as in the varying combinations of a stock repertoire of motifs to form new varieties of composition; and new, too, as far as we can tell, is the idea of placing these gaudy, overbearing architectural decorations within the intimacy of the private house. Some of the grand, large-scale, figured fresco cycles, such as the figures from another room at Boscoreale, or the frieze from which the Villa of the Mysteries at Pompeii takes its name, are also likely to owe much to lost Greek painting; but the adaptation of original models to suit both individual room sizes and the demands of the patron led in each case to a good deal of innovation and variation of the prototype or prototypes. Contemporary mosaic work tended to be somewhat sober, in order not to compete with the riot of colour and decorative detail on the walls, but the taste continued for set-piece, small-scale, figured panels of great intricacy (*emblemata*) in the centre of the floors of the more important rooms. This, however, was wholly a legacy of the Hellenistic tradition; Roman mosaic only begins to show major originality with the gradual development of a quite different black-and-white technique from Augustan times onward.

In the architecture of late Republican Italy, too, the impact of the Greek world was not inconsiderable. The regular town grid, with streets intersecting at right-angles, which first the Etruscans (from *c.* 500) and then the Romans adopted for their new foundations, was with only minor adjustments the legacy of Greek orthogonal planning; and both the garden peristyle of the Roman house, introduced in the course of the second century B C, and many building-types in Roman public architecture, such as the stoa / portico, the theatre, and probably the basilica (its name means 'royal' in Greek), were more or less closely derived from Hellenistic Greek models. Much more significant, however, was the emergence in Italy of the new building technique of concrete, which (for once) owes nothing to the Greeks. In the second half of the third century B C, Italian architects discovered that when mortar was made with the volcanic brick-earth known as pozzolana, widely available in central and central-southern Italy, and added with lime and water to rubble aggregate, the result was an enormously strong (and waterproof) mass capable of bearing great stress. Expensive and cumbersome large-block ashlar construction could now be discarded in favour of concrete walling, the facing material of which was of no significant structural importance. At the same time the Romans first made use of another architectural feature they were to adopt very much as their own, the arch—an invention, in fact, of the Greeks, but never fully exploited by them. The more or less simultaneous discovery in central Italy of concrete and of the potential of the arch, prompted in turn the creation of the semicircular barrel vault in concrete, a revolutionary means of spanning a space which broke utterly free from the conventional timber beam-and-truss roof. An early maturity in the handling of serried ranks of barrel vaults with interconnecting arched openings is displayed in the gigantic warehouse in Rome of 193 B C, the Porticus Aemilia (some 487 m. long), and later in the second century it was concrete that made possible the creation of the finest surviving architectural complex of the Roman Republic, the great sanctuary of Fortuna at Palestrina. Here barrel vaulting was used to fashion a series of orderly terraces and retaining walls out of a rugged hillside, although, in contrast to the Porticus Aemilia, the concrete structures were for the most part concealed behind respectable colonnades in time-honoured Greek fashion. The traditional Greek orders were also used as a decorative frame for arched openings, an idea soon picked up and repeated in many other buildings (the Theatre of Marcellus, for example: p. 365). Concrete also played a vital role in the development of the Roman bath-house, in which concrete vaults were a more practical alternative to timber for roofing the heated rooms with their steamy atmosphere. The first surviving examples come from Campania, where the amphitheatre, another quintessentially Roman building, also made its earliest appearance, before the end of the second century B C (Pompeii's of *c.* 80 B C being a well-preserved early example); but it was only after further advances in concrete architecture under the Empire that both building-types were to reach full maturity.

The Augustan Principate

When C. Octavianus (soon to take the title Augustus) emerged triumphant from the battle of Actium in 31 B C, he lost little time in embarking on a building programme the like of which Rome had never seen before. The reign of Augustus was an age of enormous architectural and artistic fervour, in which cautious conservatism was combined with revolutionary new ideas. The establishment of the Principate created for the first time a stability which enabled a long-term, coherent planning programme to be worked out for the monuments of the capital. The Emperor, with his family and associates, provided a motivated patronage which drew architects, sculptors, and painters to the capital, a patronage which was vital for creating the right conditions for works of art and buildings on the grand scale; and with that imperial patronage came the centralized control of state funds. Such conditions had of course existed before in the ancient world—in Periclean Athens, for example, and especially in the Hellenistic kingdoms such as Pergamum—but for Rome they were essentially new. Augustus was also not slow to realize the political overtones of a lavish architectural and sculptural programme: Caesar had already shown the way with his great vision of a monumental reorganization of the heart of Rome, and some of his projects were duly completed by Augustus. Caesar's adoptive son launched a building programme on an even more ambitious scale which, by his death in AD 14, had totally transformed the physical appearance of the capital. Mobilizing the building industry was one way of stimulating the economy; building theatres and amphitheatres, baths and basilicae, *fora* and temples, curried favour with a restless populace; and in the showpieces of the Augustan programme the potential for using monuments as vehicles of elaborate propaganda was exploited to the full.

Some idea of the scale of the new building programme can be judged from Augustus' astonishing claim that he built or restored no less than eighty-two temples in one year alone, quite apart from other types of building; add to that the projects sponsored by other energetic builders in his family, and one can gain some impression of the building fever that gripped Augustan Rome. Many of the new structures were essentially conservative, repeating the formulae already tried and tested in the late Republic. The theatre of Marcellus, for example, begun by Caesar but not finished until *c*.13–11 BC, with its seats raised on concrete substructures and with an outer façade of superimposed arcades (each row framed by a continuous colonnade of engaged columns, a formula which much influenced architects from the sixteenth century onwards), was essentially the type of building already established at Rome by the earlier theatre of Pompey (55 BC). Many of the temples, too, continued to use traditional materials, either travertine (a hard white limestone quarried near Tivoli) or one of the variety of local volcanic stones liberally covered with stucco. Such conservatism in the Augustan building programme would have delighted the contemporary architect, Vitruvius, whose ten books *On Architecture*, written between about 28 and 23 BC, enjoyed enormous fame from the Renaissance onwards, especially as a sourcebook for the Classical Greek orders. Conscious, but disapproving, of the radical changes going on around him, Vitruvius issues strictures against the haste and the boldness of the new generation of architects, while lavishing undiluted praise on the use of ashlar, on the materials of local quarries, even on the usefulness of mud-brick. Vitruvius was no progressive; his writings are more important for the light they shed on Greek and Roman Republican architectural practice than as a commentary on his own age.

For the materials on which Vitruvius pinned his faith were not to be those of the future. The Augustan age was an age of experiment, in using new materials

INTERIOR OF THE SO-CALLED 'TEMPLE OF MERCURY' AT BAIAE, actually a circular bathing hall in a thermal complex (late first century BC or early first century AD). The building is notable for its hemispherical concrete dome, the earliest large-scale example in Roman architecture. Owing to the sinking of the earth-level in the region, the hall is now half submerged in water.

and in exploring fresh uses for old. The quality of concrete, for example, was constantly being improved, and innovatory architects were trying out a new method of roofing, the hemispherical dome in concrete, which was to play such a vital part in the Roman architectural revolution of the next 150 years: the earliest surviving example, probably Augustan, is the so-called 'Temple of Mercury' at Baiae. Another arrival of lasting significance was kiln-fired brick, not a newly-invented material as such, but employed now for the first time as a continuous facing for concrete. In Rome it appears to have been used only modestly until after Augustus' death; real confidence in handling the new material was gained elsewhere, especially in Italian cities such as Turin. With brickwork, as with the dome, the significant developments were yet to come, but Augustan architects deserve credit for pointing the way forward.

PORTA PALATINA AT TURIN, one of the monumental gateways of the Augustan colony founded *c*.25 BC, and an early instance of brickwork on the grand scale. In form it belongs to a familiar North Italian and Gaulish type of the early-imperial period, with projecting towers at the sides and an arcaded corridor above. Originally there would have been a rectangular inner courtyard.

A more immediate impact on the architectural scene was made by marble. Augustus boasted, according to Suetonius, 'that he found Rome a city of (mud-)brick and left it a city of marble'; and it is clear from the sheer number of marble-faced buildings which sprang up in the capital that this was no idle boast. Caesar had probably been the first to realize the potential of the rich Carrara marble quarries near Luna in north Italy, but their full-scale exploitation began only with Augustus' reign. Dead-white, crystalline, and clean-breaking (and therefore excellent for crisp carving and cutting), this handsome material won immediate and widespread popularity. Alongside Luna appeared an increasing range of polychrome marbles from abroad: yellow African marble, salmon-pink marble from Chios, and greeny-blue *cipollino* from Euboea, as well as Phrygian marble from Asia Minor. Marble had come to stay; and although the Augustan use of polychromatic effects, both for columns and in paving and wall veneers, remained restrained by comparison with later fashions, the new material gave a welcome touch of elegance and sophistication, as well as a splash of colour, which the architecture of the capital had hitherto lacked.

COMPOSITE CAPITAL re-used in the Church of Santa Costanza in Rome. Dated on stylistic grounds to the early Augustan period (*c*.40–20 BC), this is one of the earliest examples of the new hybrid order which combines Ionic volutes with Corinthian acanthus leaves. The first examples in position on a dated building are those of the Arch of Titus (soon after AD 81).

But the exploitation of marble brought with it a problem, lack of Roman expertise in handling it. That is why an army of Greek craftsmen were drafted into the capital: their role in shaping the distinctive creations of the Augustan programme is hard to overestimate. A new, precise language of architectural ornament, based on that of classical Greece, but with fresh variations and combinations, set the tone for the rest of the Empire and in turn was a source of inspiration for generations of Renaissance and Neo-classical architects. Even the one original Roman contribution to the classical orders, the Composite, with its blending of the volutes of Ionic with the acanthus leaves of Corinthian, makes its first known appearance in Augustan Rome and is hardly to be dissociated from the creative genius of Greek craftsmen in the capital.

The marriage of Greek skills and traditions with Roman taste and demands is nowhere more clearly documented than in the two monuments which mark the culmination of the Augustan programme, the Ara Pacis Augustae (dedicated in 9 BC), and the Forum of Augustus (2 BC). The forum in concept and planning is quintessentially Roman: the great Italic-style temple of Luna marble on a lofty podium dominates an open space flanked by porticoes, a formal, axial layout following the strict principles already established in Republican architecture. Roman too is the use of the forum as a portrait gallery of the great trail-blazers of Roman history, including Augustus himself, identified as just another hero in a long line of Republicans. As an ingenious and disingenuous piece of imperial propaganda and as a blueprint for architectural planning, the forum of Augustus was unmistakably Roman; yet its detail was no less unmistakably Greek: the textbook Corinthian capitals, the zoomorphic pilaster capitals with figures of Pegasus at the corners, most obviously of all the line of Caryatids above the colonnades, are closely matched in the Classical or late-Hellenistic architecture of Attica.

The Altar of Augustan Peace is an even more eloquent witness of the cultural interchange of Greece and Rome. The altar itself, set on a stepped platform, was surrounded on all sides by lofty screen walls broken by entrances on the west and east. Mythological panels flanked each entrance—Mother Earth (above, p. 210) with children on her lap and personifications of Ocean and Water at her side, a scene carved fully in the Hellenistic tradition and exuding the blessings of tranquillity and renewed fertility that accompanied the Augustan peace; Aeneas sacrificing at the spot where he first set foot on Italian soil. Just around the corner, near the head of the procession on the south side, is Augustus in the same act of solemn sacrifice: the propaganda message is being hammered home, that Augustus is the new Aeneas, the bringer of hope and the architect of a Rome reborn. The rest of the south side shows members of his family (above, p. 150), while magistrates and their families fill up the north side; it is a commemoration in marble of an actual procession and sacrifice that took place in 13 BC in thanksgiving for the Emperor's safe return after a provincial tour. The idea of historical relief sculpture to record a specific event had been tentatively explored during

CARYATID ORDER OF THE FORUM OF AUGUSTUS (end of first century BC). The upper storey of the colonnade enclosing the new forum was articulated with a series of carved female figures copied directly from the Caryatid porch of the Erechtheum in Athens (Vol, I, p. 119)—a vivid illustration of the classical Greek element in Augustan architectural decoration.

the late Republic, but it was to find full expression only during the Empire. As an exercise in political propaganda, the Ara Pacis succeeds brilliantly in presenting some of the essential values that Augustus stood for: *grauitas* witnessed by the solemnity of the occasion; *humanitas* witnessed by such touches as a tired child pulling at his father's toga and by the overall flavour of a 'family occasion'; above all *pax*, peace both in Italy and in the world at large. As a sculptural monument, too, the friezes of the Ara Pacis are superlative, a tribute to the skills of the Greek sculptors who worked on them. The influence, above all, of Athens is paramount: in the overall form of the altar, a copy on a more monumental scale of the Altar of Pity in the Athenian *agora* (*c.* 420); in the processional friezes which inevitably recall those of the Parthenon; in the quiet solemnity reminiscent, perhaps, of Attic grave reliefs of the Classical age; and in the superbly disciplined yet exuberant floral scroll occupying the lower half of the screen wall, which, while at present most closely paralleled in Hellenistic Asia Minor, may well have been derived from now lost Attic models. The Ara Pacis epitomizes the Roman genius for borrowing freely from the Greek repertoire, but moulding it and adapting it into something new and distinctively Roman.

Another vital element of the new Roman propaganda machine was image-building; and Greek sculptors played a key role in fashioning a series of portrait-types of Augustus which were copied in vast numbers so that all corners of the Empire could be systematically bombarded with the image of the *princeps*. The types now created for Augustus and his family were not the ruthlessly realistic portraits of the late Republic, but a delicate blend of realism and states-manly ideal. The mood might vary from the grim determination of the Capi-toline Octavian, fashioned at a time before the total consolidation of his position, through the sober *auctoritas* of Augustus as *pontifex maximus*, carved some thirty years later yet with hardly a hint of ageing, to the supremely self-confident Primaporta Augustus, where the Emperor with expansive gesture harangues an unseen populace; but the overriding impression of a determined, efficient, authoritative leader is common to all.

In private life Augustus is reputed to have been a man of simple tastes who chose to dwell in a modest house unostentatiously adorned; certainly the property excavated on the Palatine and identified as his shows no greater luxury than comparable patrician residences of its day. In the fresco paintings of this and other properties of the imperial family, the overbearing architectural schemes which characterize the full-blown Second Style give way instead to decoration with a lighter touch, which favours architecture of less substantial form and an increasing emphasis on large central mythological 'panel' pictures as the focal point of each wall. The logical culmination of this trend was to deny altogether the illusion of depth and to emphasize instead the solidity of the wall. The new scheme of decor which thus emerged (the so-called Third Style) depended for its effect on intricate and often fanciful decorative detail, especially floral and abstract designs, usually interspersed with figured tableaux which varied a good deal in size and number, while architectural elements, if they survived at all, now became flimsy and unreal. The new decorative scheme can be seen fully developed at another imperial property, the country house at Boscotrecase near Pompeii. The elegance and restraint of the frescoes here, in stark contrast to the excesses of the Second Style at its most extravagant, mark the culmination of a quiet but decisive revolution in artistic taste, achieved through the skill of court painters, but dic-tated, no doubt, by the personal preferences of the imperial family itself.

The individual ingredients of the new style of painting reflect the eclecticism of Augustan art as a whole. One ingredient was unashamedly classicizing: the wall schemes adopted by Augustan decorators, with their mythological panel pictures, large and small, were ideal vehicles for the widespread copying of Classical and Hellenistic Old Masters, and in this they set the tone for Roman wall painting for the next century. Another ingredient was the Egyptianizing element. This, like copying, was not entirely new, but it received an undoubted boost after the annexation of Egypt in 30 BC, when the curiosity value of things Egyptian ran high in Italy for a time. Some of the recurrent decorative features in Third Style compositions, such as sphinxes, ibises, cult objects, and figures of

PAINTED WALL-DECORATION IN THE VILLA OF AGRIPPA POSTUMUS AT BOSCOTRECASE (*c.*10 BC). A fine example of the early Third Style: above a black socle (not shown) the wall is predominantly red, with divisions effected by delicate bands of polychrome ornament. The central panel contains a superb landscape painting of the sacro-idyllic type.

Isis, as well as vignettes of Nilotic scenes, were directly derived from the Egyptian repertoire. More controversial is the source of another popular ingredient in Augustan and later painting, the dreamy landscapes loosely referred to as 'sacro-idyllic' because they usually centre around a fanciful 'votive' column or flimsy shrine, with a variety of figures in attendance. Though they are often claimed as the products of Alexandrian mannerism, inspired by the bucolic poetry of Theocritus, no Hellenistic precedents in painting are so far known, and while some elements may well have had Hellenistic forerunners, the idea of peopling these artificial settings with shepherds, flocks, and dogs appears to begin only with the striking sacro-idyllic pictures from Boscotrecase; they may, therefore, be essentially an Augustan creation. Here the name of Studius is possibly relevant. He was the first, so Pliny tells us, who went in for the 'very charming paintings' of landscape gardens and the like filled with people engaged in the tasks of everyday life. This sounds like the sort of thing which crops up in several Augustan residences: tiny figures, depicted impressionistically in flat monochrome, walking

DETAIL OF A STUCCO VAULT-DECORATION from a suburban villa in the grounds of the Villa Farnesina, Rome. This landscape corresponds to the sacro-idyllic paintings of the same period, with both sacred and domestic buildings and both worshippers (bottom centre) and genre figures (bottom right). Certain elements, such as the house and tree at the left, suggest Egyptian influence.

and fishing and chatting and going about their daily business, in a setting of bridges, porticoes, and topsy-turvy pavilions. Certainly Studius did not invent landscape as such, nor can his name be associated with another masterpiece of Augustan painting, the 'garden of Livia' from her villa at Primaporta: here are no human figures, and so far from being impressionistic, the fruit and flowers of this wilderness of a paradise garden are executed with a loving care for naturalistic detail. Judgement must be suspended on this unique painting as to whether it, too, owes all or something to Hellenistic predecessors, or whether it is rather an exuberant product of the Augustan genius for originality.

The principal advances of Augustan art and architecture were worked out, of course, mainly in the capital; but the Augustan age saw in addition an enormous outpouring of building energy elsewhere in Italy and the Empire, especially in the western provinces. In many cases, indeed, we have to turn to these areas for preserved examples of buildings which are only fragmentary, or have vanished altogether, in Rome itself. One such is the triumphal arch, a characteristic monument of imperial propaganda of which several early examples still stand in north Italy and southern Gaul. Commemorative arches of a sort had been known in Republican Rome, but the developed form, articulated with columns, architrave, and attic bearing an inscription, is essentially an Augustan creation. Many of the buildings newly erected in the provinces at this time were based directly on metropolitan blueprints or from models elsewhere in Italy. Indeed in some instances (as at the famous Maison Carrée in Nîmes of AD 2–3) the presence of stonemasons and sculptors who had actually worked on the Augustan building programme in Rome can be argued. One of the most familiar of all Roman monuments, the stately Pont du Gard aqueduct near Nîmes, a harmonious structure which vividly demonstrates that the aesthetics of appearance need not be divorced from practical function, is also an Augustan monument, erected in the last quarter of the first century BC (plate facing p. 248). In the East, where urbanization was already deep-rooted, the impact of Augustus was less dramatic; but in the West—above all in his creation of a road system and in his establishment or refounding of innumerable, carefully chosen towns in Yugoslavia, Gaul, the Iberian peninsula, and along the north-African littoral—Augustus left a decisive and enduring stamp on the map of western Europe.

The Julio-Claudians: Tiberius to Nero (AD 14–68)

Augustus died on 19 August AD 14, and within a month he had been deified. Among the trappings of the official state cult of *diuus Augustus* was a newly created iconographical language for depicting the deceased Emperor in the company of gods. An eloquent early expression can be seen in the cameo known as the Gemma Augustea, a frank glorification of the dead Augustus, half draped, as befits his divine status, and surrounded by personifications of Rome, *Oikoumenē* (the inhabited world), Ocean, and Earth. Yet the new language rarely lost an opportunity to speak clearly also about the living, emphasizing the 'continuity factor' between the old regime and the new. On the Gemma Augustea, for example, Augustus looks across to his chosen successor Tiberius stepping from the chariot of victory, while the lower register alludes to Augustus' German wars, in which the prime architect of victory was none other than Tiberius. Some scholars claim that this and similar scenes were intended for private circulation during Augustus' lifetime; but that the man who himself shunned personal worship was instrumental in creating the new idiom seems unlikely. These scenes stand at the beginning of a long line of historical reliefs which use elaborate allegorical paraphrase to convey a political message.

Few monumental reliefs of Julio-Claudian date from Rome survive; those that do display a rather dry style entirely in the Augustan classicizing mould. The grand processional reliefs in the Villa Medici, for example, thought by some to be part of an Ara Pietatis ('Altar of Piety') of *c.* AD 22–45, are conceived and executed very much in the manner of the Ara Pacis; only in one major respect

THE GEMMA AUGUSTEA, one of the finest examples of the large sardonyx cameos carved with propagandist reliefs by artists of the imperial court. According to the most likely interpretation, the upper register shows the deified Augustus and Tiberius descending from his triumphal chariot, while in the lower register Roman soldiers erect a trophy of victory, with barbarian prisoners in attendance, for Tiberius' German campaigns of AD 10–11.

do they break fresh ground, in their detailed rendering of architectural setting, though the problem of providing this without sacrificing the prominence of the human figures has yet to be solved. A roughly contemporary relief showing a procession of city magistrates also marks an advance in its hesitant adoption of a slightly aerial perspective rather than a horizontal one: the heads of the second row are raised slightly above those in the foreground. Neither architectural setting nor vertical perspective was entirely new to the sculptural arts, but for the state reliefs of the capital they were a fresh departure, much exploited in the years to come.

Sculpture in the round was long to be dominated by the influence of Greek works and of the 'neo-Attic' school. Much of this was dreary and repetitive copying of the established Classical and Hellenistic masterpieces, in constant demand for decorating the town and country houses of the rich, as well as public *fora*, gardens, and bath-buildings; what little originality existed was usually limited to feeble pastiches. Not all of this sculpture, however, lacked vitality: witness, for example, the outstanding work produced by the Rhodians Hagesander, Athanadorus, and Polydorus. One, the Laocoon (above, p. 256), found in the Golden House of Nero, exerted a powerful influence on Michelangelo and his contemporaries; the other, a series of dramatic larger-than-life groups including the Blinding of Polyphemus and Odysseus' ship passing Scylla, adorned a grotto in Tiberius' villa at Sperlonga. None of this sculpture was probably wholly original, being best regarded as adaptations and reworkings from Hellenistic models; but nor is it derivative hack-work: it testifies to the continuing vibrancy, intensity, and superb technical quality of Hellenistic baroque at its best, well into the early years of Empire.

Magnificent sculpture of this sort was to play an increasingly important part in grandiose interior decoration; the more generous the setting, the more colossal the sculpture to suit it. Nor are other indications lacking of a growing luxury in Julio-Claudian interior decor: an expanding range of polychrome marbles for floor slabs and wall veneer, abandoning the comparative restraint of Augustan taste; wall mosaic using glass tesserae of dazzling colours, which was soon employed to good effect in sparkling fountains at Pompeii and elsewhere; mosaic work, too, to cover the soaring surfaces of concrete vaults, a medium with a

RELIEF FROM THE ARA PIETATIS IN ROME (dedicated by Claudius in AD 43 in belated thanks for the recovery of the Dowager Empress Livia from a serious illness twenty-one years earlier). A sacrifice takes place in front of the Temple of Magna Mater, one of the first instances in Roman sculpture of a precisely rendered architectural setting.

HEAD OF ODYSSEUS FROM
SPERLONGA. The hundreds
of fragments of baroque
sculptural compositions from a
grotto identified as that where
Tiberius narrowly escaped
death in a rock-fall in AD 26
have been reconstructed to
form four main groups
showing adventures of the
Greek hero Odysseus; this
head from the Blinding of
Polyphemus is a good sample
of their emotional, chiaroscuro
style.

long future down into Byzantine and early medieval times. Wall-painting, too, shared in the increasing desire for elaboration. One has only to compare some examples of the late Third Style, as in the House of Lucretius Fronto at Pompeii (c. 34–45), with the early-Augustan versions of the same style (as at Boscotrecase) to appreciate just how significant a shift in taste had taken place: there is still the horizontal wall division into three, still the prominent mythological panel in the centre, but the restraint and elegant simplicity of an earlier generation has been replaced by a riot of contrasting sweeps of colour, and by a wide range of intricate, often fussy detail; while the virtuoso pavilions in the top register with their shifting planes look forward to the even more elaborate developments of the Fourth Style.

The transition to the fully developed Fourth Style seems to belong to the 50s; certainly its use on the grand scale is brilliantly seen a decade later in the frescoes of the Domus Aurea, the Golden House of Nero (AD 64-8), inspired creations of the court painter Fabullus. It is a style marked above all by the 'opening up' of the wall to provide once more an architectural vista, usually to each side of a central panel (more rarely in an 'all-over' composition). No longer, however, in the Fourth Style are the architectural forms grounded in reality. In the Golden House they form a scintillating essay in airy and insubstantial fantasy, creating a whimsical framework around full-length figures, mythological panels, landscapes, and patches of 'solid' wall in a dazzling *tour de force*. Enlivened too by dainty arabesques, the whole series of frescoes is executed with a light touch; while some of the vignettes, displaying deft and rapid brushwork, are masterpieces of the Roman impressionistic manner. Many of these features recur in varying degrees of elaboration in countless examples of Fourth Style paintings at Pompeii and Herculaneum; and another aspect of the frescoes of the Golden House, the use of white as the background colour, was also to be of lasting influence, for it gained increasingly in favour, especially from the mid second century onwards. Even today, ravaged by the passage of time, the decoration of the Golden House makes a stunning impact on the visitor, just as it did nearly five centuries ago when

WALL-DECORATION IN THE GOLDEN HOUSE OF NERO, recorded in an eighteenth-century engraving. Above a dado veneered with coloured marbles rose a painted scheme of flimsy fantasy architecture in the manner of the Fourth Style; figures and vases were set within the pavilions as if in a real environment. The colour scheme (despite the effect of the engraving) was mainly yellow on a dark-red background.

Raphael and Giovanni di Udine, according to Vasari, 'were both seized with astonishment at the freshness, beauty, and excellent manner of these works.'

The Golden House of Nero was indeed no ordinary building. In the history of architecture, too, it represents a watershed, for the octagonal room in the east wing is roofed by the first surviving dome in the capital. This major achievement provided a novel flexibility in interior planning which at once opened up exciting possibilities for the future. The octagonal plan in itself (as also the five-sided court immediately to the west) is symptomatic of an impatience with the traditional rectangular room shapes which had long dictated architectural planning. Now, with concrete roofing a flexible tool in the hands of confident architects, the exploitation of circular, ovoid, and apsidal shapes in conjunction with stock rectangular ones created a variety in interior design that had not been possible before. In time, when the exterior shell was stripped away, the juxtaposition of widely differing room shapes with their medley of domes, semi-domes, barrel-vaults, and cross-vaults, often produced a positively ugly exterior. But the new Roman architecture is not an architecture of the exterior: rather it derives its dramatic impact from the interplay of light and space in the interior, so that the void becomes every bit as important as the solid envelope that encloses it. The dome of the Domus Aurea is but a small beginning, but it heralds the dawn of a new architectural approach which had a decisive influence on European architecture down to the present century.

The Golden House and its attendant pleasure park were created by an act of opportunism and imperial greed after the great fire of AD 64 had devastated the heart of Rome. That fire also presented Nero's city planners with a golden opportunity for revitalizing the domestic housing of the urban poor by replacing

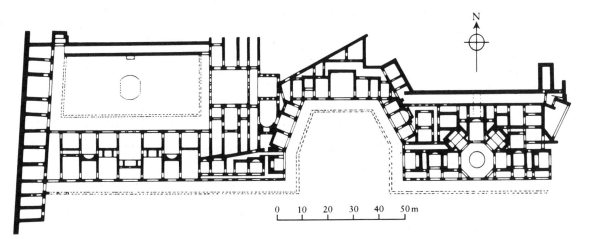

NERO'S GOLDEN HOUSE (AD 64–8): the Emperor's fabulous urban villa contained mechanical wonders and decorations 'all smeared with gold and picked out with jewels'; but more significant was its experimentation with new shapes and volumes within the basically rectangular plan. The novelty of the experiments is indicated by the presence of awkward, redundant triangular spaces between the main groups of rooms.

the sprawling tenement dwellings of the past with the tight, rational planning of the multi-storey rectangular apartment block (above, pp. 312 f.). It was a severely functional architecture, its sober façades rarely relieved by decorative detail; but it also has an uncompromisingly modern look, for the formula was repeated countless times in the urban housing of Renaissance and modern Rome. The material which made all this possible was brick-faced concrete, a winning combination which was strong, light and, as far as possible, fireproof. Having served its apprenticeship under the Julio-Claudians, brickwork was poised to sweep all before it and to take over as the principal facing material for major construction work in central Italy down to the very end of antiquity.

The Flavians, Nerva, and Trajan (AD 69–117)

In the autumn of 69 Vespasian established himself as sole master of the Roman world. A man of plebeian stock, he was a down-to-earth realist with the common touch, and it is probably not accidental that the best-known portrait of him, in Copenhagen, strips away the idealizing varnish and reveals a tough, experienced, ageing man, his leathery skin creased by long years of military campaigning. It is a frank portrayal in the Late Republican vein, shunning the blend of idealism and realism normally adopted in imperial portraits of the time (above, p. 148).

Vespasian's name is indissolubly linked with the most celebrated of all Roman buildings, the Colosseum, the amphitheatre he provided for the entertainment and gratification of the Roman people. Only in its enormous size, however, which called for great architectural ingenuity to ensure efficient crowd control, does it break fresh ground; in other respects it is essentially conservative. Two other Flavian buildings are more important as trend-setters in the brick-faced concrete style. One is the public baths of Titus, which stands at or near the head of a distinguished line of imperial bath-buildings, each rationally and symmetrically arranged around its central short axis. The other is the imperial palace built by Domitian on the Palatine hill in the 80s and early 90s, a building which later spawned numerous provincial imitations. Within its tight rectilinear exterior, the Palatine palace enunciates many of the distinctive tenets of the new architectural thinking: confident handling of enormous masses of brick-faced concrete, grouped in split-level arrangement to take maximum advantage of a complex site; a continuing interest in the dome—three examples in all, each resting on walls which open out into alternating apses and rectangular recesses, now fully integrated with the maze of rooms beyond; and a delight in the curvilinear at the expense of the rectangular. All created novel visual and spatial effects, replacing the expected with the unexpected at every turn. But Domitian's palace was designed not just to surprise, but to impress. 'The edifice is august, immense, splendid,' wrote Statius, 'an edifice to stupefy the neighbouring abode of Jupiter the Thunderer'; and awe, even intimidation, was the keynote of such halls as the palace vestibule (down in the forum) with walls 98 feet high, the vast audience

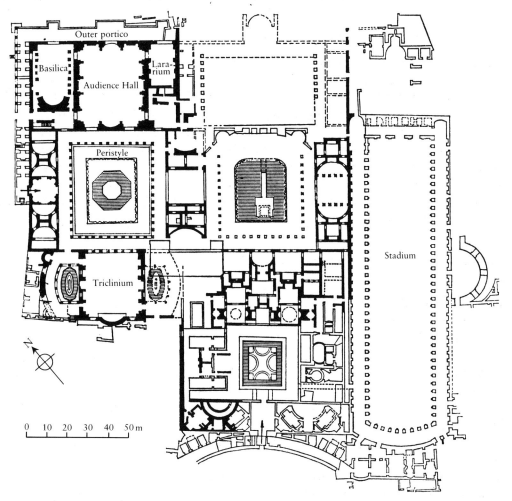

Labels in image: Outer portico, Basilica, Lara-rium, Audience Hall, Peristyle, Triclinium, Stadium

0 10 20 30 40 50m

DOMITIAN'S PALACE (the Domus Augustana) in Rome (AD 81-92). The palace consisted of three main blocks: at the left the official palace including the state rooms; in the centre the Emperor's private residence; at the right the so-called Stadium, a sunken garden in the form of a hippodrome. The detailed planning shows a new facility in the integration of curvilinear and rectilinear shapes.

chamber, the dining-room only slightly smaller, and the 'basilica' in the north-west corner where the Emperor sat in judgement. This, with its apse and double row of columns, probably derives from the palaces of Hellenistic kings, but the distinctive plan was later to have a decisive influence on the layout of the early Christian church. Ablaze with brilliant polychrome marble, adorned, too, with enormous statues, these grandiose state apartments, among the largest interiors yet created by Roman architects, were designed to overwhelm, to make the visitor feel he was in the presence of a very god. Domitian paid the price of an assassin's dagger for such overt assumption of divine honours, and his immediate successors played down this inflated image of the imperial personage, even though they continued to live amid the splendour of his palace.

Domitian's conviction of his own divine status is further emphasized by one of the reliefs from the Papal Chancellery, where he sets out for war in the exclusive company of deities. There can be no doubt that this relief was carved in the Emperor's lifetime, as his head was later reshaped with the features of his successor Nerva. No earlier relief indisputably shows a living Emperor in such divine company; but the almost contemporary relief from the Arch of Titus, erected by Domitian in his brother's memory, is an equally frank glorification of the Emperor, showing him accompanied by Rome and other personifications rather than by ordinary mortals. From now on this elaborate allegorical shorthand became a fully fledged part of the grand tradition of historical relief sculpture, and by the time of Trajan a generation later the conventions are fully established, without hubristic overtones.

The Chancellery reliefs, competently carved but overall rather dull, are still firmly shaped by the mould of Augustan classicism. By contrast the lively reliefs on the Arch of Titus are brim-full of the excitement of a triumph in progress, especially in the procession of the spoils, where the participants spring along past the spectator, placards waving, and wheel round through an archway into the distance. There is a new interest in the handling of depth here, with the figures carved in higher or lower relief according to their distance from the spectator; but the illusion of life and movement owes more, perhaps, to the Hellenistic tradition than to any immediately preceding Roman work, even though the subject matter is an entirely Roman one.

RELIEF OF DOMITIAN'S DEPARTURE FROM ROME (*PROFECTIO*). Between AD 81 and 96. The Emperor is seen off on a military campaign by an assortment of deities and personifications, including Mars, Minerva (or the Goddess Roma), Virtus (Courage), the Roman Senate, and the Genius (Spirit) of the Roman People. The mixing of historical event and allegory is typical of Roman state relief.

CAPTURED SPOILS FROM JERUSALEM, relief panel in the passageway of the Arch of Titus (soon after AD 81). The two reliefs in the arch, which represent the Emperor Titus' triumphal procession after the defeat of the Jewish Revolt in AD 70, have an unprecedented effect of bustle and movement and of being excerpts from a much larger action.

Nowhere, however, is a sense of life and movement more dramatically conveyed than on the stupendous 700-foot frieze of Trajan's Column in Rome. Dedicated in AD 113, and designed to commemorate the Dacian Wars of 101-2 and 105-6, it undoubtedly represents the very apogee of continuous narrative sculpture in the ancient world. The problem of receding space was not tackled in any consistent fashion; rather the designer's first priority was to present an almost uninterrupted flow of action-packed scenes. The constant switching between horizontal and bird's eye perspective, the frequent placing of figures 'above' and 'below' one another without perspective diminution, the incongruities of scale for some figures in relation to buildings, tend not to detract from the whole but to lend to it increased variety and vitality; the action relentlessly unfolds from bottom to top, never flagging despite its enormous length. Here, then, is a veritable textbook of the Roman army at work—gathering stores, preparing for the march, foraging for supplies, building camps, engaging the Dacian foe—delineated with supreme attention to detail. When Trajan appears it is always as the calm, authoritative commander-in-chief addressing his troops,

TRAJAN ADDRESSING HIS TROOPS (*ADLOCUTIO*). This relief from Trajan's column (dedicated in AD 113) demonstrates the concern of the artist to fill the whole height of the frieze which spiralled up the column's shaft, partly by the use of landscape elements (the tree at the left) and partly by a distribution of figures at different levels.

consulting his generals, performing sacrifices, receiving envoys: for on the column there is nothing of the majestic tone of the 'grand style' reliefs with their episodic treatment and full use of allegorical paraphrase; indeed personifications are entirely absent except when required for occasional scene-setting. The overall organization of the frieze called for imagination and dexterity of the highest order; and no less remarkable is the execution in very low relief of some 2,500 figures by a group of sculptors who (as on the Parthenon frieze) reached a uniformly high level of craftsmanship. The modelling of the figures is still firmly rooted in the Classical tradition, and some of the battle scenes can be traced back to late-Hellenistic groups, while other set-pieces are derived from the established repertoire of imperial iconography. But the overall effect is totally novel, a fully fledged product of pure Roman art, un-Greek in conception and execution. Most original of all is the use of a 100-foot column as a vehicle for propaganda sculpture, a bold stroke which marks the Column of Trajan with a touch of genius.

COVERED HALL IN TRAJAN'S MARKETS in Rome (*c*.AD 100–12). The central space is flanked on each side by six shops (*tabernae*) of the standard Roman form, with a wide door, a barrel-vaulted interior and a window to light a mezzanine storey. Above these ran galleries with further shops set back behind them; and between them rose the piers of a series of cross-vaults which spanned the central hall.

That touch of genius may well have been furnished by Apollodorus of Damascus, the architect of the forum in which the column stands. A man of forceful character, later to fall out with the Emperor Hadrian (who had strong, if idiosyncratic, architectural ideas of his own), Apollodorus was a first-rate structural engineer whose achievements included a half-mile-long bridge over the fast-flowing Danube, an amazing technical feat justly admired in antiquity. His forum too won high renown, not least for its impressive scale and the riot of gilded statues and polychrome marbles; but with the exception of the column and the integration of a basilica on the transverse axis (a novelty for the capital), the forum as a whole was closely linked with the past, consciously imitating the Forum of Augustus; and the relief sculpture, too, harks back to an Augustan dignity and simplicity of line. By contrast the friezes on a contemporary monument (the rebuilt temple in the Forum of Caesar) favour instead an ornate, highly decorative style with deep undercutting (intended to provide strong shadows and hence a powerful 'black and white' effect), a style with a longer future ahead of it in later Roman sculpture than restrained and sober classicism.

While Apollodorus' forum, however, looks decisively to the past, the accompanying market and shopping precinct terraced into the Quirinal hill looks no less emphatically to the future. Here is a complex where Apollodorus' mastery of the contemporary architectural idiom is displayed to the full: some 170 shops, offices, and storehouses, in brick-faced concrete up to four storeys high, brilliantly arranged on no less than six levels in an immensely complicated and irregular site. The jewel of the whole complex is a covered market-hall, roofed by one of the earliest large-scale examples of groined cross-vaulting to survive. This simple idea—a barrel-vault on the long axis intersected at right angles by a series of lesser barrel-vaults—marks an enormous architectural stride forward: for now the weight of the roof can be borne by great piers at intervals instead of by the entire length of the side walls, and windows can be opened up to the very crown of the vault, thus creating an imaginative, well-lit interior instead of the cavernous gloom of the usual barrel-vaulted hall. The first tentative steps in this direction were taken in the reign of Nero, but it needed the architectural ingenuity of a master-builder of Apollodorus' calibre to bring the idea to full fruition. Henceforth the cross-vault was to play a major role in Roman architecture, not least in the central halls of imperial bath-buildings with their impressive vistas opening off in all directions; and it is hardly surprising that the baths of Trajan, the first mature example of the axial type, three times the size of Titus' baths, were also the creation of Apollodorus himself.

Hadrian and the Antonines (AD 117–193)

It is tempting to link Apollodorus' name also with Hadrian's temple to all the gods, the Pantheon, the construction of which was already in full swing within a year or so of Trajan's death; but no ancient authority does so, and the creator of what is unquestionably one of the great architectural masterpieces of all time remains anonymous. Characteristically it is not the exterior which wins admiration. The façade with its conventional portico and gable was very much run-of-the-mill for the temples of its time, and the radical conjunction of a rectangular porch with massive circular *cella* is positively disharmonious. Yet this incongruity is quite forgotten once one steps inside the enormous rotunda: for the impact of the interior, as any visitor to the Pantheon knows, is breathtaking. The eye is drawn up, immediately and irresistibly, to the superb lines of its coffered concrete dome, at 148 feet in diameter the largest man-made dome in the world until modern times. Sheer size is one element in the building's appeal: surprise is another. For the Pantheon is designed not along the lines of a conventional temple building dominated by a longitudinal, horizontal axis, but around a

INTERIOR OF THE PANTHEON (*c.*AD 118–28). The great Hadrianic rotunda dedicated to the planetary gods is a fine example of the new interest in interior space and surface ornament which developed in imperial architecture. The diameter of the dome (42.50 m) was greater than that of St Peter's and remained unsurpassed till the present century.

DOMED HALL IN THE GARDENS OF SALLUST, ROME (engraving by Piranesi): a fine example of the ambitious vaulting techniques explored in Hadrianic times, especially in the emperor's villa at Tivoli. The dome consists of eight sectors alternately flat and concave. Hadrian may have had a personal interest in designing such domes: Trajan's architect Apollodorus is said to have told him in a famous exchange of words, 'Go and draw your pumpkins.'

vertical axis, an invisible line joining the centre of the floor with the opening in the summit of the dome. Nothing is allowed to distract from this vertical aspect of the building, so that the articulation of niches and *aediculae* in the cylindrical drum wall is deliberately restless. Even the impact of the apse opposite the door is muted, no longer fulfilling its usual role as the focal point of a temple building. Yet despite this apparent complexity the essential geometry of the Pantheon is based on a simple, harmonious formula: the diameter of the whole building is identical to its height. Size, surprise, simplicity—these are three keynotes of this extraordinary temple. It is a building which embodies all the principal characteristics that define the specifically Roman contribution to architecture since Augustus: controlled use of polychrome marbles for columns, floor paving, and wall veneer, from Africa, Egypt, and Asia Minor; mastery of the properties of brick-faced concrete in its 20-foot-thick walls, constructed with numerous relieving arches and recesses to lessen the chances of settlement; mastery, too, in the pouring of some 5,000 tons of concrete for the soaring dome, with carefully graded ingredients ranging from strong basalt near its spring-line to light pumice at its summit. Above all the Pantheon is a supremely eloquent essay in the creation of interior space, and in the lighting of that space, through a single, bold opening at the very crown of the dome. More than any other Roman building it has inspired countless imitations and adaptations, starting in Hadrian's own reign with the Temple of Asclepius at Pergamum, and continuing on well into the present century.

The other architectural *tour de force* of Hadrian's reign is the sprawling stately home constructed by the Emperor near Tivoli over an enormous tract of rolling countryside. The whole bears the unmistakable stamp of the personality of its self-indulgent owner, who had at his disposal both the technical resources and the bottomless purse necessary to create the succession of luxurious living quarters, baths, pavilions, banquet halls, libraries, and grandiose ornamental pools. Throughout the villa the variety of room shapes and the ingenuity shown in their interrelationship betoken a lively interest in the architecture of interiors; while in the central court of the pavilion in the Piazza d'Oro, or in the villa-in-miniature on its artificial island (where Hadrian could retreat when in reclusive mood), a delight in the curvilinear is carried to baroque extremes. Roofing, too, was the subject of fresh experiment: the dome in the vestibule of the Piazza d'Oro was no longer provided with an outer masonry skin to cloak its inner form (a frank admission that it was interior effect, not exterior appearance, which really mattered in Roman architecture); while the Serapeum has a spectacular example of the new 'pumpkin' dome, composed of distinct radiating segments alternately concave and flattened. Hadrian himself had a personal interest, possibly even a creative role, in this fresh variation of the dome, and an even more ambitious example occurs in another of his palaces, in the Gardens of Sallust at Rome.

While the architecture of Hadrian's villa was uncompromisingly Roman, the sculptural detail was no less uncompromisingly Greek. Hadrian was by far the most philhellenic of all Roman Emperors, and the enthusiasm which earned him the nickname of 'Greekling' carried him on occasion a little too far: his attempt to implant a temple of entirely Greek form, the Temple of Venus and Rome, in the very heart of the capital was widely regarded as an aesthetic failure. Sculpture, however, was a different matter; and such was the influence wielded by artistic patronage that the personal predilections of the Emperor could and did leave a decisive mark on the sculpture of the age. When Hadrian opted for a 'Classical revival' he stopped dead in its tracks for a generation the development of an authentically Roman sculptural style, such as was beginning to emerge on Trajan's Column. Instead he welcomed to Rome Greek sculptors and craftsmen on a scale not seen since Augustus' day, and evidence of their work can be detected in the embellishment of all the major projects associated with Hadrian. That evidence points to Asia Minor as the homeland of these gifted men, for the architectural ornament in Rome can sometimes be matched, detail for detail, with work at Pergamum, Ephesus, and elsewhere. Much of it was carved in the fine white marble (with a pronounced blue streak) from the quarries of Proconnesus near Istanbul, a material which arrived in Rome for the first time with these Asiatic craftsmen. Also carved by them on Italian soil was a wide range of sculpture both in relief and in the round, much of it with life and spontaneity suggestive of genuine creativity. Certainly it was to sculptors from the Greek world that Hadrian turned to perpetuate the melancholy beauty, diffident manner, and lithe and sensuous frame of his boyfriend Antinous, deified after drowning in the Nile in October 130. In original creations such as this Greek artists made a more important contribution to Hadrianic sculpture than did routine copies of Caryatids and other fifth-century Attic masterpieces which line the Canopus pool at the Tivoli villa, copies mechanically reproduced in Italian workshops long accustomed to demands of this kind.

The introduction of fresh currents from Greek lands into the mainstream of art and architecture was also symptomatic of an increasing cosmopolitanism in Rome and the Roman world under Hadrian and the Antonines. The second and third quarters of the second century were a particularly glorious age for the provincial cities of the Roman Empire, as self-confidence increased, living standards rose, and horizons widened. One graphic witness of the new outlook is provided by the rush to construct or refurbish in marble, which resulted in an astonishing boom in the export of coloured marbles. Its beginning can be dated to the early years of Hadrian's reign, and by the middle of the century nearly all new public buildings in major provincial cities were being constructed with marble columns and architraves and marble veneers. In some cases there is evidence that the imported materials were carved on arrival by craftsmen from the country of source, a process also documented later in the second century (as well as in the third) for the elaborate marble relief sarcophagi from Greece and Asia Minor, which were shipped in a roughed-out state and only worked in detail once they had reached their destination. This is no longer a Rome-centred world in which a metropolitan building type or decorative motif could be transmitted without substantial transmutation to a provincial centre: instead we are presented with an infinitely more complex and sophisticated organization which took architects, sculptors, and even jobbing masons far from their homes, with the resulting diffusion of fresh ideas and techniques into a common pool. Rome was no longer the only or even the dominant force in shaping provincial art and architecture: other vital creative centres had their part to play, leading to the emergence of an art which was no longer always individualistic along narrow provincial lines, but was common to widely separated parts of the entire Roman Empire.

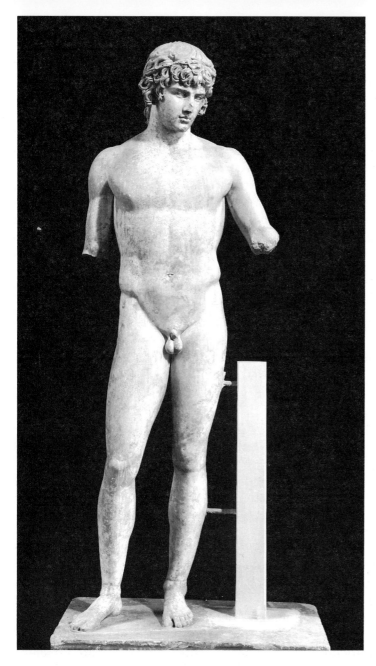

STATUE OF ANTINOUS in the museum at Delphi. The young Bithynian, Hadrian's boy-friend, drowned in mysterious circumstances in the River Nile in 130, was commemorated by numerous statues, based on a type which was the last great original creation in the classicizing style. It combined a body of mid-fifth-century form with a head which conveys a new emotional intensity.

That Asia Minor was among the most important of those creative centres has already been made clear. While art and architecture in the region generally retained its conservative, late-Hellenistic flavour during the first century, sparks of originality were also there: the recently discovered Sebasteion reliefs from Aphrodisias for example, dating to the fifties, glorify members of the imperial house in an individual style untramelled by the dictates of Italian state sculpture.

But it was in architecture that the sparks of creativity really flew: and in such marble extravaganzas as the fountain building at Miletus (*c.* 100) or the library of Celsus at Ephesus (*c.* 117–20) we are treated to a controlled display of traditional, classical architectural elements presented in new guise: simple two-columnar *aediculae* are combined in straddle formation to achieve novel visual effects, heightened by baroque detail such as segmental and volute pediments. The notion of such elaborate columnar screens won widespread popularity, especially in theatre back-drops the length and breadth of the empire; while the language of baroque architecture finally became common currency during the second century in the architectural repertoire of the East, although it only occurred spasmodically in Italy or the West until Renaissance architects discovered it in the late fifteenth century. It is possibly also to the Hellenistic East that we must look for the origins of another highly influential idea, that of springing arches direct from

CLAUDIUS OVERWHELMING BRITANNIA: relief from the Sebasteion (building of the imperial cult) at Aphrodisias in Caria (AD 54–68). The vigorous style owes a good deal to Classical and Hellenistic models, as does the heroic nudity of the Emperor. Other reliefs from the building celebrate the victories of Augustus and the remaining Julio-Claudians, concluding with Nero.

FOUNTAIN-BUILDING AT MILETUS (beginning of second century AD). The reconstruction reveals a number of features characteristic of Roman 'baroque' architecture: the elaborate play of advancing and receding entablatures, the sideways misplacement of pavilions so that those of the upper storeys straddle the spaces between those below, and the enlivenment of the whole façade with statue-niches. Such features were especially common in the eastern provinces.

columns, a device with a long and distinguished role to play from the early fourth century onwards in the architecture of the Christian church.

In fresco painting all the indications point to a decline after the end of the first century. There are some exceptions, but the monotonous frescoes from Ostia show that in general Hadrianic and Antonine interior decorators were content with repeating hackneyed decorative schemes which echo the Third and Fourth Styles of the previous century with increasing simplification and hardly a hint of originality—broad splashes of colour, especially red and yellow and white, but fewer and fewer mythological panels, which were gradually replaced completely by individual figures or motifs floating free in the centre of each zone. Ceiling decoration, by contrast, reached new heights of inspiration during the Antonine period: the strikingly detailed stuccoes from the Tombs of the 'Valerii', the Pancratii, and the Nasonii at Rome, all *c.* 160, represent the very apogee of the Roman stucco-worker's craft. But it too seems to have declined thereafter, and by the early third century we have instances of walls and ceiling in the same room being painted with identical, humdrum, compartmentalized schemes, as in some of the early catacombs. Only in the occasional 'all-over' figured composition does second-century wall painting show signs of a different approach, as in

PAINTED MARINE DECORATION from one of a pair of rooms excavated in the vicinity of the docks on the Tiber in Rome (*c.*AD 131). Painted *aquaria* appeared in the vaults of bath-suites of the first century, where fish were reflected in the water of a pool and appeared to be swimming among the bathers; but the combination of such marine creatures with mythological or idyllic scenes (the rowing boat) is a trend of the second and later centuries.

a lively Hadrianic fishing scene from near the Porto Flumentano in Rome, but this appears to have become widespread only from early in the third century.

While painting was apparently in the doldrums, second-century mosaic work took on a new lease of life. The richly coloured, intricately figured panels of Hellenistic origin had continued to be made in Italy throughout the first century, and spasmodically even later, but they had been joined by modest black-and-white figural mosaics in a silhouette style from the Augustan period onwards.

From about AD 110 fresh life was injected into this style, with ambitious and enormously successful wall-to-wall compositions, depending for their effect not on spatial depth or naturalistic detail but on superb draughtsmanship. Outstanding Hadrianic examples include lively marine tableaux in the Baths of Neptune, and animal scenes in the Baths of the Seven Sages at Ostia; but the black-and-white style flourished throughout the Italian peninsula (and occasionally elsewhere) well into the third century. Purely ornamental mosaics in black and white, also widespread in Italy, became increasingly ornate, and both complicated curvilinear patterns and delicate floral arabesques enter the repertoire now. Ornamental designs were carried further in the experiments in polychromy that followed, both in Italy and the western provinces, from the mid second century; while the floral arabesque was adopted in polychromy by African workshops, which were already preparing the way for the enormous outburst of creativity that mosaicists there were to display during the third and fourth century. That story, however, lies outside our scope; but in the prelude to the full flowering of mosaic in late antiquity, the second-century mosaicists of Italy had a vital role to play.

In state sculpture too, the second century represents a crucial transition, heralding the emergence of a late antique style which breaks free from the shackles of the Classical heritage. We have seen how the personal tastes of Hadrian left a distinctive mark on the sculpture of a generation; and an entirely classicizing spirit, technically excellent but frigid and dull, can be seen on 'official' relief sculpture from his reign, such as two panels from a demolished triumphal arch (*c.* 136–8). The subject of one depicting the apotheosis of his wife Sabina, borne to heaven by a winged female figure and watched by Campus Martius and an impassive Hadrian, is taken up again on the monumental base for Antoninus' Column, dedicated posthumously in 161. Here it is the deceased Emperor as well as his consort who are conveyed aloft on an even more preposterous winged figure, probably a personification of the Golden Age, with Campus Martius and Roma in attendance below. Again we are dealing with sculpture which shows consummate naturalistic handling of its material; yet the overall impression is static, pompous, even comic. The same serene and rather lifeless quality also pervades some of the reliefs dedicated by Marcus Aurelius, probably on an arch of 175–6; these display in addition an increasing simplification of composition and the beginning of a more frontal emphasis for the Emperor, a pose that was to become *de rigueur* by the fourth century. All these state reliefs, however, despite high technical skill, mark the very end of the road for the Classical tradition: sculptors now found themselves in a cul-de-sac, anxious for an avenue of escape from what was becoming routine and devoid of challenge. The earliest sign of the search for a new sculptural language comes on the Antonine Column base of 161, in two panels showing scenes of a funeral procession, each with ten footsoldiers of the Praetorian guard encircled by seventeen horsemen. The combination of horizontal and bird's eye perspective in a single scene is not in itself

BLACK-AND-WHITE MOSAIC in the Baths of Neptune at Ostia (*c.*AD 140). While second-century mosaicists in parts of northern Italy and the north-western provinces were moving towards a polychrome 'carpet' type of pavement decoration, the artists of central and southern Italy preferred a highly effective style of all-over figured pavements with black silhouettes on a white ground. Here the god Neptune is surrounded by sea-creatures in a grand marine *cortège*.

new, but on this scale it is novel, on a neutral background stripped of all setting; and the handling of the individual figures, with their large heads and dumpy bodies, also represents a new departure. The trend towards a fresh simplicity and abstraction of form is further developed on the Column of Aurelius, commemorating the Marcomannic Wars of 172–5 but not finished until 193. Inevitably compared unfavourably with the Column of Trajan, it lacks the involved action, the variety, the attention to detail of its forerunner. But its designer and sculptors were not seeking to make a duplicate of Trajan's Column. They intended to convey an impression of war rather than a detailed commentary on it, by presenting fewer episodes carved boldly and clearly; and instead of careful modelling we find rather flat surfaces, with grooved lines for drapery, and deep undercutting around the figures, designed to enhance the 'black-and-white' effect of the whole.

A yet further stage in the development of what might be termed impressionistic sculpture can be seen on the Arch of Septimius Severus in the Roman Forum (AD 203). It is easy to dismiss the groups of ill-proportioned two-dimensional figures with their heavily drilled hair and clothing as naive and degenerate products, representative of sculpture in decline; but as the figures of the Seasons or the Victory spandrels on the same Arch—or indeed the magnificent contemporary figured sarcophagi commissioned by private patrons—amply demonstrate, the sculptors of the period had not forgotten how to carve naturalistically; they were merely searching for a new and different means of expression. In this they paved the way for the transition to late antiquity, and ultimately, through Byzantium, to the cathedral sculpture of medieval Europe.

CAVALRY PARADE on the base of the column of Antoninus Pius (*c*.AD 161). This relief marks a sharp break with the classical style of previous state sculptures, dispensing with conventional visual perspective and with indications of setting. The foot-soldiers are supposed to be standing in the middle, with the cavalry passing in front of and behind them.

ADLOCUTIO OF MARCUS AURELIUS. This scene from Marcus's column (AD 180–95) can be compared with the same subject on the column of Trajan three quarters of a century earlier. The elimination of landscape, the more repetitive poses of the figures, the tendency to arrange figures in two distinct tiers, the reliance on drill-grooves to model drapery, the stumpy proportions of the figures, and above all the frontality of the imperial group, all foretoken the end of classical art.

Further Reading

An excellent collection of source material in translation with brief linking commentary can be found in J. J. Pollitt, *Art of Rome* (Englewood Cliffs, NJ, 1966, reissued Cambridge, 1983). There is no up-to-date translation and commentary on Vitruvius, but M. H. Morgan's translation (1914; repr. New York, 1960) remains serviceable; for a brief discussion, A. McKay, *Vitruvius, Architect and Engineer* (London, 1978). For Rome there is a collection of ancient sources in translation in D. R. Dudley, *Urbs Roma* (London, 1967), and the reference work of S. B. Platner and T. Ashby, *Topographical Dictionary of Ancient Rome* (Oxford, 1929) and the photographic archive of E. Nash, *Pictorial Dictionary of Ancient Rome* (2 vols., 2nd. edn., London and New York, 1968) remain fundamental.

The best short introduction in English to Roman art is that of J. M. C. Toynbee, *Art of the Romans* (London and New York, 1965); the most balanced longer account that of D. E. Strong, *Roman Art* (Harmondsworth, 1976, reissued with full annotation 1988), but the latter was published posthumously and shows signs of being unfinished. Neither deals with architecture. M. Henig (ed.), *Handbook of Roman Art* (Oxford, 1983), is a well illustrated up-to-date account for the general reader with essays of uneven quality from several hands. The most lavishly illustrated single-volume treatment of Roman art, with copious colour and black-and-white photographs, is B. Andreae's *The Art of Rome* (New York, 1977; London, 1978), and there are also excellent illustrations in R. Bianchi Bandinelli's *Rome, The Centre of Power* and *Rome, The Late Empire* (London and New York, 1970 and 1971). Sir Mortimer Wheeler's *Roman Art and Architecture* (London and New York, 1964) has a lively if slightly idiosyncratic text and deals mainly with architecture, thematically by building type; the chapters on painting, sculpture, and the minor arts are very sketchy. Somewhat idiosyncratic, too, is the arrangement of material adopted by R. Brilliant, *Roman Art* (London, 1974). More balanced, well-illustrated accounts include G. M. A. Hanfmann, *Roman Art* (London and New York, 1964) and H. Kähler, *Rome and Her Empire* (London and New York, 1963), but both are now slightly out of date. O. Brendel, *Prolegomena to the Study of Roman Art* (New Haven and London, 1979), is especially useful on the different attitudes to Roman art from the eighteenth century onwards.

On the Republican background see the early chapters of the books quoted in the last paragraph. There are no full-length studies, except on the architecture, for which see A. Boethius, *Etruscan and Early Roman Architecture* (Harmondsworth, 1978); this is a revised version of the first part of A. Boethius and J. B. Ward-Perkins, *Etruscan and Roman Architecture* (Harmondsworth, 1970), now reissued as two separate books. The Etruscan background is best studied in O. J. Brendel, *Etruscan Art* (Harmondsworth, 1978), and G. M. A. Richter's *Ancient Italy* (Ann Arbor, 1955) studies *inter alia* the impact of Hellenistic art on the peninsula, a theme explored in depth in P. Zanker (ed.), *Hellenismus in Mittelitalien* (Gröningen, 1976), a conference proceedings with contributions in several languages.

On Roman imperial architecture, J. B. Ward-Perkins's *Roman Imperial Architecture* (Harmondsworth, 1981) is magisterial and will long remain the standard work; this is the revised version of the second part of the 1970 book mentioned above. J. B. Ward-Perkins's *Roman Architecture* (New York, 1977) is a briefer, but no less lucid, account from the same hand. F. Sear, *Roman Architecture* (London, 1982), largely rehearses the same ground as Ward-Perkins with few fresh insights. Briefer essays include F. E. Brown, *Roman Architecture* (New York, 1961), and G. Picard, *Living Architecture: Roman* (London and New York, 1966); more specialized are W. L. MacDonald, *The Architecture of the Roman Empire* I (New Haven and London, 2nd edn., 1982), a detailed study of five buildings in Rome from Nero to Hadrian (especially good on vaulting), and the collection of essays on various topics by A. Boethius, *The Golden House of Nero* (Ann Arbor, 1960). MacDonald's essay on *The Pantheon* (Harmondsworth, 1976) provides not only a lucid analysis of that singular building but also an account of its many imitators down to the present century. On baroque there is M. Lyttelton, *Baroque Architecture in Classical Antiquity* (London and Ithaca, NY, 1974), a theme also treated in W. L. MacDonald, *The Architecture of the Roman Empire* II (New Haven and London, 1986); the latter is a geographically wide-ranging work which primarily attempts to explore the function and interrelationship of public buildings in their urban setting.

On painting there is no adequate monograph in English; G.-Charles Picard's *Roman Painting* (London and Greenwich, Conn., 1970) is superficial and, despite its title, does not deal exclusively with painting. Better concise accounts of the Pompeian material can be found in the books cited in the Bibliography of Chapter 14. W. Dorigo's *Late Roman Painting* (London and New York 1971) deals with the post-Pompeian material and includes mosaic; although well illustrated, the discussion is verbose and, at times, wayward. On mosaics, K. M. D. Dunbabin's *Mosaics Of Roman North Africa* (Oxford, 1978) includes survey chapters on more general aspects of the medium and ranges outside Africa; while on the Italian black-and-white school, there is now J. R. Clarke, *Roman Black and White Figural Mosaics* (New York 1978).

On sculpture, D. E. Strong, *Roman Imperial Sculpture* (London, 1961), remains the best introduction; A. W. Lawrence, *Greek and Roman Sculpture* (London and New York, 1972), is a fuller but more austere account. Notable essays on specific works include J. M. C. Toynbee's study of the Ara Pacis in *Proceedings of the British Academy* 39 (1953), 67-95, and her *The Flavian Reliefs from the Palazzo della Cancelleria in Rome* (Oxford, 1957). Trajan's Column has received monograph treatment in English from L. Rossi, *Trajan's Column and the Dacian Wars* (London and Ithaca, NY, 1971, with poor photographs), while I. A. Richmond's classic 1935 treatment is now available in his *Trajan's Army on Trajan's Column* (London 1982). The reliefs on the Antonine column base are fully discussed by L. Vogel, *The Column of Antoninus Pius* (Cambridge, Mass., 1973).The propaganda aspects in general of Roman sculpture are now exhaustively studied in N. Hannestad, *Roman Art and Imperial Policy* (Aarhus, 1986).

Envoi: On Taking Leave of Antiquity

HENRY CHADWICK

THE ancient classical world is a large entity to take leave of. How did it all end? Or should one ask how it survived so long? What principally distinguishes 'ancient' history from that which we label medieval or modern? One obvious difference is that the available sources, though massive enough, are on a far smaller scale, so that the writing of ancient history is a distinct operation from writing modern history where the quantity of documents overwhelms the student. But that is of the accidents rather than the substance of what makes ancient classical studies a special and unique discipline. The rock whence western civilization is hewn is the old Mediterranean world, beginning with high achievements at the eastern end in the Nile valley, in the Assyrian and Persian worlds, in Judaea, but then seeing the centre of gravity move westwards: first to the Greeks, with a high peak of excellence in the fifth and fourth centuries BC, then to the Romans, whose power ultimately yields to the energy of the despised, crude, bibulous barbarians of the north and north-west.

Yet even the barbarian invasions of the fifth century AD fail to mark a decisive ending to the structures and values of classical Greece and Rome. If by 'the end of the ancient world' we mean the loss of a uniquely privileged position for Greek and Latin classics in western education and culture, then the shift cannot be described as decisive until the twentieth century, an age in which powerful forces are inimical to the very notion of a 'classic' of the past providing a model or criterion of judgment over the present. Even as the twentieth century draws to a close, the continued centrality of Rome and of the old Mediterranean world retains at least one living and undiminished symbol in the Papacy, presiding over a community of more than 700 million people, most of whom do not live in Europe. Until very recent times the renewal of high culture in the West has been linked with some direct contact with the prime sources of this culture in antiquity: in Greek philosophy, in Roman law and administration, in the universalism stemming from biblical monotheism.

That is not to say that these three main sources are, or were at the time felt to be, wholly harmonious and co-operative friends. The Romans, from Cicero to Pope Gregory the Great, regarded the Greeks as too clever to be honest. The Greeks, as is clear from Plutarch, admired the Romans, but did not greatly appreciate being conquered by them and would have preferred their own incompetent government to Roman efficiency and justice. Christian monotheism represented a disruptive challenge to immemorial local cults and social customs throughout the Empire, and was met by vigorous resistance in the form of philosophic criticism and state harassment.

It is astonishing that the Roman Empire survived the crisis of the third century AD. Already by 200 a serious trade recession had begun to hit the Mediterranean world, and people spoke anxiously of a falling birth-rate. In the middle years of the century the legions suffered fearful defeats from Persians, Goths, and other Germanic tribes; and the ferocity of internal civil wars brought the enterprise of imperial government to the verge of disintegration. This was averted by the new deal imposed first by Diocletian (Emperor 284–306, died 316 at Split), then by Constantine the Great (Emperor 306–37). From about 250 there was drastic inflation, which Diocletian vainly tried to check by fixing prices (which drove goods off the market altogether), and which Constantine fuelled when gold from pagan temple treasuries was allowed to flood the market. The repulse of the barbarians was achieved at the price of almost total concentration of power in the Emperor's hands and the decline in political significance of the old Senate, though senators remained in possession of their great estates and served in high offices of state. A rigid caste system enforced order. The graded rank of officials in the bureaucracy was marked by insignia in their clothing, particularly shoes and girdles, and by special titles—in descending order *illustris, spectabilis, clarissimus, perfectissimus*, inferior officials in the secretariat being *deuotus* or *modestus*, and so on.

Diocletian divided the old provinces into two, thereby multiplying the costs of the civil service. Late Roman society felt the hand of bureaucracy heavy upon it, especially when even good bureaucrats, who felt themselves underpaid, took for granted a substantial tip from any whose interests they served. The worst officials expected 'protection money'. In the case of high officers of state whose support was indispensable in an important matter, a *douceur* would be substantial; we hear of petitioners landing themselves in huge debts at crushing interest rates, and perhaps even then not getting what they sought.

Usury was frowned on by Christian moralists. But the effect of making it difficult to obtain redress from a defaulter through the lawcourts must be to push interest rates higher, since the lender then spreads the risk over fewer customers. In practice loans continued with little restriction and became a target for sharp criticism when people of little means took out loans on the security of their

CONSTANTINE THE GREAT: fragments of the gigantic statue from the Basilica of Constantine, Rome (*c*.AD 313). The full-size column and doorway at the right of the picture give an idea of the scale of the statue, which showed the Emperor seated with his right hand gripping a sceptre or spear and his left hand holding symbols of power and victory.

houses or small holdings and ended by being evicted. Towards the end of the fourth century a series of infectious urban riots occurred which Jerome ascribed to the rage at wholesale evictions resulting from exorbitant interest rates. In the late Empire there was a constant tendency for land and property to be concentrated in fewer hands. Under pressure the weak sold to the strong, who competed with each other in the size of their estates.

There seems to have been no time in antiquity when corruption was excluded from the lawcourts and the tax system. Cyprian, bishop of Carthage (martyred 258), trenchantly described the system in which a man who had bought office felt justified in recouping his outlay and gathering more for the day when he fell from favour. The Emperors realized what inefficiency resulted from corruption and made intermittent attempts to stop it. One Christian preacher of about 370, probably at Edessa, illustrates the awesomeness of the last judgement by painting a word-picture of a provincial governor handing in his seals of office, standing trembling, white with fear, in the anteroom of the palace awaiting an interview with the Emperor. To check corruption Diocletian created an inspectorate, but they became merely a secret police, using power for their own advantage and at least as corrupt as anyone else.

The administration separated the Latin and Greek halves of the Empire, with two praetorian prefects in each half at the head of the civil services. They were responsible for justice and taxation, but not for the army. Under them were deputies (*uicarii*) administering groups of provinces called dioceses, and provincial governors. At court lay the central officers of State, the most influential being the Master of the Offices, responsible for intelligence services, the government postal service (not available to private individuals), arsenals, coastguards, keeping the Emperor informed, and seeing that his wishes were carried out. The civil service was organized in departments called 'cabinets' (*scrinia*). Other major officers were the Treasurer; the administrator of the Privy Purse; and, especially powerful, the Quaestor of the Palace, responsible for justice. Diocletian copied the Persian court, enhancing his authority by the mystery of elaborate ceremonial, with veils separating the anterooms from the audience chamber, and a series of silentiaries to guard the way. The number of veils to be passed was an index of the dignity of an official's place in the bureaucracy. Eunuchs became important as major-domos, not only in rich households, but also at court. In the office of High Chamberlain they would exercise an influence resented by high officers of state.

Diocletian's division of the Empire into two halves was reversed by Constantine, who by 324 had disposed of superfluous colleagues and made himself sole Emperor. But the division was later restored, and from 395 the western and eastern empires were in effect administered increasingly independently. People talked of 'both governments', recognizing the Empire to be a duality in more than language. In 476 the barbarian army commander Odovacer sent the Emperor Romulus Augustulus into pleasant retirement and assumed the insignia of regal office. The Ostrogothic king Theoderic, educated at Byzantium, was sent to remove Odovacer in 493, but he too found that his status in relation to the east-Roman Emperor Anastasius (491–518) was uneasy. There was regret at the ending of the line of Roman emperors in the West, even though they had long been controlled by barbarian generals. Anastasius, Justin (518–27), and Justinian (527–65) aspired to restore Roman control. Two decades of desolating war were the price that Italy paid for having the Goths (whose administration under Theoderic (493–526) was pre-eminent) turned out by Justinian's armies under Belisarius and Narses. Soon the Goths were succeeded by the Lombards; and in the generations after Justinian's death Slavs and Avars poured into the Balkan peninsula (the Avars leaving a lasting mark in the name Navarino). The Emperor Heraclius exhausted the Empire's military strength in beating back the Persians and left the Jordan desert frontier defenceless against the Arabs. The Arabs had long been restless and marauding in Palestine and Egypt, but were now inspired by Islam and dreams of world conquest.

But until the Arab invasions of the seventh century the peoples of the

Mediterranean world still felt themselves to be̸
Vandals at Carthage were a nuisance for a hundr̸
wars ended that. In the barbarian kingdoms of̸
lived according to their own tribal law, while Ron̸
law. The great aristocratic families served under the ̸
(the elevation of dukes above counts being one per̸
provided a civil service and lawcourts. Self-consciously ̸
new masters, whom they found hard-drinking and mai̸
in southern Gaul and the Burgundians early in the sixth ̸
codes, in the one case juxtaposing, in the other amalgam̸
Roman enactments. Thanks to the value placed on Roman i̸
Germanic kingdoms, there survives the law-code of the Empe̸
published in the East on 15 February 438 and then also accep̸
The Theodosian Code was transmitted with a supplement of add̸   ̸or
'novels' for the years 438–58.

The 'end of the western Empire' in 476 was an event that no one at the time much noticed. There was no sudden collapse of Roman resistance against external barbarians. The barbarians had long been providing the army, and all that had happened was that the man with the real power assumed the ceremonial insignia as well. But the landed aristocrats of Italy and the Byzantine Emperors soon realized that the Gothic kingdom of Theoderic was much less Roman than they liked. We hear complaints of the appalling Gothic taste in music, of trousers and hair-grease. In the West the Church increasingly came to be the vehicle of Roman culture and civic values. It is characteristic, for example, that the clergy did not adopt barbarian dress at the time when their congregations were doing so, but continued to wear the 'Sunday best' of old Roman aristocrats—which we today think of as ecclesiastical vestments. It mattered little or nothing that Rome as a city had long given place to Milan and then Ravenna as the western Emperor's residence. Ravenna had the merit of being surrounded by marshes on the landward side, with a good port at Classis. Behind its walls Emperors felt safe. From there Theoderic administered Italy, and his palace chapel is now Sant' Apollinare Nuovo. There too in Justinian's time the exquisite church of San Vitale was erected and adorned with incomparable mosaic, including portraits of Justinian and Theodora.

The barbarian domination made people assertive about *Romanitas*. In Theoderic's Italy Boethius and Cassiodorus set about preserving ancient culture and philosophy. Boethius declared his 'fear that many things which are now known soon will not be'. At Constantinople Priscian wrote a Latin grammar which long educated the medieval West. Justinian's loudest assertion of Roman values was his code of laws superseding the Theodosian Code. All imperial edicts not included were declared invalid. In the Theodosian Code some edicts ('laws of citations') prescribed the legal authorities which could be cited as argument in court: Papinian, Paulus, Ulpian, Modestinus, Gaius, a majority among them

MOSAIC OF JUSTINIAN WITH GUARDS, OFFICIALS, AND CLERICS, in the church of San Vitale at Ravenna (*c.*AD 547). The Emperor, who briefly reunited Italy to the Eastern Empire, is shown wearing a halo and carrying a gold vessel at the consecration of the church; the Archbishop Maximian stands at his side.

being decisive. Under the great quaestor Tribonian, Justinian instructed his law commission of professional jurists to make a digest of the classical authorities, and this huge book remains the main source for our knowledge of classical Roman law. The way in which Tribonian's commissioners went about the task of compiling the *Digest* has given modern legal historians an unrivalled problem in detection and decoding, to which the utmost ingenuity has been applied. Justinian also put his name to a textbook of law, *Institutiones* or elementary instructions, designed to ensure that even students at law-school had a guidebook sealed with imperial authority. Both *Digest* and *Code* are Latin texts, though produced in the Greek East. The corpus of civil law had a third part, mainly in Greek, consisting of Justinian's further edicts or 'novels' promulgated subsequently to the *Code*, which appeared in 534 with a pompous fanfare of an introduction.

Historians of the law and of architecture cannot say an *envoi* to Justinian without a salute of deep admiration for his extraordinary achievements. The *Code* and *Digest*, Sancta Sophia at Istanbul, and San Vitale at Ravenna are enough to put the person responsible among the greater giants of western civilization. But one cannot help feeling about him as the Anglican John Bramhall in 1658 felt about Henry VIII—that great good can come of the deeds of dreadful men. In

INTERIOR OF THE CATHEDRAL OF ST SOPHIA, ISTANBUL (AD 532-7), the crowning architectural achievement of Justinian's reign. The most lavish of all Byzantine churches, it incorporated materials from all over the Mediterranean and outdid the buildings of pagan Rome in the daring of its structure: the first dome collapsed in 558 and had to be replaced.

the Church, especially in the West, many found the Emperor hard to bear. He loved to issue elaborate edicts on orthodox dogma, and then to summon large synods to ratify what he had prescribed. The horribly maltreated Pope Vigilius experienced Justinian as a disaster. Pagan intellectuals, not accustomed to agreeing with the Pope, found reason to dislike the Emperor very much. In 529 the Platonic Academy at Athens was led by the militantly anti-Christian Neoplatonist Damascius. Justinian closed the place down and confiscated the endowments, leaving Damascius, with Simplicius and other philosophers, to emigrate to the Persian Empire in a hope for liberty which was sadly unrealized. They all soon returned. At Alexandria the Neoplatonic school kept a much lower profile, writing commentaries on Aristotelian logic. Justinian did not interfere there at all. Moreover, among the Alexandrian exegetes of Aristotle was the Christian John Philoponus, with an intelligence that anticipated many of Galileo's discoveries. The most significant evidence of the way Justinian was regarded is the attitude of the principal chronicler of his military and architectural glories, Procopius of Palestinian Caesarea, an eloquent writer with a sardonic pen who served under Belisarius. How intense was his hatred of Justinian and Theodora stands out from every line of his *Anecdota* or 'Secret History', a portrait of a Stalin-like tyrant married to a grimly penitent harlot. Procopius thought the apotheosis of arbitrary autocracy unspeakable and appalling.

The imperial absolutism of Diocletian, Constantine, and their successors had long been presupposed by the Roman legal system. In the second century AD the jurist Gaius says explicitly that imperial decrees have the full force of law without needing further legitimation from the Senate. The supreme sovereignty of the Emperor was enhanced by the confusions and contradictions of edicts, of which the fourth-century historian Ammianus Marcellinus complains. Fourth-century Emperors were surrounded by lawyers, both civil and ecclesiastical, assuring them that their will was the sole source of valid law, and that they stood above it in the sense of not being bound by the enactments of their predecessors.

When those enactments were so full of contradictions, autocracy was no doubt a necessary doctrine. Naturally the Emperor was expected to preserve law and order and to defend the frontier. Tyrannical government made men remember old Stoic vindications of the right to tyrannicide. Christian writers like Ambrose of Milan, on the other hand, could appeal to the Emperor's status above the law to justify the Emperor Gratian (376–83) in suspending pagan cult at the Altar of Victory. If the Emperor Julian (355–63) chose to sit among the senators and spoke of himself as the enforcer of laws by which he felt himself bound, this was a criticism of his predecessor Constantius II, whose language and actions were at times absolutist, dangerously fortified by the belief that he was called to represent divine monarchy on earth, rather than a restatement of an older and more collegial political theory. In practice Julian's reversion to polytheism imposed on him a necessity to assert his unique position as the embodiment of public law and as principal exponent of a philosophical theology designed to vindicate pagan cults. Many students have been struck by the resemblance in political theory and practice between Julian and Justinian, both Emperors regarding religious dissent as a treason to society and the Empire. Paradoxical though it may seem, the 'democratic' ideal of populist participation came to our modern world more from Christian beliefs in the share of all the faithful in the society of the people of God than from Aristotle, the Stoics, or the Greek experience generally. Likewise surprising is the recognition that the Anglo-Saxon tradition of the common law owes more to the operations of ecclesiastical canon law than to classical Roman law.

The ancient political ideal was certainly very slow to die. When early in the fifth century Augustine of Hippo came to describe his ideal society, he did so in anachronistic terms of the classical city-state, with an autonomy that no city of the Empire had enjoyed for some centuries past—an antiquarianism which emerges again in his description of Roman religion on the basis of Varro's work, in tactful silence about the contemporary scene. Augustine's attitude to imperial power was considerably indebted to the sombre pages of Sallust, and he writes with a hot and cold ambivalence about Rome's domination of the Mediterranean world: a manifestation of cupidity and lust to dominate on the one hand, yet, on the other, a beneficent force for centralized order and peace, without which human society would degenerate into jungle warfare. Augustine was well informed about Roman law, whose maxims and principles he cited with admiration. Friends to whom he turned for advice when questions of arbitration in civil cases were referred to him for judgement, included jurisconsults. He was aware that good Emperors can enact laws with unfortunate and unfair consequences, that bad Emperors may enact legislation that has a wholly beneficent effect, and that the problems of social justice are anything but simple.

Like his elder contemporary Jerome, Augustine was master of the classical literary tradition. Both men's writings abound in echoes and allusions to Cicero and Seneca, or the poets Virgil, Horace, Juvenal, and Tibullus. Terence was especially familiar. Though Augustine came from a small provincial town where a single schoolmaster taught all subjects to every child, the ancient educational system was not ineffective for him. He tells of one lifelong friend named Simplicius who 'knew Virgil backwards'; cite a line and he could tell you the preceding line, and he knew by heart several of Cicero's orations. A century later Boethius' prose and verse in the *Consolation of Philosophy*, written without access to a library in prison at Pavia, abounds in reminiscences of classical texts in which his mind was soaked. At one time in his youth Augustine taught grammar, and even wrote a textbook on the subject, together with other guides to the liberal arts of rhetoric, dialectic, geometry, and music (rhythm and metre, not pitch, on which he never wrote—Boethius was to take it up later). His writings show a sustained interest in grammar and diction. He could not but be acutely aware of the gulf between Ciceronian usage and the colloquial Latin of the Hippo waterfront.

Language

Before Diocletian introduced elaborate court ceremonial on the Persian model, Emperors were already being addressed as abstractions such as 'Your Majesty'. Powerful bureaucrats would be addressed as 'Your Excellency' or 'Your Eminence'. A tendency to verbal inflation went hand in hand with the debauch of the currency in the third century. Style became elaborate and formal. It was an indication of a person's importance if he was addressed in the third person rather than the second (a feature still apparent in Italian and German and in English etiquette for formal invitations). In the letters of Cyprian of Carthage, a man of upper-class origin, we see the use of similar courtesies entering ecclesiastical forms of address—'Your Holiness', or 'Your Beatitude'. By the fifth century the epithet 'venerabilis' is used for either Popes or Emperors. An Emperor is often 'serenissimus' or 'christianissimus', while a bishop is 'religiosissimus' and/or 'reverentissimus'. The plural form of self-designation and of address is adopted by Emperors and by Popes, who speak of themselves as 'we' and of their correspondent as 'you' (plural). Government chancellery formulas speak not of 'him', but of 'the aforesaid' or 'the above-mentioned', 'suprascriptus', 'memoratus', and so on. Instead of saying 'this', they write 'the present', 'praesens'. These and similar pedantries of formal style, familiar still in the formula books of European and American administrators, were established in this age.

The barbarian invasions of the fifth century had moments of tense military crisis, especially with the Vandals crossing the Rhine in 406, and later with the arrival of Attila, but for the most part the infiltration of the Germanic tribes was fairly gradual. Through service in the army a Vandal, Stilicho, could attain the summit of effective power. Such men learnt to speak and write fluent Latin; and in the West Latin remained a principal medium of communication among all well-educated men until the end of the medieval period, only gradually yielding to the vernacular. It required the zealous advocacy of Thomas More and William Tyndale (highly educated men who did not otherwise agree about much) to persuade English people that their language could be a proper medium for discussing serious subjects.

But at the everyday level Latin was by 700 in process of undergoing transformation into Romance. The travel diary of the pilgrim lady Egeria who in 384 journeyed from Spain to the Holy Land and ascended Sinai, or the sixth-century Rule of St Benedict, illustrates a colloquial idiom indifferent to the forms and syntax of Cicero. In the Carolingian renaissance after Alcuin had sent men back to school to learn formal Latin again, the rough colloquialisms of Benedict seemed vulgar and distressing to monks of high culture, so that a version of the Rule in correct Latinity had to be provided, saying, for instance, 'ausculta', not 'obsculta', for 'listen'. By Benedict's time plural nouns of the first declension use the accusative form for the subject of the sentence. Verbal forms have long become largely periphrastic; in fact, the auxiliary verb 'to be' mainly drops out of use, so that in some writers one meets long sentences with chains of participles and apparently no main verb. The spoken language in Italy was on the way to becoming Italian: one Roman inscription of the seventh century has 'essere abetis' for 'eritis'. The French definite article, in the forms *lo, la, lis*, is first attested in eighth-century Gaul. A council of bishops at Tours in 813 ruled that sermons be not in Latin but in 'rustica Romana lingua' so that everyone can understand. (The rest of the service evidently remained in Latin.) In sixth-century Merovingian Gaul the Latinity of Gregory of Tours, historian of the Franks, feels like a conscious act of resistance to demotic speech. Naturally, to admit the rustic Frankish form of pidgin Latin to the pulpit was to make possible a more rigorous purity of Latin for the educated élite in the government and the Church. From Alcuin on, a correct Latin was the preserve of this élite. To know it well, to be able to decorate a letter with a tag from Horace's *Ars Poetica* or the *Aeneid*, was to be elevated above the common herd and to have access to positions of considerable emolument.

Pronunciation of Latin varied regionally. When Augustine moved from Carthage to Milan, his African vowels brought comment from his Italian hearers. Africans made no distinction, as Italians still did, between long and short vowels. He astringently remarks that whether the third syllable of *ignoscere* is long or short is a matter of sublime indifference to a man crying to God for pardon. But only the educated in North Africa knew anyway, because the pronunciation would have been identical without regard to the quantity. In Gaul, on the other hand, there came to be a habit of making *c* before *i* or *e* to sound *ts*. But among the northern barbarians in Britain the older hard *k* sound was kept for *c*. In the tenth century Abbo of Fleury (no mean logician) came to England to live for two years at Ramsey Abbey, and was pained by what seemed to him sad evidence of the uncivilized ways of the English who, though hospitable, were so uncultured as to pronounce *ce* and *ci* as *ke* and *ki*. It would have provoked incredulous astonishment to inform him that the crude barbarians of the north had preserved a more original usage than his own. It is likely that both Bede and Alcuin were accustomed to use the hard *k*, which was usual in the Irish schools, the isolation of which after the barbarian invasions produced deep conservatism.

In Augustine's mercantile congregation at Hippo (mainly sailors, dockers, and farm workers—very unlike Carthage, where he could address people who knew what a Stoic or Epicurean was), popular speech said 'dolus' for 'pain' when a grammarian would have prescribed 'dolor'. Having an identical pronunciation for both ōs, mouth and ŏs, bone, the people had replaced the latter by ossum. Although by training and every acquired reflex Augustine was acutely conscious of grammatical correctitude, he also knew, and liked to quote Horace to reinforce the point, that what is correct usage is determined by custom, the *consuetudo loquendi* which has a way of defying both logicians and grammarians with indifferent serenity. He reserved special scorn for people more offended by a linguistic vulgarism than by a fundamental breach of ethical principle. He admired the spontaneous vigour of popular Latin. While the Latinity of the *Confessions* is highly elaborate rhyming prose, never more sophisticated in rhetorical skill than when denouncing the meretricious arts of rhetoric, his sermons are in a direct style using short sentences and everyday idioms, usually with some apology and occasionally a swipe at scornful secular grammarians who did not know what was important in human life. In both Jerome and Augustine we find classical literature regarded as essentially secular. In Jerome's famous nightmare he dreamt of being arraigned before the Judgement Seat on a charge of being a Ciceronian, not a Christian. His promise of reform was ineffective. Augustine could also express reserve ('a certain Cicero', he wrote in the *Confessions*), but the Virgil who had first inflamed his heart as a schoolboy remained a lifelong love, together with Plotinus. He thought it very possible that the fourth *Eclogue* was a prophecy of Christ, the poet being inspired without being aware of the fact, and hoped the great sages and poets of the classical world had not only a providential role in the preparation for the gospel, but also a place in God's kingdom.

Augustine knew how to write moving Latin prose, whether simple or sophisticated. In the later Roman Empire there was a strong taste for a rococo style with out-of-the-way words and neologisms to challenge the reader's erudition and flatter his ingenuity in discovering the author's meaning. At its worst it became a tendency to say nothing as elaborately as possible. Literary allusions could provide a kind of esoteric code in letters between cultivated friends conscious of living in an increasingly unappreciative world. The Latinity of the pagan Martianus Capella, writing in Vandal Carthage about 470, or Ennodius, bishop of Pavia (*d.* 521), is not intended to communicate in the most direct terms with the ordinary reader. In Capella the technique is used as a mask for his essentially pagan sympathies. This mannerist style long continued. In the seventh century the Italian Jonas, educated in the Irish monastery at Bobbio, composed a *Life* of his hero St Columban. His Latin style is full of poetic reminiscences and neologisms of the most *outré* kind, extravagant etymologies in which he takes special pleasure, and an impressive sprinkling of Greek words. All this is mingled with richly demotic usages—*pluriores* for *plures*, present participles used with passive force, confusions between similar-sounding words, and malapropisms such as *limes* for *limen*.

Nevertheless Jonas shows that classical literature was still being taught in schools. Augustine shows that the level of culture varied very much from place to place. At Carthage there were those who had read the *Aeneid* and could pick up an allusion. At Hippo no one except the bishop had read Virgil. His Hippo congregation knew the story of Dido, or ('a specially popular theme') the Judgement of Paris, from attending the local theatre, not from reading any books.

In the writing of Latin prose an awareness of the old rhythmic *cursus* was not lost. Schools continued to teach the rules. In Monte Cassino during the eleventh century proper prose rhythm even became something of an obsession. The replacement of quantity by accent, first seen coming in the third century, had decisive consequences for the writing of verse. Monastic and episcopal schools transmitted Latin through the most precarious age of the barbarian kingdoms, until they in turn gave ground to the newly founded universities. Medieval universities were directed towards vocational training in theology, law, medicine, and the *artes*. In them the study of classical Latin did not necessarily prosper better than it had done in the older episcopal schools. Until the twelfth century what was known in the Latin West about Plato came indirectly through Apuleius, Calcidius, Macrobius, Martianus Capella, and Boethius, who had also provided translations of Aristotle's *Organon* (only his versions of the *Categories* and *Interpretation*, and of Porphyry's *Isagoge* being generally known). The schoolmen's fascination with logic, stimulated further by contact with Muslim writers such as Avicenna and Averroes, also led them to coin neologisms of a repellent kind to meet their needs when negotiating a hesitant way over the *pons asinorum*.

The Renaissance reacted against the Schoolmen and their continual moulding of Latin to contemporary needs. Lorenzo Valla treats Boethius with a patronizing mixture of admiration and distaste—the last man to write decent Latin, but sadly tolerant of barbarisms. The Renaissance enthusiastically demanded classical Latin in its purity and beauty. Thereby, paradoxically, it reduced Latin to the status of a dead language. Once the churches of the Reformation required the vernacular, there was a further dethronement of the language from any ordinary employment. In the twentieth century even the Roman Catholic Church capitulated, and the Latin mass went the way of the steam engine.

The Greek language did not have so many problems to contend with, but underwent nevertheless a comparable development. The conquests of Alexander the Great might have made *koinē* Greek the normal means of communication in government administration and trade, but it was not used everywhere in the same way. The language of the Alexandrian waterfront or Syrian bazaars was very different from anything known to Aeschylus or Thucydides. One has only to pick up St Mark's Gospel to see that; he writes the demotic language of the streets. Pronunciation too varied in different regions. Lucian of Samosata was strongly conscious of his tell-tale accent; anyone could deduce he came from Syria. The educational system prescribed certain texts as pre-eminently suitable for educational purposes. The main corpus of classical Greek literature familiar to us today is the selection made by some anonymous schoolmasters, perhaps at Alexandria or Pergamum or Athens in the third century BC. The vast amount that is lost to us is what they omitted from their selection as unfitted for ordinary level work. The tension between poetry and philosophy, which surfaces in Plato's *Republic* and to which Plutarch devoted a tract, long continued into the Roman period.

The supreme model in poetry always remained Homer. Even in eleventh-century Byzantium, according to the express testimony of Michael of Ephesus, schoolboys learnt each day between thirty and fifty lines of Homer by heart. An elementary school course normally included the first book of the *Iliad* and one play each of Sophocles, Euripides, and Aristophanes, with a few bits of Pindar and Theocritus thrown in. Byzantine schoolmasters of the twelfth century are found still debating the question keenly discussed a millennium earlier (for instance, by Dio Chrysostom) whether the superhuman elements in Homer's poetry required disbelief in the historicity of Odysseus and even of the Trojan War—a debate which Origen in 248 invokes as analogous to the debate about the miraculous element in the gospel narrative. A Homeric allusion always added a touch of class to the prose of any Byzantine author other than the most radically world-rejecting monk. In the fifth century Theodoret, bishop of Cyrrhus in Syria, who wrote a *Life* of the contemporary pillar saint Simeon Stylites, also composed urbane letters decorated with Homeric echoes to officers of the imperial consistory. Michael Psellos tells in his *Chronicle* how when the Emperor Constantine IX first introduced his mistress at court, one courtier quoted just two words from the Trojan elders' awe at the beauty of Helen. Everyone got the allusion except the lady, whose inferior education was revealed by the need to explain the highly sophisticated reference to her.

High style in the Byzantine world was necessarily marked by a self-conscious archaism. The demotic usages of the streets and farmyards were not appropriate for anyone with pretensions to be read in polite society. But the presence of the demotic element exerted a mounting pressure. Early in the seventh century a Cilician monk named John Moschos, intimate confidant of Sophronius the sophist, author of *Anacreontica*, and then first patriarch of Jerusalem under the Arab occupation, compiled an anthology of unusual, sometimes macabre stories about monastic heroes, entitled *Leimonarion*, the spiritual 'Meadow'. The work is fascinating not only for its folklore elements (one story reappears in the *Thousand and One Nights*), but also for the colloquial diction and syntax. Words and phrases characteristic of modern demotic Greek can go back a long way: *nero* for cold water appears in the apophthegms of the Desert Fathers of the fourth century. The eleventh-century epic *Digenes Akritas* ('the Borderer') used popular idioms, and regularly said *na* for *hina*. Beneath the surface veneer of high Byzantine style there was a popular speech uninfluenced by upper-class archaizing. Gradually poets and then prose writers came to have the confidence to use the demotic idiom. The twentieth-century tensions between demotic and *katharevousa* are in part a distant legacy of the divergence between the self-conscious correctness of the city of Constantinople with its literary élite and the everyday language of colloquial usage. Even in the second century AD the grammarian Phrynichus was warning aspiring writers against admitting barbarous or uneducated words into their prose. A number of the usages which he specifically vetoes appear in the New Testament as ordinary unselfconscious speech. Throughout the history of the language, the conservative preservation of a pure and more archaizing or classical Greek is connected with the acknowledgement that in the classical age lie the supreme achievements of all Greek literature, history, and philosophy. To make the demotic language standard usage is obviously to weaken a link that gives wide access to that classical world, though at the same time it may prevent contemporary Greeks from thinking that they have inherited with their mother's milk a capacity to understand Aeschylus or Lycophron. In the continuous development of the Greek language since antiquity, an élite has always existed which wished to recite Homer and to write prose in the manner of Thucydides. Such a manner can be achieved only by some degree of affectation, and sophisticated Byzantine prose of the late-medieval period can be uncommonly difficult to interpret. It must have been found so at the time. Some neo-Latin writers of the Renaissance offer obvious parallels.

Philosophy and Religion

The Christian mission in the Graeco-Roman world, initially led by a Christian Jew from Tarsus whose followers were at times baffled by the profundity and dynamism of his understanding of Christ and the Church, met with a success sufficient to provoke government persecution and philosophical criticism. To their persecutors the Christians replied when in co-operative mood that an ethic which demanded stable family life and honesty in trade deserved encouragement, and that, provided one had no part in polytheistic cult which they thought honouring evil spirits, one could render to both God and Caesar whatever was their due. Indeed they recognized a religious obligation to pay taxes. They further claimed that the intellectual tradition of the classical past was not alien to them. They soon found ways to make it their own. Stoic ethics required attitudes to slavery or wealth that they found congenial. 'Seneca saepe noster' ('Seneca is often one of us'), said Tertullian. Platonic metaphysics affirmed divine transcendence, the freedom of the will, the immortality of the soul, and that virtue is necessary and sufficient for happiness. In Justin, Clement of Alexandria, and Origen, Platonism and Christian thought come to keep house together.

The marriage went with allegorical or symbolist exegesis of parts of the Pentateuch, already worked out in detail by the Jew Philo of Alexandria. This principle was soon extended to any part of the authoritative corpus of biblical writings accepted for reading in church lectionaries (this acceptance being a criterion of 'canonicity'). How deeply the first Christians pondered the complex relation between faith and history is apparent in St John's Gospel, where it is a general rule of interpretation that if anything can have two or more levels of meaning, it does: the history is a sacramental vehicle of spiritual truth. The Christians were not the first to discern a pattern in history that discloses the nature and meaning of human existence (Thucydides had already travelled that way); but symbolist writing in literature has its principal springs in the New Testament.

The dialogues of Plato that fascinated the Neoplatonists were *Timaeus*, *Parmenides* and *Republic*. The *Timaeus* set out Plato's cosmogony and therefore a doctrine of the relation between the Creator and the cosmos. The *Parmenides* dealt with dialectical problems about being, identity, and difference. These two dialogues and the Neoplatonic commentaries on them were read by Christians with obvious sympathy.

The marriage of Platonism and Christianity, however, had its tiffs. The pagan Platonists were not in the least grateful for the hand of intellectual sympathy which the Christians stretched out towards them, and asked awkward questions about the compatibility of the notion of incarnation with divine immutability, which Plato had argued to be necessary to the concept of perfection. From the Christian side there was fierce criticism of the Platonic axiom of the eternity of the world, the belief that the soul possesses an eternity and immortality independent of the Creator, and, above all, the fatalism inherent in the notion of reincarnation.

Clement of Alexandria speaks of the Church as a river emerging from the confluence of Bíblical faith with Greek philosophy. Apocalyptic hope, passing from late Judaism into early Christian preaching, is that element in Christianity which to a Platonist critic (Celsus) seemed most bizarre. Yet from apocalyptic the Christians brought to the western world the sense that the historical process is moving to a divine event—whether near or far off they disputed. In Romans 8 Paul sees the sufferings of this life as the birth-pangs preceding a new age.

Apocalyptic language implies a negative view of much of the world's way of going about its business. Neoplatonic ethics also encouraged world rejection and withdrawal. 'Plotinus always seemed ashamed of being in the body.' Before Plotinus' time Clement and Origen were articulating an ascetic ladder of the soul's ascent from passion and pleasure to a training and discipline of the character whose final goal is expressed in mystical terms of the vision of God granted to the pure in heart.

An accurate delineation of the distinctive features of early Christian ethics in comparison with the philosophical ethics of antiquity is intricate, certainly not susceptible of simplistic formulas. When the pagan Celsus dismisses Christian ethical teaching as having 'nothing new', Origen in reply is delighted to concede; for the gospel is a gift of the Creator for the realization of those duties or goods which the informed conscience recognizes, imprinted by the creative reason, the light that lightens every man coming into the world. The early Christians had not read Kant (though John Chrysostom anticipates verbatim Kant's dictum that God is discerned through the moral law within and the starry heavens above). They did not think moral reasoning a special way of exercising rational judgment separate from other deployments of the reason. They did not talk about the moral imperative as command coming from an alien force outside the soul and asking for blind obedience. The doctrine of man made in God's image, fused with Platonic language about the soul's 'affinity' with God, helped them to say that the soul naturally recognizes how right and rational it is to be good and just. The imperatives in the conscience are signposts to what the source of all goodness is like. But the Christians dissented deeply from the Socratic principle that none errs knowingly or deliberately, and saw human nature as a noble ruin whose self-inflicted misery called for a restoration transcending human powers. The stress on redemption and grace went with an insistence on obedience and humility of which Christ is model. But the main shift in ethical concern resulting from conversion to Christianity comes to lie in an intense interest in motive as the source of value. Augustine was especially fascinated by the fact that circumstances and motives are primary in evaluating the moral significance of an act.

The most striking manifestation of Christian detachment from the secular appears in the monastic movement of the fourth century. In a sermon of the mid third century Origen observed that renunciation of the world is not achieved by physically moving oneself out into the desert, a remark which suggests that already somebody thought otherwise. The complex motives that drove men and women to become hermits or, more commonly, to join communities of ascetics living under obedience are only partly visible to us. The fourth-century Church experienced the movement as a shock to its sytem. Many bishops opposed the weakening of urban or village congregations which resulted from the exodus of the most dedicated members into special separate communities owing an allegiance to their abbot and often showing a cool reserve to the ordinary life of the Church. The earliest document yet found to mention a monk is a papyrus from the Fayum of 6 June 324. Athanasius of Alexandria portrayed the hermit Antony in a *Life* which owed something to Pythagorean hagiography about their founder. In the Nile valley from about 320 the Copt Pachomius was establishing large communities of monks under virtually military discipline, some of which were embarrassingly successful in agriculture. In Asia Minor in the 360s and 370s Basil of Caesarea composed rules for communities under rule with a common habit and dedicated to the service of the outside community.

The monks enraged writers such as Libanius or the Alexandrian schoolmaster Palladas, whose embittered epigrams won a place in the *Palatine Anthology*, or in the West the poet Rutilius Namatianus. The Platonic Christian, Synesius of Cyrene, disliked their rejection of culture, and much misgiving was provoked by the readiness of some monks to form bands for the dismantling of pagan shrines. Augustine begs his people to win the minds and hearts of their pagan neighbours, not to infuriate them by insulting matters they held dear, even if obviously corrupt and superstitious.

The Church and the End of the Ancient World

The change of religion had some social consequences which affected the world from which the Church wished to be detached and independent. The capture of society, in principle largely achieved by 400 (though pockets of pagan resistance long continued), also affected the Church itself. Could the Church be respectable in class terms without losing its sense of obligation to and identification with the poor? The first charge on the local church chest was the maintenance of those whose names stood in the 'register of the poor' (the phrase is first attested in 422, but the thing is much earlier). Augustine knew that the alms of the faithful were inadequate to the problem of destitution, and longed for the imperial government to provide subsistence benefit, financed by redistributive taxation that, he felt sure, good men would be happy to pay. Rich benefactors usually preferred to see their money put into buildings or mosaic and marble decoration in basilicas. Then there were questions about compromise with the political and social system. Gregory of Nyssa boldly attacked the institution of slavery. Augustine thought the domination of man over his neighbour an inherent wrong, but saw no way of ending it and concluded that, since the ordering of society prevented the misery of anarchic disintegration, slavery was both a consequence of the fall of man and at the same time a wrong that providence prevented from being wholly harmful. Slaves were not a very large proportion of the ancient labour force, since the cost of a slave to his owner exceeded that of employing free wage-labourers. Slaves in a good household with a reasonable master enjoyed a security and standard of living that seldom came the way of free wage-labourers. But not all slaves had good masters, and in special cases bishops used the church chest to pay the costs of emancipation. Refusal on moral grounds to own slaves became a rule for monasteries.

The ancient Church deeply disapproved of capital punishment and judicial torture. A Roman church-order of about 200 forbids a Christian magistrate to order an execution on pain of excommunication. No Christian layman could tolerably bring a charge against anyone if the penalty might be execution or a beating with lead-weighted leather thongs. There was a tendency, first apparent in the fifth century, to modify rigorism against capital punishment in all circumstances; Pope Innocent I (405) ruled against excommunicating magistrates who imposed it, which was not to say that such penalties were welcome. Torture forced so many innocent people to confess to crimes they had not committed that the Christian hatred of it commanded wide assent. Nevertheless, by what were deemed necessities of state it continued. In the Merovingian period conciliar canons had to be content with forbidding clergy to be present in the torture chamber. The Bulgar king was probably little moved when in 866 Pope Nicolas I told him that torture is contrary to both divine and human law. The military impact of Islam first made some Christians argue the controversial thesis that one could resort to violence to withstand the infidel. Even after that had been admitted and implemented in the Crusades, in the west it was not effectively until the age of the papal monarchy that torture and execution began to be deployed against heretics, and there were those at the time who noted the break with immemorial tradition. Although Augustine justified coercion against the Donatist schismatics of north Africa, seeing how successful the policy was, nevertheless he laid down strict limits to the penalties that might be imposed, and refused all resort to force. The pain of his legacy arose from his need to reason out a theoretical justification of the coercion, and this survived the particular situation and his mitigating hand.

People bequeathed estates to churches and monasteries, and landownership brought responsibilities for the work-force and for correct financial trusteeship which were a source of anxiety to bishops and abbots, but nevertheless gave them powers of patronage. As the barbarian kingdoms took control in the West, aristocratic and cultured Romans, such as Sidonius Apollinaris in Gaul, found a bishopric a vantage-point for preserving independence and for protecting the secular interests of church members before an unsympathetic government. A bishop was not expected to confine himself to preaching good expository sermons. He had to be a community leader. In Syria Theodoret of Cyrrhus built porticos, baths, two bridges, and an aqueduct for his little town. Christianity never shrugged off its origins as an urban religion moving from the town out into the surrounding countryside which was slow to be converted and tenacious of old peasant superstitions. The Church was joined by many women and manual workers, but never had a proletarian ethos. From the start (as I Corinthians shows) it contained a proportion of well educated people, capable of private Bible study at home. In a society where rhetoric was a part of the school curriculum eloquent sermons were appreciated, but it was often observed that sincerity and personal passion in the preacher mattered more than a fine turn of phrase. The bishops, based in the city, became identified with the city community in a way which, after the barbarian invasions, became socially important. Even by the third century bishops signed their names appending an adjectival form of the name of their town.

Among bishops the level of education varied by extremes. They were elected by their congregations subject to the veto of the consecrating bishops of the province under the metropolitan; they were local people, not brought in from outside or overseas, and closely reflected the style of their laity. Illiterate bishops— a favourite butt for the mockery of the half-educated, as Augustine once observed—were rare. By the mid fifth century a bishopric could be the destiny of a voluntarily retired praetorian prefect or a forcibly retired emperor. When Cyrus of Panopolis, a pagan poet who rose to be city prefect of Constantinople, fell foul of the chamberlain Chrysaphius, he saved himself by baptism and a Phrygian bishopric where the enraged population had lynched his four predecessors. Although individual bishops were occasionally unpopular, we hear more of the respect and affection in which their people held them. Like a rich patron, a bishop was expected to intercede with magistrates or tax authorities on behalf of his people and even to get employment for them. Augustine liked to quote a wise man's aphorism, that he had too much regard for his own reputation to vouch for other people's. He feared the dangers of his social role. When an acquaintance was elected to a bishopric, he wrote to warn him of the trappings of office, the raised throne with embroidered cloth, and the choir of nuns singing to welcome him; 'the honour of this world is passing away.'

The storms of the fifth-century invasions made all honour in this world seem infinitely precarious. The establishment of the barbarian kingdoms formalized a take-over which had long been reality. Even before Constantine's time Germanic tribes were providing some of the best soldiers for the legions. Julian's hymn of hate against Constantine includes the charge that he elevated barbarians to great offices of state. To the distress of the Roman aristocrats, Julian himself found it necessary to put a barbarian general into the prestigious post of consul. At the beginning of the fifth century the Vandal Stilicho held all real power in the West. Long before 476 collaboration had gone so far that resistance was no option. When the Goths poured into the Balkan peninsula to escape the Huns in 375, and shattered the imperial army of Valens at Adrianople (378), Ambrose of Milan saw the fulfilment of biblical prophecies of Gog and Magog coming from the north to ravage the city of God. Augustine would not accept this exegesis: 'the city of God has as much room for Goths as for Romans.'

The question has been repeatedly asked. Did Rome's conversion to Christianity directly cause or indirectly contribute to the end of the ancient world? Is there truth (even if now to be drastically reformulated in secular terms) in the contention of those whom Augustine sought to refute in the *City of God*, who thought Alaric's capture of Rome in 410 a consequence of Rome's abandonment of the old gods, the closing of the temples in 391, and the prohibition of pagan sacrifices?

In 412 the proconsul of Africa, Volusianus, later a Christian, but at that time still pagan, asked a friend of Augustine if the ethic of the Sermon on the Mount would bring the collapse of the Empire. Was war justifiable in self-defence or to recover stolen property? Augustine thought so, for it was in the cause of justice, and 'those who desire peace must first love justice.' Yet the wars of the Empire must be so conducted that afterwards the vanquished can enjoy justice and peace. Likewise mercy to prisoners of war is a fundamental principle. (The redemption of prisoners of war was a ground on which bishops thought it right to sell church plate given by wealthy benefactors.) There is no evidence that the Church denounced or discouraged the defence of the Empire against Attila. At this period we meet the first evidence for military chaplains attached to units of the Roman army. Augustine observed that Christ did not ask the centurion in the gospel to find a new career. But he might have felt strong misgivings had he seen the order of service prescribed for Toledo cathedral about 500 'when the Visigothic king goes forth to war'.

A more plausible answer than pacifism (or what Gibbon memorably called the Christian preaching of patience and pusillanimity) is that the Church provided an alternative society with a rival career structure and different loyalties. Warnings in ascetic texts betray awareness that bishoprics could be sought for reasons not exclusively religious. The Church competed for the available talent. It drew into its power structure men ambitious, not necessarily for themselves, but for the cause they served, who might well have been useful soldiers or administrators or traders or manufacturers increasing the material wealth of society instead of channelling it into poor relief or noble basilicas like the Ravenna churches. Even this answer to the question evidently rests on a concealed value judgement. In the second century Celsus thought the Church had too few educated people ready to accept public office. Was it that in the fourth and fifth century it employed too many?

The evidence of the time shows that the churches of late antiquity were desperately understaffed. Successive north-African councils deplored the shortage of clergy. Those whom they did have seem from Augustine's correspondence to be altogether unremarkable. There are obvious exceptions. Ambrose left a provincial governorship to become bishop at Milan, where his sermons instructed Valentinian II in his duties. He served as special envoy in matters of state. In that age bishops were often so used; there was an assumption that as negotiators they might be successful because they had divine aid. The millionaire Paulinus sold most of his estates to retire to Nola to write religious verse in honour of St Felix. His renunciation was not well regarded by all Christians; when he asked for a papal audience to tell the glad tidings, he was abruptly refused.

One could move from high positions in the world to become a bishop, but it was not socially proper to move in the reverse direction. In late antiquity bishops did not, like their successors in the late Middle Ages or the Renaissance, combine spiritual office with major secular administration. It was thought highly unusual when Cyrus, the patriarch who surrendered Alexandria to the Arab invaders in 641, combined his patriarchate with the post of prefect of Egypt. He wore one shoe with the insignia of the patriarch, the other with those of the prefect—the ancient equivalent of wearing two hats.

There is one unquestionable respect in which conversion to Christianity brought to the administration of the Empire complexities it would prefer to have done without. The Christians tended to quarrel about ever more refined points of dogma and to take their disagreements to the crucial point of suspending eucharistic communion. That meant a denial that those with whom one refused to hold communion were part of the commonwealth of God; they were to be held as strangers and outsiders. From 311 until the coming of Islam at the end of the seventh century the great Church of north Africa was split between two rival groups, whose theological disagreement was enforced by rancour, by prohibitions on mixed marriages, and by one side wholly rejecting the validity of orders and sacraments on the other side. In the East also there were successive splinter-groups, some only small but others very substantial. The followers of Nestorius flourished outside the Empire in Persia and across central Asia into China. At the opposite end of the theological spectrum the Monophysites, unable to accept the decisions of the fourth General Council at Chalcedon (451), set up a rival hierarchy against those in communion with the Orthodox patriarchates. The government harassed them in Egypt and Syria, and as a result, when these provinces first met the force of the Arab invaders from 634, the capacity of the Byzantine army and administration to resist was weakened by the deep alienation of many of its Monophysite citizens, who soon found their new rulers, though not always tolerant, at least much easier to live with than the Constantinople straitjacket. In Egypt the scale of apostasy to Islam so saddened one seventh-century monk on Sinai that in despair he took his life, and in the circumstances even suicide incurred no censure.

The Arab conquest of Syria, Egypt, north Africa, and then southern Spain and Sicily, ended the unity of the old Roman world as no other factor did. The Mediterranean was no longer a Roman lake.

Further Reading

The classic study of the 'end of the ancient world' remains Edward Gibbon's *Decline and Fall of the Roman Empire* (1776-88, best read in J. B. Bury's edn., London 1909-14); it is good until the sixth century, though Gibbon lacked a sense of history as process and had a complex personal attitude to sex and to Christianity. (Richard Porson's judgement stands: 'Mr Gibbon's humanity never slumbers unless when women are ravished or the Christians persecuted.') See also the early volumes of the *Cambridge Medieval History*. On the fourth century: N. H. Baynes, *Constantine the Great and the Christian Church* (2nd edn. London 1973); D. Bowder, *The Age of Constantine and Julian* (London, 1978); T. D. Barnes, *Constantine and Eusebius* (Cambridge, Mass., 1981). On Julian: specialized studies by R. Browning: *The Emperor Julian* (London, 1975); G. W. Bowersock, *Julian the Apostate* (London, 1978); and P. Athanassiadi-Fowden, *Julian and Hellenism* (Oxford, 1981), which supplement the symposium edited by A. Momigliano, *The Conflict Between Paganism and Christianity in the Fourth Century* (Oxford, 1963). On social and economic history, especially the bureaucracy, see A. H. M. Jones, *The Later Roman Empire* (Oxford, 1964). On the barbarians, see J. B. Bury, *The Invasion of Europe by the Barbarians* (London, 1928); J. M. Wallace-Hadrill, *The Barbarian West* (3rd edn. London, 1967); *The Frankish Church* (Oxford, 1983); E. A. Thompson, *The Visigoths in the Time of Ulfila* (Oxford, 1966); *The Goths in Spain* (Oxford, 1969). C. E. Stevens, *Sidonius Apollinaris and his Age* (Oxford, 1933). On Spain, H. Chadwick, *Priscillian of Avila* (Oxford, 1976).

Of Augustine there is a striking portrait by Peter Brown: *Augustine of Hippo* (London, 1967). For his ideas see John Burnaby, *Amor Dei* (London, 1938 and repr.); É. Gilson, *The Christian Philosophy of St. Augustine* (ET London, 1961); H. A. Deane, *The Political and Social Ideas of St Augustine* (New York-London, 1963). On the sixth century: R. Browning, *Justinian and Theodora* (London, 1971); A. M. Honoré, *Tribonian* (paperback, London, 1981). Averil Cameron, *Agathias* (Oxford, 1970); H. Chadwick, *Boethius; The Consolations of Music, Logic, Theology, and Philosophy* (Oxford, 1981); M. Gibson (ed.), *Boethius* (Oxford, 1981).

On the development of the languages: E. Löfstedt, *Late Latin* (ET Oslo, 1959); R. Browning, *Medieval and Modern Greek* (2nd edn. Cambridge, 1983).

Monks: Owen Chadwick, *John Cassian* (2nd edn. Cambridge, 1968); D. J. Chitty, *The Desert a City* (London, 1966); P. Rousseau, *Ascetics, Authority and the Church* (Oxford, 1978). On the Church in ancient society: H. Chadwick, *The Early Church* (Harmondsworth, 1967); *History and Thought of the Early Church* (London, Variorum, 1982).

TABLES OF EVENTS

TABLES OF EVENTS

GREECE

Only those events of importance to the Greeks in the west are mentioned here.

775–650	Greek colonization in the West
700–650	The diffusion of hoplite tactics
657–570	The age of tyrants
600	Foundation of Greek city of Massalia (Marseilles)
546–480	The flight of Ionian Greeks from Persia brings Greek philosophy and culture to the west: Xenophanes, Pythagoras, Parmenides active as philosophers, Alcmaeon of Croton as a doctor
540	Battle of Alalia; Carthaginians and Etruscans check Greek expansion in the western Mediterranean
524	Etruscans defeated at Cumae
508	Reforms of Cleisthenes at Athens

ROME

Early Rome

The dates and the reality of events in early Roman history are quite uncertain. Rome began as a community on the fringes of Etruscan culture; under the later kings she was in effect an Etruscan city dominating Latium. The establishment of the republic caused a decline in her power as she fought for survival against the Etruscans and sought to re-establish her dominance in Latium. The fifth century was a period of acute social tension. The destruction of Veii ended the Etruscan threat, and the sack of Rome by the Gauls proved only a temporary setback. By 338 Rome had incorporated Latium and moved into Campania.

753	Traditional date for foundation of Rome
753–509	Period of kings
616–579	Tarquinius Priscus
579–534	Servius Tullius; military reforms and creation of *comitia centuriata*; treaty with the Latins and foundation of Temple of Diana on the Aventine
534–509	Tarquinius Superbus; draining of Roman forum suggests creation of an urban centre
509	Foundation of the Republic; first treaty with Carthage; foundation of Temple of Jupiter on the Capitoline

496	Latins defeated at battle of Lake Regillus; treaty with Latins
494–440	Struggle of the Orders
450	Publication of Laws of Twelve Tables
405–396	Siege and capture of Veii
390	Sack of Rome by the Gauls
366	First plebeian consuls
340	Latin War; Latin League dissolved
338	Campania incorporated into the Roman state

491–466	Tyrannies of Gelon and Hieron create a Greek power based on Syracuse
480	Great Persian Expedition by land to Greece; Carthaginians invade Sicily and are defeated at the battle of Himera
461	Radical reforms of the legal system at Athens by Ephialtes
431–404	Great Peloponnesian War between Athens and Sparta
415–413	Athenian expedition to Sicily is destroyed
405	Dionysius I becomes tyrant of Syracuse; peace between Syracuse and Carthage
367	Death of Dionysius I; Dionysius II becomes tyrant of Syracuse
359–336	Philip II of Macedon establishes Macedonian power over Greece
356–354	Dion, uncle of Dionysius and pupil of Plato, controls Syracuse
346–344	Second tyranny of Dionysius II
344–338	Timoleon arrives in Sicily, ends the tyrannies, and defeats the Carthaginians at Crimisus (341); revival of Greek Sicily
336–323	Alexander the Great overthrows the Persian Empire, and establishes Greek control as far as Russia, Afghanistan, the Punjab, and Egypt

THE HELLENISTIC WORLD

POLITICAL EVENTS	CULTURAL DEVELOPMENTS	ROME
Age of the Successors		*The Colonization and Conquest of Italy*
The struggles of the generals who divided Alexander's empire centred on the attempts of first Perdiccas and then Antigonus the One-Eyed to maintain the empire's unity. By 306 the family of Alexander had been eliminated, and the contenders felt sure enough to claim the title of king in their own areas; by 276 the three great powers of the Hellenistic world, Macedon, Egypt, and the Seleucid Empire were firmly established.		The period from 334 to 264 saw the gradual expansion of Rome to control by colonization, conquest, and alliance of all Italy south of the Po valley.
323–320 Perdiccas tries to maintain unity through his regency, but is killed in Egypt	325–300 Pytheas of Massilia circumnavigates Britain	327–304 Second Samnite War against Samnites in the central Apennines
323–322 Athens and her allies attempt to free themselves from Macedon in the Lamian War	322 Deaths of Aristotle and Demosthenes Theophrastus becomes head of Lyceum	
	321–289 Career of Menander (poet of New Comedy)	
320–301 Antigonus the One-Eyed aims at universal empire	320–05 Hecataeus of Abdera writes first Hellenistic cultural history of Egypt	
317–289 Agathocles tyrant of Syracuse	317–07 Demetrius of Phaleron (Peripatetic philosopher) is Macedonian governor of Athens	
317 Philip III half-wit half-brother of Alexander murdered	317 *Dyscolus* of Menander performed End of Attic gravestone series	
315 Olympias mother of Alexander murdered		
315–311 Coalition of satraps against Antigonus	314 Polemo becomes head of Academy on death of Xenocrates	
312 Seleucus captures Babylon; beginning of Seleucid era		

Date	Event	Date	Event	Date	Event
311	Peace between the successors recognizes in effect the division between Antigonus (Asia), Macedon/Greece (Cassander), Thrace (Lysimachus), Egypt (Ptolemy), and by omission the eastern satrapies (Seleucus)	310	Clearchus of Soli (Peripatetic philosopher) visits Aï Khanoum in Afghanistan(?)	310	Roman advance into Etruria
311–306	War between Agathocles and Carthage; invasion of Africa	310	Zeno of Citium establishes the Stoic school in *Stoa Poikilē* at Athens		
310	Murder of Alexander IV, son of Alexander the Great and last member of the dynasty	309	Philitas of Cos (scholar and founder of Alexandrian poetry) appointed tutor to future Ptolemy II		
307	Demetrius the Besieger, son of Antigonus, 'liberates' Athens	307–306	Exile and recall of Theophrastus from Athens		
306–304	Antigonus, Ptolemy, and Seleucus call themselves kings	307	Epicurus establishes his philosophical school at Athens		
305–304	Siege of Rhodes by Demetrius				
303	Seleucus cedes Indian territories to Chandragupta founder of Mauryan dynasty for 500 war elephants	302–290	Megasthenes (author on India) at court of Chandragupta		
301	Destruction of power of Antigonus and Demetrius at battle of Ipsus; Antigonus killed	300	Ptolemy I founds Museum of Alexandria on advice of Demetrius of Phaleron; Zenodotus royal tutor and first head of the library Euhemerus writes his utopian romance Euclid (mathematician) active		
297	Death of Cassander ruler of Macedon			298–290	Third Samnite War
297–272	Career of Pyrrhus of Epirus	295	Tyche of Antioch; Colossus of Rhodes		

THE HELLENISTIC WORLD (cont.)

ROME (cont.)

POLITICAL EVENTS

285	Demetrius the Besieger captured by Seleucus, dies of drink in 283
283	Ptolemy I Soter dies; Ptolemy II Philadelphus succeeds
281	Lysimachus killed
280	Seleucus assasssinated; his son Antiochus I succeeds
	Foundation of Achaean League
279	Invasion of Macedon and Greece by Gauls
276	Antigonus Gonatus, son of Demetrius, defeats the Gauls and becomes king of Macedon, founding the Macedonian dynasty

CULTURAL DEVELOPMENTS

290	Berossus (Babylonian priest) writes history of Babylonia
287	Theophrastus dies; Strato head of Lyceum
280	Duris of Samos (leading exponent of 'tragic history') active
	Bion of Borysthenes (satirist) active
276	Death of Polemo, head of the Academy

ROME

280–275	Pyrrhus of Epirus crosses into south Italy to help the Greek cities against Rome, and is defeated by the Romans
	Earliest Roman coinage
272	Surrender of Tarentum; alliance with Greek cities in south Italy
272–215	Hiero, lieutenant of Pyrrhus, elected general and then king (270) at Syracuse; Syracusan age of prosperity and building

The Balance of Power

The third century saw the creation of an uneasy balance of power between the great kingdoms, with conflict confined to disputed areas: the Ptolemies and the Seleucids fought over Syria and Palestine, while the Greek cities of the Aegean area sought to manipulate the great powers in order to achieve independence. This was the great age of Hellenistic culture: philosophy was centred on Athens, while the patronage of Ptolemy II created Alexandrian literature and science. From the 230s there are signs of the re-emergence of non-Greek forces on the political scene.

274–271	First Syrian War between Ptolemy II and Antiochus I

271	Death of Epicurus
270–242	Arcesilaus converts the Academy to scepticism
270	Callimachus, Theocritus, Lycophron (or a century later), Aratus, and Posidippus active as poets

The First Punic War

Rome begins to emerge on the western Mediterranean scene with her expansion into Sicily, Corsica, and Sardinia, and her response to the Carthaginian expansion in Spain

264 First gladiatorial show at Rome
Roman army enters Sicily to help Mamertines against Carthage: First Punic War begins

263 Hiero of Syracuse becomes ally of Rome

Manetho (historian and Egyptian priest) lays foundations of Egyptian history
Ctesibius of Alexandria (engineer) and Herophilus of Chalcedon (doctor) active
Aristarchus of Samos proposes heliocentric theory of universe

269 Death of Strato, last head of Lyceum

265–235 Archive of Zeno illuminates economic life of Egypt

262 Cleanthes succeeds Zeno as head of Stoics

260 Hieronymus of Cardia (historian of the Successors) dies aged 104;
Timaeus of Tauromenium (historian of the west) dies aged ninety-six

267–262 Chremonidean War: Ptolemy unsuccessfully supports Greek independence from Macedon. Antigonus Gonatas enters Athens

263–241 Eumenes ruler of Pergamum founds independent power and begins building programme

261 Antiochus II succeeds to Seleucid kingdom

260–253 Second Syrian War between Ptolemy II and Antiochus II

THE HELLENISTIC WORLD (*cont.*)

POLITICAL EVENTS		CULTURAL DEVELOPMENTS	
251–213	Career of Aratus of Sicyon statesman and general of Achaean League	260	Apollonius of Rhodes writes *Argonautica* (epic) Herodas (author of mimes) active Erasistratus of Ceos (doctor) understands action of heart and distinguishes motor and sensory nerves
246	Ptolemy III succeeds to kingdom of Egypt Seleucus II succeeds to Seleucid kingdom	260–212	Archimedes (mathematician and inventor) active
246–241	Third Syrian War between Ptolemy III and Seleucus II	256	Asoka, king of Mauryans (269–232), proclaims his Buddhist mission to the Greek world
244–241	Agis IV attempts to reform Sparta and is executed	250	Ariston of Chios (Stoic philosopher) active at Athens
239	Demetrius II succeeds Antigonus Gonatas as king of Macedon War between Macedon and the Achaean and Aetolian Leagues	246	Eratosthenes becomes head of Library at Alexandria; literary scholar and pioneer of scientific geography, he calculates the circumference of the earth correctly
239–130	Independent Greek kingdom established in Bactria		
238	Emergence of Parthia		
238–227	War of Attalus of Pergamum against Galatians; he becomes master of Asia Minor and takes royal title		

ROME (*cont.*)

256–255	Expedition of M. Regulus to Africa ends in disaster
255–249	Series of Roman naval disasters
247	Hamilcar Barca begins Carthaginian offensive in Sicily
241	Roman victory off Aegates Islands; end of First Punic War
240–207	Livius Andronicus (earliest Roman poet and playwright) active

237	Roman occupation of Corsica and Sardinia Hamilcar begins Carthaginian expansion in Spain, followed by Hasdrubal				
236	Naevius' first play produced	235	Apollonius of Perge (mathematician) active	235–222	Cleomenes III king of Sparta; he reforms Spartan state in 227
		232	Chrysippus succeeds Cleanthes as head of Stoics		
228	Rome establishes protectorate over the Illyrian coast			223	Antiochus III succeeds to Seleucid kingdom
227	Sicily and Sardinia are made provinces	225	Eratosthenes of Cyrene (polymath) and Ariston of Ceos (Peripatetic philosopher) active	221	Philip V succeeds to kingdom of Macedon Ptolemy IV succeeds to kingdom of Egypt
221	Hannibal, aged twenty-five, takes command of Carthaginian forces in Spain Rome allies with Saguntum in Spain				
219	Siege and capture of Saguntum by Hannibal			219–217	Fourth Syrian War between Ptolemy IV and Antiochus III Egypt is saved from conquest by Egyptian native troops at battle of Raphia

ROME

THE EAST	THE WEST	CULTURAL DEVELOPMENTS

The Conquest of the Mediterranean

'There can surely be no-one so petty or so apathetic in his outlook that he has no desire to discover by what means and under what system of government the Romans succeeded in less than fifty-three years (220–167) in bringing under their rule almost the whole of the inhabited world, an achievement which is without parallel in human history' (Polybius). About 200 Rome began to develop a culture of its own, heavily dependent on Greek models.

THE EAST	THE WEST	CULTURAL DEVELOPMENTS
	218–201 Second Punic War Hannibal invades Italy	
	217 Hannibal defeats Romans at Lake Trasimene	
	216 Hannibal defeats Romans at Cannae	
215 Philip V of Macedon allies with Carthage	215 Hannibal in south Italy Roman victories in Spain	
214–205 First Macedonian War between Rome and Philip	213 Carthage allies with Syracuse Romans besiege Syracuse	
212–205 Antiochus III campaigns in the east in an unsuccessful attempt to reconquer Parthia and Bactria	212 Romans besiege Capua	
211 Roman alliance with Aetolian League	211 Hannibal marches on Rome Capua and Syracuse fall Roman defeats in Spain	
209 Attalus I of Pergamum allies with Rome against Philip	211–206 Scipio Africanus defeats Hasdrubal in Spain Spain divided into two provinces	
206–185 Revolt and independence of Upper Egypt	204 Scipio invades Africa	204–169 Ennius active at Rome as poet and teacher
204 Ptolemy V succeeds in Egypt	203 Hannibal recalled from Italy	204 Plautus' *Miles Gloriosus* performed Career of Plautus 204–184
203–200 Philip and Antiochus make a secret alliance against Egypt; fifth Syrian War: Antiochus seizes Syria	202 Scipio defeats Hannibal at battle of Zama Carthage becomes a dependent of Rome	202 Fabius Pictor writes first prose history of Rome in Greek

200–197 Second Macedonian War between Rome and Philip	202–191 Roman conquest of Cisalpine Gaul	200 onwards Greek art begins to become known to the Romans
196 Rome declares the freedom of the Greeks at the Isthmus of Corinth		200 Aristophanes of Byzantium (scholar) becomes head of Library at Alexandria
196–179 Philip rebuilds the power of Macedon		
194 Romans evacuate Greece		
192–188 Syrian War between Rome and Antiochus		
187 Antiochus III dies		186 Senatorial edict against Bacchic rites
		184 Censorship of the Elder Cato
179 Philip V dies and is succeeded by his son Perseus		179 Basilica Aemilia and Aemilian Bridge built at Rome
175 Antiochus IV Epiphanes succeeds to Seleucid empire		
171–167 Third Macedonian War		
170–168 Sixth Syrian War		
167 Battle of Pydna ends kingdom of Macedon; Rome divides territory into four republics	167 Direct taxation of Roman citizens abolished	167 Polybius the historian arrives in Rome
Rome orders Antiochus IV out of Egypt		
Rome declares Delos a free port		
Desecration of Temple at Jerusalem brings to a head Jewish resistance against Antiochus' policy of hellenizing the Jews; Maccabean Revolt		
164 Death of Antiochus IV; book of Daniel composed		166–159 Plays of Terence produced Great Altar of Zeus and Athena built at Pergamum

ROME (cont.)

THE EAST	THE WEST	CULTURAL DEVELOPMENTS
		155　Carneades (head of the Academy) comes to Rome on an embassy and introduces the Romans to philosophy
		150　Agatharchides of Cnidus (Ptolemaic geographer) flourished
	149–146　Third Carthaginian War: Carthage, destroyed by Romans; Africa becomes a province	149　Publication of Cato's *Origines* or history of Rome
148　Fourth Macedonian War and war against Achaean League Corinth is sacked and Macedonia becomes a Roman province		

The Late Republic

The history of this period is the history of Rome *domi militiaeque*, at home and abroad. Rome exploited ruthlessly her control of the Mediterranean world; her generals led her citizens to ever richer conquests. But at home the strains of empire began to destroy republican government. Culturally Rome became the centre of patronage, and Latin literature flourished.

AT HOME	ABROAD	CULTURAL DEVELOPMENTS
		145　Aristarchus (scholar and head of the Library) and other intellectuals flee from Alexandria on accession of Ptolemy VIII
		144　Panaetius (Stoic philosopher c.185–109) arrives in Rome
	142　Independence of the Jews	
	141　Parthians attack Babylon	
	137　Roman army defeated at Numantia in Spain	
136–132　First Sicilian Slave War		135　Nicander (medical poet) active
133　Tribunate of Tiberius Gracchus	133　Attalus III of Pergamum bequeaths his kingdom to Rome; it becomes the province of Asia (129)	133　Calpurnius Piso (Roman historian) consul; his work covered Roman history down to 146　　Lucilius (Roman satirist) active

Date	Event	Date	Event
130	Antiochus VII dies fighting the Parthians		
125	M. Fulvius Flaccus proposes enfranchising the Latins		
123–122	Tribunates of C. Gracchus		
121	First use of *senatusconsultum ultimum* to authorize massacre of Gracchan supporters	120–110	Temple of Fortuna at Praeneste built Circular temple in Forum Boarium, Rome
121	Gallia Narbonensis becomes a Roman province	118	Polybius dies soon after this
		106	Cicero born
118–117	Roman campaigns in Dalmatia		
114–110	Series of Roman defeats		
112–106	War against Jugurtha of Mauretania ended by Marius	100	Philo of Larissa becomes head of the Academy
107–100	C. Marius consul six times; he reforms the army	99	Lucretius born
104–102	Second Sicilian Slave War	95	Meleager of Gadara (poet and collector of earliest epigrams in the Greek Anthology) active
102–101	Marius defeats the Teutones and Cimbri		
100	Caesar born		
91–88	Attempted reforms of M. Livius Drusus lead to Social War between Rome and her Italian allies. Rome defeats the allies by force and offers of citizenship	88–68	Antiochus of Ascalon becomes head of the Academy at Athens; Philo of Larissa leaves for Rome
88	L. Sulla marches on Rome	87–51	Posidonius (philosopher, historian, and polymath) active in Rhodes and at Rome
88–85	Mithridates VI of Pontus massacres Roman citizens in Asia and seeks to free the Greeks from Rome	84	Catullus born
87	Marius seizes Rome, but dies in 86		
86	Sulla in the East captures Athens and Greece		
83–82	Sulla returns to Italy; civil war		
83–82	Second Mithridatic War		

ROME (*cont.*)

AT HOME		ABROAD		CULTURAL DEVELOPMENTS	
82–80	Sulla appointed dictator of Rome; Sullan reforms. He resigns in 80 and dies in 78	80–72	Sertorius, Marian supporter, controls Spain	81	Cicero's earliest extant speech
				78	Sisenna (Roman historian) praetor The Tabularium (record house) on the Capitoline built
73–71	Slave Revolt of Spartacus	74–63	Third Mithridatic War	75–35	Philodemus (poet and Epicurean philosopher) active at Rome Aenesidemus (Sceptic philosopher) active
70	Consulate of Crassus and Pompey Trial of Verres			70	Cicero's *Verrine Orations* delivered Virgil born Valerius Antias (Roman historian) active
				68	Cicero's correspondence begins
				65	Horace born
63	Consulate of Cicero Catilinarian conspiracy Caesar elected *pontifex maximus*	66–63	Pompey defeats Mithridates and reorganizes the East. End of Seleucid monarchy (64) and of independent kingdom of Judaea; provinces of Bithynia, Cilicia, Syria, Crete organized, and client kings established elsewhere	63	Cicero's *Catilinarian Orations* delivered Augustus born
62	Pompey returns to Italy and disbands his army			62	Cicero's *pro Archia* delivered
61	Trial and acquittal of P. Clodius on religious charge				
60	'First triumvirate' formed between Pompey, Crassus, and Caesar			60–30	Diodorus of Sicily compiles his *Historical Library*
59	Consulate of Caesar; legislation in favour of the triumvirs; Pompey marries Caesar's daughter, Julia			59–54	Catullus' poems to Lesbia
58–57	Cicero's exile and return	58–49	Caesar campaigns in Gaul	58–52	Caesar writes his account of the *Gallic Wars*
56	Agreement between triumvirs renewed at Luca				

54	Julia dies; the link between Caesar and Pompey is severed	55–54	Caesar's invasions of Britain	55	Death of Lucretius; his poem published posthumously Theatre of Pompey completed

54	Julia dies; the link between Caesar and Pompey is severed	55–54 Caesar's invasions of Britain	55 Death of Lucretius; his poem published posthumously Theatre of Pompey completed
52	Clodius murdered by Milo in gang warfare	55–53 Crassus in the East, killed by Parthians at battle of Carrhae (53); his army destroyed	54 Cicero's *pro Caelio* delivered Catullus dies
		51 Parthian invasion of Syria	52 Cicero's *pro Milone* written
			51 Cicero writes his *de Republica*
			50 Andronicus of Rhodes discovers and begins editing the lost works of Aristotle; foundation of our modern knowledge of Aristotle
49	Civil War: Caesar crosses the Rubicon and Pompey leaves for East		49–27 M. Terentius Varro (antiquarian) active
48	Caesar defeats Pompey at battle of Pharsalus Pompey murdered in Egypt	47–45 Caesar campaigns against Republicans in the East, Africa, and Spain	
47–44	Dictatorship of Caesar		
45	Caesar returns from Spain		46 Forum of Caesar begun in Rome Cicero's *pro Marcello* delivered
44	(15 March) Caesar is murdered		45–44 Cicero's main philosophical works published
			44 Cicero's *de Officiis* written

THE ROMAN EMPIRE

POLITICAL EVENTS   CULTURAL DEVELOPMENTS

The Second Triumvirate and the Age of Augustus

Caesar's heirs struggled for control of the Roman world; the final victory of his nephew Octavian (later Augustus) saw the establishment of monarchy under the guise of a 'restored Republic'. His long reign was marked by consolidation and reform in every sphere of politics and culture. The great age of Latin poetry began with the Triumvirate and continued into the Augustan age.

44	M. Antonius, surviving consul, controls Rome	44	Cicero attacks Antony in his *Philippics*
		44–AD 21	Strabo (geographer and historian) active

THE ROMAN EMPIRE (*cont.*)

	POLITICAL EVENTS		CULTURAL DEVELOPMENTS
43	Octavian seizes the consulate	43	Murder of Cicero
	Second triumvirate of Antony, Lepidus, and Octavian formed; their opponents murdered in the proscriptions		Birth of Ovid
42	Republicans defeated at battle of Philippi; Brutus and Cassius commit suicide		
	Cisalpine Gaul incorporated into Italy		
41–32	Antony in the East	40	Didymus (last great Alexandrian literary scholar) active
40	Antony marries Octavia; pact of Brundisium		Virgil's fourth *Eclogue*
37	Renewal of Triumvirate	38	*Eclogues* of Virgil published
36–35	Campaigns against Sextus Pompeius, son of Pompey	37–30	Horace's *Satires* written
32	Final breach between Antony and Octavian		
31	Octavian defeats Antony at battle of Actium		
30	Antony and Cleopatra commit suicide	30	Horace's *Epodes* published
	Annexation of Egypt by Rome	29	Virgil's *Georgics* and Propertius' *Elegies* I completed
27	'The Republic restored': the first constitutional settlement.	28–23	Vitruvius *On Architecture* written
	Octavian given the name *Augustus*		Mausoleum of Augustus begun
27–19	Agrippa completes conquest of north-west Spain	26–16	Propertius' *Elegies* 2–4 written
		25	Ovid begins writing *Amores*
23	Conspiracy against Augustus and second constitutional settlement	24–23	Publication of Horace *Odes* 1–3
		23	Effective end of Maecenas' patronage of poetry
20	Settlement with Parthia: Parthians return Roman standards	20	Building of Temple of Mars the Avenger begun
19	Constitutional readjustment of Augustus' powers		Horace's *Epistles* I published
18	Augustan marriage and social reforms	19	Tibullus (elegiac poet) and Virgil die
		17	Horace writes *carmen saeculare* for performance at Secular Games
12	Death of M. Agrippa, heir apparent	13–11	Theatre of Marcellus
	Augustus becomes *pontifex maximus* on death of Lepidus the triumvir	12	Horace *Epistles* 2.1 to Augustus published
		9	First edition of Ovid's *Art of Love*
12–9	Tiberius campaigns in Pannonia		End of Livy's history of Rome
6–AD 2	Tiberius in retirement on Rhodes		Dedication of Ara Pacis Augustae
2	Scandal of the elder Julia	8	Death of Maecenas and Horace
		2	Second edition of Ovid's *Art of Love*
			Forum of Augustus dedicated

AD 2-4	Lucius and Caius Caesar die
	Final dynastic settlement: Tiberius is given tribunician power and adopts his nephew Germanicus
8	Scandal of the younger Julia
6-9	Pannonian Revolt
9	Disaster in Germany: Rhine becomes Roman frontier

AD 1-4	Ovid's *Fasti* written
3	Maison Carrée at Nîmes built
8	Ovid banished to the Black Sea

The Julio-Claudian Dynasty

Despite the excesses of individual Emperors in Rome, the imperial governmental system was consolidated under a dynasty which claimed hereditary descent from Augustus.

TIBERIUS (14-37)

19	Death of Germanicus	Manilius (astronomical poet) and Velleius Paterculus (historian) active
23	Death of Drusus, Emperor's son	
26	Tiberius retires to Capri	
31	Sejanus, praetorian prefect and effective ruler of Rome, executed	

GAIUS (CALIGULA) (37-41)

Philo (Jewish writer) active
Death of Elder Seneca (writer on oratory)

CLAUDIUS (41-54)

43	Invasion of Britain under Aulus Plautius	
		49 Seneca (philosopher and tragedian) made tutor to future Emperor Nero

NERO (54-68)

54-62	Burrus and Seneca control the young Emperor	54 Seneca's *Apocolocyntosis* published; Lucan (epic poet) and Persius (satirist) active
58-62	Conquest and loss of Armenia	
59	Murder of Agrippina on Nero's orders	
61	Revolt of Iceni in Britain under Boudicca	
62	Death of Burrus and end of Seneca's influence	
64	Fire in Rome for nine days; persecution of Christians	64-8 Building of Nero's Golden House
65	Pisonian Conspiracy against Nero	65 Suicides of Seneca and Lucan
66-73	Jewish Revolt	66 Suicide of Petronius (author of *Satyrica*)
		67 Josephus, rebel leader in Judaea and future author, deserts to the Romans

THE ROMAN EMPIRE (*cont.*)

POLITICAL EVENTS		CULTURAL DEVELOPMENTS	

The Flavian Dynasty

With the Flavian dynasty power shifted to the bourgeoisie of Italy; luxury became unfashionable at Rome as the Emperor displayed 'old-fashioned standards'. Literature gives way to government as the art of Rome.

69	The Year of the Four Emperors: Galba, Otho, Vitellius, and Vespasian struggle for power		
VESPASIAN (69–79)			
70	Destruction of Temple at Jersalem	74	Frontinus (administrator and technical writer) consul
TITUS (79–81)			
79	Eruption of Vesuvius; destruction of Pompeii and Herculaneum	79	Death of Elder Pliny (administrator, naturalist, and encyclopedist) investigating eruption
80	Fire at Rome: destruction of Capitoline Temple	80	Inauguration of Colosseum
DOMITIAN (81–96)			Domitian's palace on Palatine hill built
78–85	Campaigns of Agricola in Britain		Statius, Silius Italicus, Martial (poets), and Quintilian (writer on rhetoric) active
86–92	Domitian's wars against Dacians		

The Age of the Antonines

'If a man were called to fix the period in the history of the world, during which the human race was most happy and prosperous, he would, without hesitation, name that which elapsed from the death of Domitian to the accession of Commodus' (Edward Gibbon). Culturally the Greek world began to revive as city life prospered.

NERVA (96–8)		97	Tacitus consul
TRAJAN (98–117)			
101–6	Trajan conquers Dacia (modern Rumania)	100–11	Dio Chrysostom (Greek orator), Epictetus (moralist), and Plutarch (essayist and biographer) active in Greek literature
			Pliny the Younger (orator and letter-writer) consul and governor of Bithynia
			Tacitus writes *Histories* and *Annals*

112–13	Forum of Trajan and Trajan's Column dedicated
	Appian (historian), Lucian (satirist), and Ptolemy (astronomer) active in Greek literature; Suetonius (biographer) and Juvenal (poet) in Latin
	The Pantheon (Rome), Hadrian's Villa (Tivoli), and Hadrian's Wall (Britain) built
143	Pausanias writes his description of Greece
	Herodes Atticus (Greek orator) and Fronto (Latin orator) consuls
144	Speech of Aelius Aristides (Greek orator) in praise of Rome
148	900th anniversary of founding of Rome
165	Apuleius (Latin writer) and Galen (doctor) active
	Justin (Christian apologist) martyred
174–80	*Meditations* of Marcus Aurelius
193	Column of Marcus Aurelius completed

114–17	Trajan's Parthian War: Armenia and Mesopotamia annexed
115–17	Jewish Revolt

HADRIAN (117–38)

131	Hadrian establishes the Panhellenion, based on Athens, as a league of the Greek cities
132–5	Bar Kochba's revolt leads to final dispersal of Jews

ANTONINUS PIUS (138–61)

MARCUS AURELIUS (161–80)

162–6	Parthian Wars of L. Verus
165–7	Plague spreads through the Roman Empire
168–75	German Wars of Marcus

COMMODUS (180–92)

193	With the murder of Commodus four Emperors contend for power.

THE ROMAN EMPIRE (*cont.*)

POLITICAL EVENTS		CULTURAL DEVELOPMENTS	

The Severan Dynasty

'Our history and the affairs of the Romans descend from an age of gold to one of iron and rust' (Cassius Dio, contemporary historian). The causes of the decline and subsequent transformation of the Roman world are complex. Militarization of the Empire and a shift of power from centre to outlying frontiers as barbarian pressure increased, brought strains which began to emerge under the Severans.

SEPTIMIUS SEVERUS (193–211)

			Philostratus (literary biographer), Herodian (historian), Marius Maximus (biographer), Sextus Empiricus (sceptic philosopher), Alexander of Aphrodisias (commentator on Aristotle),
208–11	Severus campaigns in Britain and dies at York		Tertullian and Clement of Alexandria (Christian writers) active
			Severus lavishly rebuilds his home town of Leptis Magna and builds the Arch of Septimius Severus in the Roman Forum

CARACALLA (212–17)

212	The *constitutio Antoniniana* grants citizenship to all inhabitants of the Empire	216	Baths of Caracalla completed
		200–54	Origen (Christian philosopher) active

ELAGABALUS (218–22)

SEVERUS ALEXANDER (222–35)

226	Ardashir the Sassanian, crowned King of Kings in Iran, inaugurates 400 years of intermittent war with the Roman Empire	223	Murder of Ulpian, praetorian prefect and jurist, by his troops
		229	Cassius Dio (historian) consul for the second time with the Emperor

The Late Empire

Fifty years of military anarchy (235–84, with nearly twenty Emperors) were ended by Diocletian's reforms and the establishment of the Tetrarchy. But intractable problems of frontier defence, heavy taxation, inflation, and excessive bureaucracy remained, and were not affected by Constantine's conversion to Christianity. The Late Empire was a new world in which from time to time Emperors such as Julian, or literary figures, sought to recapture the values of a lost society. Only a few leading events are mentioned in this brief list.

267	Heruli invade Greece
249–51	Decius' persecution of the Christians
258	Martyrdom of Cyprian
270	Death of Plotinus (Neoplatonist philosopher)
271	Aurelian Walls of Rome built
284–306	Diocletian re-establishes central power and founds the Tetrarchy
303–5	Great Persecution
306–37	Career of Constantine the Great
307–12	Basilica of Maxentius in Rome, completed by Constantine
312	Constantine wins battle of Milvian Bridge under the sign of the Cross: Christianity declared official state religion
313–22	First Christian basilica built in Rome
324	Foundation of Constantinople
360–3	Julian the Apostate Emperor
378–95	Theodosius the Great Emperor
395	Division of the Empire between the sons of Theodosius
410	Sack of Rome by Alaric the Visigoth
	Rome formally renounces Britain
430	Death of Saint Augustine
439	Vandals conquer Carthage and Africa
476	End of Roman Empire in the West
527–65	Justinian, eastern emperor, seeks to reconquer Italy and Africa
529	Justinian orders the closure of the Academy at Athens
	The *Digest* of Roman Law is compiled
633–55	Arab conquest of Syria, Egypt, and the Sassanid Empire
1453	Conquest of Constantinople by the Turks and end of the Eastern Roman Empire

LIST OF ILLUSTRATIONS

COLOUR PLATES

BLACK-AND-WHITE ILLUSTRATIONS

INDEX

References followed by grid letters (e.g. 10 Bd) are to maps. References in italics are to illustrations.